The Challenge of Communicating

Guiding Principles and Practices

Isa N. Engleberg
Prince George's Community College

Dianna R. Wynn
Nash Community College

PEARSON

Boston • New York • San Francisco
Mexico City • Montreal • Toronto • London • Madrid • Munich • Paris
Hong Kong • Singapore • Tokyo • Cape Town • Sydney

Editor-in-Chief: *Karon Bowers*

Associate Development Editor: *Jenny Lupica*

Series Editorial Assistant: *Jessica Cabana*

Marketing Manager: *Suzan Czajkowski*

Production Editor: *Claudine Bellanton*

Editorial-Production Service: *Publishers' Design and Production Services, Inc.*

Composition Buyer: *Linda Cox*

Manufacturing Buyer: *JoAnne Sweeney*

Electronic Composition: *Publishers' Design and Production Services, Inc.*

Interior Design: *Ellen Pettengell*

Photo Researchers: *Julie Tesser and Rachel Lucas*

Cover Administrator/Designer: *Kristina Mose-Libon*

For related titles and support materials, visit our online catalog at www.ablongman.com.

Between the time Website information is gathered and then published, it is not unusual for some sites to have closed. Also, the transcription of URLs can result in typographical errors. The publisher would appreciate notification where these errors occur so that they may be corrected in subsequent editions.

Library of Congress Cataloging-in-Publication Data

Engleberg, Isa N.
   The challenge of communicating : guiding principles and practices / Isa N. Engleberg, Dianna R. Wynn.
     p. cm.
   Includes bibliographical references and index.
   ISBN-13: 978-0-205-55476-8 (alk. paper)
   ISBN-10: 0-205-55476-8
   1. Communication. 2. Interpersonal communication. 3. Decision making. I. Wynn, Dianna. II. Title.
   HM1166.E54 2008
   302.2—dc22   2007035654

10 9 8 7 6 5 4 3 2 1   Q-WC-V 11 10 09 08 07

Brief Contents

Contents

Part Two The Challenge of Interpersonal Communication

Part Three The Challenge of Group Communication

Part Four The Challenge of Presentational Communication

MyCommunicationLab Chapters

(Only available on www.mycommunicationlab.com [access code required].)

Preface

We wrote this textbook with one overriding question in mind: *If this is the first or only communication course students take, what do they need to know to communicate more effectively?* The search for answers to this question produced what we believe is an innovative, basic communication textbook well-suited for the complex world in which we live. Research has confirmed our conclusion. A study commissioned by the Association of American Colleges and Universities (AAC&U) polled several hundred employers and recent college graduates to identify the intellectual and practical skills needed by college students entering the world of work. Here are the top four preferences:

1. Teamwork skills and the ability to collaborate with others in diverse group settings

2. The ability to communicate effectively orally and in writing

3. Critical thinking and analytical reasoning skills

4. The ability to locate, organize, and evaluate information from multiple sources[1]

The AAC&U study results present several challenges. Is there a best way to learn these intellectual and practical skills? Is there an academic discipline that can legitimately claim all four competency areas as its own? Is there a basic course that identifies these four areas as student learning outcomes? The answer to this last question is yes: Only the basic human communication course has the potential to encompass the theory, research, strategies, and skills that meet the identified intellectual and practical challenges of the 21st century.

The Key Elements and Guiding Principles of Human Communication

Many communication textbooks appear to be four separate mini books under a single cover—one on basic communication principles, one on interpersonal communication, one on group communication, and one on public speaking. Rarely do these sections "speak" to one another. Separating the four areas does a disservice to communication students, instructors, and scholars by implying that the four areas have little or nothing to do with one another. Rather than separating the four areas, we have unified them with a set of common elements and guiding principles that apply to *all* areas of human communication.

[1]Peter D. Hart Research Associates, *How Should Colleges Prepare Students to Succeed in Today's Global Economy?* 2006, p. 5 [Conducted on behalf of The Association of American Colleges and Universities]. Also see Association of American Colleges and Universities, *College Learning for the New Global Age* (Washington, DC: Association of American Colleges and Universities, 2007).

At the heart of *The Challenge of Communicating: Guiding Principles and Practices* is a unique decision-making system based on seven key elements and guiding principles of human communication derived from well-established axioms found in the literature of communication studies. Regardless of the context (intrapersonal, interpersonal, group, or presentational communication), these key elements and guiding principles will help you make decisions about the nature of a communication challenge, select the strategies that effectively address that challenge, and demonstrate the skills needed to achieve your communication goal. The seven key elements and guiding principles form a unified, comprehensive model of the communication process that can be applied to every communication challenge.

Key Elements of Communication	Communication Axioms	Guiding Principles of Communication
Self	Communication Is Personal	Recognize how *your* characteristics and attitudes affect the way you communicate.
Others	Communication Is Relational	Understand, respect, and adapt to other communicators.
Purpose	Communication Is Intentional	Determine your communication goal.
Context	Communication Is Contextual	Adapt to the communication circumstances and setting.
Content	Communication Is Symbolic	Select appropriate message content.
Structure	Communication Is Structured	Organize message content.
Expression	Communication Is Irreversible	Plan how to convey your message to others.

Do these seven guiding principles represent everything you need to know about effective and ethical communication? Of course not. Rather, the seven key elements and guiding principles provide a framework for strategic decision making about the complex process of communicating.

Textbook Overview

PART ONE

The Challenge of Communicating

Chapter 1 introduces you to the communication process, the seven key elements and guiding principles of human communication, and the importance of ethical communication. Chapter 2 focuses on the first key element: *self*. We examine how your perceptions, self-concept, and level of confidence affect your ability and willingness to communicate. Chapter 3 examines the second element: *others*. Whenever you communicate with others, you should strive to understand, respect, and adapt to differences in others—their characteristics and cultures—and appreciate how *your* characteristics and culture affect your interactions with others.

Chapter 4 discusses how effective listening, critical thinking, and sound argumentation are prerequisites for effective communication. Chapter 5 takes a sophisticated look at language through the eyes of linguistic and rhetorical scholars. Lastly, Chapter 6 explores the multifaceted challenge of understanding nonverbal communication and its significant effects on the meaning of messages.

PART TWO

The Challenge of Interpersonal Communication

Part Two applies the key elements and guiding principles of human communication to improving *interpersonal* communication. Chapter 7 introduces basic interpersonal concepts, including how your personal needs and personality type affect the way you communicate, how to initiate interpersonal relationships and conversations, and how to deal with conflict and anger. Chapter 8 shifts the focus from basic interpersonal concepts to strategies for improving personal, romantic, family, and friend relationships. The chapter also looks at the interplay of personal privacy issues, self-disclosure, sensitivity to feedback, and emotional expression. Chapter 9 focuses on professional relationships. In addition to a detailed discussion of effective interviews, the chapter looks at several types of professional relationships and strategies for handling work-related communication challenges.

PART THREE

The Challenge of Group Communication

Part Three applies the key elements and guiding principles of human communication to group communication. Chapter 10 focuses on the challenge of working in groups and teams by examining group development, group participation, group leadership, and group diversity. Chapter 11 concentrates on strategies and skills for making effective decisions and solving problems in groups as well as guidelines for running effective meetings.

PART FOUR

The Challenge of Presentational Communication

The five chapters in Part Four address the challenges of effective presentational speaking. Chapter 12 provides guidelines for planning a presentation by focusing on the key elements of *self* (speaker credibility and ethics), *others* (audience analysis and adaptation), *purpose* (clear goals and appropriate topics), and *context* (adapting to the logistics and occasion). Chapter 13 presents strategies that focus on the key element of *content* (how to gather and select relevant information for a presentation) and *structure* (how to organize presentation content to engage audience interest and comprehension). Chapter 14 is devoted to the element of *expression* and focuses on two components: language and delivery. Strategies for using clear, oral, rhetorical, and eloquent language are described. In addition to different modes of delivery, the chapter also provides detailed instructions for improving both vocal and physical delivery techniques as well as designing and using presentation aids effectively.

Chapter 15 goes well beyond the usual organizational format and tips in other textbooks by presenting a unified theory of informative speaking that offers specific strategies based on the speaker's purpose and the type of informative topic. The chapter also discusses how to use humor, storytelling, and audience participation to generate listener interest. Chapter 16 looks at several theories of persuasion and how they can be used to develop messages that influence audience opinions and behavior. Sections on building and structuring persuasive arguments complete the chapter.

MYCOMMUNICATIONLAB CHAPTERS

Two additional chapters are available on MyCommunicationLab (for more information, please see the description of MyCommunicationLab in the supplements section discussed later) and are recommended as useful supplements to the textbook. MyCommunicationLab Chapter A, *Research Strategies and Skills*, recommends strategies and skills for using and evaluating researched information in interpersonal, group, and presentational contexts. MyCommunicationLab Chapter B, *Effective Presentation Aids*, goes beyond simple descriptions and techniques for using presentation aids. In addition to advice on choosing appropriate media, the chapter offers a comprehensive set of design principles to enhance the quality and effectiveness of presentations aids.

Textbook Innovations and Features

The Challenge of Communicating moves through a series of traditional topics in much the same order as other basic textbooks do. At the same time, we offer unique features designed to help you learn about communication theories, strategies, and skills. The following features represent a few of the unique benefits in *The Challenge of Communicating.*

THE SEVEN KEY ELEMENTS AND GUIDING PRINCIPLES OF HUMAN COMMUNICATION

The Challenge of Communicating: Guiding Principles and Practices is the first basic course textbook to incorporate a set of key elements and guiding principles that apply to *all* communication contexts, and give intellectual unity and academic coherence to the study of communication. Although each guideline is written to accommodate the content of a specific chapter, the key elements and axioms always remain the same. For example, regardless of whether you are talking to a friend, chairing a meeting, or speaking to an audience, your communication will be more effective if you consider all seven key elements: self, others, purpose, context, content, structure, and expression.

IMPROVING PROFESSIONAL RELATIONSHIPS (CHAPTER 9)

Although other basic communication textbooks usually include a section or chapter on interviewing, Chapter 9, "Interpersonal Communication: Professional Relationships," makes *The Challenge of Communicating* the only textbook to examine *other* communication challenges in the workplace, such as superior–subordinate relationships, coworker relationships, customer relationships, organizational culture, office gossip, workplace romances, working with friends, sexual harassment, and resigning from a job.

THEORY-BASED INFORMATIVE SPEAKING STRATEGIES (CHAPTER 15)

The Challenge of Communicating breaks new ground for this important type of presentational speaking. Whereas the chapters on informative speaking in most basic textbooks offer little more than sample organizational patterns and a list of tips, Chapter 15, "Presentations: Speaking to Inform," examines four types of informative messages: (1) reporting new information, (2) explaining difficult concepts, (3) explaining complex processes, and (4) overcoming confusion and misunderstanding, accompanied by appropriate informative speaking strategies for each type of message.[2]

---

[2]Based on Katherine E. Rowan, "Informing and Explaining Skills: Theory and Research on Informative Communication," in *Handbook of Communication and Social Interaction Skills*, ed. John O. Greene and Brant R. Burleson (Mahwah, NJ: Lawrence Erlbaum Associates, 2003), pp. 403–438.

Chapter 15 also examines strategies for generating audience interest, a subject missing from most other textbooks. Strategies include techniques for overcoming disinterest as well as methods for telling stories, using humor, and involving the audience.

UNIQUE AND RARELY COVERED THEORIES, RESEARCH, STRATEGIES, AND SKILLS

The Challenge of Communicating includes subjects that are *not* or are *rarely* covered in most basic communication textbooks:

- Argumentation
- Aristotle's ethics
- Group members' decision-making styles
- Emotional support and comforting skills
- Emotions and critical thinking
- Fundamental Interpersonal Relationships Orientation (FIRO) Theory
- Heuristics and persuasion
- Informatory and explanatory speaking strategies
- Linguistics
- Model of leadership effectiveness
- Motivating group members
- Mythos: Narrative Theory
- Personality theories
- Persuasive evidence research
- Psychological Reactance Theory
- Storytelling strategies and skills
- Toulmin's Model of Argument
- Workplace communication issues

In-Text Student Learning Features

Student learning takes place in many places—in classrooms, in study groups, online, through websites, and in private places where you study and prepare for class. *The Challenge of Communicating* includes a variety of in-text pedagogical features designed to help students analyze communication challenges, choose appropriate communication strategies, and master communication skills. In-text pedagogical features accommodate the different learning styles and cultures of today's diverse student population. *Every* chapter includes the following in-text pedagogical tools:

- *Chapter-opening graphic of key elements, axioms, and guiding principles*

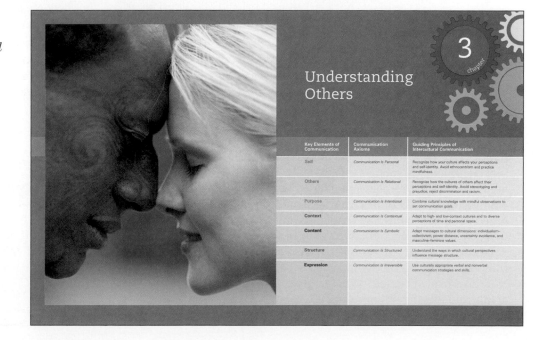

CommFAQ Do Fear Appeals Work?

Many advertisements, public service announcements, political ads, and magazine articles "go negative" by using fear as a persuasive tool. Persuasion scholar Richard Perloff writes, "Appealing to people's fears is, to a considerable degree, a negative communication strategy. The communicator must arouse a little pain in the individual, hoping it will produce gain."[1] Fear appeals work because they try to scare listeners into changing their attitudes or behavior by suggesting how bad things will be if they fail to take the speaker's advice.

Kathleen Hall Jamieson studies political campaign ads with a special focus on attack ads. She concludes that these ads have a bad reputation because most reporters and the public believe that candidates use them to spread deceptions about a rival. Ironically, the ads that *brag* about the candidate running for office often contain more distorted information than the ads that blast the opponents. Like it or not, attack ads designed to arouse negative emotions succeed in changing opinions and behavior.[2]

Fear appeals directed toward people we care about also work. Think of how many advertisements use this approach. Life insurance ads suggest that you invest not for yourself but for those you love. Political ads tell you to vote for particular candidates because they will make the world safer for you and your family.

[1]Richard M. Perloff, *The Dynamics of Persuasion: Communication and Attitudes in the 21st Century*, 2nd ed. (Mahwah, NJ: Lawrence Erlbaum, 2003), p. 186.
[2]Kathleen Hall Jamieson, "Shooting to Win," *Washington Post*, September 26, 2004, pp. B1, B2.

- *CommFAQs.* Short answers to some of the most commonly asked student questions. Examples: "Do fear appeals work?" "How can a person be a chair?" "Do women talk more than men?" "Can you detect a lie?" "How can I keep my voice from shaking?"

- *CommFYIs.* Advice, cautionary notes, and reminders about effective communication. Examples: "Listening keeps couples together." "Beware of self-fulfilling prophecies." "Learn how to apologize." "Inoculate your audience." "Practice like the pros."

CommFYI Listening Keeps Couples Together

In his best-selling book, *Emotional Intelligence*, Daniel Goleman presents the following interchange between two people:

He: You're shouting!
She: Of course I'm shouting—you haven't heard a word I'm saying. You just don't listen.

Goleman maintains that "listening is a skill that keeps couples together." Couples headed for divorce, however, "become absorbed in the anger and fixate on the specifics of the issue at hand, not managing to hear—let alone return—any peace offerings."[1] Sadly, feuding couples often become highly defensive. Each partner ignores or immediately refutes the spouse's complaint, reacting to it as though it were an attack rather than an attempt to express feelings or to change injurious behavior.[2]

[1]Daniel Goleman, *Emotional Intelligence: Why It Can Matter More Than IQ* (New York: Bantam Books, 1997), p. 145.
[2]Ibid.

CommQuiz Fill in the Abstract-to-Concrete Words

Superordinate Terms (most abstract)	Basic Terms	Subordinate Terms (most concrete)
Visual entertainment	Film	*Gone with the Wind*
	Chair	
Seafood		
		Blue Spruce
Sport		
	Dress	

- *CommQuiz.* Short surveys and quizzes to help students apply chapter content to everyday life experiences. Examples: "Do you have the right stuff for the job?" "How emotionally intelligent are you?" "How can I become a leader?" "How argumentative are you?" "How do I find common ground?"

- *CommTech.* How to communicate in virtual environments such as e-mail, bulletin boards, chat rooms, audio conferences, videoconferences, text-based computer conferences, electronic meeting systems, and collaborative presentation technology. Examples: "Hoaxes, rumors, and myths on the Internet." "Cultures in cyberspace." "Online interaction and identity." "Love online."

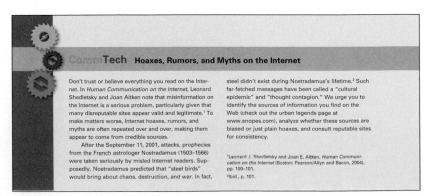

CommTech Hoaxes, Rumors, and Myths on the Internet

Don't trust or believe everything you read on the Internet. In *Human Communication on the Internet*, Leonard Shedletsky and Joan Aitken note that misinformation on the Internet is a serious problem, particularly given that many disreputable sites appear valid and legitimate.[1] To make matters worse, Internet hoaxes, rumors, and myths are often repeated over and over, making them appear to come from credible sources.

After the September 11, 2001, attacks, prophecies from the French astrologer Nostradamus (1503–1566) were taken seriously by misled Internet readers. Supposedly, Nostradamus predicted that "steel birds" would bring about chaos, destruction, and war. In fact, steel didn't exist during Nostradamus's lifetime.[2] Such far-fetched messages have been called a "cultural epidemic" and "thought contagion." We urge you to identify the sources of information you find on the Web (check out the urban legends page at www.snopes.com), analyze whether these sources are biased or just plain hoaxes, and consult reputable sites for consistency.

[1]Leonard J. Shedletsky and Joan E. Aitken, *Human Communication on the Internet* (Boston: Pearson/Allyn and Bacon, 2004), pp. 100–101.
[2]Ibid., p. 101.

- *CommEthics.* In addition to examining and applying the National Communication Association's Credo for Ethical Communication, this feature examines ethical issues and their consequences related to discussions of plagiarism, self-disclosure, leadership, principled persuasion, cultural sensitivity, and more. Examples: "The ethics of caring." "Ethics and implicit biases." "Ethical conflict resolution." "Don't take it out of context."

CommEthics   The Ethics of Caring

The NCA Credo for Ethical Communication includes a principle that speaks directly to interpersonal relationships: "We promote communication climates of caring and mutual understanding that respect the unique needs and characteristics of individual communicators."[1] Philosopher and educator Nel Noddings believes we make moral choices based on an ethic of caring. For example, a mother picks up a crying baby, not because of a sense of duty or because she is worried about what others will say if she doesn't, but because she cares about the baby. Relationship theorists emphasize that this is not a gender-based ethic. Rather, it is based on a way of thinking that honors two fundamental characteristics of ethical behavior: avoiding harm and providing mutual aid. Most of us have a basic and universal aversion to harm, both physical and psychological. We also have a basic and universal urge to help others, particularly when they suffer from harm. Interpersonal ethics calls for rational justifications, flexibility, self-control, and self-monitoring in our communication and interactions with others. As ethical communicators, we must accept the difficult challenge of defending our choices and the consequences of our actions.[2]

[1] www.natcom.org/aboutNCA/Policies/Platform.html.
[2] Elaine E. Englehardt, "Introduction to Ethics in Interpersonal Communication," in *Ethical Issues in Interpersonal Communication*, ed. Elaine E. Englehardt (Fort Worth, TX: Harcourt, 2001), pp. 1–25. In the same volume, see also Carol Gilligan, "Images of Relationship," and Nel Noddings, "An Ethics of Care," pp. 88–96 and 96–103.

What are the telltale signs that the man in this photograph is not listening to the woman?

- *Photo Questions.* Captions serve as mini case studies and pose questions for student deliberation and discussion.

- *End-of-Chapter Communication Challenges.* Individual or group activities that demonstrate or help students practice communication strategies or skills discussed in the chapter. Communication Challenges also help students practice interacting in a collaborative learning environment.

Communication Challenge

What Is Culturally Normal?

Directions: Respond to each of the following twelve items by putting a checkmark in the column that describes the behavior; descriptions range from "Quite Ordinary" to "Quite Strange." Then use the comment section to explain your response briefly.

Item	Quite Ordinary	Ordinary	Neutral	Strange	Quite Strange
1. A man wearing a skirt in public	☐	☐	☐	☐	☐
Comment:					
2. Two women holding hands in a park	☐	☐	☐	☐	☐
Comment:					
3. A woman breast-feeding her child in public	☐	☐	☐	☐	☐
Comment:					
4. Talking with someone who does not look you in the eye	☐	☐	☐	☐	☐
Comment:					
5. A woman refusing to shake hands with a man	☐	☐	☐	☐	☐
Comment:					
6. A family taking a communal bath	☐	☐	☐	☐	☐
Comment:					
7. Interacting with professors on a first-name basis	☐	☐	☐	☐	☐
Comment:					
8. Praying to many gods	☐	☐	☐	☐	☐
Comment:					
9. A man wearing Bermuda shorts to a fine restaurant	☐	☐	☐	☐	☐
Comment:					
10. Eating a formal meal without utensils	☐	☐	☐	☐	☐
Comment:					
11. A man who stands so close you can smell his breath	☐	☐	☐	☐	☐
Comment:					
12. People who will not eat the food in your home	☐	☐	☐	☐	☐
Comment:					

Review your ratings and comments. All twelve behaviors are customary (and normal) in another culture or country. Consider how individuals from other cultures might find some of your "normal" behaviors unusual (and even abnormal).

Source: Activity based on Myron W. Lustig and Jolene Koester, *Instructors Manual to Accompany Intercultural Competence*, 2nd ed. (New York: HarperCollins, 1996), pp. 72–74.

Communication Assessment

Writing Apprehension Test (WAT)

Directions: The following statements about writing attempt to measure how you feel about the process of putting your ideas and opinions on paper. There are no right or wrong answers to these statements. Please indicate the degree to which each statement applies to you by marking whether you (1) strongly agree, (2) agree, (3) are uncertain, (4) disagree, or (5) strongly disagree with the statement. Although some of these statements may seem repetitious, take your time and try to be as honest as possible.

_____ 1. I avoid writing.

_____ 2. I have no fear of my writing being evaluated.

_____ 3. I look forward to writing down my ideas.

_____ 4. My mind seems to go blank when I start to work on a composition.

_____ 5. Expressing ideas through writing seems to be a waste of time.

_____ 6. I would enjoy submitting my writing to magazines for evaluation and publication.

_____ 7. I like to write my ideas down.

_____ 8. I feel confident in my ability to express my ideas clearly in writing.

_____ 9. I like to have my friends read what I have written.

_____ 10. I'm nervous about writing.

_____ 11. People seem to enjoy what I write.

_____ 12. I enjoy writing.

_____ 13. I never seem to be able to write down my ideas clearly.

_____ 14. Writing is a lot of fun.

_____ 15. I like seeing my thoughts on paper.

_____ 16. Discussing my writing with others is an enjoyable experience.

_____ 17. It's easy for me to write good compositions.

_____ 18. I don't think I write as well as other people write.

_____ 19. I don't like my compositions to be evaluated.

_____ 20. I'm not good at writing.

Scoring: To determine your score on the WAT, complete the following steps:

1. Add the scores for items 1, 4, 5, 10, 13, 18, 19, and 20.
2. Add the scores for items 2, 3, 6, 7, 8, 9, 11, 12, 14, 15, 16, and 17.
3. Complete the following formula:

$$\text{WAT} = 48 - \text{total from step 1} + \text{total from step 2}$$

Your score should be between 20 and 100 points. If your score is less than 20 or more than 100 points, you have made a mistake in computing the score. The higher your score, the more apprehension you feel about writing.

Score	Level of Apprehension	Description
20–45	Low	Enjoy writing; seek writing opportunities
46–75	Average	Some writing creates apprehension; other writing does not
76–100	High	Troubled by many kinds of writing; avoid writing in most situations

Source: From Richmond, Virginia P. & James C. Mc Croskey _Communication Apprehension, Avoidance And Effectiveness, 5/e._ Published by Allyn and Bacon, Boston, MA. Copyright © 1998 by Pearson Education. Reprinted by permission of the publisher. See also John Daly and Michael Miller, "The Empirical Development of an Instrument to Measure Writing Apprehension," _Research in the Teaching of English_ 12 (1975), pp. 242–249.

143

- _End-of-Chapter Communication Assessments._ Self-assessment, group assessments, and presentation speaking assessment instruments that evaluate student or group understanding of communication theories, strategies, and/or skills.

In addition, a glossary at the back of the book includes every term or phrase defined in the book. Key terms printed in bold type are defined within the chapters as well as in the glossary.

Supplements for the Instructor

PRINT RESOURCES

- _Instructor's Manual_ prepared by the text authors. This text-specific ancillary is comprehensive, rigorous, and easily used. The manual includes a sample syllabus, course outlines, more than 125 chapter-by-chapter class activities, and more than 20 oral and written assignments with matched assessment instruments.

- _Test Bank_ prepared by the textbook authors. The test bank contains multiple-choice, true/false, and essay questions for each chapter. More than 1,200 questions are referenced by page number and associated with a difficulty level to make question selection easier.

- _A&B Public Speaking Transparency Package, Version II_ contains 100 full-color transparencies created with PowerPoint software to provide visual support for classroom lectures and discussions.

- *The Blockbuster Approach: Teaching Interpersonal Communication with Video, 3/e,* by Thomas Jewell, Bergen Community College. This guide provides lists and descriptions of commercial videos that can be used in the classroom to illustrate interpersonal concepts and complex interpersonal relationships. Sample activities are also included.

- *Great Ideas for Teaching Speech (GIFTS), 3/e,* by Raymond Zeuschner, California Polytechnic State University, San Luis Obispo. This instructional booklet provides descriptions of and guidelines for assignments successfully used by experienced public speaking instructors in their classrooms.

- *A Guide for New Teachers of Introduction to Communication, 2/e,* by Susanna G. Porter, Kennesaw State University. This instructor's guide is designed to help new teachers effectively teach the introductory communication course. Topics such as choosing a text, structuring your course, effectively using group work, dealing with classroom challenges, and giving feedback are included, as well as a number of sample materials in the appendix.

ELECTRONIC RESOURCES

- *MyCommunicationLab* (www.mycommunicationlab.com). Where students learn to communicate with confidence! As an interactive and instructive online solution designed to be used as a supplement to a traditional lecture course or completely administered as an online course, MyCommunicationLab combines multimedia, video, communication activities, research support, tests, and quizzes to make teaching and learning more relevant and enjoyable. Students benefit from a wealth of video clips that include student and professional speeches, small group scenarios, and interpersonal interactions—some with running commentary and critical questions—all geared to help students learn to communicate with confidence. (Access code required).

- *Computerized Test Bank.* The printed test questions are also available electronically though our computerized testing system, TestGen EQ. The test-generating software, which is capable of being placed on a network, is now available on a multiplatform CD-ROM. The user-friendly interface enables instructors to view, edit, and add questions; transfer questions to tests; and print tests in a variety of fonts. Search and sort features allow instructors to locate questions quickly and arrange them in a preferred order.

- *PowerPoint Presentation Package,* prepared by the textbook authors and Larry Edmonds, Arizona State University. This text-specific package consists of more than 500 slides, many of which are interactive and challenging. Available for download at www.ablongman.com/irc.

- *Allyn & Bacon Communication Digital Media Archive, Version 3.0,* available on CD-ROM, offers more than 200 still images, video excerpts, and PowerPoint slides that can be used to enliven classroom presentations.

- *VideoWorkshop for Introduction to Communication, Version 2.0* (www.ablongman.com/videoworkshop), by Kathryn Dindia, University of Wisconsin. *VideoWorkshop for Introduction to Communication* is a new way to bring video into your course for maximized learning. This total teaching and learning system includes quality video footage on an easy-to-use CD-ROM, plus a *Student Learning Guide* and an *Instructor's Teaching Guide.* The result? A program that brings textbook concepts to life with ease that helps your students understand, analyze, and apply the objectives of the course. *VideoWorkshop* is available for your students as a value-pack option with this textbook.

- *Lecture Questions for Clickers: Introduction to Communication* by Keri Moe, El Paso Community College. An assortment of questions and activities covering culture, listening, interviewing, public speaking, interpersonal conflict and more are presented in PowerPoint. These slides will help liven up your lectures and can be used along with the Personal Response System to get students more involved in the material. Available on the Web at www.ablongman.com/irc.

- *PowerPoint Presentation for Public Speaking.* This course-specific Power-Point outline adds visual punch to public speaking lectures with colorful screen designs and clip art. Our expanded Public Speaking PowerPoint™ package now includes 125 slides and a brief User's Guide. Book-specific PowerPoint Presentations also are available for many texts. Available on the Web at www.ablongman.com/irc.

VIDEO MATERIALS

- *New Video Case Studies, Scenarios, and Presentation Program.* A professionally produced set of video clips presents realistic, contemporary portrayals of interpersonal, group, and presentational communication. The interpersonal and group communication videos employ skilled actors playing creative, scripted roles in a variety of communication contexts. As a result, the case studies and group scenarios enable viewers to suspend disbelief and focus full attention to the ways in which the scenarios demonstrate a wide range of communication theories, strategies, and skills. The videos lend themselves to several uses:

  - An introduction or overview to textbook chapters
  - A source of examples to supplement class lectures
  - A source of examples for class or online discussions
  - A review of key terms and concepts
  - An opportunity to observe and analyze nonverbal communication
  - The basis for multiple-choice, true/false, and essay/short answer exam questions
  - The basis for analysis in student papers

- *A&B Public Speaking Video Library.* Allyn & Bacon's Public Speaking Video Library contains a range of videos from which adopters can choose. The videos feature different types of speeches delivered on a multitude of different topics, allowing you to choose the speeches best suited for your students. Please contact your Allyn & Bacon representative for details and a complete list of videos and their contents to choose which would be most useful to in your class. Each video has its own ISBN and must be ordered separately.

- *A&B Small Group Communication Library.* This small group communication collection presents video case studies of groups working in diverse contexts and highlights key concepts of communication including group problem-solving, leadership roles, diversity, power, conflict, virtual group communication, and more. Please contact your Allyn & Bacon representative for details and a complete list of videos and their contents to choose which would be most useful to in your class. Each video has its own ISBN and must be ordered separately.

- *Allyn & Bacon's Interpersonal Communication Video Library* contains a range of videos from which adopters can choose. Each of the videos features a variety of scenarios that illustrate interpersonal concepts and relationships, including topics such as nonverbal communication, perception, conflict and listening. Please contact your Allyn & Bacon representative for details and a complete list of videos and their contents to choose which would be most useful to in your class. Each video has its own ISBN and must be ordered separately.

- *A&B Contemporary Classic Speeches DVD.* This exciting supplement includes more than 120 minutes of video footage in an easy-to-use DVD format. Each speech is accompanied by a biographical and historical summary that helps students understand the context and motivation behind each speech. *It may also be packaged with participating Allyn & Bacon texts.*

Student Supplements

PRINT RESOURCES

- *Student Learning Manual* prepared by the textbok authors. A preface introduces students to the textbook and basic learning principles. Each chapter in the *Student Learning Manual* includes the following features:

  - Guiding Principles Model
  - Chapter outline
  - Key terms review
  - Activities and exercises including surveys, worksheets, group activities, and assessments instruments
  - Applying the Guiding Principles Scenarios
  - Sample quiz questions
  - Textbook Features Review
  - Evaluation guidelines and peer evaluation forms

- *ResearchNavigator.com Guide: Speech Communication.* This updated booklet by Steven L. Epstein of Suffolk County Community College includes tips, resources, and URLs to aid students conducting research on Pearson Education's research website, www.researchnavigator.com. The guide contains a student access code for the Research Navigator database, offering students unlimited access to a collection of more than 25,000 discipline-specific articles from top-tier academic publications and peer-reviewed journals, as well as the *New York Times* and popular news publications. The guide introduces students to the basics of the Internet and the World Wide Web, and includes tips for searching for articles on the site, and a list of journals useful for research in their discipline. Also included are hundreds of Web resources for the discipline, as well as information on how to cite research correctly. *The guide is available packaged with new copies of the text.*

- *Study Card for Introduction to Communication.* Colorful, affordable, and packed with useful information, Allyn & Bacon's study cards make studying easier, more efficient, and more enjoyable. Course information is distilled down to the basics, helping you quickly master the fundamentals, review a subject for understanding, or prepare for an exam. Because they are laminated for durability, you can keep these study cards for years to come and pull them out whenever you need a quick review. *Sold separately or packaged with participating Allyn & Bacon texts.*

- *Speech Preparation Workbook*, by Jennifer Dreyer and Gregory H. Patton, San Diego State University. This workbook takes students through the stages of speech creation—from audience analysis to writing the speech—and includes guidelines, tips, and easy-to-complete pages. *Sold separately or packaged with participating Allyn & Bacon texts.*

- *Preparing Visual Aids for Presentations*, 4/e, by Dan Cavanaugh. This brief booklet provides a host of ideas for using today's multimedia tools to improve presentations, including suggestions for how to plan a presentation, guidelines for designing visual aids and storyboarding, and a walkthrough that shows how to prepare a visual display using PowerPoint. *Sold separately or packaged with participating Allyn & Bacon texts.*

- *Public Speaking in the Multicultural Environment, 2/e*, by Deborah Lieberman, Portland State University. This two-chapter essay focuses on speaking and listening to a culturally diverse audience and emphasizes preparation, delivery, and how speeches are perceived. *Sold separately or packaged with participating Allyn & Bacon texts.*

- *Multicultural Activities Workbook*, by Marlene C. Cohen and Susan L. Richardson, both of Prince George's Community College. This workbook is filled with hands-on activities with a multicultural focus, such as checklists, surveys, and writing assignments. *Sold separately or available packaged with the text.*

- *The Speech Outline: Outlining to Plan, Organize, and Deliver a Speech: Activities and Exercises*, by Reeze L. Hanson and Sharon Condon, Haskell Indian Nations University. This brief workbook includes activities, exercises, and answers to help students develop and master the critical skill of outlining. *Sold separately or packaged with participating Allyn & Bacon texts.*

- *The Speech Preparation Workbook*, by Suzanne Osborn, University of Memphis, contains forms to help students prepare a self-introductory speech, analyze the audience, select a topic, conduct research, organize supporting materials and outline speeches. *Sold separately or packaged with participating Allyn & Bacon texts.*

ELECTRONIC RESOURCES

- *MyCommunicationLab* (www.mycommunicationlab.com). Where students learn to communicate with confidence! As an interactive and instructive online solution designed to be used as a supplement to a traditional lecture course or completely administered as an online course, MyCommunicationLab combines multimedia, video, communication activities, research support, tests, and quizzes to make teaching and learning more relevant and enjoyable. Students benefit from a wealth of video clips that include student and professional speeches, small group scenarios, and interpersonal interactions—some with running commentary and critical questions—all geared to help students learn to communicate with confidence. (Access code required).

- *Introduction to Communication Study Site*, accessible at www.abintrocomm.com. This website features communication study materials for students, including flashcards and a complete set of practice tests for interpersonal communication, group communication, and public speaking. Students also will find Web links to valuable sites for further exploration of major topics.

- *Allyn & Bacon Communication Studies Website*, by Terrence Doyle, Northern Virginia Community College; Tim Borchers, Moorehead State University; and Nan Peck, Northern Virginia Community College. This site includes modules on interpersonal communication, small group communication, and public speaking. It includes links, enrichment materials, and interactive activities to enhance students' understanding of key concepts. Access this site at www.ablongman.com/commstudies.

- *VideoLab CD-ROM*. This interactive study tool for students can be used independently or in class. It provides digital video of student speeches that can be viewed in conjunction with corresponding outlines, manuscripts, notecards, and instructor critiques. A series of drills to help students analyze content and delivery follows each speech. *Sold separately or packaged with participating Allyn & Bacon texts.*

- *Speech Writer's Workshop CD-ROM, Version 2.0*. This exciting public speaking software includes a *Speech Handbook* with tips for researching and preparing speeches; a *Speech Workshop*, which guides students step-by-step through the speech-writing process; a *Topics Dictionary*, which gives students hundreds of ideas for speeches; and the *Documentor* citation database, which helps students format bibliographic entries in either MLA or APA style. *Sold separately or packaged with participating Allyn & Bacon texts.*

- *VideoWorkshop for Introduction to Communication, Version 2.0* (www.ablongman.com/videoworkshop), by Kathryn Dindia, University of Wisconsin. *VideoWorkshop for Introduction to Communication* is more than just video footage you can watch. It's a total learning system. Our complete program includes quality video footage on an easy-to-use CD-ROM, plus a *Student Learning Guide* and an *Instructor's Teaching Guide*. The result? A program that brings textbook concepts to life with ease that helps your students understand, analyze, and apply the objectives of the course. *VideoWorkshop* is available for your students as a value-pack option with this textbook.

Acknowledgments

We extend our sincere appreciation to the following reviewers, whose excellent suggestions and comments helped shape the content in *The Challenge of Communicating*:

Linda Atwell, George Mason University
Glenda Boling, Danville Area Community College
Maryann Brohard, University of Northwestern Ohio
Rex Butt, Bronx Community College
Marcia Dixson, Indiana State University
Charles Korn, George Mason University
Shirley Maase, Chesapeake College
Edie MacPherson, Suffolk Community College
Carel Neffenger, Jr., Highline Community College
Kim Parker, Palm Beach Community College, Boca Raton Campus
Ané Pearman, ECPI College of Technology
Evelyn Plummer, Seton Hall University
Beth Waggenspack, Virginia Polytechnic Institute and State University
John T. Warren, Bowling Green State University

Although the title page of this book puts our names front and center, this textbook would never have been completed without the work of talented editors. If it takes a village to raise a child, it takes another village of editors, designers, copyeditors, graphic artists, marketing experts, and a host of assistants to produce a good textbook. We thank everyone at Allyn & Bacon, with special attention to a few exceptional individuals.

First we give a standing ovation to Karon Bowers, our talented, insightful, and dynamic Editor-in-Chief at Allyn & Bacon. We also thank the highly effective team of professionals who guided us through the production and marketing process: Jenny Lupica, Suzan Czajkowski, and Jessica Cabana. Their contributions personify the principle of effective group work we promote in the textbook.

Special thanks go to Claudine Bellanton, who took on the daunting task of piloting this book through the choppy seas of production. Her patience, good sense, and professionalism helped us transform a lost-at-sea manuscript into a highly coherent, cutting-edge textbook.

Finally, we thank Bill Barke, CEO of the Addison Wesley Higher Education Group at Pearson Education, for making a major commitment to us by supporting this project.

Isa N. Engleberg and Dianna R. Wynn

Understanding Human Communication

Key Elements of Communication	Communication Axioms	Guiding Principles of Human Communication
Self	*Communication Is Personal*	Recognize how *your* characteristics and attitudes affect the way you communicate.
Others	*Communication Is Relational*	Understand, respect, and adapt to other communicators.
Purpose	*Communication Is Intentional*	Determine your communication goal.
Context	*Communication Is Contextual*	Adapt to the communication circumstances and setting.
Content	*Communication Is Symbolic*	Select appropriate message content.
Structure	*Communication Is Structured*	Organize message content.
Expression	*Communication Is Irreversible*	Plan how to convey your message to others.

A Lifetime of Communicating

The instant you were born, you began communicating about your needs. You squirmed, cried, and even screamed when you were hungry or hurt. You smiled and gurgled when you were happy and content. And as you fussed and cooed, you also began learning how to speak and listen. From a very early age, you faced hundreds of communication challenges—and still do.

Communication occupies more of your waking time than anything else you do. You listen to the equivalent of a book a day, you speak a book a week, you read the equivalent of a book a month, and you write a book a year.[1] Although you communicate all the time, you can always learn how to do it better. In fact, your personal, academic, and professional success throughout your lifetime will depend on how well you learn to communicate.[2] Personal relationships are richer and more rewarding when both parties communicate effectively. Colleagues who express respect for one another and argue constructively are more likely to enjoy productive interactions. Work groups that understand member roles and use appropriate problem-solving strategies are more likely to achieve their goals in a positive, social climate. And if you are a good speaker, you are often selected for leadership roles.

COMMUNICATION CHALLENGES

The challenge of communicating requires more than learning a set of rules or "tricks of the trade." Effective communicators use communication theories to guide them as they choose appropriate strategies and skills for a variety of communication situations. They also accept responsibility for the outcomes of their choices. The following questions address several of the everyday communication challenges you face.

- *Personal.* How can you develop more meaningful personal relationships with close friends, family members, and partners?
- *Professional.* How can you communicate more effectively within and on behalf of a business, organization, or work team?
- *Educational.* How can you demonstrate what you have learned in collegiate, corporate, and other training settings?

How does the communication among members of a surgical team differ from communication in personal, business, and educational settings?

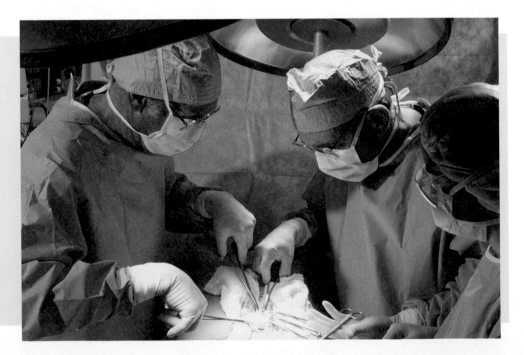

The growth of online learning takes education far beyond the physical boundaries of campuses and classrooms. Successful online learning, however, requires special kinds of knowledge, motivation, and communication skills. If you are taking any portion of this course online or are using online resources to access course content and complete assignments, make sure you have "the right stuff" to succeed.

1. *Knowledge.* Online learning requires an understanding of course content, course requirements, and online technology.
2. *Motivation.* Online learning requires self-discipline and a major commitment to keep up with the class and its assignments. You must be willing and able to spend many hours per week on each course.
3. *Skills.* Online learning requires effective communication skills:

   - The ability to communicate through writing (if you do not like writing or have limited writing skills, online learning may not be for you)
   - The ability to think critically and make decisions on your own and explain your reasoning to your instructor and others

- The ability to work electronically with others on a regular basis to complete an assignment
- The ability to use communication technology properly

If you enjoy campus life and face-to-face learning, you may not be happy in a virtual classroom. Although the level of social interaction can be high online, it's not the same as in a traditional classroom. In virtual classrooms, instructors cannot see whether students are engaged, confused, frustrated, or bored. Thus, if you are having problems with the technology or with course content, you should communicate with your instructor immediately. Before entering the "virtual" classroom, make sure you are ready, willing, and able to succeed as an online communicator and learner.[1]

[1]Based on information from the Illinois Online Network, July 23, 2004, http://illinois.online.uillinois.edu/IONresources/onlineLearning/StudentProfile.asp

- *Intercultural.* How can you understand, respect, and adapt to people from diverse backgrounds?
- *Intellectual.* How should you analyze and evaluate the meaning of multiple and complex messages in an ever-changing world?
- *Societal.* How should you critically analyze and appropriately respond to public and mediated messages?
- *Ethical.* How should you apply ethical standards to personal and public communication in a variety of situations?

One of your challenges will be communicating at work when you get a job; in fact, effective communication is crucial for both keeping a job and succeeding at it. The *Chronicle of Higher Education* reports that college faculty members identify speaking, listening, problem solving, interpersonal skills, working in groups, and leading groups as essential skills for every college graduate.[3] A national survey of one thousand human resource managers concludes that oral communication skills are the *most* critical factors for obtaining jobs and advancing in a career.[4] Executives with Fortune 500 companies claim that the college graduates they employ need better communication skills as well as the ability to work in teams and with people from diverse backgrounds.[5]

The Association of American Colleges and Universities commissioned a study that asked business executives to rank the skills most needed in potential employees. The top three intellectual and practical skill areas are (1) teamwork skills and the ability to collaborate with others in a diverse group, (2) critical thinking and analytical reasoning skills, and (3) the ability to communicate effectively orally and in writing. Recent college graduates, 80 percent of whom are currently employed, rated the same three skills as most important to their career success.[6]

In the private sector, communication training has become big business. Hundreds of companies and thousands of consultants offer group seminars and private coaching sessions to help employees and clients learn communication skills—from conflict resolution and employee motivation to teamwork and public speaking. Instruction in communication also is available at most colleges and universities. Regardless of the challenge, you *can* become a more effective communicator by learning how to choose and use appropriate strategies and skills.

DEFINING COMMUNICATION

You know what communication is. After all, you do it every day, and most of the time you do it well. But what about the other times—when you're in the middle of a heated argument, when you can't think of what to say to a troubled friend, or when an important presentation falls short? In such situations you need more than common sense. Like most complex processes, effective communication requires knowledge, skills, and motivation.

Communication is the process of using verbal and nonverbal messages to generate meaning within and across various contexts, cultures, and channels.[7] This seemingly simple sentence provides a rich definition for understanding human communication. The key phrase is *generating meaning*. You generate meaning not only when you speak, write, act, and create visual images, but also when you listen, read, and react to messages. All the words in the world are literally "meaningless" unless someone makes sense out of them. Furthermore, as the definition of communication suggests, the meaning of a message can be very clear or completely misinterpreted depending on

- the context (where, when, with whom, and under what circumstances you communicate)
- the culture (the predominant characteristics, attitudes, and behaviors of the communicators)
- the channels (transmission via sight, sound, taste, smell, and/or touch)

The Seven Elements of Human Communication

In basic chemistry courses, you often begin by studying the elements—more than one hundred of them—starting with well-known favorites such as hydrogen, helium, carbon, and oxygen. Each element is a fundamental building block of chemistry with its own unique configuration of atomic particles. When studying communication, you should also begin by learning the **key elements**: the fundamental building blocks of human communication, which are listed in Figure 1.1.

When you learn about the chemical elements, you also learn about the physical laws that govern their nature and behavior. Chemical laws explain physical events that occur with *unvarying* uniformity under the *same* conditions. The "laws" of human communication are not as exact. They attempt to explain communicative acts that occur with *general* uniformity under *similar* conditions. We call these "laws" **axioms**: self-evident or universally recognized truths or beliefs. Functioning much like the laws of chemistry, communication axioms govern the nature of human communication. Just as the laws of chemistry tell us how hydrogen and oxygen act and react in certain conditions, communication axioms tell us how key elements such as *self* and *others* may act and react in a variety of contexts.

If we combine chemicals correctly, we can produce a myriad of results (e.g., two hydrogen atoms and one oxygen atom give us water). What happens if we put the *self* (you) and *others* (employer) together in a job interview context? We know that each element will affect the other. If the elements are combined skillfully, the result should be a successful job interview. In communication studies, we use **guiding principles** to help us select and apply the best strategies and skills for specific situations. Guiding principles go beyond axioms related to the nature of communication. They answer questions about *how* to communicate and *why* certain communication strategies succeed or fail.[8]

Communication is a complex, interactive process in which decision making is the one constant. As you can see in Figure 1.2, the phrase *decisions about* precedes every communication element. Effective communication requires much more than identifying seven elements. Your success requires the ability to make strategic decisions about each of those elements. For example, every communicative act occurs in a particular context and conveys specific content. Your decisions about adapting to

---

Figure 1.1   The Seven Key Elements of Human Communication

Key Elements	When You Communicate . . .
Self	you reveal aspects of your *self*.
Others	you share messages with *others*.
Purpose	you and others try to achieve a *purpose*.
Context	you interact within a *context*.
Content	you develop message *content*.
Structure	you *structure* your message.
Expression	you *express* yourself verbally and nonverbally.

that context and developing appropriate content for your message will influence whether and how well you achieve your communication purpose.

Figure 1.2 puts *you* (self) and *others* in an "inner sphere." Your *self* is relatively stable over time and instrumental in determining how you think and make decisions about communication.[9] Decisions about *others* (the person or persons with whom you communicate) influence how well you adapt to their characteristics and attitudes. Closely aligned with your *self* and *others* are decisions about your *purpose—* what you and others want to achieve through interaction. These relationships and intentions fuel the communication process.

Figure 1.2 also illustrates that *purpose* influences how you and others make decisions about the *context, content,* and *structure* of messages. *Expression* surrounds the communication process and represents how you decide to convey your messages to others.

Do decisions about the key elements represent everything you need to know about effective and ethical communication? Of course not. Rather, the seven elements provide a framework for strategic decision making about a complex process. If you believe there are only seven things you need to know about communication, you will be disappointed *and* unprepared to interact with others effectively.

Communication is a kind of chemistry in which you and others interact to create relationships and generate meaning. Regardless of what, where, when, why, or with whom you communicate, your ultimate success depends on how well you understand the interaction of the key elements, how well you make communication decisions informed by communication axioms, and how skillfully you apply the guiding principles of human communication. The following sections of this chapter discuss

| **Figure 1.2** | Interaction of the Seven Key Elements |

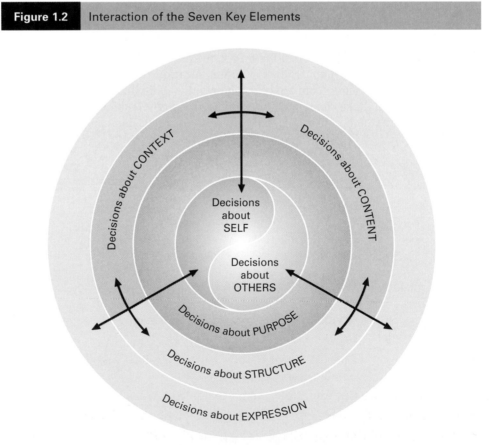

You are always communicating with your self. That is what you do when you think. You ask and answer simple, routine questions ranging from when to set the alarm or what to have for lunch to complex, consequential questions such as whether to accept a job offer or how to achieve your purpose in a presentation.

In communication studies, we refer to the process of communicating with your self as *intrapersonal communication*. The prefix *intra* means "within" or "inside," as in *intramural sports* (rather than *intercollegiate*) or *intravenous* (within a blood vessel). Thus, **intrapersonal communication** is the way in which you communicate within your self about your self to your self.[1]

[1]Graeme Burton and Richard Dimbley, *Between Ourselves: An Introduction to Interpersonal Communication*, 2nd ed. (London: Arnold, 1995), p. 2.

the seven key elements of communication, their related axioms (recognized assumptions or generalized laws about communication), and their associated guiding principles (how to select and apply communication strategies and skills effectively).

SELF

Self, the first key element of human communication, derives from this axiom *Communication Is Personal*. Your **self** is part of an invisible and unique inner sphere in which your unique characteristics and attitudes influence how effectively and ethically you communicate. Your *self* shares a nucleus with *others* at the center of the communication process (Figure 1.2). Without you, communication does not happen.

Just as no two people look alike, so no two people communicate alike. Your genetic code is one of a kind among the billions of genetic codes on earth. Your communication abilities and instincts are also one of a kind. Because you are the person inside your own skin, only you can understand your uniqueness and decide how to present it to others. Therefore, the guiding principle for the element of *self* is "Recognize how *your* characteristics and attitudes affect the way you communicate."

Key Element	Communication Axiom	Guiding Principle of Human Communication
Self	*Communication Is Personal*	Recognize how *your* characteristics and attributes affect the way you communicate.

The way you view your *self* is largely determined by your interactions with others. If you think you're smart, attractive, compassionate, funny, or brave, it's probably because others have told you so. If someone hugs you affectionately, you may feel loved and safe. If your boss or a colleague praises you, you may believe you are a valued employee.

Several questions related to the key element of *self* can help you appreciate why communication is unique to every individual:

- How do your characteristics, traits, skills, attitudes, values, and self-concept influence your communication goals and style?
- How credible are you when you communicate?
- Can you accurately recognize and assess a communication challenge?
- What is your ethical responsibility as a communicator?

OTHERS

In most successful communication situations, other people interact with you to share meaning. Just as it takes "two to tango," it takes at least two to communicate. The **other** can be one person or a large audience. Others can be listeners, readers, or observers. Your relationships with others affect what, when, where, why, and how you communicate, as expressed in the second axiom: *Communication Is Relational*.

Key Element	Axiom	Guiding Principle of Human Communication
Others	*Communication Is Relational*	Understand, respect, and adapt to other communicators.

A comment such as "Let's grab a drink after work" can mean one thing if the invitation comes from your best friend, a colleague who's been trying to date you, or your boss. When you share a message or respond to another person's message, you also are negotiating your relationship with that person. The nature of that relationship affects how you choose specific communication strategies and skills.

To connect with and adapt to others, you must understand your relationship with them. Ask yourself these questions:

- With whom are you communicating?
- How do their characteristics, traits, skills, attitudes, and beliefs affect the way they listen and respond?
- How can you learn more about them?
- How can you adapt to others and improve your communication with them?

PURPOSE

Purpose is closely connected to your *self* and *others*. It directs decision making about the other elements of human communication. The third axiom, *Communication Is Intentional*, recognizes that when you knowingly communicate with another person or group of people, you usually have a reason to create and send specific messages with specific purposes and meanings. That reason, or goal, can be as weighty as proposing marriage, securing a lucrative business contract, or resolving a world crisis. Understanding **purpose**—what you and others are trying to accomplish by communicating—is essential when deciding what and how to communicate.

Key Element	Axiom	Guiding Principle of Human Communication
Purpose	*Communication Is Intentional*	Determine your communication goal.

Even when you're not fully conscious of your intentions, your communication is purposeful. When you say, "Hi, how ya doin'?" as you pass a friend in the hallway, unconsciously nod as someone talks to you, or touch the arm of a colleague who has received bad news, you are maintaining and strengthening your friendships and working relationships. Even when you have no intention of communicating, someone else may perceive that you have sent a purposeful message. For example, if Fred overhears you talking about a good film you have seen, have you communicated with Fred? If you see your boss frowning, should you assume she wants you to know she is unhappy, worried, or angry? Thus, in a very general sense, some communication occurs regardless of whether you intend it to.

We take the position that *most* communication is intentional, but recognize that unintended communication can and does occur. Thus, effective communicators understand and take into account the fact that some of their behaviors may be perceived as communication when it was not intended as such.[10] We cannot predict or prescribe a formula for unintentional communication, other than making you aware that every time you use verbal and nonverbal messages to generate meaning, there may be unintended consequences. Although the best-intended messages may go astray, we can help you become a more effective, *intentional* communicator.

The following questions about purpose focus on the intentional nature of human communication while recognizing that some communication may not be understood as intended:

- Why are you communicating?
- What do you want others to know, think, believe, feel, or do as a result of communicating with them?
- How might others misunderstand or misinterpret your purpose?
- Can you identify the purpose of other communicators?

CONTEXT

All communication occurs within a **context**, the circumstances and setting in which communication takes place. Although this definition may appear simple—after all, communication must occur somewhere—context is anything but simple. The obvious but frequently overlooked fourth axiom, *Communicational Is Contextual*, deserves special attention.

Key Element	Axiom	Guiding Principle of Human Communication
Context	*Communication Is Contextual*	Adapt to the communication circumstances and setting.

Consider how the physical and psychological contexts in the following examples affect the implied meaning of this short question: Why are you here?

In the classroom: "Why are you here?" (Meaning: I can help you achieve your goals if I know why you have enrolled in this course.)

At work: "Why are you here?" (Meaning: We need to determine how your department will contribute to and benefit from this meeting.)

At a funeral: "Why are you here?" (Meaning: I thought you didn't like Gloria.)

How do the logistics of a setting affect the ways in which a speaker adapts to the circumstances and location of a presentation?

At the doctor's office: "Why are you here?" (Meaning: Tell me how you're feeling.)

At a political rally: "Why are you here?" (Meaning: What issues are most important to you?)

At home: "Why are you here?" (Meaning: You're late for school and need to get going.)

In each case, the meaning of "Why are you here?" differs depending on the context. There are three types of context to consider: psychosocial, logistical, and interactional.

TYPES OF CONTEXT
▶ Psychosocial
▶ Logistical
▶ Interactional

Psychosocial Context **Psychosocial context** refers to the overall psychological and cultural environment in which you live and communicate. When addressing the psychosocial context, consider your relationship with other communicators, their psychological traits, and the extent to which they share cultural attitudes, beliefs, values, and behaviors. Look at variables such as age, gender, race, ethnicity, religion, sexual orientation, levels of ability, and socioeconomic class.

The psychosocial context also includes your emotional history, personal experiences, and cultural background. Thus, if you have a history of conflict with a work colleague, your feelings, experience, and culture may influence your response to a suggestion made by that colleague.

Logistical Context **Logistical context** refers to the physical characteristics of a particular communication situation and focuses on a specific time, place, setting, and occasion. Are you talking to your friend privately or in a busy hallway? Are you speaking informally to colleagues in a staff meeting or welcoming guests to an important celebration? Is there a time limit for your oral report? Is the place where you are speaking comfortable?

Interactional Context **Interactional context** refers to the composition of the interaction—that is, whether communication occurs one-to-one, in groups, or between a speaker and an audience. There are three major types of interactional contexts: interpersonal, group, and presentational.

Context can be mediated; that is, it may include some*thing* that enables the communication to take place. When you and a friend talk on the phone, the telephone is the mediator; you can't communicate without it. Communication scholars Marianne Dainton and Elaine D. Zelley use the term **mediated communication** to describe any communication in which something exists between communicators. This "something" can be technology (such as a phone), or it can be a sign-language interpreter who helps a person who is deaf communicate with a hearing person. **Mass communication** is mediated communication between a person and a large, often unknown audience. Radio, television, film, and websites are forms of mass communication, as are newspapers, magazines, and books.

Usually, the person who shares a message using mass communication cannot see or hear how audience members react as they look and listen. Dainton and Zelley note that all mass communication is mediated, but not all mediated communication is for the masses. A personal e-mail message and a private telephone call are mediated by a computer and a telephone, but they are not used to communicate with large and often unknown audiences.[1]

[1]Marianne Dainton and Elaine D. Zelley, *Applying Communication Theory for Professional Life* (Thousand Oaks, CA: Sage, 2005), p. 197.

Interpersonal communication occurs when a limited number of people, usually two, interact for the purpose of sharing information, accomplishing a specific goal, or maintaining a relationship. Chapters 7, 8, and 9 focus on the fundamentals of interpersonal communication and strategies for effective communication in personal and professional relationships.

Group communication refers to the interaction of three or more interdependent people who interact for the purpose of achieving a common goal. A group is more than a collection of individuals who talk to one another; it is a complex system in which members depend upon one another. In other words, the actions and reactions of one group member affect everyone else in the group as well as the outcome of the group's work. Not only do you develop interpersonal relationships in groups, but you also rely on those relationships to achieve the group's common goal. Family members and friends, work groups, neighborhood associations, self-help groups, social clubs, and athletic teams engage in group communication. Chapters 10 and 11 focus on understanding how groups work and discuss strategies for effective group participation, leadership, decision making, and problem solving.

Presentational communication occurs when speakers generate meaning with audience members, who are usually present at the delivery of a presentation.[11] Presentational communication comes in many forms, from formal commencement addresses, campaign speeches, and conference lectures to informal class reports, staff briefings, and PowerPoint-aided training. You will make many presentations in your lifetime—at school, at work, at family and social gatherings, or at community events. Most businesses, organizations, and associations value the contributions of effective presenters. Chapters 12 through 16 explain how to use the guiding principles of communication to prepare and deliver successful presentations.

Several questions can help you understand the influence of context on communication:

- Under what circumstances will you communicate?
- What role are you assuming when communicating in this setting and situation?
- How can you adapt to the logistics of the place where you will be communicating?
- Does the specific situation or occasion require special adaptations?

INTERACTIONAL CONTEXTS
► Interpersonal Communication
► Group Communication
► Presentational Communication

Many people assume that creating messages that generate meaning is the sole responsibility of a speaker. This notion is not an accurate description of what happens when people communicate. Rather, communication is a highly interactive and collaborative process in which you and others construct meaning together. Thus, if you do not actively participate in the co-construction of a conversation, you may be seen as disinterested, aloof, and noncommunicative.[1]

Communication is a transaction between you and others. Rob Anderson and Veronica Ross put it this way: "Meaning emerges from relationships because it is in relationships, not in our heads, that our lives are led."[2] For example, say two students receive a grade of B. The grade represents the instructor's message to students about their performance. One student may be

delighted with the B, but the other may be disappointed. The "happy" B student may also decide that the instructor is pleased with his work, whereas the "disappointed" B student may worry that the instructor doesn't like her. No matter how carefully you construct a message you believe is clear and appropriate for others, your purpose, the context, and its ultimate meaning depend on others who see, hear, read, or experience it.[3]

[1]Rae Sonnenmeier, "Co-construction of Messages During Facilitated Communication," *Facilitated Communication Digest* 2 (February 1993), p. 7.

[2]Rob Anderson and Veronica Ross, *Questions of Communication: A Practical Introduction to Theory*, 3rd ed. (New York: St. Martin's, 2002), p. 66.

[3]Ibid.

CONTENT

Content refers to the ideas, information, and opinions you collect and select for inclusion in a message. Your content can be an original thought or something from a report, article, website, television show, or speech. Animals and humans communicate content using messages. However, the symbolic nature of human language is "unique in its ability to communicate or convey an open-ended volume of concepts."[12] Put another way, humans can invent new words, say sentences that have never been said before, and communicate creative ideas. Most animals only have a limited number of messages they can send and comprehend. Our unique ability to generate meaning by combining letters and/or sounds is expressed in the fifth axiom: *Communication Is Symbolic.*

Key Element	Axiom	Guiding Principle of Human Communication
Content	*Communication Is Symbolic*	Select appropriate message content.

A symbol is something that represents something else. In language, a **symbol** is a grouping of letters or words used to represent an object, idea, quantity, quality, concept, relationship, element, or function. A symbol can also be a nonverbal image or action, such as a corporate logo, a recognizable hand gesture, or a universal road sign.

Symbols are *not* the things they represent. There is absolutely nothing in the letters *c*, *a*, and *t* that looks, smells, sounds, or feels like a cat. And even though dictionaries may define *cat* as a carnivorous mammal domesticated as a catcher of rodents and as a pet, you would be hard pressed to imagine what a cat looks, smells, sounds, or feels like if you had never seen one. Moreover, your likes or dislikes about cats have no connection to the selection of the letters *c*, *a*, and *t* to represent this species of animal. You may have great affection for and interest in cats, but someone else may find them a nuisance responsible for serious allergic reactions.

Because there is no tangible relationship between a symbol and the thing it represents, you always have the potential to be misunderstood. For example, what does it mean to you if someone says that it's cold outside? If you live in the far north, "cold" can mean more than forty degrees Fahrenheit below zero. If you live at sea level near the equator, "cold" can mean forty degrees Fahrenheit above zero.

The symbolic nature of communication leads to questions about how to develop and interpret the content of verbal and nonverbal messages:

- What ideas, information, and opinions should you include in a message?

- How should you support your ideas and opinions?

- What strategies will enhance others' comprehension, analysis, empathy, and appreciation of your messages?

- How well do you interpret messages from others?

STRUCTURE

The sixth axiom claims that *Communication Is Structured*. When you understand your self and others, have a purpose for communicating, have analyzed the context, and have selected relevant content, you face the challenge of organizing these elements into a coherent message.

Key Element	Axiom	Guiding Principle of Human Communication
Structure	*Communication Is Structured*	Organize message content.

The word *structure* refers to "the way in which parts are arranged or put together to form a whole."[13] You would not build a house without knowing something about who will live in it, the location and setting, and the materials needed to assemble it. House construction involves putting all these elements together into a well-designed, durable structure. The same is true in communication. **Structure** involves organizing appropriate content into a coherent and purposeful message.

Questions about structure recognize that messages are composed of many parts. Ask yourself these questions:

- What are the most effective ways to organize your message given your purpose, others, the context, and the content?

- How can your organizational structure generate attention and interest?

- In what order should you share your ideas and information?

- What skills and techniques will improve your ability to structure your message?

EXPRESSION

When two children argue on a playground, one child may yell, "Take it back!" and the other shrieks, "I will not!" The fact that you can't "take it back" is embodied in the seventh axiom: *Communication Is Irreversible*. Whether you say something you regret or mistakenly hit the "Send" key on your e-mail before you're ready, you can't undo communication. At best, you can try to clarify what you've said or try to repair unintended consequences. You can sincerely apologize to someone about something you've said, but you can't literally "take it back."

Key Element	Axiom	Guiding Principle of Human Communication
Expression	*Communication Is Irreversible*	Plan how to convey your message to others.

How does the context of a videoconference affect the nature and outcome of participant communication?

The **expression** of a message requires deciding how that message will be conveyed to others. Communication **channels** are the various physical and electronic media through which messages are transmitted. You can transmit messages using one or more of your sensory channels: sight, sound, touch, taste, and smell. Although we use sight and sound most frequently when we speak and listen to others, do not dismiss the power of the other three senses. Perfumes and colognes are designed to communicate attractiveness or mask offensive odors. Being asked to join someone for a carefully prepared dinner or expensive restaurant meal can communicate a great deal about how the other person feels about you. Most powerful of all is touch, be it a warm hug or a rough shove.

However, the communication channels you use today extend well beyond a face-to-face environment and into the far reaches of cyberspace. As Bob Johansen of the Institute for the Future notes, "the personal computer is gradually becoming the interpersonal computer."[14] Technology enables you to enlist a variety of electronic media: telephones, television, computers, and the World Wide Web. Whether you're engaged in an online chat or participating in a videoconference, the media you choose and use affect the nature and outcome of your communication.

Because communication cannot be undone, effective communicators carefully choose strategies and skills that will help them express their intended messages. Questions about expression focus on how well you deliver and receive messages:

- Which channels are most appropriate given your purpose, the other communicators, the context, the content, and the message's structure?
- What skills and techniques will improve your ability to express your message?
- How effectively do you express and listen to verbal and nonverbal messages?
- How can practice help you prepare for a communication experience?

Applying the Seven Guiding Principles of Communication

The seven guiding principles derive from the key elements and axioms to form a unified, comprehensive model of the communication process that can be applied to almost every communication challenge (Figure 1.3). These principles apply regardless of whether you are talking to a friend, delivering a speech to a large audience, planning a business meeting, or crafting an online presentation. They will help you make decisions about the nature of a communication challenge, the strategies that effectively address that challenge, and the skills needed to achieve your communication goal.

When you communicate, analyze your own characteristics and attitudes (self), the characteristics and attitudes of the people with whom you communicate (others), and what you and others hope to achieve when communicating (purpose). Consider when and where you are communicating (context), the substance of your message (content), how you will organize your message (structure), and the different ways to deliver your message (expression).

Keep in mind that the seven guiding principles provide a framework for strategic decisions about communication. You can evaluate how well you engage in this decision-making process by converting each guiding principle into a question. For example, to assess decisions about your *self*, you can ask: Have I considered and adapted to the ways in which my characteristics and attitudes affect how I communicate? To assess your decisions about *others*, ask yourself: Have I made decisions that will help me connect with and adapt to others?

The guiding principles are more than a "To Do" list for effective communication. No matter how well you structure the content of your message, you won't achieve your purpose if you make poor decisions about the other guiding principles. If you offend your listeners or use words they don't understand, you won't achieve your purpose or enhance your credibility. If you dress perfectly for a job interview but fail to speak clearly and persuasively, you may lose out on a career opportunity. If you hug someone who dislikes being touched, you've chosen the wrong communication channel.

Figure 1.4 offers scenarios in each of the three interactional contexts (interpersonal, group, and presentational communication). Review each scenario and observe how the key elements and guiding principles provide a foundation for making critical communication decisions in each situation.

Figure 1.3	Communication Elements, Axioms, and Guiding Principles

Key Elements	Communication Axioms	Guiding Principles of Communication
Self	*Communication Is Personal*	Recognize how *your* characteristics and attitudes affect the way you communicate.
Others	*Communication Is Relational*	Understand, respect, and adapt to other communicators.
Purpose	*Communication Is Intentional*	Determine your communication purpose.
Context	*Communication Is Contextual*	Adapt to the communication circumstances and setting.
Content	*Communication Is Symbolic*	Select appropriate message content.
Structure	*Communication Is Structured*	Organize message content.
Expression	*Communication Is Irreversible*	Plan how to convey your message to others.

Figure 1.4	Key Elements across Communication Contexts		
	Interpersonal Communication	**Group Communication**	**Presentational Communication**
SCENARIO	*You hear that your boss is dissatisfied with the quality of a project you just finished. You share some of her concerns given the last-minute complications and staff problems you encountered. The boss wants to meet with you in private at the end of the day.*	*You are appointed to serve as the student representative on a screening committee charged with reviewing and recommending candidates for the job of college president. Committee members include administrators and faculty as well as local business and community leaders.*	*In addition to turning in a major research report, you have been assigned the task of presenting your results to the class in a ten-minute oral report. The instructor has invited other professors to drop in on the class to listen to student presentations.*
Self	• How do you feel about this upcoming meeting—anxious or eager? How can you develop your boss's trust in you and your competence?	• How do you feel about serving on this committee—intimidated, honored, or ego-boosted? Why do you think you were chosen for this committee?	• How do you feel about presenting to this particular audience—nervous or confident? How do you think your report will compare with others that will be presented?
Others	• How well do you know and get along with your boss? What kind of pressure is she experiencing? How can you adapt to your boss's characteristics and opinions? Are there cultural differences you should take into account?	• What do you know about the other committee members? How can you get to know them better? What do they expect from you? How can you adapt to their personal agendas? How will their status affect your comfort level and ability to interact?	• How will you adapt to your professor, classmates, and visiting faculty members? Is the instructor most important? Can adapting to students help boost your confidence? How can you impress the visiting professors?
Purpose	• What do *you* want to accomplish? Do you want to show you did a good job despite the problems, discuss bigger issues, and/or preserve your good name and good will with management?	• What do you hope to achieve? Do you want to make sure student perspectives are considered? Do you want to impress faculty and business leaders and secure good references from them in the future?	• What are your goals? What's the purpose of the assignment? Should you highlight an interesting finding, demonstrate your mathematical prowess, and/or make sure you get an A?
Context	• Can you be prepared by the end of the workday? How will your boss's office environment and your previous dealings with her affect the interactions? How long will the meeting last?	• Where and when will the group meet? How long will the meetings last? Is the psychosocial climate conducive to open interaction and effective collaboration? Will the group have access to communication technology?	• How can you adapt a major research paper to a 10-minute talk? Does the classroom have the technological resources you need for the presentation? When will you speak—first, third, or last?
Content	• What information and explanations do you need? How will you gather and analyze information that supports your ideas? What arguments will you develop and/or support?	• What ideas and opinions should you share with the committee? How will you phrase student concerns and positions? Are you prepared to ask and answer questions?	• What parts of the report should you include? What is the central idea of your presentation? How can you make the presentation interesting? How can you promote audience comprehension and appreciation?
Structure	• How should you begin the conversation? How will you organize your explanation (best reason first or chronologically)? What should you emphasize at the end of the conversation?	• Does the committee have an agenda for its business? What kind of decision-making procedures will be used? When will you contribute your ideas and opinions in the process? How will you organize your comments?	• How will you gain and maintain audience interest? What organizational pattern should you use? Which ideas or key points should you emphasize? How will you conclude?
Expression	• Would it be appropriate to use notes when you speak? Should you shake hands with your boss at the beginning of the meeting? Should you assume a relaxed or formal posture? Will your speaking style be formal or informal?	• Should you speak formally and respectfully or casually? Should you e-mail members to further advocate and reinforce your positions? How will you regulate your tone of voice and body language during the meetings? What should you wear to the meetings?	• Will you use a manuscript or notes when you speak? What visual aids would be appropriate? Will you hand out an outline or summary? Have you practiced your presentation? Can you maintain eye contact with your audience for most of your talk?

The Communication Process

Many of us have photos of friends and family standing around talking at a wedding or party. Suppose you see a photo of a guest holding up a broken wine glass. Although the person in the photo is captured in a moment of communication, the picture tells you very little about the background, complexity, and outcome of the communication situation. Why is the glass broken? Was it an accident or a tradition? What about the context of the situation might tell you more? What can you learn from examining the person's facial expression and posture? As this example illustrates, communication is not a "thing" you can hold in your hand like a photograph. Communication is an ongoing, dynamic process that develops and changes over time.

A **process** is a set of constantly changing actions, elements, and functions that bring about a result. For example, the digestive process includes ever-changing, interacting body functions that change food into life-giving nutrients. Communication pioneer David Berlo described a process as something that is constantly moving and in which the elements interact with one another.[15] Thus, the characteristics of other communicators can affect your purpose, your choice of content can affect decisions about expression, and your personal values can determine how you adapt to the context in which you communicate. Unlike a physical process, which may follow an established pathway or predictable set of steps, communication is a psychological and behavioral process that asks you to decide on the right course of action.

COMMUNICATION MODELS

To talk about communication, we often use **communication models**, or pictures that simplify and illustrate the process. Communication scholars Rob Anderson and Veronica Ross write that "a model of communication—or any other process, object, or event—is a way of simplifying the complex interactions of elements in order to clarify relevant relationships, and perhaps to help predict outcomes."[16] Communication models

- identify the basic components involved in the communication process
- show how the various components relate to and interact with one another
- help explain why a communicative act did or did not achieve its intended purpose

EARLY COMMUNICATION MODELS

Since the mid 1950s, numerous models have been offered to explain how communication works as a process. Throughout the years, these models have become more sophisticated, more comprehensive, and more useful. Figure 1.5 depicts two early models.

The earliest type of communication model, a **linear communication model**, functions in only one direction: a source creates a message and sends it through a channel to reach a receiver. Linear models identify several important components but do not directly address the interactive nature of human communication.

Theorists next devised **interactive communication models**, which include the concepts of noise and feedback to show that communication is not an unobstructed or one-way street. When feedback is added, each communicator becomes both the source and receiver of messages. When noise is added, every component becomes susceptible to disruption.

Feedback   **Feedback** is any verbal or nonverbal response you can see or hear from others. A person giving feedback may smile or frown, ask questions or challenge your

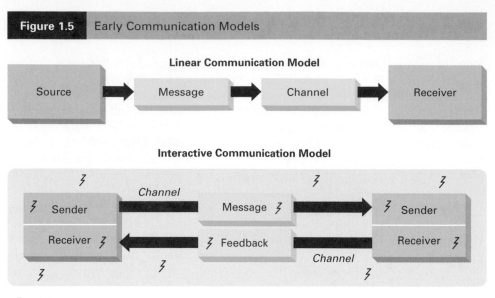

Figure 1.5   Early Communication Models

Linear Communication Model

Source → Message → Channel → Receiver

Interactive Communication Model

Channel

Sender → Message → Sender

Receiver ← Feedback ← Receiver

Channel

⚡ = Noise

ideas, listen intently or tune out. If you accurately interpret feedback, you can assess how well your message is being received and whether it is likely to achieve your purpose. Feedback is also a control mechanism that can help you adjust your message while you are speaking.

The president of a New York marketing and design company, in telling us how much he relies on feedback, said, "You *know* when they are with you." Another chief executive officer confessed that when he fumbled through a talk and rambled, he noticed that he was losing listeners and then became even more unnerved. Expert communicators are sensitive to listener reactions. They use feedback—positive or

What kinds of noise does Nobel Peace Prize laureate Muhammad Yunus (first left) of the Grameen Bank of Bangladesh encounter as he interacts with sponsors, participants, and media at a conference in Beijing, China?

Noise can affect every key element in the communication process. As you consider each guiding principle of human communication, be prepared to deal with noise that may threaten the intended outcome of your communication.

- *Noise and Self.* Personal problems and anxieties can impede your ability to communicate.
- *Noise and Others.* Inaccurate analysis of others' characteristics and opinions can prevent you from achieving your purpose.
- *Noise and Purpose.* Unclear thinking about your purpose can make your message difficult to understand.

- *Noise and Context.* Distraction within and outside a room can divert the attention and interest of others.
- *Noise and Content.* Invalid research and unclear explanations can make a message difficult to comprehend and accept.
- *Noise and Structure.* A poorly organized message can decrease comprehension and influence.
- *Noise and Expression.* A weak voice, defensive posture, or faulty computer hookup can distort the interpretation of a message.

negative—to evaluate whether and how well they are achieving their purpose, and then they adjust their message accordingly.

Noise   Interactive communication models also recognize obstacles that can prevent a message from reaching its receivers as intended. **Noise** is a communication term used to describe these inhibiting factors. It is a lot more than static on a telephone line. Generally, there are two sources of noise: external and internal. **External noise** consists of elements in the environment or communication context that interfere with effective communication. Noise is often an audible problem: a police siren outside the window, a soft speaking voice, or a difficult-to-understand accent. However, noise is not limited to only the sounds you hear. An uncomfortably warm setting, an unpleasant odor, a crowded room, or even bright and distracting wall hangings can all interfere with your ability to be an attentive and effective communicator.

Although external noise can be any distracting element within your environment, internal noise is a mental distraction within your *self*. **Internal noise** consists of thoughts, feelings, and attitudes that interfere with your ability to communicate and understand a message as it was intended. A listener preoccupied with personal thoughts can miss or misinterpret a message. As a speaker, you may be distracted and worried about how you look during a presentation instead of focusing your attention on your audience. Or, you may be thinking about your upcoming vacation plans rather than listening carefully to a coworker's instructions. Such preoccupation can inhibit your ability to speak and listen effectively.

Encoding and Decoding   With these early models, communicators have two important functions: they serve as both the source and receiver of messages. The communication **source** is a person or group of people who create a message intended to produce a particular response. Your message has no meaning until it arrives at a **receiver**, another person or group of people who interpret and evaluate your message. These two actions, sending and receiving, are called *encoding* and *decoding*.

Most of this textbook is devoted to strategies for effectively encoding and decoding messages. When you communicate with others, you *encode* your ideas; you transform them into verbal and nonverbal messages, or "codes." Thus, **encoding** is the decision-making process by which you create and send **messages** that evoke meaning.

To encode messages effectively, you need to consider all seven elements of human communication.

Decoding converts a "code" or message sent by someone else into a form you can understand and use. Decoding is the decision-making process you use to interpret, evaluate, and respond to the meaning of verbal and nonverbal messages. Certainly your own unique characteristics and attitudes influence the decoding process. Other factors that affect decoding are your perceptions of other communicators, their purpose, the context, the message content and structure, and how the message is expressed.

A TRANSACTIONAL MODEL OF HUMAN COMMUNICATION

Communication is more complex than the processes depicted in linear or interactive models. In reality, communication is a *simultaneous* transaction in which we continuously exchange verbal and nonverbal messages and share meanings. Transactional communication is also fluid, not a "thing" that happens. The nature and history of your relationships as well as your hopes and expectations affect how you interact with other communicators. **Transactional communication models** recognize that we send and receive messages at the same time within specific contexts. Even when we listen to someone, our nonverbal reactions send messages to the speaker.

The transactional model illustrates the interrelationships among the key elements of human communication. Figure 1.6 "freezes" the communication process to reveal the model's interacting components.

With the transactional model, encoding and decoding messages require decisions about all seven guiding principles. Your ability to make strategic decisions about every element affects whether and how well you achieve your communication goal.

In an ideal communication transaction, you have a clear purpose in mind. You have adapted your message to others and the context. Your message contains appropriate and well-structured content as it is expressed through one or more channels with a minimum of interfering noise. Effective communicators accept the fact that they may never create or deliver a perfect message, but they never stop trying to reach that ideal.

Figure 1.6	Transactional Communication Model

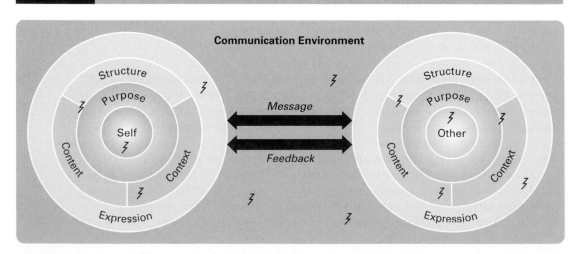

⚡ = Noise

Communication Theories, Strategies, and Skills

Most of us would laugh if someone tried to become a champion tennis player, a professional airline pilot, or a gourmet chef just by reading a book. Likewise, no textbook or classroom lecture alone can teach you to become a more effective communicator. The best way to study communication is to apply an understanding of communication theories to appropriate strategies and skills. Communication theories, strategies, and skills are inseparable. Mastering isolated skills will not help you resolve a conflict, lead a discussion, or plan a presentation. Understanding the relationship among theories, strategies, and skills will.

LEARN ABOUT THEORIES

Theories are statements that explain how the world works. They try to describe, explain, and predict events and behavior. Karl Popper describes theories as "nets to catch what we call 'the world': to rationalize, to explain, and to master it."[17] Communication theories have emerged from extensive observation, empirical research, and rigorous scholarship. They help you understand what is happening when you communicate, and why communication is sometimes effective and sometimes ineffective.

However, learning about theories in isolation will not make you a more effective communicator. Theories do not necessarily tell you what to do or what to say. Nevertheless, without theories, we would have difficulty understanding why or how a particular strategy works or how strategies and skills interact.

CHOOSE APPROPRIATE STRATEGIES

Strategies are the specific plans of action you select to help you communicate. The word *strategy* comes from the Greek word *strategia* and refers to the office of a military general. Like great generals, effective communicators marshal their "forces" to achieve a specific purpose: to comfort a friend, resolve a conflict, lead a group discussion, or deliver an informative presentation. Throughout this textbook, you will read about individual and group strategies, including ways to listen more effectively, procedures for managing group discussions, and guidelines for organizing the key points of a presentation.

However, learning about strategies is not enough. Effective strategies are based on theories. If you don't understand theory, you won't know why strategies work in one situation and fail in another. Strategies based on theory help you understand when, where, why, and how to use a particular strategy most effectively.

DEVELOP SKILLS

Communication **skills** refer to your acquired ability to accomplish communication goals during the course of an interaction.[18] Communication skills are the tools or techniques you use to collaborate with a colleague, prepare a meeting agenda, and speak loudly enough to be heard by a large audience. Throughout this textbook you will read about many communication skills: how to be more assertive, how to think critically, how to resolve conflicts, how to speak clearly, how to do research, how to organize a message, and how to explain complex concepts or persuade others.

Like strategies, skills are most effective when grounded in theory. Without that grounding, you may not understand when and why to use a particular strategy or skill to its best advantage. For example, in the hope of improving group morale, you decide to forgo using a well-structured, problem-solving agenda at a critical meeting when, in fact, group morale is low because your approach to problem solving is disorganized and wastes their time. However, if you are familiar with the theory of

A habit is something you do so frequently and for so long that you've stopped thinking about why, when, how, and whether you do it. Effective and ethical communication can become a habit—something that is second nature to you. Stephen R. Covey, author of *The Seven Habits of Highly Effective People*, gives us a definition of habit that also describes good communication. In Covey's opinion, **habits** require knowledge, skills, and desire. Knowledge plays a role similar to theories and strategies; it describes *what* to do and *why* to do it. Skills represent *how* to do it. And motivation is the desire to communicate effectively and ethically; you *want* to do it. Covey maintains that to make something a habit, you have to have all three. Effective and ethical communication relies as much on your attitude (*want to do it*) as it does on your knowledge and skills.[1]

Covey addresses the challenge of listening to illustrate the three components of a habit:

1. *Knowledge.* I may be ineffective in my interaction with my work associates, my spouse, or my children because I constantly tell them what I think but I never really listen to them. Unless I search out correct principles of human interaction, I may not even *know* I need to listen.
2. *Skills.* Even if I do know that to interact effectively with others I really need to listen to them, I may not have the skill. I may not know how to listen deeply to another human being.
3. *Desire.* But knowing I need to listen and knowing how to listen is not enough. Unless I *want* to listen, unless I have the desire, it won't be a habit in my life. Creating a habit requires work in all three dimensions.

[1]Stephen R. Covey, *The Seven Habits of Effective People* (New York: Simon and Schuster, 1989), p. 48.

reflective thinking, you will know that using a standard agenda helps a group to follow a series of practical steps to solve problems. In our eagerness to communicate effectively, we may grab ready-made, easy-to-use "tricks of the trade" that are inappropriate or ineffective. Enlisting skills without an understanding of theories and strategies can make communication inefficient and ineffective as well as a frustrating experience for everyone.

Ethical Communication

How would you feel if you learned that

- a corporate executive hid lavish, personal expenditures while laying off employees
- a teacher gave higher grades to students he liked and lower grades to students who annoyed him
- a close friend shared your most intimate secrets with people you don't know or like
- a politician used racial slurs in private to describe a disgruntled group of constituents

Most of these behaviors are not illegal. They are, however, unethical.

Theories answer *why* (Why does communication work this way?), strategies answer *what* (What should work in this communication situation?), and skills answer *how* (How should I express myself?). An effective communicator also must be able to answer the *whether* questions. That is, whether you should communicate as planned: Is it right? Is it fair? Is it deceptive?[19]

Ethical issues arise whenever we communicate because communication has consequences. What we say and do can help or hurt others. Sadly, the theories,

The National Communication Association Credo for Ethical Communication

Questions of right and wrong arise whenever people communicate. Ethical communication is fundamental to responsible thinking, decision making, and the development of relationships and communities within and across contexts, cultures, channels, and media. Moreover, ethical communication enhances human worth and dignity by fostering truthfulness, fairness, responsibility, personal integrity, and respect for self and others. We believe that unethical communication threatens the well-being of individuals and the society in which we live. Therefore we, the members of the NCA, endorse and are committed to practicing the following principles of ethical communication:

- We advocate truthfulness, accuracy, honesty, and reason as essential to the integrity of communication.
- We endorse freedom of expression, diversity of perspective, and tolerance of dissent to achieve the informed and responsible decision making fundamental to a civil society.
- We strive to understand and respect other communicators before evaluating and responding to their messages.
- We promote access to communication resources and opportunities as necessary to fulfill human potential and contribute to the well-being of families, communities, and society.
- We promote communication climates of caring and mutual understanding that respect the unique needs and characteristics of individual communicators.
- We condemn communication that degrades individuals and humanity through distortion, intimidation, coercion, and violence, and through the expression of intolerance and hatred.
- We are committed to the courageous expression of personal conviction in pursuit of fairness and justice.
- We advocate sharing information, opinions, and feelings when facing significant choices while also respecting privacy and confidentiality.
- We accept responsibility for the short- and long-term consequences of our own communication and expect the same of others.[1]

---

[1]The NCA Credo for Ethical Communication was developed at a 1999 summer conference sponsored by the NCA. The credo was adopted and endorsed by the Legislative Council of the NCA in November 1999 (www.natcom.org/aboutNCA/Policies/Platform.html).

---

strategies, and skills in this textbook can and have been used for less-than-ethical purposes. Unscrupulous speakers have misled trusting citizens and consumers. Bigots have used hate speech to oppress and discriminate against those who are "different." Self-centered people have destroyed the reputations of their rivals by spreading cruel rumors among friends and colleagues.

Ethics requires an understanding of whether communication behaviors meet agreed-upon standards of right and wrong.[20] The National Communication Association (NCA) provides a Credo for Ethical Communication (see CommEthics feature). In Latin, the word *credo* means "I believe." Thus, an ethics credo is a belief statement about what it means to be an ethical communicator.

The ancient Greek philosopher Aristotle offered the "doctrine of the mean" as a practical way of looking at ethical communication.[21] He suggested that when you face an ethical decision, you should select an *appropriate* reaction somewhere between two extremes—such as a response somewhere between expressing mild annoyance at one extreme or uncontrolled rage at the other extreme. Aristotle maintained that anyone can become angry; that is easy. But to be angry at the right things, with the right people, to the right degree, at the right time, for the right purpose, and in the right way—is worthy of praise.[22]

All of us face decisions about whether we should communicate in a particular way at a particular time for a particular purpose. Is this an appropriate way to let my friend know I'm angry? Is this an appropriate way to persuade this particular audience? Is this the most appropriate way to motivate the members of my group? The answers to these questions have ethical dimensions and far-reaching consequences.

How do Liberian President Ellen Johnson Sirleaf's ethical decisions about communicating in a particular way at a particular time for a particular purpose affect her credibility as a world leader?

If expressing your personal conviction has the potential to harm rather than help others, Aristotle would urge you to reconsider your actions. However, there are no "ten commandments" of ethics. In the end, you must decide whether you have communicated appropriately and ethically.

Effective communicators accept and practice ethical communication. They understand that their personal credibility and the believability of their messages depend on others seeing them as honest and ethical. Ethical decision making focuses on all seven key elements of human communication. The guiding principles in Figure 1.7 can help you practice and assess the ethical dimensions of communication.

Figure 1.7   Guiding Principles of Ethical Communication

Key Elements	Guiding Principles of Ethical Communication
Self	Value truthfulness, accuracy, honesty, and reason.
Others	Strive to understand and respect others before evaluating their messages.
Purpose	Seek communication goals that benefit both you *and* others. Accept responsibility for the consequences of your communication.
Context	Promote a climate of caring and mutual understanding.
Content	Use valid information and opinions to support your ideas. Respect privacy and confidentiality.
Structure	Structure messages to promote comprehension and minimize misunderstandings.
Expression	Openly express your personal convictions. Condemn intolerance and deception.

Communication Challenge

Elements in Action

Directions: Use the following alphabet letters to identify the *primary* communication element operating in the twelve scenarios that follow.

a. Self   e. Content
b. Others   f. Structure
c. Purpose   g. Expression
d. Context

_____ 1. Although Marge wants to use PowerPoint at the afternoon staff meeting, she knows that the sun will create a glare in the unshaded room. Instead, she decides to print her key ideas onto several flip chart pages.

_____ 2. Because Kentry knows that he is respected and trusted by his friends, he feels confident that he can get them to change their minds about going downtown after midnight.

_____ 3. Ross likes to wear all-black outfits and his black leather jacket to class. On the day of an oral report, however, he decides to wear a pair of tan slacks, blue shirt, and striped tie to gain attention and look more earnest and professional.

_____ 4. When Jessie realizes that her parents are reluctant to let her study in Russia during the summer, she collects several Study Abroad brochures and selects the three companies that emphasize student safety and supervision as their highest priority. She shares these brochures with her parents in the hopes they will change their mind.

_____ 5. Cheryce spends several hours preparing an agenda for an upcoming meeting. Although she has many other things to do before the meeting begins, she wants everyone to have a working agenda to guide them through the discussion.

_____ 6. Lawrence knows that he will have difficulty pronouncing *Weyerhaeuser* during his upcoming job interview with the company. He calls the corporate headquarters and asks the receptionist to sound out the correct way to pronounce the company's name.

_____ 7. Nicole knows that most audience members won't change their minds about gun control after hearing her speak. Instead, she decides to talk about why she and her colleagues changed *their* minds about gun control. She will consider her speech a success if the audience leaves respecting her position.

_____ 8. Uzoma understands that his way of doing business in Nigeria may be misunderstood in the United States. He consults with two of his American colleagues before meeting with potential clients to make sure that he understands, respects, and adapts to their perspectives.

_____ 9. Eric knows that his audience won't be very interested in listening to his logical arguments about recycling. Instead of sharing statistics on the need for and benefits of recycling, he decides to tell a funny story about his first research "dumpster dives" and then to describe well-known communities that transformed their neighborhoods—physically and socially—by joining forces to recycle.

_____ 10. Grace has just had an argument with her friend Tasha. When another friend calls and asks Grace to help plan a surprise birthday party for Tasha, Grace agrees. She hopes that her actions will show Tasha that she wants to continue their friendship.

_____ 11. Allan and Lisa have just bought a piece of furniture that must be assembled. As Lisa starts pulling apart the box to get at the pieces, Allan asks her to stop so he can read the directions out loud. He reminds her that the last time they didn't follow a set of step-by-step instructions, they ended up with a door hung backward.

_____ 12. Jay has been invited to present his research findings at a public seminar. Although he could spend all of his time explaining the complexities of the research methods he used, he decides to put the methodology and resulting data on his public website. For his talk, he will only describe how his research findings could be used to improve health care.

Communication Assessment

Oral Communication Survey

Directions: On a 5-point scale, where 5 is "Extremely Important" and 1 is "Not at All Important," how would you rate the following types of knowledge, strategies, and skills as important to you in becoming a more effective oral communicator? Please circle one number for each item.

Item	Extremely Important	Very Important	Somewhat Important	Not Very Important	Not at All Important
1. Understanding the communication process—how and why it works	5	4	3	2	1
2. Reducing nervousness, apprehension, or speaking anxiety	5	4	3	2	1
3. Learning about and adapting to others	5	4	3	2	1
4. Communicating sensitively and ethically	5	4	3	2	1
5. Influencing others to modify their attitudes and/or behavior	5	4	3	2	1
6. Using and interpreting nonverbal communication effectively	5	4	3	2	1
7. Using humor appropriately	5	4	3	2	1
8. Listening effectively to others	5	4	3	2	1
9. Developing good interpersonal relationships	5	4	3	2	1
10. Holding an interesting conversation	5	4	3	2	1
11. Using your voice effectively	5	4	3	2	1
12. Managing and resolving interpersonal conflicts	5	4	3	2	1
13. Using gestures, body language, and eye contact effectively	5	4	3	2	1
14. Being a good interviewer (conducting the interview)	5	4	3	2	1
15. Being a good interviewee (the person interviewed)	5	4	3	2	1
16. Adapting to people from different backgrounds and cultures	5	4	3	2	1
17. Serving as a group or team leader	5	4	3	2	1
18. Researching information for a group discussion or presentation	5	4	3	2	1
19. Using visual aids and presentation software	5	4	3	2	1
20. Telling stories effectively	5	4	3	2	1

Item	Extremely Important	Very Important	Somewhat Important	Not Very Important	Not at All Important
21. Chairing or conducting a meeting	5	4	3	2	1
22. Holding the attention and interest of others when you speak	5	4	3	2	1
23. Preparing and delivering an effective presentation or speech	5	4	3	2	1
24. Explaining complex ideas to others	5	4	3	2	1
25. Inspiring or motivating others	5	4	3	2	1
26. Asserting your ideas and opinions	5	4	3	2	1
27. Deciding what to say to a person, group, or audience	5	4	3	2	1
28. Involving other people in a productive discussion	5	4	3	2	1
29. Organizing the content of a presentation or speech	5	4	3	2	1
30. Improving communication with close friends, romantic partners, and family members	5	4	3	2	1
31. Beginning and ending a presentation or speech	5	4	3	2	1
32. Understanding how your beliefs and perceptions communicate	5	4	3	2	1
33. Using appropriate and effective words	5	4	3	2	1
34. Developing strong, valid arguments	5	4	3	2	1
35. Improving communication in business and professional settings	5	4	3	2	1
36. Comforting others	5	4	3	2	1
37. Other: _____	5	4	3	2	1

Key Terms

axiom	guiding principle	other
channel	habit	presentational communication
communication	interactional context	process
communication model	interactive communication model	psychosocial context
content	internal noise	purpose
context	interpersonal communication	receiver
culture	intrapersonal communication	self
decoding	key element	skill
encoding	linear communication model	source
ethics	logistical context	strategy
expression	mass communication	structure
external noise	mediated communication	symbol
feedback	message	theory
group communication	noise	transactional communication model

Notes

1. Marilyn H. Buckley, "Focus on Research: We Listen to a Book a Day; Speak a Book a Week: Learning from Walter Loban," *Language Arts* 69 (1992), pp. 101–109.

2. See Sherwyn P. Morreale, Michael M. Osborn, and Judy C. Pearson, "Why Communication Is Important: A Rationale for the Centrality of the Study of Communication," *Journal of the Association for Communication Administration* 29 (2000), pp. 1–25. The authors of this article collected and annotated nearly one hundred articles, commentaries, and publications that call attention to the importance of studying communication in contemporary society.

3. Robert M. Diamond, "Designing and Assessing Courses and Curricula," *Chronicle of Higher Education*, 1 August 1997, p. B7.

4. Jerry L. Winsor, Dan B. Curtis, and Ronald D. Stephens, "National Preferences in Business and Communication Education: A Survey Update," *Journal of the Association for Communication Administration*, 3 (September 1997), pp. 170–179. Winsor et al. conclude that a stronger emphasis should be given to training in listening and interpersonal communication in addition to developing competencies in group communication and presentation speaking.

5. "Graduates Are Not Prepared to Work in Business," *Association Trends* (June 1997), p. 4.

6. Peter D. Hart Research Associates, *How Should Colleges Prepare Students to Succeed in Today's Global Economy?* Conducted on behalf of The Association of American Colleges and Universities, 2006, p. 5. Also see Association of American Colleges and Universities, *College Learning for the New Global Age* (Washington, DC: Association of American Colleges and Universities, 2007).

7. In association with the NCA, the Association for Communication Administration's 1995 Conference on Defining the Field of Communication produced the following definition: "The field of communication focuses on how people use messages to generate meanings within and across various contexts, cultures, channels and media. The field promotes the effective and ethical practice of human communication." See www.natcom.org/nca/Template2.asp?bid=344.

8. The Seven Key Elements and Guiding Principles of Human Communication as well as the accompanying communication model are copyrighted by Engleberg and Wynn, 2004.

9. David W. Johnson, *Reaching Out: Interpersonal Effectiveness and Self-Actualization*, 7th ed. (Boston: Allyn & Bacon, 2002), p. 65.

10. See Brant R. Burleson, "Taking Communication Seriously," *Communication Monographs* 59 (1992), pp. 79–86. Burleson suggests that communication occurs only when the sender intends to send a message and the receiver recognizes the sender's intent. An excellent description of the intentionality debate can be found in Dominic A. Infante, Andrew S. Rancer, and Deanna F. Womack, *Building Communication Theory*, 2nd ed. (Prospect Heights, IL: Waveland, 1993), pp. 13–18. Also see a series of essays on the intentionality debate in *Communication Studies* 42 (1990).

11. In this textbook, we prefer and use the broader term *presentational communication* rather than *public speaking* to describe the act of speaking before an audience. Public speaking is one type of presentational communication that occurs when a speaker addresses a public audience. See Isa N. Engleberg and John A. Daly, *Presentations in Everyday Life: Strategies for Effective Speaking*, 2nd ed. (Boston: Houghton Mifflin, 2005), p. 6.

12. John McWhorter, *The Power of Babel: A Natural History of Languages* (New York: A.W.H. Freeman, 2001), p. 5.

13. *American Heritage Dictionary of the English Language*, 4th ed. (Boston: Houghton Mifflin, 2000), p. 1718.

14. Robert Johansen, *Groupware: Computer Support for Business Teams* (New York: Free Press, 1988), p. 20.

15. David Berlo, *The Process of Communication: An Introduction to Theory and Practice* (New York: Holt, Rinehart and Winston, 1960), p. 24.

16. Rob Anderson and Veronica Ross, *Questions of Communication: A Practical Introduction to Theory*, 3rd ed. (New York: St. Martin's, 2002), p. 69.

17. Karl R. Popper, *The Logic of Scientific Discovery* (New York: Basic Books, 1959), p. 59.

18. Brant R. Burleson, Sandra Metts, and Michael W. Kirch, "Communication in Close Relationships," in *Close Relationships: A Sourcebook*, ed. Clyde Hendrick

and Susan S. Hendrick (Thousand Oaks, CA: Sage, 2000), p. 249.

19. Anderson and Ross, p. 301.

20. Richard L. Johannesen, *Ethics in Human Communication*, 5th ed. (Prospect Heights, IL: Waveland, 2002), p. 1.

21. D.S. Hutchinson, "Ethics," in *The Cambridge Companion to Aristotle*, ed.

Jonathan Barnes (Cambridge: Cambridge University Press, 1995), pp. 217–227.

22. Aristotle, *Nicomachean Ethics*, trans. W.D. Ross, rev. J.O. Urmson, in *The Complete Works of Aristotle: The Revised Oxford Translation*, ed. Jonathan Barnes. (Princeton: Princeton University, 1984), p. 1776.

Understanding Self

chapter 2

Key Elements of Communication	Communication Axioms	Guiding Principles of Intrapersonal Communication
Self	*Communication Is Personal*	Recognize how *your* characteristics, perceptions, self-concept, and confidence affect the way you communicate.
Others	*Communication Is Relational*	Monitor and interpret feedback from others to promote self-awareness.
Purpose	*Communication Is Intentional*	Develop communication strategies for becoming your ideal self.
Context	*Communication Is Contextual*	Recognize how social and cultural contexts affect the way you perceive yourself and others.
Content	*Communication Is Symbolic*	Develop messages that communicate confidence and a positive personal impression.
Structure	*Communication Is Structured*	Recognize how message structure affects others' perceptions of and reactions to you.
Expression	*Communication Is Irreversible*	Practice verbal and nonverbal communication strategies and skills to enhance your confidence and personal image.

Intrapersonal Communication

Effective communication begins with a clear understanding of your *self* and the world around you. In Chapter 1, we place *self* at the core of the communication process. In other words, communication begins with *you*. Who you are and how you think determines how you perceive and interact with others. Your sense of self also determines how you make decisions about the purpose, context, content, and structure of communication. Ultimately, who you are influences how you express your thoughts and emotions.

As we note in Chapter 1, **intrapersonal communication** refers to communication *within* yourself *about* yourself *to* yourself.[1] The saying "know thyself" captures the fundamental meaning of intrapersonal communication. In this chapter we examine three major aspects of intrapersonal communication: perception, self-concept, and confidence. Understanding how these intrapersonal variables affect one another will help you become a more effective and ethical communicator in interpersonal, group, and presentational settings.

The Process of Perception

Why does one person find great satisfaction in a job whereas someone else in the same job dreads coming to work each day? Why do you find a speech inspiring whereas another audience member leaves the room offended? The answer to these questions lies in one word: *perception.*

Imagine that you and a friend are chatting after a meeting. You say, "That was a good session. We got through all the issues and ended early." Your friend responds with "Are you kidding? Didn't you notice that Lynn rushed us through the agenda to avoid any serious discussion or disagreement?" What happened here? You both attended the same meeting, but each of you perceived the experience quite differently.

The American Heritage Dictionary of the English Language defines *perception* as the act of becoming aware through any of the senses, particularly sight or hearing; or the recognition and interpretation of sensory stimuli based chiefly on memory.[2] From a communication point of view, we define **perception** as the process through which you select, organize, and interpret sensory stimuli in the world around you. Your perceptions determine how you interpret and evaluate the things, events, and people you encounter.

Figure 2.1 demonstrates the power of perception. What do you see? Do you see a young, fashionable woman with a dainty nose? Or do you see an elderly woman who has a large nose and her chin tucked into her coat? Depending on how your eyes selected graphic details, how you organized that information, and how you interpreted the results, you decided that you saw a young woman or an old woman. Take another look at the picture. Can you see the other woman? It's often difficult to switch perceptions once you've drawn a conclusion.

Generally, we trust our perceptions and treat them as accurate and reliable. We say things such as, "Seeing is believing," "I call it as I see it," or "I saw it with my own eyes." However, as Figure 2.1 shows, we can't always rely on what we see. Others may see things quite differently than you do and may be just as certain about their conclusions. As police officers know very well, three witnesses to a traffic accident may provide three different descriptions of the cars involved, the estimated speed they were traveling, and the physical characteristics of the drivers. In fact, eyewitness testimony, although persuasive, is often one of the least reliable forms of courtroom evidence.

| **Figure 2.1** | Do You See an Old Woman or a Young Woman? |

How does the outcome ... breaking a wishbone affect each person's perception of the contes...

In addition to the flaws in eyewitness testimony, studies of traditional police line-ups show that they lead witnesses to make more mistaken IDs than lineups showing suspects and ringers one at a time. Even videotaped confessions can bias juries and judges. Several studies report that we are more likely to believe a voluntary confession when the camera only focuses on the suspect rather than when it focuses on both the suspect and the police officer doing the interrogation. New Zealand requires a two-person camera perspective to avoid such bias.[3]

Even though you run the risk of drawing incorrect conclusions, you would be lost in a confusing world without your perceptions. Given the millions of bits of information that bombard your senses daily, perception helps you select, organize, and interpret that information. Not only does perception help you make sense out of other people's behavior, it helps you decide what you will say or do. Suppose you notice that your boss keeps track of employees who arrive late and leave early, and that she rarely grants these employees the special privileges given to those who put in their full workday. These perceptions help explain and predict her behavior when employees ask for a favor. They also tell you that it is a good idea to arrive early and stay late if you want a positive evaluation or a future promotion.

There are three stages to perception: selection, organization, and interpretation. The following sections discuss these stages.

THREE STAGES OF PERCEPTION

► *Selection:* You use your senses to notice and choose from many stimuli.

► *Organization:* You sort selected stimuli into messages.

► *Interpretation:* You interpret the meaning of messages.

SELECTION

You use your senses (sight, sound, taste, smell, and touch) to notice and choose from the many stimuli around you. Your needs, wants, interests, moods, and memories largely determine which stimuli you will select. For example, when your eyes and ears detect something familiar or potentially interesting as you flip through television channels, you stop. Or you may be daydreaming in class, but when your professor says, "The following chapters will be covered on the next test," you find yourself paying full attention again.

Figure 2.2 illustrates the importance of selection in the process of perception. Do you see a vase or two people facing each other in the figure? Depending on which elements of the figure you focus on, or select, you will perceive different images.

| Figure 2.2 | Reversible Images |

Neuroscientists have found evidence that what you see can influence what you taste, and what you touch can change what you see. In other words, your senses "talk" to and influence one another because your brain can "glue" your senses together.[1] Here are a few examples of how the boundaries between your senses are blurred:

• If you put red food coloring in a glass of white wine, some of the most accomplished wine experts will believe they're drinking red wine.
• If you show a friend a single flash on a computer screen while playing two beeps, she may swear she saw two flashes.

• If you ask someone to rub his hands together while listening to an audiotape of rubbing dry skin, his skin may feel rough and parched.
• If you dye a delicious strawberry blue, it's likely to smell strange too.

Even with the best intentions and the sharpest senses, your perceptions of the world around you may be misinterpreted.

[1]Lila Guterman, "Do You Smell What I Hear? Neuroscientists Crosstalk among the Senses," *The Chronicle of Higher Education* (December 14, 2001), pp. 17–18.

This optical illusion illustrates the **figure–ground principle** of perception: We focus on certain features (the figure) while deemphasizing less relevant background stimuli (the ground).[4] Thus, you see a person standing against a building, not a building with a person-shaped hole in it.[5] In communication, you see your friend smile and hear her tell you everything is okay. However, you focus your attention on her red and swollen eyes, suspect she has been crying, and conclude that she is upset. Her smile and verbal assurances are relegated to the background. When talking to a friend in a noisy restaurant, you focus on hearing your friend and try to push less relevant noises to the background. Ultimately, what you select to focus on will affect how you organize and interpret the events around you *and* how well you communicate in those situations.

ORGANIZATION

Suppose you see a middle-aged woman wearing a suit walking across campus. You conclude she is a professor. You also observe a young man entering a classroom wearing a school sweatshirt and carrying a backpack that appears to be loaded with textbooks. You assume he is a student. You took the information, or stimuli, you observed and categorized it into "professor" and "student." Not surprisingly, context influences how you organize information. For example, you could conclude that a woman in a suit on campus is a professor, but in a different context, you might conclude that she is a business executive. You may conclude that a young man wearing a school sweatshirt and carrying books on campus is a student, but backstage in a theater, you may decide that he is an actor in costume for a play.

You sort and arrange the sensory stimuli you select into useful categories based on your knowledge and past experiences with similar stimuli. There are four principles that influence how you organize or categorize information: the proximity principle, the similarity principle, the closure principle, and the simplicity principle.[6]

The Proximity Principle   The closer objects, events, or people are to each other, the more likely you will perceive them as belonging together.[7] You go to a restaurant to eat lunch alone, and another person who you do not know gets in line behind you. The host asks, "Two for lunch?" When you don't want to be perceived as associated with an individual, you may even find yourself moving away from that person to create greater physical distance.

ORGANIZING PRINCIPLES

▶ The Proximity Principle
▶ The Similarity Principle
▶ The Closure Principle
▶ The Simplicity Principle

CommFYI   Your Culture Influences Your Perception

In addition to individual differences in perception, the culture in which you live or were raised influences how you select and organize the information you encounter. Psychologist Richard Nisbett argues that each culture can "literally experience the world in very different ways."[1] For example, people from western and eastern Asian cultures organize information differently. Look at the three objects depicted below. Which two objects would you pair together?

Westerners are more likely to put the chicken and cow together because they are both animals. East Asians, however, are more likely to pair the cow and the grass because cows eat grass. According to Nesbitt, East Asians perceive the world in terms of relationships whereas westerners are inclined to see objects that can be grouped into categories. As Chapter 3, "Understanding Others," explains, many cultures—and East Asian cultures in particular—are more sensitive to the context in which communication takes place.

The mental process of perception, however, is the same across cultures. Everyone selects, organizes, and interprets stimuli. However, your culture influences what you notice, how you organize that information, and how you interpret information and situations. Learning more about the values, beliefs, history, and teachings of another culture will help you understand how a person from another culture can reach very different conclusions than you do.

[1]Richard E. Nisbett, *The Geography of Thought: How Asians and Westerners Think Differently . . . and Why* (New York: Free Press, 2003), p. 87.

The Similarity Principle   Similar elements or people are more likely to be perceived as part of a group. When two individuals share one characteristic or trait, you may conclude that they also have other things in common. For example, you meet a person from Texas and assume that she enjoys country music because other Texans you know listen to that kind of music. Unfortunately, the similarity principle can lead to stereotyping and inaccurate conclusions. Your new acquaintance may dislike country music but love jazz.

How do your perceptions of this photograph of United Airlines pilots demonstrate the Similarity Principle?

| Figure 2.3 | How Many Triangles Do You See? |

The Closure Principle   We often fill in missing elements to form a more complete impression of an object, person, or event. Look at Figure 2.3. How many triangles do you see? Some people will see as many as eleven triangles. However, given that a triangle is a figure with three *attached* sides, there are no triangles in the figure. If you saw triangles, you mentally filled in or "closed" the image's elements.

The Simplicity Principle   We tend to organize information in a way that provides the simplest interpretation. For example, on a cloudy day you look out the window and see that the sidewalk is wet and think that it must have rained. This is a reasonable and simple conclusion. However, there may be other explanations for the wet sidewalk, like automatic sprinklers or a leak in a water pipe, but you chose the simplest one first.

These four principles of organization explain some of the ways in which you try to make sense out of the information around you. Although these organizing principles can result in reasonable assumptions, they can just as easily promote inaccurate perceptions.

INTERPRETATION

Imagine you are among hundreds of people attending a basketball game. You notice one man reading a newspaper (selection). Because he is sitting on the other side of the court, you categorize him as a fan of the opposing team (organization). You then conclude that he is not a very loyal supporter of his team (interpretation). This example illustrates how you interpret and evaluate the stimuli you select and organize to reach conclusions about their meaning.

A number of factors influence your interpretation of people or events. Suppose that a friend asks you to volunteer your time over the weekend to help build a house for Habitat for Humanity. The following factors may affect your interpretation and reaction to your friend's request:

- *Past Experiences.* After volunteering at a soup kitchen last year, you felt really good about yourself.
- *Knowledge.* You spent a summer working as a house painter and believe that you have something useful to contribute.
- *Expectations.* It sounds like fun, and you might meet some interesting people.
- *Attitudes.* You believe that volunteering in the community is important.
- *Relational Involvement.* This is really important to your friend.

These same factors may also lead to inaccurate perceptions. For example, suppose your best friend's ex-husband is hired to work in your department. You believe that he treated your friend badly and now you will have to endure his inconsiderate attitude and careless work. However, everyone else—supervisors, coworkers, and customers—seem pleased with him. Clearly, your previous experience may be responsible for an unfair or erroneous perception of his work.

PERCEPTION CHECKING

Improving the accuracy of your perceptions can help you avoid misunderstandings and improve your communication with others. Psychologists Richard Block and Harold Yuker point out that "perception often is a poor representation of reality. Yet it is important to recognize that a person's behavior is controlled less by what is actually true, than what the person believes is true. Perceptions may be more important than reality in determining behavior!"[8]

You can begin the process of improving the accuracy of your perceptions by pausing to check the basis for your conclusions. **Perception checking** requires that you become aware of how you select, organize, and interpret sensory stimuli, whether you consider alternative interpretations, and whether you try to verify your perceptions with others.[9] Consider how applying the seven guiding principles can help you improve your perception.

- *Self.* Consider personal factors that may influence your perceptions. Analyze whether you are viewing things objectively or whether you are influenced by personal biases, past experiences, or your cultural background.
- *Others.* Determine whether others perceive a situation the same way you do. Try to discover why they have reached different conclusions.
- *Purpose.* Analyze how your goals, motives, and needs may influence how you interpret information and reach conclusions.
- *Context.* Consider how the psychosocial, logistical, and interactional communication context may affect your perceptions.
- *Content.* Notice the kinds of stimuli that capture your attention and whether you are ignoring other types of information. Consider alternative conclusions that could be drawn from the same information.
- *Structure.* Notice how the organization of ideas and information may affect how you interpret a message.
- *Expression.* Notice whether the way a message is expressed affects your perception. Consider how the choice of channel may influence your perception of a message.

Perceptions of Self

The guiding principle related to *self* calls for an understanding of how *your* characteristics, perceptions, self-concept, and confidence affect the way you communicate. In short, your willingness to perceive your *self* accurately and objectively affects your ability to communicate effectively and ethically. Accurately perceiving your *self* is a daunting challenge, but it will help you understand why *self* is at the center of every communication transaction.

SELF-CONCEPT

Your **self-concept** represents the relatively stable sum total of beliefs you have about yourself. Self-concept answers two simple questions: "Who are you?" and "What makes you *you*?" In addition to cultural categories such as age, nationality, race, religion, and gender (as in "I am a 30-year old, African American Catholic female"), how would you rate yourself on the following continuum of characteristics?

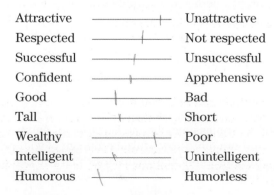

Attractive	Unattractive
Respected	Not respected
Successful	Unsuccessful
Confident	Apprehensive
Good	Bad
Tall	Short
Wealthy	Poor
Intelligent	Unintelligent
Humorous	Humorless

SOURCES OF SELF-CONCEPT

▶ Level of Self-Awareness
▶ Influence of Others
▶ Past Experiences and Personal Memories
▶ Cultural Background

When you add cultural characteristics to your self perceptions, you begin to have a sense of who you are. Your self-concept is a reflection of these perceptions.

Although your concept of self is relatively stable, it can change as you change; you are always becoming. An awkward child who discovers that training and practice can improve her physical skills may become a confident and graceful dancer or talented athlete. An average college student who learns to think critically, solve problems, write eloquently, or work on behalf of people in need may win a Nobel Prize. An unattractive, "ugly duckling" teenager can mature into a beautiful "swan."

SOURCES OF SELF-CONCEPT

So where does your self-concept come from? You certainly aren't born with one. Infants only begin to recognize themselves in a mirror between 18 and 24 months of age. Only then do they begin to express the concept of "me."[10] Although many factors influence the ways in which you develop a self-concept, here we focus on four major factors: self-awareness, social interactions, past experiences, and cultural perspective.

Level of Self-Awareness   **Self-awareness** is the ability to be conscious of your own traits, thoughts, and feelings as well as to respond appropriately to the reactions and behavior of others. Self-awareness is a personal understanding of the very core of your identity.[11]

In his best-selling book, *Emotional Intelligence*, Daniel Goleman identifies self-awareness as the first and most fundamental emotional competency: the keystone of emotional intelligence.[12] He writes,

> The ability to monitor feelings from moment to moment is crucial to psychological insight and self-understanding. An inability to notice our true feelings leaves us at their mercy. People with greater certainty about their feelings are better pilots of their lives, having a surer sense of how they really feel about personal decisions from whom to marry to what job to take.[13]

The ability to *monitor* your thoughts and feelings is crucial to self-awareness. This ability is called **self-monitoring**, a combination of introspection (thinking about yourself), careful observation (noting how others react to you), and adaptation (modifying how you present yourself). This definition focuses on three interrelated communication skills: (1) ability to identify your thoughts and feelings accurately and objectively; (2) the ability to observe and analyze accurately how *others* react to your comments, appearance, and behavior; and (3) the ability to use such observations to modify how you present yourself. Effective self-monitors correctly interpret the verbal and nonverbal feedback of others and change their behavior in response to that feedback.

Effective self-monitoring can help you realize, "This is anger I'm feeling" rather than letting rage hijack your mind and body. Self-monitoring can help you differentiate emotional responses: love versus lust, disappointment versus depression, and anxiety versus excitement. By becoming aware of your thoughts and feelings, you can avoid mistaking sexual arousal for everlasting love, avoid letting minor difficulties trigger depression, and avoid mistaking fear for anger.

People who are *high self-monitors* constantly watch other people, what they do, and how they respond to the behavior of others. Such people are self-aware, like to "look good," and usually adapt well to differing social situations.

On the other hand, *low self-monitors* are generally oblivious to how others see them and may "march to their own, different drum."[14]

Influence of Others   Although self-awareness may be the keystone of emotional intelligence, the influence of other people is a more powerful determinant of your self-concept. Such influences include significant others, the groups to which you belong, the roles you assume, and the rewards you receive from others.

- *Significant Others.* Significant others include individuals whose opinions you value, such as family, friends, coworkers, and mentors. What do trusted colleagues, good friends, and family members tell you about yourself? Do they say that you're smart, attractive, talented, outgoing, and lovable? Or do you hear the opposite? Equally important, how do they act around you? Do they seem to enjoy your company or do they seem to find excuses to be somewhere else?

- *Reference Groups.* Reference groups are groups with whom you closely identify and enjoy membership. How did belonging to a high school clique (popular, smart, artistic, or athletic) affect your self-concept and interaction with others? How does your current membership in groups (work team, church group, civic association, professional organization, social club) affect the way you see yourself? Certainly the distinct ways in which members of a legal team, a rugby club, and a self-help group view themselves affects their self-concept.

- *Roles.* A **role** is a pattern of behaviors associated with an expected function in a specific context or relationship. Thus, your behavior often changes when you shift to a different role. For example, your communication in the role of student probably differs from your behavior when interacting with your family, your boss, or your neighbor. How does your job role (teacher, mechanic, nurse, manager, clerk, artist, lawyer, police officer) affect your vision of yourself? How do your private roles (child, parent, spouse, lover, best friend) shape your self-concept?

How is children's self-esteem affected by their parents' expressions of affection and anger?

- *Rewards.* How has recognition at school, work, or in your community (academic honor, employee-of-the-month award, job promotion, community service prize) affected your self-concept? If you never receive praise or words of encouragement from others, you may not believe you are worthy or capable of achievement.

Past Experiences and Personal Memories   Without the ability to select, organize, and interpret past experiences, you would have little basis for a coherent self-concept. Sharon Brehm and her colleagues put it this way: "Who would you be if you could not remember your parents or childhood playmates, your successes and failures, the places you lived, the schools you attended, the books you read, and the teams you played for?"[15] You also have vivid memories of certain shocking events—the death of a loved one, the September 11 attacks, a serious automobile accident, the war in Vietnam or Iraq—that affect how you interpret and react to current events and circumstances.

Not surprisingly, you (and everyone else) have a tendency to distort memories. You tend to remember the past as if it were a drama in which you were the leading player.[16] When asked, many people describe high school as "terrible" or "wonderful," when they really mean it *seemed* terrible or wonderful *to them*. In reality, high school couldn't have been all good or all bad. When we tell stories about the past, we put ourselves at the center of action rather than as a bit player or observer.

Given that social interactions significantly influence the development of self-concept, online interactions provide a unique context for experimenting with and expressing your identity. In her book *Online Connections: Internet Interpersonal Relationships*, Susan Barnes explains that "although online selves emerge within the same processes by which any self emerges, changes in the symbolic environment in which persons interact will transform the boundaries and nature of self, social world, and the relationship between the two."[1]

Scholars disagree on whether online communication harms or promotes the development of a self-concept. Some suggest that cyberspace's limitless number of communities with constantly changing significant others and reference groups results in an unstable context in which the formation of a stable self-identity is difficult to develop.[2] Others argue that virtual communities provide us with opportunities to experiment with identities. For example, shy teenagers may feel more confident and comfortable communicating online rather than in face-to-face interactions. As they "try on" different selves, feedback from others online may help teenagers develop a stronger self-concept and a healthier self-esteem.[3]

Technology provides a context for experimenting with identity, but it also allows opportunities for deceptive communication. The absence of face-to-face interaction makes it easier to distort aspects of your self or completely fabricate an identity. It may be great fun and even acceptable to present a false impression of your self in some virtual communities, but many have felt betrayed and hurt when they discovered that what seemed to be a very real online relationship was built on deceptive presentations of identity.

[1]Susan B. Barnes, *Online Connections: Internet Interpersonal Relationships* (Creskill, NJ: Hampton Press, 2001), p. 234.
[2]Ibid.
[3]Ibid., p. 91.

Cultural Background Culture has a significant influence on who you are and how you understand yourself. Intercultural communication scholar Min-Sun Kim explains that culture involves "different ways of being, and different ways of knowing, feeling, and acting."[17] For example, western cultures emphasize the value of independence and self-sufficiency, whereas in East Asian cultures the self is generally defined in terms of memberships in groups and relationships to others. Thus, many people from English-speaking western cultures have a hard time recognizing how their culture shapes their self-concept. But this is exactly what you would expect from people in highly independent countries like the United States and Australia.

Cultural background significantly influences your values and beliefs, your understanding of appropriate roles and relationships, and how you view your place within the world. Chapter 3, "Understanding Others," focuses on how the characteristics and cultures of others affect how we communicate.

As you work to understand your self-concept, check your perceptions against reality by asking several questions:

- In what ways do my interactions with others verify my perceptions of myself?
- What experiences, memories, and cultural perspectives form the basis for my self-concept?
- What factors or behaviors suggest that these perceptions are accurate?

ASSESSING YOUR SELF

Understanding your self-concept only begins the process of trusting and relying on your *self* to communicate effectively and ethically. You also need to assess your self-concept in light of the many contexts in which you live and interact with others. As Nathaniel Branden writes, "[o]f all the judgments we pass in life, none is as important as the one we pass on ourselves."[18]

Self-appraisals are evaluations of your self-concept in terms of your abilities and behaviors. "I'm bad at math" or "I'm an excellent basketball player" are examples of self-appraisals. Not surprisingly, when your appraisal is positive, you are more likely to succeed. For example, positive beliefs about your abilities may make you more persuasive when asking for a promotion, or may help you deal with rejection. At the same time, be aware that your mind may try to protect you from potentially hurtful or threatening feedback from others. These ego-defense excuses can mislead you into forming a distorted self-image.[19] "What's the big deal about being late to a meeting? She's just obsessed with time and took it out on me. It's no big deal." You can minimize this kind of self-deception by using three forms of self-appraisals—actual performance, social comparison, and reflected appraisal.

Actual Performance   Your actual performance or behaviors are the most influential source of appraisals.[20] If you repeatedly fail at something, you are likely to evaluate your performance in that area negatively. On the other hand, repeated successes give you the confidence to rely on such attributes and skills in the future. For example, if you have always been an A student, you probably expect to continue earning high grades and consider yourself a good student with enough smarts to succeed. On the other hand, students with high grades in high school may be disappointed or distressed to receive much lower grades in college and, as a result, have doubts about their academic and intellectual abilities.

Social Comparison   According to social psychologist Leon Festinger, **social comparison** is the process of evaluating yourself in relation to the others in your reference groups.[21] The notion of "keeping up with the Joneses" is an example of our need to compare favorably with others. If you are the only one in the class who receives a failing grade on a test, you may evaluate yourself as less intelligent, less prepared, or less capable than your classmates. On the other hand, if everyone does poorly on the test, comparing yourself with your classmates may allow you to feel good about yourself because you did just as well as everyone else. We also compare ourselves with others in terms of appearance and physical ability. When people compare themselves with fashion models, alluring movie stars, and professional athletes, they have chosen an almost impossible ideal.

FORMS OF SELF-APPRAISAL
▶ Actual Performance
▶ Social Comparison
▶ Reflected Appraisal

How does a demonstration of like-minded people affect participants' self-concept and self-appraisal?

CommFYI   Beware of Self-Fulfilling Prophecies

A prophecy is a prediction. Thus, a *self*-fulfilling prophecy is a prediction that *you* make happen. For example, if young girls are told that boys do better in mathematics, they may believe it and stop trying to succeed. As a result, they won't do as well in math as boys, just as predicted. According to Nathaniel Branden, a **self-fulfilling prophecy** is "an impression formation process in which an initial impression elicits behavior in another that conforms to the impression."[1]

In 2005, Lawrence H. Summers, then president of Harvard University, made a speech in which he suggested that women might be underrepresented in the top ranks of science and mathematics because of inborn differences in ability from men. The resulting uproar produced a public apology from Summers and a commitment from Harvard University to develop programs to aid the advancement of female faculty members in science and mathematics.

Criticisms of Summers' comments about women contributed to his eventual resignation.[2] Interestingly Harvard University named Drew G. Faust as its new president. Dr. Faust is also the first woman to serve as president of this distinguished university.

When professors, family members, friends, and even the president of Harvard University claim that women cannot perform as well as men in science and mathematics, there is a good chance that they won't. A letter to the editor of *The Chronicle of Higher Education* signed by more than one hundred scientists, engineers, and educators noted that in 1970, women represented about 5 percent of law students and about 8 percent of medical school students. Today, women represent approximately 50 percent of students in law and medicine. Obviously, the low rate of women's participation in 1970 had nothing to do with genetic barriers to success.[3] It had everything to do with society's expectations, widespread gender bias, and women's self-fulfilling prophecies.[4]

In one study, researchers administered a math comprehension test to different groups of women. Before taking the test, one group of women was told that that men and women do math equally well. Another group was told that there is a genetic difference in math ability that explains why women are not as good at math as men. The women in the first group got nearly twice as many right answers as those in the second group. The researchers concluded that the results suggest that people tend to accept genetic explanations as powerful and permanent, which can lead to self-fulfilling prophecies.

Self-fulfilling prophecies can influence your communication with another person in two ways. First, your judgments about another person can bring about a behavior change in that person that supports your prediction. Second, your predictions can influence how you behave toward another person, thus promoting responses from that person that confirm your impression.

You can minimize the effects of self-fulfilling prophecies by asking yourself several critical thinking questions:

- What predictions am I making about the behavior of others?
- Why am I making this prediction? Is it justified?
- Am I doing anything to elicit the predicted response?
- What other behaviors could help avoid fulfilling my prophecy?

[1]Nathaniel Branden, *The Art of Living Consciously: The Power of Awareness to Transform Everyday Life* (New York: Fireside Book/Simon and Schuster, 1999), pp. 168–169.

[2]Piper Fogg, "Harvard Creates Two Panels to Advance Female Professors," *The Chronicle of Higher Education*, February 18, 2005, p. A12.

[3]Carol M. Muller, Sally K. Ride, and Jeanie M. Fouke, Letter to the Editor, *The Chronicle of Higher Education*, February 18, 2005, p. A47.

[4]"Women's Math Scores Affected by Suggestions," *The Washington Post*, October 20, 2006, p. A11. The article summarizes a study published in the October 2006 issue of *Science*.

Reflected Appraisal   As you discover others' opinions of you, you probably accept those opinions as part of your self-concept, particularly if an appraisal is frequently repeated. When someone encourages you to believe in yourself and your abilities, you often do. As a result, you may put more effort into a task or a relationship. For example, coaches give pep talks before a big game so that players will believe they can win. But, if you hear negative appraisals often enough, you may develop a negative self-concept. Tell a child that she is worthless or stupid and she may very well believe it.

Self-Esteem

Now that you know something about your self-concept, how do you *feel* about yourself? Are you satisfied, discouraged, delighted, optimistic, surprised, troubled? **Self-esteem** represents your judgments about your self. Nathaniel Branden puts it this way: "Self-esteem is the reputation we acquire with ourselves."[22] The word *esteem* comes from the Latin *aestimare*, which means to estimate or appraise.

Self-esteem involves both beliefs about yourself (e.g., "I am competent/incompetent," "I am liked/disliked") and associated emotions (e.g., joy/despair, pride/shame). Self-esteem is also expressed in our behavior (e.g., assertive/passive, confident/cautious). Finally, self-esteem can be specific to a particular dimension (e.g., "I believe I am a good writer and feel proud of that in particular") or global in extent (e.g., "I believe I am a good person and feel proud of myself in general"). Not surprisingly, people with high self-esteem are also confident and competent communicators.

Studies consistently find that people with high self-esteem are significantly happier than others. They are also less likely to be depressed. One especially compelling study surveyed more than 13,000 college students. High self-esteem emerged as the strongest factor in overall life satisfaction.[23]

IMPROVING SELF-ESTEEM

If your self-esteem isn't very high, you can take steps to improve it. Your self-esteem can change for the better if you self-monitor and are willing to learn new ways of communicating with others. There are several strategies that can help you build self-esteem.[24] Keep in mind that engaging in these practices requires diligence, effort, and self-monitoring, but that negative consequences can result if these behaviors are "practiced" to the extreme.

Practice Self-Acceptance (But Not as an Excuse)   Self-acceptance is the willingness to acknowledge and "own" your thoughts, feelings, and behaviors. You don't have to like all your actions, but you must be willing to accept them as part of who

STRATEGIES TO IMPROVE YOUR SELF-ESTEEM

▶ Practice Self-Acceptance
▶ Practice Self-Responsibility
▶ Practice Self-Assertiveness
▶ Practice Purposeful Living
▶ Practice Personal Integrity
▶ Practice Self-Talk

How would winning a coveted award affect the self-concept and self-esteem of this management team?

CommQuiz   The Rosenberg Self-Esteem Scale

Directions: The statements below describe different ways that people think about themselves. Please read them carefully and then use the scale shown to indicate how much you agree with each of them.[1]

1	2	3	4
strongly disagree	disagree	agree	strongly agree

_____ 1. I feel that I'm a person of worth, at least on an equal plane with others.

_____ 2. On the whole, I am satisfied with myself.

_____ 3. I wish I could have more respect for myself.

_____ 4. I certainly feel useless at times.

_____ 5. At times I think I am no good at all.

_____ 6. I feel that I have a number of good qualities.

_____ 7. All in all, I am inclined to feel that I am a failure.

_____ 8. I am able to do things as well as most other people.

_____ 9. I feel that I do not have much to be proud of.

_____ 10. I take a positive attitude toward myself.

Scoring: Score items 1, 2, 6, 8, and 10 in a positive direction (i.e., strongly agree = 4, agree = 3, and so on) and items 3, 4, 5, 7, and 9 in a negative direction (i.e., strongly agree = 1, agree = 2, and so forth). The highest possible score is 40 points; the lowest possible score is 10 points. Higher scores indicate higher self-esteem. Please note that there are no good or bad scores; rather, the scale gives you a chance to measure how you *perceive* your level of self-esteem.

[1]Morris Rosenberg, *Society and the Adolescent Self-Image* (Princeton, NJ: Princeton University Press, 1965).

you are. No one is perfect. At the same time, self-acceptance is no excuse for engaging in inappropriate behavior. A boss who berates or yells at employees and justifies it by saying, "I'm just an emotional person. If you can't take it, get a job somewhere else" has distorted the concept of self-acceptance by taking it to an extreme.

Practice Self-Responsibility (But Don't Try to Control Everything)   Realize that you are largely responsible for your own happiness and the fulfillment of your goals. Rather than asking, "Who's to blame?" ask yourself, "What do *I* need to do?" Taking control of your life is an important part of feeling in control of and being satisfied with your life. On the other hand, we have worked with colleagues who want to control everything. As a result, they are overburdened, frustrated, and angry with others, rather than feeling confident and satisfied.

Practice Self-Assertiveness (But Respect the Needs of Others)   Know your needs and goals and be willing to pursue them. Don't become obsessed about the disapproval of others. Self-assertiveness requires a willingness to stand up for yourself in appropriate ways to fulfill your needs. Unfortunately, it can easily become aggression if you do not acknowledge and respect the needs and goals of others. Make sure that when you stand up for yourself you are not standing on or in the way of others. In Chapter 7, "Interpersonal Communication: Understanding Relationships," we devote a major section to the strategies and skills for promoting your own needs and rights while also respecting the needs and rights of others.

Practice Purposeful Living (But Don't Be Inflexible)   Identify short-term and long-term goals and develop an action plan. As you pursue your goals, your future will look brighter and you will develop a more positive perception of yourself. At the same

Self-assertiveness and high self-esteem will not solve all your personal problems, nor will they automatically improve your ability to communicate effectively and ethically. Educators have learned this lesson much to the detriment of students. For example, some well-meaning school systems have tried to raise the self-esteem of disadvantaged and failing students by passing them to the next grade. Unfortunately, such efforts had no positive effects and demonstrated that inflating self-esteem by itself could actually decrease grades.[1]

Researchers once assumed that people acted violently toward others because they suffered from low self-esteem; rather, the opposite seems to be true. Violent people often act the way they do because they suffer from *high,* but unrealistic, self-esteem. Violent criminals often describe themselves as superior to others. Even playground bullies regard themselves as superior to other children. Low self-esteem is found among the victims of bullies, but not among bullies themselves. In fact, most violent groups generally have belief systems that emphasize their superiority over others.[2]

Someone with an overinflated sense of self-esteem may be a braggart, bully, or tyrant rather than a person with a healthy self-concept. Someone with lower self-esteem but a secure and confident sense of self can be a model of humility and goodness.

[1]Roy F. Baumeister, Jennifer D. Campbell, Joachim I. Krueger, and Kathleen D. Vohs, "Exploding the Self-Esteem Myth," *Scientific American* (January 2005), http://en.wikipedia.org/wiki/Self-esteem.
[2]Roy F. Baumeister, "Violent Pride," *Scientific American*, 284 (2001), pp. 96–101.

time, remember that life is unpredictable, and sometimes even the best-laid plans can be derailed by unexpected events and circumstances. There is nothing wrong with pausing in your pursuit of goals or even changing those goals when necessary.

Practice Personal Integrity (But Understand and Respect Others) Behave in ways that are consistent with your values and beliefs. First identify the beliefs and values that are important to you and then base your behavior on those beliefs. If you believe in honesty, don't cheat. If you value education, study. When you go beyond thinking about what you ought to do or should do and actually *do* "the right thing," you will feel more self-assured. "The right thing" for you, however, may not be "the right thing" for someone else. In Chapter 3, "Understanding Others," we note that different cultures may have customs, beliefs, and values that vary from yours. Be careful that your idea of personal integrity doesn't have serious negative consequences for others.

Practice Self-Talk (But Listen to Others Too) Changing your self-talk is another way to build self-esteem. **Self-talk** represents the silent statements you make *to* yourself *about* yourself. If you listen to what you say to yourself, you may find that you are making a lot of negative self-defeating statements: "I can't do this," "I don't know how," or "He won't like me." When you "hear" yourself engaging in negative self-talk, think of more positive and productive statements instead: "If I focus, I can do this," "I'll learn how," and "I'll give him a chance to get to know me." Behavioral researcher Shad Helmstetter points out that "if the strongest messages we receive about ourselves from the outside world are stored and acted on as though they're true, then we should be doubly careful what kind of messages we give ourselves!"[25] Listening to yourself, however, should never substitute or prevent you from listening to others.

One strategy for working toward higher levels of ethical decision making is to use the Golden Rule as a guide: "Do to others what you would have them do to you."[1] In other words, make decisions and act based on what you think would be right if you were in another person's place. However, what you would hope for is not necessarily what another would want. Follow these steps for applying the Golden Rule[2]:

- Understand how another person may perceive a situation, particularly if his or her perception could differ from your own.
- Imagine how you might feel if placed in another's situation.

- Try to find solutions that would be appropriate and just from someone else's perspective.

[1]"The Golden Rule is found in the New Testament (Matthew 7:12, NIV) but is often confused with the related admonition to "love your neighbor as yourself," which appears repeatedly in both the Hebrew Bible and the New Testament. . . . The Golden Rule has also been attributed to other religious leaders, including Confucius, Muhammad, and the first-century rabbi Hillel." Stephen Prothero, *Religious Literacy: What Every American Needs to Know—And Doesn't* (New York: HarperSanFrancisco, 2007), pp. 182–183.

[2]Adapted from Clayton E. Tucker–Ladd, *Psychological Self-Help* (2000), http://mentalhelp.net/psyhelp/chap3/chap3h.htm.

Communicating with Confidence

Your level of self-confidence directly affects how successfully you communicate.[26] Most of us see ourselves as bright and hardworking. At the same time, all of us have occasional doubts and insecurities. If you lack confidence, you are less likely to share what you know or voice your opinions. But when you feel good about yourself, you can engage in a conversation with ease, defend your ideas in a group, and give successful presentations.

Most people experience some anxiety when they are in an important communication situation. In fact, that "keyed up" feeling is a positive and normal reaction, and demonstrates that you care about what you have to say. The issue is not whether you experience anxiety in some communication situations, but how you perceive it and whether you choose to transform it. In the following sections, we discuss the nature of communication apprehension and how to express yourself with confidence.

COMMUNICATION APPREHENSION

The anxiety you may experience when speaking to others is referred to by many names: *speech anxiety*, *stage fright*, and *communication apprehension*. James McCroskey and his colleagues explore the anxieties people feel when they speak to others in a variety of contexts. McCroskey defines **communication apprehension** as "an individual's level of fear or anxiety associated with either real or anticipated communication with another person or persons."[27]

Communication apprehension is not just "in your head"; it involves real physiological responses to stress. Physical reactions such as sweaty palms, perspiring, a fast pulse, shallow breathing, cold extremities, flushed skin, nausea, trembling hands, quivering legs, or "butterflies" in the stomach are the body's response to the release of hormones such as adrenaline.[28]

The "Personal Report of Communication Apprehension" at the end of this chapter assesses your overall level of communication apprehension and identifies the communication contexts—group discussions, meetings, interpersonal conversations, public speaking—that produce the most anxiety for you. Anxieties about an upcoming job interview or a meeting with your boss can be just as fear provoking as the prospect of giving a public speech.

About 20 percent of the general population experience very high levels of communication apprehension. When that anxiety is measured in public speaking settings, the percentage is much higher. In fact, national surveys have discovered that fear of snakes and fear of speaking in public are the top two common fears among North Americans, way ahead of fear of heights, anxieties about financial problems, and even fear of death. Fortunately, you can learn how to reduce your anxieties and transform that energy into effective communication.

SOURCES OF COMMUNICATION APPREHENSION

The process of managing communication apprehension begins with recognizing why you feel anxious when speaking to an individual, a group, or an audience. Although everyone has personal reasons for nervousness, researchers have identified some of the key fears that underlie communication apprehension.[29] These include fear of failure, fear of the unknown, fear of the spotlight, fear of others, and fear of breaking the rules.

Fear of Failure   Some researchers suggest that the fear of a negative evaluation is the number one cause of communication anxiety.[30] Rather than focusing on your purpose, you may worry about what others will think of you. When you focus your thoughts on the possibility of failure, you are more likely to fail. Try to shift your focus to the positive feedback you see from others—a nod, a smile, or an alert look. When you sense that a listener likes you and your message, you may gain the extra confidence you need.

Fear of the Unknown   Most people fear the unfamiliar. Performing an uncommon or unexpected role can transform a usually confident person into a tangle of nerves. If you are attending an event as an audience member and suddenly are called on to introduce a guest to the audience, you can become very unsettled. Similarly, most people feel stressed when interviewing for a job in an office they've never been to and with a person they hardly know. If you've been promoted to a leadership position and are now "the boss," you may feel less comfortable communicating with the colleagues you now supervise. By taking a communication course, you have taken the most important step toward conquering your fear of the unknown: You are learning communication strategies and skills as well as how to think critically about new and challenging situations.

Fear of the Spotlight   Although a little attention may be flattering, being the center of attention makes many people nervous. When others are watching everything that you do, you may feel conspicuous and become self-conscious, which in turn may cause you to focus on *yourself* rather than on what you have to say. Psychologist Peter Desberg puts it this way: If you were performing as part of a choir, you'd probably feel much calmer than if you were singing a solo.[31] The more self-focused you are, the more nervous you become. This is especially true when giving a presentation to an audience. Try to stay focused on your purpose and message, rather than allowing yourself to be distracted by the spotlight.

Fear of Others   Sometimes the characteristics of your listeners can heighten your anxiety. Do you get nervous when interacting with people who have more status or power, education or experience, fame or popularity? Fear of others can be heightened when talking to a powerful person, an influential group, or a large audience. Usually this fear is based on an exaggerated feeling of being different from or inferior to others. Some students report fear of their classmates even when the class is small and regardless of who's in it. It's just a fear of the "other." If you don't know much about the people around you, you are more likely to feel apprehensive. Learning more about

SOURCES OF COMMUNICATION APPREHENSION
▶ Fear of Failure
▶ Fear of the Unknown
▶ Fear of the Spotlight
▶ Fear of Others
▶ Fear of Breaking the Rules

What factors could lead to a female's apprehension about speaking in front of a group of male colleagues?

your listeners can decrease your anxiety. You may have more in common with them than you realize.

Fear of Breaking the Rules The rules of communication are not like the rules of baseball or physics. "Three strikes and you're out" works in baseball, and "What goes up must come down" makes sense in physics. Unfortunately, some people believe the communication "rules" they read in a textbook or learn about in a class are hard and fast. At best, such rules are generalizations that can be applied to many situations. Occasionally we meet someone who follows the "rules" for effective communication as though they are enforceable laws. For example, sometimes novice speakers over-rehearse to the point of sounding robotic for fear of saying "uh" or "um" in a presentation. Good communicators learn not to "sweat the small stuff" and that, sometimes, "rules" should be bent or broken.

STRATEGIES FOR BECOMING A CONFIDENT COMMUNICATOR

Despite your worst fears, most people are kind and willing to forgive and forget a mistake. No one expects you to be perfect. Also, remember that in most cases your anxiety is invisible. We can't see your pounding heart, upset stomach, cold hands, or worried thoughts. Most of us think we display more anxiety than listeners report noticing. However, the fact that your anxiety is often invisible to others does not make it feel any less real to you. Fortunately, there are a number of strategies to reduce your anxiety and help you become a more confident communicator: Be prepared, practice relaxation and positive thinking, focus on your message instead of yourself, and practice.

Prepare Being well prepared can reduce your level of communication apprehension. Although you may not be able to predict unexpected situations or anticipate the nature of everyday conversations, you can prepare for many of the communication situations you encounter. For instance, you can prepare for a job interview or performance appraisal, a staff meeting or professional seminar, and a public speech or presentation. Thorough preparation results in more fully developed thoughts because it changes the unfamiliar into something familiar. With good preparation, you will know a great deal about the ideas you wish to discuss, the others who will be involved, the context of the situation, the content and structure of your message, and how you will be expected to express your message.

Re-lax, Re-think, Re-vision   Combining physical relaxation with a positive mental attitude is the most effective strategy for reducing communication apprehension. By learning to relax your body, you can reduce your level of communication apprehension. However, a relaxed body is only half the battle; you also need to change the way you think about communication.[32] When you have confident thoughts ("I know I can persuade this group to join the Animal Rescue League"), you begin to feel more confident. The following strategies can help you rethink your attitudes, visualize your message, and relax your body:

- *Cognitive Restructuring*. Worrisome, irrational, and counterproductive thoughts can cause anxiety. **Cognitive restructuring** is a method for reducing anxiety by replacing negative, irrational thoughts with more realistic, positive self-talk. The next time you feel anxious, tell yourself these positive statements: "My message is important" and "I am a well-prepared, skilled communicator." Whenever you have negative thoughts about communicating, respond with a positive and productive thought. Instead of the fear-provoking thought such as "The audience will think I don't know my material," substitute a positive statement such as "I know more about this than the audience does." Instead of "These budget meetings always make me nervous," substitute "I've done this before, so I'm not going to be as nervous as I've been in the past."[33]

- *Visualization*. **Visualization** is the process of imagining what it would be like to experience an entire communication act. Find a quiet place, relax, and visualize success. Imagine yourself walking into the room with confidence and energy. Think about the smiles you'll receive as you talk, the heads nodding in agreement, and the look of interest in the eyes of your listeners. By visualizing yourself communicating effectively, you are mentally practicing the skills you need to succeed while also building a positive self-image. Visualization is a powerful method for building confidence.

- *Systematic Desensitization*. **Systematic desensitization** is a relaxation and visualization technique developed by psychologist Joseph Wolpe to reduce the anxiety associated with stressful situations.[34] It begins by teaching you to achieve deep muscle relaxation. When you are in this relaxed state, you deliberately imagine yourself in a variety of communication situations ranging from very comfortable to highly stressful (Figure 2.4). By working to remain relaxed while visualizing various situations, you will gradually associate communication with relaxation rather than nervousness.

Figure 2.4   **Hierarchy of Anxiety-Producing Communication Situations**

The following is a list of communication situations ranging from the least likely to produce anxiety to situations that tend to be more stressful. You can create your own hierarchy for a specific fear or a particular situation. As you visualize each of the situations, try to remain calm and relaxed.[1]

1. You are talking to your best friend on the phone.

2. You are talking to your best friend in person.

3. You are being introduced to a new acquaintance by your best friend.

4. You have to introduce yourself to a new acquaintance.

5. You are talking to an operator about placing a long-distance phone call.

6. You are talking to a clerk in a department store.

7. You have to talk to a small group of people, all of whom you know well.

8. You are talking to a supervisor or someone who is in a supervisory role, such as a teacher, about a problem at work or school.

9. You are at a social gathering where you don't know anyone but are expected to meet and talk to others.

10. You are going to ask someone to go to a movie with you.

11. You are going to ask someone to go to a party with you.

12. You have to talk to a police officer about a ticket.

13. You are going on a job interview.

14. You have been asked to give a presentation in front of a large group of people.

15. You are getting ready to give a public speech but realize you left your notes at home.

16. You are to appear on a television show with other panelists to talk about a topic you know well.

17. You are to appear on a television show and debate another person.

18. You are ready to appear on a television show and give a speech but you lost your notes.

[1]From Richmond, Virginia P. & James C. Mc Croskey *Communication Apprehension, Avoidance And Effectiveness, 5/e.* Published by Allyn and Bacon, Boston, MA. Copyright © 1998 by Pearson Education. Reprinted by permission of the publisher.

Focus   One of the best ways to build confidence is to concentrate on your message rather than on yourself. Anxiety only takes your attention away from your message and places it on the symptoms of your fears. If you concentrate on the purpose and content of your message, you will be less nervous than if you spend time worrying about how you look or sound. When you focus on getting your message across, you don't have time to think about your fears. This strategy can reduce your level of anxiety and improve your communication.

To what extent does a comfortable and informal communication environment affect whether group members focus attention on their goals rather than on themselves?

Practice   The best way to become good at something is to practice, regardless of whether it's cooking, serving a tennis ball, or communicating. You can practice wording a request or expressing an emotion to one other person, answering questions in an interview, stating your position at a meeting, or making a presentation to an audience.

In addition to enhancing your confidence, practice stimulates your brain in positive ways. As Daniel Goleman notes in *Social Intelligence*, "when we mentally rehearse an action—making a dry run of a talk we have to give, or envisioning the fine points of a golf swing—the same neurons activate in the premotor cortex [of our brain] as if we have uttered those words or made that swing. Simulating an act is, in the brain, the same as performing it."[35] Practicing communication in our heads as well as physically is as important as practicing the piano or a gymnastic routine. Skilled pianists and award-winning gymnasts spend hours practicing. At the very least, communicators should practice what they intend to say to others.

CommFAQ How Can I Calm a Nervous Speaker?

You will often encounter people who seem far more nervous in a situation than you are. For example, when you attend social events with a friend or colleague, you may be more at ease than someone who doesn't know the other guests or is uncomfortable meeting strangers. When you interview someone for a job, the applicant is more nervous than you are. And, of course, when listening to a speaker give a presentation, you have much less to worry about. In fact, you may even feel relieved that you're not the one who is giving a speech. At the same time, you can help anxious communicators feel more confident by using the following strategies:[1]

- Encourage and assist apprehensive communicators in advance by helping them prepare.
- Include anxious communicators in a conversation or group discussion without "putting them on the spot."
- Provide supportive feedback when you listen to a nervous communicator: smile, nod, and focus your attention.

- Avoid interrupting nervous speakers while they're speaking, because such interruptions may crumble their confidence.
- Be patient.
- Provide constructive feedback after the communication event.

The most important thing you can do to help those who have difficulty speaking is to pay attention and listen carefully. In a discussion situation, for example, you may see someone take in a breath as though he or she wants to speak, only to be stifled by the comments of others. Try to curb you own comments so that others have a chance to speak. When an anxious communicator is speaking, pay attention and *look* like you're listening. Your feedback will help the speaker gain confidence.

[1]See Isa Engleberg and Dianna Wynn, *Working in Groups: Communication Principles and Strategies*, 4th ed. (Boston: Houghton Mifflin, 2007), pp. 106–108.

You *can* become a more confident communicator if you understand that it takes conscientious work to achieve this goal—and that it won't happen overnight. Experience, practice, and a positive attitude will eventually give you the tools you need to project confidence in your *self* and your message.

Positive Self-Talk

The first column in the following table provides examples of negative self-talk. In the second column, create a positive statement as a replacement. In the last two rows, identify some of your own negative self-talk and then substitute a more positive statement for each of your examples.

Negative Self-Talk

Example: *I won't be able to work as quickly as the other group members.*

Example: *Nobody will be interested in what I have to say in my presentation.*

I won't have anything interesting to talk about at the party.

I don't know why I'm going to the interview. The other applicants are probably more qualified.

The topic of my presentation isn't that interesting. My audience will be bored.

Other statement: _____
_____

Other statement: _____
_____

Positive Self-Talk

Example: *I'll do my best and ask for help if I need it.*

Example: *Others may share my opinions or come to understand another perspective better.*

_____
_____

_____
_____

_____
_____

_____
_____

_____
_____

Personal Report of Communication Apprehension[36]

Directions: The Personal Report of Communication Apprehension (PRCA) is composed of twenty-four statements concerning feelings about communication with other people. Please indicate the degree to which each statement applies to you by marking whether you (1) strongly agree, (2) agree, (3) are undecided, (4) disagree, or (5) strongly disagree. Work quickly; record your first impression.

_____ 1. I dislike participating in group discussions.

_____ 2. Generally, I am comfortable while participating in group discussions.

_____ 3. I am tense and nervous while participating in group discussions.

_____ 4. I like to get involved in group discussions.

_____ 5. Engaging in a group discussion with new people makes me tense and nervous.

_____ 6. I am calm and relaxed while participating in a group discussion.

_____ 7. Generally, I am nervous when I have to participate in a meeting.

_____ 8. Usually I am calm and relaxed while participating in a meeting.

_____ 9. I am very calm and relaxed when I am called upon to express an opinion at a meeting.

_____ 10. I am afraid to express myself at meetings.

_____ 11. Communicating at meetings usually makes me feel uncomfortable.

_____ 12. I am very relaxed when answering questions at a meeting.

_____ 13. While participating in a conversation with a new acquaintance, I feel very nervous.

_____ 14. I have no fear of speaking up in conversations.

_____ 15. Ordinarily I am very tense and nervous in conversations.

_____ 16. Ordinarily I am very calm and relaxed in conversations.

_____ 17. While conversing with a new acquaintance, I feel very relaxed.

_____ 18. I'm afraid to speak up in conversations.

_____ 19. I have no fear of giving a speech.

_____ 20. Certain parts of my body feel very tense and rigid while I am giving a speech.

_____ 21. I feel relaxed while giving a speech.

_____ 22. My thoughts become confused and jumbled when I am giving a speech.

_____ 23. I face the prospect of giving a speech with confidence.

_____ 24. While giving a speech, I get so nervous I forget facts I really know.

Scoring: The PRCA permits computation of one total score and four subscores. The subscores are related to communication apprehension in each of four common communication contexts: group discussions, meetings, interpersonal conversations, and public speaking. As you score each subcategory, begin with a score of 18 points. Then add or subtract from 18 based on the following instructions:

Subscores	Scoring Formula
Group discussions	18 + scores for items 2, 4, and 6; – scores for items 1, 3, and 5
Meetings	18 + scores for items 8, 9, and 12; – scores for items 7, 10, and 11
Interpersonal conversations	18 + scores for items 14, 16, and 17; – scores for items 13, 15, and 18
Public speaking	18 + scores for items 19, 21, and 23; – scores for items 20, 22, and 24

Communication Assessment (*continued*)

To obtain your total score for the PRCA, simply add your four subscores together. Your score should range between 24 points and 120 points. If your score is less than 24 points or more than 120 points, you have made a mistake in computing the score. Scores on the four contexts (groups, meetings, interpersonal conversations, and public speaking) can range from a low of 6 points to a high of 30 points. Any score more than 18 points indicates some degree of apprehension. If your score is more than 18 points for the public speaking context, you are like the overwhelming majority of Americans.

Norms for PRCA

	Mean	Standard Deviation
Total score	65.5	15.3
Group	15.4	4.8
Meetings	16.4	4.8
Interpersonal	14.5	4.2
Public speaking	19.3	5.1

Source: From Richmond, Virginia P. & James C. Mc Croskey *Communication Apprehension, Avoidance And Effectiveness, 5/e.* Published by Allyn and Bacon, Boston, MA. Copyright © 1998 by Pearson Education. Reprinted by permission of the publisher.

Key Terms

closure principle
cognitive restructuring
communication apprehension
figure–ground principle
intrapersonal communication
perception
perception checking
proximity principle
purposeful living
reference group

reflective appraisal
role
self-acceptance
self-appraisal
self-assertiveness
self-awareness
self-concept
self-esteem
self-fulfilling prophecy
self-monitoring

self-responsibility
self-talk
significant other
similarity principle
simplicity principle
social comparison
systematic desensitization
visualization

Notes

1. Graeme Burton and Richard Dimbley, *Between Ourselves: An Introduction to Interpersonal Communication*, 2nd ed. (London: Arnold, 1995), p. 2.

2. *The American Heritage Dictionary of the English Language*, 4th ed. (Boston: Houghton Mifflin, 2000), pp. 1303, 1304.

3. Sharon Begley, "Angle of Questioning," *Newsweek* (March 19, 2007), p. 13.

4. Douglas A. Bernstein et al., *Psychology*, 7th ed. (Boston: Houghton Mifflin, 2006), p. 161.

5. Ibid., p. 172.

6. Ibid., p. 162.

7. Ibid.

8. J. Richard Block and Harold Yuker, *Can You Believe Your Eyes?* (New York: Gardner Press, 1989), p. 239.

9. Ronald B. Adler, Lawrence B. Rosenfeld, and Russell F. Proctor II, *Interplay: The Process of Interpersonal Communication*, 8th ed. (Fort Worth, TX: Harcourt Brace, 2001), p. 114.

10. Sharon S. Brehm, Saul M. Kassin, and Steven Fein, *Social Psychology*, 6th ed. (Boston: Houghton Mifflin, 2005), p. 57.

11. January 11, 2006, http://en.wikipedia.org/wiki/Self-awareness.

12. Daniel Goleman, *Emotional Intelligence* (New York: Bantam, 1995), pp. 43, 47.

13. Ibid., p. 43.

14. http://changingminds.org/explanations/theories/self-monitoring.htm

15. Brehm et al., p. 65.

16. Anthony G. Greenwald, "The Totalitarian Ego: Fabrication and Revision of Personal History," *American Psychologist* 35 (1980), pp. 603–618.

17. Min-Sun Kim, *Non-Western Perspectives on Human Communication* (Thousand Oaks, CA: Sage, 2002), p. 9.

18. Nathaniel Branden, www.nathanielbranden.com.

19. Richard E. Boyatzis, "Developing Emotional Intelligence Competencies," in *Applying Emotional Intelligence: A Practitioner's Guide*, ed. Joseph Ciarrochi and John D. Mayer (New York: Psychology Press, 2007), p. 42.

20. Albert Bandura, *Social Foundations of Thought and Action: A Social Cognitive Theory* (Englewood Cliffs, NJ: Prentice Hall, 1986), pp. 399–408. Cited in William Crain, *Theories of Development: Concepts and Applications*, 4th ed. (Upper Saddle River, NJ: Prentice Hall, 2000), p. 203.

21. Leon Festinger, "A Theory of Social Comparison Processes," *Human Relations* 7 (1954), pp. 117–140.

22. Branden, www.nathanielbranden.com

23. Roy F. Baumeister, Jennifer D. Campbell, Joachim I. Krueger, and Kathleen D. Vohs, "Exploring the Self-Esteem Myth," *Scientific American* (December 20, 2004), www.sciam.com/print_version.cfm?articleID=000CB565-F330-11BE-AD0683414B7F0000.

24. The first five strategies are found in Nathaniel Branden, *The Power of Self-Esteem* (Deerfield Beach, FL: Health Communications, 1992), pp. 168–169.

25. Shad Helmstetter, *Who Are You Really, and What Do You Want?* (New York: Park Avenue Press, 2003), p. 47.

26. The discussion of communication apprehension is based on Chapter 3 of Isa Engleberg's and John Daly's, *Presentations in Everyday Life: Strategies for Effective Speaking*, 2nd ed. (Boston: Houghton Mifflin, 2005); and Chapter 4 of Isa Engleberg's and Dianna Wynn's, *Working in Groups: Communication Principles and Strategies*, 4th ed. (Boston: Houghton Mifflin, 2007).

27. Virginia P. Richmond and James C. McCroskey, *Communication: Apprehension, Avoidance, and Effectiveness*, 4th ed. (Scottsdale, AZ: Gorsuch, Scarisbrick, 1995), p. 32.

28. Brehm et al., p. 525.

29. See John A. Daly and James C. McCroskey, eds., *Avoiding Communication: Shyness, Reticence, and Communication Apprehension* (Thousand Oaks, CA: Sage, 1984); Richmond and McCroskey; Karen Kangas Dwyer, *Conquer Your Speechfright*, 2nd ed. (Belmont, CA: Thomson Wadsworth, 2005); and Michael T. Motley, *Overcoming Your Fear of Public Speaking: A Proven Method* (Boston: Houghton Mifflin, 1997).

30. Dwyer, p. 23.

31. Peter Desberg, *Speaking Scared, Sounding Good* (Garden City Park, NY: Square One Publishers, 2007), p. 60.

32. Ibid., pp. 101–110. Desberg describes several effective relaxation exercises that readers can practice. Desberg notes that "Fortunately, it feels great to practice them." p. 100.

33. Ibid., p. 76.

34. As cited in Richmond and McCroskey, pp. 97 and 101. For more on systematic desensitization, see Richmond and McCroskey, pp. 97–102; and Dwyer, pp. 95–103 and 137–141.

35. Daniel Goleman, *Social Intelligence* (New York: Bantam, 2006), pp. 41–42.

36. Richmond and McCroskey, pp. 129–130.

Understanding Others

Key Elements of Communication	Communication Axioms	Guiding Principles of Intercultural Communication
Self	*Communication Is Personal*	Recognize how *your* culture affects your perceptions and self-identity. Avoid ethnocentrism and practice mindfulness.
Others	*Communication Is Relational*	Recognize how the cultures of others affect their perceptions and self-identity. Avoid stereotyping and prejudice; reject discrimination and racism.
Purpose	*Communication Is Intentional*	Combine cultural knowledge with mindful observations to set communication goals.
Context	*Communication Is Contextual*	Adapt to high- and low-context cultures and to diverse perceptions of time and personal space.
Content	*Communication Is Symbolic*	Adapt messages to cultural dimensions: individualism–collectivism, power distance, uncertainty avoidance, and masculine–feminine values.
Structure	*Communication Is Structured*	Understand the ways in which cultural perspectives influence message structure.
Expression	*Communication Is Irreversible*	Use culturally appropriate verbal and nonverbal communication strategies and skills.

The Many Faces of Others

The increasing diversity of the U.S. population affects us in many ways—socially, economically, artistically, and spiritually. We also reach beyond our borders to other cultures through international trade, job outsourcing, military intervention, and global politics. More than ever, we must communicate effectively with many people who are not just like us.

The "other" in a communication transaction can be one person or an audience of one thousand, a close friend or a total stranger. You and the "other" may share many beliefs and behaviors or live significantly different lifestyles. If someone is very different from yourself, it's still possible to communicate effectively, but it takes understanding, respect, and effort. To connect with and adapt to the many "others" you encounter, you need to understand how their characteristics, cultural attitudes, beliefs, and values affect the ways in which they speak, listen, and behave.

THE CHANGING FACE OF THE UNITED STATES

According to the 2000 Census, the "face" of the United States has changed significantly from the faces known by previous generations. Not only are there many more faces, but the color and characteristics of those faces have changed as well.[1]

During the 1990s, the Hispanic population increased 58 percent, and the Asian population increased 48 percent. Between 1990 and 2000, more than 13 million people immigrated to the United States, the largest immigration number in a ten-year span in the country's history. The following percentages represent the racial and ethnic makeup of people living in the United States and reported in the 2000 Census.

Whites	75.1%
Hispanics	12.5%
Blacks	12.3%
Asians	3.6%
Native American or Alaskan native	0.9%
Native Hawaiian/Pacific Islander	0.1%
Other races	5.5%
Two or more races	2.4%

How do these three new citizens (originally from Haiti, St. Vincent, and Canada) and the 40,000 noncitizens in the U.S. military reflect the changing face and future of the United States?

If you took time to add up the percentages in Census 2000, you would come up with a total of 112.4 percent. This is because, for Census 2000, the federal government considered race and Hispanic origin to be two separate categories. Hispanics are considered an ethnic group identified by their country of origin rather than race. Thus, people who list themselves as Hispanics on the Census form are also asked to designate their race.

The census shows that, in 2000, three-quarters of the people in the United States were white. By 2006, the percentage of whites had decreased to 56.6 percent.[2] Today, more than half the people living in California are nonwhite, as are the majority of individuals living in several large American cities. Moreover, the population of Hispanic, Asian, and other immigrant groups is growing and will continue to grow. Soon after the middle of this century, whites will become one of the many minority groups living in America.[3] In short, there will be no majority culture; all groups will need to understand, respect, and adapt to cultures that are not their own.

DEFINING CULTURE

When some people hear the phrase *cultural diversity*, they think about race or people from other countries. Words such as *nationality*, *race*, and *ethnicity* are often used synonymously with the term *culture*. However, the concept of culture is much more than a country of origin, skin color, or ancestral heritage. In Chapter 1, we defined **culture** as "a learned set of shared interpretations about beliefs, values, and norms which affect the behaviors of a relatively large group of people."[4]

Within most cultures there are also groups of people—members of **co-cultures**—who coexist within the mainstream society yet remain connected to one another through their cultural heritage.[5] In the United States, Native American tribes are co-cultures, as are African Americans, Hispanic/Latino Americans, Asian Americans, Arab Americans, Irish Americans, and members of large and small religious groups. Given our broad definition of culture, a Nebraska rancher and a Boston professor can have very different cultural perspectives, as would a native Egyptian, Brazilian, Indonesian Muslim, and Chippewa tribal member.

Barriers to Understanding Others

Many years ago, a white American business*man* could predict the gender, race, average age, and even religion of his neighbors, friends, and colleagues: They would look like him, speak like him, and share many of the same attitudes, beliefs, and values.

Many years ago, hospital nurses could also predict the gender, predominant race, and average age of their colleagues and the doctors for whom they worked. Very little accommodation was needed to live and work in a predictable world. Today, corporations and hospitals are multicultural communities in which a thirty-five-year-old woman from India might be an orderly, a manager, a nurse, a doctor, a clerk, or a hospital's chief executive officer.

Learning to communicate effectively in the global village that characterizes life in the twenty-first century can be a significant challenge. Culturally sensitive communicators develop effective strategies and skills for interacting with others from diverse backgrounds. Yet learning about people from other cultures will not make you a more effective and ethical communicator if you succumb to five obstacles that can inhibit your understanding of others: ethnocentrism, stereotyping, prejudice, discrimination, and racism.

ETHNOCENTRISM

Ethnocentrism is a belief that your culture is superior to others. Ethnocentrism is not just about patriotism or pride. It is a mistaken belief that your culture is a superior culture with special rights and privileges that are or should be denied to others. An ethnocentric communicator believes the following:

- My culture should be the role model for other cultures.
- People would be happier if they lived like people in my culture.
- Most other cultures are backward when compared with my culture.[6]

Ethnocentric communicators offend others when they imply that they represent a superior culture with superior values. As an ethical and culturally sensitive communicator, you should examine your own ethnocentric beliefs. You can begin by investigating how your culture and your culture-based perspectives may differ from others. At the end of this chapter, you can complete the GENE (Generalized Ethnocentrism) Scale to assess your level of ethnocentrism.

STEREOTYPING

Stereotypes are generalizations about a group of people that oversimplify their characteristics. When we stereotype others, we rely on exaggerated beliefs to make judgments about a group of people. Unfortunately, stereotyping usually attributes negative traits to an entire group when, in reality, only a few people in the group may possess those traits. A study of college students found that, even in the mid 1990s, African Americans were stereotyped as lazy and loud, and Jews were described as shrewd and intelligent.[7] Comments such as "Athletes are poor students," "Old people are boring and incompetent," and "Hispanics never arrive on time" are stereotypical statements.

In addition to negative stereotypes, we may hold positive ones. Comments such as "Asian students excel in math and science," "Females are more compassionate than males," and "Homosexual men have a great sense of style" make positive but all-inclusive generalizations. Although positive stereotypes may not seem harmful, they can lead to unfair judgments. Believing that women are more compassionate may lead students to resent assertive female professors who strictly enforce course attendance policies. Assuming that all Asian students are good in science may overlook an individual's interest or talent in the arts.

PREJUDICE

Stereotypes lead to **prejudices**: positive or negative attitudes about an individual or cultural group based on little or no direct experience with that person or group. The word *prejudice* has two parts: *pre*, meaning "before," and *judice* as in *judge*. When you believe or express a prejudice, you are making a judgment about someone before

Intercultural communication scholars Stella Ting-Toomey and Leeva C. Chung contend that the nature of our language shapes many of our stereotypes. Paired words, for example, encourage either/or thinking: straight or gay, us or them, female or male, black or white, rich or poor, old or young, red state or blue state. Such either/or perceptions lead us to interpret the social world as either good or evil, fair or unfair, and right or wrong.

The media also plays a critical role in shaping stereotypes about ourselves and others. Despite some improvements and even outstanding exceptions, television and film tend to portray certain cultural and ethnic groups in stereotypical ways. Ting-Toomey and Chung offer some examples:

- Native American males are strong warriors or sidekicks to European American male heroes.
- Native American women are maidens and princesses or symbols of ancient wisdom and harmony with nature.
- African American males are relegated to comedic or athletic and sexually powerful roles.
- African American women are either sexually alluring or asexual and nurturing mammies.
- Latino/Latina Americans work in low-status occupations.[1]

[1]Stella Ting-Toomey and Leeva C. Chung, *Understanding Intercultural Communication* (Los Angeles, CA: Roxbury, 2005), pp. 236–239.

you have taken time to get to know that person and see whether your opinions and feelings are justified. Although prejudices can be positive—"He must be brilliant if he went to Yale"—most prejudices are negative. Statements such as "I don't want a disabled person working on our group project," "I'm not hiring someone that old," or "I'm not voting for a pregnant woman" are all examples of prejudging someone based on stereotypes about people with disabilities, elders, and pregnant women. These kinds of prejudices have several characteristics:

- Biased perceptions and beliefs about group members that are not based on direct experience and firsthand knowledge
- Irrational feelings of dislike and even hatred for certain groups
- A readiness to behave in negative and unjust ways toward members of the group[8]

DISCRIMINATION

The word *discrimination* has many definitions. People with acute hearing can discriminate (that is, differentiate) one sound or tone from another. However, we use the term **discrimination** to describe how we act out and express prejudice. When we discriminate, we exclude groups of people from opportunities granted to others: employment, promotion, housing, political expression, equal rights, and access to educational, recreational, and social institutions.

Sadly, discrimination comes in many forms: racial discrimination; ethnic discrimination; religious discrimination; gender discrimination; sexual harassment; discrimination based on sexual orientation, disability, and age; and discrimination against people from different social classes and political ideologies. There has been enormous progress since the 1960s, when Congress passed far-reaching antidiscrimination laws. But the United States still has a long way to go,

To what extent, if at all, does this photograph make you uncomfortable and how does that discomfort reflect implicit biases you may have about race and female/male relationships?

CommEthics Ethics and Implicit Biases

The National Communication Association's *Credo for Ethical Communication* includes the following principle: We condemn communication that degrades individuals and humanity through distortion, intimidation, coercion, and violence, and through the expression of intolerance and hatred.[1] Practicing this principle, however, is more difficult than it seems. Despite claims of "I'm not prejudiced," most of us have positive and negative attitudes about cultural groups based on little or no direct experience with that group.

Two Harvard researchers, Mahzarin Banaji and Brian Nosek, have developed an Implicit Association Test that you can take for free on Harvard's website at www.implicit.harvard.edu. The results indicate that the majority of Americans, including people of color and other minorities, show a variety of biases they believe they do not have. Banaji and Nosek recommend that when it comes to prejudice, it is less important how biased you are and more important how willing you are to confront your unconscious thoughts about others. When you acknowledge your unconscious biases, you can take steps to confront them.[2]

If you decide to take the online Implicit Association Test, we urge you to read the background information, the answers to frequently asked questions about the test, the section on understanding and interpreting test results, and the section on ethical considerations. Why? Because the results may surprise and even upset you. For example, most people who take the test show biases for Christians over Jews, the rich over the poor, and men's careers over women's careers. Results usually contrast with what most people say about themselves—that they have no bias. Test results have also revealed another unsettling truth: Minorities internalize the same biases as majority groups. Some 48 percent of blacks show a pro-white or anti-black bias, 36 percent of Arab Muslims showed an anti-Muslim bias, and 38 percent of gays and lesbians showed a bias for straight people over homosexuals.[3]

[1]www.natcom.org/aboutNCA/Policies/Platform.html

[2]Shankar Vedantam, "For Allen and Webb, Implicit Biases Would Be Better Confronted," *The Washington Post*, October 9, 2006, p. A2. Also see www.washingtonpost.com/science and implicit .harvard.edu

[3]Shankar Vendtam, "See No Bias," *The Washington Post*, January 23, 2005, p. W12. Also see implicity.hard.edu

despite a great deal of civil rights legislation and greater tolerance of diversity. Is your opinion about discrimination "colored" by the color of your own skin, by your gender, or by the religion you profess? Figure 3.1 documents the large gap in perceptions by examining black and white viewpoints about economic inequities, racism, discrimination, and government aid for the disadvantaged.

RACISM

Racism is the result of ethnocentrism, stereotyping, prejudice, and discrimination. As you now know, stereotyping occurs when we make generalizations about a group of people that oversimplify their characteristics. Stereotyping can lead to prejudices: positive or negative attitudes about an individual or cultural group based on little or no direct experience with that group. When you act out and express prejudice, you discriminate. **Racism** entails practicing ethnocentrism, stereotyping, prejudice, and discrimination. People who are racist assume that a person with a certain inherited characteristic (usually a superficial characteristic like skin color) also has a certain character and set of abilities, and that some "races" are superior to others.

Racism usually leads to the abuse of power. When you have power, you can control, dominate, restrain, mistreat, and harm people of other races without fear of consequences. Racism enables the people who control power to keep other races at a significant disadvantage. In the Americas, white slave owners controlled their black slaves. World War II Nazis controlled and eliminated "inferior" races. Permission to torture and humiliate others unleashes the most horrible forms of racism.

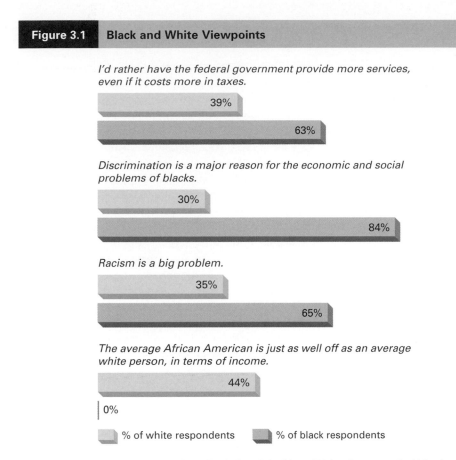

Figure 3.1   Black and White Viewpoints

I'd rather have the federal government provide more services, even if it costs more in taxes.

39%

63%

Discrimination is a major reason for the economic and social problems of blacks.

30%

84%

Racism is a big problem.

35%

65%

The average African American is just as well off as an average white person, in terms of income.

44%

0%

■ % of white respondents   ■ % of black respondents

Source: Based on a Washington Post/Kaiser Family Foundation/Harvard University survey of middle-class blacks and whites with incomes between $30,000 and $75,000, as reported in the *Washington Post National Weekly Edition,* October 16–22, 1995, p. 8. Quoted in Judith N. Martin and Thomas K. Nakayama, *Intercultural Communication in Contexts* (Mountain View, CA: Mayfield, 1997), p. 83.

Understanding Cultures

Each one of us has a certain ethnicity, gender, age, religious beliefs (including atheism), socioeconomic position, sexual orientation, and ability. We also live in or have come from a certain region or country. Here are some examples:

- A sixth-generation, female, Lutheran schoolteacher whose family still lives in the same midwestern town

- A fifty-five-year-old Jewish male scientist living in New York whose family emigrated from Russia

- An Islamic, African American female working as a researcher for the federal government in Washington, DC

- A thirty-year-old executive whose parents are Cuban refugees living in Miami

- A second-generation Japanese American teenager whose parents were detained in an internment camp during World War II and who just won the Van Cliburn piano competition

All of these characteristics contribute to our **social identity**: our self-concept as derived from the social categories to which we see ourselves belonging.[9] However, although we

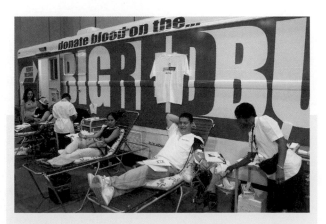

How has human genome research and biological studies affected beliefs about the blood of different races?

CommFYI   Is There Such a Thing as Race?

The question "Is there such a thing as race?" may seem dimwitted. After all, the U.S. Census asks questions about race and we have laws prohibiting discrimination on the basis of race. We've witnessed race riots, seen an increasing number of interracial marriages, and debated the fairness of race-based grants and scholarships. No wonder we believe that there is such a thing as race.

Communication professors Mark P. Orbe and Tina M. Harris define **race** as a socially constructed concept that classifies people into separate value-based categories.[1] Genetic researchers, however, see race as the natural results of genetic changes that began 50,000 years ago as many generations of people migrated out of Africa to different continents.[2]

Unfortunately, there are many people who see race as subdivisions of the human species based on *significant* genetic differences. Even in ancient times, the Egyptians, Greeks, and Romans left paintings, sculptures, and writings depicting people with perceived racial differences.[3] In general, modern ideas about race as we know it today did not exist until the eighteenth century, when a German scientist named Johann Friedrich Blumenbach classified humans based on geography and observed physical differences by using Caucasians as the ideal. The result was a racial ranking of (white) Europeans first, Malays and Native Americans second, and Africans and Asians last. The following pyramid illustrates Blumenbach's 1795 Geometry of Human Order[4]:

These classifications led to the separation of people based on skin color: white, yellow, and black.

Many anthropologists, biologists, geneticists, and ethicists, however, do not share these historical or popular beliefs about the nature of race. They have termed race as "a social construct, not a scientific classification," and a "biologically meaningless" concept.[5] They emphasize that 99.9 percent of DNA sequences are common to all humans.[6] Extensive research indicates that pure races never existed and that all humans belong to the same species, *Homo sapiens*, which originated in Africa.

Before the human genome was decoded, most systems of race classification were based on characteristics such as skin color, which often resulted in a cruel agenda that claimed one race's alleged superiority over others. The genetic definition of race has no such agenda and has absolutely nothing to do with any physical or behavioral characteristics.[7]

So what does all of this mean? Is there such a thing as race? The word *race* certainly has meaning and is very real to all of us. Those who believe that one race (depending on their ethnicity or background) is better than another have an erroneous, misguided, or biased view of race. As we see it, race should be viewed as both a socially constructed concept *and* understood as the outcome of ancient population shifts that left their mark in our genes. When race is viewed in social and genetic contexts, it becomes a very neutral and natural human characteristic.

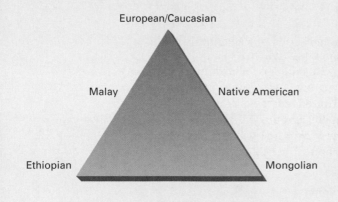

European/Caucasian

Malay   Native American

Ethiopian   Mongolian

[1]Mark P. Orbe and Tina M. Harris, *Interracial Communication: Theory into Practice* (Belmont, CA: Wadsworth, 2001), p. 6.

[2]Nicholas Wade, *Before the Dawn: Recovering the Lost History of Our Ancestor*s (New York, Penguin, 2006), p. 181.

[3]Marcel Danesi and Paul Perron, *Analyzing Cultures: An Introduction and Handbook* (Bloomington, IN: Indiana University Press, 1999), p. 25.

[4]Orbe and Harris, p. 28.

[5]Wade, p. 183.

[6]Orbe and Harris, p. 31.

[7]Wade, p. 188.

may identify ourselves as Irish, Korean, Ethiopian, or Sioux, many of us have lost touch with our family history and culture.

UNDERSTANDING YOUR CULTURE

Culture affects your life in both obvious and subtle ways. Thus, the first step in understanding others is to understand yourself. You derive a significant part of your social identity from the cultural groups you belong to as well as the groups you do not belong to: "I know who I am and that I am *not* you." This is a thoroughly natural thing

CommFAQ Is Whiteness a Culture?

If you belong to the mainstream culture in a country—in the United States, white Christian—you may not think you have a culture. When asked what *whiteness* means, white students often respond with answers such as, "Whiteness doesn't mean anything except that is what color I am," or "Whiteness means I'm like most Americans." Such beliefs undermine our ability to understand the privileges that come with being a white American, and blind us from seeing the ways others perceive and interact with people who are white.

Many white people don't think of their behavior as characteristic of a culture. Because whiteness is a norm in the United States, it is difficult to classify it as a culture. As Rita Hardiman wrote,

> Like fish, whose environment is water, we are surrounded by Whiteness and it is easy to think that what we experience is reality rather than recognizing it as the particular culture of a particular group. And like fish who are not aware of water until they are out of it, White people sometimes become aware of their culture only when they get to know, or interact with, the cultures of people of color.[1]

White people in the United States enjoy many "race"-based privileges, such as higher incomes and the assumption of more corporate and political leadership positions. Children grow up with stories praising Snow White's pure-white skin or Cinderella's golden hair. Whites can wander through stores and be fairly sure no store employee will track them as potential thieves. In fact, and until recently, Band-Aids™ were always "flesh" colored to blend with white skin.[2] By understanding the "invisibility" of whiteness, we can learn to "see" the ways in which whiteness operates as a dominant social force that mobilizes how people act and interact, not only in the United States, but around the world.[3]

[1]Rita Hardiman, "White Racial Identity Development in the United States," in *Race, Ethnicity and Self: Identity in Multi-Cultural Perspective*, ed. Elizabeth Pathy Salett and Dianne R. Koslow (Washington, DC: National MultiCultural Institute, 1994), pp. 130–131.

[2]Judith N. Martin and Thomas K. Nakayama, *Experiencing Intercultural Communication* (Boston: McGraw-Hill, 2001), pp. 84–86.

[3]Philip C. Wander et al., "Whiteness and Beyond," in *Whiteness: The Communication of Social Identity*, ed. Thomas K. Nakayama and Judith N. Martin (Thousand Oaks, CA: Sage, 1999), pp. 22–23.

to do. However, on the basis of these characteristics, we often divide our world into distinct and very opposite social groups (men and women, rich and poor, Christian and non-Christian, black and white, young and old, American and foreign) in a way that sets us in actual opposition to others. A more constructive approach is to explore your own social identity so that you can learn to communicate with people with other identities. Just as you learn about yourself by interacting with others, you also learn about the culture of your social group by interacting with *other* social groups.

In his book, *Religious Literacy*, Stephen Prothero notes that Americans are a very religious people: Ninety percent of adults in the United States believe in God, 80 percent say that religion is important to them personally, and more than 70 percent report praying daily.[10] Yet these same Americans know very little about their *own* religion, let alone the religions of others. Prothero shares the following facts from several of his surveys[11]:

- Only 50 percent of American adults can name even one of the four Gospels.
- Most Americans cannot name the first book of the Hebrew Bible.
- Ten percent of Americans believe that Joan of Arc was Noah's wife.

UNDERSTANDING THE CULTURES OF OTHERS

If you believe you can live a life in which you avoid people from other cultures, you are fooling yourself. Many remote towns have been transformed by migrant workers, religious groups that settled locally, and immigrant populations that have found a collective home. Even though you may live in a one-race or predominantly one-religion community, you may find it difficult to advance in a career unless you are willing to

CommQuiz Questions of Faith

There are more than 4,000 religions in the world. How many can you name? Like most of us, you only may be familiar with the "big" religions and a few "obscure" faiths. Yet, as Stephen Prothero explains, many of us are illiterate about our own and others' religions. He defines **religious illiteracy** as "the ability to understand and use the religious terms, symbols, images, beliefs, practices, scripture, heroes, themes, and stories that are employed in American public life."[1]

The following true/false items test your knowledge about a few of the world's major religions[2]:

T F ? 1. Muslims believe in Islam and the Islamic way of life.

T F ? 2. Judaism is an older religion than Buddhism.

T F ? 3. Islam is a monotheistic religion (belief in one God) just like Christianity and Judaism.

T F ? 4. A Christian Scientist believes that disease is a delusion of the carnal mind that can be cured by prayer.

T F ? 5. Jews fast during Yom Kippur; Muslims fast during Ramadan.

T F ? 6. Jesus Christ was Jewish.

T F ? 7. Roman Catholics throughout the world outnumber all other Christians combined.

T F ? 8. Sunni Muslims compose about 90 percent of all adherents to Islam.

T F ? 9. Hindus believe in the idea of reincarnation.

T F ? 10. The Ten Commandments form the basis of Jewish laws.

T F ? 11. Mormonism is a Christian faith founded in the United States.

T F ? 12. The Protestant reformer, Martin Luther, labeled the beliefs of Muslims, Jews, and Roman Catholics as false.

T F ? 13. One-third of the world's population is Christian.

T F ? 14. One-fifth of the world's population is Muslim.

T F ? 15. Hinduism is the oldest of the world's major religions, dating back more than 3,000 years.

Answers:

All of the statements are true.

[1]Stephen Prothero, *Religious Literacy: What Every American Needs to Know—And Doesn't* (New York: HarperSanFrancisco, 2007), p. 11. See also, Prothro's Religious Literacy Quiz, pp. 27–28 and 235–239.

[2]Questions are based on three sources: Robert Pollock, *The Everything World's Religions Book* (Avon, MA: Adams Media, 2002); Leo Rosen (ed.), *Religions of America: Fragment of Faith in an Age of Crisis* (New York: Touchstone, 1975); *Encyclopedia Britannica Almanac 2004* (Chicago: Encyclopedia Britannica, 2003).

---

work in a diverse environment. Even religious communities that flee the "evils" of American culture often find themselves dependent on that culture for food, jobs, and medical care.

Regardless of whether you are a Catholic, a Mormon, a Jew, a Muslim, a Buddhist, a Baptist, a Hindu, a Sikh, a Janist, or an atheist, "you must remember that people feel strongly about their religion, and that differences between religious beliefs and practices do matter."[12] For example, among the Oriya Brahman of India, it is considered shameless if a husband and wife eat a meal together. In France, religious attire, including headscarves for Muslim girls, Christian crosses, and skullcaps for Jewish boys have been banned from public high schools.[13]

You are surrounded and dependent on diverse groups of people who deserve the same understanding and respect you bestow on your own culture. The sooner you learn about the people around you, the better you will communicate with the range of people in our pluralistic society.

There are more than three hundred ethnic cultures in the United States. At many colleges, dozens of languages are spoken. When we recommend that you become well informed and knowledgeable about other cultures, we may seem to be asking for the impossible. But you only need to learn about the major cultural groups that you are likely to encounter in your studies, at work, and when you travel within this country or throughout the world.

THE DIMENSIONS OF CULTURE

We owe a great deal to a social psychologist and an anthropologist for identifying several important dimensions of culture. Dutch social psychologist Geert H. Hofstede's groundbreaking research on cultural characteristics has transformed our understanding of others. He defines **intercultural dimension** as "an aspect of a culture that can be measured relative to other cultures."[14] His work on cultural variability identifies four dimensions that characterize cultural groups: individualism–collectivism, power distance, uncertainty avoidance, and masculine–feminine values. Anthropologist Edward T. Hall adds a fifth and sixth dimension: high-context and low-context cultures and monochronic–polychronic time.

Individualism–Collectivism   According to Hofstede and many contemporary researchers, those of us in the United States accept **individualism** as a cultural value. As a whole, we believe that the individual is important, that independence is worth pursuing, that personal achievement should be rewarded, and that individual uniqueness is an important value.[15] In the United States, an "I" orientation prevails. However, the value of individualism is not shared by most other cultures. As much as 70 percent of the world's population regards interdependence or **collectivism** as a more important value.[16] In these cultures, "we" is much more important than "I." The following features are characteristic of collectivist cultures:

- There is greater emphasis on the views, needs, and goals of the in-group than on the individual's views, needs, and goals.
- Social norms and duty are defined by the in-group rather than by the individual's personal pleasure or personal benefits.
- Beliefs that are shared with the in-group are more important than beliefs that distinguish yourself from the in-group.
- There is greater readiness to cooperate with in-group members.[17]

Individualism–collectivism may be the most important factor distinguishing one culture from another.[18] For instance, many Japanese see babies as overly individualistic and in need of training to become connected; in the United States, babies are often seen as too connected and in need of training to become more individualistic.[19] Figure 3.2 illustrates the most individualistic and collectivist cultures.

Given the top ranking of the United States in terms of individualism, should you assume that all Americans are individualistic? If you answer yes, you are stereotyping. In fact, many African Americans have the characteristics of collective societies, as do Mexican Americans and other Hispanic/Latino co-cultures. Even so, the focus of the United States on individual achievement and personal rewards can make interaction with people from collectivist cultures quite difficult. The U.S. communicator's style and behavior may be viewed as selfish, arrogant, antagonistic, power hungry, ruthless, and impatient. Interestingly, as poor nations gain wealth, they begin to shift toward greater individualism.[20]

Power Distance   Is it easy to make a personal appointment with the president of your college or university? Can you walk into your boss's office or do you have to navigate your way through an army of secretaries and administrative assistants? Does our society truly believe in the sentiments expressed in the U.S. Declaration of Independence that all people are created equal? These are the questions addressed in Hofstede's power distance dimension. **Power distance** refers to the physical and psychological distance between those who have power and those who do not have power in relationships, institutions, and organizations. It also represents "the extent to which the less powerful person in society accepts inequality in power and considers it normal."[21]

SIX DIMENSIONS OF CULTURE

▶ Individualism–Collectivism
▶ Power Distance
▶ Uncertainty Avoidance
▶ Masculine–Feminine Values
▶ High–Low Context
▶ Monochronic–Polychronic Time

| **Figure 3.2** | Individualism and Collectivism |

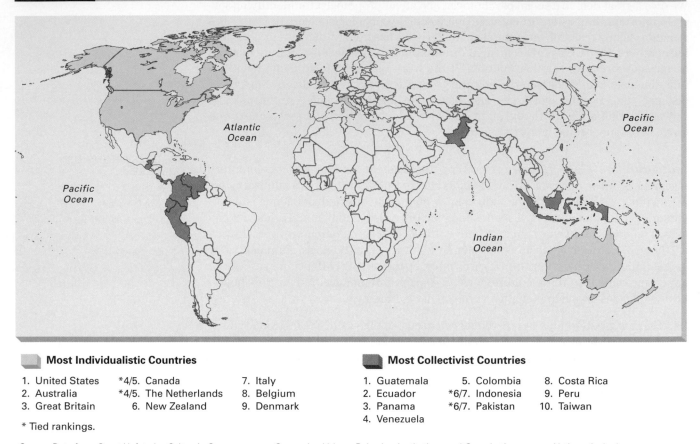

Most Individualistic Countries

1. United States	*4/5. Canada	7. Italy
2. Australia	*4/5. The Netherlands	8. Belgium
3. Great Britain	6. New Zealand	9. Denmark

* Tied rankings.

Most Collectivist Countries

1. Guatemala	5. Colombia	8. Costa Rica
2. Ecuador	*6/7. Indonesia	9. Peru
3. Panama	*6/7. Pakistan	10. Taiwan
4. Venezuela		

Source: Data from Geert Hofstede, *Culture's Consequences: Comparing Values, Behavior, Institutions and Organizations across Nations,* 2nd ed. (Thousand Oaks, CA: Sage, 2001), p. 215.

In cultures with **high power distance**, individuals accept differences in power as normal, that all people are *not* created equal. In such cultures, the privileged have much more power and use it to guide or control the lives of people with less power. In a high-power distance culture, you accept and do not challenge authority. Parents have total control over their children. Husbands may have total control over their wives. And government officials, corporate officers, and religious authorities may dictate rules of behavior and have the power to ensure compliance.

In cultures with **low power distance**, power distinctions are minimized: supervisors work with subordinates, professors work with students, elected officials work with constituents. Figure 3.3 ranks the top cultures in each category of this dimension. Despite the fact that the United States claims to be the greatest democracy on earth and an equal opportunity society, it is sixteenth on the list of low-power-distance cultures such as Finland, Switzerland, Great Britain, Germany, Costa Rica, Australia, The Netherlands, and Canada.

Power distance has enormous implications for communicators. For example, in Australia (a low-power-distance country), students and professors are often on a first-name basis, and lively discussions are the norm in most classes. However, in Malaysia (a high-power-distance country), students show up and are seated *before* class begins; almost no one comes late. Students are polite and appreciative but rarely challenge a professor's claims. In a high-power-distance culture, you do not

Figure 3.3	Power Distance

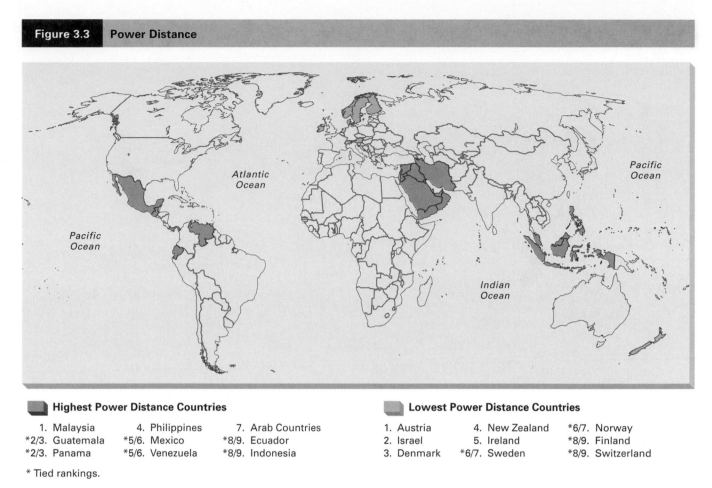

Highest Power Distance Countries

1. Malaysia	4. Philippines	7. Arab Countries
*2/3. Guatemala	*5/6. Mexico	*8/9. Ecuador
*2/3. Panama	*5/6. Venezuela	*8/9. Indonesia

Lowest Power Distance Countries

1. Austria	4. New Zealand	*6/7. Norway
2. Israel	5. Ireland	*8/9. Finland
3. Denmark	*6/7. Sweden	*8/9. Switzerland

* Tied rankings.

Source: Data from Geert Hofstede, *Culture's Consequences: Comparing Values, Behavior, Institutions and Organizations across Nations,* 2nd ed. (Thousand Oaks, CA: Sage, 2001), p. 87.

openly disagree with teachers, elders, bosses, law enforcement officials, or government agents.

If you compare Figures 3.2 and 3.3, you will notice a strong correlation between collectivism and high power distance, and between individualism and low power distance. If you are individualistic and strongly encouraged to express your own opinion, you are more willing to challenge authority. If, on the other hand, your culture is collectivist and your personal opinion is subordinate to the welfare of others, you are less likely to challenge the collective authority of your family, your employer, or your government.

Uncertainty Avoidance How well do you handle unexpected changes or uncertainty? Do you feel more comfortable if your future is predictable? Hofstede defines **uncertainty avoidance** as the extent to which people within a culture are made nervous by situations that they perceive as unstructured, unclear, or unpredictable. If uncertainty makes them very nervous, they avoid these situations by maintaining strict codes of behavior and a belief in absolute truths.[22]

In cultures with **high uncertainty avoidance**, members "feel threatened by uncertain or unknown situations." This feeling is expressed through nervous stress and in a need for predictability—a need for written and unwritten rules.[23] Hofstede puts it this way: "What is different, is dangerous."[24] Cultures with **low uncertainty**

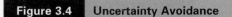

| Figure 3.4 | Uncertainty Avoidance |

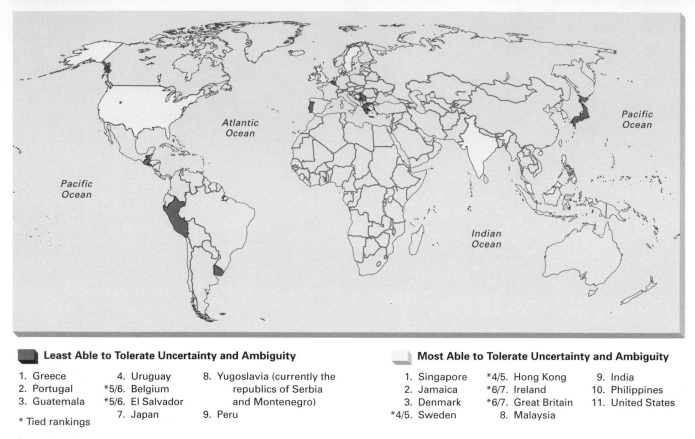

■ Least Able to Tolerate Uncertainty and Ambiguity

1. Greece	4. Uruguay	8. Yugoslavia (currently the
2. Portugal	*5/6. Belgium	republics of Serbia
3. Guatemala	*5/6. El Salvador	and Montenegro)
	7. Japan	9. Peru

* Tied rankings

□ Most Able to Tolerate Uncertainty and Ambiguity

1. Singapore	*4/5. Hong Kong	9. India
2. Jamaica	*6/7. Ireland	10. Philippines
3. Denmark	*6/7. Great Britain	11. United States
*4/5. Sweden	8. Malaysia	

Source: Data from Geert Hofstede, *Culture's Consequences: Comparing Values, Behavior, Institutions and Organizations across Nations,* 2nd ed. (Thousand Oaks, CA: Sage, 2001), p. 151.

avoidance accept change as part of life, tolerate nonconformity, take risks, and view rules and regulations as restricting and counterproductive (see Figure 3.4). Members of low-uncertainty avoidance cultures tend to live day to day. Change, conflict, and competition are natural. Dissent and deviance are not threatening.[25] Rather than seeing differences as dangerous, these cultures take the position: "What is different, is curious."[26]

The United States is eleventh on the list of countries that feel comfortable with uncertainty, following countries like Malaysia, India, and the Philippines. Imagine the communication challenge you face if you are comfortable with change and ambiguity but have to work with someone from a culture with a strong desire to avoid uncertainty. Although you are willing to take risks, the other person finds your attitude unconventional and even threatening. At the same time, you may see the other person as rigid, uncompromising, and fearful to break or bend rules. Yet even in the United States, some institutions shun uncertainty and resist change with all their might. Just try asking some government agencies or public school systems to bend a rule or risk dissent.

Masculine–Feminine Values   Hofstede uses the terms *masculine* and *feminine* to describe whether masculine or feminine traits are valued by a culture. The terms are used to describe a societal perspective, rather than individuals.

Figure 3.5   **Masculine and Feminine Values**

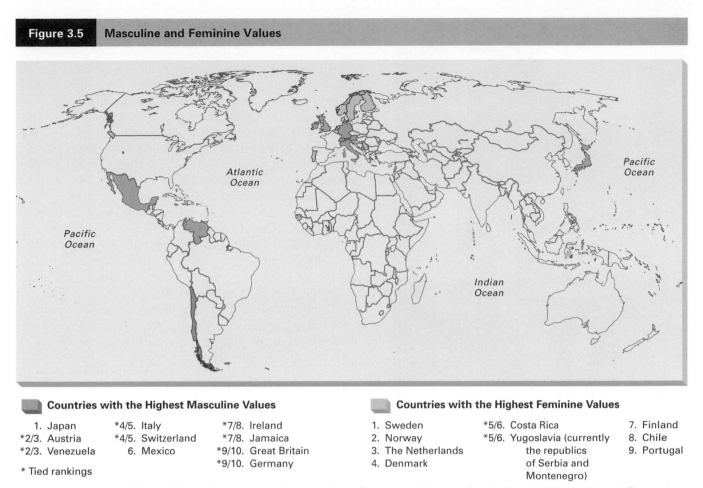

Countries with the Highest Masculine Values

1. Japan	*4/5. Italy	*7/8. Ireland
*2/3. Austria	*4/5. Switzerland	*7/8. Jamaica
*2/3. Venezuela	6. Mexico	*9/10. Great Britain
		*9/10. Germany
* Tied rankings		

Countries with the Highest Feminine Values

1. Sweden	*5/6. Costa Rica	7. Finland
2. Norway	*5/6. Yugoslavia (currently	8. Chile
3. The Netherlands	the republics	9. Portugal
4. Denmark	of Serbia and	
	Montenegro)	

Source: Data from Geert Hofstede, *Culture's Consequences: Comparing Values, Behavior, Institutions and Organizations across Nations,* 2nd ed. (Thousand Oaks, CA: Sage, 2001), p. 286.

In **masculine societies**, men are supposed to be assertive, tough, and focused on material success whereas women are supposed to be more modest, tender, and concerned with the quality of life. In **feminine societies**, gender roles overlap: Both men and women are supposed to be modest, tender, and concerned with the quality of life.[27] Figure 3.5 highlights the countries that differ in terms of masculine–feminine values.

Hofstede ranks the United States as fifteenth in terms of masculine values, but less masculine than Australia, New Zealand, and Greece. In masculine societies, personal success, competition, assertiveness, and strength are admired. Unselfishness and nurturing may be seen as weaknesses or "women's work." Although women have come a long way from the rigid roles of past centuries, they have miles to go before they achieve genuine equality in a masculine-oriented culture.

High-Low Context   In Chapter 1 we defined *context* as the psychosocial, logistical, and interactional environment in which communication occurs. Anthropologist Edward T. Hall sees context as the information that surrounds an event as inextricably bound up with the meaning of the event. He claims that a message's context—in and of itself—may hold more meaning than the actual words in a message.[28] Like Hofstede's dimensions, we can place cultures on a continuum from high context to low context.

How does this photograph of a Swedish father and his children reflect Geert Hofstede's concept of masculine–feminine values?

In a **high-context culture**, very little meaning is expressed through words. Gestures, silence, and facial expressions as well as the relationships among communicators have meaning. In high-context cultures, meaning can be conveyed through status (age, gender, education, family background, title, and affiliations) and through an individual's informal network of friends and associates.

In a **low-context culture**, meaning is expressed primarily through language. As members of a low-context culture, people in North America tend to speak more, speak louder, and speak more rapidly than a person from a high-context culture. We "speak up," "spell it out," "just say no," and "speak our mind." Figure 3.6 contrasts the characteristics of high- and low-context cultures.

High-context communication usually occurs in collectivist cultures in which members share similar attitudes, beliefs, and values. As a result, spoken communication can be indirect, implied, or vague because everyone *gets* the meaning by understanding the context, the person's nonverbal behavior, and the significance of the communicator's status. Notice how the following sayings capture the nature of high-context communication:

Seeing is better than hearing. (Nigeria)

Silence is also speech. (West Africa)

It is the duck that squawks that gets shot. (Japan)

Once you preach, the point is gone. (Zen phrase)

The one who raises her/his voice has already lost. (Japan)

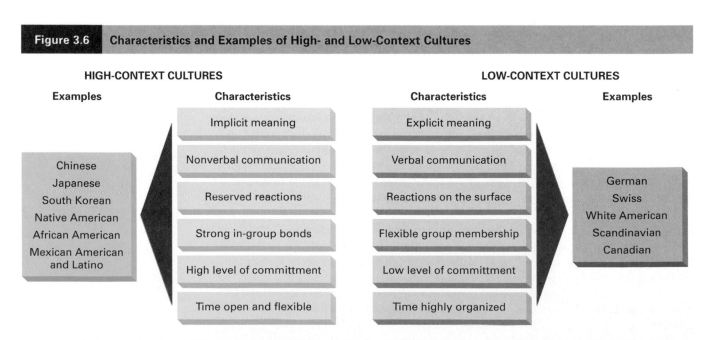

Figure 3.6   Characteristics and Examples of High- and Low-Context Cultures

HIGH-CONTEXT CULTURES		LOW-CONTEXT CULTURES	
Examples	Characteristics	Characteristics	Examples
Chinese, Japanese, South Korean, Native American, African American, Mexican American and Latino	Implicit meaning	Explicit meaning	German, Swiss, White American, Scandinavian, Canadian
	Nonverbal communication	Verbal communication	
	Reserved reactions	Reactions on the surface	
	Strong in-group bonds	Flexible group membership	
	High level of committment	Low level of committment	
	Time open and flexible	Time highly organized	

Source: Peter Andersen et al., "Nonverbal Communication across Cultures," in William B. Gudykunst and Bella Mody (Eds.), *Handbook of International and Intercultural Communication*, 2nd ed. (Thousand Oaks, CA: Sage, 2002), p. 99.

CommFAQ Why Don't We Hear Others' "Voices"?

Muted Group Theory observes that powerful, wealthy groups at the top of a society determine who will communicate and be listened to. For this reason, women, the poor, and people of color have trouble participating and being heard.[1] The following three assumptions in Muted Group Theory explain how women's voices are subdued or silenced in many cultures:

1. Women perceive the world differently than men because of traditional divisions of labor. Examples: Homemaker versus breadwinner, nurse versus doctor.
2. Women's freedom of expression is limited by men's dominance in relationships and institutions. Examples: Women in the United States only gained the right to vote in 1920. The "glass ceiling" prevents women from achieving professional advancement.
3. Women must transform their thinking and behavior to participate fully in society. Examples: Women have

become politically active and even militant to make sure that sexual harassment, date and marital rape, and spousal abuse are seen as serious crimes against women rather than practices that may be excused or tolerated.

Although Muted Group Theory focuses on women, its assumptions apply to many cultures. People of color, recent immigrants, the disabled, and the poor are also muted.

[1]Richard West and Lynn H. Turner, *Introducing Communication Theory*, 3rd ed. (Boston: McGraw-Hill, 2007), pp. 515–532. See Cheris Kramarae, *Women and Men Speaking: Framework for Analysis* (Rowley, MA: Newbury House, 1981).

Shirley van der Veur, a former Peace Corps worker and now a professor in a North American university, relates a story about a scholar from Kenya who was invited to dinner at an American colleague's home. Even though he ate ravenously, not leaving a morsel of food on his plate, the American hosts were not convinced that he liked his dinner because he had not *said* so. In Kenya, if his hosts saw him appreciatively eating his meal, they would know that he was enjoying it without necessarily needing him to express his pleasure verbally.[29]

How could cultural dimensions such as individualism, power distance, feminine values, and high/low context affect negotiations among world leaders such as Chinese President Hu Jintao, German Chancellor Angela Merkel, and Indian Prime Minister Manmohan Singh?

In their book, *Mastering Virtual Teams*, Deborah L. Duarte and Nancy Tennant Snyder contend that culture has an impact on how we use communication technology based on Hofstede's dimensions and Hall's research on context[1]:

- *Individualism–Collectivism*. Members from highly collectivistic cultures may prefer face-to-face interactions, whereas individualistic communicators may like having the screen to themselves as they share ideas and opinions.
- *Power Distance*. People from high-power distance cultures may communicate more freely when technologies are asynchronous (do not occur in real time) and when they allow anonymous input. These people sometimes use technology to indicate that they have a higher status.
- *Uncertainty Avoidance*. People from cultures with high uncertainty avoidance may be slower to adopt technology. They may also prefer technology that produces permanent records of discussions and decisions.
- *Masculinity–Femininity*. People from cultures with more feminine values may use technology in a nurturing way—that is, as a way of encouraging, supporting, and motivating others.
- *High–Low Context*. People from high-context cultures may prefer more information-rich technologies (such as videoconferences), as well as those that offer the feeling of social presence. They may resist using technologies with low social presence to communicate with people they have never met. People from low-context cultures may prefer more asynchronous communication.

[1]Deborah L. Duarte and Nancy Tennant Snyder, *Mastering Virtual Teams*, 3rd ed. (San Francisco: Jossey-Bass, 2007), p. 61.

Monochronic–Polychronic Time In northern European and North American cultures, time is a very valuable commodity. As a result, we fill our time with multiple commitments and live a fast-paced life. However, the pace of life in cultures such as India, Kenya, and Argentina and among African Americans is driven less by a need to "get things done" than by a sense of participation in events that create their own rhythm.[30]

Anthropologist Edward T. Hall classifies time as a form of communication. He claims that cultures organize time in one of two ways: as either monochronic or polychronic.[31] In **monochronic time**, events are scheduled as separate items—one thing at a time. M-time people like to concentrate on one job before moving to another and may become irritated when someone in a meeting brings up a personal topic unrelated to the purpose of the meeting.

In **polychronic time**, schedules are not as important and are frequently broken. People in polychronic cultures are not slaves to time and are easily distracted and tolerant of interruptions. P-time people are frequently late for appointments or may not show up at all.[32] If you are a P-time person, you probably like doing several tasks at one time, find it stimulating to think about several different problems at the same time, and feel comfortable holding two or three conversations simultaneously.

Hall maintains that these two time orientations are incompatible. When monochronic and polychronic people interact, the results can be frustrating. Hall notes that monochronic Americans become distressed by how polychronic people treat appointments. Being on time in some countries simply doesn't mean the same thing as it does in the United States. For P-time people, schedules and commitments, particularly plans for the future, are not firm, and even important plans may change right up to the last minute.[33]

If you are an M-time person, you can try to modify and relax your obsession with time and scheduling. If you are a P-time person, you can do your best to respect and adapt to a monochronic person's need for careful scheduling and promptness. Figure 3.7 depicts several differences between monochronic and polychronic perspectives and cultures.

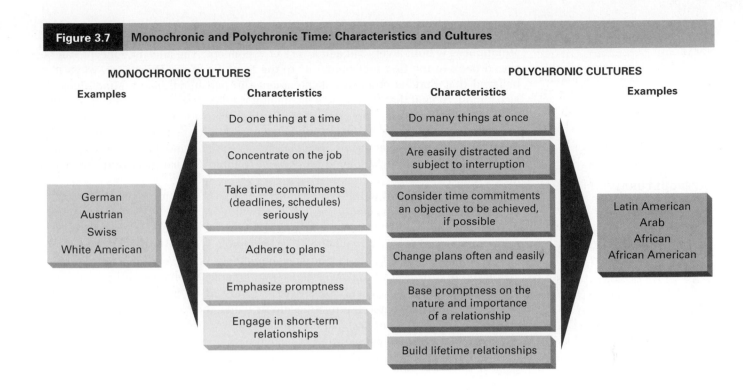

Figure 3.7 Monochronic and Polychronic Time: Characteristics and Cultures

Intercultural Communication Strategies

Intercultural communication trainers often urge their trainees to "see the world through other people's eyes" as a way of understanding the perspectives of others. But how do you do that? If your skin isn't dark, it may be impossible to know what it's like to look at the world through dark skin. If you do not use a wheelchair, it is very difficult to see the world from that vantage point. And men will never experience childbirth. Nevertheless, we should not give up in our search for new perspectives and should look for ways to understand, respect, and adapt to what others see and experience.

Joanne Koenig Coste, author of a book titled *Learning to Speak Alzheimer's*, provides an excellent example. Although she does not have Alzheimer's disease, her husband did. Coste describes how she discovered a clue to her husband's perspective:

> You have to put yourself in the patient's place and figure out what they need. When Charles [her husband, now deceased] first started to get incontinent, it was at the same time I was potty training Jason [her young son]. . . . I had this idea of painting the wall behind the toilet bright red, leaving the door open, and hoping that Jason might respond to that. Well, Charles saw it and started to use the toilet again. His problem had been one of perception, I realized. He didn't see the toilet anymore, and that is why he'd become incontinent.[34]

Clues like this are visible only for those who are constantly looking. The fundamental purpose of understanding others—seeing the world through their eyes—is to reduce miscommunication and prejudice. We must balance well-informed cultural expectations with mindful observations and appropriate adaptation. Thus, learning about and adapting to others may require changes in longstanding habits of thought and action. Three communication strategies can help you understand, respect, and adapt to the many "others" you encounter in everyday life: being mindful, adapting to others, and actively engaging others.

BE MINDFUL

Mindfulness is both a very old and a very new concept. The ancient concept can be traced back to the first millennium BC to the foothills of the Himalayas, when it is believed that Buddha attained enlightenment through mindfulness. Mindfulness is also a modern skill that counteracts the mental rigidity associated with cultural misunderstandings and discrimination.[35] **Mindfulness** means being fully aware of the present moment without making hasty judgments. Mindful communicators are fully aware of what they experience *inside themselves* (body, mind, heart, spirit) and pay full attention to what is happing *around them* (people, the natural world, surroundings, events).[36]

Before explaining mindfulness in more detail, let's take a look at its opposite: mind*less*ness. **Mindlessness** occurs when we allow rigid categories and false distinctions to become habits of thought and behavior.[37] For example, you approach a sales counter and say "Excuse me" to the salesperson. Why did you say that? Are you apologizing for interrupting someone who should have been paying more attention to you in the first place? All of us engage in some mindless behavior without any serious consequences. But when mindlessness occurs in an important situation, the results can be detrimental to a relationship or damaging to an important project. If you are mindless, you are trapped in a rigid, biased world in which your religion is always right and good, people from other cultures are inferior and untrustworthy, boys will always be boys and girls will always be girls, and change is a terrible and scary thing.[38]

Mindfulness is the opposite of mindlessness. Rather than behaving automatically and with little thought, mindfulness requires you to pay attention to how you and another person are communicating. It also asks you to observe what is happening as it happens, without forming opinions or taking sides as you learn more about someone else.[39] When you are mindful, you recognize stereotypical thinking and personal prejudices, and you try to overcome them. After the 9/11 tragedy, many Americans' ignorance of Islam led to stereotyping, prejudice, and discrimination against patriotic U.S. citizens who also were Islamic. Mindfulness gives you the freedom and motivation to understand, respect, and adapt to others.

Two concepts from Chapter 2—perception checking and self-talk—can also be used to promote mindfulness. Use perception checking to make sure you understand the basis for your conclusions about others and consider whether your conclusions are open to alternate interpretations. You can also "listen" to and critique the self-talk statements you make about others. Ask yourself if these thoughts are based on mindless categories and distinctions or mindful consideration. Two additional strategies can help promote mindfulness: Be receptive to new information and be responsive to more than one perspective.[40]

Be Receptive to New Information Mindful communicators learn more about others and their cultures by being open to new information. Too often, we dismiss another person's belief or behavior as irrational or bizarre when more information about that belief or behavior would help us understand it. Once you learn why some Muslims and Jews won't eat pork products or why Hindus won't eat the meat of sacred cows even under famine conditions, you may become more mindful and tolerant of their customs. There are plenty of resources that can help you become culturally literate:

- Watch cable and public television educational programs about different cultural groups: gender, social class, sexuality, ability, age, religion, ethnic groups, and nations.

- Read the literature of other cultures. Hours of enlightenment await those who pick up books from other cultures.

Among India's Hindus, cows are a sacred symbol of life. There is no greater sacrilege for a Hindu than killing a cow. At first, this belief may seem irrational, particularly in light of India's food shortage and poverty. If you have visited or seen pictures of India, you've seen cows wandering city streets and sidewalks, highways and railroad tracks, gardens and agricultural fields. You've also seen pictures of extreme poverty and hunger.

In his book, *Cows, Pigs, Wars, and Witches: The Riddles of Culture*, Marvin Harris offers a justification for Hindus' treatment of cows.[1] He even suggests that India may not have enough cows. Cows give birth to oxen, which are the principal source for plowing fields. Unfortunately, there are too few oxen for India's 60 million farms. Without oxen to plow fields, farmers cannot farm, food shortages result, and people go hungry. If you kill a cow, you eliminate your source of oxen. During the worst famines, killing a cow only provides tem-porary relief. Once a cow is killed, there will be no more oxen to plow the field in future years. The long-term effect may be a much more devastating famine. Harris offers this conclusion:

> What I am saying is that cow love is an active ele-ment in a complex, finely articulated material and cultural order. Cow love mobilizes the latent capac-ity of human beings to persevere in a low-energy ecosystem in which there is little room for waste or indolence.[2]

In light of Harris's anthropological explanation, we can begin to understand and respect why hungry peasants in India refuse to eat the cows that surround them.

[1]Marvin Harris, *Cows, Pigs, Wars, and Witches: The Riddles of Culture* (New York: Vintage Books, 1975), pp. 11–34.

[2]Ibid., p. 30. Also see an article about Hindu monks in Wales trying to protect their sacred but tuberculosis-infected bull in *The Week*, August 10, 2007, p. 8.

- Read nonfiction books about international politics or history, comparative reli-gious beliefs, international cooking, global trade, and working with others in culturally diverse organizations.

- Seek opportunities to interact with people from different cultures. Your college may have international student organizations that sponsor public events. Your employer may provide intercultural training for employees.

- Seek the company of trusted individuals willing to teach you something about their culture. Conversations between Jews and Muslims, blacks and whites, young and old can be informative and enjoyable.

Be Responsive to Other Perspectives   In addition to being open to new informa-tion, mindful communicators are open to other points of view. People from cultures different from your own may also reason differently than you do. Psychologist Richard Nisbett credits a graduate student from China with helping him understand such differences. After he and the student tried to work together and communicate successfully with each other, his Chinese student said, "You know, the difference between you and me is that I know the world is a circle, and you think it's a line. The Chinese believe in constant change, but with things always moving back to some prior state. . . . Westerners live in a simpler world . . . and they think they can control events because they know the rules that govern the behavior of objects."[41]

To western ears, the Chinese student's explanation may seem odd. How do you think in a circle? According to Nisbett, rather than using a western-style logic, the Chinese use contradictions as a way of understanding the relationship of one thing to another as a way of learning about the world's complexity.[42] Figure 3.8 notes some of the differences between western and East Asian ways of thinking.

"The Ballad of East and West," written in 1889 by Rudyard Kipling, includes this famous line: "Oh, East is East and West is West, and never the twain shall meet."

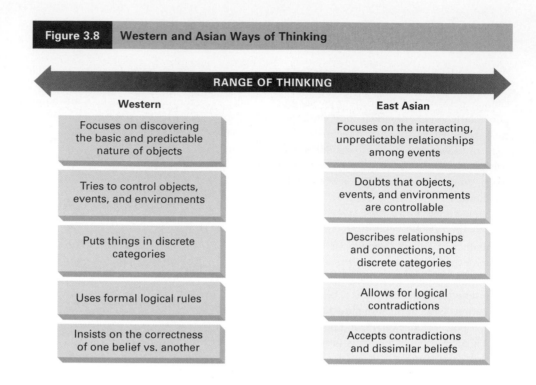

Figure 3.8   Western and Asian Ways of Thinking

RANGE OF THINKING

Western	East Asian
Focuses on discovering the basic and predictable nature of objects	Focuses on the interacting, unpredictable relationships among events
Tries to control objects, events, and environments	Doubts that objects, events, and environments are controllable
Puts things in discrete categories	Describes relationships and connections, not discrete categories
Uses formal logical rules	Allows for logical contradictions
Insists on the correctness of one belief vs. another	Accepts contradictions and dissimilar beliefs

Today, international trade, political alliances, and travel among nations challenge that pronouncement and encourage diverse cultures to understand, respect, and adapt to much broader ways of perceiving and thinking about the world and each other.

When you cling to one way of seeing a person or interpreting an event, you have stopped being mindful. Every idea, person, or object can be many things, depending on the perspective from which it is viewed. A steer is steak to a rancher, a sacred creature to a Hindu, a collection of genes and proteins to a biologist, and a mistreated animal to members of PETA (People for the Ethical Treatment of Animals).[43] When you are willing to consider more than one perspective, you have much to gain as a human being and as an effective communicator.

ADAPT TO OTHERS

You probably feel most comfortable when you "fit in" with the people around you. To fit in, you may modify the way you talk to family members, friends, colleagues, authority figures, and strangers. For example, two people may be from different areas of the country, one from the New York/New Jersey area and the other from Texas. When they go "home," their dialects, vocabulary, sentence structure, rate of speech, and even volume change to accommodate their home culture. Yet, when they speak in professional settings, they may be less "down home" and more formal in style and substance.

Communication researcher Howard Giles explores these adaptive tendencies in **Communication Accommodation Theory**,[44] which states that in every communication situation we compare ourselves with speakers from other groups. If we believe that another group has more power or has desirable characteristics, we tend to "accommodate" our conversations to the accepted speech behaviors and norms in that group. Four principles of Communication Accommodation Theory can help you understand and adapt to others:

1. *Communication similarities and differences exist in all conversations.*
   Regardless of whether you talk to an international student or your grandmother, you will encounter differences. For example, an international student

may speak English poorly and with great difficulty, and your grandmother may speak and behave more modestly than you do.

2. *The manner in which we perceive the communication of others will determine how we evaluate our interaction with others.* Chapter 2 explains that perception is the process of selecting, organizing, and interpreting sensory stimuli in the world around you. However, evaluation is the process of determining whether you like, value, and accept what you perceive. Effective communicators avoid stereotyping by carefully listening to others and attentively observing what they do.

3. *Language and behavior convey information about social status and group membership.* Usually, the person or group with more status and power establishes the "accepted" type of talk and behavior. If you are being interviewed for a job by someone who behaves formally, you are likely to behave the same way. If you like working with a party-loving group, you probably will join in on the festivities with enthusiasm.

4. *Accommodation varies in its degree of appropriateness, and norms guide the accommodation process.* If you interact with a culture that values respect for elders, you may be hesitant to question the views of an older person or senior official. However, there are times when accommodating others is not appropriate. For example, if the party-loving colleagues you like have not finished their assigned work, you may not feel comfortable joining them for a party.

ACTIVELY ENGAGE OTHERS

Are you willing to spend time and energy interacting with others, particularly when they represent a culture very different from yours? Are you willing to tolerate differences even when you do not approve of them? Can you respect someone whose beliefs, values, norms, and behaviors are different? If you answer yes to these questions, you exhibit openness and a positive attitude about communicating with others.

Direct engagement in face-to-face cultural interactions with people from culturally diverse backgrounds benefits everyone.[45] You and others may transform long-held negative beliefs about each other's cultures into positive affirmations. Through mindful communication, you can reduce the likelihood of ethnocentrism, stereotyping, prejudice, discrimination, and even racism. If you succeed in reducing your level of anxiety and uncertainty when encountering others, you may discover new worlds with fascinating people who can enrich your life. In this way you can achieve the fundamental purpose of understanding others: to reduce miscommunication and prejudice by balancing well-informed cultural expectations with mindful observations and appropriate adaptation.

After reading this chapter and thinking about the differences among people, you may assume you have nothing in common with others, perhaps even those within your own culture. In fact, all people, regardless of culture, have many similar behaviors.[46] Here's a quick look at what all of us do:

- We smile when happy.
- We wave as a greeting.
- We laugh when amused.
- We blush when embarrassed.
- We cry when sad or in pain.
- We frown when concerned or ill at ease.
- We adopt a fetal position when dejected, cold, or in a hopeless situation.
- We shrug to express, "I don't know."
- We slump when dejected or tired.
- We stand straight when alert or confident.

How does this interaction between a New Guinea villager and a Peace Corps volunteer demonstrate the benefits of direct, face-to-face engagement with people from culturally diverse backgrounds?

Just consider the smile, a facial expression common to *all* human beings. Regardless of culture, everyone smiles. For example, blind children, who cannot copy facial expressions, smile spontaneously. Contrary to some popular beliefs and even a few song lyrics, smiling does *not* make you happy unless it is a genuine smile. Researchers describe a genuine smile as a facial expression in which we raise the corners of our mouth while also crinkling the corners of our eyes into crow's feet. So smiling can make you happy, but only the right kinds of smile, one that matches the happy—even joyous—feelings that elicit a smile.[47]

Regardless of culture, nationality, gender, religion, age, and ability, all of us share the traits unique to the amazing human condition. By being more mindful, adapting to others, and actively engaging those who are "different," we can also become a more effective and ethical communicator.

What Is Culturally Normal?

Directions: Respond to each of the following twelve items by putting a checkmark in the column that describes the behavior; descriptions range from "Quite Ordinary" to "Quite Strange." Then use the comment section to explain your response briefly.

Item	Quite Ordinary	Ordinary	Neutral	Strange	Quite Strange
1. A man wearing a skirt in public	☐	☐	☐	☐	☐
Comment:					
2. Two women holding hands in a park	☐	☐	☐	☐	☐
Comment:					
3. A woman breast-feeding her child in public	☐	☐	☐	☐	☐
Comment:					
4. Talking with someone who does not look you in the eye	☐	☐	☐	☐	☐
Comment:					
5. A woman refusing to shake hands with a man	☐	☐	☐	☐	☐
Comment:					
6. A family taking a communal bath	☐	☐	☐	☐	☐
Comment:					
7. Interacting with professors on a first-name basis	☐	☐	☐	☐	☐
Comment:					
8. Praying to many gods	☐	☐	☐	☐	☐
Comment:					
9. A man wearing Bermuda shorts to a fine restaurant	☐	☐	☐	☐	☐
Comment:					
10. Eating a formal meal without utensils					
Comment:					
11. A man who stands so close you can smell his breath	☐	☐	☐	☐	☐
Comment:					
12. People who will not eat the food in your home	☐	☐	☐	☐	☐
Comment:					

Review your ratings and comments. All twelve behaviors are customary (and normal) in another culture or country. Consider how individuals from other cultures might find some of your "normal" behaviors unusual (and even abnormal).

Source: Activity based on Myron W. Lustig and Jolene Koester, *Instructors Manual to Accompany Intercultural Competence*, 2nd ed. (New York: HarperCollins, 1996), pp. 72–74.

Communication Assessment

The Generalized Ethnocentrism (GENE) Scale

Directions: Read the following statements concerning your feelings about your culture and other cultures. In the space provided, indicate the number that reflects the degree to which each statement applies to you by marking whether you (5) Strongly Agree, (4) Agree, (3) Are Undecided, (2) Disagree, or (1) Strongly Disagree with the statement.

There are no right or wrong answers. Some of the statements may seem very similar to another. Remember, everyone experiences some degree of ethnocentrism. Be honest. Work quickly and record your first response.

_____ 1. Most other cultures are backward compared with my culture.

_____ 2. My culture should be the role model for other cultures.

_____ 3. People from other cultures act strangely when they come to my culture.

_____ 4. Lifestyles in other cultures are just as valid as those in my culture.

_____ 5. Other cultures should try to be more like my culture.

_____ 6. I'm not interested in the values and customs of other cultures.

_____ 7. People in my culture could learn a lot from people in other cultures.

_____ 8. Most people from other cultures just don't know what's good for them.

_____ 9. I respect the values and customs of other cultures.

_____ 10. Other cultures are smart to look up to our culture.

_____ 11. Most people would be happier if they lived like people in my culture.

_____ 12. I have many friends from different cultures.

_____ 13. People in my culture have just about the best lifestyles anywhere.

_____ 14. Lifestyles in other cultures are not as valid as those in my culture.

_____ 15. I am very interested in the values and customs of other cultures.

_____ 16. I apply my values when judging people who are different.

_____ 17. I see people who are similar to me as virtuous/good.

_____ 18. I do not cooperate with people who are different.

_____ 19. Most people in my culture just don't know what is good for them.

_____ 20. I do not trust people who are different.

_____ 21. I dislike interacting with the values and customs of other cultures.

_____ 22. I have little respect for the values and customs of other cultures.

To determine your ethnocentrism score, complete the following four steps:

1. Add your responses to items 4, 7, and 9.

2. Add your responses to items 1, 2, 5, 8, 10, 11, 13, 14, 18, 20, 21, and 22.

3. Subtract the sum from step 1 from 18 (i.e., 18 minus step 1 sum).

4. Add results from step 2 and step 3. This is your generalized ethnocentrism score. Higher scores indicate higher ethnocentrism. Scores more than 55 points are considered high ethnocentrism.

Source: The GENE Scale, developed by James Neuliep and James C. McCroskey. See James W. Neuliep, _Intercultural Communication: A Contextual Approach_, 2nd ed. (Boston: Houghton Mifflin, 2003), pp. 29–30.

Key Terms

co-culture
collectivism
Communication Accommodation
    Theory
culture
discrimination
ethnocentrism
feminine society
high-context culture
high power distance

high uncertainty avoidance
individualism
intercultural dimension
low-context culture
low power distance
low uncertainty avoidance
masculine society
mindfulness
mindlessness
monochronic time

Muted Group Theory
polychronic time
power distance
prejudice
race
racism
religious illiteracy
social identity
stereotype
uncertainty avoidance

Notes

1. The statistics and their interpretation in this section come from two sources: *Encyclopedia Britannica Almanac 2004* (Chicago: Britannica Almanac, 2003), pp. 770–775; United States Census Bureau, Census 2000, www.census.gov/population.

2. "The 300 Millionth Footprint on U.S. Soil," *The New York Times*, October 8, 2006, p. WK 2. U.S. Census Bureau; National Center for Education Statistics; Social Security Administration.

3. U.S. Census Bureau, www.census.gov/population.

4. Myron W. Lustig and Jolene Koester, *Intercultural Competence: Interpersonal Communication across Cultures*, 5th ed. (New York: Longman, 2006), p. 25.

5. Intercultural authors use a variety of terms (*co-cultures, microcultures*) to describe the cultural groups that coexist within a larger culture. Using either of these terms is preferable to using the older, somewhat derogatory term *subcultures*. The combined co-cultures living in the United States will, by mid century, make up the majority population.

6. Items from Neuliep and McCroskey's Generalized Ethnocentrism (GENE) Scale, in James W. Neuliep, *Intercultural Communication: A Contextual Approach*, 2nd ed. (Boston: Houghton Mifflin, 2003), pp. 29–30. Also, see Chapter 3 in Neuliep for a general discussion of ethnocentrism and stereotyping.

7. Data from Patricia G. Devine and A.J. Elliot, "Are Racial Stereotypes Really Fading? The Princeton Trilogy Revisited," *Personality and Social Psychology Bulletin* 21 (1995), pp. 1139–1150.

8. Based on Lustig and Koester, p. 151.

9. Brenda J. Allen, *Difference Matters: Communicating Social Identity* (Long Grove, IL: Waveland, 2004), p. 10

10. Stephen Prothero, *Religious Literacy: What Every American Needs to Know—And Doesn't* (New York: HarperSanFrancisco, 2007), p. 23.

11. Ibid., p. 30.

12. J. Richard Hoel, Jr. "Developing Intercultural Competence," in *Intercultural Communication with Readings*, ed. Pamela J. Cooper, Carolyn Calloway-Thomas, and Cheri J. Simonds (Boston: Allyn & Bacon, 2007), p. 305.

13. Ibid.

14. Geert Hofstede, *Cultures and Organizations: Software of the Mind* (New York: McGraw-Hill, 1997), p. 14. Also see Geert Hofstede, *Culture's Consequences*, 2nd ed. (Thousand Oaks, CA: Sage, 2001), p. 29. In addition to the four intercultural dimensions included in this chapter, Hofstede identifies a fifth dimension: long-term versus short-term orientation, which relates to the choice of focus for people's efforts—either the future or the present. Cultures in Asia rank at the top of the list of long-term orientations whereas those with shorter orientations include English-speaking countries (Australia, New Zealand, United States, Britain, Canada) as well as Zimbabwe, Philippines, Nigeria, and Pakistan. We have not included this fifth dimension in the textbook because fewer cultures have been examined than those for the other four dimensions.

15. Harry C. Triandis, *Individualism and Collectivism* (Boulder, CO: Westview, 1995).

16. Harry C. Triandis, "The Self and Social Behavior in Different Cultural Contexts," *Psychological Review* 96 (1989), pp. 506–520. Also see Harry C. Triandis, 1995.

17. Harry C. Triandis, "Cross-Cultural Studies of Individualism and Collectivism," in *Cross-Cultural Perspectives*, ed. J.J. Berman (Lincoln, NE: University of Nebraska Press, 1990), p. 52.

18. William B. Gudykunst and Carmen M. Lee, "Cross-Cultural Communication Theories," in *Handbook of International and Intercultural Communication*, 2nd ed., ed. William B. Gudykunst and Bella

Mody (Thousand Oaks, CA: Sage, 2002), p. 27.

19. Anne C. Klein, *Meeting the Great Bliss Queen: Buddhists, Feminists, and the Art of the Self* (Boston: Beacon, 1995) quoted in Min-Sun Kim, *Non-Western Perspectives on Human Communication* (Thousand Oaks, CA: Sage, 2002), pp. 13–14.

20. Hofstede, 1997, p. 53.

21. Ibid., p. 28.

22. Geert Hofstede, "The Cultural Relativity of the Quality of Life Concept," in *Cultural Communication and Conflict: Readings in Intercultural Relations*, 2nd ed., ed. G.R. Weaver (Boston: Pearson, 2000), p. 139.

23. Geert Hofstede, *Culture's Consequences: Comparing Values, Behavior, Institutions and Organizations across Nations*, 2nd ed. (Thousand Oaks, CA: Sage, 2001), p. 161.

24. Hofstede, 1977, p. 119.

25. Ibid., pp. 119 and 125.

26. Ibid., p.119.

27. Ibid., pp. 81–82 and 96.

28. Edward T. Hall, "Context and Meaning," in *Beyond Culture* (Garden City, NY: Anchor, 1997).

29. Shirley van der Veur, "Africa: Communication and Cultural Patterns," in *Intercultural Communication: A Reader*, 10th ed., ed. Larry A. Samovar and Richard E. Porter (Belmont, CA: Wadsworth, 2003), p. 84.

30. Edward T. Hall, *The Silent Language* (Garden City, NY: Doubleday, 1959). See also Lustig and Koester, p. 226.

31. Edward T. Hall and M. R. Hall, *Understanding Cultural Differences: Germans, French and Americans* (Yarmouth, ME: Intercultural Press, 1990), p. 6.

32. Dean Allen Foster, *Bargaining across Borders* (New York: McGraw-Hill, 1992), p. 280.

33. Edward T. Hall, *The Dance of Life: Other Dimensions of Time* (New York: Anchor/Doubleday, 1983), p. 42.

34. Claudia Dreifus, "A Wife Learns to See with Alzheimer's Eyes," *The New York Times*, March 23, 2004, p. D6.

35. www.users.vioicenet.com/~howard/mindful.html.

36. Richard Boyatzis and Annie McKee, *Resonant Leadership* (Boston: Harvard Business School Press, 2005), p. 112.

37. Ellen J. Langer, *Mindfulness* (Cambridge, MA: Da Capo, 1989), p. 11.

38. Based on examples in Langer, p. 12.

39. www.users.vioicenet.com/~howard/mindful.html.

40. Langer, p. 62. Langer subsequently describes the three key qualities of mindfulness on pp. 63–77.

41. Richard Nisbett, *The Geography of Thought: How Asians and Western Think Differently . . . and Why* (New York: Free Press, 2003) p. xiii.

42. Ibid., p. 27.

43. Langer, p. 69.

44. See the following references: Howard Giles et al., "Speech Accommodation Theory: The First Decade and Beyond," in *Communication Yearbook*, ed. Margaret L. McLaughlin (Newbury Park, CA: Sage, 1987), pp. 13–48; Howard Giles et al., "Accommodation Theory: Communication, Context, and Consequence," in *Contexts of Accommodation: Developments in Applied Sociolinguistics*, ed. Howard Giles et al. (Cambridge: Cambridge University Press, 1991), p. 1–68.

45. See Campinha-Bacote's model of cultural competence as published in Josepha Campinha-Bacote, *The Process of Cultural Competence in the Delivery of Healthcare Services: A Culturally Competent Model of Care*, 4th ed. (Wyoming, OH: Transcultural C.A.R.E. Associates, 2003).

46. James Leigh, "Teaching Content and Skills for Intercultural Communication: A Mini Case Studies Approach," *The Edge: The E-Journal of Intercultural Relations* 2 (Winter 1999), www.interculturalrelations.com/v2ilWinter1999leigh.htm.

47. Stefan Klein, *The Science of Happiness* (New York: Marlowe, 2006), pp. 6, 20–21.

Understanding Listening and Critical Thinking

Key Elements of Communication	Communication Axioms	Guiding Principles of Listening and Critical Thinking
Self	*Communication Is Personal*	Analyze your listening and critical thinking strengths and weaknesses.
Others	*Communication Is Relational*	Analyze and adapt to others' listening and critical thinking styles.
Purpose	*Communication Is Intentional*	Use appropriate types of purposeful listening and critical thinking to achieve your communication purpose.
Context	*Communication Is Contextual*	Adapt your listening and critical thinking to diverse communication contexts. Minimize distractions.
Content	*Communication Is Symbolic*	Listen for the meaning of both verbal and nonverbal messages. Separate facts from inferences and analyze the validity of arguments.
Structure	*Communication Is Structured*	Organize messages to facilitate listening. Construct valid arguments based on sound evidence and warrants.
Expression	*Communication Is Irreversible*	Paraphrase and ask appropriate questions to enhance message comprehension and argument analysis. Present arguments clearly.

Listening and Critical Thinking

In *The Lost Art of Listening*, Michael Nichols describes listening as an indispensable communication skill:

> The feeling of not being understood is one of the most painful in human experience. Not being appreciated and responded to depletes our vitality and makes us feel less alive. When we're with someone who doesn't listen, we feel shut down. When we're with someone who's interested and responsive—a good listener—we perk up and come alive. . . . [Listening] involves learning how to suspend our own emotional agenda and then realizing the rewards of genuine empathy.[1]

In *Critical Thinking*, Brooke Noel Moore and Richard Parker explain the challenge of critical thinking in everyday life:

> One of the advantages of living in a free society is the opportunity to think for oneself. But having the *opportunity* to do it is one thing, and having the *ability* to do it is quite another. Thinking—especially clear, reasoned thinking—is not easy work, and it doesn't always come naturally.[2]

Successful communicators listen effectively and think critically. After all, if no one listens to you, why communicate? And if you have not given serious thought to your message, why *should* they listen?

The Challenge of Listening

Speaking and listening are two sides of a single coin, twin competencies that rely on and reflect one another. Whether you are communicating interpersonally, in group settings, or in front of an audience, you need effective listening skills to succeed.

THE NATURE OF LISTENING

Listening is the ability to understand, analyze, respect, and respond appropriately to the meaning of another person's spoken and nonverbal messages.[3] At first, listening may appear to be as easy and natural as breathing. In fact, just the opposite may be closer to the truth. Although most of us can *hear*, we often fail to *listen* to what others say. Hearing only requires physical ability; listening requires complex thinking ability. People who are hearing impaired may be better listeners than those who can hear the faintest sound.

In Chapter 1, we emphasized the importance of making effective communication an enduring habit and used listening as an example. To become an effective and ethical listener, you need knowledge, skills, and desire. Knowing about listening and knowing how to listen are not enough. Unless you *want* to listen—unless you have the desire—it won't become an enduring habit.

Listening is our number one communication activity. A study of college students found that listening occupies more than half of their communicating time.[4] Although percentages vary from study to study, Figure 4.1 shows how most of us divide up our daily communicating time.

Listening and Interpersonal Relationships   According to psychologist John M. Gottman, "good listening skills can help you feel easy in social situations, and build rapport that leads to solid emotional bonds."[5] Listening effectiveness can even influence how and whom you love. As one marriage counselor notes: "Without wholehearted, selfless listening to your spouse, there is no respect. And without respect, there is no happiness in marriage."[6]

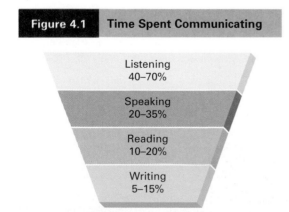

Figure 4.1   Time Spent Communicating

Listening
40–70%

Speaking
20–35%

Reading
10–20%

Writing
5–15%

In his best-selling book, *Emotional Intelligence*, Daniel Goleman presents the following interchange between two people:

He: You're shouting!

She: Of course I'm shouting—you haven't heard a word I'm saying. You just don't listen.

Goleman maintains that "listening is a skill that keeps couples together." Couples headed for divorce, however, "become absorbed in the anger and fixate on the specifics of the issue at hand, not managing to hear—let alone return—any peace offerings."[1] Sadly, feuding couples often become highly defensive. Each partner ignores or immediately refutes the spouse's complaint, reacting to it as though it were an attack rather than an attempt to express feelings or to change injurious behavior.[2]

[1]Daniel Goleman, *Emotional Intelligence: Why It Can Matter More Than IQ* (New York: Bantam Books, 1997), p. 145.

[2]Ibid.

Listening and Professional Relationships   In the business world, many executives devote more than 60 percent of their workday listening to others.[7] Between 2002 and 2003, more than 20,000 workers participated in a comprehensive listening test and most were found to have listening skills well below the level required by their jobs.[8] Listening, in fact, is cited as the communication skill most lacking in new employees.[9] A study of hundreds of businesses by researchers at Loyola University in Chicago concludes that listening is a manager's most important skill.[10] Another study identifies listening as a key characteristic of exemplary leaders.[11] No wonder Tom J. Peters, author of *In Search of Excellence* and *Thriving on Chaos*, contends that "excellent companies are not only better at service, quality, and reliability . . . they are also better listeners."[12]

Listening and Presentational Communication   Too often speakers entrust listening to the audience. Highly effective speakers know better: They listen and adapt to audience feedback as they speak. Feedback tells them whether the audience is responding positively or negatively to their message.

How do good listening skills help you feel comfortable with and close to others?

Regardless of whether you are speaking to a small group or a large audience, note their reactions. Do they look interested or uninterested, pleased or displeased, captivated or confused? If an audience seems confused, slow down and reexplain the concept. If they look bored, add a fascinating or amusing story. Learning how to listen as a speaker is just as important as learning to listen as an audience member.[13]

MISCONCEPTIONS ABOUT LISTENING

Even if you understand the importance of listening, you may have misconceptions about its nature. Frequently heard misconceptions about listening often reflect a lack of knowledge about listening rather than an unwillingness to listen or learn listening skills. Correcting these misleading notions can help you improve your listening effectiveness.

MAJOR MISCONCEPTIONS ABOUT LISTENING

► Most People Know How to Listen

► Listening Is Easy

Misconception: Most People Know How to Listen   We often take listening for granted and think we're better listeners than we really are.[14] For instance, immediately after listening to a short talk, most of us cannot accurately report 50 percent of what was said. Without training, we listen at about 25 percent efficiency.[15] And, of that 25 percent, most of what we remember is distorted or inaccurate.[16] A study of Fortune 500 company training managers concludes that "ineffective listening leads to ineffective performance or low productivity." The study also notes that "poor listening performance is ranked as a serious problem during meetings, performance appraisals, and superior–subordinate communication." These same problems also appear in studies of sales professionals, educators, health practitioners, lawyers, and religious leaders.[17] When physicians listen to patients describe their symptoms, they may arrive at the wrong diagnosis if they haven't listened carefully. Similarly, poor listening by the person who cuts your hair can result in a month of "bad hair days."

Misconception: Listening Is Easy   Effective listening is hard work and requires a great deal more than keeping quiet and recognizing individual words. Researchers note that active listeners register an increase in blood pressure, a higher pulse rate, and even more perspiration.[18] Active listening techniques involve more than using your intellect, but your emotions as well. Active listeners try to understand what a speaker is saying, the emotions behind the content, and the conclusion the speaker is making without stating it openly.[19]

Listening requires the kind of preparation and concentration required of attorneys trying a case, psychologists counseling a client, and physicians seeking a diagnosis based on patients' reported symptoms. Intensive listening can be an exhausting experience. If you are not willing to work at listening, you will not be a good listener.

Types of Purposeful Listening

Different situations require different types of listening. For example, if you are listening to a speech by a political candidate, you may engage analytical listening skills. However, if you are watching a funny movie, you may put aside analytical listening to enjoy the entertainment. Researchers have identified several types of listening, each of which calls upon unique listening skills: discriminative listening, comprehensive listening, empathic listening, analytical listening, and appreciative listening.

TYPES OF PURPOSEFUL LISTENING

► Discriminative Listening

► Comprehensive Listening

► Empathic Listening

► Analytical Listening

► Appreciative Listening

DISCRIMINATIVE LISTENING

In Chapter 3, "Understanding Others," we defined discrimination as the way in which people act out and express prejudice. The meaning of discriminative listening is very different. In fact, the first definition of *discriminate* in *The American Heritage Dic-*

Preparing to listen can be just as important as planning to speak. Here are four suggestions that can help you use your planning-to-listen time wisely:

1. *Do some prior study.* The more you know about a topic, the more you will get out of listening to someone talk about it. Read important reports before you go to a meeting. Review an applicant's resume before you meet the candidate. Learn about a political candidate's background and positions on important issues before listening to a campaign speech.
2. *Identify your listening goals.* Broadly speaking, ask yourself this question: What do I want to get out of listening? If you can find a personal reason for listening, you will be a better listener.
3. *Generate and ask questions.* Generate questions in advance. When you begin listening with questions in mind, you will listen better. If you discover that a speaker has omitted important information, ask a question about its absence.
4. *Share the message.* Make a point of telling someone else what you have heard. If you know that you will be summarizing what you hear, you will listen more attentively.

---

tionary of the English Language is "to make a clear distinction; distinguish," as in, "Can you discriminate among the different sounds of orchestra instruments?"[20] Thus, **discriminative listening** is the ability "to distinguish auditory and/or visual stimuli."[21]

Discriminative listening answers the question: Do I hear accurately? At its simplest level, it involves the ability to make clear, aural distinctions among the sounds and words in a language. Discriminative listeners also notice nonverbal stimuli such as a smile, a groan, or the shrug of a shoulder.

More than 13 million people in the United States have some form of hearing loss, many of them older adults.[22] If you do not hear well, you may miss the vocal cues that distinguish a particular word and its meaning. If you are distracted or there is competing noise in a room, you may not hear the differences between similar words (Did she say she *hit* the ball or *hid* the ball?) or the vocal inflection that changes the meaning of a word (When he said he'd *love* to do it, was he serious or sarcastic?).

A news report told the story of a dentist in New Zealand who asked a patient whom he had prepared for surgery: "So, how many teeth are we removing today?" The patient, whose mouth was numb from the local anesthetic said, "Four teeth." The dentist's ears, however, picked up "fourteen," not "four teeth." As a result and without double-checking his chart, he pulled all of her lower teeth.

Discriminative listening comes first among the five types of listening because it forms the basis for the other four. If you cannot hear the difference between an on-key or off-key note, you may not be able to listen appreciatively to a singer. If you cannot hear or recognize the distress in a person's voice, you may not be able to listen empathetically.

COMPREHENSIVE LISTENING

Comprehensive listening answers the question: What does the speaker mean? **Comprehensive listening** focuses on accurately understanding the meaning of another person's spoken and nonverbal messages. After all, if you don't comprehend what a person says, you can't be expected to respond appropriately. You use comprehensive listening when someone presents a critical report at a meeting, describes the supposed benefits of buying a new car, or speaks on behalf of a public interest group at a hearing.

In *How to Start a Conversation and Make Friends*, Don Gabor claims that the sweetest sound in any language is a person's name. People feel flattered, important, and special when you remember their name. Remembering names also builds rapport with new acquaintances. Gabor maintains that one reason we forget names is that we don't focus on the moment we hear a person's name. In other words, we're not listening effectively. We're too busy thinking about ourselves, what we're going to say, whether we make a good impression, and how other people will react to us. Add to that the physical distractions in a room and it's no wonder we can't remember a person's name.[1]

Gabor suggests a five-step method for remembering names:

1. Focus on the moment of introduction.
2. Don't think about what to say—listen for the name.
3. Repeat the name aloud.
4. Think of someone you know or someone famous with the same name.
5. Use the name during and at the end of the conversation.

Most of these suggestions make sense, but step 4 can present the greatest challenge. When you hear a person's name, who is the first person that comes to mind who has the same or a similar name? Use that same person each time you meet someone new with that name. For example, if you meet someone named Jon and your brother-in-law's name is Jon, always think of that Jon.[2]

There are other similar techniques. Does the person's name rhyme with something that will help you remember? Curly Shirley or Slim Jim. Can you associate the person's name with an event or item? Tom's Toe (Tom's toe was bandaged when you met him), or Chris Christmas (You met Chris at your neighbor's Christmas party). Does the person's first name begin with the same letter as a personal characteristic or interest? Strong Steve, Laughing Lou, Cathy the Cook, and Dianna the Debater.[3]

Sales professionals know that remembering a name and key facts about a person can help close a sale. Here are three simple steps that salespeople use to help them remember names:

1. Say the person's name five times aloud or to yourself and it's yours.
2. Visualize the name by writing it in your mind.
3. Make an association by linking the name with something that would remind you of it.[4]

[1] Don Gabor, *How to Start a Conversation and Make Friends* (New York: Fireside, 2001), p. 64.

[2] Ibid., pp. 66–68.

[3] Ibid., pp. 70–71.

[4] Joy J.D. Baldridge, *The Fast Forward MBA in Selling* (New York: John Wiley, 2000), p. 312.

Suppose a speaker is trying to persuade you to participate in a voter registration drive. As a comprehensive listener, you may wonder whether "Join the voters registration drive" means (1) you should, in general, support voter registration, (2) you should volunteer and help register voters, or (3) you should register to vote. How you interpret the meaning of a single comment can determine your response to an entire message.

EMPATHIC LISTENING

Empathic listening answers the question: How does the speaker feel? **Empathic listening** goes beyond understanding what a person means, and focuses on understanding and identifying with a person's situation, feelings, or motives.

You may overlook the most important part of a message if you do not listen for feelings. Even if you understand every word a person says, you can miss the anger, enthusiasm, or frustration in a speaker's voice. Empathic listening does not require you to agree with or feel the same as a speaker. Rather, you try to understand the type and intensity of feelings the person is experiencing without judging whether the message is good or bad, right or wrong.[23]

What kinds of questions might be on these listeners' minds?

Suppose someone says that voting is a waste of time. An empathic listener may wonder whether the speaker means that (1) she is stressed and has more important things to do than vote, (2) she is frustrated because there aren't any good candidates to vote for, or (3) the lines are so long at the polling station that voting will waste her time.

You can be an empathic listener in simple ways. For instance, smiling and nodding at someone who is speaking communicates attention and interest. If you act as though you're listening, you actually end up listening more effectively and retaining more information.

ANALYTICAL LISTENING

Analytical listening asks: What's my opinion? Of the four types of listening, **analytical listening** most closely relates to critical thinking because it focuses on evaluating a message. Later in this chapter we take a detailed look at critical thinking theories, strategies, and skills. Like good critical thinkers, analytical listeners are open-minded. They put aside any biases or prejudices about the speaker or message.

Analytical listening requires you to make a judgment based on your evaluation of another person's message. Is the speaker right or wrong, logical or illogical? Should I accept or reject the speaker's ideas and suggestions?

Imagine that a speaker makes the following proposal: "Suppose we post signs and offer free rides to the voting polls." An analytical listener might have questions such as (1) Will voters misinterpret the ride as pressure to vote for a particular candidate? (2) Wouldn't we have to check that all drivers have adequate car insurance? and (3) Is there enough time to design, print, and post the signs before the election? Depending on how you answer one or more of these questions, you may decide either to reject or accept the proposal.

Asking good questions can enhance listening comprehension.[1] Here are a few strategies that can help you become a more effective listener:

Have a plan. Make sure you know what you want to accomplish and what types of questions you need. If you don't know your purpose, your questions may be worthless.

Keep the questions simple. Ask for one answer at a time and make sure it's applicable to what the speaker says.

Ask nonthreatening questions. Questions that begin with "Why didn't you . . . ?" or "How could you . . . ?" can make speakers defensive and unwilling to continue a conversation. Use a positive tone. Critical questions run the risk of alienating another person, as well as any others who may have overheard that question.

Ask permission. If a topic is sensitive, explain why you are asking the question and ask permission before continuing. "You say you're worried about Tom's recent behavior. Would you mind telling me . . . ."

Avoid biased or manipulative questions. Tricking someone into giving you the answer you want can destroy trust. There's a big difference between "How fast was the car going when you drove past the school?" and "How fast was the car going when you sped past the school?"

Wait for the answer. In addition to asking good questions, make sure you respond appropriately. After you ask a good question, give the other person time to think and then wait for the answer.

[1]Based on Tony Alessandra and Phil Hunsaker, *Communicating at Work* (New York: Fireside, 1993), pp. 76–77.

APPRECIATIVE LISTENING

Appreciative listening answers the question: Do I like, value, or enjoy what I am hearing? **Appreciative listening** applies to *how* someone thinks, performs, and speaks—how a person chooses and uses words or how a singer interprets a song. An appreciative listener values the speaker's ability to use humor, tell stories, argue persuasively, or demonstrate understanding. Appreciative listening rewards a speaker who eloquently describes a complex idea or personal experience. When someone's words, stories, or sense of humor delight us, we listen appreciatively.

Appreciative listening is very personal. While listening to a singer, you and a friend may use discriminative listening and agree that the singer has hit a wrong note. As appreciative listeners, however, you may disagree. Although you think the melody is lovely and memorable, your friend may find it oversweet and tedious.

Suppose that a speaker suggests that there is no greater duty in a democracy than that of expressing your opinion at the polling booth on election day. An appreciative listener might think (1) that's an eloquent way of phrasing that idea, (2) it seems worthwhile when seen as a patriotic duty rather than a time-consuming chore, or (3) the tone of the speaker's voice communicates genuine sincerity.

Improving Listening

Chapter 1 described the three components of an enduring communication habit: knowledge, skills, and desire. Hopefully, you have met two of these requirements: knowledge and desire. You *know* why good listening is essential for effective and ethical communication, and you *want* to listen. Now we turn to specific strategies for developing effective listening skills.[24]

In this section we offer six listening strategies that can improve your listening ability and help you develop effective listening habits. When and how you use these strategies depends, in part, on whether you are the speaker or the listener (or both) and whether you are speaking to one person or a large group of people.

Use Your Extra Thought Speed Most people talk at about 125 to 150 words per minute. But most of us can *think* at three to four times that rate.[25] Thus, we have about 400 extra words of spare thinking time during every minute a person talks to us.

Thought speed is the speed (words per minute) at which most people can think compared with the speed at which they can speak. Poor listeners use their extra thought speed to daydream, engage in side conversations, take unnecessary notes, or plan how to confront a speaker. Good listeners use their extra thought speed productively; they do the following:

- Identify and summarize key ideas and opinions.
- Pay extra attention to the meaning of nonverbal behavior.
- Analyze the strengths and weaknesses of arguments.
- Assess the relevance of a speaker's comments.

Conscientious listeners don't waste their extra thought speed; they use it to enhance comprehensive and analytical listening. We place this skill first on our list of listening strategies and skills because it provides the time you need to engage other important listening skills.

Listen for the Big Ideas Good listeners use their extra thought speed to identify a speaker's overall purpose. Poor listeners tend to listen for and remember isolated facts rather than identify big ideas.

Sometimes listening for big ideas can be very difficult when the fault lies with the speaker. For example, listeners may lose track and drift off when listening to a speaker whose message lacks relevant content and a clear structure or whose voice lacks expressiveness. In a group setting, good listeners who sense such problems may interrupt a speaker and politely ask, "Could you help me out here and summarize your point in a couple of sentences?" Although it is tempting to blame poor speakers when you can't comprehend a person's message, good listeners try to cut through irrelevant facts and opinions to identify the most important ideas.

Listen to Feedback One of the most important and challenging communication skills is listening to and providing appropriate feedback to others during a conversation, meeting, or presentation. As we indicated in Chapter 1, **feedback** is the verbal and nonverbal responses others communicate as they listen to a speaker. Feedback tells you how your listeners react—negatively or positively—to you and your message.

All listeners react in some way. They may smile or frown, or they may nod "yes" or "no." They may break into spontaneous applause or refuse to applaud. They may sit forward at full attention or sit back and look bored, skeptical, or annoyed. Analyzing their feedback helps determine how you and your message influence others.

LISTENING STRATEGIES AND SKILLS
- ► Use Your Extra Thought Speed
- ► Listen for the Big Ideas
- ► Listen to Feedback
- ► Listen to Nonverbal Behavior
- ► Listen before You Leap
- ► Listen for Distractions

How are these women "listening" to the unhappy child? What might be causing the little girl's distress?

If most of us only listen at 25 percent efficiency, why not take notes and write down important facts and big ideas? Research has found that note takers recall messages in more detail than nonnotetakers.[1] Taking notes makes a great deal of sense, but only if it is done skillfully.

The inclination to take notes is understandable. After all, that's what you do (or probably should do) when an instructor lectures. However, if you are like most listeners, only one-fourth of what is said may end up in your notes. Even if you copy every word you hear, your notes will not include the nonverbal cues that often tell you more about what a person means and feels. And if you spend all your time taking notes, when will you put aside your pen and ask an important question or respond?

Many listeners believe there is only one way to take notes: by making an outline. Unfortunately, most people do not speak in perfect outline form. Ralph Nichols summarizes the dilemma of balancing note taking and listening when he concludes that "there is some evidence to indicate that the volume of notes taken and their value to the taker are inversely related."[2] This does not mean you should stop taking notes, but you should learn how to take *useful* notes. Effective note taking reinforces comprehension *and* provides a valuable study guide.

Adaptability is the key to taking useful notes. Effective listeners have more than one system for taking notes. They adjust their note taking to the content, style, and organizational pattern of a speaker. So, if someone tells stories to make a point, jot down a brief reminder of the story and its point. If someone provides a list of tips, do's and don'ts, or recommendations, include those lists in your notes. If someone asks and answers a series of questions, your notes should reflect that pattern. If someone discusses a new concept or complex idea, try to paraphrase the meaning in your notes or jot down questions you want to ask. Good listeners are flexible and adaptable note takers.

[1]Paul J. Kaufmann, *Sensible Listening: The Key to Responsive Interaction*, 5th ed. (Dubuque, IA: Kendall/Hunt, 2006), p. 115.

[2]Ralph Nichols, "Do We Know How to Listen? Practical Help in a Modern Age," *Speech Teacher* (March 1961), p. 122.

As you speak, look and listen to the ways in which people react to you. Do they look interested or bored, pleased or displeased? If you can't see or hear reactions, ask for feedback. You might even stop in the middle of a conversation, meeting, or presentation to ask whether others understand you. This feedback helps you adapt to your listeners and tells your listeners that you are interested in their reactions. Asking for feedback also helps others listen. By asking questions and seeking confirmation, you help everyone understand and respond to the same message.

Listen to Nonverbal Behavior As you will read in Chapter 6, "Understanding Nonverbal Communication," we don't put everything that's important into words. Very often, another person's meaning is expressed through nonverbal behavior. For example, a change in vocal tone or volume may be another way of saying, "Listen up! This is very important." A person's sustained eye contact may be a way of saying, "I'm talking to you!" Facial expressions can reveal whether a person is experiencing pain, joy, excitement, or fear. Even gestures express a level of excitement that words cannot convey. Research indicates that the face is the primary source of information next to human speech.[26] So you are missing a lot of important information if you fail to "listen" to nonverbal behavior.

A successful courtroom attorney tells this story about how jurors' feedback told him that a client had no chance of avoiding jail time. When the attorney made his final argument to the jury, one juror, almost imperceptibly, moved her head back and forth, signifying "no." When the attorney stated that his client had no idea that a crime had been committed, another juror raised one eyebrow with a look that said, "Okay, you've done your best to defend your client, but you and I know he's guilty as sin." The jury found the defendant guilty as charged.

Listen before You Leap   Ralph Nichols, often called the "father of listening research," writes: "We must always withhold evaluation until our comprehension is complete."[27] He counsels listeners to make sure they understand a speaker before reacting, either positively or negatively, to the message.

Sometimes when we become angry, friends may tell us to "count to ten" before reacting. The same caution is good advice when we listen. Counting to ten, however, implies more than withholding evaluation until you understand completely; it also means taking time to bring your emotions under control. You may comprehend a speaker perfectly, but be infuriated or offended by what you hear. If an insensitive speaker refers to women in the room as "girls" or a minority group as "you people," it may take a count to twenty to collect your thoughts and maintain your ability to listen comprehensively. If a speaker tells an offensive joke, you may have a double reaction: anger at the speaker and disappointment with those who laughed. Try to understand the effects of offensive comments and emotion-laden words without losing your composure or concentration.

When you listen before you leap, you are not approving of or condoning what someone says. Instead, you are using your extra thought speed to decide how to react to controversial, prejudiced, or offensive comments. Listening before you leap gives you time to adjust your reaction and therefore to clarify and correct a statement rather than offend, disrupt, or infuriate others.

Listen for Distractions   Have you ever attended a lecture where the room was too hot, the seats uncomfortable, or people were talking loudly in the hallway? It's not easy to listen with so many distractions. Physical distractions can take many forms.[28] Loud and annoying noises, uncomfortable room temperature and seating, frequent interruptions, or distracting decor and outside activities are logistical distractions. A speaker's delivery can be distracting: It's hard to listen to someone who talks too softly, too rapidly, or too slowly, or speaks in a monotone or with an unfamiliar accent. Even a speaker's mannerisms and appearance can cause distracting "noise."

When a distraction is physical, you are well within your rights as a listener or speaker to shut a door, open a window, or turn on more lights. In large groups you may need to ask permission to improve the group's surroundings. For example, if you are sitting in a packed, standing-room-only meeting room where the heat index is creeping into the intolerable zone, do something about it. Open a window, turn on the air conditioner, or find someone who knows how to adjust the room temperature. Be a hero. Help people listen by taking action to overcome distractions.

Depending on the circumstances and setting, you can also take direct action to reduce behavioral distractions. If someone's behavior is creating noise, ask that person to stop talking or moving around. After all, if someone is distracting you, he or she is probably distracting others. If someone speaks too softly, you should ask the presenter to speak up.

THE ART OF PARAPHRASING

Paraphrasing (also called *reflective listening* or *mirror responses*) is the ability to restate what people say in a way that indicates you understand them. When you paraphrase, you go beyond the words you hear to understand the feelings and underlying meanings that accompany the words. Too often, we jump to conclusions and incorrectly assume we know what a speaker means and feels.

Paraphrasing is a listening check that asks, "Am I right? Is this what you mean?" It requires finding *new* words to describe what you hear, rather than repeating what a

Speaking to a rude or poor listener can be frustrating and discouraging. The International Listening Association offers a list of the ten most irritating listening habits.[1] How would you feel if someone behaved in any of the following ways while you were speaking? Try to add a few more irritating listening habits to this list.

1. Interrupting you while you're speaking.
2. Not looking at you when you're speaking.
3. Rushing you as you're speaking.
4. Showing interest in something else.
5. Finishing your thoughts for you.
6. Not responding to requests you make.
7. Saying, "Yes, but . . ." when you state a fact or opinion.
8. Topping your story with one of theirs.
9. Forgetting what you were talking about.
10. Asking too many questions during and after you speak.
11. *Another irritating listening habit:* Looking around the room for someone more important to talk to.
12. *Another irritating listening habit:* _____
    _____
13. *Another irritating listening habit:* _____
    _____
14. *Another irritating listening habit:* _____
    _____

[1]International Listening Association (www.listen.org). Quoted in Sandra D. Collins, *Listening and Responding Managerial Communication Series* (Mason, OH: Thomson, 2006), p. 21.

person says. In addition to rephrasing another person's message, a paraphrase usually includes a request for confirmation. Paraphrasing can be used for many purposes:

- To ensure comprehension before evaluation
- To reassure others that you want to understand them
- To clear up confusion and ask for clarification
- To summarize lengthy comments
- To help others uncover thoughts and feelings
- To provide a safe and supportive communication climate
- To help others reach their own conclusions[29]

If you want to clarify someone's meaning, you might say: "When you said you were not going to the conference, did you mean that you want one of us to go instead?" If you want to make sure that you understand a person's feelings, you might say, "I know you said you approve, but I sense you're not happy with the outcome. Am I way off?" If you are summarizing someone's lengthy comments, you might say, "What you seem to be saying is that it's not the best time to change this policy, right?"

Paraphrasing is difficult. Not only are you putting aside your own interests and opinions, but you are also finding *new* words that best match someone else's meaning. The phrasing of an effective paraphrase can vary in four critical ways: content, depth, meaning, and language.[30]

Content   Content refers to the words used. If you only repeat the exact same words you hear, you are not paraphrasing; you are parroting. "Repeating a person's words actually gets in the way of communicating an understanding of the essential meaning of a statement."[31] And, as depicted in the following example, it sounds foolish.

Susan: I never seem to get anywhere on time, and I don't know why.

You: Ah, so you don't know why you never seem to get anywhere on time?

Susan: Yeah, that's what I just said.

Depth   Depth refers to the degree to which you match the importance and emotions of the speaker's message in your response. Try to avoid responding lightly to a serious problem and vice versa. Responses that match a speaker's depth of feeling or that lead the person to a slightly greater depth of feeling are most effective.[32]

> Susan: People, including my boss, bug me about it, and sometimes I can tell they're pretty angry.
>
> You: In other words, you worry that other people are upset by your lateness.

Notice that the words *bug me* and *pretty angry* are not repeated. Instead you looked for comparable words—*worried* and *upset by*—that try to match the same depth of feeling.

Meaning   Even experienced listeners may miss another person's meaning when paraphrasing. Sometimes we may add unintended meaning to a person's message if we become impatient and complete a sentence or thought for the speaker. What if Susan tried to say, "I really don't know what I can do to change," and you interrupted as follows:

> Susan: I really don't know . . .
>
> You: . . . how to manage your time?

In this case you would be denying Susan the opportunity to describe her doubts about resolving the problem. We also may add meaning by responding to ideas the speaker uses only as an example. Suppose Susan said, "I have an important project coming up at work and worry that I'll be late getting there and getting it done on time." Responding with "You seem to be very upset about getting an important project done" would be an inaccurate paraphrase because it only responds to one specific example that Susan gives, instead of responding to her much larger lateness problem.

Language   Finally, use clear and simple language to ensure accurate communication. If you doubt how important word choice can be, imagine the perplexity and frustration if you responded to Susan as follows:

> Susan: I never seem to get anywhere on time, and I don't know why.
>
> You: Ahh, your persistent perplexities about punctuality are inextricably linked.
>
> Susan: Huh?

Effective paraphrasing requires mindful listening. Paraphrasing says, "I want to hear what you have to say and I want to understand what you mean." If you paraphrase accurately, the other person will feel grateful for being understood. And if you don't quite get the paraphrase right, your feedback provides another opportunity for the speaker to explain.[33]

There are many ways to paraphrase. Here we offer three ways of opening a paraphrase that help you find the right words and understand the meaning of another person's message:

1. Begin with a question: "Do I understand you to say that . . . ?" or "Is it your opinion that . . . ?"

2. Begin with a statement expressed in a questioning tone: "You think we should . . . ?" or "You want us to . . . ?"

3. Begin with a statement followed by a tag question at the end: "You believe . . . , right?" or "You feel we should . . . , correct?"[34]

The **golden listening rule** is easy to remember: *Listen to others as you would have them listen to you.* Unfortunately, this rule can be difficult to follow. It asks you to suspend your own needs and opinions to listen to someone else's.[1]

The golden listening rule is not so much a "rule" as it is an ethical listening practice. It reflects a principle in the National Communication Association's Ethics Credo: "We strive to understand and respect other communicators before evaluating and respond-

ing to their message."[2] When you follow the golden listening rule, you communicate interest, patience, and open-mindedness. The key is understanding that both "players" must have a positive and ethical listening attitude.

[1]Isa Engleberg and Dianna Wynn, *Working in Groups: Communication Principles and Strategies*, 4th ed. (Boston: Houghton Mifflin, 2007), p. 158.

[2]www.natcom.org/aboutNCA/Policies/Platform.html

Listening to Differences

Adapting to the diverse listening skills, types, and levels of others can be a challenging task, particularly when gender and cultural differences are taken into account. Keep in mind that there are many exceptions to the research summaries we present about listening differences. As you read, you may say, "But I know women who don't listen this way." The existence of exceptions does not mean the basic claim is false. Diversity research provides important insights that help explain common differences in listening behavior.

GENDER DIFFERENCES

The listening behavior of women and men often differ. Researchers tell us that men are more likely to listen to the content of what is said whereas women focus on the relationship between the speaker and listener. Males tend to hear the facts whereas females are more aware of the mood of the communication. In other words, men generally focus on comprehensive and analytical listening whereas women are more likely to be empathic and appreciative listeners.

What are the telltale signs that the man in this photograph is not listening to the woman?

Many women complain that their male partners and colleagues don't listen to them. Interestingly, men sometimes make the same complaint about women. Linguist Deborah Tannen explains that the accusation "You're not listening" often means, "You don't understand what I said" or "I'm not getting the response I want." Being listened to can become a metaphor for being understood and valued.[1]

Tannen offers an explanation for why it may *seem* that men don't listen. Quite simply, many men don't *show* they are listening, whereas women do. In general, women provide more feedback when listening: They provide listening responses, like *mhm, uh-huh*, and *yeah*. And women respond more positively and enthusiastically by nodding and laughing. To a man (who expects a listener to be quiet and attentive), a woman giving a stream of feedback and support will seem to be talking too much for a listener. To a woman (who expects a listener to be active and show interest, attention, and support), a man who listens silently will seem to have checked out of the conversation. The bottom line is this: Women may get the impression that men don't listen when, in fact, they are listening. Unfortunately, there are men who really don't want to listen because they believe it puts them in a subordinate position to women.[2]

[1]Deborah Tannen, *You Just Don't Understand: Women and Men in Conversation* (New York: Ballantine Books, 1990), pp. 141–142.
[2]Ibid., pp. 142–143.

Research also claims that men often tune out things they can't solve, or wonder why they should even listen if there isn't a problem to solve. Women may become more involved and connected to the speaker and see listening as something important to do for the other person.[35] Although men use talk to establish status, women are more likely to use listening to empower others. Unfortunately, people who listen much more than they talk are often viewed as subordinate and subservient, rather than powerful.[36]

CULTURAL DIFFERENCES

Cultural differences influence the ways in which people listen. For example, in Chapter 3, "Understanding Others," we introduced the concept of high- and low-context cultures. In high-context countries such as Japan, China, and Korea, and in African American, Native American, and Arab cultures, very little meaning is expressed through words. Much more attention is given to nonverbal cues as well as the relationships among the communicators. As a result, listeners from high-context cultures "listen" for meanings in your behavior and who you are, rather than the words you say. However, most listeners from Germany, Switzerland, Scandinavia, and the United States focus on words. They expect speakers to be direct. When high-context speakers talk to low-context listeners—and vice versa—messages may generate misunderstanding, offense, and even conflict. In many Asian cultures, the amount of time spent talking and the value placed on talking are very different than they are in the United States, Latin America, and the Middle East. For example, consider the Buddhist expression, "There is a truth the words cannot reach."

The Challenge of Critical Thinking

After many years of teaching, coaching, and consulting, we have learned that effective communicators are also excellent critical thinkers. They know how to analyze a communication situation and to select the strategies and skills that will help them achieve their purpose. **Critical thinking** is the kind of thinking you use to analyze what you read, see, or hear to arrive at a justified conclusion or decision. It is a conscious process that, when effective, always has an outcome. Critical thinking can result in a conclusion, decision, opinion, or behavior.[37] It can also result in a more effective conversation, group discussion, or presentation.

At every stage of the communication process, you will need to make critical decisions: What is my purpose? How should I adapt to other communicators? How should I structure my message? What words should I use? Critical thinking can help you answer these important questions. Throughout this textbook, we provide theories, strategies, and skills that will help you become a more critical thinker and, as a result, a more effective communicator. Here we introduce a useful model and a set of communication strategies and skills that will help you analyze the claims, facts, inferences, arguments, and thinking errors you encounter every day.

THINKING CRITICALLY ABOUT CLAIMS

Critical thinking requires the "careful, deliberate determination of whether we should accept, reject, or suspend judgment about a claim—and the degree of confidence with which we accept or reject it."[38] A **claim** is a statement that identifies your belief or position on a particular issue or topic. For example, claims answer the question: What am I trying to explain or prove? There are several types of claims, as shown in Figure 4.2. You might claim that something is true or false, probable or improbable, good or bad, or reasonable or unreasonable.

THINKING CRITICALLY ABOUT FACTS AND INFERENCES

In addition to understanding the different types of claims, critical thinkers know how to separate claims of fact (a statement that can be proved true or false) from inferences. An **inference** is a conclusion based on claims of fact. For example, "Julia has been late to the last three project meetings" is a claim of fact. You can document the

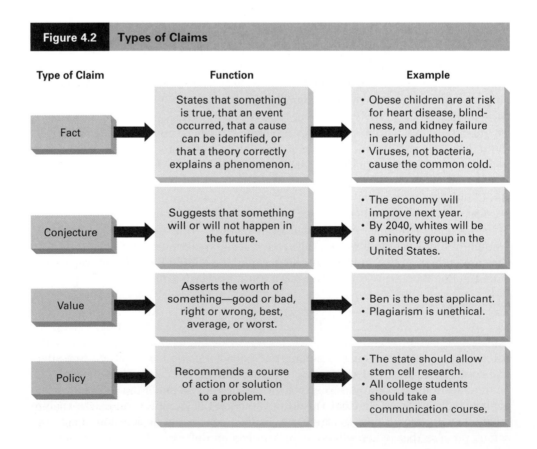

Figure 4.2 **Types of Claims**

Type of Claim	Function	Example
Fact	States that something is true, that an event occurred, that a cause can be identified, or that a theory correctly explains a phenomenon.	• Obese children are at risk for heart disease, blindness, and kidney failure in early adulthood. • Viruses, not bacteria, cause the common cold.
Conjecture	Suggests that something will or will not happen in the future.	• The economy will improve next year. • By 2040, whites will be a minority group in the United States.
Value	Asserts the worth of something—good or bad, right or wrong, best, average, or worst.	• Ben is the best applicant. • Plagiarism is unethical.
Policy	Recommends a course of action or solution to a problem.	• The state should allow stem cell research. • All college students should take a communication course.

A common misunderstanding about critical thinking is that it means the same as criticizing. Definitions of the word *criticize* include "to find fault with" and "to judge the merits and faults of."[1] The word *critical* is a broader, less fault-finding term. *Critical* comes from the Greek word for critic (*kritkos*), which means to question, to make sense of, or to be able to analyze.[2] Critical thinking is a way of analyzing what you read, see, hear, and experience to make intelligent decisions about what to believe or do. It is not the same as tearing down someone's argument or criticizing a person. Critical thinkers must identify what they are being asked to

believe or accept, and to evaluate the evidence and reasoning given in support of the belief. Good critical thinkers can develop and defend a position on an issue, ask probing questions, be open-minded, and draw reasonable conclusions.[3]

[1]*The American Heritage Dictionary of the English Language*, 4th ed. (Boston: Houghton Mifflin, 2000), p. 432.

[2]John Chaffee, *Thinking Critically*, 7th ed. (Boston: Houghton Mifflin, 2003), p. 51.

[3]Robert H. Ennis, "Critical Thinking Assessment," *Theory into Practice* 32 (1993), p. 180.

truth of this statement. However, the statement "Julia does not care about our team's project" is an inference.

Critical thinking helps you separate verifiable facts from unverifiable inferences. When you accept an inference as a fact, you are jumping to conclusions that may not be justified. When you assume that an inference is true, you may be led down a path that leads to a poor decision. Julia's tardiness might instead be the result of car trouble, unreliable childcare, or the needs of an elderly parent. More facts are needed to make a justifiable inference.

THINKING CRITICALLY ABOUT ARGUMENTS

Suppose someone approaches you and claims that stricter controls should be placed on the sale and possession of handguns. Do you know how to argue effectively for or against this policy claim?

We often think of an argument as a disagreement or hostile confrontation between two people. In critical thinking and communication terms, an argument is not a dispute. Rather, an **argument** is a claim supported by evidence or reasons for accepting it. For example, "The Latino/Latina Heritage Club should be given more funds next year" is simply a claim of policy, whereas "The Latino/Latina Heritage Club should be given more funds next year because it has doubled in size and cannot provide the same number or quality of programs without an increase in funding" is an argument.

Stephen Toulmin, a British philosopher, presents a model that depicts the structure of an argument that reflects and can be applied to real-life arguments.[39] The **Toulmin Model** is a framework for developing and analyzing arguments that includes the following components: data, claim, warrant, backing, reservation, and qualifier.[40]

Data, Claim, and Warrant   The data, claim, and warrant make up the three primary elements of an argument. The first component, the claim, is simply a conclusion or a position you advocate. For example, the statement "My group will do well on our class project" is a claim of conjecture. **Data**, the second component, constitute the evidence you provide to support your claim: "During the first meeting, all group members said they would work hard on the project."

The third component of the model is the **warrant**, which explains how and why the data support the claim. For example, the warrant might say that when group members are willing to work hard, a successful outcome is usually the result. The

CommQuiz   Is That a Fact?

Directions: Read the story carefully and assume that all the information presented is accurate and true while understanding that the story has ambiguous parts designed to lead you astray. Next, read the statements about the story and indicate whether you consider the statements to be true, false, or unclear, using the following options:

> T: The statement is definitely true on the basis of the information presented.
>
> F: The statement is definitely false.
>
> ? The statement may be true or false, but it is unclear from the information available.

Answer each statement in order, and do not go back to change previous answers. Don't reread any statements after you have answered them (this will distort your score), but reread the story, if you wish.

Story: A businessman had just turned off the lights in the store when a man appeared and demanded money. The owner opened a cash register. The contents of the cash register were scooped up and the man sped away. A member of the police force was notified promptly.

Statements about the Story:

T F ? 1. A man appeared after the owner had turned off his store lights.

T F ? 2. The robber was a man.

T F ? 3. The man who appeared did not demand money.

T F ? 4. The man who opened the cash register was the owner.

T F ? 5. The store owner scooped up the contents of the cash register and ran away.

T F ? 6. Someone opened the cash register.

T F ? 7. After the man who demanded the money scooped up the contents of the cash register, he ran away.

T F ? 8. While the cash register contained money, the story does not state how much.

T F ? 9. The robber demanded money of the owner.

T F ? 10. A businessperson turned off the lights when a man appeared in the store.

T F ? 11. It was broad daylight when the man appeared.

T F ? 12. The man who appeared opened the cash register.

T F ? 13. No one demanded money.

T F ? 14. The story concerns a series of events in which only three persons are referred to: the owner of the store, a man who demanded money, and a member of the police force.

T F ? 15. The following events occurred: someone demanded money, a cash register was opened, its contents were scooped up, and a man dashed out of the store.

Answers: (1) ?, (2) ?, (3) F, (4) ?, (5) ?, (6) T, (7) ?, (8) ?, (9) ?, (10) ?, (11) ?, (12) ?, (13) F, (14) ?, (15) ?.

Before becoming frustrated by the many question marks among the answers, take time to think critically about why the author stands by these answers. Here are his justifications for the first two answers:

1. Do you *know* that the "businessman" and the "owner" are one and the same?
2. Was there necessarily a robbery involved here? Perhaps the man was the rent collector or the owner's son—they sometimes demand money.

Source: William V. Haney, *Communication and Interpersonal Relationships: Text and Cases* (Homewood, IL: Irwin, 1992), pp. 231–232, 241.

definition of the word *warrant* may help you understand this concept. A warrant can mean "justification for an action or belief" as in, "Under the circumstance, the actions were warranted." A warrant is also something that provides assurance or confirmation as in a *warrant of authenticity* or a *product warranty*. In legal terms, a warrant gives an officer the right to make a search, seizure, or arrest.[41] In arguments, a warrant justifies your claim based on evidence. Also, as the definitions suggests, it authorizes or confirms the validity of a conclusion and gives you the right to make your claim.

What components of argumentation and elements of communication does an attorney consider when addressing a jury?

In their book *The Well-Crafted Argument*, Fred White and Simone Billings write that "Compelling warrants are just as vital to the force of an argument as are compelling data" because they reinforce validity and trustworthiness of both the data and claim. "Unsuccessful warrants often seem disconnected from, or even contradictory to, the evidence."[42] Here's an example of an unwarranted argument:

> Girlfriend (to boyfriend):   You only saw me walking to my car with your friend Dale and jumped to the conclusion that we were seeing each other behind your back. That inference is *unwarranted!*

In this argument, the evidence (she is walking to her car with Dale) is insufficient to make the claim (she's seeing Dale without her boyfriend's knowledge), because the warrant is unreasonable (If a woman is seen talking to a man, she must be romantically or sexually interested in him).[43]

Backing, Reservation, and Qualifier   Beyond the three primary elements of an argument, there are three additional components to the Toulmin Model: backing, reservation, and qualifier. **Backing** provides support for the argument's warrant. In the preceding example, backing for the warrant might be: "The group that worked hardest last time received the best grade." However, not all claims are true all the time. The **reservation** recognizes exceptions to an argument or concedes that a claim may not be true under certain circumstances: "Even though group members say they will work hard, the group won't do well if members miss meetings or make mistakes." The final component is the **qualifier**, which states the degree to which a claim appears to be true. Qualifiers are usually words or phrases such as *likely, possibly, certainly, unlikely,* or *probably.* A claim with a qualifier might state, "The group will probably do well on the project."

Using Toulmin's Model of Argument   Toulmin's model depicts a complete argument. In everyday communication, however, we rarely express all six components. We're more likely to say, "I'm sure we'll get an A on this project because we're all

How do United Nations delegates use critical thinking to analyze what they hear in order to arrive at a justified conclusion, decision, opinion, or behavior?

working so hard." This claim and evidence, however, has built-in assumptions about the warrant, backing, reservations, and qualifier. The entire Toulmin Model of Argument is illustrated in Figure 4.3.

In some situations, your arguments will be more powerful and persuasive if you include all six components. In other cases, you may need nothing more than a claim

Figure 4.3   **The Toulmin Model of Argument**

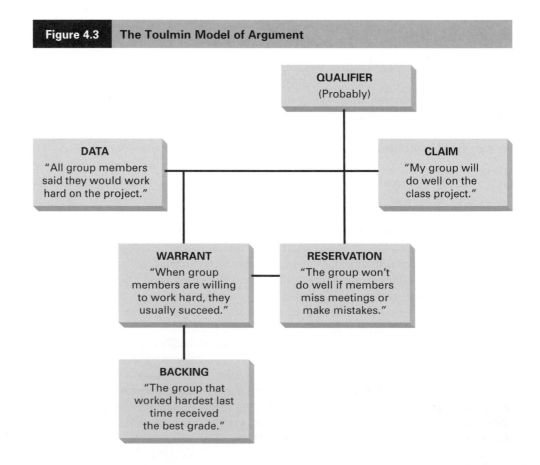

Although the Internet provides access to a tremendous amount of information, there is no guarantee that the information is accurate. Unlike most traditional information sources, not all information on the Web is scrutinized by editors or experts in a field. The following guidelines can help you determine the reliability of information on a website:

- *What is the site's purpose?* Generally, websites sponsored by government agencies or educational institutions are aimed at providing the public with useful information. However, commercial or political sites often have their own agendas.[1]

- *Can the facts be confirmed?* Remember that anyone can state anything on the Internet. Regardless of whether it is intentional, inaccurate information is commonly posted online. Verify any facts with other sources.[2]

- *Does the site include a recent posting or revision date?* Information posted on a website can often remain indefinitely. The result is that information can be outdated and no longer accurate.

[1]Vincent Ryan Ruggiero, *Becoming a Critical Thinker*, 4th ed. (Boston: Houghton Mifflin, 2002), p. 165.

[2]Ibid., p. 166.

to secure agreement. Yet, even if you don't express every component, the Toulmin Model provides a way to diagram and evaluate arguments. Understanding the model lets you know what critical thinking questions to ask.

- *Claim.* What type of claim is being made?
- *Data.* What evidence supports this claim?
- *Warrant.* How does the evidence lead to the claim?
- *Backing.* How strong and valid are the warrant and evidence?
- *Reservation.* Under what circumstances might the claim not be warranted or true?
- *Qualifier.* With how much certainty can the claim be made (e.g., *definitely, possibly, unlikely, probably*)?

If you encounter an unsupported claim, ask for evidence or data to support the argument. If the warrant is questionable, ask for backing to support it. If a situation alters the certainty of a claim, suggest a more reasonable position. When developing your own arguments, the Toulmin Model can help you test the strength of your ideas. Thinking critically about someone else's message helps you decide whether to accept an idea, reject it, or ask for more information.

CRITICAL THINKING ERRORS

Critical thinkers understand and look for misleading messages and obstacles to clear thinking. One way to recognize invalid arguments or unjustified claims is to identify fallacies. A **fallacy** is an error in thinking that has the potential to mislead or deceive others. Fallacies can be intentional or unintentional. However, when an unethical communicator misuses evidence or reasoning, or when a well-meaning person misinterprets evidence or draws erroneous conclusions, the result is still the same—inaccuracy and deception.

After you've learned to identify fallacies, don't be surprised if you begin noticing them everywhere—in television commercials, in political campaigns, on talk radio, and in everyday conversations. What, for example, is fallacious about advertisers' claims that "No other aspirin is more effective for pain than ours" and "Buy America's best-selling pickup truck"? Are fallacies involved when a political candidate talks about an opponent's past as an antiwar protester or drunk driver? The following section describes several of the most common fallacies.

COMMON FALLACIES OF ARGUMENT

- ► Attacking the Person
- ► Appeal to Authority
- ► Appeal to Popularity
- ► Appeal to Tradition
- ► Faulty Cause
- ► Hasty Generalization

When a celebrity such as Oprah praises a movie she likes, the books she chooses, and the diet she champions, do you go out a see the movie, read the book, or begin dieting? Why or why not?

Attacking the Person The fallacy of **attacking the person** also has a Latin name—*ad hominem*—which means "against the man." An *ad hominem* argument makes irrelevant attacks against a person rather than against the content of a person's message. Responding to the claim "Property taxes should be increased" with "What would you know? You don't own a home!" attacks the person rather than the argument. Name calling, labeling, and attacking a person rather than the substance of an argument are unethical, *ad hominem* fallacies. Political campaign ads are notorious for attacking candidates in personal ways rather than addressing important public issues.

Appeal to Authority Expert opinion is often used to support arguments. However, when the supposed expert has no relevant experience on the issues being discussed, the fallacy of **appeal to authority** occurs. Here's an example of a claim that makes this fallacy: "I'm not a doctor, but I play one on TV, and I recommend that you use Nick's Cough Syrup." Unless the actor has expert credentials on medical issues, the argument is fallacious. You often see television and magazine advertisements in which celebrities praise the medicines they use, the companies that insure them, the financial institutions that manage their money, and the beauty products that make them look young and attractive.

Appeal to Popularity An **appeal to popularity** claims that an action is acceptable or excusable because many people are doing it. "Most of your neighbors have agreed to support the rezoning proposal" is an appeal to popularity. Just because a lot of people hold a particular belief or engage in an action does not make it right. If most of your friends overindulge on alcohol, should you? If lots of people tell you that penicillin can cure your common cold, should you ask your physician for a prescription? Instead, it may mean that a lot of people are wrong. Unfortunately, appeals to popularity have been used to justify hate speech, unscrupulous financial schemes, and abusive behavior.

Appeal to Tradition Claiming that a certain course of action should be followed because it was done that way in the past is an **appeal to tradition**. "We must have our annual company picnic in August because that's when we always schedule it" appeals to tradition. Just because a course of action was followed for a time does not mean it is the best option.

Faulty Cause "We are losing sales because our sales team is not working hard enough." This statement may overlook other causes for low sales, such as a price increase that made the product less affordable or a competitor's superior product. The **faulty cause** fallacy occurs when you claim that a particular situation or event is the cause of another event before ruling out other possible causes. Will you catch a cold if you don't bundle up when you go outside? Will you have bad luck if you break a mirror? If you answer yes to either of these questions, you are not thinking critically. *Viruses* cause colds, although a chill can weaken your immune system. Beliefs about breaking a mirror or walking under a ladder or allowing a black cat to cross your path are nothing more than superstitions.

CommFAQ Do Emotions Matter in Critical Thinking?

Critical thinkers understand that effective decision making is an art, not an exact science. They also appreciate the important role that emotions play in everyday decisions. Sometimes our emotions trigger a response that defies rational thinking. In such cases, our instincts may be more reliable than a conclusion based on detailed analysis. Antonio Damasio, a neurologist, maintains that emotions play a crucial role in critical thinking. In his studies of patients with damage to the emotional centers of their brains, Damasio found that a lack of feelings actually impaired rational decision making.[1]

Emotions, gut feelings, instincts, hunches, and practical wisdom can help you make good decisions. They help you understand how decisions affect others and provide a way of assessing value when considering competing options.

Of course, although emotions should be heeded, they can also act as a barrier to critical thinking and decision making. Your intuitions and hunches are not always correct. For this reason, emotions must be balanced with critical thinking. Think about these popular sayings: "Opposites attract" and "Absence makes the heart grow fonder." Are these statements true? As much as your personal experiences or conventional wisdom may confirm both of these maxims, social science research suggests that both are usually wrong.

[1]Antonio R. Damasio, *Descartes' Error: Emotion, Reason, and the Human Brain* (New York: Penguin U.S.A., 1994); and Antonio R. Damasio, *The Feeling of What Happens: Body and Emotion in the Making of Consciousness* (San Diego, CA: Harvest/Harcourt, 1999).

Hasty Generalization   All it takes to commit a **hasty generalization** fallacy is to jump to a conclusion based on too little evidence or too few experiences. The fallacy argues that if it is true for some, it must be true for all. "Don't go to that restaurant. I went once and the service was awful" is a hasty generalization. One negative experience does not mean that other visits to the restaurant would not be enjoyable.

Claims about Claims

Directions: Read the following claims and indicate whether, in your opinion, they are claims of fact, conjecture, value, or policy. If you believe that the claim cannot be classified or qualifies as more than one type of claim, check N.

F = Claim of Fact　　　　C = Claim of Conjecture
V = Claim of Value　　　 P = Claim of Policy
N = None of the above or more
　　 than one type of claim

Claim	F	C	V	P	N
1. Only two U.S. senators have ever been elected as president of the United States.	☐	☐	☐	☐	☐
2. Freedom of expression, diversity of perspective, and tolerance of dissent are fundamental to a democratic society.	☐	☐	☐	☐	☐
3. The Declaration of Independence was signed in 1772.	☐	☐	☐	☐	☐
4. Watching violent TV shows harms children.	☐	☐	☐	☐	☐
5. The personal use of marijuana should be decriminalized.	☐	☐	☐	☐	☐
6. Despite personal scandals, Bill Clinton was an excellent U.S. president.	☐	☐	☐	☐	☐
7. Sea turtles often become entangled in trash or eat floating debris they mistake for food.	☐	☐	☐	☐	☐
8. Despite controversy over the war in Iraq, George Bush will be judged an excellent U.S. president.	☐	☐	☐	☐	☐
9. Audiences tend to remember vivid, dramatic information as well as negative or distressing information.	☐	☐	☐	☐	☐
10. The death penalty deters criminals.	☐	☐	☐	☐	☐
11. The first inhabitants of Sanibel Island were the Calusa Indians.	☐	☐	☐	☐	☐
12. Most people cannot remember 50 percent of what they hear immediately after hearing it.	☐	☐	☐	☐	☐

Communication Assessment

Student Listening Inventory

Directions: This inventory helps identify your listening strengths and weaknesses within the context of a college classroom. Remember that "speaker" can mean the instructor or another student. Use the following numbers to indicate how often you engage in these listening behaviors:

1 = Almost never   2 = Not often   3 = Sometimes   4 = More often than not   5 = Almost always

Listening Behavior	1	2	3	4	5
1. When someone is speaking to me, I purposely block out distractions such as side conversations and personal problems.	☐	☐	☐	☐	☐
2. I am comfortable asking questions when I don't understand something a speaker has said.	☐	☐	☐	☐	☐
3. When a speaker uses words I don't know, I jot them down and look them up later.	☐	☐	☐	☐	☐
4. I assess a speaker's credibility while listening.	☐	☐	☐	☐	☐
5. I paraphrase and/or summarize a speaker's main ideas in my head as I listen.	☐	☐	☐	☐	☐
6. I concentrate on a speaker's main ideas rather than the specific details.	☐	☐	☐	☐	☐
7. I try to understand people who speak indirectly as well as I understand those who speak directly.	☐	☐	☐	☐	☐
8. Before reaching a conclusion, I try to confirm with the speaker my understanding of his or her message.	☐	☐	☐	☐	☐
9. I concentrate on understanding a speaker's message when she or he is explaining a complex idea.	☐	☐	☐	☐	☐
10. When listening, I devote my full attention to a speaker's message.	☐	☐	☐	☐	☐
11. When listening to someone from another culture, I factor in my knowledge of cultural differences to interpret meaning.	☐	☐	☐	☐	☐
12. I watch a speaker's facial expressions and body language for additional information about the speaker's meaning.	☐	☐	☐	☐	☐
13. I encourage speakers by providing positive nonverbal feedback—nods, eye contact, vocalized agreement.	☐	☐	☐	☐	☐
14. When others are speaking to me, I establish eye contact and stop doing other nonrelated tasks.	☐	☐	☐	☐	☐
15. I avoid tuning out speakers when I disagree with or dislike their message.	☐	☐	☐	☐	☐
16. When I have an emotional response to a speaker or the message, I try to set aside my feelings and continue listening to the message.	☐	☐	☐	☐	☐

Communication Assessment (continued)

Listening Behavior	1	2	3	4	5
17. I try to match my nonverbal responses to my verbal responses.	☐	☐	☐	☐	☐
18. When someone begins speaking, I focus my attention on the message.	☐	☐	☐	☐	☐
19. I try to understand how past experiences influence the ways in which I interpret a message.	☐	☐	☐	☐	☐
20. I attempt to eliminate outside interruptions and distractions.	☐	☐	☐	☐	☐
21. When I listen, I look at the speaker, maintain some eye contact, and focus on the message.	☐	☐	☐	☐	☐
22. I avoid tuning out messages that are complex, complicated, and challenging.	☐	☐	☐	☐	☐
23. I try to understand the other person's point of view when it is different from mine.	☐	☐	☐	☐	☐
24. I try to be nonjudgmental and noncritical when I listen.	☐	☐	☐	☐	☐
25. As appropriate, I self-disclose a similar amount of personal information as the other person shares with me.	☐	☐	☐	☐	☐

Scoring: Add up your scores for all the questions. Use the following general guidelines to assess how well you think you listen. Please note that your score only represents your personal *perceptions* about your listening behavior and skills.

Score	Interpretation
0–62	You perceive yourself to be a poor classroom listener. Attention to all the items on the inventory could improve your listening effectiveness.
63–86	You perceive yourself to be an adequate listener in the classroom. Paying attention to some types of listening could improve your overall listening effectiveness.
87–111	You perceive yourself to be a good listener in the classroom, but there are some steps that could use improvement.
112–125	You perceive yourself to be an outstanding listener in the classroom.

Note: Several questions in this inventory have been modified to ensure clarity or facilitate scoring.

Source: Andrew Wolvin and Laura Janusik, "Janusik/Wolvin Student Listening Inventory," in *Instructor's Manual for Communicating: A Social and Career Focus*, 9th ed., ed. Roy M. Berko, Andrew D. Wolvin, and Darlyn R. Wolvin (Boston: Houghton Mifflin, 2004), pp. 129–131.

Key Terms

analytical listening
appeal to authority
appeal to popularity
appeal to tradition
appreciative listening
argument
attacking the person
backing
claim

comprehensive listening
critical thinking
data
discriminative listening
empathic listening
fallacy
faulty cause
feedback
golden listening rule

hasty generalization
inference
listening
paraphrasing
qualifier
reservation
thought speed
Toulmin Model of Argument
warrant

Notes

1. Michael P. Nichols, *The Lost Art of Listening* (New York: Guilford, 1995), pp. 36–37.

2. Brooke Noel Moore and Richard Parker, *Critical Thinking*, 5th ed. (Mountain View, CA: Mayfield, 1998), p. 3.

3. Sections of this chapter are based on the listening chapter (Chapter 6) in Isa N. Engleberg and Dianna R. Wynn, *Working in Groups: Communication Principles and Strategies*, 4th ed. (Boston: Houghton Mifflin, 2007), pp. 148–172.

4. Larry L. Barker et al., "An Investigation of Proportional Time Spent in Various Communication Activities by College Students," *Journal of Applied Communication Research* 8 (1980), pp. 101–109.

5. John M. Gottman and Joan DeClaire, *The Relationships Cure* (New York: Three Rivers Press, 2001), p. 198.

6. Rebecca Z. Shafir, *The Zen of Listening* (Wheaton, IL: Quest Books, 2003), p. xiii.

7. Andrew D. Wolvin and Carolyn G. Coakley, *Listening*, 5th ed. (Madison, WI: Brown and Benchmark, 1996), p. 15.

8. Reported in Sandra D. Collins, *Listening and Responding Managerial Communication Series* (Mason, OH: Thomson, 2006), p. 2.

9. Ibid.

10. Tony Alessandra and Phil Hunsaker, *Communicating at Work* (New York: Fireside, 1993), p. 54.

11. James M. Kouzes and Barry Z. Posner, *The Leadership Challenge* (San Francisco: Jossey-Bass, 1995), p. 146.

12. Tom Peters, *In Search of Excellence* (New York: Harper and Row, 1982), p. 196.

13. Isa N. Engleberg and John A. Daly, *Presentations in Everyday Life: Strategies for Effective Speaking*, 2nd ed. (Boston: Houghton Mifflin, 2005), p. 39.

14. Michael P. Nichols, p. 11.

15. Ralph G. Nichols, "Listening Is a 10-Part Skill," *Nation's Business* 75 (September 1987), p. 40.

16. S.S. Benoit and J.W. Lee, "Listening: It Can Be Taught," *Journal of Education for Business* 63 (1986), pp. 229–232.

17. Florence I. Wolff and Nadine C. Marsnik, *Perceptive Listening*, 2nd ed. (Fort Worth, TX: Harcourt Brace Jovanovich, 1992), pp. 9–16.

18. Alessandra and Hunsaker, p. 55.

19. Jim Collins, *Good to Great* (New York: Harper Collins, 2001), p. 14.

20. *The American Heritage Dictionary of the English Language*, 4th ed. (Boston: Houghton Mifflin, 2000), p. 517.

21. Wolvin and Coakley, p. 158.

22. Lester Lefton, *Psychology*, 5th ed. (Boston: Allyn and Bacon, 1994), p. 104.

23. Paul J. Kaufmann, *Sensible Listening: The Key to Responsive Interaction*, 5th ed. (Dubuque, IA: Kendall/Hunt, 2006), p. 133.

24. Stephen R. Covey, *The Seven Habits of Effective People* (New York: Simon and Schuster, 1989), p. 48.

25. Ralph G. Nichols, 1987, p. 40.

26. Mark L. Knapp and Judith A. Hall, *Nonverbal Communication in Human Interaction*, 6th ed. (Belmont, CA: 2006), p. 296.

27. Ralph G. Nichols, "Do We Know How to Listen? Practical Help in a Modern Age," *Speech Teacher* (March 1961), p. 121.

28. Madelyn Burley-Allen, *Listening: The Forgotten Skill*, 2nd ed. (New York: Wiley, 1995), pp. 68–70.

29. Adapted from Wolvin and Coakley, p. 299.

30. David W. Johnson's Questionnaire on Listening and Response Alternatives in *Reaching Out: Interpersonal Effectiveness and Self-Actualization*, 7th ed. (Boston: Allyn and Bacon, 2000), pp. 234–239.

31. Ibid., p. 234.

32. Ibid., p. 235.

33. Michael P. Nichols, p. 126.

34. Wolvin and Coakley, p. 253.

35. See Deborah Tannen, *You Just Don't Understand: Women and Men in Conversation* (New York: Ballantine Books, 1990), pp. 123–148; see also Diana K. Ivy and Phil Backlund, *Exploring Gender-Speak* (New York: McGraw-Hill, 1994), pp. 224–225.

36. See Tannen, pp. 149–151; Ivy and Backlund, pp. 206–208, 224–225; and Teri Kwal Gamble and Michael W. Gamble, *The Gender Communication Connection* (Boston: Houghton Mifflin, 2003), pp. 122–128.

37. For other definitions and discussions of critical thinking, see Moore and Parker; John Chaffee, *Thinking Critically*, 6th ed. (Boston: Houghton Mifflin, 2000); Richard W. Paul, *Critical Thinking: How to Prepare Students for a Rapidly Changing World* (Santa Rosa, CA: Foundation for Critical Thinking, 1995); and Vincent Ryan Ruggero, *Becoming a Critical Thinker*, 4th ed. (Boston: Houghton Mifflin, 2002).

38. Moore and Parker, p. 5.

39. Jay Verlinden, *Critical Thinking and Everyday Argument* (Belmont, CA: Wadsworth/Thomson Learning, 2005), p. 79.

40. Stephen Toulmin, *The Uses of Argument*. (London: Cambridge University Press, 1958). Based on an example in Stephen Toulmin, Richard Rieke, and Allan Janik, *An Introduction to Reasoning* (New York: Macmillan, 1979), p. 45.

41. *The American Heritage Dictionary of the English Language* (Boston: Houghton Mifflin, 2000), p. 1940.

42. Fred D. White and Simone J. Billings, *The Well-Crafted Argument: A Guide and Reader*, 2nd ed. (Boston: Houghton Mifflin, 2005), p. 93.

43. Based on an example in Toulmin et al., p. 45.

Understanding Verbal Communication

Key Elements of Communication	Communication Axioms	Guiding Principles of Verbal Communication
Self	*Communication Is Personal*	Monitor how the words you use affect how you think and generate messages. Recognize the inherent biases in your language.
Others	*Communication Is Relational*	Select language appropriate to the cultural perspectives of others. Use personal pronouns. Avoid exclusionary and offensive words.
Purpose	*Communication Is Intentional*	Choose words and phrases that accurately reflect and reinforce your communication purpose.
Context	*Communication Is Contextual*	Use language and grammar appropriate for the circumstances, setting, and psychological context.
Content	*Communication Is Symbolic*	Consider the denotative and connotative meanings of words. Use appropriate vocabulary, an oral style, and metaphors to enhance message comprehension and impact.
Structure	*Communication Is Structured*	Organize the words you select in clear and grammatically appropriate forms.
Expression	*Communication Is Irreversible*	Speak clearly and expressively. Use appropriate nonverbal behaviors to support your message.

Although the chimpanzee can communicate with humans using simple sign language, what other kinds of communication does a chimpanzee use in the wild?

Human Language

Human beings do not share the remarkable communication skills of many animals. You cannot track a faint scent through a forest trail or camouflage your skin color to hide from a predator. Many mammals do a much better job of interpreting the meaning of body movement than you do.[1] Yet you can do something that no animal can do: You use language. We would not be human without our words. Without words, we could not tell stories that live for thousands of years, follow or give directions, or explain our feelings.

Even though animals use sophisticated communication systems, they do not use a language as complex and powerful as the one you are reading right now. In fact, the ability to learn words and to combine, invent, and give meaning to new words is one of the things that make humans different from animals.[2]

Human **language** is a system of arbitrary signs and symbols used to communicate thoughts and feelings. Every one of the 5,000 to 6,000 languages spoken on this planet is a *system:* an interrelated collection of words and rules used to construct and express messages that generate meaning. In addition to the meanings of words, all languages have grammatical rules to describe how words should be arranged, modified, and even punctuated. "The went store he to" makes no sense until you rearrange the words: "He went to the store." And although "Him go to store" may be understandable, it breaks several grammatical rules.

Linguists Victoria Fromkin and Robert Rodman note that "whatever else people do when they come together—whether they play, fight, make love, or make automobiles—they talk. We live in a world of language."[3] Well-chosen words lie at the heart of effective communication, regardless of whether you are chatting with a friend, leading a group, addressing an audience, or writing a novel. The right words teach ("Two plus two equals four"), persuade ("Don't drink and drive"), inspire ("We hold these truths to be self-evident that all men are created equal"), and delight ("Peter Piper picked a peck of pickled peppers").

Although words have great power, they also pose many challenges. As Mark Twain, the great American humorist, observed, "The difference between the almost right word and the right word is really a large matter—'tis the difference between the

Linguistics and *linguists* are related words with different meanings. The Latin word *lingua* is a noun that refers to the tongue. The word *language* has the same Latin root. **Linguistics** is an academic discipline that studies the nature and structure of human speech. It explores how language functions as

- a system of communication
- a medium for thought
- a vehicle for literary expression
- a social institution
- a matter for political controversy
- a significant social and intellectual activity[1]

Throughout this chapter we refer to research and writings by distinguished linguists. However, the word *linguist* has two meanings. A statement such as "She's quite a linguist" can mean that she speaks or can understand several languages. The second definition refers to a specialist in the field of linguistics. For the purposes of this textbook, when we identify someone as a **linguist**, we use the second definition: a scholar who studies the nature and structure of speech.

[1]William O'Grady, Michael Dobrovolsky, and Mark Aronoff, *Contemporary Linguistics: An Introduction*, 2nd ed. (New York: St. Martin's Press, 1993), p. 1.

lightning bug and the lightning."[4] Moreover, humans communicate nonverbally as well as verbally. This chapter focuses on **verbal communication**—the ways in which we use the words in a language to generate meaning. Verbal communication can be expressed face-to-face, fax-to-fax, over the phone, or through e-mail.[5] In Chapter 6, "Understanding Nonverbal Communication," we take a detailed look at the nonverbal components of communication—physical appearance, body movement, vocal qualities, and environmental factors—rather than the nature and meaning of words.

THE ORIGINS OF LANGUAGE

No one knows exactly when or how human language began. We do know, however, that humans are anatomically specialized to speak and that our human ancestors combined sounds into words that generated meaning long before they developed writing.

Researchers estimate that the first humans to speak language as we know it lived in East Africa about 150,000 years ago.[6] In a 100,000-year-old skull, anthropologists found a modern-shaped hyoid bone, which fits right at the top of the windpipe and resembles part of the apparatus we need to speak. Fully modern language probably evolved only 50,000 years ago.[7] Thus the ability to speak is relatively modern, particularly given that our earliest known ancestors lived about 3.3 million years ago in what is now Ethiopia.[8]

Our early ancestors also walked upright rather than hunched over like apes. Standing up on their own two feet made it possible for humans to use their hands to carry things, make tools, and gesture in complicated ways. Equally important, it contributed to physiological changes in the larynx, lungs, throat, and vocal cavity that enabled them to talk. As a result, we are the only species specialized for speech and complex language development. Figure 5.1 compares the speech functions of our major speech organs with their primary survival functions in both humans and other animals.

THE FUNCTIONS OF LANGUAGE

In *Rhetorical Criticism and Theory in Practice*, Dann L. Pierce describes the need to understand verbal communication like this: While we often recognize that word-based language is an important tool or device, we don't often probe under the hood to see how that tool or device works. Pierce also notes that the language you learn in

| **Figure 5.1** | **Organs for Survival and Speech** |

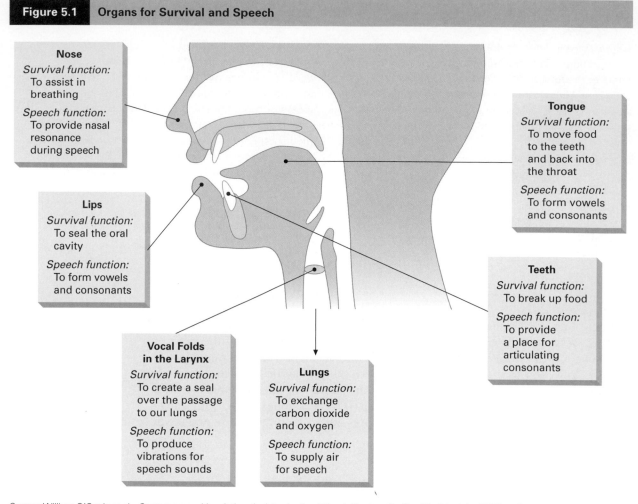

Nose
Survival function: To assist in breathing

Speech function: To provide nasal resonance during speech

Tongue
Survival function: To move food to the teeth and back into the throat

Speech function: To form vowels and consonants

Lips
Survival function: To seal the oral cavity

Speech function: To form vowels and consonants

Teeth
Survival function: To break up food

Speech function: To provide a place for articulating consonants

Vocal Folds in the Larynx
Survival function: To create a seal over the passage to our lungs

Speech function: To produce vibrations for speech sounds

Lungs
Survival function: To exchange carbon dioxide and oxygen

Speech function: To supply air for speech

Source: William O'Grady et al., *Contemporary Linguistics: An Introduction,* 5th ed. (Boston: Bedford/St. Martin's, 2005), p. 2.

your native culture is first and foremost a filter for perception and experience. Words help you select, deflect, and reflect what you experience in the world around you.[9] Figure 5.2 charts several of the most important language functions, all of which are necessary for everyday life. A term you may not understand in the figure is *phatic*. **Phatic language** is socially predictable small talk used in everyday conversations, such as "Hi," "Have a nice day," and "See ya' around."

Generating Meaning

When you don't know the meaning of a word, you may look it up in a dictionary. Depending on the word, however, you may find many definitions. In fact, no two people share exactly the same meaning of the same word. Words do not have meanings; people have meanings for words.[10] Just think of the many ways in which people define the word *love:* romantic love, love for your family and friends, love for a sport or hobby, love of country.

Linguistics devotes an entire area of academic study—**semantics**—to understanding the various meanings of words and phrases. Semantic scholars also study the relationships between the signs and symbols in a language as well as the different types and levels of meaning.

Figure 5.2	The Functions of Language

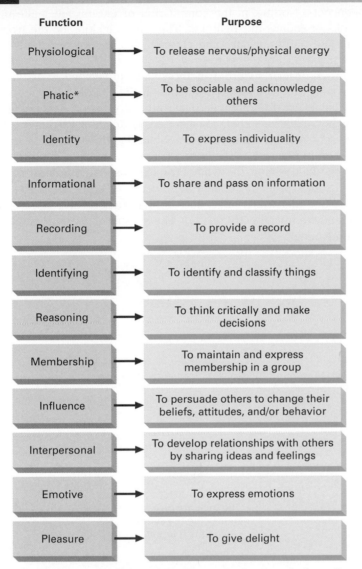

Function	Purpose
Physiological	To release nervous/physical energy
Phatic*	To be sociable and acknowledge others
Identity	To express individuality
Informational	To share and pass on information
Recording	To provide a record
Identifying	To identify and classify things
Reasoning	To think critically and make decisions
Membership	To maintain and express membership in a group
Influence	To persuade others to change their beliefs, attitudes, and/or behavior
Interpersonal	To develop relationships with others by sharing ideas and feelings
Emotive	To express emotions
Pleasure	To give delight

* Phatic language is socially predictable small talk or meaningless talk used in everyday conversations. Examples: Hi. Have a nice day. How ya' doin'? Excuse me. See ya' around.

Sources: Based on and adapted from discussions of language uses and functions in R.L. Trask, *Language: The Basics,* 2nd ed. (London: Routledge, 1995), p. 122; Geoffrey Finch, *Word of Mouth: A New Introduction to Language and Communication* (New York: Palgrave, 2003), p. 112.

SIGNS AND SYMBOLS

Like walking or breathing, language seems an entirely natural function. But all languages are inventions: The words we speak or write, and the system that underlies their use, have all been made up by people.[11] All languages are also composed of signs and symbols. A **sign** stands for or represents something specific and often looks like or depicts the thing it represents. Thus it has a visual relationship to that thing. For example, the graphic depictions of jagged lightning and dark clouds on a weather map are signs of a storm. Such graphic depictions are also used as international traffic signs to help drivers navigate the roads in foreign countries.

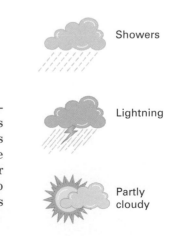

Showers

Lightning

Partly cloudy

Unlike signs, **symbols** do not have a direct relationship to the things they represent. Instead, they are an *arbitrary* collection of sounds that in certain combinations stand for concepts. Nothing in the compilation of letters that make up the word *lightning* looks or sounds like lightning. The letters making up the word *cloud* are neither white and puffy nor dark and gloomy. You cannot be struck by the word *lightning* nor get wet from the word *rain*.

When you see or hear a word, you apply your knowledge, experience, and feelings to decide what the word means. For example, if someone talks about a steak dinner, you may have very different reactions to the word *steak* depending on whether you are a rancher, a gourmet chef, a vegetarian, or an animal rights activist.

Language scholars C.K. Ogden and I.A. Richards provide a classic explanation of this phenomenon in Figure 5.3. They use a triangle to explain the three elements of language: the thinking person, the symbol (or sign) used to represent something, and the actual thing, idea, or feeling being referenced.[12]

The Ogden and Richards triangle does not have a solid base because the symbol and the referent are *not* directly related. The symbol must be mentally processed before it has meaning.

Figure 5.3	Odgen and Richards' Triangle of Meaning

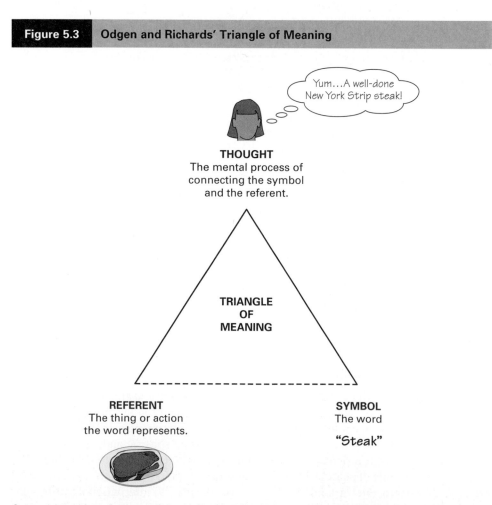

Source: Adapted from Ogden and Richards, *The Meaning of Meaning* (New York: Harcourt, Brace, 1936).

Our ability "to name" is uniquely human. It has been considered a holy privilege as well as a magical gift. In Judaism and Christianity, the first honor God confers on Adam, even before the creation of Eve, is that of naming the animals.[1]

In act II, scene 2, of Shakespeare's tragedy *Romeo and Juliet*, Juliet laments that because Romeo's last name is Montague and hers is Capulet, they cannot be married because their families are mortal enemies. She begs Romeo to "refuse thy name" and laments, "'Tis but thy name that is my enemy." Shakespeare's tragedy suggests that names can kill.

Before Shakespeare's time, most people only had one name (what we think of as a person's first name, such as George, Enrico, or Margaret). Because duplications occurred, surnames (literally "names on top of a name") were adopted. "Last" names often reflected a place of origin ("John where-the-apples-grow" became John Appleby) or parentage (son of John became Johnson), or occupation (Smith, Farmer, Carpenter, Tailor, Weaver).[2]

[1]Geoffrey Finch, *Word of Mouth: A New Introduction to Language and Communication* (New York: Palgrave, 2003), p. 28.

[2]Marcel Danesi and Paul Perron, *Analyzing Cultures* (Bloomington, IN: Indiana University Press, 1999), p. 151.

DENOTATIVE AND CONNOTATIVE MEANING

The multiple meanings of words can be further understood by examining two types of meaning: denotative and connotative. **Denotation** refers to the objective, dictionary-based meaning of a word. For example, the word *steak* has at least two possible denotations: (1) a slice of meat, typically beef, usually cut thick and across the muscle grain and served broiled, grilled, or fried; or (2) a thick slice of a large fish, such as a swordfish and salmon steak.

Connotation refers to the emotional response or personal thoughts connected to the meaning of a word. Semanticist S.I. Hayakawa refers to connotation as "the aura of feeling, pleasant or unpleasant, that surrounds practically all words."[13] Connotation, rather than denotation, is more likely to influence your response to words. Thus, the word *steak* can mean a delicious, mouth-watering meal to a hungry

What do the names of your friends and family members tell you about their characteristics and culture?

121

diner or chef, or a disgusting slab of dead flesh to a vegetarian or animal rights activist.

Words that have similar dictionary definitions can have very different connotations to your listeners. How would you describe an overweight person: *fat, heavy built, plump,* or *obese?* Is a sexy person *attractive, seductive, irresistible,* or *alluring?* If you choose a word with inappropriate connotations, your listener may be confused or offended. Effective communicators consider the possible connotations of every word they use.

GENERAL AND SPECIFIC LANGUAGE

The choice of a general word or a more specific word can also have an enormous impact on meaning. Even a general word such as *football* might cause misunderstandings with a British listener who uses the same word to mean rugby or soccer. Similarly, *freedom* might mean something different to a prison inmate than it does to you. You can minimize misinterpretations about words by paying careful attention to the different levels of meaning in our language.

Some words are very concrete. This type of word is called a **concrete word**. These words refer to specific things that can be perceived by your senses—things you can smell, taste, touch, feel, or hear. The words *table, Paris, giraffe,* and *rose* are concrete because, unlike *furniture, city, animal,* and *flower,* they narrow the number of possible meanings and decrease the likelihood of misinterpretation. An **abstract word** refers to an idea or concept that usually cannot be observed or touched because it is a generality that covers a host of examples and often requires interpretation. The word *animal* is more abstract than *giraffe* because there are a huge number of different kinds of animals. Moreover, we can see a giraffe in our mind, but what does an animal look like? A crayfish and a giraffe are both animals. Similarly, words such as *fairness, freedom,* and *evil* can have an almost endless number of different meanings and don't specifically refer to something we can see, hear, feel, taste, or touch. The more abstract your language is, the more likely your listeners may interpret your meaning other than the way you intended.[14]

There are three levels of meaning in language, ranging from the most abstract words to concrete words.[15] **Superordinate terms** are words that group objects and ideas together very generally, such as *vehicle, animal,* or *location.* **Basic terms** are words that immediately come to mind when you see an object that exemplifies a superordinate term, such as *car, van, truck; cat, chicken, mouse;* or *Bay Area, New England, Deep South.* **Subordinate terms** are even more concrete and specialized.

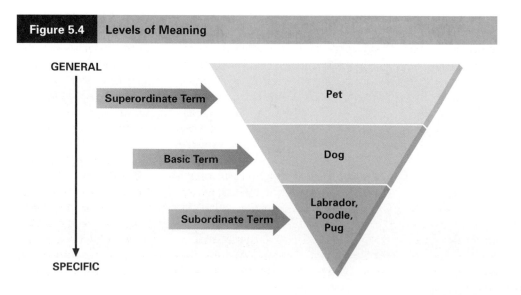

Figure 5.4 **Levels of Meaning**

GENERAL

Superordinate Term → Pet

Basic Term → Dog

Subordinate Term → Labrador, Poodle, Pug

SPECIFIC

Superordinate Terms (most abstract)	Basic Terms	Subordinate Terms (most concrete)
Visual entertainment	Film	*Gone with the Wind*
	Chair	
Seafood		
		Blue Spruce
Sport		
	Dress	

The vehicle parked outside is not just a *car*. It is a 1988 red Mercedes sports car convertible. The cat purring on your lap is not just a cat; it is a blue-eyed Siamese cat named Gatsby. If you want to see the Golden Gate Bridge and Alcatraz, don't search the entire Bay Area; go directly to San Francisco. Figure 5.4 provides an example of the three levels of meaning.

The Language of Others

There are approximately 5,000 to 6,000 languages spoken in the world, all of them with different vocabularies and rules of grammar.[16] Have you ever tried to talk to or understand someone who speaks very little English? The experience can be frustrating, comical, enlightening, or even disastrous.

LANGUAGE, MEANING, AND THINKING

One of the most significant and controversial language theories attempts to explain why people from different cultures speak and interpret messages differently from one another. Linguist Edward Sapir and his student Benjamin Whorf spent decades studying the relationship between language, culture, and thought. Whorf's most controversial theory contends that the structure of a language *determines* how we see, experience, and interpret the world around us. For example, if we don't have a word for *red*, we won't be able to see red or separate it from other colors we do see.

Whorf observed that the Hopi Indians of Arizona make no distinction in their language between past, present, and future tenses. In English, we understand the grammatical differences between "I saw the girl," "I see the girl," and "I will see the girl." The Hopi do not make such clear distinctions in their words. Whorf concluded that therefore they must perceive the world very differently. He also noted that the Hopi have a single word, *masa'ytaka*, for everything that flies, from insects to airplanes. Does that mean the Hopi cannot think about tomorrow and cannot see the differences between an airplane and a fly? Originally, many linguists believed that the answer was yes. Now linguists understand that the Hopi do think about tomorrow, but they perceive it quite differently than those of us who have the word *tomorrow*.

Would many of the Native American students in this photograph speak a language in addition to English? How does the nature of each language affect the way we see the world around us?

Language does not determine everything we think. At the same time, it does influence the way we perceive others and the world around us.[17]

Like many controversial theories, the Whorf Hypothesis (also referred to as the Sapir–Whorf Hypothesis) has been accepted, rejected, resurrected, and amended—several times. Today, most linguists accept a more moderate version of the **Whorf Hypothesis**: Language *reflects* cultural models of the world, which in turn influence how the speakers of a language come to think, act, and behave.[18] For example, in English, terms that end with *man*, such as *chairman*, *fireman*, and *policeman*, may lead us to view certain roles and jobs as only appropriate for men. Substituting words such as *chairperson*, *firefighter*, and *police officer* may change perceptions about who can work in these careers.

LANGUAGE AND CULTURE

The Whorf Hypothesis, even in its most moderate form, highlights the profound connections between language and culture, particularly in the areas of vocabulary, the use of pronouns, and verbal directness.

Unique Vocabularies   Language often reflects what is important to the people in a specific culture. In one of Tony Hillerman's mystery novels, a Navaho tribal police officer asks an FBI agent to describe the rocks at a murder scene. When the agent cannot come up with anything better than the word *rocks*, the Navaho officer explains that a Navaho would do better: "It's said the Inuits up on the Arctic Circle have nine words for snow. I guess, living in our stony world, we're that way with our rocks."[19] If there are hundreds of words used to describe camels in Arabic languages and snow in Eskimo languages, there are hundreds of English words to describe the many kinds of vehicles driven in the United States, as well as the extraordinary number of names for coffee drinks served at a local Starbucks.

The fact that many words are unique to a particular culture can make translation very difficult. Even if you are not speaking to someone from another country, there are regionalisms and special vocabulary words unique to different parts of the country and to various careers and professions. For example, a sandwich on a large roll with a variety of meats and cheeses on it may be called a *grinder*, a *hero*, a *sub(marine)*, a *hoagie*, or a *poorboy*, depending on the region of the country.[20]

In the Hebrew Bible, the descendants of Noah tried to build the Tower of Babel so they could reach heaven. God hindered the builders by making them speak different languages, thus preventing them from working together harmoniously. The word *babel* has since come to mean a confusion of meaningless voices and sounds.

Some people believe that the world and the United States would be a happier, more peaceful, and better place to live if everyone spoke the same language. But scholars dismiss this notion, with good reason. The conflicting parties in northern Ireland speak the same language, as do rival enemies in Rwanda, Bosnia, Iraq, and the two Koreas. The armies of both the northern and southern states in the U.S. Civil War spoke English.

Actually, we need many languages. Andrew Dalby, author of *Language in Danger: The Loss of Linguistic*

Diversity and the Threat to Our Future, contends that every language that disappears will take its rich cultural background with it. He predicts that within two hundred years the earth will almost certainly be down to 200 languages—from some 5,000 or more now in existence—and that English will become more common. As languages disappear, we will lose the knowledge they preserve and transmit. We also will lose the insights that other languages give us into alternative worldviews and explanations of human nature. Furthermore, we need a multiplicity of languages, because the interaction of languages keeps our own language flexible and creative.[1]

[1]Michael Dirda, Book review of *Languages in Danger: The Loss of Linguistic Diversity and the Threat to Our Future*, by Andrew Dalby, *Washington Post*, May 25, 2003, p. 15.

Pronouns   As we noted in Chapter 3, intercultural scholars view individualism–collectivism as the single most important dimension of cultural difference and the most important factor for distinguishing one culture from another. Individualistic cultures have an "I" orientation; collectivist cultures have a "we" orientation. Interestingly, "English is the only language that capitalizes the pronoun *I* in writing. English does not, however, capitalize the written form of the pronoun *you*."[21] By contrast, people of the Athabaskan-speaking community in Alaska speak and think in a collective plural voice. The word for *people*, *dene*, is used as a kind of *we*, and is the subject for almost every sentence requiring a personal pronoun.[22]

When speaking to others, pay attention to the individualistic or collectivist tendencies in the way they use languages. Although frequent use of the words *I* and *you* may be appropriate for a group of ambitious corporate executives in the United States, the word *we* might be more appropriate for African Americans or people from Central and South America, who are less individualistic.

Verbal Directness   Most people living in the United States have a very low-context, direct way of speaking. In the eyes of other cultures, we get to the point with blunt, straight talk. When we say no, we mean no! Many other cultures view this direct use of language as a disregard for others that can lead to embarrassment and injured feelings.[23] At a news conference, President George W. Bush acknowledged that his all-American speaking style may be too direct when dealing with the leaders of other nations. " 'I explained to the prime minister (Tony Blair of Great Britain) that the policy of my government is the removal of Saddam,' said President Bush. Catching himself, Bush added: 'Maybe I should be a little less direct and be a little more nuanced, and say we support regime change.' "[24]

Most North Americans learn to say yes or no when expressing their opinions; however, the Chinese, as a collectivist culture, usually use yes or no to express respect for the feelings of others. Thus, a Chinese person may say yes to a suggestion or business proposal because it is what you want to hear when, in fact, the real response is no.

In light of the subtle but profound influences of language, it is important to pay careful attention to how you express yourself and respond to others. If you suspect that you are speaking to someone from a collectivist, high-context culture, you may want to use language that is more suggestive than direct, more vague than specific, and more respectful than critical.

LANGUAGE AND GENDER

Most languages reflect a gender bias and other disparities based on gender. These differences can be minor or major depending on the language and context in which communication takes place.[25]

Gender Bias   Most languages differ in the number and use of gender-related pronouns. In English, we struggle with the words *he* and *she*. For many years, the pronoun *he* was used to refer to an unspecified individual. Older textbooks used sentences such as: *Every speaker should pay attention to his words.*

Why do women and men often separate at social gatherings? Does the nature of their talk explain this division?

Some languages have greater gender-related challenges. French, for example, has separate third-person plurals: masculine and feminine versions of *they*. Japanese distinguishes gender in both the first and second person; it has different versions of *you* for men and women. The language of Finland may have the best solution. All pronouns are gender neutral; there is only one word for *he* and *she*.[26]

Today, effective communicators of English use several techniques to avoid bias in pronouns.

- *Use plural forms.* Instead of saying, "Every speaker should pay attention to his words," you could substitute, "All speakers should pay attention to their words."

- *Avoid using any pronoun.* In some cases, you can reword a sentence and remove the pronoun, as in "Good speakers pay careful attention to language."

- *Use variations on the phrase "he or she" as well as "his and hers."* The following sentences avoid bias, but they are somewhat awkward to say: "Every speaker should pay attention to his or her words," and "Every speaker should pay attention to her or his words."

Also make sure you use gender-neutral terms to describe jobs and professions. In the theater and film industries, the word *actor* is replacing *actress* for female performers. The following are some gender-biased terms and their gender-neutral substitutes:

Gender-Biased Terms	Gender-Neutral Terms
Stewardess	Flight attendant
Fireman	Firefighter
Female soldier	Soldier
Chairman	Chairperson
Male nurse	Nurse
Mankind	People, humanity, human beings

Although some languages, such as Finnish, make very few distinctions between men and women, English favors men over women. Most gender-related word pairings begin with the male term: male and female, boys and girls, husband and wife, Jack and Jill, Romeo and Juliet, Mr. and Mrs.[27] If you doubt this preference, think about the married couples you know. Would you address a letter to Mrs. and Mr. Smith? How do you talk about a couple when using their first names? Is it Dick and Jane or Jane and Dick? Adam and Eve or Eve and Adam?

Unfortunately, because of the male bias in English and in American society, female terms tend to take on demeaning connotations. The connotations of the second word in the following pairings are negative or outdated for women: *wizard/witch, governor/governess, master/mistress, sir/madam.* Women are also compared with animals: *bitch, cow, shrew, crow, vixen, dog.*[28] Single men are *bachelors* or even *studs*, whereas single women may be called *old maids* or *spinsters.* In fact, one study lists more than five hundred English slang terms for *prostitute*, but only sixty-five for the men who are their willing clients.[29]

Gender Differences   Linguist Deborah Tannen contends that women and men use language differently. Many women speak tentatively. Their sentences are more likely to contain qualifiers and tag questions, as in "I guess it may be time to move on to my next point, don't you think so?" Men, however, tend to use language to assert their ideas and compete with others. Their speech is generally characterized as more direct and forceful. Although one style of communication is not better than another, the result is that women speakers may be seen as less powerful than their male counterparts.[30]

CommFAQ Do Women Talk More Than Men?

One of the great language myths is that women talk more than men. This belief is neither new nor confined to the United States. Many proverbs and sayings express this pervasive myth[1]:

Where there are women and geese there's noise. (Japanese)

The woman with active hands and feet, marry her. But the woman with overactive mouth, leave well alone. (New Zealand Maori)

In actuality, most research studies portray a different picture. A recent study of 400 college students found that the number of words uttered by males and females were virtually the same. An analysis of sixty-three studies of gender differences in talkativeness found that men actually "yakked slightly more than women, especially when interacting with spouses or strangers and when the topic was non-personal." Women talked more with classmates, with parents and children, and in situations where the topic of conversation required disclosure of feelings.[2]

When women and men are together in work settings, men may do most of the talking. Even when women hold influential positions, they often find it hard to contribute to a discussion as much as men do. This pattern is also evident in educational settings (from kindergarten through university), where males dominate classroom talk. Sadly, when women talk as much as men do, they may be perceived as talking "too much."[3]

After reviewing the literature on the amount of male and female talk, linguist Janet Holmes concludes that the answer to the question "Do women talk more than men?" is "It depends." It depends on the social context, the kind of talk, the confidence of the speaker, the social roles, and the speaker's expertise. Generally, men are more likely to dominate conversation in formal, public contexts where talk is highly valued and associated with status and power. Women, on the other hand, are likely to contribute more in private, informal interactions, when talk functions to maintain relationships and in situations where women feel socially confident.[4]

[1]Janet Holmes, "Myth 6: Women Talk Too Much," in *Language Myths*, ed. Lauri Bauer and Peter Trudgill (London: Penguin, 1998), p. 41.

[2]David Brown, "Stereotypes of Quiet Men, Chatty Women Not Sounds Science," *The Washington Post*, July 6, 2007, p. A2. See also, Donald G. McNeill, Jr. "Yada, Yada, Yada. Him? Or Her?" *The New York Times*, July 6, 2007, p. A13.

[3]Holmes, pp. 42–47.

[4]Ibid., pp. 48–49.

Linguist Robin Lakoff was one of the first linguists to write about gender differences in *Language and Woman's Place*.[31] She contends that women tend to use language that expresses uncertainty, lack of confidence, and excessive deference or politeness. Here are some of the features she identifies as characteristic of women's speech:

- *Tag Questions.* Use of questions tagged onto sentences to gain approval, such as "don't you agree?" and "haven't you?"

- *Superpolite Forms.* Avoidance of direct requests, as in "Could you please close the door?" or "Would you mind closing the door?"

- *Hedges.* Use of "fillers" such as *like, you know, well*, and *kind of*, which make statements more tentative.

We would be guilty of stereotyping if we didn't note the exceptions to such tendencies. Certainly, many men speak tentatively and cooperatively whereas many women speak directly and assertively. As we explain later in this chapter, both men and women often use highly powerful language when their communication goal is significant and personally important.

A new computer program can determine (in most cases) the gender of an author by detecting subtle differences in the words men and women prefer to use. For example, female writers tend to choose terms that apply to personal relationships, such as *for* and *with*, more frequently than men do. Perhaps not surprisingly, women write the pronoun *she* more often than men do, although both sexes use *he* about equally.

According to the researcher who developed the program, "Women have a more interactive style. They want to create a relationship between the writer and the reader." Men, on the other hand, seem to care more than women do about conveying specific information. Male writers seem to be saying: "Here's something I want to tell you about, and here are some things about it." The words favored most heavily by men are what grammarians call determinative words, such as *the, a, as, that,* and *one.* Female writers favor *she* and relationship words such as *for, with, in, and,* and *not.*[1]

[1]Knight Ridder/Tribute Service, "Program Determines the Gender of Authors," *The Sun,* May 23, 2003, p. 6A. Based on a report published by Shlomo Argamon, Moshe Koppel, and Anat Shimoni, *Literary and Linguistic Computing* (April 2003).

Language and Context

What kind of language would you use in a college classroom, at a beloved family member's funeral, at a critical job interview, at a political or pep rally, at home with your parents, or at a party with your friends? There would be subtle and not-so-subtle differences in your choice of words and grammar. We naturally change our language based on our relationships with other communicators, their psychological traits and preferences, and the extent to which they share our cultural attitudes, beliefs, values, and behaviors.

CODE SWITCHING

Code switching is a common and usually successful strategy for adapting to the many contexts in which we communicate. If you can speak more than one language, you already code switch as you move from one language to another. In fact, the term *code switching* was first used to describe the ability to use more than one language in different contexts, such as when immigrants speak English as well as their native language. Here we use the term **code switching** in a much broader sense: to describe how, depending on the context, we often modify how we use verbal and nonverbal communication to generate meaning.

Effective communicators learn to adapt their language to the communication context. Although a swear word would never pass your lips at a job interview, during a church service, or in a formal public speech, you may curse in the company of close friends and like-minded colleagues.

African Americans often switch their linguistic codes depending on the context. They may speak one way in the world of white people (Standard English) and quite differently at home (Black English). In his book *Word on the Street*, linguist John McWhorter notes that many middle-class African Americans typically speak both Black English and Standard English, switching constantly between the two, often in the same sentence.[32] For example, a Black English speaker may use double negatives ("He don't know nothing") and delete verbs based on *to be* ("She fine") within statements made in Standard English. McWhorter also notes that African Americans

How does context affect what is considered appropriate language in each of these situations?

usually code switch between Standard and Black English when the topic or tone is informal, lighthearted, or intimate. As a result, African Americans are competent in two sophisticated dialects of English.[33]

LANGUAGE OVER TIME

All languages change over time. With every new edition of a dictionary, new words are added. For example, after computers became common in most businesses and homes, we added words such as *software* and *modem* as well as new meanings for words such as *mouse*, *bulletin board*, and *CD*. Many well-respected dictionaries now include words such as *phat*, *dot-commer*, *identity theft*, *mosh pit*, and *shopaholic*.

When teaching or coaching speakers from other countries, we are often asked, "How can I get rid of my accent?" The honest answer is that in most cases, you can't. The better response is: Why do you want to? Most of the time, an accent or a dialect won't hinder your ability to communicate.

Accents and dialects are not the same. An **accent** is the sound of one language imposed on another. For example, some Asian speakers have difficulty producing the "r" and "v" sounds in English.

Dialects differ from accents because they represent regional and cultural differences within the same language. What people call a southern accent is really a southern dialect.[1] In general, dialects refer to the use of different words for a similar object or idea as well as variations in the pronunciation of common words.

Linguists have identified eighteen regional dialects of American English. For example, a carbonated soft drink is called *soda* in the Northeast, *pop* in the inland areas and the Northwest, *tonic* in eastern New England, and *soda pop* in parts of southern West Virginia, eastern Kentucky, the western Carolinas, and eastern Tennessee.

Dialects may also have a distinctive sound. Northeast dialects, for example, range from the unique sound of New York City residents to the loss of "r" sounds in New England (in words such as *park, car, Harvard*, and *yard*). Southern dialects are also marked by the loss of the "r" sound as well as distinctive phrases such as *y'all*.

A consistent finding across several studies is that Standard American English speakers are judged as more intelligent, ambitious, and successful, even when the judges themselves speak a nonstandard American dialect.[2] However, having an accent or dialect does not stop anyone from being an effective communicator. What matters is that you speak loud enough and clear enough for others to hear and understand, and that is true no matter what language you speak.

[1]Isa Engleberg and John Daly, *Presentations in Everyday Life: Strategies for Effective Speaking*, 2nd ed. (Boston: Houghton Mifflin, 2005), pp. 347–349; William O' Grady et al., *Contemporary Linguistics*, 5th ed. (Boston: Bedford/St. Martin's, 2005), pp. 627, 635.

[2]Ethel C. Glenn, Phillip J. Glenn, and Sandra Forman, *Your Voice and Articulation*, 4th ed. (Boston: Allyn and Bacon, 1998), p. 10.

Longstanding words also change their meanings slightly or even dramatically over the centuries. For example, the word *awful* originally meant "inspiring awe," which explains the origins of the popular word *awesome*. Now the word *awful* means "extremely bad" or "very" as in the phrase "awfully good." Connections to the notion of "awe" have been lost.[34] Linguist Peter Trudgill writes that "meanings can and do change as they are modified and negotiated in millions of everyday exchanges over the years between one speaker and another. Languages are self-regulating systems because their speakers want to understand each other and be understood."[35]

Misunderstanding Meaning

Despite our best efforts to understand the complex relationship between language and meaning, misunderstandings are inevitable. Three common language barriers to effective communication are bypassing, exclusionary language, and offensive language.

BYPASSING

When two people have different meanings for the same word or phrase, they risk bypassing one another. **Bypassing** is a form of miscommunication that occurs when people "miss each other with their meanings."[36] A friendship can be damaged, a meeting can be doomed, and a presentation can backfire if there are differences in the interpretations of a single word or phrase. If you have ever found yourself saying, "But, that's not what I meant," you have experienced bypassing. Note the problem created in the following example of bypassing.

LANGUAGE BARRIERS
- ▶ Bypassing
- ▶ Exclusionary Language
- ▶ Offensive Language

At a routine staff meeting, a vice president asks her managers to "survey the members of your department to find out whether they are satisfied with the new e-mail system." During the following week, the vice president receives a copy of a memo from one manager requesting that everyone in his department fill out a two-page questionnaire about the e-mail system. The vice president telephones the manager and asks, "What's this questionnaire all about?" The manager replies, "I thought you said I had to survey everyone in my department."

What the vice president had in mind was an informal poll rather than a detailed, questionnaire-based analysis of the new system. Although the manager heard the vice president's words accurately, the communicators "missed" each other's meaning.

William Haney, an organizational communication scholar, maintains that effective "communicators who habitually look for meanings in the *people* using words, rather than in the words themselves, are much less prone to bypass or be bypassed" (emphasis added).[37] In other words, it's not what words mean to you, but what speakers mean when they use words.

EXCLUSIONARY LANGUAGE

Exclusionary language uses words that reinforce stereotypes, belittle other people, or exclude others from understanding an in-group's message. Exclusionary language emphasizes differences by separating the world into *we* to refer to people like you, and *they* or *these people* to refer to people different from you. Be aware of terms that could widen the social gap or offend others. You don't have to be excessive in your zeal to be "politically correct," using *underachieve* for *fail*, or *vertically challenged* for *short*, but you should try to avoid alienating others by using language that excludes them. Pay special attention to the following subjects when you choose words to describe people[38]:

- *Age.* Avoid derogatory, condescending, or disrespectful terms associated with age. Refer to a person's age or condition neutrally, if at all: not *well-preserved little old lady* but *woman in her eighties* or just *woman*.

- *Politics.* Words referring to politics are full of connotations. The word *liberal*, for instance, has positive and negative connotations. Take care with words like *radical*, *left wing*, and *right wing*.

- *Religion.* Devout Christians, Jews, and Muslims should not be labeled as *extremist* or *fanatic*. Never use the term *these people* when referring to different religions, because it emphasizes differences and sounds derogatory. Even the word *we* should be avoided when it implies that all your listeners share (or should share) your religious beliefs.

- *Health and Abilities.* Avoid saying *confined to a wheelchair* and *victim* (of a disease). Instead, say *someone who uses a wheelchair* and *person with* (a disease). Never use the word *retarded* to refer to mental ability.

- *Sexual Orientation.* Refer to a person's sexual orientation only if the information is necessary to your content. Also, do not assume that the sexual orientation of others is the same as your own.

- *Race and Ethnicity.* Use the names people prefer to describe their racial or ethnic affiliations. For example, *black* and *African American* are preferred terms; *Asian* is preferred over *Oriental*. Avoid using stereotypical terms and descriptions of people based on their race or ethnicity. You gain nothing by saying that the "new supervisor is an Asian woman with a degree from Yale" or that "a Polish guy who owns several repair shops bought Frank's garage."

Instead say, "The new supervisor has a degree from Yale" or "A guy who owns several repair shops bought Frank's garage."

In addition to stereotyping others, exclusionary language can prevent others from participating or joining a discussion that relies on specialized jargon and gobbledygook. **Jargon** is the specialized or technical language of a profession or homogenous group. English professor William Lutz points out that we all use jargon as "verbal shorthand that allows members to communicate with each other clearly, efficiently, and quickly."[39] In some settings and on some occasions, such as at a meeting of psychiatrists, attorneys, information technology professionals, or educators, the ability to use jargon properly is a sign of group membership and it speeds communication among members. In other settings, such as with a general audience, jargon can make ideas difficult to understand and may even be used to conceal the truth. Some speakers use jargon to impress others with their specialized knowledge. For example, a skilled statistician may bewilder an audience by using unfamiliar terms to describe cutting-edge methodologies for establishing causality. In other situations, people use jargon when they have nothing to say; they just string together a bunch of nonsense and hope no one notices their lack of content.[40] Such tactics fail to inform others, and often result in misunderstandings and resentment.

Semanticist Stuart Chase defines **gobbledygook** (the sound of which is supposed to imitate the nonsense gobbling of a turkey) as "using two or three or ten words in place of one, or using a five-syllable word where a single syllable would suffice." He gives us this example: The word *now* has been replaced by the five-word, seventeen-letter phrase "at this point in time."[41]

The worst kind of gobbledygook occurs when speakers use big, multisyllable words in an attempt to impress listeners. Rudolf Flesch published a sixty-word blacklist in his book, *Say What You Mean*. He contends that long words are a curse, a special language that comes between a speaker and listener. According to Flesch, people use such words to cloak themselves in a mantle of false dignity or to make themselves appear more powerful.[42] Why say *affirmative* when you mean *yes?* Why say *anticipate* instead of *expect?* Why use *obtain, procure,* or *secure* when *get* works just as well? Flesh writes, "*Get* is always better. It's the way we all talk. Get it?"[43]

Movie director Spike Lee rejects being labeled as a black filmmaker. "I want to be known as a talented young filmmaker. That should be first. But the reality today is that no matter how successful you are, you're black first."

Two problems occur when you label someone or accept a label you hear or see. First, you reduce an entire person into a label: black filmmaker, dumb blond, deaf cousin, or rich uncle. Second, the label can affect your perceptions or relationship with that person. For example, if you label a person as inconsiderate, you may make excuses for an act of kindness: "I wonder what prompted her to do that?" When you label

someone as near perfect, you may go to great lengths to justify or explain less-than-perfect behavior: "Tiger Woods is still the best player in golf; he's just having an off year." Labels also influence how we interpret the same behavior:

- I'm energetic; you're overexcited; he's out of control.
- I'm laid-back; you're untidy; she's a slob.
- I'm smart; you're intelligent; Chris is brilliant!

OFFENSIVE LANGUAGE

During the first half of the twentieth century, many words were considered inappropriate, particularly those that referred to private body parts and functions. Women went to the *powder room* and men to the *lavatory*. Even the word *pregnant* was once considered improper. Instead, a woman was "in a family way" or "with child." In 1952, Lucille Ball became the first pregnant woman to appear on a television show. The scripts called her an "expectant mother," never using the word *pregnant*. All of the *I Love Lucy* scripts were reviewed by a priest, a rabbi, and a minister to make certain they were in good taste.[44] And until quite recently, swear words were literally unheard of on radio and television. Today, however, you might hear dozens of swear words on cable television shows, and you might easily witness steamy sexual scenes that would have given the *I Love Lucy* censors heart attacks.

Why People Swear Do you swear? Frequently, occasionally, never? If you *never* swear, are you ever tempted to express yourself with a swear word? People who swear do so for many reasons. In his book, *Cuss Control: The Complete Book on How to Curb Your Cursing*, James O'Connor describes several reasons people engage in what he calls "recreational swearing"[45]:

- Swearing is lazy language that is easy to call on.
- Swearing can be fun if it's used humorously or in the right company.
- Our peers (or parents, or bosses, or role models) do it.
- Men swear to show they're naturally aggressive and strong.
- Women swear to appear equal to and competitive with men.
- Swearing helps emphasize a point.
- Swearing shows we are unhappy or depressed.
- Swearing is a habit we're not motivated to break.

Controlling Cursing There are good reasons to stop swearing or, at least, to control where, when, and with whom you use such language. For example, swearing frequently offends others. One study reported that 91 percent of respondents ranked foul language as "the most ill-mannered type of workplace behavior."[46] Moreover, people

CommFYI Avoid Clichés

A **cliché** (pronounced klŭ-shāy) is a trite or overused expression. Clichés are usually phrases or ideas that have lost their originality or force through overuse.[1]

Nonnative speakers of Standard American English often have difficulty understanding clichés. For example, we heard a college vice president who was born in the former Yugoslavia describe a problem brewing in one of her academic departments as a "storm in a teacup." It took several moments for colleagues to figure out that she meant to use the cliché "tempest in a teapot."

In general, clichés should be avoided because they lack force and are predictable rather than original. So, how do you decide if you're using a cliché? Try this simple test: Say the beginning of the phrase and see if you or others can guess the last word. If most people can guess the ending, you may be using a worn-out cliché.[2]

Beginning of Phrase	End of Phrase
He's blind as a . . .	bat.
The plan is dead as a . . .	doornail.
It's selling like . . .	hotcakes.
I'm as cool as a . . .	cucumber.

A critical look at these and other clichés reveals another weakness. They often make little sense. Are cucumbers always cool? Do hotcakes always sell well? Is a doornail deader than a floor nail? And although bats may not see well with their eyes, their radar system is far superior to our vision.

[1]See Ann Raimes, *Keys for Writers: A Brief Handbook*, 3rd ed. (Boston: Houghton Mifflin, 2003), p. 271.

[2]Based on Diana Hacker, *The Bedford Handbook*, 5th ed. (Boston: Bedford, 1998), p. 279.

who do *not* swear are seen as more intelligent (because they can find more accurate and appropriate words) and more pleasant (because they don't offend anyone). They are also perceived as effective communicators who have greater control over their emotions.

When President Bush was talking to former British Prime Minister Tony Blair about violence in the Middle East, an open microphone picked up Bush's comment that Syria should press Hizbollah to "stop doing this sh*t." Was the resulting criticism of Bush justified?

When you use a **euphemism**, you substitute a mild, indirect, or vague term for a harsh, blunt, or offensive one.[1] Rather than say someone has died, we may say he or she has "passed away." In Victorian England, the word *limb* was used for *leg*, a word that had sexual connotations. Even a chair leg wasn't referred to as such because it might spark thoughts of sexuality. In restaurants, we usually ask for directions to the restroom rather than asking where the toilet is.[2]

Some euphemisms substitute a letter in a word to make it less offensive. You frequently hear people say "jeeze" instead of "Jesus," "darn" instead of "damn," and "heck" rather than "hell." Can you think of any other examples like these?

Euphemisms, however, can be used to mask the truth. President Clinton claimed he had never "slept" with Monica Lewinski even though the word *slept* is frequently used as a euphemism for having sex with someone. Pentagon spokespersons referred to the treatment of Iraqis in Abu Ghraib prison as *interrogation*, whereas many critics described these "interrogation" treatments, such as food and sleep deprivation, stress positions, hooding, and attack dogs, as *torture*.[3]

[1] *The American Heritage Dictionary of the English Language*, 4th ed. (Boston: Houghton Mifflin, 2000), p. 614.

[2] William O'Grady, Michael Dobrovolsky, and Mark Aronoff, *Contemporary Linguistics*, 2nd ed. (New York: St. Martin's Press, 1993), pp. 235–236.

[3] "The Leaked Memos: Did the White House Condone Torture?" *The Week*, June 25, 2004, p. 6.

When offensive language is a problematic habit of speech, the solution lies in understanding the nature of that habit and taking steps to break it. Like any habit— biting your nails, overeating, or abusing alcohol—you must *want* to stop doing it. Here are some suggestions:

- When you feel like swearing, use a euphemism such as *Darn* or *Good grief.*
- Take the swear word out of sentences where it's not needed. For example, rather than saying, "Who the @%*$ cares?" say, "Who cares?"
- Look for better, more interesting words. Rather than saying, "This place looks like *&%$!" try, "This place looks like an infantry company camped here *and* partied" or "This place is so cluttered, we'll have to put up emergency exit signs."
- Describe what you hear rather than jumping to a conclusion that accuses. Say, "That sounds like an exaggeration" rather than the upsetting "That's a f***ing lie."

Improving Your Way with Words

In the previous section, we emphasized what *not* to do if you want to be understood and respected by others. Here we take a more positive approach by examining six ways in which you can use language to express messages clearly and appropriately: expand your vocabulary; use oral language; use active language; use *I*, *you*, and *we*; know your grammar; and use metaphorical language.

EXPAND YOUR VOCABULARY

How many words do you know? By the age of five, you probably knew about 10,000 words, which means that you learned about ten words a day. Children have an inborn ability for learning languages that diminishes at around age twelve or thirteen. Although children can learn a second or third language with relative ease, adults struggle to become fluent in a second language.[47]

Even though we may have difficulty learning a second language, we continue to learn more words in our first language. By the time we are adults, our vocabularies have expanded to include tens of thousands of words. Not surprisingly, finding the "right" word is a lot easier if you have many words from which to choose. When your only ice cream choices are vanilla or chocolate, you miss the delights of caramel butter pecan, mocha fudge swirl, and even plain old strawberry. When you search for words in the English language, you have more than a million choices.

As you learn more words, make sure you understand their meaning and usage. For example, you should be able to make distinctions in meaning among the words in each of the following groups[48]:

- Absurd, silly, dumb, preposterous, ridiculous, ludicrous, idiotic
- Abnormal, odd, eccentric, foreign, strange, peculiar, weird
- Pretty, attractive, gorgeous, elegant, lovely, cute, beautiful

As mentioned earlier, the difference between the almost-right word and the right word is a very large matter. You may not mind being called "silly," but may have serious objections to being called "idiotic." Improving your vocabulary will be a lifelong task—and one that will be made much easier if you are an avid reader.

USE ORAL LANGUAGE

Usually, there is a big difference between the words we use for written documents and the words we use orally in conversations, group discussions, and oral presentations. In his book *How to Win Any Argument*, Robert Mayer writes: "The words you'll craft for a listener's ears are not the same as the words you'll craft for a reader's eyes. Readers can slow their pace to reread, to absorb, and to understand—luxuries listeners don't have."[49] Our advice: *Say what you mean by speaking the way you talk, not the way you write.*

- Use shorter familiar words. Example: Say *home* rather than *residence*.
- Use shorter, simpler sentences. Example: Say *He came back* rather than *He returned from his point of departure.*
- Use more informal colloquial expressions. Example: Say *Give it a try* rather than *You should attempt it.*

USE ACTIVE LANGUAGE

Effective communicators use active language: vivid, expressive verbs, rather than bland forms of the verb *be* (*be, am, is, are, was, being, been*) or verbs in the passive voice. Consider the difference between "Cheating is a violation of the college's plagiarism rules," "One violation of the college's plagiarism rules is cheating." "Cheating violates the college's plagiarism rules." The third sentence is strongest because it doesn't use the word *is* and avoids the passive voice.

Voice is a term that refers to whether the subject of a sentence performs or receives the action of the verb. If the subject performs the action, you are using an **active voice**. If the subject receives the action, you are using a **passive voice**. A strong, active voice makes your message more engaging, whereas a passive voice takes the focus away from the subject of your sentence. "The *Iliad* was read by the student" is passive. "The student read the *Iliad*" is active. Because an active voice requires fewer words, it also keeps your sentences short and direct. Simply state who is doing what, not what was done by whom.

Less committed and confident speakers often have trouble using the active voice because they worry about sounding too direct. Look at the differences in these sentences:

> Active verb: Sign this petition.
>
> Passive verb: The petition should by signed by all of you.

The more passive the sentence, the less powerful the message. With the passive voice, the subject is the recipient of the action. With the active voice, the subject performs the action.

USE *I, YOU,* AND *WE* LANGUAGE

The kinds of pronouns you use can affect the quality and meaning of your verbal communication. Understanding the nature and power of these pronouns can help you improve your way with words.

I *and* You *Language*   When you use the word *I*, you take responsibility for your own feelings and actions: *I* feel great. *I* am a straight A student. *I* am not pleased with the team's work on this project. Some people avoid using the word *I* because they think they're showing off, being selfish, or bragging. Other people use the word *I* too much and appear self-centered or oblivious to those around them.

Unfortunately, some people avoid *I* language when it is most important. Instead, they shift responsibility from themselves to others by using the word *you*. *You* language can be used to express judgments about others. When the judgments are positive—"You did a great job" or "You look marvelous!"—there's rarely a problem. When *you* is used to accuse, blame, or criticize, however, it can arouse defensive-

Why does using *I* language rather than *you* language defuse a disagreement or confrontation?

Even the U.S. government has taken on the language clarity challenge by creating the Plain English Network (PLAIN-US), an interagency committee with its own website. President Clinton created PLAIN-US in a quest for language ordinary people can understand. He called for "Logical organization, easy-to-read design features," and the use of "common, everyday words" whenever possible. He pushed the use of "you" and "other pronouns," short sentences, and the active voice ("the director wrote the memo," not "the memo was written by the director").

John Strylowski, of the U.S. Department of the Interior and a frequent speaker at plain language seminars, provides an example that demonstrates the value of plain language. He rewrote the Cape Cod National Seashore regulations pamphlets, which were so convoluted and complex, they came with a separate user's guide. He pared down the regulations, made them readable, and was able to eliminate a second pamphlet. It saved them both time and money. "Now that's the kind of thing that makes an impression." Here are some of Strylowski's recommendations:

- Never write a sentence with more than forty words.
- Treat only one subject per sentence.
- Don't include information just because you know it. Think about what the reader needs.
- Use shorter words and phrases such as "now" rather than "at the present time."

If you doubt the need for plain language, try to decipher the following example of gobbledygook from former Secretary of Defense Donald Rumsfeld: "Reports that say something hasn't happened are always interesting to me, because as we know, there are known knowns; there are things we know we know. We also know there are known unknowns; that is to say we know there are some things we do not know. But also unknown unknowns—the ones we don't know we don't know."[1]

[1]Excerpts from Jonathan Pitts, "At a D.C. Workshop, Participants in the Plain Language Conference Plead for End to Convoluted Communication," *The Sun*, November 7, 2005, pp. 1C, 6C.

---

ness, anger, and even revenge. Consider the following statements: "You make me angry." "You embarrass me." "You drive too fast." Sometimes the word *you* is implied, as in "Mind your own business," and "What a stupid thing to do."

When you use *you* language, you are saying that another person makes you feel a certain way rather than admitting that you control how you feel. *You* language often expresses your frustration rather than the behavior of another person. To take personal responsibility and decrease the probability of defensive reactions, try to use *I* language when your impulse tells you to use *you*. A statement using *I* language usually has three components:

1. Identify your feelings.
2. Describe the other person's behavior.
3. Explain the potential consequences.

The following examples demonstrate how these three components can help you express yourself in *I* language by describing someone's behavior and explaining how it affects you. Also note that the *you* statements are short. The *I* statements are longer because they offer more information to explain the speaker's feelings.

You Statement	*I* Statement
You embarrassed me last night.	I was really embarrassed last night when you interrupted me in front of my boss and contradicted what I said. I'm afraid she'll think I don't know what I'm doing.

A *Wall Street Journal* article warns that you risk "derailing your career" when you use language incorrectly.[1] Evidence for this claim took the form of personal stories:

- A recruiter refused to recommend a financial manager for a chief financial officer position in another company because he often said "me and so-and-so," followed by the wrong verb form.
- The president of a publication company often rejects sales and editorial candidates because they exhibit grammatically incorrect speech. The president complained that such behavior "reflects a low level of professionalism."

A growing number of businesses now retain speech coaches for rising stars with speech flaws—a service that costs between $250 and $400 an hour. If you believe that your way of speaking holds you back, ask your friends and colleagues to provide frequent feedback about your communication competency. At first, you will find it difficult to change longstanding habits. In the long run, however, you will improve your way with words—and your career prospects.

[1]Joann S. Lubin, "To Win Advancement, You Need to Clean up Any Bad Speech Habits," *Wall Street Journal*, October 5, 2004, p. B1.

You Statement	*I* Statement
What a stupid thing to do!	When you turn on the gas grill and let it run, I'm terrified that it will blow up in your face when you light it.

We *and Plural* You *Language* In her book *Team Talk*, Anne Donnellon examines how language affects group communication. She notes that successful teams use the plural pronouns *we* and *you* when talking to one another.[50] Plural pronouns are inclusive; they announce that the group depends on everyone rather than a single member. Plural pronouns also share credit for team achievements. Donnellon suggests that successful teams use pronouns in special ways.[51] Members say *we, us*, and *our* when talking about the group and its work. When members say *you*, they are usually addressing the whole group. Donnellon's observations are useful well beyond the confines of a work group. Plural pronouns also play an important role in intimate relations and before large public audiences, because they invite listeners to take an active rather than a passive role.

USE GRAMMATICAL LANGUAGE

In his book *If You Can Talk, You Can Write*, Joel Saltzman notes that when you're talking, you rarely worry about grammar or let it stand in the way of getting your point across. You probably never say to yourself, "Because I don't know if I should use *who* or *whom*, I won't even ask the question." According to Salzman, when you're talking, 98 percent of the time your grammar is fine and not an issue. For the 2 percent of time your grammar is a problem, many of your listeners won't even notice your mistakes.[52]

We are not saying that grammar isn't important. However, worrying about it all the time may make it impossible for you to write or speak. If you have questions about grammar, consult a good writing handbook.[53] Although most listeners miss or forgive a few grammatical errors, consistent grammatical problems can distract listeners and seriously harm your credibility.

Your ability to use grammar correctly makes a public statement about your education, social class, and even intelligence. In television shows and films, many scriptwriters have the dumb characters break grammatical rules: "Him and I was out partying" or "I don't know nothin'."

Both similes and metaphors are powerful figures of speech that highlight striking resemblances. They compare two things that are different in most ways but have at least one quality in common. A **simile** differs from a metaphor in that it makes a direct comparison between two things or ideas by using the words *like* or *as*. The great boxer Muhammad Ali described his technique using a simile: "Float like a butterfly, sting like a bee."

Metaphors make a comparison between two things or ideas without connective words such as *like* and *as*. In a famous speech, British prime minister Winston Churchill created a lasting metaphor: "An iron curtain has descended across the continent of Europe."

All similes and metaphors are based on comparisons. For example, the statement "If a copilot must be qualified to pilot the plane, a U.S. vice president should be qualified to govern the country" can be expressed as a simile: "The U.S. vice president is *like* a copilot." It could also work as a metaphor: "The U.S. vice president is our nation's copilot."

USE METAPHORICAL LANGUAGE

A **metaphor** is a word or phrase that ordinarily designates one thing but is used to designate another thing by making an implicit comparison. Shakespeare's famous line "All the world's a stage" in *As You Like It* has become a classic metaphor. The world is not a theatrical stage, but we do play and act many parts during a lifetime.

Many linguists contend that metaphors are the most powerful figures of speech. They are much more than literary devices reserved for the use of authors and poets.[54] Metaphors are so deeply embedded in our language that we use them without realizing what we are doing. Many linguistic scholars and psychologists believe that metaphors are a window into the workings of the human mind.[55]

You may not realize how often you use metaphors in everyday speech. But you've probably tried something new by "getting your feet wet" or held a "dead-end" job or perhaps contributed money to a consumer "watchdog" group. Some of our common metaphors borrow the names of body parts: *teeth* of a comb, *mouth* of a river, *foot* of a mountain, *tongue* of a shoe, *eye* of a needle (or storm), and *head* of a corporation.[56]

Metaphors are much more than a language technique; they help us move from one realm of thought to another. For example, we often hear people use baseball references used to describe the experience of love: "I made it to first base." "I struck out." "Our separation is just a seventh-inning stretch." We also use journey images: "We're at a crossroads." "Our relationship has hit a dead end." "We can't turn around now." So when you find yourself at a loss for words, consider using a metaphor.

Everyone Knows What I Mean

Directions: Write your answers to each of the questions on the following *Everyone Knows What I Mean* worksheet. Work quickly and put down the first answer that comes to mind. When you finish, consider how similar or different your responses might be compared with the responses of others. In what ways might your age, gender, culture, college and work experience, or economic status affect your answers?

Statement and Question   **Answer**

1. Diego is middle-aged. How old is he?   _____

2. Mary makes an excellent salary. How much does she
   make per year?   _____

3. John is a heavy smoker. How much does he smoke
   a day?   _____

4. Mike has a very good grade point average. What is
   his GPA?   _____

5. Kay bought an expensive car. How much did
   it cost?   _____

6. Linda has several close friends. How many close
   friends does she have?   _____

7. Susan applied to several colleges. How many
   applications did she send?   _____

8. Hong reads quite a few books each year. How many
   books does he read?   _____

9. Leticia wants the project report on her desk soon.
   When does she want it?   _____

10. Bob makes an excellent salary. How much does he
    make a year?   _____

Writing Apprehension Test (WAT)

Directions: The following statements about writing attempt to measure how you feel about the process of putting your ideas and opinions on paper. There are no right or wrong answers to these statements. Please indicate the degree to which each statement applies to you by marking whether you (1) strongly agree, (2) agree, (3) are uncertain, (4) disagree, or (5) strongly disagree with the statement. Although some of these statements may seem repetitious, take your time and try to be as honest as possible.

_____ 1. I avoid writing.

_____ 2. I have no fear of my writing being evaluated.

_____ 3. I look forward to writing down my ideas.

_____ 4. My mind seems to go blank when I start to work on a composition.

_____ 5. Expressing ideas through writing seems to be a waste of time.

_____ 6. I would enjoy submitting my writing to magazines for evaluation and publication.

_____ 7. I like to write my ideas down.

_____ 8. I feel confident in my ability to express my ideas clearly in writing.

_____ 9. I like to have my friends read what I have written.

_____ 10. I'm nervous about writing.

_____ 11. People seem to enjoy what I write.

_____ 12. I enjoy writing.

_____ 13. I never seem to be able to write down my ideas clearly.

_____ 14. Writing is a lot of fun.

_____ 15. I like seeing my thoughts on paper.

_____ 16. Discussing my writing with others is an enjoyable experience.

_____ 17. It's easy for me to write good compositions.

_____ 18. I don't think I write as well as other people write.

_____ 19. I don't like my compositions to be evaluated.

_____ 20. I'm not good at writing.

Scoring: To determine your score on the WAT, complete the following steps:

1. Add the scores for items 1, 4, 5, 10, 13, 18, 19, and 20.
2. Add the scores for items 2, 3, 6, 7, 8, 9, 11, 12, 14, 15, 16, and 17.
3. Complete the following formula:

$$\text{WAT} = 48 - \text{total from step 1} + \text{total from step 2}$$

Your score should be between 20 and 100 points. If your score is less than 20 or more than 100 points, you have made a mistake in computing the score. The higher your score, the more apprehension you feel about writing.

Score	Level of Apprehension	Description
20–45	Low	Enjoy writing; seek writing opportunities
46–75	Average	Some writing creates apprehension; other writing does not
76–100	High	Troubled by many kinds of writing; avoid writing in most situations

Source: From Richmond, Virginia P. & James C. Mc Croskey *Communication Apprehension, Avoidance And Effectiveness, 5/e.* Published by Allyn and Bacon, Boston, MA. Copyright © 1998 by Pearson Education. Reprinted by permission of the publisher. See also John Daly and Michael Miller, "The Empirical Development of an Instrument to Measure Writing Apprehension," *Research in the Teaching of English* 12 (1975), pp. 242–249.

Key Terms

abstract word
accent
active voice
basic term
bypassing
cliché
code switching
concrete word
connotation
denotation

dialect
euphemism
gobbledygook
jargon
language
linguist
linguistics
metaphor
passive voice
phatic language

semantics
sign
simile
subordinate term
superordinate term
symbol
verbal communication
Whorf Hypothesis

Notes

1. William O' Grady et al., *Contemporary Linguistics: An Introduction*, 4th ed. (Boston: Bedford/St. Martin's, 2001), p. 659.

2. Nicholas Wade, *Before the Dawn: Recovering the Lost History of Our Ancestors* (New York: Penguin, 2006), pp. 36–37.

3. Victoria Fromkin and Robert Rodman, *An Introduction to Language*, 6th ed. (Fort Worth, TX: Harcourt Brace, 1998), p. 3.

4. Mark Twain, Letter to George Bainton, October 15, 1888, www.twainquotes.com/Lightning.html.

5. Anne Donnellon, *Team Talk: The Power of Language in Team Dynamics* (Boston: Harvard Business School Press, 1996), p. 6.

6. John H. McWhorter, *The Power of Babel: A Natural History of Language* (New York: Times Books/Henry Holt, 2001), pp. 4–5.

7. Wade, p. 226.

8. Geoffrey Finch, *Word of Mouth: A New Introduction to Language and Communication* (New York: Palgrave, 2003), pp. 5–10; William O'Grady, Michael Dobrovolsky, and Mark Aronoff, *Contemporary Linguistics*, 2nd ed. (New York: St. Martin's Press, 1993), p. 9.

9. Dann L. Pierce, *Rhetorical Criticism and Theory in Practice* (Boston: McGraw-Hill, 2003), p. 282.

10. Nelson W. Francis, *The English Language: An Introduction* (London: English University Press, 1967), p. 119.

11. Finch, p. 1.

12. C.K. Ogden and I.A. Richards, *The Meaning of Meaning* (New York: Harcourt, Brace, 1936), p. 11.

13. S.I. Hayakawa and Alan R. Hayakawa, *Language and Thought in Action*, 5th ed. (San Diego, CA: Harcourt Brace Jovanovich, 1990), p. 43.

14. Isa N. Engleberg and Dianna R. Wynn, *Working in Groups: Communication Principles and Strategies*, 4th ed.

(Boston: Houghton Mifflin, 2007), pp. 123–124.

15. Vivian J. Cook, *Inside Language* (London: Arnold, 1997), p. 91.

16. Finch, p. 2.

17. See Finch, www.aber.ac.uk/media/Documents/short/whorf.html, and www.users.globalnet.co.uk/~skolyles/swh.htm.

18. Marcel Danesi and Paul Perron, *Analyzing Cultures: An Introduction and Handbook* (Bloomington, IN: Indiana University Press, 1999), p. 61.

19. Tony Hillerman, *The Wailing Wind* (New York: HarperTorch, 2002), p. 126.

20. William O'Grady et al., *Contemporary Linguistics*, 5th ed. (Boston: Bedford/St. Martin's, 2005), p. 509.

21. Myron W. Lustig and Jolene Koester, *Intercultural Competence: Interpersonal Communication across Cultures*, 5th ed. (New York: Longman, 2006), p. 193.

22. Ibid., p. 194.

23. Larry A. Samovar and Richard Porter, *Communication between Cultures*, 5th ed. (Belmont, CA: Wadsworth, 2004), pp. 146–147.

24. *Washington Post*, April 6, 2002, p. A1. www.whitehouse.gov/news/release/2002/04/print/20020406-3.html

25. Finch, p. 134.

26. Ibid., p. 135.

27. Ibid., p. 136.

28. Ibid.

29. M. Schultz, "The Semantic Derogation of Woman," in *Language and Sex: Difference and Dominance*, ed. B. Thorne and N. Henley (Rowley, MA: Newbury House, 1975), as quoted in Finch, p. 137.

30. Deborah Tannen, *You Just Don't Understand: Women and Men in Conversation* (New York: Morrow, 1990).

31. Robin Lakoff, *Language and Woman's Place* (New York: HarperCollins, 1975).

32. John McWhorter, *Word on the Street: Dubunking the Myth of a "Pure" Stan-

dard English* (Cambridge, MA: Perseus, 1998), p. 143.

33. Ibid., pp. 145, 146.

34. Peter Trudgill, "Myth 1: The Meaning of Words Should Not Be Allowed to Vary or Change," in *Language Myths*, ed. Laurie Bauer and Peter Trudgill (London: Penguin, 1998), p. 2.

35. Ibid., p. 8.

36. William V. Haney, *Communication and Interpersonal Relations: Text and Cases*, 6th ed. (Homewood, IL: Irwin, 1992), p. 269.

37. Ibid., p. 290.

38. Isa Engleberg and Ann Raimes, *Pocket Keys for Speakers* (Boston: Houghton Mifflin, 2004), p. 224.

39. William Lutz, *Doublespeak* (New York: HarperPerennial, 1990), p. 3.

40. Lyn Miller, "Quit Talking Like a Corporate Geek," *USA Today*, March 21, 2005, p. 7B.

41. Stuart Chase, quoted in Richard Lederer, "Fowl Language: The Fine Art of the New Doublespeak," *AARP Bulletin* (March 2005), p. 27.

42. Rudolf Flesch, *Say What You Mean* (New York: Harper and Row, 1972), p. 70.

43. Ibid., p. 88.

44. James V. O'Conner, *Cuss Control: The Complete Book on How to Curb Your Cursing* (New York: Three Rivers Press, 2000), p. 3.

45. Ibid., pp. 18–27.

46. "Cleaning Up Potty-Mouths," *The Week*, August 18, 2006, p. 35.

47. R.L. Trask, *Language: The Basics*, 2nd ed. (London: Routledge, 1995), pp. 170, 179.

48. Based on Melinda G. Kramer, Glenn Leggett, and C. David Mead, *Prentice Hall Handbook for Writers*, 12th ed. (Englewood Cliffs, NJ: Prentice Hall, 1995), p. 272.

49. Robert Mayer, *How to Win Any Argument* (Franklin Lakes, NJ: Career Press, 2006), p. 187.

50. Anne Donnellon, *Team Talk: The Power of Language in Team Dynamics* (Boston: Harvard Business School Press, 1996), p. 33.

51. Ibid., pp. 40–41.

52. Joel Saltzman, *If You Can Talk, You Can Write* (New York: Time Warner, 1993), pp. 48–49.

53. See Ann Raimes, *Keys for Writers: A Brief Handbook*, 3rd ed. (Boston: Houghton Mifflin, 2003), pp. 282–284.

Also see Engleberg and Raimes, pp. 227–264.

54. O'Grady et al., 2001, p. 255.

55. Danesi and Perron, p. 174.

56. Trask, p. 128.

Understanding Nonverbal Communication

6 *chapter*

Key Elements of Communication	Communication Axioms	Guiding Principles of Nonverbal Communication
Self	*Communication Is Personal*	Monitor how your nonverbal behavior affects the way you generate and respond to messages.
Others	*Communication Is Relational*	Appropriately use and accurately interpret nonverbal communication with others. Identify, respect, and adapt to culture-specific nonverbal cues.
Purpose	*Communication Is Intentional*	Match your nonverbal behavior to your communication goal.
Context	*Communication Is Contextual*	Recognize how context affects nonverbal communication and the behavioral norms in diverse circumstances and settings.
Content	*Communication Is Symbolic*	Recognize how nonverbal behavior affects the meaning of messages. Provide appropriate nonverbal feedback when listening.
Structure	*Communication Is Structured*	Organize nonverbal strategies to repeat, contradict, complement, accent, regulate, and substitute for verbal messages.
Expression	*Communication Is Irreversible*	Use nonverbal behaviors that complement and strengthen verbal messages. Make use of appropriate immediacy strategies.

The Challenge of Nonverbal Communication

Can you recall a situation in which someone's actions spoke louder than words? Maybe it was a hug from a friend, a coworker's nod of approval, or the applause of an audience. Perhaps it was a situation in which someone's appearance, body movement, or facial expression communicated more than the words that were spoken.

Nonverbal communication refers to message components other than words that generate meaning. Some researchers suggest that 60 to 70 percent, or about two-thirds, of the meaning we generate may be conveyed through nonverbal behaviors.[1] Yet we usually devote most of our time and effort to choosing and interpreting words. Given the importance of nonverbal communication, we should give equal consideration to selecting the most appropriate behavior for expressing our ideas, opinions, and feelings.

Everyone uses nonverbal communication every day. People who are aware of their own nonverbal behavior and are sensitive to others' nonverbal messages tend to have more academic and occupational success, better social relationships (and, consequently, less loneliness, shyness, depression, and mental illness), more satisfying marriages, and less stress, anxiety, and hypertension.[2] Because effective nonverbal communication is crucial to being a skilled social being, improving such skills benefits everyone engaged in communication.

THE NATURE OF NONVERBAL COMMUNICATION

We usually choose words to express the content of a message and use nonverbal behaviors to express the emotional element of a message.[3] This nonverbal component can promote understanding as well as express your affection for a friend, your desire to collaborate with others, and your ability to persuade and motivate an audience. Not surprisingly, nonverbal communication includes many forms of expression:

Physical appearance	Clothing and accessories
Posture and gestures	Physical movement
Facial expression	Touch
Eye contact	Vocal characteristics
Use of time	Personal space and territory
Environment	Smell and taste

Compared with verbal communication, nonverbal communication is less structured, learned informally, highly contextual, continuous, and even more convincing.

Less Structured   Language is highly structured and governed by rules related to grammar, spelling, and pronunciation. Nonverbal communication, in contrast, has very few agreed-upon rules. For example, language rules tell us that the verb form is incorrect in the statement "Robert is smiled." However, there is no rule that tells Robert precisely when and how to smile. Nor are there rules that define the meaning of a particular smile. Consequently, nonverbal behavior can communicate multiple and ambiguous meanings, and can be difficult to interpret.

Learned Informally   You probably spent hours learning how to read and write in elementary and secondary school, but you probably did not spend time learning how to express and interpret nonverbal messages. Instead, you learned about nonverbal communication informally by watching others and interpreting feedback about your own nonverbal behavior. At best, adults may have told you what *not* to do nonverbally: Don't stare at strangers, don't stick out your tongue, and don't make body noises in front of others.

NONVERBAL VERSUS VERBAL COMMUNICATION

▶ Nonverbal Communication Is Less Structured

▶ Nonverbal Communication Is Learned Informally

▶ Nonverbal Communication Is Highly Contextual

▶ Nonverbal Communication Is Generally Continuous

▶ Nonverbal Communication Is More Convincing

How does classroom communication influence what children learn about nonverbal behavior?

Highly Contextual   The meaning of nonverbal messages is highly dependent on a situation's psychosocial, logistical, and interactional context. For example, depending on the context, a laugh can express amusement, approval, contempt, scorn, or embarrassment.

Chapter 3, "Understanding Others," explains how different cultures rely on the context of communication to generate and interpret meaning. In low-context cultures like the United States, we rely on language to express meaning. High-context cultures like those in Asia convey meaning primarily through nonverbal communication. No matter how carefully you choose your words, a person from a high-context culture will give more attention and assign more credibility to your nonverbal behavior.

Generally Continuous   When you communicate with others, you rarely do all the talking (although there are exceptions). During a conversation, you take turns speaking, and in most meetings you interact with several other people—sometimes speaking, sometimes listening. Even when delivering a presentation, you may pause to check audience reactions or use visual aids to support ideas. In other words, although verbal communication is usually discontinuous (it may stop and go), nonverbal communication often continues uninterrupted.[4] Even when you stop talking, you do not stop communicating. When listening to someone, your facial expressions, posture, and body movement communicate meaning. If you are angry at a friend and decide not to speak to her, you are still communicating through your silence.

More Convincing   For many people, nonverbal communication is more believable because it represents "spontaneous expressions of internal thoughts and feelings that reveal our inner selves."[5] However, such perceptions can be inaccurate. Think of the times you've heard someone complain, "He *seemed* so honest when I met him," or "She behaved as though she really cared." Champion poker players claim that their success depends on the ability to read nonverbal behavior, yet many expert players have been fooled by amateurs.

Just as a smile or a pat on the back can communicate, so too can an angry shove or a slap. Unfortunately, some people use violent nonverbal communication to express negative emotions or exert power over others. Each year approximately 1.5 million women and more than 800,000 men are victims of violence from an intimate partner such as a husband, wife, boyfriend, girlfriend, or date.[1] Although female victims are more likely to need medical attention, research reveals that women hit men as often as men hit women.[2] Violence also occurs in the workplace between coworkers and by frustrated customers. Fifteen percent of homicides in the workplace are committed by coworkers.[3]

Physical **intimidation** and violence have been referred to as the "darkest side of communication."[4] Violent communication includes acts such as hitting, restraining, and shoving as well as behavior that stops short of physical contact, such as throwing things, pounding on a desk, or destroying property. Intimidating nonverbal communication can also take more sub-

tle forms, such as physically blocking another's path, moving aggressively and too close, or creating a threatening presence. The use of unjustified physical aggression violates the National Communication Association's *Credo for Ethical Communication,* which specifically condemns communication that is intimidating, coercive, or violent.[5]

[1]Centers for Disease Control and Prevention, *Intimate Partner Violence: Fact Sheet,* www.cdc.gov/ncipc/factsheets/ipvfacts.htm.

[2]ABC News, "Battle of the Sexes: Spousal Abuse Cuts Both Ways," February 7, 2004, abcnews.go.com/sections/2020/dailynews/ 2020_batteredhusbands030207.html.

[3]Eric F. Sygnatur and Guy A. Toscano, "Work-Related Homicides: The Facts," in *Compensation and Working Conditions* (Spring 2000), bls.gov/opub/cwc/archive/spring2000art1.pdf.

[4]Linda Marshall, "Physical and Psychological Abuse," in *The Dark Side of Interpersonal Communication,* ed. William R. Cupach and Brian H. Spitzberg (Hillsdale, NJ: Lawrence Erlbaum, 1994), p. 281.

[5]National Communication Association, *Credo for Ethical Communication,* 1999, www.natcom.org/nca/Template2.asp? bid=374.

THE IMPORTANCE OF NONVERBAL COMMUNICATION

You rely on nonverbal communication to share your thoughts and feelings and to interpret the messages of others. Because nonverbal communication allows you to send and receive messages through all five of your senses, you have more information to draw upon to generate or interpret a message. Beyond promoting understanding of a single message, effective nonverbal communication can help you achieve the following communication goals:

What nonverbal factors draw everyone's attention to the woman in this photograph?

- *Create Impressions.* As soon as you walk into a room, your physical appearance, clothing, posture, and facial expression create an impression. When attorneys prepare witnesses to testify in court, they often advise them about how to dress and how to look and sound confident, knowing that jurors begin forming opinions of witnesses before they utter a word. Whether it's a first date, a job interview, or a meeting with a new client, your nonverbal messages create strong impressions.

- *Express Emotions.* We use nonverbal communication to express the emotional components of a message. For example, if Jason says, "I'm angry," he simply labels an emotion, but his nonverbal behavior—vocal intensity, facial expression, and body movement—tell you how to interpret his anger. Expressing emotions by smiling, laughing, frowning, crying, and hugging often makes words unnecessary.

- *Define Relationships.* The nature of a relationship is often expressed nonverbally. For example, the closeness

CommFAQ Can You Detect a Lie?

A parent says, "Look me in the eye and tell me what happened" as a way to assess the truth of a child's suspicious story. Expert poker players decide whether an opponent is bluffing by looking for "tells," or nonverbal habits that suggest a player's true hand. Yet Paul Ekman, a leading researcher in deception and nonverbal communication, points out that there is no single facial expression or body movement that is a reliable sign of deceit.[1]

Research does suggest that *combinations* of leaked nonverbal cues may signal deception in some instances.[2] **Leakage cues** are unintentional nonverbal behaviors that may reveal deceptive communication. They fall into three categories: nervousness, negative affects, and decreased communication skill:

1. Nervousness may be revealed through higher pitch, vocal tension, fidgety movements, or longer pauses.
2. Negative affects include behaviors such as reduced eye contact and less pleasant facial expressions.
3. Decreased communication skill is often signified by increased speech errors, rigid posture, hesitations, or exaggerated movements.

Leakage cues are not the same for everyone. For example, a skillful liar may look you in the eye while someone telling the truth may avoid eye contact because she fears she won't be believed. Some nonverbal behaviors provide better clues to deception than others.[3] Vocal elements such as pitch seem to be a better indicator of deceit than facial expressions because it is much easier for most of us to control our facial muscles.

The research on deception and nonverbal behavior is clear on one thing: Most of us aren't very good at accurately detecting deception.[4] Judee Burgoon, a noted communication researcher studies human deceptions. She reports that "[c]opious evidence documents that deception is pervasive. . . . At the same time, deception detection accuracy is poor."[5] Overall, most people's ability to detect deception accurately is equivalent to the flip of a coin: about fifty/fifty.

[1]Paul Ekman, *Telling Lies: Clues to Deceit in the Marketplace, Politics, and Marriage* (New York: W.W. Norton, 1992), p. 80.

[2]H. Dan O'Hair and Michael J. Cody, "Deception," in *The Dark Side of Interpersonal Communication,* ed. William R. Cupach and Brian H. Spitzberg (Hillsdale, NJ: Lawrence Erlbaum, 1994), p. 190.

[3]Daniel Goleman, "Can You Tell When Someone Is Lying to You?" in *The Nonverbal Communication Reader: Classic and Contemporary Readings*, 2nd ed., ed. Laura K. Guerrero, Joseph A. DeVito, and Michael L. Hecht (Prospect Heights, IL: Waveland Press, 1999), pp. 360–362.

[4]Ibid., p. 360.

[5]Judee Burgoon, "Truth, Lies, and Virtual Worlds," *The National Communication Association's Carroll C. Arnold Distinguished Lecture*, 2005 annual convention of the National Communication Association, Boston, MA, November 2005.

and duration of a hug can reveal the level of intimacy between friends. A group member may take a central position at the head of a conference table to establish leadership or authority.

- *Interpret Verbal Messages.* "Nonverbal communication provides us with a message about the message," or a **metamessage**,[6] by offering important clues about how to interpret the verbal portion of a message. For example, you may doubt a person who says he's feeling fine after a fall, because he winces when he walks. If someone says she's glad to see you, but is looking over your shoulder to see who else is in the room, you may distrust her sincerity.

THE FUNCTIONS OF NONVERBAL COMMUNICATION

Psychologist Paul Ekman's research identifies the functions of nonverbal cues in relation to verbal messages. He notes that most nonverbal behaviors repeat, contradict, complement, accent, regulate, or substitute for verbal messages.[7]

Repeat **Repetitive nonverbal behaviors** visually repeat a verbal message. For example, when a waiter asks if anyone is interested in dessert, Elaine nods as she says, "Yes." She then points at a selection on the dessert tray and says, "I want the cheesecake." Ralph says he would like the same, so Elaine holds up two fingers and says, "Make it two slices, then." Nodding, pointing, and holding up two fingers repeats some of Elaine's words nonverbally.

FUNCTIONS OF NONVERBAL COMMUNICATION

▶ Repeat Verbal Messages
▶ Contradict Verbal Messages
▶ Complement Verbal Messages
▶ Accent Verbal Messages
▶ Regulate Verbal Messages
▶ Substitute for Verbal Messages

Contradict **Contradictory nonverbal behaviors** conflict with the spoken words. Upon receiving a birthday gift from a coworker, Sherry says, "It's lovely. Thank you." However, her forced smile, flat vocal expression, and lack of eye contact suggest that Sherry does not appreciate the gift. This is a classic example of a **mixed message**: a contradiction between verbal and nonverbal meanings. When nonverbal behavior contradicts spoken words, messages are confusing and difficult to interpret. In addition to the fact that nonverbal channels carry more information than verbal ones, we usually rely on the nonverbal elements of communication to determine the true meaning of a message. In some instances we may use contradictory nonverbal cues to create a desired effect. Sarcasm uses positive words combined with negative nonverbal behaviors.[8] As Sherry shows the gift to her husband that evening, she rolls her eyes as she says, "Isn't it just lovely?" Although the coworker is confused by Sherry's earlier response, her husband will understand Sherry's sarcasm.

Complement **Complementary nonverbal behaviors** are consistent with the verbal message. During a job interview, your words state that you are a confident professional, but what you say will be more believable if nonverbal elements such as clothing, posture, facial expressions, and vocal quality send the same message. Even the meaning of a simple *hello* can be strengthened if your facial expression and tone of voice communicate genuine interest and pleasure in greeting someone.

Accent **Accenting nonverbal behaviors** emphasize important elements in a message by highlighting the focus or emotional content. Saying the words "I'm angry" may fail to make the point, so you may couple this message with louder volume, forceful gestures, and piercing eye contact, all of which will make your point much more clearly. Stressing a word or phrase in a sentence also focuses meaning. Consider how stressing the following words change the meaning of two sentences: "She was *born* in Texas" (meaning she may have grown up and lived elsewhere) and "She was born in *Texas*" (meaning she wasn't born in the state where she now lives).

Regulate We use **regulating nonverbal behaviors** to manage the flow of a conversation. Nonverbal cues tell us "when to begin a conversation, whose turn it is to speak, how to get a chance to speak, how to signal others to talk more, and how to end a conversation."[9] If you lean forward and open your mouth as if to speak, you are signaling that you want a turn in the conversation. In a classroom or large meeting, you may raise your hand when you want to speak. When your friend nods her head as you speak, you may interpret her nod as a sign to continue what you're saying.

Substitute In many instances, nonverbal communication can substitute for verbal language or take its place; in this case we are using **substituting nonverbal behaviors**. When we wave hello or goodbye, the meaning is usually clear even in the absence of words. Without saying anything, a mother may send a message to a misbehaving child by pursing her lips, narrowing her eyes, and moving a single finger to signal "stop." Even if the child fails to obey, the message of disapproval is probably clear.

EXPECTANCY VIOLATION THEORY

Read the following two scenarios, and then decide what they have in common *and* what makes them different.

> *Scenario 1.* You have stopped at a local convenience store for a cup of coffee on your way to work, and you notice a poorly dressed man looking at you as you walk into the store. You've never seen him before. While you are preparing your coffee, he approaches and stands right next to you, smiling. As he reaches for a cup, his hand brushes against your arm. You turn to leave. Now he is standing directly behind you to pay for the coffee—and smiles again. As you leave, he follows you out the door.

Scenario 2. You have stopped at the office snack bar to get a cup of coffee, and you notice a well-dressed man looking at you. He's a valued friend and colleague you've worked with for many years. While you are preparing your coffee, he approaches and stands right next to you, smiling. As he reaches for a cup, his hand brushes against your arm. You turn to leave. Now he is standing directly behind you to pay for the coffee—and smiles again. As you leave, he follows you out the door.

Both scenarios are similar. Yet, in the first case, you may react with suspicion and disapproval, whereas in the second case you may feel more relaxed and positive. According to **Expectancy Violation Theory**, your expectations about nonverbal behavior have a significant effect on how you interact with others and how you interpret the meaning of nonverbal messages. When you enter an elevator, you probably conform to nonverbal expectations: You turn around and face front, avoid eye contact with others, avoid movement, refrain from talking or touching others, and stare at the numbers as they go up or down. But how would you react if someone entered a cramped elevator with three unruly dogs and lit a cigar? You'd probably disapprove or object, because this is not the kind of behavior you'd expect in a confined public space.

At least three characteristics influence how one communicator reacts to the nonverbal behavior of another communicator.[10] Think of the previous two scenarios as you consider these characteristics.

1. *Communicator Characteristics.* Similarities and differences in physical and demographic characteristics, such as age, gender, ethnicity, and physical appearance as well as personality and reputation

2. *Relational Characteristics.* Level of familiarity, past experiences, relative status, and type of relationship with another person, such as close friend, romantic partner, business associate, service provider, or stranger

3. *Contextual Characteristics.* Physical, social, psychological, cultural, and professional settings and occasions, such as football games, funerals, religious services, or business meetings

Clearly, the first scenario highlights differences in communicator, relational, and contextual characteristics, whereas the second scenario highlights similarities. In the first scenario, the man violates a number of nonverbal expectations: Don't stare, follow, or touch strangers. In the second scenario, the man is "allowed" to violate the same nonverbal expectations because you know him well.

When someone "violates" your nonverbal expectations you may react positively or negatively, as illustrated in Figure 6.1. A positive reaction may occur when the

Figure 6.1	**Effects of Nonverbal Expectancy Violation**		
	SCENARIO 1	SCENARIO 2	SCENARIO 3
Context and Expectation	Movie theater: only passing, impersonal gaze from others	Psychiatrist's office: slightly formal demeanor	CEO's office: expensive suit
Violation	Strong and sustained eye gaze	Slouching in chair with feet up on desk	CEO wears blue jeans
Positive Effect	Means the person may be attracted to you	Means the psychiatrist is your friend	Means the CEO is not going to pull rank on you
Negative Effect	Means the person may be rude or unstable	Means the psychiatrist doesn't take your problems seriously	Means the CEO is out of touch or arrogant

violation comes from someone you know, like, or admire. In some cases positive violations can even enhance the other person's credibility, power, and attractiveness. However, a negative reaction may result when the violation comes from someone you don't know or don't like (even when it's the same nonverbal behavior), and can reduce the other person's credibility, power, and attraction.[11]

When communicating with a friend we generally view eye contact as positive and averted gazes as negative. From a general acquaintance, we may accept nonintimate, brief touches but recoil from too much touching.[12] Your decision to "violate" a nonverbal expectation should be based on a careful analysis of your self and others, your purpose, message content, context, and structure as well as how you express yourself nonverbally.

TYPES OF NONVERBAL COMMUNICATION

▶ Physical Appearance

▶ Body Movement

▶ Touch

▶ Facial Expression

▶ Eye Contact

▶ Vocal Cues

▶ Space and Distance

Types of Nonverbal Communication

Nonverbal communication is undeniably complex. To interpret nonverbal meaning accurately, you must pay attention to many elements: physical appearance, body movement, touch, facial expression, eye contact, vocal cues, space and distance, and much more. As you read about the many categories of nonverbal communication, keep in mind that meaning is rarely reflected in a single behavior. Effective communicators consider the totality of their own and others' nonverbal behavior.

PHYSICAL APPEARANCE

When you first meet someone, you probably rely on physical appearance to form an impression. Although it seems unfair to judge a person's personality and character based on characteristics determined, in large part, by genetics, physical attractiveness, clothing, and even hairstyles strongly influence beliefs about ourselves and others.

Attractiveness   For better or worse, attractive individuals tend to be perceived as kinder, more interesting, more sociable, more successful, and sexier than those considered less attractive.[13] One study found that good-looking people tend to make more money and get promoted more often than those with average looks.[14] In their quest to be more attractive, many Americans try to alter their physical appearance. One study found that approximately 75 to 80 percent of women in the United States are unhappy with their body weight, and most of these women are on a diet or have dieted in the past.[15] Others alter the color of their skin by tanning or with cosmetics. Hair color and style can easily be changed, and plastic surgery and chemical enhancements allow people to alter their facial structure and body shape.

Certainly the images of attractive men and women on television and in popular magazines and film influence how we see others. But the standards of beauty found in the media create yearnings for unachievable goals.[16] Most of us were not born with movie star features and never will meet those standards of "beauty." Yet, there is no question that physical attraction plays a significant role in selecting dating and marriage partners, getting and succeeding in a job, persuading others, and maintaining high self-esteem.[17]

How can your clothing and accessories send messages about your economic status, education, social position, and level of sophistication?

Clothing and Accessories   Your clothing and accessories can send messages about your economic status, education, trustworthiness, social position, level of sophistication, and moral character.[18] For example, a person wearing a stylish suit and carrying an expensive leather briefcase suggests a higher

CommFAQ   Do Tattoos and Body Piercings Damage Your Credibility?

In many cultures, both past and present, people have pierced and tattooed their bodies. These markings often commemorated a rite of passage such as puberty, marriage, or a successful hunt. However, in most western cultures, tattoos have traditionally been associated with people of lower social status and membership in groups such as gangs, "bikers," and lower ranked military personnel. "Traditional religions have generally prohibited tattoos on the ground that they encourage superficial thinking (what's on the surface is not what matters)."[1]

Today, pierced ears on women and a few men are fairly common. Piercing the nose, tongue, eyebrow, lip, navel, and other body parts was virtually unheard of in mainstream society a short time ago; however, that too has changed. Tattooing and body piercing have become a popular trend, especially among adolescents and young adults. A study published by the American Academy of Dermatology reports that 36 percent of eighteen- to twenty-nine-year olds have a tattoo. David Brooks observes that "a cadre of fashion-forward types thought they were doing something to separate themselves from the vanilla middle class but are now discovering that the signs etched into their skins are absolutely mainstream."[2]

Tattoos and body piercings create an impression that may not serve you well or be what you intended. In one survey, 42 percent of people polled said that they have negative perceptions of employees who display tattoos or body piercings. More than 50 percent of employees with tattoos or body piercings conceal them on the job.[3] Public perception may change as a younger generation of tattooed and pierced college graduates rise to leadership positions in their companies and communities. In the meantime, recognize that a tattoo or body piercing can distract from and misrepresent the impression you want to create. As many young job seekers have learned, they may have to conceal tattoos and remove body piercings for job interviews and in professional settings.[4]

[1]David Brooks, "Nonconformity Is Skin Deep," *The New York Times*, August 27, 2006, WK p. 11.

[2]Ibid.

[3]"Tattoos, Body Art and Piercing" (February 2003). Available from FindArticles, Inc., San Francisco, CA. Copyright National Recreation and Park Association and Gale Group.

[4]Mark Hickson III, Don W. Stacks, and Nina-Jo Moore, *Nonverbal Communication: Studies and Applications*, 4th ed. (Los Angeles: Roxbury Publishing, 2004), p. 187.

income, a college education, and more status within a company than a person wearing a uniform and carrying a mop. Accessories such as a college ring, a wedding band, or a religious necklace reveal a great deal about another person.

However, judging others based on their clothing can lead to inaccurate assumptions. For example, what type of clothing does a millionaire wear? In their book, *The Millionaire Next Door: The Surprising Secrets of America's Wealthy*, marketing researchers Thomas Stanley and William Danko reveal that the vast majority of millionaires do not dress as you might expect. They do not purchase expensive suits, shoes, or watches.[19] Stanley and Danko point out that "it is easier to purchase products that denote superiority than to actually be superior in economic achievement."[20] In the case of clothing, the old adage is often true: You can't always judge a book by its cover.

Hair   Hair is something of an obsession in the United States. In *Reading People,* jury consultant Jo-Ellan Dimitrius and attorney Mark Mazzarella use hair as a predictor of people's self-image and lifestyle. They claim that your hairstyle can reveal "how you feel about aging, how extravagant or practical you are, how much importance you attach to impressing others, your socioeconomic background, your overall emotional maturity, and sometimes even the part of the country where you were raised or now live."[21] If you doubt their claim, think about the ways in which very long hair on men communicated antiwar rebellion and hippy lifestyles in the late 1960s and early 1970s.

However, be careful when drawing conclusions about others based on their hairstyle. A man who wears short hair may be an ultraconservative or a rebel, an athlete or a cancer patient, a police officer or a fashion model. Women with very short hair may be as different as men with little hair. Short, chic, carefully cut hair can signify an artistic, creative, and expressive nature or may indicate a more practical nature.

Finally, we must note that, in the United States, the cultural norm for women is to shave their legs and armpits, pluck shabby eyebrows, and remove other facial hair. Women in most other countries do not share this antihair obsession; nor do women who want to signal their rebellion against traditional fashion norms.[22]

BODY MOVEMENT

Jamal points to his watch to let the chairperson know that the meeting time is running short. Karen gives a thumbs-up gesture to signal that her friend's speech went well. Robin stands at attention as the American flag is raised. How you sit, stand, position the body, or move your hands generates nonverbal messages. Even your posture can convey moods and emotions. Slouching back in your chair may be perceived as lack of interest or dislike, whereas sitting upright and leaning forward communicates interest and is a sign of active listening.

Gestures are body movements that communicate an idea or feeling. They can emphasize or stress parts of a message, reveal discomfort with a situation, or convey a message without the use of words. The hands and arms are used most frequently for gesturing, although head and foot movements are also considered types of gestures.[23]

Many people have difficulty expressing their thoughts without using gestures. Why else would we gesture when speaking to someone on the phone? Research suggests that gesturing helps ease the mental effort when communication is difficult.[24] For example, we tend to gesture more when using a language that is less familiar or when describing a picture that a listener cannot see. As Figure 6.2 indicates, gestures serve three major functions as emblems, illustrators, and adaptors.[25]

Emblems An **emblem** is a gesture that has the same meaning as a word and has a meaning that is clear to most members of a group or culture. For example, most Americans recognize that an index finger placed over the lips means "be quiet," that making a circle with the thumb and index finger signals "okay," and that raising your hand in class indicates "I would like to speak."

Emblems can also send offensive messages. For example, the intended meaning of an extended middle finger is abundantly clear. Although the meanings of most emblems are recognized within a culture, many emblems can only be understood within a certain context. For example, holding up the index and middle finger of one hand could mean *two*, *peace*, or *victory*. Furthermore, the meaning of emblematic gestures varies from culture to culture. Although forming a circle with the thumb and

How would you classify this pilot's gesture? Is it an emblem, illustrator, or adaptor?

"A Walk across Cultural Lines" is the title of an article about the "deliberate swagger and exaggerated dip" that some black males use when they walk. La Vonne Neal, an African American scholar, studies this "stroll" and the reaction of white teachers. She reports that when *she* sees the walk, she says it's simply a young man saying, "Here I am in my uniqueness."[1]

Research indicates that many white teachers, however, see it quite differently and very negatively. When Neal asked teachers to evaluate black and white students who use a standard walk or the "stroll," the results showed that teachers

- considered both white and black teens using the stroll *lower* in achievement than when they used the standard walk.
- considered white youth with a stroll even *lower* in achievement than black youth with a stroll.
- viewed teens with a stroll *higher* in aggression than when they used the standard walk.
- perceived teens with a stroll as more likely to need special education services.[2]

Given these results, you may wonder why students use the stroll walk at all. In his 1994 autobiogra-phy, *Makes Me Wanna Holler*, Nathan McCall describes the importance of perfecting the stylized walk among some black males:

> The [walk] was a proud, defiant, bouncy stride. You take a regular step with one leg, then sort of hop or drag the other on the second step. The best . . . twisted their torso slightly and swung their arms in unison with that hop. It made guys look cool and tough.[3]

Body movement is culturally conditioned, and our reactions to those movements are also culturally conditioned. Understanding this can help you avoid stereotyping and prejudice about the ways in which people from other cultures and co-cultures communicate through movement.

[1]Quoted in Tamara Henry, "A Walk across Cultural Lines," *USA Today*, April 23, 2001, p. 6D.

[2]Ibid.

[3]Nathan McCall, *Makes Me Wanna Holler* (New York: Vintage Books, 1994), p. 26.

---

index finger represents an okay signal to Americans, in Brazil it is an obscene gesture, and in Japan it signifies money.[26]

Illustrators   **Illustrators** are nonverbal signs that are used with verbal messages but lack meaning without the words. If you hold your hands two feet apart and say, "The fish I caught was this big," the gesture alone does not have any meaning. To understand what the speaker means, you need both the words and the gesture.[27]

Figure 6.2	Functions of Gestures	
Type of Gesture	**Function**	**Examples**
Emblems	Gestures that have the same meaning as a word	V for victory/peace, wave goodbye, be quiet (finger to lips)
Illustrators	Gestures that help explain or highlight an action or emotion	Point in a direction, indicate size and shape, signal excitement
Adaptors	Habitual gestures that satisfy a need or reveal an emotion	Tapping a pencil, scratching your head, wringing your hands

Source: Paul Ekman and Wallace V. Friesen, "Hand Movements," in *The Nonverbal Communication Reader: Classic and Contemporary Readings*, 2nd ed., ed. Laura K. Guerrero, Joseph A. DeVito, and Michael L. Hecht (Prospect Heights, IL: Waveland Press, 1999), p. 49.

Unlike emblems, illustrators have no verbal equivalent. Consider how both words and nonverbal behavior are needed to communicate meaning in the following examples:

- Striking a desk with your hand or fist while saying the "not" in "I will *not* put up with this!"
- Counting out the steps of a procedure with your hand while orally describing each step.
- Snapping your fingers while saying, "It happened just like that," to indicate that an event occurred quickly.
- Spatial movement to show the size or shape of something, such as holding your arm out, palm down, in front of you while saying, "My dog is now this tall."

Adaptors   Have you ever clenched your fists in anger? Or chewed your nails because you were worried or anxious? These gestures are **adaptors**—gestures that help us manage and express our emotions. Adaptive gestures accompany emotions such as anxiety, worry, excitement, anger, or boredom. Drumming your fingers on a table, scratching your head, wringing your hands, clenching your fist, twisting your hair, or twiddling your thumbs may help you cope with an emotional situation.

We often develop our own adaptive behaviors even if we are not aware of them. For example, some people tap their feet when bored or impatient, whereas others fidget with their jewelry. During an important meeting or presentation where appearing confident is important, adaptors can reveal nervousness, distract your listeners, and get in the way of your message.

TOUCH

Touch is one of the most potent forms of physical expression. It not only has the power to send strong messages, but it also affects your overall well-being. Being deprived of touch can adversely affect your physical and psychological health.[28] For example, we know that infants need human touch to survive. In looking for the causes of infant deaths, researchers conclude that babies need to be touched and carried to develop. When new parents and hospital nurses engage in more touching behavior, infant death rates decrease.

We use touch to express a wide range of emotions. An encouraging pat on the shoulder from a coworker, a hug from a friend, or a lover's embrace can convey encouragement, appreciation, affection, empathy, or sexual interest. Playful touches tend to lighten the mood without expressing a high degree of emotion. A light nonthreatening punch in the arm between friends or covering another's eyes and asking, "Guess who?" is a playful touch.

Touch is also used to express control or dominance. In some instances, only a minor level of control is needed, such as when we tap someone on the shoulder to get his or her attention. In other cases, touch sends very clear messages about status or dominance. Research shows that individuals with more power and status are more likely to touch someone of lesser status, but subordinates rarely initiate touch with a person of higher status.[29]

Some people are more comfortable with touch than others. **Touch approachers** tend to be comfortable with touch and initiate touch more often. A touch approacher is more likely to initiate a hug or a kiss when greeting a friend. Some touch approachers even touch or hug people they don't know very well. At the extreme end of the continuum are touch approachers who touch too much and violate nonverbal expectations.

Touch avoiders are less comfortable initiating or being touched. They are also more conscious of when, how, and by whom they are touched. Extreme touch avoiders avoid any physical contact even with loved ones. Most of us are somewhere in the middle of the continuum. Obviously, misunderstandings can result when touch approachers and avoiders meet. Approachers may view avoiders as cold and unfriendly, and avoiders may perceive approachers as invasive and rude.

Not surprisingly, norms for touch depend on the context. For example, violating touch norms in the workplace can result in misunderstandings or allegations of sexual harassment. Norms for touch also vary according to gender and culture. Studies show that most North American men tend to avoid same-sex touch, with the exception of expressions of camaraderie in settings such as team sports.[30] But this avoidance behavior is not displayed in all cultures. A photo of President George W. Bush shows him holding hands with a Middle Eastern ruler whose culture accepts and even expects such behavior between trusted male friends. Women are generally more comfortable using touch to express warmth or affection to a female friend.

FACIAL EXPRESSION

The face is composed of complex muscles capable of displaying well more than a thousand different expressions.[31] Facial expressions let you know if others are interested in, agree with, or understand what you have said. Generally, women tend to be more facially expressive and smile more often than men.[32] But although men are more likely to limit the amount of emotion they reveal, everyone relies on a person's facial expressions to comprehend the full meaning of a message.

We learn to manage facial expressions to convey or conceal an emotion and to adapt our facial expressions to particular situations. The most common techniques for adapting facial expressions are masking, neutralization, intensification, and deintensification.[33]

FACIAL MANAGEMENT TECHNIQUES

▶ Masking
▶ Neutralization
▶ Intensification
▶ Deintensification

Masking **Nonverbal masking** conceals true emotions by displaying facial expressions considered more appropriate in a particular situation. When a friend excitedly announces her engagement to a man you dislike, you may smile and congratulate her

Facial Expressions in Cyberspace

When you communicate face-to-face, you can listen to how words are said and observe nonverbal behavior. However, we increasingly rely on technology for communication. For example, many of us use e-mail daily to communicate with coworkers and to keep in touch with friends. In the workplace, virtual groups rely on technologies that don't allow members to hear each other or to see the facial expressions, head nods, gestures, or posture of others. An **emoticon** is an ordinary typographical character that is used to convey a nonverbal expression. The following are examples of common emoticons:[1]

:-)	Happiness, sarcasm, joking	:-(	Unhappy or sad
:-o	Surprise	:-P	Sticking out tongue
;-)	Wink	:-D	Laughing

We also use other visual elements of written language to help communicate nonverbal meaning. For example, repeated letters can help emphasize a point, as in "I'm sooooo happy" or "Noooooooo way!" Capital letters may signal shouting or anger. Putting a word between asterisks can highlight its importance, as in "He is *not* going to be invited."

In theory, emoticons serve as substitutes for nonverbal behavior. However, research suggests that emoticons have become less and less useful as nonverbal cues and have little or no effect on the interpretation of a typed message.[2] We are more likely to rely on the words rather than the emoticons when interpreting the intention of the text portion of a message. Apparently this is because emoticons are "now over-used, and the impact that [they are] supposed to have diminished, either culturally/historically, or as an individual user is first entertained, and later bored, with the cuteness of them all."[3] In their book *Rules of the Net*, Thomas Mandel and Gerard Van der Leun contend that "nothing—especially the symbols on the top row of your keyboard—can substitute for a clear idea simply expressed. Avoid :-)s or ☺ and all associated emoticons as you would avoid clichés."[4] We temper Mandel and Van der Leun's conclusion by offering this advice: Generally, avoid emoticons. However, if emoticons are the norm in your group or relationship, ☺ away.

[1] The Primitive Baptist Web Organization, *Common Emoticons and Acronyms*, pb.org/emoticon.html; and ComputerUser.com, *Emoticons*, computeruser.com/resources/dictionary/emoticons.html.

[2] Joseph B. Walther and Kyle P. D'Addario, *The Impacts of Emoticons on Message Interpretation in Computer-Mediated Communication* (paper presented at the meeting of the International Communication Association, Washington, DC, May 2001).

[3] Ibid., p. 13.

[4] Thomas Mandel and Gerard Van der Leun, *Rules of the Net: Online Operating Instructions for Human Beings* (New York: Hyperion, 1996), p. 92.

rather than displaying your disapproval. A parent may expend great effort to look stern when reprimanding a toddler who has dumped a bowl of spaghetti on his head.

Neutralization **Nonverbal neutralization** is an effort to eliminate any display of emotions. When Micah learns that the accounting job he interviewed for went to a former colleague, he conceals his disappointment by shrugging his shoulders as if to say it doesn't matter. Although Micah's true emotion is disappointment and some anger, he chooses to display neither positive nor negative emotion.

Intensification Masking and neutralization conceal emotion, but **nonverbal intensification** exaggerates your facial expressions. We often do this to fulfill others' needs. For example, you may like the gift you've received from a friend, but decide to express more pleasure than what you feel so your friend feels fully appreciated. You may exaggerate your display of anger when others seem to be ignoring you or your stated disagreement.

Deintensification **Nonverbal deintensification** involves reducing the amount of emotion you display. Downplaying emotion may be appropriate in a number of situations. For example, a committee chairperson may be outraged at the rude behavior of a group member but only displays mild disapproval because fully expressing anger could create an uncomfortable situation for everyone in the room.

EYE CONTACT

Your eyes may be the most revealing and complex of all your facial features. Two-thirds of the approximately three million sensory fibers entering the brain are related to the eyes.[34] Eye contact can aid comprehension, signify status or leadership, express emotion, and indicate a willingness to communicate.[35] To comprehend fully what another person is saying, most of us will look at a speaker more than 80 percent of the time. A group member who wants to be viewed as a leader may choose a seat at the head of the table to gain more visual attention. We tend to increase gaze in response to positive emotions such as surprise or interest and avert our eyes in response to negative experiences like disgust or horror. We also use eye contact to let others know if we're willing to communicate. For example, we try to establish eye contact to get a server's attention in a restaurant. Students who don't want the instructor to call on them in class will typically avert their eyes.

As with all nonverbal behavior, norms for eye contact vary according to gender and culture. Women tend to engage in more eye contact when listening than men. North Americans perceive eye contact as an indicator of attitude. Lack of eye contact is frequently perceived as signifying rudeness, indifference, nervousness, or dishonesty. However, this is not true across all cultures. For example, "direct eye contact is a taboo or an insult in many Asian cultures. Cambodians consider direct eye contact an invasion of one's privacy."[36]

VOCAL CUES

How you *say* a word significantly influences its meaning. Your vocal quality also affects others' perceptions of you. For example, it can be difficult to listen to a person with a very high-pitched or monotone voice. A loud voice can convey anger, excitement, irritation, or dominance.

Some of the most important vocal characteristics are pitch, volume, rate, and word stress. **Volume** refers to the loudness of the voice. Whispering can indicate that the information is confidential; yelling suggests urgency or anger. **Pitch** refers to how high or low your voice sounds. In the United States, Americans seem to prefer low-pitched voices. Men and women with deeper voices are seen as more authoritative and effective. Men with a naturally high pitch may be labeled effeminate or weak, and women with very high pitches may be labeled as childish, silly, or anxious.[37]

Rate is the speed at which you speak. A speaking rate that is too fast makes it difficult to understand a message. On the other hand, we become bored by or stop listening to a person who speaks too slowly. In Chapter 14, "Language and Expression," we take a closer look at these vocal characteristics and see how they contribute to the success of a public speech or presentation.

When pitch, volume, and rate are combined, they can be used to vary the stress you give to a word or phrase. **Word stress** refers to the "degree of prominence given to a syllable within a word or words within a phrase or sentence."[38] Notice the differences in meaning as you stress the italicized words in the following sentences:

Is *that* the report you want me to read?

Is that the report you want *me* to read?

Is that the report you want me to *read*?

Although the same words are used in all three sentences, the meaning of each question is quite different.

SPACE AND DISTANCE

The use of space and distance can significantly influence nonverbal communication. The Paris peace talks that helped end the war in Vietnam were bogged down for eight months until delegates from South Vietnam, the National Liberation Front, and the

The well-known phrase "silence is golden" may be based on a Swiss saying "*Sprechen ist silbern; Swchweigen ist golden*," which means "speech is silver; silence is golden." This metaphor contrasts the value of speech and silence. Although speech is important, silence may be even more significant in certain contexts. The power of silence is recognized and embraced in many cultures, as shown by the following sayings.

> Those who know, do not speak. Those who speak, do not know. (Tao Te Ching)
>
> Silence is also speech. (African proverb)
>
> Silence is a friend who will not betray. (Confucius)

A loud voice shows an empty head. (Finnish proverb)

The cat that does not meow catches rats. (Japanese proverb)

Understanding the value of silence is important for several reasons. We use silence to communicate many things: to establish interpersonal distance, to put our thoughts together, to show respect for another person, or to modify others' behaviors.[1]

[1]Virginia P. Richmond and James C. McCroskey, *Nonverbal Behavior in Interpersonal Relationships*, 5th ed. (Boston: Allyn and Bacon, 2004), p. 103.

United States agreed to a round table as the setting for negotiation. When the leaders of Bosnia, Croatia, and Serbia met at Wright-Patterson Air Force Base in Ohio, the United States made sure that each party had equal seating space around a modest but perfectly round table. **Territoriality** is the sense of personal ownership attached to a particular space. For instance, most classroom students sit in the same place everyday. If you have ever walked into a classroom to find another person in *your* seat, you may have felt that your territory had been violated. Ownership of territory is often designated by objects acting as **markers** of territory. Placing a coat on a chair or books on a table can send a clear message that a seat is taken or saved.

Anthropologist Edward T. Hall uses the term **proxemics** to refer to the study of spatial relationships and how the distance between people communicates information about their relationship. Hall maintains that we have our own personal portable

What are the ways in which people signal that they own a space that others should not enter or occupy?

"air bubble" that we carry around with us. This personal space is culturally determined. For example, the Japanese, who are accustomed to crowding, need less space around them whereas "wide open spaces" North Americans need more space around them to feel comfortable.[39]

Hall contends that most Americans interact within four spatial zones or distances.[40] Figure 6.3 describes the spatial zones and distances used by mainstream culture in the United States.

Not surprisingly, we reduce the distance between ourselves and others as our relationships become more personal. Intimate distance is usually associated with love, comfort, protection, and increased physical contact. In most situations, you encounter a mixture of distances. You may feel comfortable using an intimate or personal distance with a good friend at work, but use social distance with other colleagues.

Nonverbal Context

Do you behave the same way in the classroom as you do at work? How do you behave in a business meeting as opposed to a social gathering with a group of friends and family members? As we note at the beginning of this chapter, nonverbal

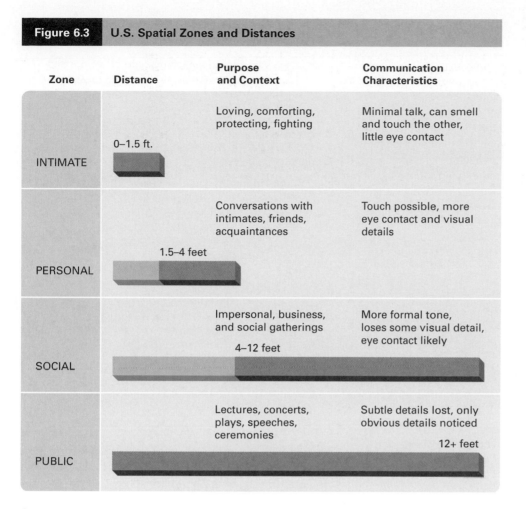

Figure 6.3   U.S. Spatial Zones and Distances

Zone	Distance	Purpose and Context	Communication Characteristics
INTIMATE	0–1.5 ft.	Loving, comforting, protecting, fighting	Minimal talk, can smell and touch the other, little eye contact
PERSONAL	1.5–4 feet	Conversations with intimates, friends, acquaintances	Touch possible, more eye contact and visual details
SOCIAL	4–12 feet	Impersonal, business, and social gatherings	More formal tone, loses some visual detail, eye contact likely
PUBLIC	12+ feet	Lectures, concerts, plays, speeches, ceremonies	Subtle details lost, only obvious details noticed

Source: Based on a figure in Myron W. Lustig and Jolene Koester, *Intercultural Competence: Interpersonal Communication across Cultures,* 5th ed. (New York: Longman, 2006), p. 219.

communication is highly contextual. Therefore, understanding context helps you make decisions about your nonverbal communication.

Context does more than influence nonverbal communication; it is a part of nonverbal communication. In other words, context alone can communicate a message. For example, an office with stacks of unorganized papers crowding the room, a stale smell, uncomfortable chairs, and ugly orange walls may create a negative impression of the occupant, but it may also affect how comfortably you interact in that space. Environmental elements such as furniture arrangement, lighting, color, temperature, and smell communicate.

Figure 6.4 presents six dimensions of communication environments that affect how we are likely to behave. For example, a weekly staff meeting may be informal, warm, usually private, familiar, regularly scheduled, and set in a room where people are physically close to one another. At a courtroom trial, however, you may find yourself in an environment that is more formal, less comfortable, open or private (depending on your role), unusual, temporary, and set in a place where people are more physically separated from one another.[41]

You can examine the six dimensions in almost any context. For example, think of the environment you are in right now, or your classroom environment. How would you rate your environment in terms of the six dimensions? Now consider another environment and do the same. If the two environments have been designed for the same purpose, they should have similar "ratings." If not, you will find you communicate differently in each.[42]

Feng Shui (pronounced "fung schway") is the ancient Chinese practice of arranging your surroundings to attract positive life energy. It is based on a belief that people are affected—for better or worse—by the shapes, colors, textures, sound, light, images, and furniture arrangements in their surroundings.[1] Feng Shui has become a popular practice when buying a home, choosing and arranging furniture, and selecting items to adorn rooms. It also has been used to determine furniture arrangement in corporate settings.

Here are a few of the interesting suggestions provided by a Feng Shui website:

- Place pink, red, or white flowers in the rear right corner of your bedroom to enhance your marriage or love life.
- Design an area of your home as a Health Area. Place items there that represent long life, such as a statue of a crane or elephant (or any animal or plant that lives a long time).

- Keep valuables in the left rear corner of your bedroom to amplify or draw more wealth to you.
- A blue or black rug at your front door will symbolically allow opportunities to flow like water.[2]

Feng Shui has become big business for some interior designers. In one California town, Feng Shui enthusiasts convinced the city council to change the system for numbering home addresses to conform to Feng Shui principles. Many clients insist that Feng Shui is miraculous because it helps make their home or business more comfortable, healthy, and productive. Others contend that the process of making any home more comfortable and less cluttered is well worth the effort no matter what you call the theory.

[1]Stephanie Roberts, *Fast Feng Shui* (Kahului, HI: Lotus Pond Press, 2001), p. 3. Also see www.webterrace.com/fengshui and www.internationalfengshuiguild.org.

[2]www.webterrace.com/fengshui.

Most environments are designed with a purpose in mind. An expensive restaurant's dining room may separate tables at some distance to offer diners privacy. The restaurant's atmosphere may be comfortable, quiet, and only subject to the mouthwatering aroma of good food. How does this differ from the environmental features at your local fast-food restaurant? There the environment is designed to get you in and out as fast as possible.

Figure 6.4	Dimensions of Nonverbal Context

Level of Formality

Informal ⟷ Formal

Warmth

Comfortable ⟷ Uncomfortable

Privacy

Open ⟷ Private

Familiar

Unusual ⟷ Usual

Distance

Others close ⟷ Others far

Improving Nonverbal Expression

Most people learn to communicate nonverbally by imitating others and by paying attention to and adapting to feedback. Thus, when someone responds positively to a particular nonverbal behavior, you tend to keep using it. If you receive negative reactions, you may choose a more effective behavior next time. Training and practice can help you develop more effective nonverbal communication skills.[43]

BE "OTHER" ORIENTED

People who are effective self-monitors and sensitive to others are usually accurate observers and interpreters of nonverbal communication. **Other orientation** means giving serious "attention to, concern for, and interest in" other communicators.[44] For example, during face-to-face encounters, "listen" to the nonverbal messages: *Look* while you listen. The more of your five senses you use, the more nonverbal cues you will notice. During a telephone conversation the tone of your voice may be more communicative than the words spoken. In face-to-face interactions, you can also see facial expressions and gestures. Pay attention to other nonverbal communication elements as well, such as how people are dressed, their choice of perfume or cologne, their handshakes, and the ways in which they've decorated a room.

Not only should you look *while* you listen, but you should also look like you *are* listening. Nodding your head, leaning forward, and engaging in direct eye contact are just some of the nonverbal cues that let others know that you are paying attention and interested. Furthermore, your nonverbal feedback lets a speaker know your response to a message. For example, if your nonverbal behaviors suggest you don't understand or that you disagree with what is being said, the other person may try to clarify information or present a better argument.

USE IMMEDIACY STRATEGIES

Generally, we avoid individuals who appear cold, unfriendly, or hostile. Similarly, we tend to feel more comfortable and want to approach people who seem warm and friendly. **Immediacy** is the degree to which a person seems approachable or likable. Imagine approaching a customer service counter where you see two workers, both available to help you. One of the workers leans away from the counter, does not make eye contact with you, and is frowning. The other worker looks directly at you and smiles. The principle of immediate communication suggests that you will walk up to the worker who appears friendly. Perceptions of another person's approachability will also influence your own nonverbal behavior. For example, if the only person available at the counter is an unfriendly-looking worker, your expectations about how that person will behave toward you may elicit cold and defensive behaviors on your part before a single word is even spoken.

A variety of nonverbal behaviors can promote immediacy.[45] Neat, clean, and pleasant-smelling people are generally more approachable than those that are dirty, sloppy, and smelly. Other nonverbal immediacy behaviors are more subtle. The degree to which you are perceived as likable and approachable may be the difference between a smile and a frown, leaning toward rather than away from another person, direct eye contact versus looking away, a relaxed rather than a rigid body posture, or animated instead of neutral vocal tones. When you use nonverbal immediacy behaviors, other people are more likely to want to communicate with you, and those interactions will be warmer and friendlier for everyone involved.

STRATEGIES FOR IMPROVING NONVERBAL COMMUNICATION
▶ Be "Other" Oriented
▶ Use Immediacy Strategies
▶ Adapt to Cultural Differences

What nonverbal behaviors indicate that a person is highly focused on what someone else is saying?

Several studies find positive links between immediacy and learning. Teachers who are immediate generate more interest and enthusiasm about the subject matter.[1] This also applies to anyone seeking to inform, persuade, or entertain others. Verbal immediacy is associated with expressing a sense of humor, self-disclosing, offering feedback, and using inclusive language such as *we* and *us*. Some of the nonverbal characteristics of high immediacy include

- consistent and direct eye contact
- smiling
- appropriate and natural body movement
- vocal variety
- maintaining closer physical distance[2]

Think of some of the most effective and memorable teachers you've had. Were their bodies glued to their desk or lectern, or did they come from behind that barrier, gesture openly, and move closer to you and the other students? Did they smile and look at you directly, use an expressive voice, and listen actively? If they did, you probably liked them and, even more important, learned more from them.[3]

[1]John A. Daly and Anita Vangelisti, "Skillfully Instructing Learners: How Communicators Effectively Convey Messages," in *Handbook of Communication and Social Interaction Skills,* ed. John O. Greene and Brant R. Burleson (Mahwah, NJ: Lawrence Erlbaum, 2003), pp. 892–894.

[2]Timothy G. Plax and Patricia Kearney, "Classroom Management: Contending with College Student Discipline," in *Teaching Communication: Theory, Research, and Methods ,* ed. Anita L. Vangelisti, John A. Daly, and Gustav W. Friedrich (Lea's Communication Series), 2nd ed. (Mahwah, NJ: Lawrence Erlbaum, 1999), p. 276.

[3]Isa N. Engleberg and John A. Daly, *Presentations in Everyday Life: Strategies for Effective Speaking*, 2nd ed. (Boston: Houghton Mifflin, 2005), p. 132.

ADAPT TO CULTURAL DIFFERENCES

Nonverbal communication varies dramatically across cultures. A friendly gesture in one culture may be offensive in another. People from other cultures may feel comfortable standing much closer or much farther away than you are accustomed. Likewise, direct eye contact may be expected in one culture but viewed as rude in another. In Italy people typically gesture while speaking, but in China extensive hand gestures are less common. In Saudi Arabia, the right hand is used for gesturing because the left hand is considered unclean.[46] Just as a culture's language may be different from your own, so too might its nonverbal communication be different.

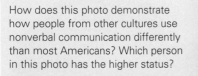

How does this photo demonstrate how people from other cultures use nonverbal communication differently than most Americans? Which person in this photo has the higher status?

Just as nonverbal behaviors vary across cultures, there are also differences in nonverbal behavior among men and women. To a large extent, these differences are the result of traditional male and female roles. For example, little girls are told to "sit like a lady" and little boys are told that "men don't cry." Generally, men are expected to create impressions of dominance, assertiveness, strength, and independence. Traditional female behavior is supportive, accommodating, and subordinate. Certainly, male and female roles have changed dramatically during the past few decades. However, many of our behaviors continue to be based on traditional gender roles. Research offers the following examples of male and female differences in nonverbal communication[1]:

- Women tend to take up less personal space when interacting with men.
- Men tend to use larger and more sweeping gestures than women.
- Women often use a rising intonation that turns statements into questions and thus weakens their power.
- Men are more likely than women to conceal emotion by masking their facial expressions.
- Generally, women tend to use more eye contact during a conversation than men.

- During a conversation, a man is more likely to interrupt a woman when she is speaking than vice versa.
- Women tend to smile more often than men.[2]
- Women are more sensitive to nonverbal cues and more accurately interpret behavior.[3]

These examples are only broad generalizations, particularly as gender roles and behavior continue to change. Many men smile, are facially expressive, and limit their interruptions in conversations. Women often use animated gestures, assert their need for personal space, and interrupt men. Effective communicators are able to draw on a variety of behaviors, both feminine and masculine, as they adapt to different situations.

[1]Virginia P. Richmond and James C. McCroskey, *Nonverbal Behavior in Interpersonal Relations*, 5th ed. (Boston: Allyn & Bacon, 2004), pp. 224–233.

[2]Judith A. Hall, "How Big Are Nonverbal Sex Differences? The Case of Smiling and Sensitivity to Nonverbal Cues," in *Sex Differences and Similarities in Communication: Critical Essays and Empirical Investigations of Sex and Gender in Interaction*, ed. Daniel J. Canary and Kathryn Dindia (Mahwah, NJ: Lawrence Erlbaum, 1998), p. 155.

[3]Ibid., p. 159.

Nobody is expected to learn all the nonverbal communication norms for every culture. However, you can learn to adapt to and interpret effectively the nonverbal behavior of those you do encounter by listening to and carefully observing their behavior. Notice how someone's nonverbal communication is different from your own. You can also learn about another culture by reading and asking questions. Finally, look for opportunities to interact with people of different cultures. Effective communicators welcome and learn from their intercultural encounters.

Your Way without Words

Directions: The following table lists seven types of nonverbal cues across the top. Five types of emotional messages are listed in the far left column: warmth, fear, joy, anger, and boredom. As in the example for *warmth*, write down the kind of nonverbal behavior you would use to express these feelings to another person.

Types of Nonverbal Cues

Emotional Message	Facial Expression	Eye Contact	Tone of Voice	Touch	Gestures	Distance	Posture
Example: Warmth	Smiling, calmness	Direct	Soft	Gentle, reassuring	Open, slow	Intimate or personal	Alert, relaxed
Fear							
Joy							
Anger							
Boredom							

Source: Based on an exercise in David W. Johnson, *Reaching Out: Interpersonal Effectiveness and Self-Actualization,* 7th ed. (Boston: Allyn and Bacon, 2000), pp. 201, 206.

Communication Assessment

Nonverbal Effectiveness Rating Scale

Directions: Rate yourself or someone else's nonverbal effectiveness by circling the appropriate number on the following scale: (1) ineffective, (2) somewhat ineffective, (3) adequate, (4) good, or (5) excellent.

Rating	Nonverbal Behavior
Self	
1 2 3 4 5	1. Is knowledgeable about nonverbal communication
1 2 3 4 5	2. Self-monitors nonverbal communication and behavior
1 2 3 4 5	3. Is motivated to improve nonverbal communication
Others	
1 2 3 4 5	4. Is knowledgeable about cultural differences in nonverbal behavior
1 2 3 4 5	5. Adapts nonverbal behavior to others
1 2 3 4 5	6. Displays other-oriented nonverbal behavior
Purpose	
1 2 3 4 5	7. Understands functions of nonverbal communication
1 2 3 4 5	8. Matches nonverbal communication to message purpose
Context	
1 2 3 4 5	9. Adapts nonverbal behavior to the situation and environment
1 2 3 4 5	10. Adapts to various nonverbal expectations
Content	
1 2 3 4 5	11. Identifies potential nonverbal communication strategies
1 2 3 4 5	12. Provides effective nonverbal feedback to others
Structure	
1 2 3 4 5	13. Organizes nonverbal elements to support a message
1 2 3 4 5	14. Uses nonverbal behavior to signal transitions from one idea to another
Expression	
1 2 3 4 5	15. Uses appropriate facial expression and eye contact
1 2 3 4 5	16. Uses appropriate body movement and gestures
1 2 3 4 5	17. Uses appropriate vocal characteristics and quality
1 2 3 4 5	18. Uses appropriate touch, space, and distance

Key Terms

accenting nonverbal behavior
adaptor
complementary nonverbal behavior
contradictory nonverbal behavior
emblem
emoticon
Expectancy Violation Theory
gesture
illustrator
immediacy
leakage cue

marker
metamessage
mixed message
nonverbal communication
nonverbal deintensification
nonverbal intensification
nonverbal masking
nonverbal neutralization
other orientation
pitch
proxemics

rate
regulating nonverbal behavior
repetitive nonverbal behavior
substituting nonverbal behavior
territoriality
touch approacher
touch avoider
volume
word stress

Notes

1. Mark Hickson III, Don W. Stacks, and Nina-Jo Moore, *Nonverbal Communication: Studies and Applications*, 4th ed. (Los Angeles, CA: Roxbury Publishing, 2004), p. 7. Note: The percent of meaning generated by nonverbal communication is often overestimated in research. For example, Mehrabian and Ferris' widely quoted study is often misinterpreted to mean that 90 percent of all meaning is conveyed nonverbally. See David Lapakko, "Three Cheers for Language: A Closer Examination of a Widely Cited Study of Nonverbal Communication," *Communication Education* 46 (January 1997), pp. 63–67. For Mehrabian's explanation of how his nonverbal percentages have been misunderstood, see Max Atkinson, *Lend Me Your Ears* (New York: Oxford University Press, 2005), pp. 342–345.

2. Judee K. Burgoon and Aaron E. Bacue, "Nonverbal Communication Skills," in *Handbook of Communication and Social Interaction Skills*, ed. John O. Greene and Brant R. Burleson (Mahwah, NJ: Lawrence Erlbaum, 2003), pp. 208–209.

3. Virginia P. Richmond and James C. McCroskey, *Nonverbal Behavior in Interpersonal Relations*, 5th ed. (Boston, MA: Allyn & Bacon, 2004), p. 5.

4. Ibid., p. 4.

5. Michael L. Hecht, Joseph A. DeVito, and Laura K. Guerrero, "Perspectives on Nonverbal Communication: Codes, Functions, and Contexts," in *The Nonverbal Communication Reader: Classic and Contemporary Readings*, 2nd ed., ed. Laura K. Guerrero, Joseph A. DeVito, and Michael L. Hecht (Prospect Heights, IL: Waveland Press, 1999), pp. 4–5.

6. Hickson et al., p. 23.

7. Paul Ekman, "Communication through Nonverbal Behavior: A Source of Information about an Interpersonal Relationship," in *Affect, Cognition and Personality*, ed. Silvan S. Tompkins and C.E. Izard (New York: Springer, 1965).

8. Mark L. Knapp and Judith A. Hall, *Nonverbal Communication in Human Interaction*, 5th ed. (Belmont, CA: Wadsworth, 2002), p. 14.

9. Hecht et al., p. 9.

10. Judee K. Burgoon, David B. Buller, and W. Gill Woodall, *Nonverbal Communication: The Unspoken Dialog* (New York, McGraw-Hill, 1996), p. 286. See also Richard West and Lynn H. Turner, *Introducing Communication Theory* (Boston: McGraw Hill, 2007), pp. 152–153.

11. Judee K. Burgoon and Aaron E. Bacue, "Nonverbal Communication Skills," in *Handbook of Communication and Social Interaction Skills*, ed. John O. Greene and Brant R. Burleson (Mahwah, NJ: Lawrence Erlbaum Associates, 2003), p. 206.

12. Ibid.

13. Glenn Wilson and David Nias, "Beauty Can't Be Beat" in *The Nonverbal Communication Reader: Classic and Contemporary Readings*, 2nd ed., ed. Laura K. Guerrero, Joseph A. DeVito, and Michael L. Hecht (Prospect Heights, IL: Waveland Press, 1999), p. 102.

14. From The Federal Reserve Bank of St. Louis, *The Regional Economist* (April 2005) quoted in "Good Looks Can Mean Good Pay, Study Says," *The Sun*, April 28, 2005, p. D1.

15. Richmond and McCroskey, p. 33.

16. Knapp and Hall, p. 175.

17. Ibid., pp. 175–180.

18. Richmond and McCroskey, p. 38.

19. Thomas J. Stanley and William D. Danko, *The Millionaire Next Door: The Surprising Secrets of America's Wealthy* (Atlanta, GA: Longstreet Press, 1996), pp. 31–35.

20. Ibid., p. 28.

21. Jo-Ellan Dimitrius and Mark Mazzarella, *Reading People: How to Understand People and Predict Their Behavior—Anytime, Anyplace* (New York: Ballantine, 1999), p. 52.

22. Ibid., pp. 56–58.

23. Knapp and Hall, p. 229.

24. Sharon Begley, "Gesturing as You Talk Can Help You Take a Load off Your Mind," *Wall Street Journal*, November 14, 2003, www.online.wsj.com/article_print/SB10686987621722900.html.

25. Paul Ekman and Wallace V. Friesen, "Hand Movements" in *The Nonverbal Communication Reader: Classic and Contemporary Readings*, 2nd ed., ed. Laura K. Guerrero, Joseph A. DeVito, and Michael L. Hecht (Prospect Heights, IL: Waveland Press, 1999), p. 49.

26. Roger E. Axtell, *Do's and Taboos Around the World*, 2nd ed. (New York: John Wiley and Sons, 1990), p. 47.

27. http://ilc.2.doshisha.ac.jp/users.kkitao/library/student/reading/communication theory/theory_3.htm. Last updated, 3/08/2004.

28. Guerrero et al., p. 174.

29. Larry Smeltzer, John Waltman, and Donald Leonard, "Proxemics and Haptics in Managerial Communication" in *The Nonverbal Communication Reader: Classic and Contemporary Readings*, 2nd ed., ed. Laura K. Guerrero, Joseph A. DeVito, and Michael L. Hecht (Prospect Heights, IL: Waveland Press, 1999), p. 190.

30. Knapp and Hall, p. 282.

31. Remland, *Nonverbal Communication in Everyday Life*, 2nd ed. (Boston: Houghton Mifflin, 2003), p. 175.

32. Richmond and McCroskey, p. 84.

33. Richmond and McCroskey, pp. 75–77.

34. Gerald W. Grumet, "Eye Contact: The Core of Interpersonal Relatedness" in *The Nonverbal Communication Reader: Classic and Contemporary Readings*, 2nd ed., ed. Laura K. Guerrero, Joseph A. DeVito, and Michael L. Hecht (Prospect Heights, IL: Waveland Press, 1999), p. 63.

35. Ibid., pp. 67–69.

36. Guo-Ming Chen and William. J. Starosta, *Fundamentals of Intercultural Communication* (Boston, MA: Allyn & Bacon, 1998), p. 91.

37. Isa N. Engleberg and John A. Daly, *Presentations in Everyday Life: Strategies for Effective Speaking*, 2nd ed. (Boston: Houghton Mifflin, 2005), p. 342.

38. Lyle V. Mayer, *Fundamentals of Voice and Diction*, 13th ed. (Boston: McGraw Hill, 2004), p. 229.

39. Allan Pease and Barbara Pease, *The Definitive Book of Body Language* (New York: Bantam, 2004), pp. 193–194.

40. Based on figure in Myron W. Lustig and Jolene Koester, *Intercultural Competence: Interpersonal Communication across Cultures*, 5th ed. (New York: Longman, 2006), p. 219.

41. Hickson et al., pp. 130–131.

42. Hickson et al., p. 130.

43. Remland, pp. 99–100.

44. Brian H. Spitzberg, "Perspectives on Nonverbal Communication Skills" in *The Nonverbal Communication Reader: Classic and Contemporary Readings*, 2nd ed., ed. Laura K. Guerrero, Joseph A. DeVito, and Michael L. Hecht (Prospect Heights, IL: Waveland Press, 1999), p. 22.

45. Richmond and McCroskey, pp. 199–212.

46. Ibid., pp. 297–298.

Interpersonal Communication: Understanding Relationships

7

chapter

Key Elements of Communication	Communication Axioms	Guiding Principles of Interpersonal Communication
Self	*Communication Is Personal*	Recognize how your interpersonal needs and personality affect how you communicate.
Others	*Communication Is Relational*	Understand, respect, and adapt to the interpersonal needs and personalities of others.
Purpose	*Communication Is Intentional*	Use appropriate communication strategies and skills to initiate, maintain, and strengthen interpersonal relationships.
Context	*Communication Is Contextual*	Adapt to the ways in which psychosocial and cultural contexts affect your relationships.
Content	*Communication Is Symbolic*	Choose appropriate message strategies to manage your personal impression, assert your needs, and resolve conflict.
Structure	*Communication Is Structured*	Select and organize appropriate strategies for beginning, maintaining, and ending relationships.
Expression	*Communication Is Irreversible*	Use verbal and nonverbal strategies that promote positive personal impressions, cooperation, and assertiveness.

The Challenge of Interpersonal Communication

Consider your interactions with other people on an average day. Who is the first person you talk to? Who do you see when you leave home in the morning? How many people do you talk with on a typical day? Like most people, you may discuss your plans for the day with a family member or roommate, ask a classmate about an upcoming exam, discuss your grade with a professor, share gossip with a close friend, talk to coworkers and customers at work, or phone your auto mechanic or doctor's office. All these interactions are examples of interpersonal communication.

Interpersonal communication occurs when a limited number of people, usually two, interact by using verbal and nonverbal messages to generate meaning for the purpose of sharing information, achieving a goal, or maintaining a relationship. There are many types of interpersonal relationships—perhaps as many as there are people you know. The most common types, shown in Figure 7.1, fall under the headings of impersonal, personal, and professional relationships.

Impersonal relationships involve occasional interactions with people in predictable social or business roles, or in random encounters. They usually involve someone you see infrequently or don't know well, such as a stranger at a party, a clerk at the dry cleaners, or a new neighbor. **Personal relationships** are characterized by a higher level of emotional connection and commitment, such as you have with friends, romantic partners, and family members. Chapter 8, "Interpersonal Communication: Improving Personal Relationships," deals with these important relationships. **Professional relationships** involve connections with people you associate and work with to accomplish a goal or perform a task. Chapter 9, "Interpersonal Communication: Professional Relationships," focuses on communication in professional and workplace contexts.

As you might expect, some of your relationships fall into more than one category. For example, you may have an impersonal relationship with a bank teller who has processed your transactions for several years. When his daughter joins the same

Figure 7.1	Types of Interpersonal Relationships

Impersonal Relationships
- Encounters with people who nod or say hello when passing in a hallway or on the street
- Encounters with clerks or cashiers in stores or businesses
- Encounters with people in line at grocery stores, concerts, bus stops, or theme parks

Personal Relationships
- Interaction with family members
- Interaction with friends
- Interaction with romantic partners

Professional Relationships
- Superior–subordinate relationships
- Coworker relationships
- Customer relationships

sports team as your daughter or young sister, you begin having regular conversations with him at games. After years of interacting with "the teller" on an *impersonal* basis, you have begun to develop a *personal* relationship. In other situations, you may have both a personal and professional relationship with someone. Your best friend also may be a colleague or supervisor at work. Like many people, you may develop long-lasting interpersonal relationships that began with impersonal, role-based interaction.

Interpersonal Needs and Preferences

Should you stay home and read a book or go to a movie with a friend? Should you volunteer to chair a committee or are you more comfortable letting someone else take the lead? Should you confide a personal secret to a new friend or wait until you're better acquainted? Two significant psychological theories—Schutz's FIRO Theory and the Myers-Briggs Type Indicator Theory—can help you understand how such decisions reflect your interpersonal needs and preferences.

SCHUTZ'S INTERPERSONAL NEEDS THEORY

Psychologist William Schutz's **Fundamental Interpersonal Relationship Orientation (FIRO) Theory** concentrates on three basic interpersonal needs: the needs for inclusion, control, and affection.[1] Schutz maintains that we interact with others to satisfy one or more of these basic needs.[2]

What type of interpersonal relationship is depicted in this photograph?

Inclusion   **Inclusion** represents a need to belong, to be involved, and to be accepted. When inclusion needs are met, the result is what Schutz calls an **ideal social person**: a person who enjoys being with others but is also comfortable being alone.

If, however, your inclusion needs are not met, you may not feel accepted or valued by others. As a result, you may engage in undersocial or oversocial behavior. An **undersocial person** feels unworthy or undervalued. Such people may withdraw and become loners. Because they believe that no one values them, they avoid interpersonal relationships. An **oversocial person** also feels unworthy and undervalued but tries to attract attention to compensate for feelings of inadequacy. These people seek companionship and can't stand being alone. As a result, they try to impress others with what and who they know. Thus, if a friend constantly seeks attention or tends to withdraw from social situations, a strong but unmet inclusion need may be responsible. You can satisfy this need by praising your friend's accomplishments.

Control   **Control** refers to whether you feel competent and confident. When control needs are met, the result is what Schutz calls a **democratic person**: someone who has no problems with power and control and who feels just as comfortable giving orders as taking them.

Unmet control needs can result in the emergence of an abdicrat or autocrat. The **abdicrat** wants control but is reluctant to pursue it and therefore is often submissive. The **autocrat** also wants control but tries to take over or dominate others. Autocrats may criticize other people and force decisions on them. Dealing with abdicrats and autocrats is a challenge. You may need to grant them a sense of control appropriate to their needs. For example, if someone at work has a strong but unmet control need, you may ask her to suggest a plan of action or to take on an important responsibility.

SCHUTZ'S FUNDAMENTAL INTERPERSONAL RELATIONSHIP ORIENTATION THEORY

► Need for Inclusion
► Need for Control
► Need for Affection

Giving someone even a small amount of responsibility can satisfy that person's need for control.

Affection   Affection[3] refers to the need to feel liked. When we need affection, we seek close friendships, intimate relationships, and expressions of warmth from others. When affection needs are met, the result is what Schutz calls an **ideal personal type**: a person who wants to be liked but who also is secure enough to function in situations in which social interaction and affection are not high priorities.

According to Schutz, when affection needs are not met, people tend to react in two ways: by establishing superficial relationships or by getting too close to everyone. **Underpersonal types** believe they are not liked and may establish only superficial relationships with others. When pressed, they rarely share their honest feelings or opinions and may appear aloof and uninvolved. **Overpersonal types** try to get close to everyone. They may seek an intimate relationship despite the disinterest of the other person. Dealing with underpersonal and overpersonal types requires expressing fondness for them. Showing affection to someone has the potential to satisfy that person's affection need.

Figure 7.2 illustrates the potential outcomes when interpersonal needs are met or not met.

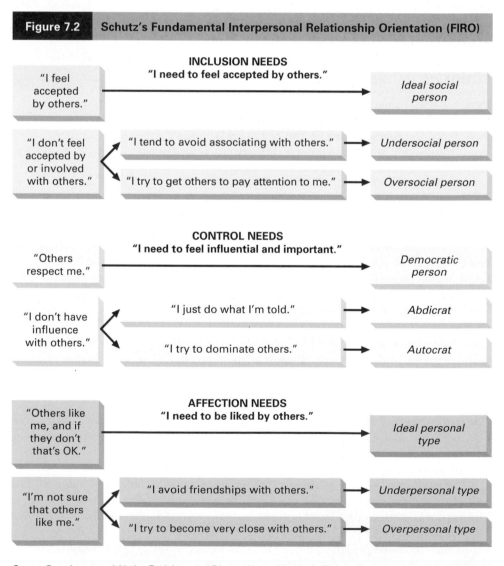

| Figure 7.2 | Schutz's Fundamental Interpersonal Relationship Orientation (FIRO) |

INCLUSION NEEDS
"I need to feel accepted by others."

"I feel accepted by others." → *Ideal social person*

"I don't feel accepted by or involved with others."
→ "I tend to avoid associating with others." → *Undersocial person*
→ "I try to get others to pay attention to me." → *Oversocial person*

CONTROL NEEDS
"I need to feel influential and important."

"Others respect me." → *Democratic person*

"I don't have influence with others."
→ "I just do what I'm told." → *Abdicrat*
→ "I try to dominate others." → *Autocrat*

AFFECTION NEEDS
"I need to be liked by others."

"Others like me, and if they don't that's OK." → *Ideal personal type*

"I'm not sure that others like me."
→ "I avoid friendships with others." → *Underpersonal type*
→ "I try to become very close with others." → *Overpersonal type*

Source: Based on material in Isa Engleberg and Dianna Wynn, *Working in Groups: Communication Principles and Strategies*, 4th ed. (Boston: Houghton Mifflin, 2007), pp. 39.

MYERS-BRIGGS TYPE INDICATOR

Isabel Briggs Myers and her daughter, Katherine Briggs, developed a personality type measure that examines the ways in which we perceive the world around us as well as how we reach conclusions and make decisions.[4] The **Myers-Briggs Type Indicator** is used by thousands of corporations, including most Fortune 100 companies, "to identify job applicants whose skills match those of their top performers," whereas others use it "to develop communication skills and promote teamwork among current employees."[5]

According to Myers-Briggs, all of us have preferred ways of thinking and behaving that can be divided into four categories, with two opposite preferences in each category, as indicated in Figure 7.3. As you read about the types and their traits, ask yourself which preferences best describe how you communicate.[6]

Extrovert or Introvert   Extrovert and introvert are two traits that describe where you focus your attention: outward or inward. **Extroverts** are outgoing; they talk more, gesture more, and can become enthusiastic during a discussion. They get their energy by being with people. Extroverts enjoy solving problems in groups and like to involve others in projects and activities. They also have a tendency to dominate conversations without listening to others. At the same time, however, they can be terrific energizers.

Introverts think before they speak and usually are not as talkative as extroverts. They prefer socializing with one or two close friends rather than spending time with a large group of people. Introverts are also comfortable spending time alone. Although they may have a great deal to offer others in a discussion, they may find the experience exhausting. Introverts recharge by being alone and often prefer to work by themselves.

Knowing whether you or another person is an extrovert or introvert can be valuable. Although an extrovert may want to go to a party, an introvert may prefer a quiet evening with a friend. "Extroverts complain that introverts don't speak up at the right

Figure 7.3	Myers-Briggs Type Indicator Preferences

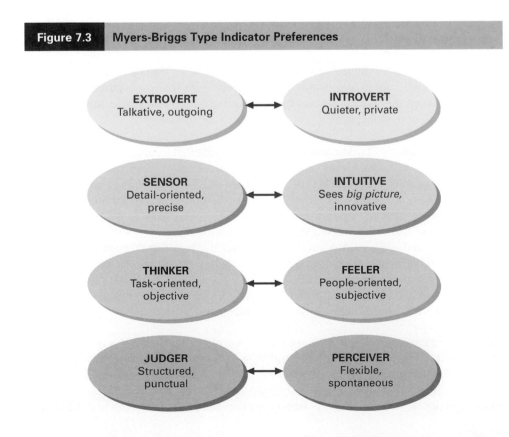

Are you comfortable spending time alone? Who would feel more comfortable having a meal alone and/or working alone—an introvert or an extrovert?

time in meetings. Introverts criticize extroverts for talking too much and not listening well."[7] In classrooms, extroverts like to participate in heated discussions whereas introverts hate being put on the spot.

Sensor or Intuitive   How do you look at the world around you? Do you see the forest (the big picture) or the trees (the details)? **Sensors** focus on details and prefer to concentrate on one task at a time. They may uncover minor flaws in an idea and request detailed instructions for completing a task. **Intuitives** look for connections and concepts rather than rules and flaws. They like to come up with big ideas but are bored with details. Sensors focus on regulations, step-by-step explanations, and facts, whereas intuitives focus on outwitting regulations, supplying theoretical explanations, and skipping details.

Both personality types are needed in the workplace. Management communication experts Carl Larson and Frank LaFasto emphasize the importance of having a balance between the "nuts and bolts types" and those individuals who are capable of being creative and conceptual.[8]

Thinker or Feeler   Thinker and feeler are two traits that explain how you go about making decisions. **Thinkers** are analytical and task oriented. They take pride in their ability to think objectively and logically. Thinkers often enjoy arguing and making difficult decisions; they want to get the job done, even if the cost is poor feelings among others. **Feelers** are more people oriented. They want everyone to get along. Feelers will spend time and effort helping others.

Thinkers and feelers often misunderstand each other. Thinkers may appear unemotional and aggressive, whereas feelers may annoy others by "wasting time" with social chit-chat. However, when thinkers and feelers appreciate their differences, they can form a strong relationship. Although the thinker makes decisions and moves things forward, the feeler makes sure everyone gets along and works together harmoniously.

Judger or Perceiver   Do you approach the world and its challenges in a structured and organized way? If so, you are most likely a judger. **Judgers** are highly structured people who plan ahead, are very punctual, and become impatient with others who show up late or waste time. **Perceivers** are less rigid than judgers. Because they like open-endedness, being on time is less important than being flexible and adaptable.

Perceivers are risk takers who are willing to try new options. They often procrastinate and end up in a frenzy to complete a task on time.

Judgers and perceivers often have difficulty understanding each other. To a judger, a perceiver may appear scatterbrained. To a perceiver, a judger may appear rigid and controlling. Although judgers are prepared to make decisions and solve problems, perceivers "aren't comfortable with things being 'decided'; [they] want to reopen, discuss, rework, argue for the sake of arguing."[9] In classroom settings, judgers usually plan and finish class assignments well in advance, whereas perceivers may pull all-nighters to get their work done. It's important to note that both types get their work done—the difference is when and how they go about doing it.

Initiating Interpersonal Relationships

All interpersonal relationships begin somewhere. Your best friend's sister or brother may have been an annoyance when you were in elementary school, but she or he may become your prom date in high school. Someone you meet on an airplane may eventually offer you a job.

Is there a "best" way to get relationships started? Do you just let things happen or do you make them happen? Two communication strategies and skills are crucial for developing relationships with others: effective conversations and impression management.

EFFECTIVE CONVERSATIONS

A **conversation** is an interaction, often informal, in which two people exchange speaking and listening roles as they discuss information, thoughts, or feelings. Most interpersonal communication takes place through conversations. On any given day you may have a conversation with a classmate in the hallway, a coworker at the next desk, or someone you've just met at a reception or party. Context influences the nature of interactions. For example, you may wait until others aren't around or until a championship game on television is over to have a serious and private conversation with a close friend. The nature of a relationship also influences what you talk about in a conversation. You may discuss highly personal issues with a close friend, but you probably don't share as much with someone you've just met.

Starting a Conversation   When you begin a conversation with someone you don't know, you can create a basis for engaging in further discussion by offering information about yourself, asking questions, and listening for "iceberg" statements.

Introducing yourself is the most obvious way to begin a conversation: "I'm Allison; my family and I are here on vacation from Nebraska." The other person will usually reciprocate by offering similar information or following up on your information: "I have cousins in Nebraska and visited them one summer when I was a kid." A second approach to opening a conversation is to ask questions: "Do you know anything about the professor?" "Have you been to this club before?" "Your name tag says you work for the Special Olympics. Do you know Julie Borchard?"

Finally, follow up on the other person's response. In particular, listen for **iceberg statements**, which Don Gabor describes in *How to Start a Conversation and Make Friends* as "a comment or piece of free information where ninety percent is under the surface waiting to be asked."[10] In other words, a simple comment may be just the tip of the communication iceberg. For example, a classmate sits down next to you and says, "You won't believe who I just saw in the parking lot." The response "Who was it; what happened?" may be all you need to get a good conversation going.

Maintaining a Conversation   One of the best ways to keep a conversation going is to ask open-ended questions. A **closed-ended question** requires only a short and

WAYS TO BEGIN A CONVERSATION
- ▶ Offer Information about Yourself
- ▶ Ask Questions
- ▶ Listen for "Iceberg" Statements

Countless newspaper articles have been written regarding cell phone etiquette—and for good reasons. There is almost nothing as annoying and even embarrassing as being forced to listen in on someone elses cell pho ne conversation. "Placing a cell phone call in public instantly transforms the strangers around you into unwilling listeners."[1] A survey of workplace pet peeves found that 30 percent of working adults are annoyed by ringing cell phones (particularly when they have cute ring tones). Besides the distracting ring, they don't like the ensuing conversations in which people discuss more personal topics in front of coworkers.[2] We're sure you've heard people complain to their spouses and employees or have heard boyfriends and girlfriends express their puppy love for one another. We've even heard a speaker in a panel answer his cell phone in the middle of another person's presentation!

Robbie Blinkoff, an anthropologist who studies consumer behavior for Context-Based Research Group, suggests that "people are defining new rules and new behavior for what's personal and what's private."[3] Surveys indicate that the majority of cell phone users believe that loud or private calls made in public settings are inappropriate. However, "that same majority indulges in such calls themselves."[4]

To avoid embarrassing yourself, annoying others, or humiliating the person you're talking to, follow a few simple rules when talking on a cell phone[5]:

- Avoid personal calls during business meetings.
- Maintain a distance from others of at least ten feet when talking on the phone.
- Avoid cell phone conversations in enclosed public spaces such as elevators, waiting rooms, or buses.
- Avoid cell phone conversations in public places where side talk is considered bad manners, such as libraries, museums, theaters, restaurants, and places of worship.
- Avoid loud and distracting ring tones.
- Control the volume of your voice. Don't force everyone around you to listen to your private conversation. Tilt your chin downward so that you're speaking toward the floor. That way, your voice won't carry as far.
- Avoid cell phone conversations when engaging in other tasks such as driving or shopping.
- Take advantage of the phone's many features, such as vibrate mode and voice mail. When you step into your workplace or a classroom, put your cell phone on vibrate and let your calls roll to your voice mail.

We believe you're well within your rights to interrupt a friend or acquaintance who is carrying on an extended conversation on a cell phone in a public place such as a restaurant, during a meeting, or at a small social gathering. Try this: "Can I ask you a favor? Would you mind turning off your cell phone while we're here?" Someone who wants to be on good terms with you will comply.

[1]Christine Rosen, "Bad Connections," *New York Times Magazine* (March 20, 2005), p. 18.

[2]"What Drives Co-Workers Crazy," *The Week*, February 23, 2007, p. 40.

[3]Joanna L. Krotz, "Cell Phone Etiquette: 10 Dos and Don'ts" (Microsoft Small Business Center, 2004), www.microsoft.com/smallbusiness/issues/technology/communications/cell_phone.

[4]Ibid.

[5]Ibid. See also "Proper Cell Phone Etiquette," www.cellphonecarriers.com/cell-phone-etiquette.html.

---

direct response. "Is this class required for your major?" could be answered with a yes or no. **Open-ended questions** encourage more specific or detailed responses. "What did you think of the professor the first day of class?" invites someone to share an observation or opinion.

When you are asked questions during a conversation, avoid responding with simple answers. Rather, give an answer that provides the other person with more information about your thoughts or experiences. An engaging conversation requires the effort of two people. Otherwise, the conversation will quickly deteriorate into an awkward silence.

Good conversations seek **common ground**: beliefs, attitudes, or experiences that both of you share. Two people in the same situation (stuck in a long line for class registration or theater tickets) have some common ground. If you meet someone at a concert, you may share the same taste in music. Have you read the same books, seen the same movies, visited some of the same places? Seeking common ground can take some time and effort, but eventually you should find a topic that interests both of you.

Finally, make sure you balance talking with listening. A successful conversation involves taking turns. We negotiate conversational turn taking primarily through our nonverbal behavior. **Turn-requesting cues** are verbal and nonverbal messages that signal a desire to speak, such as leaning forward, providing direct eye contact, and lifting one hand as if beginning to gesture. **Turn-yielding cues** are verbal and nonverbal messages that signal that you are completing your comments and are preparing to listen, such as slowing down your speaking rate, relaxing your posture or gestures, and leaning slightly away. Good conversationalists are sensitive to turn-taking cues. If someone dominates a conversation and forces you to interrupt to get a turn, you may avoid future interactions. Talking with someone who never seems willing to speak or make a contribution can be equally frustrating and awkward.

Ending a Conversation   Ending a conversation abruptly can send a rude message to the other person. It is better to take advantage of a moment in the conversation where ending seems natural. This often occurs at the point when you feel that you have exhausted a topic. You can also use the nonverbal cues that signal the end of a conversation.[11] For example, shifting to the edge of a chair, standing up, looking away, leaning away, or picking up your things can signal it's time to stop talking. The following strategies can help you effectively conclude a conversation:

How do the woman and man in this photograph demonstrate some of the ways people negotiate conversational turn taking?

- *End on a positive and courteous note.* Refer to comments the other person made as a way of showing you were listening and interested. "I've really enjoyed talking to you about . . . ."
- *Make plans to meet again.* Let the other person know you'd like to talk again. Even better, extend an invitation for meeting at a specific date, time, and place.
- *Make a concluding statement.* Describe how the conversation has affected you or how you might use the information you gained. "As soon as I get home, I'm going to look that up on the website you mentioned."
- *State the need to leave.* When there is no good time to end a conversation or the other person is ignoring your hints, state clearly and directly that you must leave, as in "I hate to cut our conversation short, but I really have to get going."

IMPRESSION MANAGEMENT

You know from experience that first impressions count. If you don't make a good impression on a first date, it may be your last date with that person. If you don't impress group members at a first meeting, you probably won't be chosen to chair the committee. In other words, you don't get a second chance to make a first impression.

According to the **primacy effect**, the first information you receive about someone is highly influential in forming an enduring impression. However, although first impressions are powerful, they are not the only factor influencing your impressions. The **recency effect** suggests that the last information you receive can also create a lasting impression. For example, when couples break up, they often share stories about the final fight or "last straw" rather than focusing on the good qualities that brought them together. Similarly, the conclusion of a presentation can have a powerful and long-lasting impact on an audience.

Which principle—primacy or recency—is more powerful? As is often the case, it depends on the situation. For example, being the first to be interviewed for a job allows you to set the standard for applicants that come after you. On the other hand,

CommFAQ How Do I Handle Conversational Dilemmas?

A **conversational dilemma** occurs when you or another person violate expectations about acceptable conversational behavior.[1] The following examples illustrate common conversational dilemmas[2]:

- *Getting Caught in a Lie*. You tell your friend you can't go out with her because you have too much homework, but then you bump into her at the movies that night.
- *Choosing between Your Own and Someone Else's Needs*. You and George are applying for the same supervisory position at work. George asks your advice about how to handle the job interview.
- *Moral Dilemma*. A close friend lies about his work experience on a job application and, without asking, lists you as a reference. The company has called you to verify his work history.
- *Putting Your Foot in Your Mouth*. After telling someone over the phone what sloppy work another coworker does, you discover that that coworker has been standing behind you the entire time.
- *Pressure to Choose Sides*. Two of your good friends are having an argument and each demands that you get involved.

- *Tact or Truth*. If you tell a coworker her casual outfit is not appropriate for the company banquet, she could be offended by your comment. If you say it looks nice, she could embarrass herself by wearing the outfit.

It's difficult to avoid conversational dilemmas. Often, by the time the dilemma presents itself, you are already involved in the conversation. The following strategies can help you when confronted with a conversational dilemma[3]:

- Ask someone else to intervene or give advice.
- Give in to someone else's needs to avoid conflict.
- Save face by apologizing or by giving an excuse.
- Conceal harmless information.
- Change the subject or use humor to avoid the discussion.
- Confront the issue directly and honestly.

[1]John A. Daly, Carol A. Diesel, and David Weber, "Conversational Dilemmas," in *The Dark Side of Interpersonal Communication*, ed. William R. Cupach and Brian H. Spitzberg (Hillsdale, NJ: Lawrence Erlbaum, 1994), p. 130.

[2]Ibid., pp. 131–134.

[3]Ibid., p. 142.

---

you may be more memorable if you interview last. In many situations, creating good first and last impressions are equally important.

Once you create an initial impression, your subsequent behavior can reinforce and maintain that impression or can weaken and even reverse what you want others to think about you. Sociologist Erving Goffman claims that we assume a social identity that others help us maintain.[12] This perspective is useful in understanding **impression management**: the strategies people use to shape others' impressions of them to gain influence, power, sympathy, or approval.[13] Impression management strategies that can help shape your image in positive ways include ingratiation, self-promotion, exemplification, supplication, and intimidation.[14]

Ingratiation (But Not Phony Flattery) When you ingratiate yourself with others, you agree, give compliments, and do favors so another person will like you. Complimenting someone with whom you disagree can ease tensions and reopen communication channels. But ingratiation should be used sparingly and appropriately. If you always agree or give undeserved compliments, you can damage rather than enhance your image. Honest flattery ingratiates yourself with others; insincere flattery has the opposite effect.

Self-Promotion (But Not Big-Headed Bragging) Tell others about your successes and the things you do well. For example, "I'm a fast writer" can earn you a place on an important work team that has short-deadline projects and reports. At the same time, you should promote yourself honestly and appropriately, because no one likes a braggart. Overselling yourself or making promises you can't keep may create a negative impression that is difficult to change.

IMPRESSION MANAGEMENT STRATEGIES

▶ Ingratiation
▶ Self-Promotion
▶ Exemplification
▶ Supplication
▶ Intimidation

182

Exemplification (But Not Just in Public)   When you exemplify, you offer yourself as a good example or model of behavior. But make sure you practice what you preach. If you claim it's wrong to pirate CDs but you photocopy entire books rather than buy them, no one will believe your claims about honesty and moral values. Don't declare you're on a strict diet and then get caught with your hand in the cookie jar.

Supplication (But Not Endless Whining)   Supplicants make others feel resourceful and helpful. When you express a need for help, you demonstrate that you are human like everyone else. But don't become a perpetual sufferer. In *Gone with the Wind*, Scarlett O'Hara plays helpless as a way of getting what she wants from others, but she ends up alone.

Intimidation (But Not Brutality)   To be perceived as powerful, you may demonstrate that you are willing and able to cause harm. "If you speak to me that way again, I will file a formal grievance against you." In most communication situations, we do *not* recommend intimidation as a strategy for impression management. In some instances, however, you may need to establish your authority and willingness to use power. If people take advantage of you, you may need to show them that you won't take it anymore. But be careful, because intimidation can backfire.

How does this t-shirt message affect your impression of the man in this photograph? Which impression management strategy is illustrated?

Interpersonal Conflict

All healthy relationships, no matter how important or well managed, experience interpersonal conflict. Conflict is often associated with quarreling, fighting, anger, and hostility. Although these elements can be present, conflict does not have to involve the expression of negative emotions. **Conflict** is the disagreement that occurs in relationships when differences are expressed.

Many people avoid conflict because they do not understand the differences between destructive and constructive conflict. **Destructive conflict** is the result of behaviors that create hostility or prevent problem solving.[15] Constant complaining, personal insults, conflict avoidance, and loud arguments or threats all contribute to destructive conflict.[16] This kind of conflict has the potential to harm a relationship permanently. In contrast, **constructive conflict** occurs when you express disagreement in a way that respects others' perspectives and promotes problem solving. Figure 7.4 summarizes the differences between constructive and destructive conflict.

Kenneth Cloke and Joan Goldsmith of the Center for Dispute Resolution explain how your perceptions of conflict affect the outcome:

> Each of us has a choice about how to describe the conflicts in our lives. We can describe them as experiences that imprison us or lead us on a journey, as a battle that embitters us or an opportunity for learning. Our choice between these contrasting attitudes and approaches will shape the way the conflict unfolds.[17]

CONFLICT STYLES

When you are faced with conflict, do you jump into the fray or run the other way? Do you marshal your forces and play to win, or do you work with everyone involved to find a mutually agreeable solution? Psychologists Kenneth Thomas and Ralph Kilmann claim that we use one or two of five conflict styles in most situations: avoidance, accommodation, competition, compromise, and collaboration.[18] These five styles can be understood by examining the extent to which you focus on achieving personal needs or mutual needs. People who are motivated to fulfill their own needs tend to choose more competitive approaches, whereas collaborative people usually are more concerned with achieving mutual goals. Figure 7.5 illustrates the relationship of each conflict style to an individual's motivation.

Avoidance   If you are unable or unwilling to stand up for your own needs or the needs of others, you may rely on the **avoidance conflict style**. People who use this

Figure 7.4   **Constructive and Destructive Conflict**

Constructive Conflict →
- Focuses on issues
- Respects others
- Supportive
- Flexible
- Cooperative
- Committed to conflict management

Destructive Conflict →
- Attacks others
- Insults others
- Defensive
- Inflexible
- Competitive
- Avoids or aggravates conflict

Source: Based on Isa Engleberg and Dianna Wynn, *Working in Groups: Communication Principles and Strategies*, 4th ed. (Boston: Houghton Mifflin, 2007), p. 177.

Figure 7.5	Conflict Styles

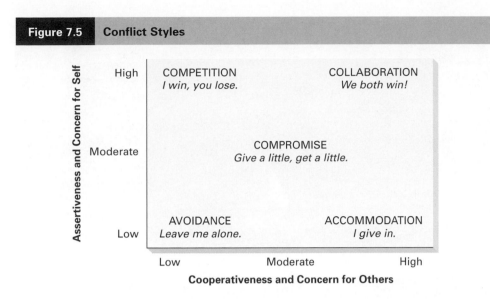

Source: Based on Isa Engleberg and Dianna Wynn, *Working in Groups: Communication Principles and Strategies,* 4th ed. (Boston: Houghton Mifflin, 2007), p. 179.

style change the subject, avoid bringing up a controversial issue, and even deny that a conflict exists. Avoiding conflict can be counterproductive because it fails to address a problem and can increase tension in a relationship. Furthermore, ignoring or avoiding conflict does not make it go away.

However, in some circumstances, avoiding conflict is an appropriate approach. Consider avoiding conflict when the issue is not that important to you, when you need time to collect your thoughts or control your emotions, when the consequences of confrontation are too risky, or when the chances of resolution are remote.

Accommodation   Do you give in to others at the expense of meeting your own needs? If so, you use the **accommodating conflict style**. You may believe that giving in to others preserves harmony even when the relationship could benefit from discussion. People who always approach conflict by accommodating others may become less influential when making decisions in personal or professional relationships.

On the other hand, an accommodating conflict style can be an appropriate and effective approach when the issue is very important to the other person but not very important to you. Accommodation is also appropriate when it is more important to preserve harmony in a relationship than to resolve a particular issue, when you realize you are wrong, or if you have changed your mind.

Competition   The **competitive conflict style** occurs when you are more concerned with fulfilling your own needs than with meeting mutual needs in a relationship. Quite simply, you want to win because you believe that your ideas are better than the alternatives suggested by others. When used inappropriately, the competitive style can be characterized by hostility, ridicule, and personal attacks against others. Approaching conflict competitively tends to reduce people to winners and losers.

In certain situations, however, the competitive approach may be the most appropriate style. Approach conflict competitively when you have strong beliefs about an important issue or when immediate action is needed in an urgent situation. The competitive approach is particularly appropriate when the consequences of a bad decision may be very serious, harmful, unethical, or illegal.

Compromise   The **compromising conflict style** is a "middle ground" approach that involves conceding some goals to achieve others. Many people believe that compromise is an effective and fair method of resolving problems, particularly given that

Which of the Thomas and Kilmann conflict styles is probably used when two attorneys approach the bench to discuss or debate an issue before a judge?

each person loses and wins equally. However, if everyone is only partially satisfied with the outcome, no one may be committed to supporting or implementing the solution.

The compromise approach should be used when you are unable to reach a unanimous decision or agree upon an acceptable solution. Consider compromising when other methods of resolving the conflict will not be effective, when you have reached an impasse, or if there is not enough time to explore more creative solutions.

Collaboration   The **collaborative conflict style** searches for new solutions that will achieve both your goals and the goals of others. Also referred to as a *problem-solving* or *win–win approach*, the collaborative conflict style avoids arguments about whose ideas are superior. Instead, the parties collaborate and look for creative solutions that satisfy everyone.

There are two potential drawbacks to the collaborative approach. First, collaboration requires a lot of time and energy, and some issues may not be important enough to justify the extra time and effort. Second, in order for collaboration to be successful, everyone—even the avoiders and accommodators—must fully participate in the process.

Approach conflict resolution collaboratively when you want a solution that will satisfy both your own needs and the needs of others. Collaboration works best when new and creative ideas are encouraged, when both parties must commit to the final decision, and when you have enough time to spend on creative problem solving.

CONFLICT RESOLUTION STRATEGIES

Effective communicators are flexible and use a variety of approaches to resolving conflict. In this section we describe two conflict resolution strategies: the A-E-I-O-U Model and negotiation. The A-E-I-O-U Model can help you identify critical attitudes, beliefs, and values about conflict. Negotiation involves bargaining as a way to settle differences.

The A-E-I-O-U Model   To resolve conflict, you must fully understand the attitudes, beliefs, and values of those involved. The **A-E-I-O-U Model** focuses on communicating personal concerns and suggesting alternative actions to resolve a conflict.[19] The steps in the A-E-I-O-U Model are as follows:

CommQuiz   How Argumentative Are You?

Directions: This questionnaire contains statements about how you feel about arguing with others, particularly on controversial topics. Indicate how often each statement is true for you by placing the appropriate number in the blank. Use the following ratings to respond to each statement: (1) almost never true, (2) rarely true, (3) occasionally true, (4) often true, (5) almost always true.

_____ 1. While in an argument, I worry that the person I am arguing with will form a negative impression of me.

_____ 2. Arguing over controversial issues improves my intelligence.

_____ 3. I enjoy avoiding arguments.

_____ 4. I am energetic and enthusiastic when I argue.

_____ 5. After I finish an argument, I promise myself that I will not get into another.

_____ 6. Arguing with a person creates more problems for me than it solves.

_____ 7. I have a pleasant, good feeling when I win a point in an argument.

_____ 8. When I finish arguing with someone, I feel nervous and upset.

_____ 9. I enjoy a good argument over a controversial issue.

_____ 10. I get an unpleasant feeling when I realize I am about to get into an argument.

_____ 11. I enjoy defending my point of view on an issue.

_____ 12. I am happy when I keep an argument from happening.

_____ 13. I do not like to miss the opportunity to argue a controversial issue.

_____ 14. I prefer being with people who rarely disagree with me.

_____ 15. I consider an argument an exciting intellectual challenge.

_____ 16. I find myself unable to think of effective points during an argument.

_____ 17. I feel refreshed after an argument on a controversial issue.

_____ 18. I have the ability to do well in an argument.

_____ 19. I try to avoid getting into arguments.

_____ 20. I feel excitement when I expect that a conversation I am in is leading to an argument.

Scoring:

1. Add your scores on items 2, 4, 7, 9, 11, 13, 15, 17, 18, and 20.
2. Add 60 to the sum obtained in step 1.
3. Add your scores on items 1, 3, 5, 6, 8, 10, 12, 14, 16, and 19.
4. To compute your argumentativeness score, subtract the total obtained in step 3 from the total obtained in step 2.

Interpretation:

> 73–100 pt = high in argumentativeness
> 56–72 pt = moderate in argumentativeness
> 20–55 pt = low in argumentativeness

Individuals vary in how comfortable they feel engaging in argument. **Argumentativeness** is the willingness to argue controversial issues with others.[1] It is a constructive trait that does not promote hostility or personal attacks. The argumentative person tends to focus on the most important issues and has little desire to make personal attacks.[2] Highly argumentative individuals enjoy the intellectual challenge of an argument and show a genuine interest in promoting a constructive discussion.

[1]Dominic A. Infante and Andrew S. Rancer, "A Conceptualization and Measure of Argumentativeness," _Journal of Personality Assessment_ 46 (1982), pp. 72–80. Reproduced by permission of Society for Personality Assessment. www.personality.org.

[2]Daniel J. Canary and William R. Cupach, _Competencies in Interpersonal Conflict_ (New York: McGraw-Hill, 1997), p. 58.

A: Assume the other person means well and wants to resolve the conflict. "I know that both of us want to do a good job and complete this project on time."

E: Express your feelings. "I'm frustrated when you ask me to spend time working on a less important project."

I: Identify what you would like to happen. "I want to share the responsibility _and_ the work with you."

O: Outcomes you expect should be made clear. "If both of us don't make a commitment to working on this full time, we won't do a good job or get it done on time."

U: Understanding on a mutual basis is achieved. "Could we divide up the tasks and set deadlines for completion or bring in another person to help us?"

Negotiation   **Negotiation** is a process of bargaining to settle differences or reach solutions. Normally, negotiation takes the form of compromise, with each person giving in on some issues to achieve agreement on other points. Some people are more willing to bargain if they believe that they will be no worse off and might even be better off by the end of the negotiation process.

Roger Fisher, William Ury, and Bruce Patton of the Harvard Negotiation Project suggest that conflict can be resolved through a process of "principled negotiation."[20] However, negotiation can become deadlocked if we fail to appreciate the needs of others or are unwilling to make concessions. Figure 7.6 summarizes effective negotiation strategies.

Effective negotiation requires that you balance a variety of needs, your own as well as others', by openly communicating your willingness to give in on some points without sacrificing your critical needs or personal beliefs. You must balance the need to accomplish your own short-term goal against the benefits of mutually desirable long-term conflict resolution.

ASSERTIVENESS

In any relationship, you experience competing needs. Your boss wants you to work longer hours, but you want more time with your family. Your friend wants to go to a party, but you need to stay home and study. The insurance agent wants you to protect your business, but you need to trim your budget. To balance these competing needs and resolve potential conflicts, it is helpful to practice **assertiveness**, which involves promoting your own needs and rights while also respecting the needs and rights of others. In *Asserting Yourself*, Sharon and Gordon Bower describe several characteristics of assertiveness, including the ability to express your feelings, to accept compliments graciously, to choose how you will act, to speak up for your rights when appropriate, to enhance your self-esteem, to develop self-confidence, to

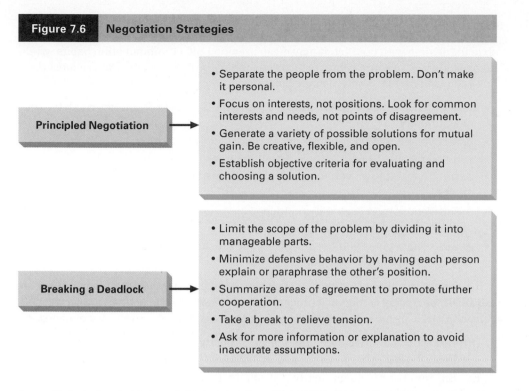

Figure 7.6   Negotiation Strategies

Principled Negotiation
- Separate the people from the problem. Don't make it personal.
- Focus on interests, not positions. Look for common interests and needs, not points of disagreement.
- Generate a variety of possible solutions for mutual gain. Be creative, flexible, and open.
- Establish objective criteria for evaluating and choosing a solution.

Breaking a Deadlock
- Limit the scope of the problem by dividing it into manageable parts.
- Minimize defensive behavior by having each person explain or paraphrase the other's position.
- Summarize areas of agreement to promote further cooperation.
- Take a break to relieve tension.
- Ask for more information or explanation to avoid inaccurate assumptions.

Source: Strategies for principled negotiation based on Roger Fisher, William Ury, and Bruce Patton, *Getting to Yes: Negotiating Agreement without Giving In* (Boston: Houghton Mifflin, 1991), p. 15. Strategies for breaking a deadlock based on Myra W. Isenhart and Michael Spangle, *Collaborative Approaches to Resolving Conflict* (Thousand Oaks, CA: Sage, 2000), p. 58.

disagree on important issues, to modify your own behavior, and to ask others to change their inappropriate or offensive behavior.[21]

Passivity and Aggression   Assertiveness is best understood in relation to three alternatives: passivity, aggression, and passive aggressiveness. **Passivity** involves giving in to others at the expense of your own needs or avoiding conflict and disagreement altogether. For example, Joe's boss asks him to work over the weekend. Joe agrees and says nothing about his plans to attend an important family event. Not surprisingly, passive individuals often feel taken advantage of by others and blame them for their unhappiness. As a result, they fail to take responsibility for their own actions and the consequences of those actions.[22]

The opposite of passive behavior is **aggression**, which puts personal needs first and often at the expense of someone else's needs. Aggressive communication includes demands for compliance and personal attacks on others. It is the technique used by bullies. Although in extreme instances aggressive behavior can be violent, usually it is more subtle. Raising your voice, rolling your eyes, or glaring at someone else can all signal aggressive behavior.[23]

Some individuals may seem passive while engaging in more covert forms of aggressive behavior. **Passive aggressiveness** only *appears* to accommodate another person's needs, but actually it is combined with more subtle aggressive behavior. It is also referred to as *hidden aggression.* For example, a passive–aggressive person might agree to give you a ride to the library but may pick you up so late that you have little time left to do research. Passive–aggressive individuals may also make you feel manipulated into agreeing with them. For example, when you refuse to do a favor for your brother, he mopes around the house until you finally give in to his request.

Assertiveness Skills   Aggressive, passive, and passive–aggressive behavior can be effective in the short term, but in the long term such behaviors usually result in poor personal and professional relationships. Assertiveness can be difficult to learn, particularly if you've always relied on an avoiding, accommodating, even compromising style for dealing with conflict. It may mean breaking old communication habits, while recognizing that in some contexts those styles may be appropriate. For the most part, however, assertiveness offers many benefits:

- Assertiveness allows you to interact with others with less conflict, anxiety, and resentment.
- Assertiveness allows you to be more relaxed around others, because you know you will be able to handle most situations reasonably well.
- Assertiveness allows you to retain your self-respect without trampling that of others.
- Assertiveness increases self-confidence by reducing the need for approval from others.
- Assertiveness gives you control over your life and reduces helplessness, defensiveness, and even depression.[24]

An effective strategy for becoming more assertive is to use what Bower and Bower call **DESC scripting**, a four-step process that addresses another person's objectionable behavior. DESC is an acronym for Describe, Express, Specify, and Consequences.[25]

D: **D**escribe the unwanted situation or offensive behavior. Use concrete terms. Describe the other person's action, not their perceived motive.

E: **E**xpress your feelings clearly and calmly. Direct your comments to the specific offending behavior, not to the whole person.

S: **S**pecify what you want to happen or the behaviors you want the other person to change. Take into account whether the other person can do what you request and what changes you're willing to make.

C: Clarify the **C**onsequences of accepting or denying your request. Focus on both positive and negative consequences. Ask yourself: What rewarding consequences can I provide?

The DESC script can be used in both personal and professional relationships. Consider the following examples:

I understand that the car is becoming unreliable. (Describe) However, I feel uncomfortable with the expense of a new car payment. (Express). We should instead look at used vehicles. (Specify) A new car payment could put us in real financial trouble. (Consequences).

Even though I explained the importance of arriving to work on time, you've repeatedly arrived late this past month. (Describe) I am disappointed. (Express) You must start arriving to work on time. (Specify) If you don't, I may demote or fire you. (Consequences)

Initially, assertive behavior may feel strange or uncomfortable because asserting your rights can open the door to conflict. Aggressive individuals may be frustrated if you no longer accommodate their every request. However, by being assertive, you may force passive–aggressives to deal with issues more honestly and openly. Practicing assertive behavior will ultimately improve your self-esteem, your ability to resolve conflicts, and the quality of your interpersonal relationships.

ANGER

Anger is a natural, human reaction. Everyone feels angry at times. In fact, in many instances, anger may be fully justified. If a friend lies to you, a coworker takes credit for your work, or an intimate partner betrays you, anger is a natural response. Thus, the issue is not whether you are angry, but how well you understand and manage your anger.

Anger is an emotional response to unmet expectations that ranges from minor irritation to intense rage. If, for example, you expect an A in a course but don't get it, you may become angry—at your teacher, at a friend who lured you away from studying, or at yourself. If you expect your best friend to be loyal and find out that he or she has been making fun of you behind your back, you may feel intense anger directed toward someone you've always liked. In her book, *Calming the Anger Storm*, Kathy Svitil lists a host of common anger triggers.[26] How many of these do you recognize? How many can you add?

- Unfair treatment
- Powerlessness
- Offense to personal morals and values
- Thoughtlessness or incompetence
- Cannot control something or someone
- Interfering with personal goals and plans
- Delays (traffic, long lines, slow service)
- Property damage or destruction

- Unmet expectations
- Stress and pressure
- Criticism
- Disrespectful treatment
- Harassment
- Fatigue
- Threats to self-esteem
- Irresponsibility of others

Anger Myths Just about everyone knows what anger is when they feel it. Many of us, however, have mistaken beliefs about anger that hinder our ability to deal with such feelings. The authors of *ACT on Life Not on Anger* present several myths that inhibit our ability to manage anger effectively. Here are three of them:

1. *Anger and aggression are human instincts.* There is no scientific evidence to support the belief that humans are innately aggressive. Rather, our survival depends on cooperation, not destructive conflict and aggression.[27]

2. *Anger is always helpful.* Anger can be beneficial when it warns you of danger and prepares your body for a fight-or-flight response. However, anger fueled by hostility to others (as opposed to anger that serves as a warning) is bad for your health, particularly for your heart.[28]

3. *Anger is caused by others.* When you're angry, you may say "She made me angry when she showed up late" or "The boss made me angry when he forgot to give me credit for writing the report." How you react to your angry thoughts and feelings is up to you. By blaming others for your anger, you don't have to change your own behavior in any way. As a result, you stay angry.[29]

Anger Management Effective anger management requires that you know how to communicate your angry feelings appropriately while treating others with respect. The following guidelines describe ways of expressing anger constructively[30]:

- *State your anger verbally.* Shouting may let others know you are angry, but *calmly* stating "I am very angry" will let them know how you feel and pave the way for resolving conflict constructively.

- *Acknowledge anger rather than venting it.* Although you have a right to your feelings and screaming at someone in anger may feel good, such behavior is often unfair and disrespectful to others. Exploding in rage rarely addresses the source of your anger.

- *Avoid expressing your anger as personal attacks.* Personal attacks only escalate a conflict. Use "I" statements ("I expected you to . . .") instead of "you" statements ("You messed up when you . . .").

- *Identify the source of your anger.* Help others understand why you are angry. "Because the report isn't finished, I'm now in a bind with my supervisor."

What are some of the ways in which you can communicate your angry feelings appropriately and constructively?

We can look at anger from two perspectives. Some people believe that anger is always destructive and should be suppressed. They also believe that expressing anger is not "nice" and that things will probably blow over if we don't make a big deal or become angry. Suppressing justified anger, however, can be counterproductive. Your anger may fester or build while recurring problems go unresolved. Psychotherapist Bill DeFoore compares suppressed anger with a pressure cooker. "We can only suppress or apply pressure against our anger for so long before it erupts. Periodic eruptions can cause all kinds of problems."[1]

At the other extreme, people believe that anger should be fully expressed, regardless of how intense or potentially damaging it is. They also believe that an angry outburst releases the tension and lets the person calm down. Psychologists maintain that venting anger to let off steam can be "worse than useful. Expressing anger does not reduce anger. Instead it functions to make you even angrier."[2] Moreover, people on the receiving end of angry outbursts usually get angry right back—which only makes the problem worse. If you decide to vent your anger by letting it out for everyone to see and hear, you have made a communication choice that has the potential for long-lasting, negative consequences. "Acting on anger is not inevitable, instinctual, or something you need to do."[3]

Both of these extreme views about anger can be counterproductive. Expressing anger inappropriately or not expressing it at all can damage interpersonal relationships and may even contribute to serious health problems such as heart disease and hypertension.[4]

[1]Bill DeFoore, *Anger: Deal with It, Heal with It, Stop It from Killing You* (Deerfield Beach, FL: Health Communications, 1991), p. viii.

[2]Georg H. Eifert, Matthew McKay, and John P. Forsyth, *ACT on Life Not on Anger* (Oakland, CA: New Harbinger, 2006), p. 19.

[3]Ibid.

[4]William R. Cupach and Daniel J. Canary, *Competencies in Interpersonal Conflict* (New York: McGraw-Hill, 1997), p. 78.

Although it is important to express anger appropriately, it is equally important to respond to another's anger constructively. The following guidelines and examples describe appropriate ways of reacting to someone else's anger[31]:

- *Acknowledge the other person's feelings of anger.* "I understand how angry you are."

- *Identify the issue or behavior that is the source of the anger.* "I don't believe I promised to work both your shifts next weekend, but you seem to think we made this agreement."

- *Assess the intensity of the anger and the importance of the issue.* "I know that it's important for you to find someone to cover your shifts so that you can attend your friend's wedding."

- *Encourage collaborative approaches to resolving the conflict.* "I can only cover one of your shifts this weekend. Why don't we work together to find someone else who will take the second shift?"

- *Make a positive statement about the relationship.* "I enjoy working with you and hope we can sort this out together."

How you express or respond to anger can escalate a conflict or redirect it in a positive way. Social psychologist Carol Tavris writes that anger "requires an awareness of choice and an embrace of reason. It is knowing when to become angry—'this is wrong, this I will protest'—and when to make peace; when to take action, and when to keep silent; knowing the likely cause of one's anger and not berating the blameless."[32]

ADAPTING TO DIFFERENCES

Conflict can be more complex and difficult to resolve when diverse cultures or genders clash. Ignoring cultural diversity and gender differences when attempting to resolve conflict in personal or professional relationships can make matters worse. Companies that fail to respect and adapt to differences are likely to have more strikes and lawsuits, lower morale among workers, less productivity, and higher employee turnover.[33]

Cultural Differences   Cultural values can significantly influence the degree to which individuals are comfortable with conflict and the way conflict is resolved. Chapter 3, "Understanding Others," explains that a culture can be characterized as either promoting individualism or valuing collectivism. Although individualistic cultures value independence and personal achievement, collectivistic cultures emphasize the needs of the group and stress cooperation.

Collectivist cultures also place a high value on "face." From a cultural perspective, **face** is the positive image that you wish to create or preserve. Thus, cultures that place a great deal of value on "saving face" discourage personal attacks and outcomes in which one person "loses." Figure 7.7 summarizes individualistic and collectivist perspectives about conflict.

Members of cultures that value conformity are less likely to express disagreement than those from cultures that place a higher value on individualism. Japanese, German, Mexican, and Brazilian cultures value conformity, whereas Swedish and French cultures are generally more comfortable expressing differences.[34] Cultural differences may be regional rather than international. For example, Franco-Canadians are often more cooperative during negotiation than Anglo-Canadians, who are slower to agree to a resolution.[35]

Culture also may dictate who should argue. Many cultures give enormous respect to their elders. In these cultures, a young person arguing with an older adult is viewed as disrespectful. Among several Native American and African cultures, the elderly are considered wiser and more knowledgeable, and young people are expected to accept the views of elders rather than challenging or rebelling against them.

Gender Differences   According to sociolinguist Deborah Tannen, men and women approach argument differently.[36] In general, men tend to be competitive arguers, whereas women are more likely to seek consensus. Men tend to view issues as only

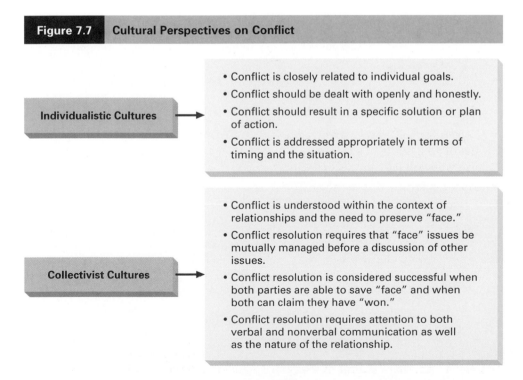

| **Figure 7.7** | **Cultural Perspectives on Conflict** |

Individualistic Cultures →
- Conflict is closely related to individual goals.
- Conflict should be dealt with openly and honestly.
- Conflict should result in a specific solution or plan of action.
- Conflict is addressed appropriately in terms of timing and the situation.

Collectivist Cultures →
- Conflict is understood within the context of relationships and the need to preserve "face."
- Conflict resolution requires that "face" issues be mutually managed before a discussion of other issues.
- Conflict resolution is considered successful when both parties are able to save "face" and when both can claim they have "won."
- Conflict resolution requires attention to both verbal and nonverbal communication as well as the nature of the relationship.

Source: William R. Cupach and Daniel J. Canary, *Competencies in Interpersonal Conflict* (New York: McGraw-Hill, 1997), p. 133.

two sided: for or against, right or wrong. Women are more likely to search out many perspectives on a subject. In general, men tend to use a competitive style whereas women are more likely to compromise or avoid conflict altogether.[37] On the other hand, research aimed at predicting divorce has found that unhappy marriages are often characterized by wives who feel comfortable engaging in conflict and husbands who withdraw from conflict.[38]

Gender differences in conflict styles, however, are generalizations. Overall, men and women are more similar in how they approach conflict than they are different. Both can and do use all five conflict resolution styles. In most instances, the context of the communication and the nature and history of the relationship will be as influential in conflict resolution as any gender differences.

What Is Your Personality Type?

Directions: Read the pairs of descriptions for each personality type. For example, the first pair is "I am outgoing, sociable, and expressive" *and* "I am reserved and private." For each pair, put a check mark next to the *one* phrase that *best* describe you.

When you have completed each set of personality types, add up the check marks and note the personality type with the most check marks—extrovert or introvert, sensing or intuition, thinking or feeling, judging or perceiving. Answer as you really are, not as you wish you were or wish you could be in the future.

1. Are you an extrovert or an introvert?

    ___ I am outgoing, sociable, and expressive.   ___ I am reserved and private.

    ___ I enjoy groups and discussions.   ___ I prefer one-to-one interactions.

    ___ I often talk first, think later.   ___ I usually think first, then talk.

    ___ I can do many things at once.   ___ I focus on one thing at a time.

    ___ I think out loud.   ___ I think to myself.

    ___ Other people give me energy.   ___ Other people often exhaust me.

    _____ **Total** (Extrovert)   _____ **Total** (Introvert)

2. Are you a sensor or an intuitive?

    ___ I focus on details.   ___ I focus on the big picture.

    ___ I am practical and realistic.   ___ I am theoretical.

    ___ I like concrete information.   ___ I like abstract information.

    ___ I like facts.   ___ I get bored with facts and details.

    ___ I trust experience.   ___ I trust inspiration and intuition.

    ___ I value common sense.   ___ I value creativity and innovation.

    ___ I want clear, realistic goals.   ___ I want to pursue a vision.

    _____ **Total** (Sensor)   _____ **Total** (Intuitive)

3. Are you a thinker or a feeler?

    ___ I am task oriented.   ___ I am people oriented.

    ___ I am objective, firm, analytical.   ___ I am subjective, humane, appreciative.

    ___ I enjoy arguing.   ___ I think arguing is disruptive.

    ___ I prefer businesslike meetings.   ___ I prefer social interchange in meetings.

    ___ I value competence, reason, justice.   ___ I value relationships and harmony.

    ___ I am direct and firm-minded.   ___ I am tactful and tenderhearted.

    ___ I think with my head.   ___ I think with my heart.

    _____ **Total** (Thinker)   _____ **Total** (Feeler)

4. Are you a judger or a perceiver?

    ___ I value organization and structure.   ___ I value flexibility and spontaneity.

    ___ I am in control and definite.   ___ I go with the flow.

    ___ I like having deadlines.   ___ I dislike deadlines.

    ___ I will work now, play later.   ___ I will play now, work later.

    ___ I like standards and expectations.   ___ I feel constrained by rules.

    ___ I adjust my schedule to complete work.   ___ I do work at the last minute.

    ___ I plan ahead.   ___ I adapt as I go.

    _____ **Total** (Judger)   _____ **Total** (Perceiver)

Summarize your decisions by indicating the letter that best describes your personality traits and preferences:

_____   _____   _____   _____

  E or I   S or N   T or F   J or P

Think about your personal characteristics and preferences *based on your four-letter personality type* and answer the following questions:

1. Name two of the personality traits you value most. (Example: I am tactful and tenderhearted.)

    • _____

    • _____

2. Name two ways in which others see you in most situations. (Example: Others see me as very task oriented.)

    • _____

    • _____

3. Name two ways in which you can improve your effectiveness as a communicator in light of your personality traits and preferences. (Example: I need to put more focus on meeting deadlines so I don't annoy or frustrate others so much.)

    • _____

    • _____

Note: The Myers-Briggs Type Indicator is for licensed use only by qualified professionals whose qualifications are on file and have been accepted by Consulting Psychologists Press, Inc. This Communication Challenge is only a quick self-test and is not a licensed instrument.

Communication Assessment

Ross-DeWine Conflict Management Message Style Instrument

Directions: The following statements represent eighteen messages made by people in conflict situations. Consider each message separately and decide how closely it resembles those that you have used in conflict settings, even if the language may not be exactly the same as yours. There are no right or wrong answers, nor are these messages designed to trick you. Answer in terms of responses you make, not what you think you should say. Give each message a 1- to 5-point rating according to the following scale. Mark one answer only.

1	2	3	4	5
Never say things like this	Rarely say things like this	Sometimes say things like this	Often say things like this	Usually say things like this

_____ 1. "Can't you see how foolish you're being with that thinking?"

_____ 2. "How can I make you feel happy again?"

_____ 3. "I'm really bothered by some things that are happening here; can we talk about them?"

_____ 4. "I really don't have any more to say on this . . . [silence]."

_____ 5. "What possible solutions can we come up with?"

_____ 6. "I'm really sorry that your feelings are hurt. Maybe you're right."

_____ 7. "Let's talk this thing out and see how we can deal with this hassle."

_____ 8. "Shut up! You are wrong! I don't want to hear anymore of what you have to say."

_____ 9. "It is your fault if I fail at this, and don't you ever expect any help from me when you're on the spot."

_____ 10. "You can't do (say) that to me. It's either my way or forget it."

_____ 11. "Let's try finding an answer that will give us both some of what we want."

_____ 12. "This is something we have to work out; we're always arguing about it."

_____ 13. "Whatever makes you feel happiest is okay by me."

_____ 14. "Let's just leave well enough alone."

_____ 15. "That's okay . . . it wasn't important anyway. . . . Are you feeling okay now?"

_____ 16. "If you're not going to cooperate, I'll just go to someone who will."

_____ 17. "I think we need to try to understand the problem."

_____ 18. "You might as well accept my decision; you can't do anything about it anyway."

Scoring: Use the following grid to determine your score. Next to each item, list the rating (from 1–5) you gave to that item. When you have entered all ratings, total the ratings for each column and divide by six. Enter the resulting score in the space provided.

Self Items	Issue Items	Other Items
1. _____	3. _____	2. _____
8. _____	5. _____	4. _____
9. _____	7. _____	6. _____
10. _____	11. _____	13. _____
16. _____	12. _____	14. _____
18. _____	17. _____	15. _____
Total = _____	Total = _____	Total = _____
Score = _____ (Total ÷ by 6)	Score = _____ (Total ÷ by 6)	Score = _____ (Total ÷ by 6)
Average score = 13.17 pt	Average score = 24.26 pt	Average score = 21.00 pt

Most of us have a predominant style (self, issue, other) that influences the kinds of messages we send during conflict situations. The following section describes each style:

- _Self._ These messages suggest that your primary concern in resolving conflict is that your personal view is accepted by others. This is an "I win" approach to conflict resolution.
- _Issue._ These messages emphasize an overriding concern about content issues rather than the personal relationship. This is a "Let's do what's best regardless of how we feel" approach to conflict resolution.
- _Other._ These messages emphasize maintaining the relationship even at a cost of resolving the conflict. This is a "Let's stay friends even if it means we can't resolve this problem" approach to conflict resolution.

Sources: Roseanna G. Ross and Sue DeWine, _Management Communication Quarterly_, 2 1988; vol. 1: pp. 389–413, copyright 2007 by Sage Publications, Inc. Reprinted by Permission of Sage Publications, Inc.

Key Terms

abdicrat
accommodating conflict style
A-E-I-O-U Model
affection
aggression
anger
argumentativeness
assertiveness
autocrat
avoidance conflict style
closed-ended question
collaborative conflict style
common ground
competitive conflict style
compromising conflict style
conflict
constructive conflict
control
conversation
conversational dilemma
democratic person

DESC scripting
destructive conflict
dialogue
exemplification
extrovert
face
feeler
Fundamental Interpersonal Relationship
    Orientation (FIRO) Theory
iceberg statement
ideal personal type
ideal social person
impersonal relationship
impression management
inclusion
ingratiation
interpersonal communication
intimidation
introvert
intuitive
judger

monologue
Myers-Briggs Type Indicator
negotiation
open-ended question
overpersonal type
oversocial person
passive aggressiveness
passivity
perceiver
personal relationship
primacy effect
professional relationship
recency effect
self-promotion
sensor
supplication
thinker
turn-requesting cue
turn-yielding cue
underpersonal type
undersocial person

Notes

1. William Schutz, *The Human Element: Productivity, Self-Esteem, and the Bottom Line* (San Francisco: Jossey-Bass, 1994).

2. This section is based on material in Isa Engleberg and Dianna Wynn, *Working in Groups: Communication Principles and Strategies*, 4th ed. (Boston: Houghton Mifflin, 2007), pp. 38–41.

3. In his more recent works, Schutz refers to this need as *openness*. However, we find that students understand this concept better when we use Schutz's original term—*affection*.

4. Isabel B. Myers with Peter B. Myers, *Gifts Differing: Tenth Anniversary Edition* (Palo Alto, CA: Consulting Psychologists, 1990).

5. Annie Murphy Paul, *The Cult of Personality* (New York: Free Press, 2004), pp. 125–127.

6. Exercise caution in accepting and applying psychological theories as "laws" of interpersonal communication. They are other theories that try to explain human behavior and communication decisions. "Most people's personalities, psychologists note, do not fall neatly into one category or another, but occupy some intermediate zone. . . . [Nor are these traits necessarily] inborn or immutable types." Annie Murphy Paul, *The Cult of Personality* (New York: Free Press, 2004), pp. 125–127.

7. Robert E. Levasseur, *Breakthrough Business Meetings: Shared Leadership*

in Action. (Holbrook, MA: Bob Adams, 1994), p. 79.

8. Carl E. Larson and Frank M.J. LaFasto, *TeamWork: What Must Go Right/What Can Go Wrong* (Newbury Park, CA: Sage, 1989), p. 63.

9. Otto Kroeger and Janet M. Thuesen, *Type Talk: Or How to Determine Your Personality Type and Change Your Life* (New York: Delacorte, 1988), p. 80.

10. Don Gabor, *How to Start a Conversation and Make Friends* (New York: Simon and Schuster, 2001), p. 42.

11. Maria J. O'Leary and Cynthia Gallois, "The Last Ten Turns in Conversations between Friends and Strangers," in *The Nonverbal Communication Reader: Classic and Contemporary Readings*, 2nd ed., ed. Laura K. Guerrero, Joseph A. DeVito, and Michael L. Hecht (Prospect Heights, IL: Waveland Press, 1999), pp. 415–421.

12. Erving Goffman, *The Presentation of Self in Everyday Life* (New York: Doubleday, 1959).

13. Sharon S. Brehm, Saul Kassin, and Steven Fein, *Social Psychology*, 6th ed. (Boston: Houghton Mifflin, 2005), p. 86.

14. Sandra Metts and Erica Grohskopf, "Impression Management: Goals, Strategies, and Skills," in *Handbook of Communication and Social Interaction Skills*, ed. John O. Greene and Brant Burleson (Mahwah, NJ: Lawrence Erlbaum, 2003), pp. 358–359. We have

added the parenthetical cautions to Metts and Grohskopf's list of strategies.

15. Isa N. Engleberg and Dianna R. Wynn, *Working in Groups: Communication Principles and Strategies*, 4th ed. (Boston: Houghton Mifflin, 2007), pp. 176–177.

16. Ronald T. Potter-Efron, *Work Rage: Preventing Anger and Resolving Conflict on the Job* (New York: Barnes and Noble Books, 2000), pp. 22–23.

17. Kenneth Cloke and Joan Goldsmith, *Resolving Conflicts at Work: A Complete Guide for Everyone on the Job* (San Francisco: Jossey-Bass, 2000), p. 23.

18. See Kenneth W. Thomas and Ralph W. Kilmann, "Developing a Forced-Choice Measure of Conflict-Handling Behavior: The MODE Instrument," *Educational Psychological Measurement* 37 (1977), pp. 390–395; William W. Wilmot and Joyce L. Hocker, *Interpersonal Conflict*, 5th ed. (Boston: McGraw-Hill, 1998), pp. 111–141.

19. Jerry Wisinski, *Resolving Conflicts on the Job* (New York: American Management Association, 1993), pp. 27–31.

20. Roger Fisher, William Ury, and Bruce Patton, *Getting to Yes: Negotiating Agreement without Giving In* (Boston: Houghton Mifflin, 1991), p. 15.

21. Sharon Anthony Bower and Gordon H. Bower, *Asserting Yourself: A Practical Guide to Positive Change* (Cambridge, MA: Perseus Books, 1991) pp. 4–5.

22. Ibid., p. 9.

23. Madelyn Burley-Allen, *Managing Assertively: How to Improve Your People Skills* (New York: John Wiley, 1983), p. 45.

24. Based on Randy J. Paterson, *The Assertiveness Workbook* (Oakland, CA: New Harbinger Publications, 2000), p. 20.

25. Bower and Bower, p. 90. See also Augsburg College Academic Skill Center, www.augsburg.edu/acskills/Being%20Assertive.rtf.

26. Kathy A. Svitil, *Calming the Anger Storm* (New York: Alpha, 2005), pp. 14–15.

27. Georg H. Eifert, Matthew McKay, and John P. Forsyth, *ACT on Life Not on Anger* (Oakland, CA: New Harbinger, 2006), pp. 15, 16.

28. Ibid., pp. 19, 20.

29. Ibid., p. 21.

30. Wilmot and Hocker, p. 221.

31. Ibid., p. 222.

32. Carol Tavris, *Anger: The Misunderstood Emotion* (New York: Simon and Schuster, 1982), p. 253.

33. Bren Ortega Murphy, "Promoting Dialogue in Culturally Diverse Workplace Environments," in *Innovation in Group Facilitation: Applications in Natural Settings*, ed. Larry R. Frey (Creskill, NJ: Hampton, 1995), pp. 77–93.

34. Russell Copranzano, Herman Aguinis, Marshall Schminke, and Dina L. Denham, "Disputant Reactions to Managerial Conflict Resolution Tactics: A Comparison among Argentina, the Dominican Republic, Mexico, and the United States" *Group and Organization Management* 24 (1999), p. 131.

35. Laura E. Drake, "The Culture–Negotiation Link: Integrative and Distributive Bargaining through an Intercultural Communication Lens," *Human Communication Research* 27 (2001), p. 321.

36. Deborah Tannen, *You Just Don't Understand: Women and Men in Conversation* (New York: William Morrow, 1990).

37. Wilmot and Hocker, p. 25.

38. Ibid., p. 26.

Interpersonal Communication: Improving Personal Relationships

Key Elements of Communication	Communication Axioms	Guiding Principles of Communication in Personal Relationships
Self	*Communication Is Personal*	Recognize the value of appropriate self-disclosure, receptivity to feedback, and emotional intelligence.
Others	*Communication Is Relational*	Understand, respect, and adapt to the personal and emotional needs of others, and respect privacy boundaries.
Purpose	*Communication Is Intentional*	Monitor and effectively negotiate dialectic tensions with friends, romantic partners, and family members.
Context	*Communication Is Contextual*	Adapt to the breadth and depth of personal relationships and to diverse communication climates.
Content	*Communication Is Symbolic*	Use self-disclosure appropriately. Focus on the present with descriptions rather than judgments.
Structure	*Communication Is Structured*	Select appropriate communication strategies for building, strengthening, or ending personal relationships.
Expression	*Communication Is Irreversible*	Express your emotions clearly, appropriately, and ethically. Use verbal and nonverbal communication strategies to listen and respond effectively.

The Nature of Personal Relationships

Your ability to communicate effectively in personal relationships influences your psychological and physical health, your personal identity and happiness, your social and moral development, your ability to cope with stress and misfortunes, and the quality and meaning of your life.[1] Medical researchers have found "a link between relationships and physical health. . . . People with rich personal networks—who are married, have close family and friends, are active in social and religious groups—recover more quickly from disease and live longer."[2]

Equally important, interpersonal effectiveness profoundly affects the quality, depth, and stability of your friendships, intimate relationships, and family life. Meaningful and lasting personal relationships do not just happen. *You* make them happen. And that depends, in large part, on how well you communicate. In this chapter we examine the complex and contradictory nature of personal relationships as well as strategies for strengthening and sustaining the personal relationships you value.

RELATIONAL DIALECTICS

Leslie Baxter and Barbara Montgomery's Relational Dialectics Theory claims that personal relationships are characterized by dialectics.[3] The word *dialectics* refers to the interplay of opposing or contradictory forces.[4] Thus, **Relational Dialectics Theory** focuses on the ongoing tensions between contradictory impulses in personal relationships. The following pairs of common folk sayings illustrate several contradictory beliefs about personal relationships:

"Opposites attract" *but* "Birds of a feather flock together."

"Out of sight, out of mind" *but* "Absence makes the heart grow fonder."

"Two's company; three's a crowd" *but* "The more, the merrier."[5]

"To know him is to love him" *but* "Familiarity breeds contempt."[6]

In addition to physical closeness, how can two people in a romantic relationship seek intimacy and grant each other the time they need to be apart—even in as romantic a city as Paris?

Rather than trying to prove that one of these contradictory proverbs is truer than the other—an "either/or" response—relational dialectics takes a "both/and" approach. For example, two people in a romantic relationship seek togetherness, but they also need time to be alone—time to think about personal needs, to escape the daily routine, and to engage in personal interests not shared by the other person. In many close relationships you want *both* intimacy *and* independence. You want *both* the comfort of a stable relationship *and* the excitement of change. You can appreciate these dialectic tensions in the way a student wrote about her three-month romantic relationship: "Every relationship is a meeting of two people and however hard you try, you're not gonna form one sort of unified whole; you need the unity but there also has to be individuality for a relationship to be really close."[7] Leslie Baxter identifies three major dialectics in personal relationships: integration versus separation, stability versus change, and expression versus privacy.[8]

Integration versus Separation   Interpersonal relationships survive when we successfully negotiate the **integration–separation dialectic**: our desire for *both* connection *and* in-

Relational dialectic theory suggests that a couple's private names for one another illustrates the presence of both connection and independence in relationships. For example, pet names and nicknames often highlight a unique personal trait (as in Big Guy, Champ, or Sweetness). Because distant friends do not have "permission" to use pet names, they also indicate a relational closeness.[1]

In her Pulitzer Prize–winning novel, *The Namesake*, Jhumpa Lahiri describes the two kinds of names given to Indian children—one private, one public. The private (pet) name, or *daknam*, is used by friends, family, and other intimates at home and in other private, unguarded moments. Every pet name is paired with a "good" name, a *bhalonam*, for the outside world. Good names appear on envelopes, on diplomas, in telephone directories, and in all other public places. They tend to represent dignified and enlightened qualities. Pet names have no such aspirations; they are private terms of affection known by a relatively close circle of friends and family members.[2]

[1]Leslie A. Baxter and Barbara M. Montgomery, *Relating: Dialogues and Dialectics* (New York: The Guilford Press, 1996), p. 170.

[2]Jhumpa Lahiri, *The Namesake* (Boston: Houghton Mifflin, 2003), pp. 25–26.

dependence. As you grow up, you may want to remain closely connected to your parents *and* live an independent life free from parental intrusion. Or you may want to apply for a promotion that will take you out of town on many business trips, but your spouse wants you to spend more time with the family. In both of these cases, you must address the tension of wanting togetherness as well as independence. As much as you want to be close to others, you also need to be your separate self.

Stability versus Change   Most of us like the security of a stable relationship *and* the novelty and excitement of change, the predictability of day-after-day interactions *and* an occasional change in routine. To achieve this *both/and* result, we negotiate the **stability–change dialectic**. For example, an engaged couple might decide to follow several wedding traditions—formal invitations, a wedding reception, flowers and traditional wedding music, and even the bride in white—but also decide to hold the wedding in a riding stable with the bride, groom, and presiding official on horseback.[9]

Expression versus Privacy   The **expression–privacy dialectic** focuses on your conflicting desire to reveal personal information openly and honestly to another person and also to protect your privacy. In other words, this dialectic addresses your conflicting urges to tell your secrets and to keep them hidden.[10]

Do your best friends, romantic partner, and closest family members know every secret you have? Should they? Later in this chapter we discuss the expression–privacy dialectic in more detail. The question at the heart of this dialect is: How do I maintain a reasonable balance between my need for privacy and the benefits of self-disclosure?

RELATIONAL DIALECTICS

▶ Integration versus Separation
▶ Stability versus Change
▶ Expression versus Privacy

MANAGING INTERPERSONAL DIALECTICS

Although Relational Dialectics Theory does not offer foolproof guidelines for improving interpersonal communication, it does help explain your experiences in ongoing personal relationships. Relational dialectics offers a strong justification for seeking the "both/and" focus when you communicate with others. Figure 8.1 presents six strategies for negotiating dialectic tensions in close personal relationships.[11]

Figure 8.1	Managing Dialectics	
STRATEGY	DESCRIPTION	EXAMPLE
Cyclical Alteration	We choose different options at different points in our lives.	We are close to siblings when we're young, but less close when we're married and/or raising a family.
Segmentation	We choose different options for different psychosocial contexts.	We are less connected and open when we interact with a close friend in a work environment.
Selection	We choose one aspect of the dialectic and ignore the other.	We decide that being close to our family is more important than socializing with lots of nonfamily friends.
Neutralizing	We compromise between opposite options.	We invite relatives to travel with us to a vacation destination rather than only visiting with them in their home.
Reframing	We change our view of the opposite option so it no longer *appears* opposite.	We decide we can only be close if we put a little time and distance between us.
Disqualifying	We do not talk about certain topics in order to avoid dialectic tension.	We decide to be totally open about all topics except sex, finances, and certain personal habits.

Sharing Self

Being willing to share your self with others is essential for developing and improving any significant relationship. Whether you are talking about your favorite movies with a new acquaintance or revealing your deepest fears to a loved one, both of you must be willing and able to share personal information with one another.

Self-disclosure is the process of sharing personal information, opinions, and emotions with others that would not normally be known to them. We are *not*, however, suggesting that you reveal the most intimate details of your life to everyone you meet. Rather, you must judge whether and when sharing is appropriate by understanding and adapting to the other person's attitudes, beliefs, values, and feelings.[12]

Determining what, where, when, how, and with whom to self-disclose may be one of the most difficult communication decisions you face in a personal relationship. Fortunately, three theories and models can help you make this decision wisely: Social Penetration Theory, Communication Privacy Management Theory, and the Johari Window Model.

SELF-DISCLOSURE THEORIES AND MODELS

▶ Social Penetration Theory
▶ Communication Privacy Management Theory
▶ The Johari Window Model

SOCIAL PENETRATION THEORY

Two psychologists, Irwin Altman and Dalmas Taylor, offer Social Penetration Theory as a way of understanding the connections between self-disclosure and interpersonal closeness. **Social Penetration Theory** describes the process of relationship bonding in which individuals move from superficial communication to deeper, more intimate communication.[13]

Altman and Taylor use the metaphor of an onion to illustrate their theory. They explain that the process of developing an intimate relationship is similar to peeling an onion. The outer skin of the onion represents superficial information about yourself. The inner layers—those closest to the core—represent intimate information. Figure 8.2 illustrates the components of the social penetration process.

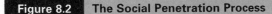

| Figure 8.2 | The Social Penetration Process |

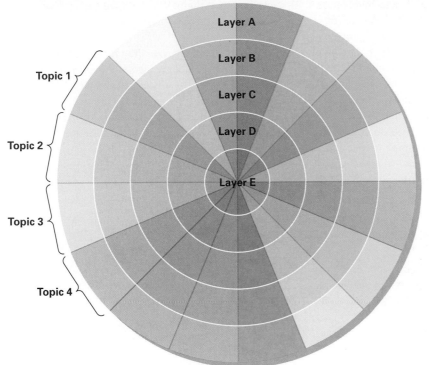

EXAMPLES OF LAYERS

Layer A: Most impersonal layer
(music, clothing, food preferences)

Layer B: Impersonal layer
(job, politics, education)

Layer C: Middle layer
(religious beliefs, social attitudes)

Layer D: Personal layer
(personal goals, fears, hopes, secrets)

Layer E: Most personal layer
(inner core, self-concept)

EXAMPLES OF TOPICS

Topic 1: Leisure activities

Topic 2: Career

Topic 3: Family

Topic 4: Health

Social Penetration Theory explains that self-disclosure has three interconnected dimensions: depth, breadth, and frequency.[14] Thus, relationships are closest when communication is

- *deep* (intimate and near the core of the "onion"). For example, there's a big difference between telling someone "I like you" and telling someone "I love you."

- *broad* (covers many topic areas—some very personal, some impersonal). For example, in addition to sharing information about your hobbies or job, you may also share your strong beliefs about family responsibilities and religion.

- *frequent* (increases as both depth and breadth in a relationship develop). For example, blurting out a personal secret or pent-up feeling may seem odd if it's not part of an ongoing pattern of self-disclosure.

The animated film *Shrek* captures the underlying premise of Social Penetration Theory. As Shrek, a large, lumbering, green ogre, and his hyperactive companion, Donkey, trek through fields and forests, Shrek tries to explain himself to Donkey:

Shrek: For your information, there's a lot more to ogres than people think.

Donkey: Example?

Shrek: Example? Okay. Um. Ogres are like onions.

Donkey: They stink?

Shrek: No.

Donkey: Oh, they make you cry?

Shrek: No.

Donkey: Oh, you leave them out in the sun and they get all brown and start sprouting little white hairs?

Shrek: No! Layers. Onions have layers. Ogres have layers. You get it? We both have layers![15]

The theories, models, strategies, and skills involved in the self-disclosure process are closely linked to intimacy. However, self-disclosure is not the same as intimacy. **Intimacy** is the feeling or state of knowing someone deeply in physical, psychological, emotional, and/or collaborative ways because that person is significant in your life. Disclosure, on the other hand, refers to the process of sharing private information and feelings with others. You do not have to be or want to be intimate with someone to disclose personal information.[1] At the same time, what, where, when, and how you disclose private information is critical to determining your level of intimacy with another person.[2] Intimacy can occur in many forms:

- *Physical Intimacy.* In most romantic relationships, physical intimacy is an expectation and a means for communicating affection, love, and passion. An infant, however, also benefits from the physical intimacy of being hugged, kissed, fed, cleaned, and held by family members and caregivers.
- *Emotional Intimacy.* We usually share our most private thoughts and feelings with intimates because we love and trust them. We also give and receive emotional support from others when a personal tragedy or crisis occurs.
- *Intellectual Intimacy.* We often feel an intellectual connection to people whose attitudes, experiences, interests, and artistic tastes are similar to our own. You may experience intellectual intimacy during an energizing conversation, an absorbing discussion about a controversial issue, or a moment of shared appreciation for a passage of music.
- *Collaborative Intimacy.* When people join forces to achieve a common goal, they may develop an intimacy that comes from productive collaboration. Successful sports teams, research teams, and work teams may develop a physical and emotional closeness. The members of a military combat unit often develop lifelong loyalties based on shared experiences.

[1]Sandra Petronio, *Boundaries of Privacy: Dialectics of Disclosure* (Albany: State University of New York Press, 2003), pp. 5–6.
[2]Ibid., p. 143.

As mentioned, Social Penetration Theory contends that people are like onions, with concentric layers. The thin outer layer is your public image. Relationships develop systematically and predictably by progressing from this outer layer (nonintimate information) to inner layers (more intimate information). As two people get to know one another better, they reveal information, feelings, and experiences below the public image layer. Relationships develop when this process is reciprocal—that is, when one person's openness leads to another's openness, and so on.

COMMUNICATION PRIVACY MANAGEMENT THEORY

Sandra Petronio's **Communication Privacy Management Theory** uses the metaphor of *boundaries* to describe the disclosure process.[16] Although we may share private information with another person, we also establish boundaries or borders that we do not want others to cross. We regulate the openness or closeness of these boundaries to bring some people closer to us and to keep others at a distance. Petronio describes this process as a "mental calculus" that helps us "decide whether to tell or keep information private."[17]

Depending on your privacy needs, your feelings about another person, and the context in which you are communicating, you may build solid, thick boundaries that no one can penetrate. Or, you may open portions of these boundaries to develop a close personal relationship with someone. Figure 8.3 represents how two people can form a collective boundary in which they share private information with one another.[18]

Even though you may be clear about where *your* personal boundaries begin and end, you may not be so clear about *other* people's boundaries. Other people may have very different boundaries and hold different values about privacy than you do. **Boundary turbulence** arises when two people cannot jointly develop and follow compatible rules about the boundaries of self-disclosure, either because they do not

Figure 8.3   **Personal and Collective Boundaries**

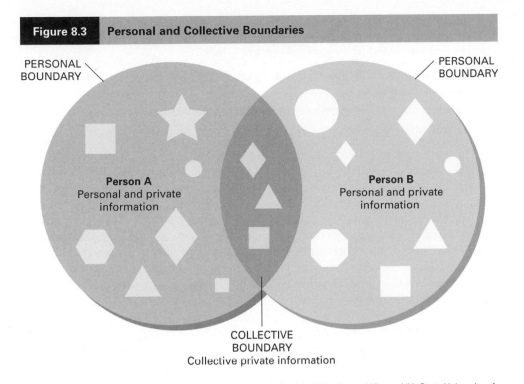

PERSONAL
BOUNDARY

PERSONAL
BOUNDARY

Person A
Personal and private
information

Person B
Personal and private
information

COLLECTIVE
BOUNDARY
Collective private information

Source: Based on Sandra Petronio, *Boundaries of Privacy: Dialectics of Disclosure* (Albany, NY: State University of New York Press, 2000), p. 7.

understand each other's boundaries or because they are well aware of the boundaries but do not respect them. For example, if a close friend shares your most private secrets with a third person you barely know, you may feel betrayed, embarrassed, and enraged.

When boundary turbulence occurs, we become much more aware of our privacy rules. Betrayal, spying, gossip, and violating confidences can damage or end a relationship. However, when two people deeply care about each other and want to maintain a close relationship, honest self-disclosure and frequent discussions about a distressing situation or incident can become the foundation for restoring order and strengthening the relationship.[19]

THE JOHARI WINDOW MODEL

Psychologists Joseph Luft and Harrington Ingham provide a model for understanding how the connections between self-disclosure and feedback can produce greater self-awareness.[20] They use the metaphor of a window and, by combining their first names (Joe and Harry), call their model the **Johari Window**. Everything about your self—your needs, preferences, experiences, interests, likes, and dislikes—is contained within Joe and Harry's window.

The Johari Window looks at two interpersonal dimensions: willingness to self-disclose and receptivity to feedback. **Willingness to self-disclose** describes the extent to which you are prepared to disclose personal information and feelings:

- Are you willing to share your thoughts and opinions regarding both public and personal topics with others?

- Are you willing to describe your past experiences and future ambitions?

- Are you willing to express your most personal feelings to others—from love to disgust or joy to jealousy?

Although self-disclosure may be risky, it also improves your chances of strengthening a relationship.

Receptivity to feedback describes your awareness, interpretation, and response to someone else's self-disclosure about you. If you are receptive to feedback, you are open to and interested in how others react to you:

- Do you effectively listen to, accurately interpret, and appropriately respond to feedback from others?
- Do you accept and respect or avoid and reject constructive criticism?
- Do you adjust your behavior appropriately based on feedback from others?

As we noted in Chapter 2, "Understanding Self," people who are high self-monitors constantly observe other people and especially how they react during an interaction. Not surprisingly, effective self-monitors accurately interpret, learn from, and appropriately respond to feedback about themselves.

To develop and build close personal relationships, you should express a willingness to be open *with* other people (appropriately self-disclosing to them) and open *to* others (accurately interpreting their disclosures about you in an accepting way).[21] When these two dimensions are graphed against one another, the result is a figure that resembles a four-paned window (Figure 8.4). Each pane means something different, and each pane can vary in size.

Four Different Panes   Each pane in your Johari Window reflects something about you and your level of self-awareness. The panes also reveal a great deal about the nature of your relationship with others.

- *Open Area.* This pane contains information you are willing to share with others as well as information you have learned about yourself by accurately interpreting feedback from others. For example, suppose you wonder whether it's okay to tell an embarrassing but funny personal story to a group of new colleagues.

Figure 8.4	The Johari Window Model

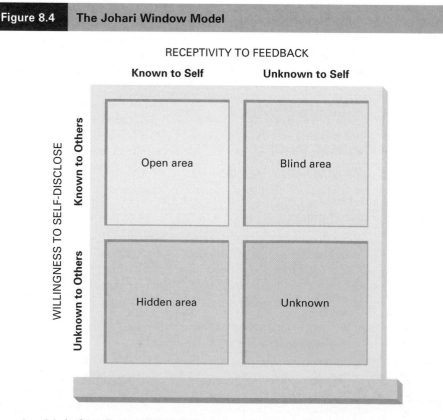

Source: Joseph Luft, *Group Process: An Introduction to Group Dynamics,* 3rd ed. (Palo Alto, CA: Mayfield, 1984).

You decide to take the risk. If your listeners laugh and seem to appreciate your sense of humor, you've learned two things: It's safe to tell jokes and you are, in fact, funny.

- *Hidden Area.* This area represents your private self, which includes information you know about yourself ("I am attracted to you," "I was once arrested") but that you are not willing to share with others. The hidden area contains your secrets. Some people retain a lot of personal information in their hidden area that could improve their relationships and likeability if it were shared.

- *Blind Area.* The blind area contains information others know about you but that *you* do not know about yourself because you don't correctly interpret feedback from others. We sometimes call this pane *the bad breath area.* If you don't notice that people are pulling back when you speak to them directly, you may not understand that they are reacting to the garlic-rich salad you had for lunch. The problem is much more serious when you don't notice that someone disapproves of your behaviors or wants your praise for a job well done.

- *Unknown Area.* This pane contains information unknown to both you and others. For example, suppose you avoid doing any writing at work because you don't consider yourself a good writer. And yet, when working with a group of colleagues on an interesting project, you end up doing most of the writing. As time passes, you and your coworkers recognize and appreciate your writing talent. This "discovery" about yourself now moves from your unknown area to your open area. Certainly at the beginning of a relationship, there is a lot of unknown information. As you get to know yourself and others better—and vice versa—this pane decreases in size.

Varying Size of Panes Depending on how willing you are to self-disclose and how receptive you are to feedback, each pane of the Johari Window will differ in size. Although this makes a very unusual-looking window, it does a good job of reflecting your level of self-awareness. As a relationship develops, you disclose more, enlarging your open area and reducing your hidden area. As you become more receptive to feedback, you reduce your blind area and enlarge your open area.[22] And as your open area expands, your unknown area gets smaller. Figure 8.5 displays four windows, each of which has a different meaning for your personal relationships.

Window A illustrates a large open area. This window is the most "open" and reflects trust, honesty, and sensitivity in a relationship. It means that the person is very willing to self-disclose and very sensitive to feedback. However, in every relationship there are elements that are blind, hidden, and unknown. Even in the closest relationship, we need privacy, time-out from others, and hope for new and exciting developments.

Window B illustrates a relationship in which the blind area is the largest. We often call this kind of relationship *the bull-in-the-china-shop window.* Someone with a large blind area is not aware of others' reactions and, as a result, may hurt another person's feelings without being aware of it.

Window C illustrates a relationship in which someone is very receptive to feedback from others (thus, a small blind area) but unwilling to disclose personal information or feelings. Helping professionals such as ministers, psychologists, counselors, and teachers may reflect this Johari Window because they often avoid sharing a great deal of personal information. In a close relationship, however, a large hidden area denies a great deal of the "real you" to someone else.

Window D depicts someone who is unwilling to self-disclose and is not receptive to feedback. Two things could be happening. The relationship may be new—it's not appropriate to self-disclose and not easy to interpret the other person's feedback. However, if the relationship is longstanding, it may be shallow because both people are shutting each other out.

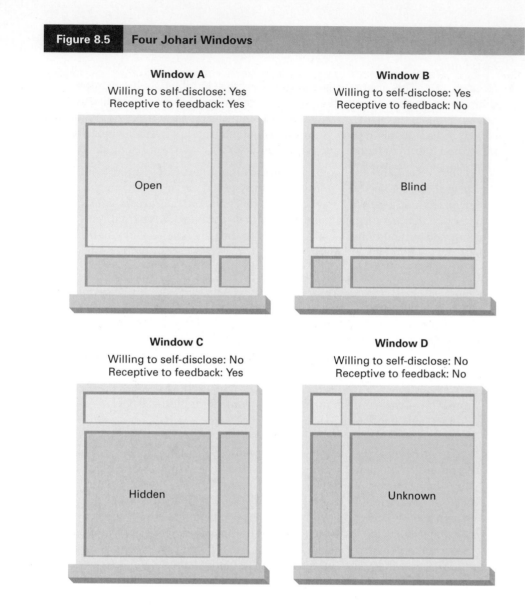

| Figure 8.5 | Four Johari Windows |

Window A
Willing to self-disclose: Yes
Receptive to feedback: Yes

Open

Window B
Willing to self-disclose: Yes
Receptive to feedback: No

Blind

Window C
Willing to self-disclose: No
Receptive to feedback: Yes

Hidden

Window D
Willing to self-disclose: No
Receptive to feedback: No

Unknown

SHARING YOUR SELF APPROPRIATELY

Social Penetration Theory, Communication Privacy Management Theory, and the Johari Window Model stress the importance of appropriate and effective self-disclosure. Each theory suggests guidelines for disclosing personal information about your self and providing constructive feedback to another person.

Effective Self-Disclosure   When you self-disclose, you reveal how you perceive and react to a situation by providing information about yourself and your past that is relevant to understanding what is happening. To accomplish this goal, you should[23]

- *Focus on the present.* Although the history of a relationship is important, don't obsess on past problems and experiences. Share your thoughts and feelings about what is happening *now*.

- *Be descriptive, not judgmental.* Describe what occurred, not your judgment of whether the other person is right or wrong, good or bad.

- *Disclose your feelings as well as facts.* Do more than tell someone that you've lost your job or received a great promotion. Sharing your feelings helps the

Many people develop and maintain close relationships via the Internet. Maybe you have. Good friends, romantic partners, and family members often rely on the Internet to stay in touch. Today, there are also more and more online dating services and chat rooms designed to help you find a "mate." By eliminating physical appearance and face-to-face awkwardness, the Internet provides a relatively safe way to develop a close relationship. This is especially true for teenagers, for whom "intimate conversations and awkward situations are easier to handle online than in person."[1]

In *Computer-Mediated Communication*, Susan Barnes discusses the most intimate of all online exchanges. "**Cybersex**," she writes "is the exchange of real-time sexually explicit messages through the Internet. Most people who engage in cybersex do it for fun and do not use their real names. However, the innocent sharing of fantasies can lead to more serious relationships."[2]

The Internet offers both great promise and great peril for people seeking meaningful relationships. The problem, of course, is deciding whether the other person is "real" or the product of a deception. Magazines, newspapers, and television shows relate tragic tales of young people being seduced by sexual predators, of spouses suing for divorce on the basis of Internet adultery, and of someone's most intimate sexual fantasies being distributed to an employer or a wide online audience.[3]

Fortunately, most people who use the Internet with frequency report that they develop interesting and close relationships with the people they meet online. However, you should use caution when deciding to share your self and intimate feelings with a new and eager cyberfriend.

[1] Susan B. Barnes, *Computer-Mediated Communication* (Boston: Allyn & Bacon, 2003), p. 140.

[2] Ibid., p. 139.

[3] Ibid., pp. 139–140.

---

other person understand why those facts are important to you and to the relationship.

- *Adapt to the person and context.* Revealing an intimate medical problem to a mere acquaintance or in a public place can embarrass everyone and achieve none of the benefits of self-disclosure.

- *Be sensitive to others' reactions.* If, when disclosing personal information, you sense that the person is reacting with extreme emotions (intense anger, overwhelming grief, humiliating embarrassment), modify what you are saying or stop disclosing.

- *Engage in reciprocal self-disclosure.* Successful self-disclosure is not a solo activity. If the other person does not self-disclose or respond to your self-disclosure, then rethink the relationship or stop sharing your thoughts and feelings.

- *Increase your disclosure during a crisis in a relationship.* Ignoring or walking away from an interpersonal problem won't solve it. Although it can be painful and risky, self-disclosure can benefit a relationship in significant ways when the emotional stakes are high.

- *Gradually move disclosure to a deeper level.* As Social Penetration Theory suggests, effective disclosure involves breadth, depth, and frequency.

Effective Feedback   Effective interpersonal communication relies on giving and receiving feedback from others. No matter where or when you provide feedback, it should not be threatening or demanding. David W. Johnson provides useful advice for understanding the characteristics of giving and receiving helpful feedback.[24] Give and ask for feedback about the following:

- Behavior, not personality
- Actions in a specific situation, not general or abstract behavior
- Immediate behavior, not behavior from the past

- Perceptions and feelings, not advice
- Actions that you and others can change

At the same time, remember that there is only so much that you and another person can comprehend and process at one time. Too much information can overwhelm a relationship.

Effective Communication Climates Finally, it is important to establish the appropriate communication climate. Jack R. Gibb suggests strategies to reduce the risks in self-disclosure and feedback.[25] In Gibb's view, there are six behaviors that create a supportive climate for communication and six that cause defensiveness. **Defensive behaviors** reflect our instinct to protect ourselves when we are being physically or verbally attacked by someone. Even though such reactions are natural, they discourage reciprocal self-disclosure. On the other hand, **supportive behaviors** create a climate in which sincere self-disclosure and responsiveness to feedback benefit both parties. In Figure 8.6, the behaviors come in pairs, one the opposite of the other, with defensive behaviors on the left and supportive behaviors on the right.

Figure 8.6	**Gibb's Defensive and Supportive Behaviors**

DEFENSIVE BEHAVIORS   SUPPORTIVE BEHAVIORS

DEFENSIVE BEHAVIORS	SUPPORTIVE BEHAVIORS
Evaluation: Judges another persons behavior. Makes critical statements. "Why did you insult Sharon like that? Explain yourself!" "What you did was terrible."	**Description:** Describes another person's behavior. Makes understanding statements. Uses more *I* and *we* language. "When we heard what you said to Sharon, we were really embarassed for her." "I'm sorry about that."
Control: Imposes your solution on someone else. Seeks control of the situation. "Give me that report and I'll make it better." "Since I'm paying for the vacation, we're going to the resort I like rather than the spa you like."	**Problem Orientation:** Seeks a mutually agreeable solution. "Okay. Let's see what we can do to get that report finished to specifications." "Let's talk and figure out how both of us can enjoy our vacation."
Strategy: Manipulates others. Hides hidden agendas or personal motives. "Frankie's going to Florida over spring break." "Remember when I helped you rearrange your office?"	**Spontaneity:** Makes straightforward, direct, open, honest, and helpful comments. "I'd like to go to Florida with Frankie over spring break." "Would you help me move some heavy boxes?"
Neutrality: Appears withdrawn, detached, indifferent. Won't take sides. "You can't win them all." "Life's a gamble." "It doesn't matter to me." "Whatever."	**Empathy:** Accepts and understands another person's feelings. "I can't believe she did that. No wonder you're upset." "It sounds as though you're having a hard time deciding."
Superiority: Implies that you and your opinions are better than others. Promotes resentment and jealousy. "Hey—I've done this a million times—let me have it. I'll finish in no time." "Is this the best you could do?"	**Equality:** Suggests that everyone can make a useful contribution. "If you don't mind, I'd like to explain how I've handled this before. It may help." "Let's tackle this problem together."
Certainty: Believes that your opinion is the only correct one. Refuses to consider the ideas and opinions of others. Takes inflexible positions. "I can't see any other way of doing this that makes sense." "There's no point in discussing this any further."	**Provisionalism:** Offers ideas and accepts suggestions from others. "We have a lot of options here—which one makes the most sense?" "I feel strongly about this, but I would like to hear what you think."

Source: Based on Jack R. Gibb, "Defensive Communication," *Journal of Communication* 2 (1961), pp. 141–148; also see http://lynn_meade.tripod.com/id61_m.htm.

Gibb's twelve supportive and defensive behaviors should not be viewed as "good" and "bad" behaviors. Rather, they represent dialectic tensions. There may be times when you should express yourself in evaluative, controlling, strategic, neutral, superior, or certain terms. For example, you may behave strategically when you have important and strong personal motives. You may behave with certainty when your expertise is well recognized and a critical decision must be made. And you may respond neutrally when the issue is of little consequence to you or others. Gibb's categories offer both a strategy and set of skills for developing a supportive communication climate that fosters self-disclosure and responsiveness to feedback—two communication skills that can increase your self-awareness and the quality of your personal relationships.

Personal Relationships in Context

There are three major personal relationships in most people's lives: friend relationships, romantic relationships, and family relationships. Because these three kinds of relationships function in different contexts, we need specialized communication strategies and skills to enhance their quality and longevity.

FRIEND RELATIONSHIPS

The ancient Roman statesman Cicero wrote, "If you take friendship out of life, you take the sun out of the world." Modern researchers confirm Cicero's outlook: Having friends increases life satisfaction and helps increase your life expectancy.[26]

Just about everyone has friends, but all friendships are not alike. To begin with, friendships differ depending on your age. What did you do when you were with your closest elementary school friends? Are they still your friends? Communication scholar Wendy Samter notes that, for young children, play and friendship are the same. The process of becoming a friend is as simple as sharing toys and playing together; when these activities are absent, friendship and liking cannot occur.[27] By the age of two, most children seem to have a concept of "friend" as someone who plays with them.[28] As children get older, they learn that friendship means more than playing a game; it also involves being a fun and nice person to play with as well as refraining from being mean.[29]

In adolescence and young adulthood, we establish enduring and intimate relationships with best friends. We learn that it's okay to share personal thoughts, secrets, hopes, and fears. However, sharing personal information with friends at this stage in life depends on our ability (1) to disclose personal information in a way that maintains the relationship; (2) to recognize that most of these disclosures center on mundane, everyday issues; and (3) to respect that some topics are taboo, such as negative life events and serious relationship issues.[30]

During late adolescence and young adulthood, most children leave home—to work, go to college, or raise a family. The dual tasks of developing new friendships while adapting to a new job, new living conditions, or new academic settings can present enormous practical, emotional, and communication challenges. Even though adolescents and young adults have more opportunities to make friends than any other age group, more of them express loneliness at this stage than at any other life stage.[31] Many college freshmen feel lonely and view leaving their family and hometown friends as the principal reason for their loneliness.

MAJOR PERSONAL RELATIONSHIPS

▶ Friend Relationships
▶ Romantic Relationships
▶ Family Relationships

How does this photograph capture the distinctive nature of friendship among young children?

In adolescence as well as young, middle, and older adulthood, men report less intimacy, less complexity, and less contact in their same-gender friendships than women. In contrast, women report greater continuity in their long-term friendships than men and see these friendships as having played an important role in their lives over time. One interesting study notes that throughout middle and older adulthood, women often value talk with their friends more than talk with their husbands.[1]

Talking together is a fundamental purpose and practice of women's friendships. Some researchers describe mutual and confirming talk as both the substance and central feature of women's friendships. Male friendships, on the other hand, tend to focus on common interests, shared activities, and sociability. According to William Rawlins's research, male friendships are "often geared toward accomplishing things and having something to show for their time spent together—practical problems solved, the house painted or deck completed, wildlife netting, cars washed or tuned, tennis, basketball, poker, or music play, and so on."[2]

Despite these differences, both adult men and women view close friendship as a mutually dependent, accepting, confidential, and trusting relationship.

[1]Wendy Samter, "Friendship Interaction Skills across the Life Span," in *Handbook of Communication and Social Interaction Skills,* ed. John O. Greene and Brant R. Burleson (Mahwah, NJ: Lawrence Erlbaum, 2003), p. 662.

[2]William K. Rawlins, *Friendship Matters: Communication, Dialects, and the Life Course* (New York: Aldine De Gruyter, 1992), p. 181.

ROMANTIC RELATIONSHIPS

Researchers have confirmed that the song lyric, "People who need people are the luckiest people in the world," is quite true. "People who are in loving relationships with another adult have better hormonal balance and better health, and are of course happier."[32] Learning how to develop and strengthen loving relationships is an important communication skill.

Why do some friends become romantically involved while others remain "just" friends? How do you let another person know that you like her or him? How do you find out whether that person likes you? The process of romancing another person begins with generating and assessing liking.

Communicating liking can be accomplished nonverbally and verbally. In Chapter 6, "Understanding Nonverbal Communication," we introduce the concept of immediacy. Nonverbal cues such as increased eye contact, touch, standing closer, and leaning forward can signal liking. When it comes to expressing liking verbally, most people don't take the direct route. We don't walk up to someone and say, "I like you." Instead, we tend to use some of the following strategies to show and generate liking[33]:

- Include the other person in a variety of social activities.
- Ask questions and encourage the other person to share personal information.
- Share your own personal information appropriately.
- Present yourself as positive, interesting, and dynamic.
- Do favors for or provide assistance to the other person.
- Seek and demonstrate similarities in tastes, interests, and attitudes.

Taken one at a time, these strategies may not seem significant or romantic, but when combined, they let the other person see that the relationship is becoming closer and has the potential for future development.

Romantic jealousy has the power to damage and end a relationship irreparably. Although jealousy occurs among friends, it plays a much more significant role in romantic relationships. **Jealousy** is an intense feeling caused by a perceived threat to a relationship. That threat may be seen as a partner's passion for work, a partner spending more time with friends, or signs of sexual unfaithfulness. Highly jealous people may interpret an innocent look or a conversation with a potential rival as flirting and seduction, or may see a partner's professional achievement as a threat.

People express jealousy in several ways. They may look hurt and resentful when the object of jealousy is discussed or present. The behavior can escalate into accusations and sarcasm or plunge a jealous person into depression expressed as physical withdrawal and the "silent treatment." Worst of all, jealousy may result in threatening, aggressive, and violent behavior. There are several communication strategies you can use to address and reduce your own or someone else's

jealousy, particularly when you are highly motivated to maintain the relationship[1]:

- *Integrative Communication.* Provide direct but nonaggressive communication about your jealousy in an effort to work things out. In other words, talk about it calmly and compassionately.
- *Compensatory Restoration.* Work to improve the relationship or make yourself more desirable. Strategies such as sending flowers or a gift, appearing more attractive and affectionate, and being extra nice can reduce or counteract jealous feelings.
- *Negative Affect Expression.* Express yourself nonverbally so the jealous person can see how it affects you (e.g., appearing hurt, distressed, or crying).

[1]Laura K. Guerrero et al., "Coping with the Green-Eyed Monster: Conceptualizing and Measuring Communicative Responses to Romantic Jealousy," *Western Journal of Communication* 59 (1995), pp. 270–304; Laura K. Guerrero and Walid Afifi, "Toward a Goal-Oriented Approach for Understanding Communicative Responses to Jealousy," *Western Journal of Communication* 63 (1999), pp. 216–248.

FAMILY RELATIONSHIPS

There was a time when an ideal nuclear family was viewed as a mother, father, and their biological children. *The New York Times* reports that in 1960 about 45 percent of U.S. families were nuclear families but that by 2001 only 23 percent of families could be described as nuclear families.[34] By 2007, more women (51 percent) were living without a husband than with one. The U.S. Census Bureau also notes that only about 30 percent of African American women were living with a spouse compared with about 49 percent of Hispanic women, 55 percent of non-Hispanic white women, and more than 60 percent of Asian women.[35] So what *is* a family? In their book on family communication, Lynn H. Turner and Richard West define a **family** as "a self-defined group of intimates who create and maintain themselves through their own interactions and their interactions with others."[36] A family may include both involuntary relationships (you don't get to choose your biological parents) and voluntary relationships (you choose your spouse). As Figure 8.7 illustrates, there are many types of families.

All of us face the challenge of understanding family communication patterns and developing communication strategies and skills that meet our own and our family's needs. Here we examine two communication variables that affect all types of families: (1) family roles and rules, and (2) parenting skills.

Family Roles and Rules   When you watch children play "house," they take on roles—mother, father, and children. Even at an early age, children learn that certain patterns of behavior and expectations are characteristic of each family member.

How does assignment of household chores affect family relationships?

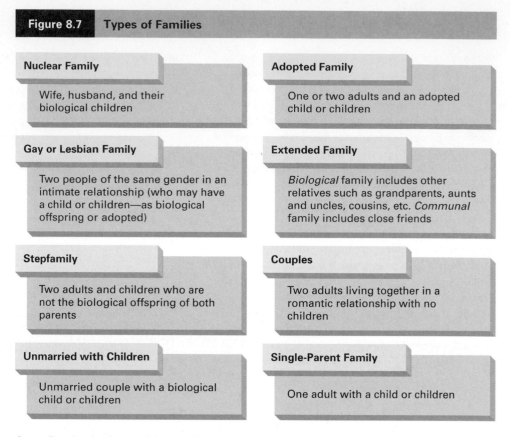

Figure 8.7   Types of Families

Nuclear Family

Wife, husband, and their biological children

Adopted Family

One or two adults and an adopted child or children

Gay or Lesbian Family

Two people of the same gender in an intimate relationship (who may have a child or children—as biological offspring or adopted)

Extended Family

Biological family includes other relatives such as grandparents, aunts and uncles, cousins, etc. *Communal* family includes close friends

Stepfamily

Two adults and children who are not the biological offspring of both parents

Couples

Two adults living together in a romantic relationship with no children

Unmarried with Children

Unmarried couple with a biological child or children

Single-Parent Family

One adult with a child or children

Source: Based on family types in Lynn H. Turner and Richard West, *Perspectives on Family Communication*, 2nd ed. (Boston: McGraw Hill, 2002), p. 33, pp. 18–37.

Family roles are often linked to family rules. For example, "Dad will deal with the car problem" may be interpreted as a rule, which in turn suggests that dad's role is vehicle caretaker. Family rules are contextual; they vary according to the situation and family culture. In some cultures, a daughter may not date until her parents meet the young man and approve her choice. In other cultures, grandparents are revered as the wisest members of the family, and their advice and approval are sought by all family members.[37]

The following examples of communication rules may be characteristic of your family:

- Tell the truth.
- Say "please" and "thank you."
- Be nice to your brothers and sisters.
- Share your toys.
- Don't talk back to your parents or grandparents.
- Say your prayers before going to bed.[38]

Family rules serve an important purpose: They allow family members to make sense out of family episodes. Rules also help family members understand one another's behavior. Although some family rules may seem unfair or arbitrary, they do help families define and maintain themselves.[39]

Parenting Skills   In supportive, healthy families, parents give children love, values, and social skills. Socially skilled children are better at understanding and appropriately reacting to the emotions of others, understand how their behavior impacts others in interpersonal conflict situations, and communicate more effectively.[40]

Do parents really make a major difference in the way children behave outside the home—and the way they grow up? Developmental psychologist Judith Rich Harris believes that parenting has almost no long-term effects on a child's personality, intelligence, or mental health. Instead, children are most influenced by two factors: their genes and their peers. Harris uses this example to make her point: Children born of immigrant parents (who speak English poorly) quickly learn to speak Standard English. They learn this from their peers, who have more influence on how they speak and sound.[1]

Same-age peers also show children how to fit in and behave—in the classroom, on the ball field, or at parties. Children adopt certain behaviors in social settings to win acceptance from their peers, and it's those behaviors outside the home that remain steadfast through adulthood. Blame your peers, Harris says, not your parents.[2]

Do you believe Harris's claims? Or do you give more credit to good parenting? How do you explain what happens when the child of two "good" parents turns out "bad"? Should parents be more concerned about the kind of neighborhood they live in than how they parent? Judith Harris's research raises many questions and has created considerable controversy and debate among psychologists, communication scholars, and family members.[3]

[1] Judith R. Harris as quoted in several online chats and interviews. See the Washington Post's online chat, September 30, 1998, http://discuss.washingtonpost.com/wp-srv/zforum/98/harris093098.htm; and *Edge 58,* June 29, 1999, www.edge.org/documents/archive/edge58.html.

[2] "Blame Your Peers, Not Your Parents, Authors Says," *APA Monitor* (October 1998), www.snc.edu/psych/korshavn/peer01.htm.

[3] For analysis and criticism of Harris's research, see Craig H. Hart, Lloyd D. Newell, and Susanne Frost Olsen, "Parenting Skills and Social–Communicative Competences in Childhood," in *Handbook of Communication and Social Interaction Skills,* ed. John O. Greene and Brant R. Burleson (Mahwah, NJ: Lawrence Erlbaum, 2003), pp. 774–776.

Not all parents can raise such children. One key factor is their parenting style. **Parenting styles** are stable sets of behaviors that characterize the psychosocial climate of parent–child interactions over a wide range of situations. Notice the considerable differences in the following three parenting styles:

1. *Authoritative.* Parent is respected, trustworthy, reliable, firm, confident, and flexible.

2. *Authoritarian/Coercive.* Parent is strict, severe, demanding, controlling, and rigid.

3. *Permissive.* Parent is lenient, tolerant, nonjudgmental, indulgent, and accepting.

In your opinion, which parenting style is most effective? As you might guess, there is no "correct" answer. However, research suggests that authoritative parenting is the most flexible and therefore has the potential to be the most effective. **Authoritative parenting** adapts to the individual characteristics and needs of children by being *both* compassionate *and* firm. Children are given the freedom to make decisions within a reasonable limit. Authoritative parents prepare children for life rather than regulating and controlling them.[41] They are more likely to help their children develop effective and ethical communication skills that will enable them to become socially skilled in a wide range of personal interactions.[42]

Authoritarian/coercive parenting is less flexible. Children are expected to follow a set of rigid rules that may not account for their individual characteristics and needs. Authoritarian/coercive parents are very strict, may use physical punishment, and may ridicule their children by putting them down or holding power over them. Although this can result in immediate compliance and "good" behavior, these

Some researchers contend that parents do not make a major difference in the way children behave outside the home and the way they grow up. Why do you agree or disagree with this claim?

217

children may never learn to regulate their own behavior from within or take responsibility for their decisions and actions.[43]

Permissive parenting is perhaps too flexible. Permissive parents are often less involved in their children's lives and may overindulge or neglect them. They tolerate their children's impulses (including aggression), encourage children to make decisions without providing limits, and refrain from imposing structure on children's time for such activities as bedtime and television watching. They make few demands for mature behavior and they do not impose consequences for misbehavior. Children raised by highly permissive parents may have difficulty respecting others, coping with frustration, delaying gratification, and following through with their plans.[44]

Relationship Stages

Close personal relationships do not happen by chance. Rather, you start, develop, maintain, strengthen, and end relationships. Mark Knapp and Anita Vangelisti describe ten predictable stages in intimate relationships.[45] Their model is heavily oriented toward male–female romantic couples, yet they also account for many child–parent relationships as well as close work relationships.[46] The model is divided into two major phases: coming together and coming apart. Figure 8.8 describes the ten interaction stages using the example of a romantic relationship.

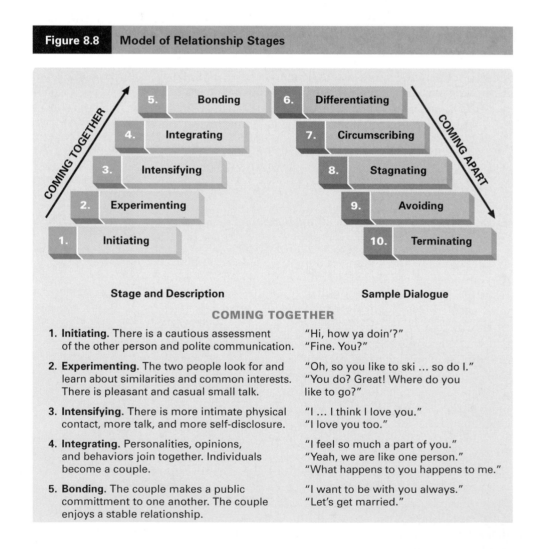

Figure 8.8	Model of Relationship Stages

Stage and Description | **Sample Dialogue**

COMING TOGETHER

1. **Initiating.** There is a cautious assessment of the other person and polite communication.
   "Hi, how ya doin'?"
   "Fine. You?"

2. **Experimenting.** The two people look for and learn about similarities and common interests. There is pleasant and casual small talk.
   "Oh, so you like to ski ... so do I."
   "You do? Great! Where do you like to go?"

3. **Intensifying.** There is more intimate physical contact, more talk, and more self-disclosure.
   "I ... I think I love you."
   "I love you too."

4. **Integrating.** Personalities, opinions, and behaviors join together. Individuals become a couple.
   "I feel so much a part of you."
   "Yeah, we are like one person."
   "What happens to you happens to me."

5. **Bonding.** The couple makes a public commitment to one another. The couple enjoys a stable relationship.
   "I want to be with you always."
   "Let's get married."

In *Uncoupling: How Relationships Come Apart*, sociologist Diane Vaughan notes that a couple's breakup is rarely sudden. It all begins, she writes, with a secret. For some reason, one of the partners starts to feel uncomfortable in the relationship. The world the two of them have built together no longer "fits."[1]

The secret is rarely about daily life, financial problems, or visits from the in-laws. It begins when a partner feels dissatisfied, uncomfortable, unhappy, or fearful about the future of the relationship. Rather than sharing these private concerns and feelings, the partner leaves them unspoken, for various reasons: He or she may be uncertain regarding their cause, their depth, and their implications, or afraid to share them for fear of hurting the other person or discovering that the other harbors much worse "secrets."[2]

If you cannot articulate your true feelings, thoughts, and moods easily, you will have difficulty addressing a problem in a relationship ("I am unhappy in the relationship and this is why"). Instead, you may display discontent through subtle hints and deeds (e.g., a disgruntled glance, a goodnight kiss omitted, an activity schedule that permanently conflicts with a time understood to be *our* time). When discontent surfaces in words, complaints are often attached to the problems of everyday life. "You laugh too loud." "You should get home in time for dinner." The emphasis is on the other person's daily failings. Not surprisingly, the other person may respond to them on the level at which they are raised—as small problems, not serious trouble.[3] But secrets about the nature of a relationship are serious trouble, and they are often the first step toward permanent and even painful uncoupling.

[1] Diane Vaughan, *Uncoupling: How Relationships Come Apart* (New York: Vintage Books, 1986), p. 3.

[2] Ibid., p. 6.

[3] Ibid., pp. 8–9.

Knapp and Vangelisti's model only scratches the surface of each stage in a relationship. Just because your partner doesn't like big social gatherings as much as you does not mean your relationship will "come apart."

Figure 8.8	Continued

COMING APART

6. **Differentiating.** Each person becomes distinct and different in character. More use of "I" and "you," than "we" and "our." There is more conflict.

"I don't like big social gatherings."
"Sometimes I just don't understand you. This is one area where I'm certainly not like you at all."

7. **Circumscribing.** There is a decrease in communication. Personal and important topics are no longer discussed.

"Did you have a good time on your trip?"
"What time is dinner?"

8. **Stagnating.** Communication shuts down. More time and attention is devoted to work and other friends.

"What's there to talk about?"
"Right. I know what you're going to say and you know what I'm going to say."

9. **Avoiding.** There is a lack of desire to spend time together. Communication may become antagonistic or unfriendly.

"I'm so busy. I just don't know when I'll be able to see you."
"I may not be around when you call."

10. **Terminating.** Psychological and physical barriers are created. Each person is more concerned about self.

"I'm leaving you … and don't bother trying to contact me."
"Don't worry. I won't."

Source: Mark C. Knapp and Anita L. Vangelisti, *Interpersonal Communication and Human Relationships* (Boston: Allyn & Bacon, 1996), p. 34.

Emotional Expression

Emotions play a major role in all relationships. An **emotion** is a transitory positive or negative experience that is felt as happening to the self, and is generated in part by a cognitive appraisal of a situation, and accompanied by both learned and reflexive physical responses.[47] In simpler terms, an emotion is the feeling you have when reacting to a situation that is often accompanied by physiological changes. Emotions are fundamental to effective and ethical communication. They play a significant role in how you develop, maintain, and strengthen interpersonal relationships.

THE BASIC EMOTIONS

For the most part, everyone experiences basic, primary emotions, but researchers disagree on the number of such emotions. Robert Plutchik's **Psychoevolutionary Emotion Theory** helps explain the development and meaning of emotions.[48] According to this theory, each basic emotion has a range of feelings (from mild to intense) as indicated in parentheses in the following list.[49]

- Fear (apprehension—terror)
- Anger (annoyance—rage)
- Joy (happiness—ecstasy)
- Sadness (pensiveness—grief)
- Acceptance (acknowledgment—trust)
- Disgust (boredom—loathing)
- Expectancy (anticipation—vigilance)
- Surprise (distraction—amazement)

What about love? Plutchik explains that some emotions, including love, are combinations of two or more of the basic emotions. Our basic emotions can be mixed—just as primary colors are mixed—to yield other emotions (colors). As Figure 8.9 shows, love is a combination of joy and acceptance. Contempt is a combination of anger and disgust.

Figure 8.9	Plutchik's Primary and Mixed Emotions

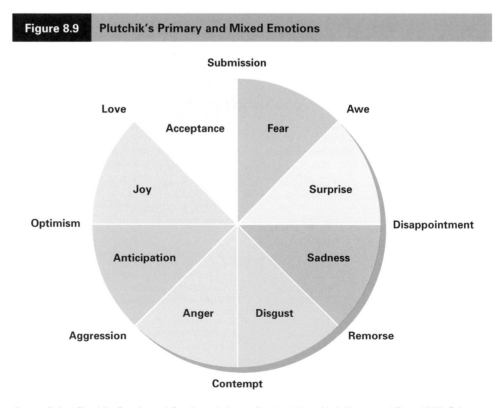

Source: Robert Plutchik, *Emotions: A Psychoevolutionary Synthesis* (New York: Harper and Row, 1980); Robert Plutchik, "Emotions: A General Psychoevolutionary Theory," in *Approaches to Emotion,* ed. K.R. Scherer and Paul Ekman (Mahwah, NJ: Lawrence Erlbaum, 1984), p. 203.

EMOTIONAL INTELLIGENCE

Psychology and science writer Daniel Goleman defines **emotional intelligence** (or EQ) as "the capacity for recognizing our own feelings and those of others, for motivating ourselves, and for managing emotions well in ourselves and in our relationships."[50] His influential book, *Emotional Intelligence: Why It Can Matter More Than IQ*, is based on the work of two psychologists, Peter Salovey and John Mayer, who coined the term *emotional intelligence* in 1990.

You can examine emotional intelligence in terms of both intra- and interpersonal communication competencies. Intrapersonal strategies include being self-aware, having some control over the expression of your emotions, and motivating yourself to keep going. Interpersonal strategies include listening skills, knowing when to share emotions, and helping others help themselves. These strategies are summarized and described in Figure 8.10.[51]

What happens when people cannot make emotions work for them? Neurologist Antonio Damasio, who studies patients with damage to the emotional center of their brains, notes that these patients make terrible decisions even though their IQ scores stay the same. So even though they test as "smart," they "make disastrous choices in business and their personal lives, and can even obsess endlessly over a decision so simple as when to make an appointment." Their decision-making skills are poor because they have lost access to their emotions. Damasio concludes that feelings are *indispensable* for rational decision making.[52] Consider whether you could answer any of these questions without taking emotions into account: Whom should I marry? What career should I pursue? Should I buy this house? What should I say to my bereaved colleague?

Figure 8.10	Emotionally Intelligent Communication

	Communication Strategies	As an Emotionally Intelligent Communicator, You...
Intrapersonal Communication Strategies	Develop Self-Awareness	Monitor and identify your feelings in order to guide your decision making. *Example:* Deciding whether you have raised your voice because you are angry or surprised.
	Manage Your Emotions	Restrain or release your emotions when the situation is appropriate. Practice relaxation to recover from emotional distress. *Example:* Deciding whether expressing your emotions will facilitate or interfere with your goals.
	Motivate Yourself	Persevere in the face of disappointments and setbacks. Seek the support of friends, colleagues, and family members to stay motivated, improve your mood, and bolster your confidence. *Example:* Seeking help from a trusted mentor.
Interpersonal Communication Strategies	Listen to Others	Engage all five types of listening to ensure you understand the nature of a situation. Use effective, empathetic listening. *Example:* Paraphrasing what you hear to make sure you understand someone else before responding emotionally.
	Develop Interpersonal Skills	Try to resolve conflicts. Use self-disclosure, assertiveness, and appropriate verbal and nonverbal communication. *Example:* Deciding whether and how to share your emotions with a close friend.
	Help Others Help Themselves	Help others become more aware of their emotions. Help them speak and listen more effectively. *Example:* Providing emotional support to a distressed friend.

Source: Based on Daniel Goleman, *Emotional Intelligence* (New York: Bantam, 1995); Daniel Goleman, *Working with Emotional Intelligence* (New York: Bantam, 1998); and Hendrie Weisinger, *Emotional Intelligence at Work* (San Francisco: Jossey-Bass, 1998).

Directions: Daniel Goleman proposes five basic emotional competencies, expressed in the following headings.[1] Use the rating scale listed here to assess your level of competence for each question: 5 = Always, 4 = Usually, 3 = Sometimes, 2 = Rarely, and 1 = Never.

Know Thy Self

_____ 1. Can you accurately identify the emotions you experience and why you experience them?

_____ 2. Do you have a strong self-concept?

_____ 3. Are you aware of your strengths and limitations?

Control Your Emotions and Impulses

_____ 4. Can you keep disruptive emotions under control?

_____ 5. Do you take responsibility for your emotions and resulting actions?

_____ 6. Are you open-minded and flexible in handling difficult situations?

Persevere

_____ 7. Do you strive to improve or meet high standards of excellence?

_____ 8. Do you persist in the face of obstacles and setbacks?

_____ 9. Can you postpone gratification and regulate your moods?

Empathize

_____ 10. Do you accurately interpret others' feelings and needs?

_____ 11. Do you provide appropriate emotional support to others?

_____ 12. Do you paraphrase appropriately?

Interact Effectively

_____ 13. Do you listen appropriately and effectively?

_____ 14. Do you make a positive social impression?

_____ 15. Do you work effectively with others to achieve shared goals?

Scoring: Add up your ratings. The higher your score, the more "emotionally intelligent" you are. Keep in mind that your ratings are only your *perceptions* of your feelings and behaviors. For example, despite what you think, you may not interpret others' feelings and needs accurately or persist in the face of obstacles. On the other hand, you may not recognize that you provide appropriate emotional support to others, even though your friends often turn to you when they need an empathetic ear.

[1]Based on Daniel Goleman, *Working with Emotional Intelligence* (New York: Bantam, 1998), pp. 26–27.

THE NEED FOR EMOTIONAL SUPPORT

How many times have you felt at a loss for words when someone needs emotional support and comfort? A colleague's home is seriously damaged by a fire. Your partner fails to get a "sure-thing" job she or he applied for. What do you say or do? As a concerned and compassionate person, you probably look for ways to comfort your friend, colleague, partner, or family member. Unfortunately, many of us feel inadequate to this task. We worry about saying the wrong thing. We search through racks of greeting cards to find a card that can "say it" better than we can.

As much as we may want to support and comfort a person in distress, many of us lack an understanding of the basic nature of emotional support as well as the communication skills needed to achieve its purpose. Communication scholar Brant Burleson defines **emotional support** as "specific lines of communicative behavior enacted by one party with the intent of helping another cope effectively with emotional distress." The "distress" can be acute (disappointment over not winning a contest, anxiety over an upcoming exam) or chronic (grief over the loss of a loved one, lingering depression over poor health) and may be mild or intense in character.[53]

CommEthics The Ethics of Caring

The NCA Credo for Ethical Communication includes a principle that speaks directly to interpersonal relationships: "We promote communication climates of caring and mutual understanding that respect the unique needs and characteristics of individual communicators."[1] Philosopher and educator Nel Noddings believes we make moral choices based on an ethic of caring. For example, a mother picks up a crying baby, not because of a sense of duty or because she is worried about what others will say if she doesn't, but because she cares about the baby. Relationship theorists emphasize that this is not a gender-based ethic. Rather, it is based on a way of thinking that honors two fundamental characteristics of ethical behavior: avoiding harm and providing mutual aid. Most of us have a basic and universal aversion to harm, both physical and psychological. We also

have a basic and universal urge to help others, particularly when they suffer from harm. Interpersonal ethics calls for rational justifications, flexibility, self-control, and self-monitoring in our communication and interactions with others. As ethical communicators, we must accept the difficult challenge of defending our choices and the consequences of our actions.[2]

[1] www.natcom.org/aboutNCA/Policies/Platform.html.

[2] Elaine E. Englehardt, "Introduction to Ethics in Interpersonal Communication," in *Ethical Issues in Interpersonal Communication,* ed. Elaine E. Englehardt (Fort Worth, TX: Harcourt, 2001), pp. 1–25. In the same volume, see also Carol Gilligan, "Images of Relationship," and Nel Noddings, "An Ethics of Care," pp. 88–96 and 96–103.

CONSTRUCTING SUPPORTIVE MESSAGES

Emotionally supportive communication strategies can help you become a more compassionate, comforting, and effective communicator. These strategies include being clear about your intentions, protecting the other person's self-esteem, and centering your messages on the other person.

Communicate Your Intentions Clearly   When someone is in great distress, you may think that this person knows you want to be helpful and supportive. You may assume that just "being there" tells the other person that you care. In some cases, your assumptions are correct. In other situations, a person in distress needs to know that you *want* to help or provide assistance. Supportive intentions should be clear and sincere. You can enhance the clarity of your supportive messages by stating them directly ("I want to help you") and by making it clear you care ("I'm here for you"). You can also intensify the perceived sincerity of your response by emphasizing your desire to help ("I really want to help however I can"), by reminding the person of the personal history you share ("You know we've always been there for each other"), and by indicating what you feel ("Helping you is important to me; I'd feel terrible if I weren't here to help").[54]

Protect the Other Person's Self-Esteem   Make sure that your offer of help does not imply that the other person is incapable of solving the problem or dealing with the situation. Otherwise, you may damage someone's self-esteem. Even with the best of intentions, expressions of sympathy ("Oh, you poor thing . . .") can convey judgments about the person's lack of competence and lack of independence. Try to encourage and praise the other person: "I know you can deal with this—as you have many times before," "I can see you're trying very hard to overcome this problem," or "I really respect what you're trying to do here."[55]

COMFORTING MESSAGE STRATEGIES

▶ Communicate Your Intentions Clearly

▶ Protect the Other Person's Self-Esteem

▶ Offer Person-Centered Messages

Offer Person-Centered Messages **Person-centered messages** reflect "the degree to which a helper validates [a] distressed person's feelings and encourages him or her to talk about the upsetting event."[56] Rather than focusing on helping someone feel better, your goal is helping others develop a deeper understanding of the problem so they take on the task of solving or coping with it.

You can help someone in distress understand the problem by encouraging that person to tell an extended, personal story about the problem or upsetting event. People in need of emotional support may want nothing more than to share the details with a trusted friend so that they can gain some insight and even explore coping options. From a communication standpoint, you can encourage such storytelling in several ways:

- Ask for your friend's version of the situation. ("What happened here? Can you tell me about it?")

- Create a supportive environment and provide enough time for the person to talk. ("Take your time. I'm not going anywhere. I want to hear the whole story.")

- Ask about the person's feelings, not just the events. ("How did you feel when that happened?" "What was your reaction when she said that?")

- Legitimize the expression of feelings. ("Be angry. It's okay." "I certainly understand why you'd feel that way.")

- Indicate that you connect with what the other person is saying. ("If that happened to me, I'd be furious too.")[57]

These communication strategies express your willingness to help, your supportive feelings, and your personal commitment. At the same time, you should avoid counterproductive strategies. For example, do not focus on or share *your* emotional experiences, as in "I know exactly how you feel. Last year, I went through a similar kind of problem. It all started when. . . ." Not only does this stop the other person from sharing, but it also shifts the focus to yourself. You should also avoid messages that criticize or negatively evaluate another person, because these can hurt more than

A church member in Texas prays with New Orleans Hurricane Katrina evacuees during a service. How does this photograph depict person-centered support and nonverbal comforting?

CommFYI Nonverbal Comforting Matters

As a child you experienced nonverbal comforting well before you understood and communicated with language. "Not surprisingly, the nonverbal behaviors first used in infancy continue as expressions of emotional support throughout a lifetime. Hugs, touches and pats, hand-holding, focused looks and soothing sounds can be remarkably effective ways of expressing reassurance, love, warmth, and acceptance."[1] This kind of nonverbal comforting—sometimes referred to as *nonverbal immediacy*—describes "behaviors such as close proximity, forward lean, facial expressiveness, and gaze, which reflect interpersonal warmth."[2] In terms of physical health, researchers note that a hospital patient's family and friends help just by visiting, regardless of whether they know what to say.[3]

Touch plays a significant role in comforting others. "Skin-on-skin touch is particularly soothing because it primes oxytocin," a neurotransmitter that causes our body to undergo many healthy changes. Blood pressure lowers and we relax. Our pain threshold increases so that we are less sensitive to discomforts. Even wounds heal faster.[4]

How would you react nonverbally if a close same-sex friend told you that she or he had just ended a serious romantic relationship? College students largely agree on what they would do. In one study, hugging emerged as the number one response. Other high-ranking responses included being attentive, moving closer to the other person, using certain facial expressions, increasing touch, and making eye contact. Not surprisingly, men and women suggested different nonverbal responses. Men were less likely than women to hug their troubled friend; they were more likely to pat their friend on the arm or shoulder and to suggest going out and doing something to take his or her mind off the problem. Women were more likely to cry with their friend and to use a variety of comforting touches.[5]

[1]Brant R. Burleson, "Emotional Support Skill," in *Handbook of Communication and Social Interaction Skills,* ed. John O. Greene and Brant R. Burleson (Mahwah, NJ: Lawrence Erlbaum, 2003), p. 553.

[2]Susan M. Jones and John G. Wirtz, "How Does the Comforting Process Work? An Empirical Test of an Appraisal-Based Model of Comforting," *Human Communication Research* 32 (2006), p. 217.

[3]Daniel Goleman, "Friends for Life: An Emerging Biology of Emotional Healing," *The New York Times*, October 10, 2006, p. D5. Also see, Daniel Goleman, *Social Intelligence* (New York: Bantam, 2006).

[4]Goleman, *Social Intelligence*, p. 243.

[5]Martin S. Remland, *Nonverbal Communication in Everyday Life*, 2nd ed. (Boston: Houghton Mifflin, 2003), p. 330.

help. Do not tell others that their feelings are wrong, inappropriate, immature, or embarrassing.

When we face a distressing or tragic situation, we may seek or want others to provide emotional support. There are, however, differences in the way men and women behave when trying to provide person-centered comforting messages. "Although men and women are similar in the type of emotional support they typically want to receive from others . . . they differ quite reliably when it comes to providing emotional support to others."[58] Men are less likely than women to use highly sensitive and effective forms of emotional support when they attempt to comfort others.

Research by Brant Burleson and colleagues investigates why men are often less effective in providing emotional support. They conclude that men may avoid highly person-centered "comforting messages (even if they have the ability to do so) because they desire to avoid engaging in behaviors they view as especially feminine"—that is, behaviors that are inconsistent with their male gender role. In addition, "stereotypical feminine behaviors (such as offering comfort) is more threatening to the gender identity of men," particularly when communicating with other men.[59] Burleson and his colleagues caution us against assuming that men cannot or will not provide effective comfort. When men care a great deal about another person and are highly motivated to provide support, they will do so. And when men use highly person-centered comforting messages, male recipients do not react negatively. In short, all of us—male or female—seek, accept, and appreciate effective emotional support from others.[60]

Communication Challenge

Perusing the Personals

Directions: Read the following samples of personal ads or find additional personal ads in newspapers, magazines, and online sources. Using the Perusing the Personals Coding Sheet, categorize the qualities sought and offered by females and males in personal ads. Note the similarities and differences between ads placed by females and males.

Sample Ads Placed by Females

- *Attractive, slender, sensual*—auburn hair, hazel eyes, 5'4", 116 lbs, professional SWF seeks educated professional gentleman, 40s, for happy light-hearted romantic summer adventures and possible LTR.

- *Christian, attractive female*—seeks old-fashioned traditional gentleman for serious LTR. Me: nonsmoker, nondrinker, commitment minded, kind-hearted conservative female seeks same. He: high morals, Christian values, honesty, financial stability.

- *Affectionate, attractive, feminine*—SBF with charm, spirit, and great personality ISO easygoing, educated, refined, ethical, tall, SM (diversity welcome) who is gainfully employed, emotionally stable, and ready to build future/family.

Sample Ads Placed by Males

- *I have it all*—except the right woman. Tall, good-looking, slender, DWM, 59, CEO, very successful Leo who loves life, knows his wine (cooks too), ISO attractive, slender, intelligent, tomboyish, fun, nonsmoking, S/DWF, 40–55 for LTR.

- *Sick of bars*—Tall, trim (in shape) handsome, bright professional, very personable, financially secure, SBM, 34, ISO pretty, slim, balanced, SWF, 21–34, for dating or LTR.

- *Seeking traditional fair lady*—who is fit, nice, age 25–42 by successful, professional DWM, 54, to pamper and help take care of her for a special relationship.

Ad Abbreviations: B, black; D, divorced; F, female; ISO, in search of; LTR, long-term relationship; M, male; S, single; W, white.

Perusing the Personals Coding Sheet

Characteristic	Females Want	Females Offer	Males Want	Males Offer
1. Attractiveness				
2. Height				
3. Weight				
4. Other body characteristics				
5. Blond hair color				
6. Other hair color				
7. Eye color				
8. Ambitious, goal oriented				
9. Independent				
10. Physically active				
11. Kind/warm/sensitive				
12. Extroverted/outgoing				
13. Introverted/introspective				
14. Good listener				
15. Talker, communicator				
16. Younger partner				
17. Older partner				
18. Education				
19. Specific occupation				
20. "Professional" status				
21. Financial status				
22. "Commitment" or "serious" relationship				
23. Other characteristics				
a. _____				
b. _____				
c. _____				

Additional Observations and Comments:

Communication Assessment

"Birds of a Feather" versus "Opposites Attract"

Directions: For each characteristic listed, place a check mark in the appropriate column or columns to indicate that the characteristic is true of yourself, your close friend, an acquaintance who is not a close friend, your current or most recent romantic partners, and/or your ideal or fantasy romantic partner.

Characteristics in Common

Characteristic	Self	Friend	Acquaintance	Romantic Partner	Romantic Ideal
Ambitious					
Assertive/dominant					
Dependent					
Good listener					
Good sense of humor					
Independent					
Intelligent					
Introspective					
Likes to take charge					
Loner					
Optimistic					
Organized, plans ahead					
Outgoing					
Passive/submissive					
Pessimistic					
Physically active					
Physically attractive					
Physically inactive					
Politically active, aware					
Responsible					
Spontaneous					
Talkative					
Warm					

Questions for Analysis

1. Are you attracted to people similar or dissimilar to you? In other words, do "birds of a feather flock together" or do "opposites attract"? For example, if you are outgoing, are your relationships with introverts or extroverts?

2. Are the characteristics of your ideal or fantasy romantic partner very different from those of your close friends and real-world romantic partner(s)?

Source: Steven Fein and Bryan L. Bonner, *Instructor's Resource Manual for Social Psychology,* 6th ed., by Sharon S. Brehm, Saul Kassin, and Steven Fein (Boston: Houghton Mifflin, 2005), pp. 319–320, 339.

Key Terms

authoritarian/coercive parenting
authoritative parenting
boundary turbulence
Communication Privacy Management
  Theory
cybersex
defensive behavior
emotion
emotional intelligence

emotional support
expression–privacy dialectic
family
integration–separation dialectic
intimacy
jealousy
Johari Window
parenting style
permissive parenting

person-centered message
Psychoevolutionary Emotion Theory
receptivity to feedback
Relational Dialectics Theory
self-disclosure
Social Penetration Theory
stability–change dialectic
supportive behavior
willingness to self-disclose

Notes

1. David W. Johnson, *Reaching Out: Interpersonal Effectiveness and Self-Actualization*, 7th ed. (Boston: Allyn & Bacon, 2000), p. 12.

2. Daniel Goleman, " 'Friends for Life': An Emerging Biology of Emotional Healing," *The New York Times*, October 10, 2006, p. D5. For a more detailed examination of this phenomenon, see Daniel Goleman, *Social Intelligence* (New York: Bantam, 2006), p. 10.

3. Leslie A. Baxter and Barbara M. Montgomery, *Relating: Dialogues and Dialectics* (New York: Guilford Press, 1996).

4. *The American Heritage Dictionary of the English Language*, 4th ed. (Boston: Houghton Mifflin, 2000), p. 501; Baxter and Montgomery, p. 19.

5. Baxter and Montgomery, p. 3.

6. Em Griffin, *A First Look at Communication Theory*, 2nd ed. (New York: McGraw-Hill, 1994), p. 161.

7. Baxter and Montgomery, p. 5.

8. See Leslie A. Baxter, "A Dialectical Perspective on Communication Strategies in Relationship Development," in *Handbook of Personal Relationships*, ed. Steve Duck (New York, Wiley, 1990), pp. 257–273.

9. Lawrence B. Rosenfeld, "Overview of the Ways Privacy, Secrecy, and Disclosure Are Balanced in Today's Society," in *Balancing the Secrets of Private Disclosures*, ed. Sandra Petronio (Mahwah, NJ: Lawrence Erlbaum, 2000), p. 5.

10. Richard West and Lynn H. Turner, *Introducing Communication Theory*, 3rd ed. (Boston: McGraw-Hill, 2007), p. 203.

11. Based on West and Turner, p. 223. Also see Dominic A. Infante, Andrew S. Rancer, and Deanna F. Womack, *Building Communication Theory*, 4th ed. (Prospect Heights, IL: Waveland, 2003), pp. 212–214; and Leslie A. Baxter, "Dialectical Contradictions in Relationships Development," *Journal of Social and Personal Relationships* 6 (1990),

pp. 69–88. The strategies of *neutralizing*, *reframing*, and *disqualifying* are subcategories of *integration*, the act of synthesizing oppositions.

12. Malcolm R. Parks, "Ideology in Interpersonal Communication: Off the Couch and into the World," in *Communication Yearbook 5*, ed. Michael Burgoon (New Brunswick, NJ: Transaction Books, 1982), pp. 79–107.

13. Irvin Altman and Dalmas Taylor, *Social Penetration: The Development of Interpersonal Relationships* (New York: Holt, Rinehart, and Winston, 1973).

14. Walid A. Afifi and Laura K. Guerrero, "Motivations Underlying Topic Avoidance in Close Relationships," in *Balancing the Secrets of Private Disclosure*, ed. Sandra Petronio (Mahwah, NJ: Lawrence Erlbaum, 2000), p. 168.

15. *Shrek*, DreamWorks, 2003.

16. Sandra Petronio, *Boundaries of Privacy: Dialectics of Disclosure* (Albany: State University of New York Press, 2002), p. xviii.

17. Ibid., p. 3.

18. Based on Petronio, 2002, p. 7.

19. Petronio, 2002, pp. 33, 177–178.

20. Joseph Luft, *Group Process: An Introduction to Group Dynamics*, 3rd ed. (Palo Alto, CA: Mayfield, 1984).

21. Johnson, p. 47.

22. Ibid., pp. 58–59.

23. Further information about self-disclosure skills are discussed in Johnson, pp. 59–61.

24. Ibid., p. 61.

25. Jack R. Gibb, "Defensive Communication," *Journal of Communication* 2 (1961), pp. 141–148.

26. Stefan Klein, *The Science of Happiness* (New York: Marlowe, 2006), pp. 151, 152.

27. Wendy Samter, "Friendship Interaction Skills across the Life Span," in *Handbook of Communication and Social Interaction Skills*, ed. John O. Greene and Brant R. Burleson (Mahwah, NJ: Lawrence Erlbaum, 2003), p. 641.

28. William K. Rawlins, *Friendship Matters: Communication, Dialects, and the Life Course* (New York: Aldine De Gruyter, 1992), p. 26.

29. Samter, pp. 641, 643.

30. Ibid., p. 661.

31. Rawlins, p. 105.

32. Richard Layard, *Happiness: Lessons from a New Science* (New York: Penguin Books, 2005), p. 66.

33. Kathryn Dindia and Lindsay Timmerman, "Accomplishing Romantic Relationships," in *Handbook of Communication and Social Interaction Skills*, ed. John O. Greene and Brant R. Burleson (Mahwah, NJ: Lawrence Erlbaum, 2003), pp. 694–697.

34. Eric Schmidt, "For the First Time, Nuclear Families Drop below 25% of Households," *The New York Times*, May 15, 2001, pp. A1, A18.

35. Sam Roberts, "51% of Women Are Now Living without Spouse," *The New York Times*, January 16, 2007, p. A1.

36. Lynn H. Turner and Richard West, *Perspectives on Family Communication*, 2nd ed. (Boston: McGraw Hill, 2002), p. 8.

37. Ibid., pp. 125–126.

38. Based on Turner and West, pp. 126–127.

39. Turner and West, p. 134.

40. Craig H. Hart, Lloyd D. Newell, and Susanne Frost Olsen, "Parenting Skills and Social–Communicative Competence in Childhood," in *Handbook of Communication and Social Interaction Skills*, ed. John O. Greene and Brant R. Burleson (Mahwah, NJ: Lawrence Erlbaum, 2003), p. 781.

41. Ibid., p. 769.

42. Ibid., p. 782.

43. Ibid., pp. 769–770.

44. Ibid., p. 771.

45. Mark C. Knapp and Anita L. Vangelisti, *Interpersonal Communication and Human Relationships* (Boston: Allyn & Bacon, 1996), pp. 33–44.

46. Ibid., pp. 33–35.

47. Douglas A. Bernstein et al., *Psychology*, 7th ed. (Boston: Houghton Mifflin, 2006), p. 430. Also see Randolph R. Cornelius, *The Science of Emotion: Research and Tradition in the Psychology of Emotion* (Upper Saddle River, NJ: Prentice Hall, 1996), pp. 9–10.

48. Robert Plutchik, *Emotions: A Psycho-evolutionary Synthesis* (New York: Harper and Row, 1980).

49. Robert Plutchik, "Emotions: A General Psychoevolutionary Theory," in *Approaches to Emotion*, ed. K.R. Scherer and Paul Ekman (Mahwah, NJ: Lawrence Erlbaum, 1984), p. 203.

50. Daniel Goleman, *Working with Emotional Intelligence* (New York: Bantam Books, 1998), p. 317.

51. See Daniel Goleman, *Emotional Intelligence: Why It Can Matter More Than IQ* (New York: Bantam, 1995); Goleman, 1998; Hendrie Weisinger, *Emotional Intelligence at Work* (San Francisco: Jossey-Bass, 1998).

52. Goleman, 1995, pp. 27–28. See also Antonio R. Damasio, *Descartes' Error: Emotion, Reason, and the Human Brain* (New York: Quill, 2000).

53. Brant R. Burleson, "Emotional Support Skills," in *Handbook of Communication and Social Interaction Skills*, ed. John O. Greene and Brant R. Burleson (Mahwah, NJ: Lawrence Erlbaum, 2003), p. 552.

54. Ibid., pp. 589–681.

55. Ibid., p. 582.

56. Susan M. Jones and John G. Wirtz, "How Does the Comforting Process Work? An Empirical Test of an Appraisal-Based Model of Comforting," *Human Communication Research* 32 (2006), p. 217.

57. Ibid., p. 583.

58. Brant R. Burleson, Amanda J. Holmstrom, and Cristina M. Gilstrap, "Guys Can't Say *That* to Guys: Four Experiments Assessing the Normative Motivation Account for Deficiencies in the Emotional Support Provided by Men," *Communication Monographs* 72 (2005), p. 469.

59. Ibid., p. 472.

60. Ibid., p. 497.

Interpersonal Communication: Professional Relationships

Key Elements of Communication	Communication Axioms	Guiding Principles of Communication in Professional Relationships
Self	*Communication Is Personal*	Identify *your* professional strengths and weaknesses as well as your role in the workplace.
Others	*Communication Is Relational*	Understand, respect, and adapt appropriately to others in the workplace.
Purpose	*Communication Is Intentional*	Identify how you can contribute to organizational goals. Develop satisfying and productive workplace relationships.
Context	*Communication Is Contextual*	Adapt appropriately to the organization's culture.
Content	*Communication Is Symbolic*	Seek and share information that promotes your own and others' work performance. Avoid gossip and offensive messages.
Structure	*Communication Is Structured*	Adapt to the organization's hierarchy. Organize messages to promote comprehension, credibility, persuasion, and motivation.
Expression	*Communication Is Irreversible*	Use verbal and nonverbal skills that promote your own and others' success. Create and maintain a positive professional image.

The Nature of Professional Relationships

Your professional relationships are among the most important in your life, and they present unique interpersonal communication challenges. Think about the number of hours most people spend at work each day. If you work full-time, you probably spend more hours interacting with coworkers, managers, clients, or customers than you do with your family and friends. Your personal relationships focus on private interactions with friends, romantic partners, and family members, whereas in **professional relationships** you interact with others to accomplish a goal or perform a task in a workplace context. Some relationships are both personal and professional. For instance, a colleague at work may become your best friend.

Professional relationships occur in a complex context defined by your role at work, the nature of your relationships with colleagues, and the organizational culture. Furthermore, many professional relationships are formed beyond the traditional workplace. You also may belong to a labor union, an academic association, a community organization, or a volunteer group. This chapter focuses on the role of communication in improving professional relationships regardless of whether you manage a work team, teach young children, work on a construction site, or volunteer at a community center.

TYPES OF PROFESSIONAL RELATIONSHIPS

Every productive workplace survives and thrives on effective interpersonal communication. However, the nature of that communication depends on how each person's role is defined. A **role** is a pattern of behaviors that is associated with an expected function in a particular context. In the workplace, interactions with your boss, employees, coworkers, and customers or clients are influenced by your roles. For example, a corporate attorney may communicate differently when interacting with her paralegal (superior–subordinate relationship), when resolving a dispute with a colleague (coworker relationship), or when counseling a client (customer relationship).

By looking at this photograph, can you determine which worker is in a superior role and which workers are in subordinate roles? Why or why not?

The nature of the workplace continues to evolve as technology enables organizations and work teams to function in virtual contexts. Because virtual communication has become a means through which many organizations function, "understanding how to work in or lead a virtual team is becoming a fundamental competency for people in many organizations."[1] Jon Katzenbach and Douglas Smith note that "today, organizations are no longer confined to team efforts that assemble people from the same location or the same time zone. Indeed, small groups of people from two or more locations and time zones routinely convene for collaborative purposes."[2]

Organizations that rely on virtual communication are complex. Employees may be from different organizations, cultures, and geographic locations—not to mention that they interact via technology. As a result, the organizational culture and the formal and informal structures are more dynamic than in organizations that primarily rely on face-to-face communication.

[1] Deborah L. Duarte and Nancy T. Snyder, *Mastering Virtual Teams: Strategies, Tools, and Techniques That Succeed*, 3rd ed. (San Francisco: Jossey-Bass, 2007), p. 4.

[2] Jon R. Katzenbach and Douglas K. Smith, *The Discipline of Teams: A Mindbook–Workbook for Delivering Small Group Performance* (New York: John Wiley, 2001), p. 23.

Superior–Subordinate Relationships **Superior–subordinate relationships** are characterized by the authority one person has over another person's work and behavior.[1] Formal roles in a work relationship influence the nature of the interaction and the content of communication. For example, superiors usually request work, explain a task, describe policies, and give feedback about a subordinate's performance, whereas subordinates are more likely to provide information about themselves, about coworkers, and about the progress of work.[2] Strained or antagonistic superior–subordinate relationships have serious consequences for everyone. Poor relationships between employees and supervisors negatively affect productivity, job satisfaction, and employee retention. Sixty percent of employees consider dealing with a supervisor the most stressful part of their job.[3] Eighty-five percent of workers who quit their jobs report doing so because they are unhappy with their boss.[4]

Usually, but not always, the more power a superior has over a subordinate, the more formal the interaction. It is natural to feel some discomfort when interacting with a person who has significant power over your destiny in an organization.

Coworker Relationships **Coworker relationships** involve interactions with people who have little or no official authority over one another but who must work together to accomplish the goals of an organization. Good relationships with coworkers are the primary source of most job satisfaction.[5] The following criteria characterize satisfying coworker relationships[6]:

- *Individual Excellence.* Do both of you perform well in the job?
- *Investment.* Do both of you devote time and resources to helping each other succeed?
- *Information.* Do both of you share information openly?
- *Integration.* Do both of you have compatible values about and styles of work?
- *Integrity.* Do you treat each other with respect?

A coworker who won't share important information can derail the performance of others. A colleague who does a poor job or is uncooperative won't be respected. Satisfying relationships with your coworkers make the difference between looking forward to or dreading another day at work.

TYPES OF PROFESSIONAL RELATIONSHIPS

▶ Superior–Subordinate Relationships

▶ Coworker Relationships

▶ Customer Relationships

Customer Relationships   Customer relations are critical to the success of any business or organization, particularly given that the average U.S. company loses half its customers within five years.[7] **Customer relationships** involve interactions between someone communicating on behalf of an organization with an individual who is external to the organization. They include the way students are treated at a college, the way patients are cared for by a doctor or hospital, and the way police officers handle crime victims. The success of both international corporations and small businesses depends on effective and ethical communication with customers and clients.

How important is it for a salesperson to meet the consumer's need to feel welcome, to get expert advice, and to be treated with respect?

CommFYI Dealing with Difficult Behavior at Work

Regardless of where you work, you are going to encounter people whose behavior makes it difficult for you to do your job and enjoy what you're doing. Difficult people at work engage in behaviors such as chronic lateness, poor performance, irritability, sniping via e-mail messages, persistent negativity, resisting needed change or shooting down new ideas, complaining constantly, neglecting commitments, and more serious forms of behavior such as harassment, work sabotage, and even physical abuse.[1]

Dealing with difficult behaviors at work is, not surprisingly, difficult. Failure to deal with such people, however, perpetuates a work environment that takes its toll on everyone. In an article titled "Feedback in the Future Tense," Hal Plotkin suggests that effective feedback is the key to dealing with people and helping them realize their full potential. Plotkin recommends a six-step approach to facilitation feedback[2]:

1. *Identify specific successes and failures.* Rather than saying, "You're always late," state the exact number of times the person has been late during a defined period of time. Be equally specific when offering praise.
2. *Stop talking and start listening.* Use all types of listening—discriminative, comprehensive, empathic, analytical, and appreciative listening—to make sure you understand the other person's point of view. And

if you listen well, maybe your colleague will do the same when you speak.

3. *Describe the implications of behavior.* Help people understand the consequences of their behavior—in both organizational and personal terms.
4. *Link past accomplishments to needed change.* Point out how the traits that have led them to successes can be applied to areas that need improvement.
5. *Agree on an action plan.* Work *together* to come up with a plan that has specific ideas or steps, clear timetables, and realistic standards for success.
6. *Follow up.* Stay engaged and set up times to meet again. Use these sessions to help the other person with problems, provide personal support, and offer praise.

Finally, change how *you* define the problem. If you talk about "difficult people" you are shifting attention from what they do to who they are. Rather, define the problem as difficult behavior and then maybe you can do something about it.[3]

[1]Hal Plotkin, "Introduction," *Dealing with Difficult People* (Boston, MA: Harvard Business School Press, 2005), p. 1.

[2]Hal Plotkin, "Feedback in the Future Tense," *Dealing with Difficult People* (Boston, MA: Harvard Business School Press, 2005), pp. 132–137.

[3]Ken Cloke and Joan Goldsmith, "How to Handle Difficult Behaviors," in *Dealing with Difficult People* (Boston, MA: Harvard Business School Press, 2005), pp. 66–67.

Unfortunately, some employees are poorly trained or have inaccurate assumptions about customer service. One study checked thousands of applications for grocery store workers and identified several false assumptions about customer service that would likely harm customer relations.[8] Almost half the applicants believed that customers should follow company policies to deserve help and should be told when they are wrong. Approximately 10 percent of would-be employees would not help a customer if it wasn't part of their job and would not volunteer to assist customers unless they asked for help.

Effective employees understand that, in a typical customer relationship, the customer has three basic communication needs.[9] First, the customer or client needs to feel welcome. Many retail staff members are trained to greet customers the moment they enter the store. Pleasant and responsive receptionists welcome outsiders as soon as they enter a lobby area. Second, customers need enough information to make a decision or solve a problem regarding a service or product. Thus, sales and customer service representatives must be product experts who offer information and ask insightful questions. Finally, customers need to be treated with respect, especially because they have the power to take their business elsewhere and to encourage others to do the same. Thus, the quality of customer relationships affects the financial health of a business and employee job security.

Dealing with dissatisfied and angry customers can be difficult and stressful, especially when customers with legitimate complaints behave in inappropriate ways. When a customer is rude or disrespectful, you may become angry. Expressing your anger, however, may only escalate the conflict. Certainly it won't help solve the problem. The Better Business Bureau points out that even when a customer isn't happy with the solution, an employee who listens and attempts to help will be perceived as cooperative.[1] The following strategies can help calm an unruly customer and promote effective problem solving[2]:

- Don't take a complaint personally.
- Listen attentively and ask questions.
- Try to separate the issues from the emotions. Rude customers may have legitimate complaints and may only be expressing frustration.

- Make statements that show you empathize: "I can understand why you would be upset" or "I don't blame you for being angry."
- Share information or explain the reasons for a decision, but do not argue with a customer.
- If the company is at fault, acknowledge it and apologize.
- Ask the customer how she or he would like the problem to be resolved.

Customers may not always be right, but they should always be treated with courtesy and respect.

[1]Council of Better Business Bureaus, "Dealing with Unruly Customers." Accessed August 7, 2007 at www.bbb.org/alerts/article.asp?ID=370.

[2]John Tschohl, Service Quality Institute, "Service, Not Servitude: Common Sense Is Critical Element of Customer Service," 2004, www.customer-service.com/articles/022502.cfm.

THE ORGANIZATIONAL CONTEXT

An organization's context significantly affects the nature of professional relationships. In many workplaces there is a structured hierarchy that establishes levels of authority and decision-making power. That hierarchy may influence who talks to whom, about what, and in what manner. In large organizations, employees are often expected to convey information and to voice concerns to their immediate supervisor. Only when a problem cannot be remedied at that level do employees have the "right" to speak to the next person up the hierarchy, and so on. Common organizational levels are illustrated in Figure 9.1.

In general, the more levels within the organization's structure, the more likely information will be distorted as communication goes up or down the hierarchy. The accuracy of the information may be reduced by up to 20 percent every time a message passes through a different level.[10]

In addition to an organizational structure, every organization has a unique culture that influences member communication. **Organizational culture** consists of the shared symbols, beliefs, values, and norms that affect the behavior of people working in and with an organization. For example, in one company employees always wear suits, spend much of their time working silently in their offices, arrive and leave promptly, and get together in small groups to socialize only after hours. Another company may have a casual dress code, open cubicles that promote social interaction during the day, and a tradition of engaging in practical jokes. Just as beliefs, norms, and traditions change when you travel from one country to another, so every organization has a unique culture.

Organizations also have subcultures. An **organizational subculture** is a group of individuals who engage in behavior and share values that are different from the larger organizational culture. The marketing department in an organization may develop different norms than that of the accounting department across the hall. The regional sales office in Texas may have different traditions than those of the Chicago office. The young associates in a law firm may develop a subculture apart from the older law partners.

Professional Communication Challenges

Maria didn't want anyone at work to know that she was dating her coworker James. Unfortunately, her officemate, Elena, overheard her talking with James on the phone and told several coworkers about the relationship. Soon there was a buzz in the office. Not only was Maria worried that she or James would have to resign, but she also feared being mocked or harassed by others.

Poor professional relationships can have serious consequences: tension in the workplace, limited advancement opportunities, or even job loss. In this section we examine some of the most difficult communication situations that occur within organizations: office gossip, workplace romances, working with friends, sexual harassment, and quitting a job.

OFFICE GOSSIP

In one survey of office workers, more than 90 percent of employees admitted to engaging in gossip.[11] The study also revealed that after learning information about a colleague intended to be secret, 75 percent of employees revealed the coworker's secret to at least two other employees that same day.

Gossip is information, usually unverified, regarding the organization, individuals, or their relationships that is communicated through informal channels in an organization. Most of us listen to gossip because we want to have as much information as everyone else. Typically, we spread gossip because we want to be perceived as "in the know."[12]

Gossip serves an important social function. Psychology professor Robin Dunbar points out that "what characterizes the social life of humans is the intense interest we show in each other's doings."[13] Consultant Annette Simmons observes that "a certain amount of small talk—sharing small details of your life—helps people feel closer to coworkers. It is what humanizes the workplace and helps people bond."[14]

However, rampant or malicious gossip can have serious consequences. Private and potentially embarrassing information, even if untrue, can damage your professional credibility. Divulging company secrets can get you fired. Time spent gossiping is time not spent doing your job. In some workplaces, gossip infects the workplace and creates a climate of hostility and distrust.

Effective communicators in a healthy organizational culture know the difference between harmless small talk and damaging gossip. The following strategies can help you manage gossip in any organization[15]:

- Do not spread unsubstantiated or malicious rumors. If you don't know whether the information is accurate, don't repeat it.
- Assess the reliability of a rumor or gossip by asking questions and checking facts.
- When others gossip, change the subject, tell them you prefer not to discuss certain topics, or say that you're too busy to talk at the moment.
- Consider the potential consequences of divulging confidential information or spreading a rumor.
- Before self-disclosing to a coworker, assume that your secret will be told to others.
- If you believe that gossip has created a serious problem, talk to someone with more power or influence.

An organization can also take measures that prevent the need for gossip.[16] The key to prevention is keeping employees well informed. Employees are more likely to

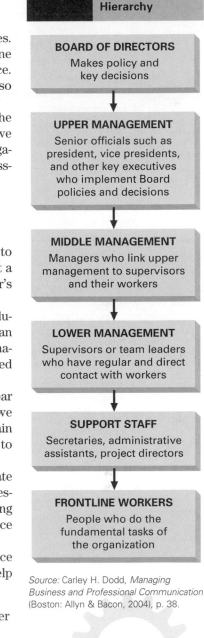

Figure 9.1 Classic Organizational Hierarchy

BOARD OF DIRECTORS Makes policy and key decisions

UPPER MANAGEMENT Senior officials such as president, vice presidents, and other key executives who implement Board policies and decisions

MIDDLE MANAGEMENT Managers who link upper management to supervisors and their workers

LOWER MANAGEMENT Supervisors or team leaders who have regular and direct contact with workers

SUPPORT STAFF Secretaries, administrative assistants, project directors

FRONTLINE WORKERS People who do the fundamental tasks of the organization

Source: Carley H. Dodd, *Managing Business and Professional Communication* (Boston: Allyn & Bacon, 2004), p. 38.

PROFESSIONAL COMMUNICATION CHALLENGES
▶ Office Gossip
▶ Workplace Romances
▶ Working with Friends
▶ Sexual Harassment
▶ Quitting a Job

CommEthics   Whistle-blowing

Employees who witness unethical or illegal practices in the workplace face a difficult choice. Should they report the wrongdoing in the hopes of correcting a problem, or should they remain silent for fear of losing a job? There are no easy answers to these questions. A **whistle-blower** is a person who reports wrongdoing in a workplace or organization to another individual or organization that has the power to expose publicly, correct, or punish the behavior.

Whistle-blowers have been responsible for shedding light on many unethical practices in corporations and government agencies. In 2002, *Time* magazine selected three prominent whistle-blowers as their Persons of the Year.[1] Sherron Watkins uncovered improper accounting methods at Enron. Coleen Rowley complained that the FBI ignored information regarding a terrorist involved in the 9/11 attack. Cynthia Cooper blew the whistle on WorldCom's unethical bookkeeping practices.

The decision to report someone else's behavior is difficult. Not only is it an awkward situation, but you may also fear repercussions. If you expose unethical actions, will the problem be corrected, or will you be resented, or worse, lose your job? Fortunately, research suggests that most whistle-blowers do not report any form of retaliation.[2] Nevertheless, you should carefully consider the potential consequences.

Consider the following guidelines for deciding whether you should blow the whistle on a wrongdoer[3]:

- Accurately assess the seriousness of the problem.
- Gather valid supporting information and present it fairly.
- Try to identify others who are also upset by the situation.

- Explore alternatives for correcting the problem.
- Decide whether you can work within the organizational structure to remedy the problem.
- If necessary, consult an attorney for advice.
- Report the problem to the appropriate individuals or organization.
- Do your best to maintain good working relationships with management, coworkers, and subordinates.
- Understand the potential consequences to you, your coworkers, or to the organization.
- Keep a careful record of events before and after blowing the whistle.

It is difficult to break ranks and voice publicly concerns that are unpopular or that have potentially serious consequences for an organization. However, Senator Joseph Biden reminds us that "only whistle-blowers can help us understand the culture that produces wrongful behavior." For that reason, he considers whistle-blowers "national assets."[4]

[1]Richard Lacayo and Amanda Ripley, "Cynthia Cooper, Coleen Rowley, and Sherron Watkins," *Time* (December 22, 2002), www.time.com/time/personoftheyear/2002/poyintro.html.

[2]Janet P. Near and Marcia Miceli, "Whistle-blowing: Myth and Reality," *Journal of Management* (1996), www.findarticles.com/p/articles/mi_m4256/is_n3_v22/ai_18764058/pg_1.

[3]J. Vernon Jensen, "Ethical Tension Points in Whistle-blowing," *Journal of Business Ethics* (1987), pp. 321–328, as cited in Richard L. Johannesen, *Ethics in Human Communication*, 4th ed. (Prospect Heights, IL: Waveland Press, 1996), pp. 185–186; Government Accountability Project, "Blowing the Whistle Wisely: 12 Survival Strategies," www.whistleblower.org/article.php?did=33&scid=72.

[4]Dave Eberhart, "Whistle-blowers Seen as Key to Corporate Crackdown," *NewsMax,* www.newsmax.com.

speculate and gossip when they are uninformed about organizational decisions. For example, when a company is purchased by a larger corporation, many—if not most—employees worry about losing their jobs, and speculate about who will stay and who will be asked to leave. If no personnel cutbacks are planned, employees should be told. When cutbacks are anticipated, an organization should inform everyone about how those decisions will be made. Although some employees will worry about their future and others may believe that their jobs are secure, everyone will have more accurate information. When organizations learn that misinformation is making its way through the rumor mill, they should address and correct it quickly before any more harm is done.

WORKPLACE ROMANCES

Approximately one-third of all romantic relationships begin in the workplace.[17] In one study, 93 percent of people surveyed report that they have worked in places where colleagues had a romantic relationship,[18] and more than 60 percent say they have been involved in at least one workplace romance.[19] Although many workplace romances result in long-lasting relationships and marriages, it can be difficult to manage the blurred distinction between our private and professional lives.

Generally, we behave differently in personal relationships than we do with most colleagues. These differences can cause problems. For example, a public display of affection in the workplace may be viewed as unprofessional and may make other colleagues feel uncomfortable. Coworkers may also suspect that a romantic partner receives preferential treatment. Romantically involved couples may find it difficult to separate issues at work from personal issues that arise after work. And if a romantic relationship ends, the professional relationship may become strained or awkward. Half the romantic relationships begun in the workplace will also end there.[20]

When Google employees meet informally or stop whizzing through the office space on scooters to see what's happening, are they likely to engage in gossip? Can gossip serve an important social function among workers?

Why do many organizations disapprove of office romance? Many corporate executives believe that office romances almost always end badly and therefore should be banned in the workplace.[21] They are concerned that an office romance may eventually result in a claim of sexual harassment or retaliatory behavior after the relationship ends.[22] Organizations also have concerns about the effect of romantic relationships on the workplace. They worry that romantically involved employees will become less productive and that their relationship will affect the morale of coworkers or create a climate of unprofessionalism.[23]

Wall Street Journal columnist Sue Shellenbarger suggests that if you can answer yes to any of the following questions, your employer may be justified in warning, reprimanding, transferring, or terminating you if you are involved in a romantic relationship at work[24]:

- Are you romantically involved with a subordinate or your boss?
- Are both of you assigned to the same team or division?
- Is the relationship negatively affecting your work?
- Will your work be negatively affected if the relationship ends?
- Could others perceive favoritism as a result of the relationship?

Shellenbarger also suggests that, if you pursue an office romance, keep in mind that in all likelihood it will eventually end. "If it does end, you have to be mature enough and professional enough to handle seeing the other person every day."[25]

WORKING WITH FRIENDS

Many coworker relationships are personal as well as professional. Mixing personal and professional relationships, however, has the potential to create difficulties in both your work and your friendship. Chapter 8, "Interpersonal Communication: Improving Personal Relationships," discusses relational dialectics—ongoing tensions between contradictory forces. Balancing a friendship with a professional relationship can be a difficult dialectic to negotiate: You want your friend to like you, but you also need coworkers, superiors, and subordinates to respect you; you want approval from your friend, but you also must make objective decisions in the workplace; you hope for your friend's professional success, but not at the expense of your own.

Figure 9.2 summarizes some of the strains that occur when friendship and work relationships collide. Many of these strains pose a dialectic challenge.

Daniel Modaff and Sue DeWine suggest that you seek your most important relationships outside the workplace and that, if you do have a personal relationship at work, you should be prepared to manage the consequences.[26] Telling a best friend that he has not met expectations on a work team can be difficult and even impossible if

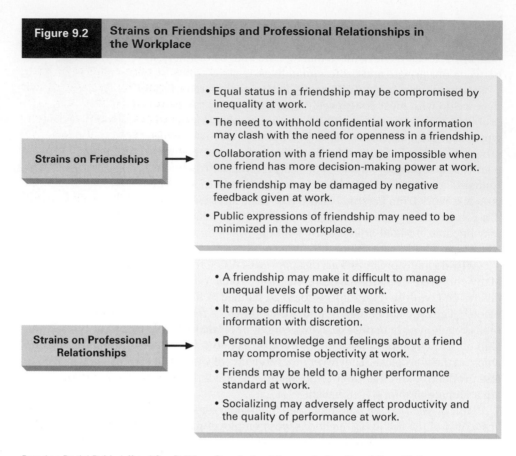

Figure 9.2	Strains on Friendships and Professional Relationships in the Workplace

Strains on Friendships

- Equal status in a friendship may be compromised by inequality at work.
- The need to withhold confidential work information may clash with the need for openness in a friendship.
- Collaboration with a friend may be impossible when one friend has more decision-making power at work.
- The friendship may be damaged by negative feedback given at work.
- Public expressions of friendship may need to be minimized in the workplace.

Strains on Professional Relationships

- A friendship may make it difficult to manage unequal levels of power at work.
- It may be difficult to handle sensitive work information with discretion.
- Personal knowledge and feelings about a friend may compromise objectivity at work.
- Friends may be held to a higher performance standard at work.
- Socializing may adversely affect productivity and the quality of performance at work.

Based on Daniel P. Modaff and Sue DeWine, *Organizational Communication: Foundations, Challenges, Misunderstandings.* (Los Angeles, CA: Roxbury, 2002), p. 202.

you want to preserve the friendship. At the same time, letting a friend get away with less-than-excellent work can destroy the morale of a group and put your reputation and leadership at risk.

SEXUAL HARASSMENT

Workplace romances should not be confused with sexual harassment. Romance in the workplace involves two individuals who agree to a personal relationship, whereas sexual harassment is the undesirable and inappropriate behavior of one person. In some cases, romantic relationships that end badly result in sexual harassment. If, for example, an employee posts embarrassing personal photographs of an "ex" in the office lunchroom as a way of getting back for a hostile breakup, the person in those photos may feel humiliated, offended, and unable to work productively with colleagues. The distressed employee also may have grounds for a sexual harassment suit.

The Equal Employment Opportunity Commission (EEOC) defines **sexual harassment** as follows:

> Unwelcome sexual advances for sexual favors, and other verbal or physical conduct of a sexual nature constitutes sexual harassment when submission to or rejection of this conduct explicitly or implicitly affects an individual's employment, unreasonably interferes with an individual's work performance or creates an intimidating, hostile or offensive work environment.[27]

The EEOC receives approximately 15,000 complaints of sexual harassment every year.[28] Thirteen percent of these are filed by men.[29]

Sexual harassment takes many forms. A supervisor may demand sexual favors from a subordinate as a guarantee of keeping a job. Making sex a prerequisite for career opportunities such as a promotion, a more lucrative sales region, or extra time off also qualifies as sexual harassment. In these instances, a supervisor or colleague uses power to coerce sexual favors.

Sexual harassment is not limited to demands for sex. It often takes the form of sexually demeaning or offensive communication, such as circulating sexually explicit messages and jokes via e-mail, posting sexual images in staff rooms, or making sexually demeaning comments about a coworker. Sexual harassment is rarely an isolated incident. Usually, it is a pattern of offensive or unwelcome behavior that takes place over a period of time. Thus, sexual harassment is a "situation and not merely an act."[30]

Identifying sexual harassment is often complicated by the fact that men and women may have differing perceptions of similar behavior. Men are less likely than women to view a behavior as harassment.[31] Thus, telling a sexually explicit joke in the office may be viewed by women as harassment, whereas men may see it as harmless. Both men and women, however, judge overt behavior, such as demands for sexual favors, as harassment.

Research indicates that victims of sexual harassment may experience a variety of reactions, including physical symptoms, "decreased work performance, anxiety, depression, self-blame, anger, feelings of helplessness, fear of further or escalating harassment, and fear of reporting the incident."[32] Although most workers indicate that they would immediately address or report harassment, research reveals that, when confronted with the situation, many people feel uncomfortable and fail to report the behavior.[33] If you believe you are the victim of sexual harassment, keep in mind that complaints are taken more seriously when brought to the attention of management immediately.[34]

Most organizations take allegations of sexual harassment very seriously to avoid costly lawsuits. Additionally, a threatening or uncomfortable organizational culture can result in low morale, decreased productivity, and employee turnover. There are many strategies organizations can use to prevent and respond appropriately to sexual harassment[35]:

- Have a clear policy against sexual harassment.
- Educate employees about sexual harassment and the complaint process.
- Educate supervisors and managers about sexual harassment and how to handle a complaint.
- Request feedback from employees about the work environment.
- Let everyone know that complaints are taken seriously.

Employees have a responsibility to treat each other with respect and to refrain from behavior that could be perceived as offensive or make others uncomfortable. Workers should not have to tolerate a sexually hostile work environment.

QUITTING A JOB

According to the U.S. Department of Labor, the typical American will change *careers* approximately seven times.[36] And according to the Bureau of Labor Statistics, before the age of thirty-two, the average American has had nine *jobs* and one-third of workers predict they will probably change jobs again within five years.[37] Just as you want to make a good first impression when interviewing and beginning a new job, it is important to leave a positive impression when quitting a job.

There are many reasons for leaving a job or changing careers. You may find a better opportunity, have to move to a new area, or not be satisfied with your current job. Whatever the reason, you should always try to leave a job on good terms and handle your resignation with professionalism and courtesy. The following practices make sense when quitting any job[38]:

- Follow company policies and procedures when resigning.
- Tell your immediate supervisor first.

Directions: For each of the following items, rate your level of satisfaction with your current or most recent job on a scale of 1 to 4: 1 = extremely dissatisfied, 2 = somewhat dissatisfied, 3 = somewhat satisfied, and 4 = extremely satisfied.

How satisfied are you with . . .

_____ 1. your job responsibilities?

_____ 2. the degree to which your skills are properly used?

_____ 3. your workload?

_____ 4. your salary or hourly pay relative to your responsibilities and experience?

_____ 5. your level of job security?

_____ 6. how your work is evaluated and rewarded?

_____ 7. the extent to which your job helps you pursue career goals?

_____ 8. the extent to which the organization helps you grow professionally?

_____ 9. the relationship you have with your boss?

_____ 10. how your boss makes decisions?

_____ 11. the extent to which you are treated fairly?

_____ 12. the relationships you have with coworkers?

_____ 13. the overall quality of work by colleagues?

_____ 14. how well coworkers cooperate with one another?

_____ 15. the degree of friendliness in the workplace?

_____ 16. the decisions of the organization?

_____ 17. your level of influence in decision making?

_____ 18. how information is shared within the organization?

_____ 19. how the organization handles dissent and disagreement?

_____ 20. the ethics of the organization's practices?

Add your responses to determine your total score. A score of less than 50 points represents general dissatisfaction with your job. The following scores represent your level of job satisfaction:

20–34 points	Very dissatisfied
35–49 points	Moderately dissatisfied
50–64 points	Moderately satisfied
65–80 points	Very satisfied

Review your responses to identify specific areas of dissatisfaction. You may enjoy your coworkers but dislike your boss. You may have a good relationship with your boss but are unhappy with organizational policies. You may enjoy a friendly work environment but believe you are underpaid.

- Resign in person, but also write a brief resignation letter.
- Give the appropriate advance notice.
- Phrase explanations positively.

Leaving on good terms is important, even when a resignation is the result of dissatisfaction with the job or a poor relationship with a boss or coworkers. Although you may feel angry or upset, keep in mind that the next employer will probably contact your previous employers. You may need a positive reference from the boss you didn't like.

After you resign, a supervisor or human resources manager may request an exit interview. Organizations gather information in exit interviews to develop strategies for retaining other employees and to improve the workplace for those who remain. Because you don't know how the information will be used or whether it will be treated confidentially, remain calm and convey a positive attitude. Focus on issues, not people. Although the interviewer's goal is to gather information, your goal is to leave a good impression. A positive exit interview has several advantages. You never know when you may encounter your exit interviewer again. Even more important, "the exit interview is not the time to burn bridges. Most industries are small, and bad behavior is not something you want people remembering about you."[39]

Unfortunately, most human resources professionals report that only 60 percent of the information provided by resigning employees is completely accurate and honest.[40] When participating in an exit interview, provide useful information rather than venting your frustrations about the job you are leaving. Honesty is best, but avoid too much negativity. As one human relations attorney put it, "Just because you're leaving the company doesn't mean your words won't live there for years to come."[41]

Types of Workplace Interviews

An **interview** is an interpersonal interaction between two parties, at least one of which has a predetermined and serious purpose, that involves asking and answering questions to share information, solve a problem, or influence one another.[42] The types of interviews you are most likely to encounter in the workplace include selection interviews, appraisal interviews, disciplinary interviews, exit interviews, and information-gathering interviews.

SELECTION INTERVIEWS

The purpose of a **selection interview** is to evaluate and choose candidates for a job. Almost all businesses use interviews as part of the hiring process. The selection interview provides employers with an opportunity to assess your knowledge, maturity, personality, attitude, and communication skills. These interviews are not limited to workplace hiring; they may also be required by colleges and scholarship committees or for membership in private groups such as fraternities, sororities, and country clubs. Selection interviews are often stressful because they can determine your ultimate acceptance by a company, an organization, or a group.

APPRAISAL INTERVIEWS

An **appraisal interview** is usually conducted to evaluate an employee's job performance. The interview may be one component in a company's performance assessment process, which may also include a written self-evaluation and evaluations from supervisors and peers. Good appraisal interviews help determine or clarify employees' professional goals, identify their training needs, determine where they can make the best contribution to the organization, and provide motivation through feedback on job performance.[43] Appraisal interviews may also contribute to decisions about promotions, salary raises, or who will remain employed.

TYPES OF WORKPLACE INTERVIEWS
► Selection Interviews
► Appraisal Interviews
► Disciplinary Interviews
► Exit Interviews
► Information-Gathering Interviews

DISCIPLINARY INTERVIEWS

Suppose that one of your employees, Brent, always arrives late and does not do his share of the work. Everyone is frustrated with having to work harder because Brent isn't pulling his weight. You decide to schedule a meeting with him to address the problem. The purpose of a **disciplinary interview** is to correct problematic behavior. An effective disciplinary interview should not focus on punishment, but on changing behavior to solve a problem.[44] Brent's disciplinary interview might include a number of questions aimed at understanding what is happening from Brent's perspective, why it is happening, his familiarity with company policies or job expectations, and how he can change his behavior to resolve the problem.[45]

EXIT INTERVIEWS

An **exit interview** solicits information about why an employee is leaving an organization and whether any problems contributed to the decision. In a survey conducted by the Society for Human Resource Management and the Bureau of National Affairs, 96 percent of human resource professionals indicated that they conduct an exit interview when an employee resigns.[46]

Exit interviews usually serve two purposes. First, "they provide closure for the departing employee and they help the company understand why the employee decided to leave."[47] Ideally, an exit interview should make employees feel as though their comments are appreciated and that they have made suggestions that could help colleagues who remain. Second and from the company's perspective, the information gained from exit interviews is used to make organizational changes that will improve employee satisfaction and retention.

INFORMATION-GATHERING INTERVIEWS

The primary purpose of an **information-gathering interview** is to "obtain facts, opinions, data, feelings, attitudes, beliefs, reactions, and feedback."[48] Fundamentally, all interviews involve information gathering. However, the previous types of interviews typically involve making decisions about individuals, whereas information-gathering interviews help interviewers understand an issue or solve a problem. Police officers interview crime witnesses and victims. Opinion research firms interview individuals about the products they like or the political candidates they prefer. Journalists interview sources to report a story. When you prepare a presentation you might interview an expert to gain insight into your topic.

Job Interviews

Although a job interview (a form of selection interview) can be a stressful communication situation, a good interview can land you the job of your dreams. Unfortunately, a poor interview can result in a major disappointment and the loss of a promising career opportunity. The saying that you never get a *second* chance to make a *first* impression is especially true for job interviews. In this section we focus on the successful preparation, presentation, and follow-up of job interviews.

BEFORE THE INTERVIEW

PREPARING FOR A JOB INTERVIEW
▶ Research the Organization
▶ Assess Your Strengths and Weaknesses
▶ Formulate Your Career Goals
▶ Practice

In a discussion of interviewing, Richard Bolles tells the story of an IBM recruiter who asked a college senior he was interviewing, "What does IBM stand for?" The senior didn't know and that was the end of the interview.[49] As with any important communication situation, a successful job interview requires careful preparation. In a survey of senior executives that rated the most common job interview mistakes, the top three related to how well a candidate prepared for an interview: (1) little or no knowledge of the company, (2) unprepared to discuss skills and experiences, and (3) unprepared to discuss career plans and goals.[50] Thus we offer the following advice: Before going to an interview, research the organization, assess your own strengths and weaknesses, formulate your career plans and goals, and practice.

In what ways is an information-gathering interview similar to or different from a job interview?

Approximately twenty to forty-five percent of applicants lie on a resume or in a job interview.[1] One study indicated that eleven percent don't tell the truth about why they left a previous job and nine percent lie about their education and responsibilities in previous jobs.[2] Not only is lying to a prospective employer unethical, but it can also backfire and have serious personal consequences.

Most organizations have become much more rigorous when screening applicants. Private detective Fay Faron explains that organizations conduct extensive background checks to avoid a lawsuit and ensure the safety of customers.[3] So count on being carefully screened, having your references checked, and being investigated for a criminal background. Furthermore, after a lie is discovered, an applicant will be rejected or, if already hired, will be fired. A survey conducted by an executive search firm revealed that ninety-five percent of employers would reject applicants who lied about a college degree and eighty percent would not hire someone who falsified previous job titles.[4] Many organizations have suffered from the high price of lawsuits resulting from the actions of unqualified employees who were poorly screened during the hiring process.

Attorney Henry Strada encourages employers to check references, contact all previous employers, and make clear that falsifying information is grounds for rejection or termination.[5] He also offers the following tips for catching liars during a job interview:

- Ask probing questions that require more specific information or explanation.
- Ask questions that are directly related to the skills needed for the job.
- Have more than one person interview the applicant.
- Compare notes with other interviewers to spot inconsistencies.

Your goal is more than getting a job, but getting a job that is right for you.[6] If you have to falsify your credentials or work experience, you are probably not qualified for the job. Moreover, the consequences of lying can be long-lasting. If your lie is discovered, "it can mean a ruined reputation not only with one company, but with an entire industry as word gets out."[7]

[1]"Lying: How Can You Protect Your Company?" www.westaff.com/yourworkplace/ywissues37_full.html.

[2]Daryl Koehn, University of St. Thomas Center for Business Ethics, "Rewriting History: Resume Falsification More Than a Passing Fiction," www.stthom.edu/cbes/resume.html.

[3]Donna Hemmila, "Tired of Lying, Cheating Job Applicants, Employers Calling in Detectives," *San Francisco Business Times*, February 27–March 5, 1998, www.erxcheck.com/articles/article22.php.

[4]Barbara Mende, "Employers Crack down on Candidates Who Lie," *Wall Street Journal Career Journal*, www.careerjournal.com/jobhunting/resumes/20020606-mende.html; "Lying: How Can You Protect Your Company?"

[5]Henry Strada, SBA Online Women's Business Center, "When Potential Employees Lie: How to Spot a Lie on a Resumé or Application," www.onlinewbc.gov/docs/manage/LyingOnApplications.html.

[6]Wallace V. Schmidt and Roger N. Conway, *Results-Oriented Interviewing: Principles, Practices, and Procedures* (Boston: Allyn & Bacon, 1999), p. 84.

[7]"Lying: How Can You Protect Your Company?"

Research the Organization Learn as much as you can about the organization. You can contact the company or organization directly and request documents they make available to the public, such as brochures, catalogs, newsletters, and annual reports. Most good libraries have publications containing information about individual businesses, public organizations, and industry-wide trends. If you know current or former employees, ask them about the organization.

A company or organization's website should tell you a great deal about the organization's mission, products and services, and achievements. If the website includes information about key employees, research the person or persons you will meet at the interview. You also may find news stories about the company or organization on other websites. The more you know, the easier it is to explain how you can make a positive contribution. Research may also uncover reasons you don't want to work for that organization, ranging from a company's policy on unions or political issues to concerns about health benefits or pension options.

Assess Your Strengths and Weaknesses Identify what *you* can bring to the job that will promote the organization's goals. Ron, a thirty-two-year-old man with some sales experience, was preparing to interview for a sales director position at a mid-size company. He found a story on the Internet reporting that the company was considering restructuring its product pricing. Although the job description did not mention needing experience with this task, Ron decided to make a point of saying that his last job involved reevaluating product pricing. Using the information he researched about the organization helped Ron demonstrate why he was the best candidate for the position.

Be prepared to explain your weaknesses as well as your strengths. How will you address unexplained gaps of time on your resumé, several jobs in a short period of time, or the lack of a skill specifically mentioned in the job description? The time to develop an acceptable answer to such reasonable concerns is not in the middle of an interview. For example, Sharon quit her graphic design job when her first child was born and was a stay-at-home mother for seven years. When she decided to reenter the workplace, she knew she would have to address concerns about being up-to-date in her field. After careful consideration, she developed an answer that focused on refresher courses she had taken during the past two years as well as the volunteer design work she had done for community groups. She also suggested that her design "eye" had matured and grown more sophisticated than it was when she was a younger artist. Whatever your weakness might be, don't assume that the interviewer hasn't noticed it on the application or resumé. Instead, be ready with a thoughtful response.

Formulate Your Career Goals How would you answer "What are your long-term goals and how do you plan to achieve them?" or "Explain why you chose this career area?" Even before you apply for a job, make sure you can answer these types of questions. If you're not satisfied with your answers, seek help at your college's career counseling center. Check your college or local library for books on career planning. A computer search of terms such as *career planning* will uncover many sites that can help you formulate your career plans and goals.

Practice During a job interview, you need to make a good impression in a limited amount of time—and during a fairly stressful communication situation. Practicing will make a difference. Create a list of interview questions that might be asked and carefully consider your answers. Figure 9.3 lists common questions asked in job interviews.

Because the interview will probably take place in a meeting room or office, sit at your desk or dining table and practice your answers out loud and confidently. After you are comfortable with your answers, ask a few friends or family members to interview you. They can give you feedback on the quality of your answers and may even suggest some additional questions to consider.

Finally, understand that nervousness during a job interview is normal. Before the interview, use the strategies discussed in Chapter 2, "Understanding Self," for coping with your fears and managing nervous tension. The more you prepare for an interview, the more confident you will appear and feel.

DURING THE INTERVIEW

An interview is a golden opportunity for both you and the interviewer. The interviewer wants to learn more about you, and you have the opportunity to learn about the job and the organization while creating a positive impression. The extent to which you accomplish these goals depends on how well you respond to questions and present yourself.

Handling Questions Most interviews are structured around a series of questions and answers. The following types of questions are often used in interviews[51]:

- *Closed-Ended Question.* A **closed-ended question** usually requires no more than a simple and direct answer or a yes or no response. Example: Are you able to work on weekends?
- *Open-Ended Question.* An **open-ended question** encourages a more detailed response beyond a simple yes or no answer. Example: What do you view as the most significant challenges facing this industry over the next few years?
- *Hypothetical Question.* A **hypothetical question** describes a set of circumstances and asks how you would respond. Example: How would you handle an

Figure 9.3	Common Interview Questions

1234 The Main Hwy., Littletown, USA 09876
(333) 555-1234
www.doublebreedlivestockcorp.com

**Doublebreed
Livestock Corp.**

INTERVIEW QUESTIONS

1. Briefly, tell us about yourself.

2. What do you hope to be doing five years from now?

3. Where do you hope to be in ten years?

4. In terms of this job, what is your greatest strength?

5. What, in your opinion, is your greatest weakness?

6. What motivates you to work hard and do your best?

7. How well do you deal with pressure? Can you give an example?

8. What are the two or three characteristics you look for in a good job?

9. Describe a major problem you encountered on the job. How did you deal with it?

10. What kind of relationship should be established between a supervisor and subordinates?

11. Why did you choose to pursue this particular career?

12. Why did you leave your last job(s)?

13. How can you contribute to our company?

14. How do you evaluate or determine success?

15. Given the fact that we have other applicants, why should we hire you?

Sources: Larry Powell and Jonathan Ambary, *Interviewing: Situations and Contexts* (Boston: Pearson/Allyn & Bacon, 2006), p. 47; Wallace V. Schmidt and Roger N. Conaway, *Results-Oriented Interviewing: Principles, Practices, and Procedures* (Boston, MA: Allyn & Bacon, 1999), p. 107; Charles J. Stewart and William B. Cash, Jr., *Interviewing: Principles and Practices* (Boston, MA: McGraw-Hill, 2003), p. 245; *Job Link USA*, "Interview," www.joblink-usa.com/interview.htm; *CollegeGrad.Com*, "Candidate Interview Questions," www.collegegrad.com/jobsearch/16-15.shtml.

employee who does good work but, even after being warned, continues to arrive late?

- *Leading Question.* A **leading question** suggests or implies the desired response. Example: Do you think the ability to work well in a group is just as important as the ability to perform routine technical tasks?

- *Probing Question.* A **probing question** is used to follow up another question and/or response by encouraging clarification and elaboration. Example: Could you explain what you mean by a "difficult client"?

Regardless of the type of question, the seven key elements and guiding principles of communication can help you develop and answer every question in an interview:

1. *Self.* How can I emphasize my positive qualities?
2. *Others.* What response will impress or convince the interviewer?
3. *Purpose.* Why did the interviewer ask this question and how can my answer address those expectations?
4. *Context.* What length and types of answer are appropriate in this interview?
5. *Content.* What ideas and information should I include in my answer?
6. *Structure.* In what order should I present my ideas and information?
7. *Expression.* What type of verbal and nonverbal behavior should I use when responding and interacting?

Consider how the following reactions illustrate the differences between an effective and an inappropriate response to commonly asked interview questions.

Question 1: Why did you leave your last job?

Answer: My boss and I just didn't get along. She expected me to do work that was really her responsibility. They didn't pay me enough to do my job and someone else's. When I complained, nobody did anything about it.

Question 2: What, in your opinion, is your greatest job-related weakness?

Answer: My natural tendency is to focus on one thing at a time until it's completed. However, most of my jobs have required me to manage several projects at once. I've had to learn how to juggle a variety of tasks, particularly when things get hectic. A couple of years ago I started using a project management software system to track projects and help me keep things organized. This has helped me shift attention back and forth among projects without losing track of priorities and deadlines.

The response to the first question—even if it is honest—is not very effective or flattering. The applicant should have considered the purpose of the question. Interviewers often ask questions like these to determine whether you had problems with a former employer and whether you will be just as troublesome in a new job. In this example, the interviewer could conclude that the applicant doesn't work well with others, resists doing required work, may complain a lot, and evaluates her or his work only in terms of a paycheck. A better approach is to focus on why a new job would offer more desirable opportunities and better match your values and goals. A job interview is not the time or place to vent frustrations about a former boss.

Unlike the response to the first question, the answer to the second question is effective and strategic. Certainly, an interviewer does not expect you to reveal information that eliminates you as a candidate for the job. The key is figuring out how to acknowledge a weakness but use it to demonstrate how you learned to deal with or overcome the problem. As a result, you transform the weakness into an example of your ability to solve problems. But don't make your response so obviously a strength that the interviewer will not take you seriously. When asked about your weakness, don't say, "I work too hard." We all do that. Being a hard worker is usually considered a strength.

In addition to preparing to answer questions, be prepared to ask some questions. Never hesitate to ask a question of clarification before giving a response. Use the interview as an opportunity to learn more about the job, its employees, and the organization. Before ending an interview, interviewers often ask if you have additional questions. Consider asking the following[52]:

- Can you tell me more about the responsibilities of this position?
- What, in your opinion, are the major challenges currently facing the organization?

CommFAQ How Do I Respond to Inappropriate Questions?

Federal and state laws prohibit discrimination in hiring. Generally, an interview should not include a discussion of race or ethnicity, gender, marital status, religion, sexual orientation, or disabilities. The following are several inappropriate questions[1]:

- What does your husband or wife do?
- Do you plan to have children?
- How many more years do you plan to work before retiring?
- Which religious holidays will you take off from work?
- Do you have any disabilities?
- What country are your parents from?

You have the right to refuse to answer a question you believe is inappropriate. However, you risk offending or embarrassing the interviewer. Be as tactful as possible and redirect the interview to a discussion of your qualifications. For example, if you are asked how many years you plan to work before retiring, you might say, "I focus my attention on accomplishing important professional goals rather than on retirement plans." Don't assume that the interviewer intends to discriminate. These types of questions are often asked out of simple curiosity or an effort to engage in conversation.

Before responding to a seemingly inappropriate question, assess the purpose of the question. What is the interviewer's underlying concern? For example, "Do you have children?" may reflect a concern that a busy parent won't work the number of hours necessary or be fully committed to the job. An appropriate response might be "If you're asking whether I can balance a demanding job with family obligations, I have always effectively done so in the past."

Finally, you always have the option of simply answering the question. The interviewer may be unaware that the question is inappropriate. For example, a hiring manager who asks whether you plan to have children could be worried that a new employee will take time off for maternity or family leave, or might not be willing to put in long hours at work. In that instance, the question is inappropriate. On the other hand, the interviewer may simply want to talk about the company's excellent maternity and childcare benefits or brag about his or her own newborn child.

Career counselor Julia Miller Vick notes that "you don't have any control over the reasons you are being asked this question, but you do have control over how you answer it and redirect the conversation."[2] The best approach depends on the situation, what information you feel comfortable revealing, and your personal communication style.

[1]Mary Heiberger and Julia Miller Vick, "How To Handle Difficult Interview Questions," *Chronicle of Higher Education,* January 22, 1999, http://chronicle.com/jobs/v45/i21/4521career.htm; Allison Doyle, "Illegal Interview Questions: Illegal Interview Question Samples," http://jobsearch.about.com/library/weekly/aa0224032/htm.

[2]Heiberger and Vick.

- What is the most important characteristic you are looking for in an employee for this position?
- How would you describe the culture of your organization?
- How will success be measured for this position?
- What other people or departments will I be working with?

Asking questions can help you learn about the job and the organization's culture. When appropriate, follow up the response with a statement about how you can meet a specific need. For example, if you are told that the job involves interacting with some important but demanding clients, describe how you would handle or have handled similar situations in the past.

Making a Good Impression   Interviews provide employers with a way of deciding whether you are the right person for a job, not just from your answers, but also from the way you speak and behave during the interview. Remember that you are being observed from the moment you arrive until the time you leave the building. In fact, it's not unusual for an interviewer to ask receptionists or secretaries for their impressions of you.

Interviewers should be well prepared, manage the interview effectively, and objectively analyze an applicant's responses and behavior after the interview is over. Before you interview anyone, make a list of the skills and qualities necessary for the job. Then develop questions and criteria for evaluating each applicant. Write down the questions in the order in which you intend to ask them. Remember that open-ended questions encourage more detailed answers and usually provide more valuable information than closed-ended questions. Also be prepared to answer questions about the organization and the position. Prior to meeting with applicants, review their applications and resumés.

When it's time to conduct the interview, consider the following tips:

- Conduct the interview in an office or conference room free of distractions and interruptions.
- Be friendly when greeting the applicant.
- Help an applicant to relax by starting with the easiest questions.
- Avoid asking personal, irrelevant, or inappropriate questions.
- Listen attentively to the applicant's responses.
- Make notes you can refer to later.
- Allow applicants to ask you questions.

The more comfortable you make the interview situation, the better you will accomplish the goals of learning about a person and creating a good impression of the organization. Management consultants Robert Heller and Tim Hindle emphasize that it is important to "always preserve the dignity and self-esteem of a candidate."[1]

[1]Robert Heller and Tim Hindle, *Essential Manager's Manual* (New York: DK Publishing, 1998), p. 677.

You can enhance your first impression by following several simple guidelines:

- Arrive a few minutes early.
- Wear appropriate business attire.
- Listen attentively.
- Use correct grammar and appropriate language.
- Smile and be facially expressive.
- Use direct eye contact.
- Use a posture that appears relaxed but not too informal.
- Avoid fidgety behavior.
- Try to appear calm and confident.
- End the interview on a positive note.

What is this job candidate doing (or not doing) to create an impression of confidence and professionalism during her interview?

A survey conducted by Northwestern University asked 153 companies why they rejected job applicants.[1] Of the fifty reasons identified, almost half are related to communication skills and creating a positive impression. The following are some of the most common mistakes made during an interview:

- Inappropriate or unprofessional appearance
- Aggressive or arrogant manner
- Poor grammar and vocal expression
- Lack of interest or enthusiasm
- Lack of confidence
- Evasiveness and tendency to make excuses
- Lack of tact
- Immaturity
- Poor manners
- Tendency to criticize past employers
- No direct eye contact
- Weak or limp handshake
- Late to the interview
- Vague responses to questions

There is one additional interview mistake worthy of attention: Don't talk too much. At first this may seem counterproductive. After all, the interviewer wants to hear your answers to questions. If, however, you talk too much you may bore your listeners or may appear insensitive to the time limits of an interview. Richard Bolles suggests that when it is your turn to speak or answer a question, plan and try "not to speak any longer than two minutes at a time if you want to make the best impression."[2] Generally, it's better to leave interviewers hungry for more information about you than wearing them out with more information than they need or want.

[1]Wallace V. Schmidt and Roger N. Conaway, *Results-Oriented Interviewing: Principles, Practices, and Procedures* (Boston: Allyn & Bacon, 1999), pp. 110–111.

[2]Richard Nelson Bolles, *What Color Is Your Parachute? A Practical Manual for Job-Hunters and Career-Changers* (Berkeley: Ten Speed Press, 2007), p. 82.

AFTER THE INTERVIEW

Immediately after an interview, send a note thanking the interviewer for his or her time and consideration. The note should briefly refer to issues discussed in the interview and emphasize that you can perform the job and help the organization meet its goals. A brief but well-written letter reinforces that you have a professional approach to and enthusiasm for the job.

Although it's natural to wonder how well you did during the interview, you may never learn how the interviewer evaluated you and your responses. An analytical self-evaluation may be more useful. To assess your own performance, ask yourself the following questions[53]:

- How well did I prepare for the interview? Was there additional information about the organization I should have known?
- Was I dressed appropriately and professionally?
- Did I use language and behavior appropriate for a professional setting?
- Which questions did I answer best?
- Which questions could I have answered better? What would have been a better answer?
- Which questions were the most difficult? Are these questions likely to be asked in other interviews?
- Did I miss any opportunities to emphasize particular strengths? How might I have incorporated those issues into my other answers?
- Are there questions I should have asked before leaving?
- What could I do differently in the next interview?

Keep in mind that you can make an excellent impression during an interview and still not be hired. There may be several excellent candidates. Regardless of whether you are selected, view each interview as an opportunity to practice your skills. The more practice you have, the more your interviewing skills will improve.

Communication Challenge

Be Strategic, Not Stupid

Directions: The questions listed here are commonly asked during job interviews. Take a few minutes to consider each question. In the Stupid Answer column, write an answer that would either disqualify you for a job or make the interviewer rank you low on the list of desired candidates. In the Strategic Answer column, craft an answer that could help you earn a job as well as the respect of the interviewer. See the example for question 1.

Interview Question	Stupid Answer	Strategic Answer
1. Why did you leave your last job?	*My boss was a jerk. She had rigid rules and never cut anyone any slack.*	*I enjoyed my job and learned a great deal. Now I'm ready for a more challenging position.*
2. What do you hope to be doing ten years from now?		
3. What, in your opinion, is your greatest weakness?		
4. What motivates you to work hard and do your best?		
5. What professional accomplishment has given you the most satisfaction?		
6. What is the ideal kind of relationship between a supervisor and subordinate?		
7. What is/was your major, and how satisfied are you with that decision?		

Job Interview Assessment

The Job Interview Assessment instrument can be used to evaluate your performance in a past interview or in a classroom interview. You can also use this instrument to help prepare for future interviews.

Directions: Use a check mark to rate yourself as an interviewee according to criteria based on the key elements of communication using the following assessment standards: E = excellent, G = good, A = average, W = weak, M = missing, or N/A = not applicable.

INTERVIEW COMPETENCIES	E	G	A	W	M	N/A
Self: Well prepared and confident, recognizes personal strengths and weaknesses						
Others: Listens and adapts to interviewer						
Purpose: Understands how hiring would promote personal and organizational goals						
Context: Adapts to the logistics and psychosocial climate of the interview setting, uses time well						
Content: Includes ideas and information relevant to and needed in the job, asks appropriate questions						
Structure: Organizes answers in a clear and memorable way						
Expression: Uses verbal and nonverbal behavior appropriately and effectively						
Overall Assessment						

Comments:

Key Terms

appraisal interview
closed-ended question
coworker relationship
customer relationship
disciplinary interview
exit interview
gossip
hypothetical question

information-gathering interview
interview
leading question
open-ended question
organizational culture
organizational subculture
probing question
professional relationship

role
selection interview
sexual harassment
superior–subordinate relationship
upward distortion
whistle-blower

Notes

1. Daniel P. Modaff and Sue DeWine, *Organizational Communication: Foundations, Challenges, Misunderstandings* (Los Angeles, CA: Roxbury, 2002), p. 175.

2. Ibid.

3. Matthew Gilbert, *Communication Miracles at Work: Effective Tools and Tips for Getting the Most from Your Work Relationships* (Berkeley, CA: Conari Press, 2002), p. 112.

4. Ibid.

5. Robert Longley, "Labor Studies of Attitudes toward Work and Leisure: U.S. Workers Are Happy and Stress Is Overstressed," August 1999, http://usgovinfo .about.com/od/censusandstatsitics/a/ labordaystudy.htm.

6. Modaff and DeWine, p. 207.

7. Gilbert, p. 153.

8. Ibid., p. 157.

9. Carley H. Dodd, *Managing Business and Professional Communication* (Boston: Allyn & Bacon, 2004), pp. 164–165.

10. Ibid., p. 40.

11. Rachel Devine, "Work and Career: Gossip Galore," iVillage Work & Career, www.ivillage.co.uk/workcareer/survive/ opolotics/articles/0,,156475_164246,00 .html.

12. Ibid.

13. Quoted in Samuel Greengard, "Gossip Poisons Business: HR Can Stop It," *Workforce* (July 2001), www.findarticles .com/p/articles/mi_m0FXS/is_7_80/ai_ 76938891.

14. Ibid.

15. Devine; Carl Skooglund and Glenn Coleman, "Advice from the Ethics Office at Texas Instruments Corporation: Gossiping at Work" (2004), Online Ethics Center for Engineering and Science, http://onlineethics.org/corp/gossip.html; Muriel Solomon, *Working with Difficult People* (New York: Prentice Hall, 2002), pp. 125–126.

16. Greengard; "Rumor Has It—Dealing with Misinformation in the Workplace,"

Entrepreneur (September 1997), www .findartcles.com/p/articles/mi_m0DTI/ is_n9_v25/ai_19892317.

17. Ed Piantek, "Flirting with Disaster," *Risk and Insurance* (May 2000), www .findarticles.com/p/articles/mi_m0BJK/ is_200_May/ai_62408701.

18. Bill Leonard, "Workplace Romances Seem to Be Rule, Not Exception," *HR Magazine* (April 2001), www.findarticles .com/p/articles/mi_m3495/is_4_46/ai_ 73848276.

19. Ibid.; "Working It—L.A. Stories—Survey Data on Office Romances," *Los Angeles Business Journal* (May 27, 2002), www.finadarticles.com/p/articles/mi_/ 5072/is_21_24/ai_91233190.

20. Piantek.

21. Work and Family Connection, "Cupid Not a Welcome Visitor at Work: A SHRM Survey Has Asked 1,221 Execs and HR Managers about Office Romances, and the Overwhelming Verdict Is Thumbs Down," *Work and Family Newsbrief* (April 2002), www.findarticles.com/p/ articles/mi_m0IJN/is_2002_April/ai_ 84543923.

22. Leonard; Judy Olian, "On the Job: Workplace Romances Are Management's Business" *Pittsburgh Post-Gazette*, November 20, 2001, www.post-gazette.com/businessnews.

23. Leonard; Olian.

24. Quoted in HaLife, "Be Cautious with a Workplace Romance," (2004), http:// halife.com/business/mayromance/html.

25. Ibid.

26. Modaff and DeWine, p. 206.

27. U.S. Equal Employment Opportunity Commission, "Facts about Sexual Harassment" (June 27, 2002), www.eeoc.gov/facts/fs-sex.html.

28. Piantek.

29. Nichole L. Torres, "Boys Will Not Be Boys: Lewdness and Rudeness Can Be Mess for Your Business—Even Without Mixed Company," *Entrepreneur* (November 2001), www.findarticles

.com/p/articles/mi_m0DTI/is_11_29/ai_ 83663647.

30. Julie A. Woodzicka and Marianne LaFrance, "Real Versus Imagined Gender Harassment," *Journal of Social Issues* (Spring 2001), www.findarticles.com/p/ articles/mi_m0341/is_1_57/ai_75140959.

31. Deborah Ware Balogh, "The Effects of Delayed Report and Motive for Reporting on Perceptions of Sexual Harassment," *Sex Roles: A Journal of Research* (April 2003), www.findarticles.com/p/ articles/mi_m2294/is_2003_April/ai_ 101174064.

32. Ibid.

33. Woodzicka and LaFrance.

34. Balogh.

35. "Preventing Sexual Harassment in the Workplace" *NOLO* (2004), www.nolo .com/lawcenter/ency/article.cfm/ ObjectID/7440C7F8-0B89-46E4-A1DE.

36. Cited in Marky Stein, "80-Day Career Change Media Challenge" (July 29, 2004), http://ca.prweb.com/releases/ 2004/7/prweb144867.htm.

37. Cited in Gilbert, p. 10; see also Humphrey Taylor, The Mood of American Workers" (January 19, 2000), www.harrisinteractive.com/harris_poll.

38. Virginia Galt, When Quitting a Job, Discretion Is the Better Part of Valor," http://globeandmail.workopolis.com/ servlet/Content/fasttrack/2004041; Peggy Post, "Rules to Live By: Quitting Your Job," http://magazines.ivillage.com/ goodhousekeeping/print/0,,636770,00.html.

39. Matt Villano, "What to Tell the Company as You Walk out the Door," *The New York Times*, November 27, 2005, p. BU 8.

40. Wallace V. Schmidt and Roger N. Conaway, *Results-Oriented Interviewing: Principles, Practices, and Procedures* (Boston: Allyn & Bacon, 1999), p. 198.

41. Villano, p. BU 8.

42. This definition is a composite statement that includes components found in most academic definitions of an interview.

See, for example, Larry Powell and Jonathan Amsbary, *Interviewing: Situations and Contexts* (Boston: Pearson/Allyn & Bacon, 2006), p. 1; Charles Stewart and William B. Cash, *Interviewing: Principles and Practices*, 10th ed. (Boston: McGraw Hill, 2003), p. 4; Jeanne Tessier Barone and Jo Young Switzer, *Interviewing Art and Skill* (Boston: Allyn & Bacon, 1995), p. 8.

43. Ibid.

44. Ibid., p. 9.

45. Ibid., p. 183.

46. Ibid., p. 198.

47. Powell and Amsbary, p. 93.

48. Stewart and Cash, p. 5.

49. Richard Nelson Bolles, *What Color Is Your Parachute? A Practical Manual for Job-Hunters and Career-Changers* (Berkeley: Ten Speed Press, 2007), p. 78.

50. Accountemps study displayed in *USA Today* Snapshots, "Most Common Job Interview Mistakes Noticed by Employers," *USA Today*, October 17, 2006, p. B1.

51. Schmidt and Conaway, pp. 34–37.

52. Stewart and Cash, pp. 254–255; "Candidate Interview Questions," CollegeGrad .Com, www.collegegrad.com/questions/ candidates.shtml; "Interview," www.joblink-usa.com/interview.htm.

53. Stewart and Cash, p. 256; Charles J. Stewart, *Teaching Interviewing and Career Preparation* (Bloomington, IN: ERIC; Annandale, VA: Speech Communication Association, 1991), p. 34.

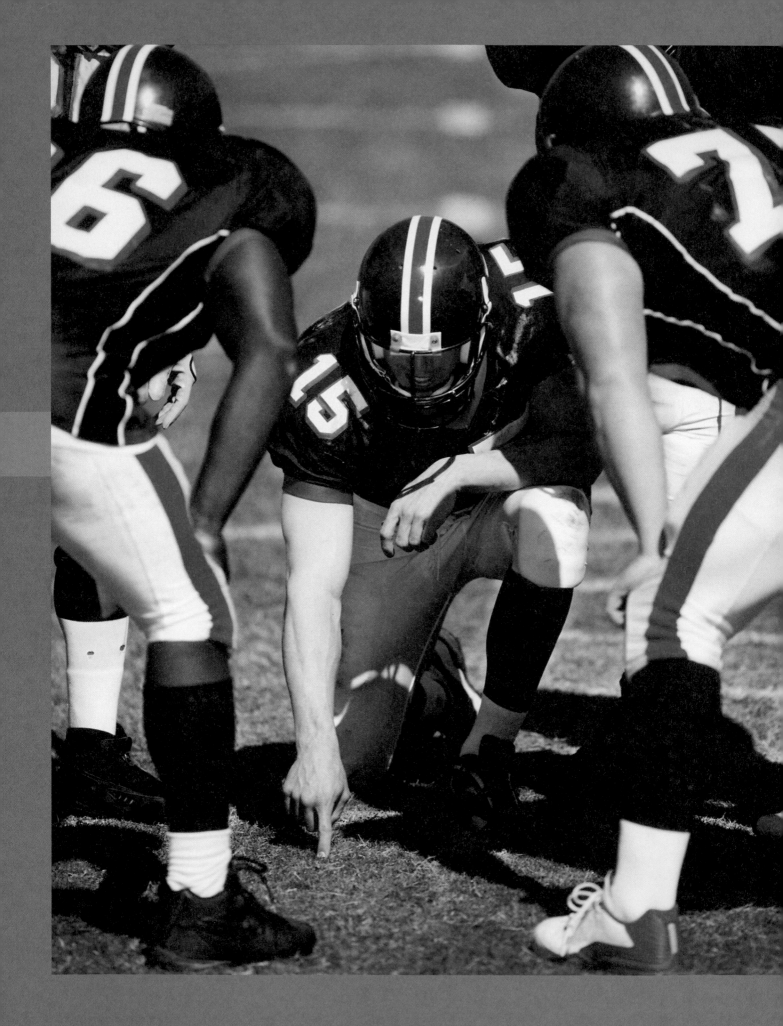

Group Communication: Working in Groups

Key Elements of Communication	Communication Axioms	Guiding Principles of Group Communication
Self	*Communication Is Personal*	Recognize how *your* characteristics and roles affect the way you communicate in groups.
Others	*Communication Is Relational*	Adapt to other members' diverse characteristics and roles to enhance group productivity and member satisfaction.
Purpose	*Communication Is Intentional*	Develop a clear understanding and commitment to the group's common goal.
Context	*Communication Is Contextual*	Adapt to the group's developmental stages, tensions, and norms. Promote group cohesiveness.
Content	*Communication Is Symbolic*	Seek constructive ideas and valid information that directly address the group's goals.
Structure	*Communication Is Structured*	Manage group size and developmental stages to maximize group effectiveness and efficiency.
Expression	*Communication Is Irreversible*	Use appropriate verbal and nonverbal strategies to support group goals and leadership.

The Challenge of Working in Groups

Everyone works in groups. You work in groups to make decisions, solve problems, share information, and resolve conflicts. You also rely on groups to produce products, provide services, and build friendships. You may be surprised by the long list of groups to which you belong. College students typically list family, friends, study groups, campus clubs, work teams, and religious groups. After graduation, you may be involved in civic organizations, management teams, work committees, and professional associations.

The need for teamwork skills extends well beyond the boundaries of a communication classroom. After surveying representatives from more than fifty companies and organizations, one study reported that most liberal arts students had "devastating" shortcomings in terms of teamwork and leadership.[1] A more comprehensive study commissioned by the Association of American Colleges and Universities asked employers to rank essential learning outcomes for college graduates entering the workplace. In two major categories—Intellectual and Practical Skills, and Personal and Social Responsibility—the top ranked outcome was "teamwork skills and the ability to collaborate with others in diverse group settings." Recent graduates ranked the same learning outcome as top priorities.[2] As one business executive wrote "I look for people that take accountability, responsibility, and are good team people over anything else. I can teach the technical."[3] In this and the next chapter we present guiding principles and practices that will help you become a more effective, efficient, and ethical group member.

THE NATURE OF GROUP COMMUNICATION

Group communication refers to the interaction of three or more interdependent people using verbal and nonverbal messages to generate meaning for the purpose of achieving a common goal.[4] A closer look at the components of this definition—three or more people, interaction and independence, and a common goal—reveals that group communication represents a unique communication context for you and others.

Group Size   The phrase "two's company; three's a crowd" recognizes that a conversation between two people is quite different from a three-person discussion. The ideal size for a problem-solving group is five to seven members. To avoid ties in decision making, an odd number of members is usually better than an even number. Groups larger than seven tend to divide into subgroups; talkative members may dominate or drown out quiet members.

GROUP COMMUNICATION INVOLVES
► Three or More People
► Interaction and Interdependence
► A Common Goal

Interaction and Interdependence   Next time you're in a group, observe the ways in which members interact with one another. A late member rushes in and apologizes. Someone poses a problem. In response, everyone starts talking at the same time. Later, the group listens intently to a member explaining an important concept or possible solution. When tensions arise, a funny comment eases the strain. Soon the group is energized as possible solutions emerge from the discussion. Finally, members exchange congratulations and good cheer as they agree on a course of action. What you have just observed is group *interaction*—a necessity for effective group communication regardless of whether members meet face-to-face or in cyberspace.

Group members are also *interdependent*—that is, the actions of an individual group member affect every other member. For example, if a member fails to provide needed background information at an important meeting, the group as a whole will suffer when it attempts to make an important decision or solve a significant problem.

Common Goal   Group members come together for a reason: a collective purpose or goal that defines and unifies the group. The importance of a group's goal cannot be underestimated. If there is one factor that separates successful from unsuccessful groups, it is having a clear goal. A study by Carl Larson and Frank LaFasto concludes

If groups were all work and no play, very few people would join or stay in groups. Fortunately, the interaction necessary to perform a group task can also make members feel socially accepted and valued. Most effective groups exhibit both task and social dimensions.

A group's **task dimension** focuses on the job—the goal or product of group effort. The more connected and committed members are to the task or group goal, the greater the potential for productive participation.

The **social dimension** focuses on the interpersonal relationships among group members. The good company of others is not the only reason people join groups, but it is a major factor in determining whether members find the group experience satisfying and significant.[1] For example, a group discussing a depart-

ment's budget may focus its attention on the difficult task of budget cutting. But at the end of the meeting, the group surprises a member with a birthday cake and shifts the focus to the social dimension.

You have probably worked with groups that took enormous tolls on your personal time, energy, and emotions—yet you continued to be active members. You may look back at many of your group experiences and remember the many good people (and a few annoying ones), the great times, the long-lasting friendships, and your collective pride in the group's achievements.

[1]Rodney W. Napier and Matti K. Gershenfeld, *Groups: Theory and Experience*, 7th ed. (Boston: Houghton Mifflin, 2004), p. 73.

that "in every case, without exception, where an effectively functioning team was identified, it was described . . . as having a clear understanding of its objective."[5] The label doesn't matter—*goal, objective, purpose, mission,* or *assignment.* Without a common goal, groups wonder: Why are we meeting? Why should we care or work hard?

ADVANTAGES AND DISADVANTAGES OF WORKING IN GROUPS

If you're like most people, you have had to sit through some long and boring meetings run by unskilled people. You may have lost patience (or your temper) with a group that couldn't accomplish a simple task you could have done better and faster by yourself. In the long run, however, the advantages of working in groups usually outweigh the potential disadvantages, as summarized in Figure 10.1.

Advantages   The reason so many groups do so much that directly affects our daily lives is fairly simple: Groups can perform better and accomplish more than individuals working alone. In *The Wisdom of Teams,* Jon Katzenbach and Douglas Smith note that groups "outperform individuals acting alone . . . especially when performance requires multiple skills, judgments, and experiences."[6] In another study, psychologists found that "approaches and outcomes of cooperating groups are not just better than those of the average group member, but are better than even the group's best problem solver functioning alone." If nothing else, the lone problem solver can't match the diversity of knowledge and perspectives of a group.[7] Despite such impressive claims,

Figure 10.1	Advantages and Disadvantages of Working in Groups

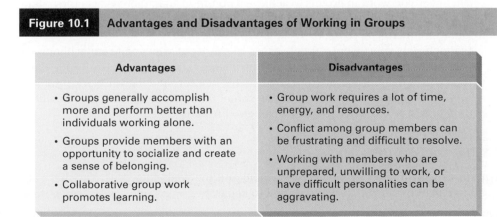

Advantages	Disadvantages
• Groups generally accomplish more and perform better than individuals working alone. • Groups provide members with an opportunity to socialize and create a sense of belonging. • Collaborative group work promotes learning.	• Group work requires a lot of time, energy, and resources. • Conflict among group members can be frustrating and difficult to resolve. • Working with members who are unprepared, unwilling to work, or have difficult personalities can be aggravating.

there are exceptions. If a task is fairly simple and routine, you may be able to do it better and faster without involving others.

Even if groups didn't accomplish more than individuals, many people would still choose to work in groups. You belong to and work in groups because you make friends, have an opportunity to socialize, and feel part of a successful team. The more opportunities we have to communicate in groups, the more satisfying the group experience.[8] Working in groups also enhances learning when members share information, stimulate critical thinking, challenge assumptions, and expect high standards of achievement.

Disadvantages Working in groups requires time, energy, and resources. The 3M Corporation studied the many factors that affect the cost of meetings, from hourly wages to overhead costs. Their research team concluded that meetings cost the 3M Corporation a staggering $78.8 million annually.[9]

Whenever you work in groups to achieve a common goal, there is also the potential for conflict. As a result, some people will do almost anything to avoid conflict and confrontation, including trying to avoid groups altogether.

As much as we may want our colleagues to share our viewpoints and willingness to work, individual members may create problems. Like anyone else in our daily lives, some group members talk too much, arrive late for meetings or work sessions, and argue aggressively. However, these same members may also be excellent researchers, effective critical thinkers, and good friends.

TYPES OF GROUPS

Groups are as different as the people in them and the goals they seek. Yet, there are common characteristics that can be used to separate groups into several categories, ranging from the most personal and informal types to more public and formal groups. You can identify each type of group by its overall purpose and its membership, as illustrated in Figure 10.2.

Two types of groups described in Figure 10.2, work groups and public groups, serve the diverse interests of organizations and public audiences. Their goal may be as complex as reengineering a global corporation or as simple as reporting their progress at a weekly staff meeting.

Work Groups If you are employed, you probably belong to several work groups: a work crew, sales staff, service department, faculty, management group, or research team. **Work groups** assume primary responsibility for making decisions, solving problems, and implementing projects in organizations. They take several forms. For example, **committees** are created by a larger group or by a person in a position of authority to take on specific tasks such as those required by social committees, budget committees, and awards committees. **Work teams** are groups that are usually given full responsibility and resources for their performance. Unlike committees, work teams are relatively permanent. They don't take time *from* work to meet—they unite *to* work. For example, a health care team attends to a particular patient, a research team focuses on a specific research project, and a legal team may defend or prosecute multiple cases.

Public Groups **Public groups** discuss issues in front of or for the benefit of the public. Their meetings usually occur in unrestricted public settings in front of public audiences. Examples include panel discussions, symposiums, forums, and governance groups.

Figure 10.2	Types of Groups

Type of Group	Purpose	Membership
Primary	To provide members with affection, support, and a sense of belonging	Families, best friends
Social	To share common interests in a friendly setting or participate in social activities	Athletic team members, hobbyists, sorority and fraternity members
Self-Help	To offer support and encouragement to members who want or need help with personal problems	Therapy group members, participants in programs such as Weight Watchers
Learning	To help members gain knowledge and develop skills	Classmates, book group members, participants in ceramic workshop
Service	To help worthy causes that help other people *outside* the group	Members of Kiwanis, Police Athletic League, charitable foundations
Civic	To support worthy causes that help other people *within* the group	Members of PTA, labor unions, veterans' groups, community associations
Work	To achieve specific tasks and routine duties on behalf of a business or organization	Committee members, department employees, task force members, management teams
Public	To discuss important issues in front of or for the benefit of the public or key decision makers	Participants in public panel discussions, symposiums, forums, governance groups

Sometimes, when groups have too much to do or have trouble making a decision or solving a problem, they will refer an issue, task, or problem to a committee, such as a membership committee, safety committee, social committee, budget committee, or some other type of committee. However, when committees spend significant amounts of time working together, members often develop the following complaints:

- They are stuck with inflexible processes or procedures that have become routine, complex, or ineffective.
- They are not appreciated.

- Members are often appointed for the wrong reasons (e.g., to get rid of an incompetent person, to let close friends work together).
- They lack the power or authority to implement decisions.

Rather than relying on ineffective committees, groups might achieve their goals better by using a task force. A **task force** has more authority and power, is appointed for a short term, develops its own procedures, and expects recommendations to be taken seriously.[1]

[1]Rodney W. Napier and Matti K. Gershenfeld, *Groups: Theory and Practice* (Boston: Houghton Mifflin, 2004), pp. 243–245.

During a **panel discussion**, several people interact about a common topic to educate, influence, or entertain an audience. During a **symposium**, group members present short, uninterrupted presentations on different aspects of a topic for the benefit of an audience. For example, a college may sponsor a symposium on eating disorders during which a doctor, medical researcher, patient, and health department official give uninterrupted talks about the causes, symptoms, and treatments of eating disorders.

Very often a panel or symposium is followed by a **forum**, which provides an opportunity for audience members to comment or ask questions. For example, a town hall meeting addressing the impact of a proposed landfill might include presentations by a scientist, an environmental activist, and a representative from the Environmental Protection Agency, and might be followed by an opportunity for citizens to make comments and ask questions. A strong moderator is needed in a forum to make sure that all audience members have an equal opportunity to speak.

Governance groups make policy decisions in public settings. State legislatures, city and county councils, and the governing boards of public agencies and educational institutions conduct their meetings in public.

How does this panel discussion by public officials (including Governor Brian Schweitzer) about Montana's educational system differ from discussions by work teams, family members, or service groups?

In addition to preparing for face-to-face discussion, you also may work in virtual groups through e-mail and discussion groups as well as telephone conferences or videoconferences. Unfortunately, when some members participate in virtual groups, they believe that it will be an easy, part-time task, especially when they do not have to attend the meetings physically. As a result, they may underestimate the time they need to spend preparing, coordinating, and collaborating.[1] In *Mastering Virtual Teams*, Deborah Duarte and Nancy Snyder describe the responsibilities of virtual team members as follows:

- Participants must prepare for the meeting by reading the background material and becoming familiar with the technology.
- During the meeting, participants should speak out (or respond using electronic methods) as well as listen to and consider others' ideas. In remote meetings, it is easier to "hide" than it is in face-to-face meetings.

- Participants must take active responsibility for making suggestions and decisions and for following up on meeting actions.[2]

In addition to these responsibilities, virtual groups may require members to assume special responsibilities, such as being virtual secretary to summarize, distribute, and edit participant comments and suggestions. Although you may not be in the same room or even on the same continent as the other group members, you are responsible for being fully prepared to contribute to the group's work.

[1]Deborah L. Duarte and Nancy Tennant Snyder, *Mastering Virtual Teams*, 3rd ed. (San Francisco: Jossey-Bass, 2007), p. 21. See also, Chapter 6, pp. 125–144.

[2]Ibid., p. 158. See also Michael McCall and Julia Szerdy, "How to Facilitate Distributed Meetings Using EMS Tools," in *Groupware: Collaborative Strategies for Corporate LANs and Intranets*, ed. David Coleman (Upper Saddle River, NJ: Prentice Hall, 1997).

Group Development

Like people, groups move through stages as they develop and mature. A "newborn" group behaves differently from an "adult" group that has worked together for a long time.

GROUP DEVELOPMENT STAGES

There are several theories of group development. As early as the 1960s, Bruce Tuckman suggested that groups develop in stages.[10] By the 1970s, he and a colleague had identified five stages: forming, storming, norming, performing, and adjourning.[11] All groups face the challenge of navigating each of these passages successfully to achieve their shared goal.

Forming   During the **forming stage**, group members may be more worried about themselves individually than about the group as a whole. Will I be accepted? Will other members like me? Will I be able to achieve my own goals? Such concerns can make initial group interaction polite, cautious, and even somewhat uncomfortable. During the early stage of group development, members need time to get oriented as the group is forming.

Storming   When the group knows what it is supposed to do and who will be involved in the effort, the second stage emerges. During the **storming stage**, groups become more argumentative and emotional as they discuss important issues and vie for leadership. Some groups are tempted to suppress this stormy phase in an effort to avoid conflict. However, conflict can help groups develop relationships, decide who's in charge and who can be trusted, and clarify the group's common goal.

Norming   During the **norming stage**, group members define their roles and determine group procedures. Members begin to work as a team and make choices about

GROUP DEVELOPMENT STAGES

▸ Forming
▸ Storming
▸ Norming
▸ Performing
▸ Adjourning

Two types of group tension may appear during the forming and storming stages: primary tension and secondary tension.[1] **Primary tension** is the social unease and inhibitions that accompany the getting-acquainted period in a new group. Because most new group members want to create a good first impression, they tend to be overly polite with one another. The following behaviors are characteristic of primary tension:

- Members rarely interrupt each other.
- There are often long, awkward pauses between comments.
- Members are soft spoken and very polite.
- Members avoid expressing strong opinions.

In most groups, primary tension decreases as members feel more comfortable with one another. But if the group is bogged down in primary tension, you can and should intervene by introducing the subject of primary tension and discussing how to break the cycle. Use assertive behavior that counteracts the symptoms of primary tension, stick to the group's agenda, and express your opinion about relevant issues.

After a group overcomes primary tension, it tries to get down to business. At this point, a different kind of tension may emerge. **Secondary tension** involves the frustrations and personality conflicts experienced by group members as members compete for social acceptance, status, and achievement. The following behaviors are characteristic of secondary tension:

- There is a high level of energy and alertness.
- The group is noisy and dynamic; members are loud and emphatic.
- Several members may speak at the same time.
- Members sit up, lean forward, and squirm in their seats.

If you sense that your group cannot resolve its secondary tension, you can let it continue or intervene. One strategy is to joke about the tension. The resulting laughter can ease individual and group stress. Another option is to work outside the group setting and discuss the personal difficulties and anxieties with individual group members. Even if you're not the group's leader, you can talk to members in private and ask them how you can help them resolve conflict and overcome problems in the group.

[1]Ernest G. Bormann, *Small Group Communication: Theory and Practice*, 6th ed. (Edina, MN: Burgess International, 1996), pp. 134–135.

the best ways to achieve a common goal. Information is freely exchanged as the group prepares to dig in and work. There is more order and direction during this third stage of group development. Later in this chapter we take a more detailed look at the development of group norms.

Performing   During the **performing stage** of group development, much of the conflict related to group organization has been resolved and members perform the tasks necessary to accomplish the group goal. Decisions are reached, problems are solved, and plans are implemented. When the performing stage is going well, members are highly energized, loyal to one another, and willing to accept every challenge that arises.

Adjourning   The **adjourning stage** describes the point at which a group goal has been achieved and the group begins to disband. Although group members may enjoy working together, the amount of interaction diminishes as their work is completed.

Group development theories help explain why and how groups and their members behave at different stages in their development. Imagine how disruptive it would be if, at your group's first meeting, a member demanded acceptance of a particular decision or solution to a problem. Moreover, if members never matured beyond the forming stage, your group would become bogged down in polite conversation and procedural details rather than dealing with its task. Understanding the natural development of a group can help explain, predict, and improve group productivity and member satisfaction.

In some situations it makes just as much sense to deviate from the group's norms as it does to conform. **Constructive deviation** is appropriate when resistance to a norm helps a group achieve its goal. The following statements are examples of constructive deviation:

> "I know we always have our annual retreat at a golf resort, but many of our new staff members don't play golf and may feel out of place or bored."

> "I can't attend any more of these meetings if they're going to last for three hours."

Constructive deviation contributes to effective group decisions and more creative solutions, because it allows members to voice serious and well-justified objections without fear of personal criticism or exclusion for taking a different position. In contrast, **destructive deviation** occurs when a member resists conformity without regard for the best interests of the group and its goal, such as by showing up late to attract attention or interrupting others to exert power.

When members deviate, a group may have to discuss the value of a particular norm and then choose to change, clarify, or continue to accept it. At the very least, deviant behavior helps members recognize and understand the norms of the group. For instance, if a member is reprimanded for leaving early, other members learn it is not acceptable to leave before a meeting is adjourned.

GROUP NORMS

The creation of group norms is a significant factor affecting a group's passage from "infant" to "adult." **Norms** are "sets of expectations held by group members concerning what kinds of behavior or opinions are acceptable or unacceptable, good or bad, right or wrong, appropriate or inappropriate."[12] Norms are the group's rules of behavior; they determine how members dress, speak, listen, and work. For example, in one group it may be rude to interrupt a member who is speaking, whereas in another group interrupting and overlapping conversations are acceptable forms of interaction. Without norms, a group lacks agreed-upon ways to organize and perform a task.

Some norms, however, can work against a group and its goals. If your group norms place a premium on friendly and peaceful discussions, members may be reluctant to voice disagreement or share bad news. If group norms permit members to arrive late and leave early, you may not have enough members to do the job. Norms that don't support your group's goals can prevent the group from succeeding.

As a responsible group member, you must decide whether you will conform to the group's norms. Before deciding to become the nonconformist or rebel, understand that there are good reasons to choose conformity, particularly if

- you want to continue your membership in the group
- you don't want to be seen as uncooperative or rebellious
- you strongly support the group's principles and goals
- you get along with and like working with the other group members
- you may be punished for violating norms and/or rewarded for compliance[13]

GROUP COHESION

Cohesion is the mutual attraction that holds members of a group together. Cohesive groups are united and committed to a common goal, have high levels of interaction, and enjoy a supportive communication climate. Their members also share

How does this parade of Marine Corps soldiers demonstrate the importance and value of group norms?

To what extent (if at all) do group celebrations, awards presentations, letters of thanks, and special gifts or bonuses enhance group cohesiveness and productivity? Can rewards decrease cohesiveness and productivity?

a sense of teamwork and pride in the group, want to conform to group expectations, and are willing to use creative approaches to achieve the group's goals.[14]

Cohesive groups are happier and get more done. Four strategies can help your group develop cohesion: establish a group identity, emphasize teamwork, reward contributions, and respect group members[15]:

- *Establish group identity.* Cohesive group members refer to the group with terms such as *we* and *our* instead of *I* and *my.* Some groups create a group name, logo, or motto, such as the "Super Sellers—We get there first." As members continue to interact with one another, they develop a common history as well as rituals and ceremonies to reinforce traditions.

- *Emphasize teamwork.* Cohesive group members feel responsible for and take pride in their work as well as the work of other members. Rather than the individual members taking personal credit for success, a cohesive group emphasizes the group's accomplishments.

- *Reward contributions.* Cohesive groups establish a climate that encourages and rewards praiseworthy contributions. Many groups use celebration dinners, letters of appreciation, certificates, and gifts to reward individual effort and initiative. Even a simple compliment can make a group member feel appreciated.

- *Respect group members.* Cohesive groups are sensitive to members' interpersonal needs. Treating members with respect, showing concern for their personal needs, and appreciating diversity will promote a feeling of acceptance.

Group Participation

Effective groups can and do succeed without leaders, but they *cannot* exist without group members who actively and responsibly participate. Ultimately, the attitudes and abilities of group members determine a group's success.

Every group member brings unique talents, preferences, and perspectives to a group. As a result, group members assume different roles depending on the nature of the group, its membership, and its goal. A **role** is a pattern of behaviors associated with an expected function within a particular group context. For example, when someone asks, "Who will get the information we need for our next meeting?" all eyes turn to Brian because researching and sharing information are tasks he performs well. If a disagreement between two group members becomes heated, the group may look to Alicia for help because she has a talent for resolving conflicts and mediating differences. Thus, a role is both a set of communication skills possessed by a group member and the expectation of other group members about those skills. Members' roles usually begin to emerge during the norming stage of group development.

GROUP TASK AND MAINTENANCE ROLES

Group member roles are divided into two functional categories: task roles and maintenance roles. Group **task roles** focus on behaviors that help manage the task and complete the job. When members assume task roles, they provide useful information, ask important questions, analyze problems, and help the group stay organized. Group **maintenance roles** affect how group members get along with each other while pursuing a shared goal. They are concerned with building relationships and keeping the group cohesive and cooperative. Members who assume maintenance roles help to create a supportive work climate, resolve conflicts, and encourage members or praise good work.

In addition to assuming roles on your own, analyze the group to determine whether important roles are missing. For example, if members are becoming frustrated because one or two people are doing all the talking, you might suggest that someone serve as a gatekeeper. If the group is having trouble tracking its progress, suggest that someone take on the role of recorder–secretary. In the best of all possible groups, all the task and maintenance roles are available as strategies to mobilize a group toward its goal.

Figures 10.3 and 10.4 (pages 268 and 269) describe several task and maintenance roles and illustrate each role with a statement that might be heard from a group member functioning in that role.[16]

DISRUPTIVE MEMBERS

Most groups can handle the occasional encounter with a difficult member, but constant problems can be disruptive. Difficult members assume several **self-centered roles** that adversely affect member relationships and the group's ability to achieve its common goal. The following list represents a few of the most common "people" problems in groups[17]:

- **Aggressor.** Puts down other members, is sarcastic and critical, takes credit for someone else's work or ideas
- **Blocker.** Stands in the way of progress, presents uncompromising positions, uses delay tactics to derail an idea or proposal
- **Dominator.** Prevents others from participating, interrupts others, tries to manipulate others
- **Recognition Seeker.** Boasts about personal accomplishments, tries to be the center of attention, pouts if not getting enough attention
- **Clown.** Injects inappropriate humor, seems more interested in goofing off than working, distracts the group from its task
- **Deserter.** Withdraws from the group, appears "above it all" and annoyed or bored with the discussion, stops contributing
- **Confessor.** Shares very personal feelings and problems, uses the group for emotional support in ways that inappropriately distract members from the group's task

Figure 10.3	Group Task Roles	

ROLE	DESCRIPTION	EXAMPLE
Initiator/ Contributor	Proposes ideas; provides direction; gets the group started	"Let's begin by considering the client's point of view."
Information Seeker	Asks for relevant information; requests explanations; points out information gaps	"How can we decide on a policy without knowing more about the cost and the legal requirements?"
Information Giver	Researches, organizes, and presents relevant information	"I checked with human resources and they said…"
Opinion Seeker	Asks for opinions; tests for agreement and disagreement	"Lyle, what do you think? Will it work?"
Opinion Giver	States personal belief; shares feelings; offers analysis and arguments	"I don't agree that he's guilty. He may be annoying, but that doesn't constitute harassment."
Clarifier/ Summarizer	Explains ideas and their consequences; reduces confusion; summarizes	"We've been trying to analyze this problem for two hours. Here's what I think we've agreed upon."
Evaluator/ Critic	Assesses the value of ideas and arguments; diagnoses problems	"These figures don't consider monthly operating costs."
Energizer	Motivates members; creates enthusiasm, and, if needed, a sense of urgency	"This is incredible! We've come up with a unique and workable solution to the problem."
Procedural Technician	Helps prepare meetings; makes room arrangements; provides materials and equipment	"Before our next meeting, let me know if you will need an overhead projector or a flip chart."
Recorder/ Secretary	Keeps accurate written records of group recommendations and decisions	"Maggie, please repeat your two deadline dates so I can get them into the minutes."

Three strategies can help you and your group deal with difficult members. You can accept, confront, or even exclude a troublesome member. Acceptance is not the same as approval. A group may allow disruptive behavior to continue when the behavior is not detrimental to the group's ultimate success or when the member's positive contributions far outweigh the inconvenience or annoyance of putting up with the negative behavior. For example, a "clown" may be disruptive on occasion but may also be the group's best report writer or a valued harmonizer.

When it becomes impossible to accept or ignore behavior that threatens the group and its members, the group needs to take action. At first, members may direct a lot of attention to the difficult person in an attempt to reason with the wayward member. For example, several members can make it clear to the difficult member that the group will progress despite his or her behavior. "Ron, I think we fully understand your strong objections, but ultimately this is a group decision." In a moment of

Figure 10.4	Group Maintenance Roles	

ROLE	DESCRIPTION	EXAMPLE
Encourager/ Supporter	Praises and encourages group members; listens empathically	"Thanks for taking all that time to find the information we needed."
Harmonizer	Helps resolve conflicts; mediates differences; encourages teamwork and group harmony	"I know we're becoming edgy, but we're almost done. Let's focus on the task, not our annoyances."
Compromiser	Offers suggestions that minimize differences; helps the group reach consensus	Maybe we ca n improve the old system rather than adopting a brand new way of doing it."
Tension Releaser	Uses friendly humor to alleviate tensions, tempers, and stress	"Can Karen and I armwrestle to decide who gets the assignment?"
Gatekeeper	Monitors and regulates the flow of communication; encourages productive participation	"I think we've heard from everyone except Michelle, who has strong feelings about this issue."
Standard Monitor	Reminds group of norms and rules; tests ideas against group-established standards	"We all agreed we'd start at 10 A.M. Now we sit around waiting for latecomers until 10:30."
Observer/ Interpreter	Monitors and interprets feelings and nonverbal communication; paraphrases member comments	"Maybe we're not really disagreeing. I think we're in agreement that..."
Follower	Supports the group and its members; willingly accepts others' ideas and assignments	"That's fine with me. Just tell me when it's due."

extreme frustration, one member may say what everyone is thinking—"Lisa, please let me finish a sentence!" Although such an outburst may make everyone uncomfortable, it can put a stop to disruptive behavior.

In Chapter 9, "Interpersonal Communication: Professional Relationships," we offer advice on dealing with difficult behavior at work. The same advice applies to disruptive members:

- Discuss *specific* successes and failures.
- Stop talking and start listening.
- Describe the implications of the member's behavior.
- Link past accomplishments to needed change.
- Agree on an action plan.
- Follow up and support the member.

When all else fails, a group may exclude a difficult member by ignoring everything the difficult member says or does. Finally, a group may expel a member to be rid of the troublemaker. Being asked to leave a group or being barred from participating is a humiliating experience that all but the most stubborn members would prefer to avoid.

Group Leadership

Without leadership, a group may be nothing more than a collection of individuals lacking the coordination and will to achieve a goal. **Leadership** is the ability to make strategic decisions and use communication to mobilize group members toward achieving a shared goal. Quite simply, leadership "means getting things done or making things happen that, without the intervention of a leader, would not occur."[18]

Even though just about everyone recognizes the importance of leadership, it is not always easy to practice effective leadership. One review of leadership studies estimates that leadership incompetence is widespread—"as high as sixty to seventy-five percent—and that our hiring practices are so flawed that more than fifty percent of leaders hired by organizations are doomed to fail."[19]

Part of the problem lies in erroneous beliefs about the qualifications and qualities of leadership. We may choose or elect a "people person" who is "nice" and sociable when the job requires a tough negotiator who can resolve conflicts and institute change. Hiring a highly skilled engineer in a supervisory position may reward someone for good work, but that person may be an ineffective supervisor with little patience and few interpersonal skills. Ineffective leaders are often indecisive, unwilling to exercise authority, or just plain irritable and insensitive.[20] It's no wonder that employees are more likely to quit because they dislike their boss than because they dislike the job.

There is another reason leaders fail. They lack or fail to demonstrate effective communication skills. In his book on leadership, Antony Bell describes communication as the mortar or glue that connects all leadership competencies. The ability to think and act, self-awareness, and self-discipline are critical leadership competencies, but it takes communication to bind these building blocks together.[21]

APPROACHES TO LEADERSHIP

Leadership is a quality that defies precise measurement. However, three leadership theories can help you understand your own and others' approaches to leadership: Trait Theory, Styles Theory, and Situational Theory.

LEADERSHIP THEORIES

▶ Trait Theory

▶ Styles Theory

▶ Situational Theory

CommFYI Participation Matters!

In almost any group setting, some members find it easier and more comfortable to limit their participation. Such members may be introverts, may experience high levels of communication apprehension, may be reluctant to express a controversial or contrary opinion, or may think that the less they speak, the less they'll have to do.

Effective group members, however, know that participation matters. Joseph Bonito conducted a study to test this assumption.[1] He reports that participation affects group effectiveness because frequent participation often has the most influence on decision making. Substantive contributions of members during the first minute of a discussion were seen as task-relevant judgments. In other words, group members who make

early, substantive comments that help a group move toward its goal are perceived as more *able*—that is, more skilled or knowledgeable than other members. As a result, members who are perceived as *able* are often given more speaking turns than members whose abilities are seen as inferior.

Bonito concludes that it is in this way that participation "matters," because it creates a context for unequal influence in groups.[2]

[1]Joseph A. Bonito, "A Longitudinal Social Relations Analysis of Participation in Small Groups," *Human Communication Research* 32 (2006), pp. 302–321.

[2]Ibid., p. 318.

Trait Theory   The Trait Theory is often referred to as the *"Great Man" Theory*. It is based on a belief that leaders are born, not made. **Trait Theory** attempts to identify individual characteristics that are associated with leadership.

What leaders do you most admire? What traits do they possess? Most of us can come up with a list of desirable traits that includes intelligence, confidence, enthusiasm, organizational talent, and good listening skills. The Myers-Briggs Type Indicator Theory discussed in Chapter 7, "Interpersonal Communication: Understanding Relationships," suggests that extroverted thinkers are natural leaders who use reasoning ability to control and direct those around them.[22] They are usually enthusiastic, decisive, confident, organized, logical, and argumentative. They love to lead and can be excellent communicators.

The weakness of the Trait Theory is that there is no guarantee that someone with all the supposedly "right" qualities will be a good leader. There are many effective leaders who possess only a few of these traits. Harriet Tubman, an illiterate slave, did little talking but led hundreds of people from bondage in the South to freedom in the North.

Styles Theory   The **Styles Theory** of leadership examines a collection of specific behaviors that constitute three distinct styles: autocratic, democratic, and laissez-faire leadership. An autocrat has a great deal of power and authority, and may maintain strict control over the group. **Autocratic leaders** try to control the direction and outcome of a discussion, make many of the group's decisions, give orders, expect followers to obey orders, focus on achieving the group's task, and take credit for successful results. An autocratic style is often best during a serious crisis when there may not be time to discuss issues or consider the wishes of all members. In an emergency, the group may want its leader to take total responsibility. However, there

How valid is the trait theory of leadership? What kinds of personal traits did Nelson Mandela have that enabled him to emerge from 27 years in prison and lead South Africa to abolish the strict segregation caused by apartheid laws?

In most groups, effective leaders use several kinds of power, depending on the needs of the group and the situation.[1] **Power** is the ability or authority to influence and motivate others. Effective leaders understand the importance of power as well as the different types of power and their functions.

- **Reward power** is the power to give group members something they value. "I have the power to award promotions."
- **Coercive power** is the power to punish, discipline, demote, or dismiss group members. "I can fire you."
- **Legitimate power** is the official power that comes with a particular job, position, or assignment. "We do it my way because I'm the senior officer."

- **Expert power** is the power associated with having a particular skill or special knowledge. "I have more training and experience with this issue."
- **Referent power** is the power and influence that result from others' respect and admiration. "I'll earn your loyalty by being a good leader and treating members with respect."

The more power a leader has, the more carefully it must be balanced with the needs of the group. If you exert too much power, your group may lose energy and enthusiasm. If you don't exert enough power, your group may flounder and fail.

[1]Based on material in Isa N. Engleberg and Dianna R. Wynn, *Working in Groups: Communication Principles and Strategies*, 4th ed. (Boston: Houghton Mifflin, 2007), pp. 203–207.

are risks to using an autocratic style. Exerting too much control can lower group morale and sacrifice long-term productivity.

A **democratic leader** promotes the social equality and task interests of group members. This type of leader shares decision making with the group, helps the group plan a course of action, focuses on the group's morale as well as on the task, and gives the entire group credit for success. In groups with democratic leadership, members are often more satisfied with the group experience, more loyal to the leader, and more productive in the long run.

Laissez-faire is a French phrase that means "to let people do as they choose." A **laissez-faire leader** lets the group take charge of all decisions and actions. Such a leader may be a perfect match for mature and highly productive groups because a laid-back leadership style can generate a climate in which communication is encouraged and rewarded. Unfortunately, some laissez-faire leaders do little or nothing to help a group when it needs decisive leadership.

Situational Theory   Rather than describing traits or styles, **Situational Theory** seeks an ideal fit between leaders and leadership roles.[23] The situational approach explains how leaders can become more effective by analyzing themselves, the group, and the context.

According to situational theory, there are two leadership styles: task motivated and relationship motivated. **Task-motivated leaders** want to get the job done. They gain satisfaction from completing a task even if the cost is bad feelings between the leader and group members. As a result, task-motivated leaders are often criticized for being too focused on the job and overlooking group morale. **Relationship-motivated leaders** gain satisfaction from working well with other people even if the cost is neglecting or failing to complete a task. Not surprisingly, they are sometimes criticized for paying too much attention to how members feel and for tolerating disruptive members.

Situational Theory requires you to match your leadership style to the situation. There are three important dimensions to every group situation: leader–member relations, task structure, and power. **Leader–member relations** can be positive, neutral, or negative. Are group members friendly and loyal to the leader and the rest of the group? Are they cooperative and supportive? **Task structure** can range from disorganized and chaotic to highly organized and rule driven. Are the goals and task clear? The third situational factor is the amount of power and control the leader possesses. Is the source of power from an outside authority, or was it earned from within the group?

| **Figure 10.5** | **Situational Model of Leadership Effectiveness** |

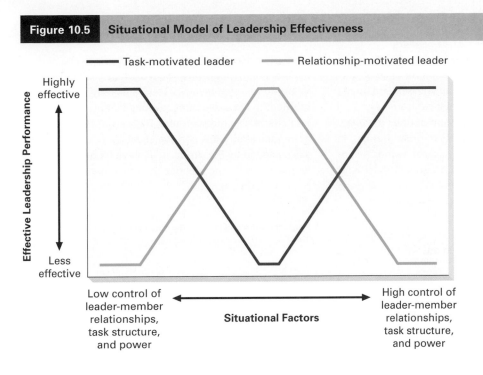

Task-motivated leaders perform best in extremes, such as when the situation requires high levels of leader control or when it is almost out of control. They also excel when there are good leader–member relationships, a clear task, and a great deal of power. Relationship-motivated leaders do well when there is a mix of conditions, such as a structured task but an uncooperative group of followers. Figure 10.5 illustrates the relationship between leadership style and situational factors.

The 4-M Model of Leadership Effectiveness

Thousands of books and articles have been published about leadership. To help you understand and balance the contributions made by these many differing approaches, we offer an integrated model of leadership effectiveness that emphasizes specific communication strategies and skills.

The **4-M Model of Leadership Effectiveness** divides leadership tasks into four interdependent leadership functions: (1) **M**odeling leadership behavior, (2) **M**otivating members, (3) **M**anaging group processes, and (4) **M**aking decisions. These strategies incorporate the features of several theories and describe the behaviors characteristic of effective leadership.[24]

MODELING LEADERSHIP BEHAVIOR

Model leaders project an image of confidence, competence, trustworthiness, and optimism. Yet, no matter how much you may want to be seen as a model leader, only your followers can grant you that honor. We recommend the following strategies for modeling effective leadership:

- Publicly champion your group and its goals. Don't focus on your personal accomplishments or ego needs.
- Speak and listen effectively and confidently.
- Behave consistently and assertively.

4-M MODEL OF LEADERSHIP EFFECTIVENESS

► Modeling Leadership Behavior
► Motivating Members
► Managing Group Processes
► Making Decisions

We place a great deal of value on leadership, but rarely do we understand or appreciate the importance of motivated followers. Our obsession with leadership is the result of the mistaken belief that extraordinary achievements are primarily the result of great leaders rather than the collaborative efforts of great groups.[1] In fact, effective groups can and do succeed without leaders, but they *cannot* exist without group members who actively and responsibly participate. Groups need good followers who are willing to accept group decisions and are motivated to carry them out.

Good followers assume critical responsibilities within a group and are prepared in advance for a dis-cussion or group task. Valuable discussion time and even entire meetings are wasted when group members fail to do their homework. Good followers make a commitment to act and accept responsibility before, during, and after a group discussion. They also possess strong communication skills and the specialized knowledge or skills needed by the group to achieve its goal. Ultimately, the attitudes and abilities of group *members* determine a group's success.

[1]Warren Bennis and Patricia Ward Biederman, *Organizing Genius: The Secrets of Creative Collaboration* (Reading, MA: Addison-Wesley, 1997), p. 5.

- Confront problems head-on and work to generate solutions.
- Demonstrate competence and trustworthiness.
- Study and improve your own leadership skills.

MOTIVATING MEMBERS

Motivating others is a critical task for leaders. Effective leaders guide, develop, support, defend, and inspire group members. They develop relationships that meet the personal needs and expectations of followers. Six leadership skills are central to motivating members:

- Secure member commitment to the group's shared goal.
- Reward the group and its members appropriately.
- Help solve interpersonal problems and conflicts.
- Adapt tasks and assignments to member abilities and expectations.
- Provide constructive and timely feedback to members.
- Give members the authority to make judgments about doing the group's work.

MANAGING GROUP PROCESSES

From the perspective of group survival, managing group processes may be the most important function of leadership.[25] If a group is disorganized, lacks sufficient information to solve problems, or is unable to make important decisions when necessary, the group cannot be effective. Five leadership skills can enhance this important function:

- Be well organized and fully prepared for all group meetings and work sessions.
- Understand and adapt to member strengths and weaknesses.
- Help solve task-related and procedural problems.
- Monitor and intervene to improve group performance.
- Secure resources and remove roadblocks to group effectiveness.

MAKING DECISIONS

An effective leader is willing and able to make appropriate, timely, and responsible decisions. When you assume or are appointed to a leadership role, you should accept the fact that some of your decisions may be unpopular, and some may even turn out

The path to a leadership position can be as easy as being in the right place at the right time or being the only person willing to take on a difficult job.[1] Although there is no foolproof method, there are ways to improve your chances of becoming a group's leader. The following strategies require a balanced approach, one that takes advantage of opportunities without abusing the privilege of leadership.

- *Talk early and often* (*and listen*). Of all the strategies that can help you attain the position of group leader, the most reliable approach is talking during the early stages of a discussion. The person who speaks first and most often is more likely to emerge as the group's leader.[2] How frequently you talk is even more important than what you say. The quality of your contributions becomes more significant after you become a leader.
- *Know more* (*and share it*). Leaders often are seen as experts: people who know more about an important topic. Even if a potential leader is only able to explain ideas and information more clearly than other group members, she or he may be perceived as knowing more. Groups need well-informed leaders; however, they do not need know-it-alls. Know-it-alls see their

own comments as most important; leaders value everyone's contributions.
- *Offer your opinion* (*and welcome disagreement*). Groups appreciate someone who offers valuable ideas and informed opinions. Offering opinions, however, is not the same as having your ideas accepted. If you are unwilling to compromise or listen to alternatives, the group may be unwilling to follow you. Effective leaders welcome constructive disagreement and discourage hostile confrontations.

The strategies for becoming a leader are not necessarily the same strategies for successful leadership. After you become a leader, you may find it necessary to listen more than talk, welcome and reward better-informed members, and criticize the opinions of others. Your focus should shift from becoming the leader to serving the group you lead.

[1]Based on material in Isa N. Engleberg and Dianna R. Wynn, *Working in Groups: Communication Principles and Strategies*, 4th ed. (Boston: Houghton Mifflin, 2007), pp. 207–210.

[2]Edwin P. Hollander, *Leadership Dynamics: A Practical Guide to Effective Relationships* (New York: Macmillan, 1978), p. 53. Also see a meta-analysis of this variable in Marianne Schmid Mast, "Dominance as Expressed and Inferred through Speaking Time," *Human Communication Research* 28 (2002), pp. 420–450.

---

to be wrong. But you still have to make them. In *The New Why Teams Don't Work: What Goes Wrong and How to Make It Right*, Harvey Robbins and Michael Finley contend that it's often better for a group leader to make a bad decision than no decision at all, "for if you are seen as chronically indecisive, people won't let you lead them."[26]

In an article titled "Building the 21st Century Leader," Carol Tice reviews the evolution of corporate leadership. Although the "top dog" leader in the 1950s "barked out orders to his dronelike workers" the leader of the 1990s wanted employees to be creative, happy, and comfortable at work even if it meant the company "went bust."[27] The successful 21st century leader must balance these two extremes. Today's leaders must be able to do *both*—collaborate with others *and* be decisive. "The desire to reach consensus or get buy-in from all parties has to be curtailed at some point, and the leader has to make a decision."[28] The following strategies can help you determine when and how to intervene and make a decision:

- Make sure that everyone has and shares the information needed to make a quality decision.
- If appropriate, discuss your pending decision and solicit feedback from members.
- Listen to members' opinions, arguments, and suggestions *before* making a decision.
- Explain the rationale for the decision you intend to make.
- Make and communicate your decision to everyone.

When President Harry S. Truman said that "the buck stops here," he was describing the ultimate responsibility of a leader. Effective leaders intervene and tell members what to do when a group lacks the confidence, willingness, or ability to make decisions. However, when group members are confident, willing, and skilled, a leader can usually turn full responsibility over to the group and focus on helping members implement the group's decision.[29] In short, as a leader, you have to decide what decision-making strategies best serve your group and its common purpose.

Diversity and Leadership

Until recently, most leadership studies concentrated on the traits, styles, and functions of white male leaders. Today, successful organizations and groups must understand, respect, and adapt to diversity if they hope to tap the potential of all their members. At the same time, female and culturally diverse leaders should understand that, even under the best circumstances, negative stereotypes about them can still hinder their ability to lead.

GENDER AND LEADERSHIP

In the early studies of leadership, there was an unwritten but additional prerequisite for becoming a leader: Be a man. Despite the achievements of exceptional women leaders, some people still question the ability of women to serve in leadership positions.

A summary of the research on leadership and gender concludes that "women are still less likely to be preselected as leaders, and the same leadership behavior is often evaluated more positively when attributed to a male than a female."[30] In other words, even when women talk early and often, are well prepared and always present at meetings, and offer valuable ideas, a man who has done the same things is more likely to emerge as the leader.

Linguist Deborah Tannen has described the difficulties that women have in leadership positions.[31] If their behavior is similar to that of male leaders, they are perceived as unfeminine, but if they act "like a lady," they are viewed as weak or ineffective. One professional woman described this dilemma as follows:

> I was thrilled when my boss evaluated me as "articulate, hard-working, mature in her judgment, and a skillful diplomat." What disturbed me were some of the evaluation comments

What qualities help or hinder a woman leader's ability to "make strategic decisions and use communication to mobilize group members toward achieving a shared goal"?

from those I supervise or work with as colleagues. Although they had a lot of good things to say, a few of them described me as "pushy," "brusque," "impatient," "disregards social niceties," and "hard driving." What am I supposed to do? My boss thinks I'm energetic and creative while other people see the same behavior as pushy and aggressive.

CULTURAL DIVERSITY AND LEADERSHIP

The ways in which a leader models leadership behavior, motivates group members, manages group processes, and makes decisions may not match the cultural dimensions of all group members. For example, if as a leader, you model leadership behavior by strongly and publicly advocating group goals, you may be upsetting members from high-context cultures who would be less direct and less open about such matters. Your way of modeling leadership may not reflect *their* view of a model leader.

A member's cultural background can also influence a leader's choice of motivational strategies. For example, individualistic western cultures (United States, Canada, Europe) assume that members are motivated by personal growth and achievement. However, a collectivist member might desire a close relationship with the leader and other group members rather than personal gain or growth. The same member may act out of loyalty to the leader and the group rather than for personal achievement or material gain.[32]

How do cultural differences among United Nations members affect the way in which the UN operates and makes decisions? When Ban Ki-moon took the oath of office as Secretary General of the UN in 2006, what kinds of leadership challenges did he face?

Managing group processes in a group composed of culturally diverse members can be difficult if, for example, you want to give the group the freedom to decide how to structure a task. Members from uncertainty–avoidance cultures will want more structure and instruction from a leader. If your leadership style is more feminine (nurturing, collaborative, caring), you may find yourself fighting a losing leadership battle with more masculine members who are competitive, independent, and aggressive. In this case, a feminine leadership style may be interpreted as weakness or indecision.

Finally, the decision-making style of a leader may not match that of a culturally diverse group. If members come from a low-power distance culture, they will not welcome an authoritarian leader who takes control of all decision making. Conversely, a leader who prefers a more democratic approach to decision making may frustrate members who come from high-power distance cultures in which leaders make all decisions with little input from group members.

Know Your Norms

Directions: The left-hand column in the following table describes several types of group norms. In the middle column, identify the group norms in your classroom. In the right column, identify the group norms in your current or a former workplace.

Types of Norms	Classroom	Workplace
1. *Verbal* (e.g., formal, casual, jargon, profanity)		
2. *Nonverbal* (e.g., formal or informal attire, seating arrangements, activity level)		
3. *Interactions* (e.g., use first or last names, nicknames, speaking turns, listening behavior, inappropriate behavior)		
4. *Content* (e.g., discussions are serious, work related, social, intimate, humorous)		
5. *Status* (e.g., who makes decisions, who has influence, whether disagreement is allowed)		
6. *Rewards* (e.g., how success is determined, how achievement is rewarded)		

Note and analyze the similarities and differences between group norms in the classroom and workplace contexts.

Communication Assessment

Group Participation and Leadership Evaluation

Directions: Evaluate the quantity and quality of participation by the members of a group to which you belong by circling the number that describes its performance. At the end, write a brief summary assessment in the space provided.

1. *Task Functions.* Members provide or ask for information and opinions, initiate discussion, clarify, summarize, evaluate, energize, and so on.

5	4	3	2	1
Excellent		Average		Poor

2. *Maintenance Functions.* Members serve as encourager, harmonizer, compromiser, tension releaser, gatekeeper, standard monitor, observer, follower, and so on.

5	4	3	2	1
Excellent		Average		Poor

3. *Group Processes.* Members avoid disruptive behavior, follow the agenda, adapt to group development stages and group norms, and so on.

5	4	3	2	1
Excellent		Average		Poor

4. *Manage Difficulties.* Members are ready, willing, and able to deal with difficult members and overall group problems.

5	4	3	2	1
Excellent		Average		Poor

5. *Leadership.* One or more members model leadership behavior, motivate others, help manage group process, make necessary decisions, and so on.

5	4	3	2	1
Excellent		Average		Poor

6. *Group's Overall Effectiveness.*

5	4	3	2	1
Excellent		Average		Poor

Summary Assessment:

Key Terms

4-M Model of Leadership Effectiveness	governance group	role
adjourning stage	group communication	secondary tension
aggressor	laissez-faire leader	self-centered role
autocratic leader	leader–member relations	Situational Theory of Leadership
blocker	leadership	social dimension
clown	legitimate power	storming stage
coercive power	maintenance role	Styles Theory of Leadership
cohesion	norming stage	symposium
committee	norms	task dimension
confessor	panel discussion	task force
constructive deviation	performing stage	task-motivated leader
democratic leader	power	task roles
deserter	primary tension	task structure
destructive deviation	public group	Trait Theory of Leadership
dominator	recognition seeker	work group
expert power	referent power	work team
forming stage	relationship-motivated leader	
forum	reward power	

Notes

1. Henry Jenkins, "From You Tube to YouNiversity," *The Chronicle of Higher Education*, February 16, 2007, p. B10.

2. Peter D. Hart Research Associates, *How Should Colleges Prepare Students to Succeed in Today's Global Economy?* (Washington, DC: Peter D. Hart Research Associates, December 28, 2006), p. 2. Also see Association of American Colleges and Universities, *College Learning for the New Global Age* (Washington, DC: Association of American Colleges and Universities, 2007).

3. Hart, p. 7.

4. This definition is modified from Isa N. Engleberg and Dianna R. Wynn, *Working in Groups: Communication Principles and Strategies*, 4th ed. (Boston: Houghton Mifflin, 2007), p. 5.

5. Carl E. Larson and Frank M.J. LaFasto, *TeamWork: What Must Go Right/What Can Go Wrong* (Newbury Park, CA: Sage, 1989), p. 27.

6. Jon R. Katzenbach and Douglas K. Smith, *The Wisdom of Teams: Creating the High-Performance Organization* (New York: HarperBusiness, 1999), p. 9.

7. Robert B. Cialdini, "The Perils of Being the Best and the Brightest," *Becoming an Effective Leader* (Boston: Harvard Business School Press, 2005), pp. 174, 175.

8. Charles Pavitt and Ellen Curtis, *Small Group Discussion*, 2nd ed. (Scottsdale, AZ: Gorsuch, Scarisbrick, 1994), p. 54.

9. 3M Meeting Management Team with Jeannine Drew, *Mastering Meetings: Discovering the Hidden Potential of Effective Business Meetings* (New York: McGraw-Hill, 1994), p. 12.

10. Bruce Tuckman, "Developmental Sequences in Small Groups," *Psychological Bulletin* 63 (1965), pp. 384–399.

11. Bruce Tuckman and Mary Ann Jensen, "Stages of Small-Group Development Revisited," *Group and Organization Studies* 2 (1977), pp. 419–427. B. Aubrey Fisher describes four similar phases of development in decision-making groups: orientation, conflict, emergence, and reinforcement. See Donald G. Ellis and B. Aubrey Fisher, *Small Group Decision Making*, 4th ed. (New York: McGraw-Hill, 1994), pp. 157–161.

12. Patricia H. Andrews, "Group Conformity," in *Small Group Communication: Theory and Practice*, 7th ed., ed. Robert S. Cathcart, Larry A. Samovar, and Linda D. Henman (Madison, WI: Brown and Benchmark, 1996), p. 185.

13. Rodney W. Napier and Matti K. Gershenfeld, *Groups: Theory and Experience*, 7th ed. (Boston: Houghton Mifflin, 2004), pp. 137–140.

14. Marvin E. Shaw, "Group Composition and Group Cohesiveness" in *Small Group Communication: A Reader*, 6th ed., ed. Robert S. Cathcart and Larry A. Samovar (Dubuque, IA: Wm. C. Brown, 1992), pp. 214–220.

15. Based on Ernest G. Bormann and Nancy C. Bormann, *Effective Small Group Communication*, 6th ed. (Edina, MN: Burgess Publishing, 1996), pp. 137–139.

16. Kenneth D. Benne and Paul Sheats, "Functional Roles of Group Members," *Journal of Social Issues* 4 (1948), pp. 41–49. We have modified the original Benne and Sheats list by adding or combining behaviors that we have observed, as well as roles identified by other writers and researchers.

17. Engleberg and Wynn, 2007, pp. 53–56. Engleberg and Wynn have modified the list of negative, self-centered roles that appears in Benne and Sheats, pp. 41–49.

18. Napier and Gershenfeld, p. 197.

19. Isa N. Engleberg and Dianna R. Wynn, *Working in Groups: Communication Principles and Strategies*, 3rd ed. (Boston: Houghton Mifflin, 2004), p. 207.

20. Ibid., p. 208.

21. Antony Bell, *Great Leadership: What It Is and What It Takes in a Complex World* (Mountain View, CA: Davies-Black, 2006), pp. 87, 91.

22. Otto Kroeger and Janet M. Thuesen, *Type Talk at Work: How the 16 Personality Types Determine Your Success on the Job* (New York: Dell, 1992), p. 385.

23. Fred E. Feidler and Martin M. Chemers, *Improving Leadership Effectiveness: The Leader Match Concept*, 2nd ed. (New York: Wiley, 1984).

24. The 4-M Model of Effective Leadership is based, in part, on Martin M. Chemers's integrative theory of leadership, which identifies three functional aspects of leadership: image management, relationship development, and resource utilization. We have added a fourth function—decision making—and have incorporated more of a communication perspective into Chemers's view of lead-

ership as a multifaceted process. See Martin M. Chemers, *An Integrative Theory of Leadership* (Mahwah, NJ: Lawrence Erlbaum, 1997), pp. 151–173. See Engleberg and Wynn, 2007, pp. 219-221.

25. Chemers, p. 160.

26. Harvey Robbins and Michael Finley, *The New Why Teams Don't Work: What Goes Wrong and How to Make It Right.* (San Francisco: Berrett-Koehler, 2000), p. 107.

27. Carol Tice "Building the 21st Century Leader," *Entrepreneur* (February 2007), pp. 66, 67.

28. Ibid., p. 68.

29. Paul Hersey and Kenneth H. Blanchard, *Management of Organizational Behavior: Utilizing Human Resources*, 5th ed. (Englewood Cliffs, NJ: Prentice Hall, 1988).

30. Susan B. Shimanoff and Mercilee M. Jenkins, "Leadership and Gender: Challenging Assumptions and Recognizing Resources," in *Small Group Communication: Theory and Practice*, 7th ed., ed. Robert S. Cathcart, Larry A. Samovar, and Linda D. Henman (Madison, WI: Brown and Benchmark, 1996), p. 327.

31. Deborah Tannen, *Talking from 9 to 5: Women and Men in the Workplace: Language, Sex, and Power* (New York: Avon, 1994).

32. Chemers, p. 126.

Group Communication: Group Decision Making and Problem Solving

Key Elements of Communication	Communication Axioms	Guiding Principles of Group Decision Making and Problem Solving
Self	*Communication Is Personal*	Recognize how *your* personal goals and decision-making style affect the way you communicate in groups.
Others	*Communication Is Relational*	Adapt to group members' diverse points of view and decision-making styles. Consider the interests of those affected by the group's decision.
Purpose	*Communication Is Intentional*	Clarify the group's decision-making and problem-solving goals.
Context	*Communication Is Contextual*	Create a collaborative climate that enhances group decision making and problem solving. Minimize the likelihood of groupthink.
Content	*Communication Is Symbolic*	Contribute high-quality information and valid arguments to group discussions. Brainstorm to generate new ideas.
Structure	*Communication Is Structured*	Select, develop, and follow appropriate decision-making methods and problem-solving procedures. Use agendas to conduct meetings.
Expression	*Communication Is Irreversible*	Use effective verbal and nonverbal strategies and skills to participate in or chair group discussions and meetings.

The Challenge of Group Decision Making and Problem Solving

You make hundreds of decisions every day. You decide when to get up in the morning, what to wear, when to leave for class or work, how to do research for a paper or report, and with whom to spend your leisure time. Many factors influence how you make these decisions—your culture, age, family, education, social status, and religion, as well as your dreams, fears, beliefs, values, interpersonal needs, and personal preferences.[1] Now take five people, put them in a room, and ask them to make a *group* decision. As difficult as it can be to make personal decisions, the challenge is multiplied many times over in groups.

Fortunately, and despite the many differences among members, effective groups have the potential to make excellent decisions because more minds are at work on the problem. As we noted in Chapter 10, "Group Communication: Working in Groups," groups generally accomplish more and perform better than individuals working alone. So, although the road may be paved with challenges, group decision making and problem solving can be more satisfying, creative, and effective.

Although the terms *decision making* and *problem solving* are often used interchangeably, their meanings differ. **Decision making** refers to the "passing of judgment on an issue under consideration" and "the act of reaching a conclusion or making up one's mind."[2] In a group setting, decision making results in a position, opinion, judgment, or action. For example, hiring committees, juries, and families decide which applicant is best, whether the accused is guilty, and whom they should invite to the wedding, respectively. Peter Drucker put it simply: "A decision is a judgment. It is a choice between alternatives."[3]

Most groups make decisions, but not all groups are asked to solve problems. **Problem solving** is a complex *process* in which groups make *multiple* decisions as they analyze a problem and develop a plan of action for solving the problem or reducing its harmful effects. For example, if student enrollment has significantly declined, a college faces a serious problem that must be analyzed and dealt with if the institution hopes to survive. Problem solving requires decision making, whereas decisions can be made in the absence of a problem. Fortunately, there are decision-making and problem-solving procedures that can help a group "make up its mind." Before trying to make a decision or solve a problem, three prerequisites should be in place: a clear purpose, quality content, and structured procedures.

GROUP DECISION-MAKING AND PROBLEM-SOLVING PREREQUISITES

▶ Clear Purpose
▶ Quality Content
▶ Structured Procedures

CLEAR PURPOSE

The first and most important task for all groups is to make sure that everyone understands and supports the group's goal or purpose. One way is to word the goal or purpose as a question. Effective groups understand the core questions they need to answer to achieve their goal. In some group contexts, the questions are dictated by an outside group or authority. For example, a work group may be asked to find ways of saving the time it takes to process an order or contact a customer. A research group may be asked to test the durability of a new product. If, however, your group has the freedom to work on its own, you should word your challenge as a question that embodies your group's purpose.

In Chapter 4, "Understanding Listening and Critical Thinking," we discuss the importance of critical thinking and how identifying claims of fact, conjecture, value, and policy helps you decide whether you should accept, reject, or suspend judgment about an idea, belief, or proposal. Groups face the same challenge when framing a discussion question.

Make sure you and your group know what kind of question you are trying to answer. Effective groups understand the differences among the following four types of questions and how discussions vary depending upon which question you ask.

1. *Questions of Fact.* Ask whether something is true or false, whether an event did or did not happen, whether something was caused by this or that. How do local colleges compare in terms of tuition costs, teacher–student ratios, and graduation rates? What causes acid rain? When a group confronts a question of fact, it must seek the best information available and subject that information to close scrutiny.

2. *Questions of Conjecture.* Ask whether something will happen. In asking a question of conjecture, the group does its best to predict what the future will bring. Will sales increase next quarter? Will there be layoffs? Who will be the next CEO? Although decisions involv-ing questions of conjecture are speculative, groups should base their decisions on valid facts and expert opinions to reach a conclusion that is most probable.

3. *Questions of Value.* Ask whether something is worth-while: Is it good or bad; right or wrong; moral or immoral; or best, average, or worst? The answer to "Are community colleges a better place to begin higher education than a prestigious university?" depends on many factors: a student's financial situa-tion, professional goals, academic achievement record, work and family situation, and beliefs about the quality of an education at each type of institution.

4. *Questions of Policy.* Ask whether a particular course of action should be taken. How can we improve cus-tomer service? Which candidate should we support as president of the student government association? However, it may be necessary to answer subques-tions of fact, conjecture, and value before tackling a significant policy question.

QUALITY CONTENT

Well-informed groups are more likely to make good decisions. The amount and accu-racy of information available to a group are critical factors in predicting its success. Group communication scholar Randy Hirokawa concludes that "the ability of a group to gather and retain a wide range of information is the single most important deter-minant of high-quality decision making."[4]

The key to becoming a well-informed group lies in the ability of members to col-lect, share, and analyze the information needed to achieve the group's goal (see MyCommunicationLab Chapter A, "Research Strategies and Skills"). When a group lacks information, responsible decision making and problem solving become diffi-cult, even impossible. During an initial meeting, a group should discuss how to become better informed. The following steps should help your group get started:

- Assess current knowledge.
- Identify areas needing research.
- Assign research responsibilities.
- Determine how to share information effectively.
- Set research deadlines.

STRUCTURED PROCEDURES

Groups need clear procedures that specify how they will make decisions and solve problems. Group communication scholar Marshall Scott Poole has called procedures "the heart of group work [and] the most powerful tools we have to improve the con-duct of meetings."[5]

There are, however, many different kinds of procedures. There are complex, theory-based, problem-solving models designed to tackle the overall problem facing a group. There are also decision-making methods and tools designed for interim tasks such as idea generation and solution implementation. The next few sections of this chapter describe how these types of procedures can and should be used to improve decision making and problem solving.

Effective Group Decision Making

All groups make decisions. Some decisions may be simple and easy; others may be complex and consequential. Regardless of the issue, effective groups look for the best way to reach a decision, one that takes into consideration the group's shared goal and the characteristics and preferences of its members.

DECISION-MAKING METHODS

▶ Voting

▶ Consensus

▶ Authority Rule

DECISION-MAKING METHODS

There are many ways for groups to make decisions, from holding secret ballots to flipping a coin. Certain methods, however, work best for groups trying to reach a decision consistent with their common goal. Groups can let the majority have its way through voting, try to find a decision or solution that everyone can live with by reaching consensus, or leave the final decision to someone else, an authority. Each approach has strengths and should be selected to match the needs and purpose of the group and its task.

Voting   Voting is the most obvious and easiest way to make a group decision. When a quick decision is needed, there is nothing more efficient and decisive. Sometimes, though, voting may not be the best way to make important decisions. When a vote is taken, some members win, but others lose.

A **majority vote** requires that more than half the members vote in favor of a proposal. However, if a group is making a major decision, there may not be enough support if only 51 percent of the members vote in favor of the project, because the 49 percent who lose may resent working on a project they dislike. To avoid such problems, some groups use a two-thirds vote rather than majority rule. In a **two-thirds vote**, at least twice as many group members vote for a proposal as against it. Voting works best when

What are the advantages and disadvantages of voting as a decision-making method? Does a unanimous vote necessarily mean that everyone fully agrees with and likes a particular decision?

- a group is pressed for time
- the issue is not highly controversial
- a group is too large to use any other decision-making method
- there is no other way to break a deadlock
- a group's constitution or rules require voting on certain issues and proposals

Consensus   Because voting has built-in disadvantages, many groups rely on consensus to make decisions. **Consensus** is reached when all group members agree to support a group decision. A consensus decision is one "that all members have a part in shaping and that all find at least minimally acceptable as a means of accomplishing some mutual goals."[6] Consensus does not work for all groups. Imagine how difficult it would be to achieve genuine consensus among pro-life and pro-choice or pro-gun control and anti-gun control group members. The guidelines shown in Figure 11.1 should be used to seek consensus.

If you decide to seek consensus, several preconditions should exist. Group members should trust one another and expect honesty, directness, and candor. If a leader dominates a group, true consensus may be impossible to achieve. Instead, everyone goes along with the leader's wishes and calls it consensus. Achieving consensus also requires time to consider everyone's opinions. If members rush to achieve consensus, no one may be satisfied. Sociologists Ralph Napier and Matti Gershenfeld put it this way: "A group that wants to use a consensual approach to decision making must be willing to develop the skills and discipline to take the time necessary to make it work. Without these, the group becomes highly vulnerable to domination or intimidation by a few and to psychological game playing by individuals unwilling to 'let go.'"[7]

Authority Rule   Sometimes a single person or someone outside the group will make the final decision. When **authority rule** is used, groups may be asked to gather information for and recommend decisions to another person or larger group. For example, an association's nominating committee considers potential candidates and recommends a slate of officers to the association. Or a hiring committee may screen dozens of job applications and submit a top-three list to the person or persons making the hiring decision.

If, however, a leader or outside authority ignores or reverses group recommendations, members may become demoralized, resentful, and unproductive on future assignments. Even within a group, a strong leader or authority figure may use a group and its members to give the appearance of collaborative decision making. The group thus becomes a "rubber stamp" and surrenders its will to authority rule.

Figure 11.1	Guidelines for Achieving Group Consensus

Do This:	Don't Do This:
✔ Listen carefully to and respect other members' points of view.	✗ Don't be stubborn and argue only for your own position.
✔ Try to be logical rather than emotional.	✗ Don't change your mind to avoid conflict or reach a quick decision.
✔ If there is a deadlock, work to find the next best alternative that is acceptable to all.	✗ Don't give in, especially if you have a crucial piece of information to share.
✔ Make sure that members not only agree but also will be committed to the final decision.	✗ Don't agree to a decision or solution you can't possibly support.
✔ Get everyone involved in the discussion.	✗ Don't use "easy" ways of reaching a solution such as flipping a coin, letting the majority rule, or trading one decision for another.
✔ Welcome differences of opinion.	

A group discussion can become a political arena in which individuals and/or special-interest groups compete to gain political influence and power. Unlike with hidden agendas, it is no secret that politically powerful people influence group decisions. They affect how and whether other members participate, whose ideas and suggestions are given serious consideration, and which solutions are chosen.

Group scholars Randy Hirokawa and Roger Pace warn that "influential members [can] convince the group to accept invalid facts and assumptions, introduce poor ideas and suggestions, lead the group to misinterpret information presented to them, or lead the group off on tangents and irrelevant discussion."[1] In short, one powerful but misguided member can be responsible for the poor quality of a group's decision.

One of the major advantages of using an established decision-making procedure is that it can protect a group from the debilitating effects of politics and power. Procedures specify the rules of engagement. Anyone violating such rules or failing to meet assigned responsibilities may justly face isolation and criticism.

[1]Randy Hirokawa and Roger Pace, "A Descriptive Investigation of the Possible Communication-Based Reasons for Effective and Ineffective Group Decision Making," *Communication Monographs* 50 (1983), p. 379.

DECISION-MAKING CHALLENGES

Regardless of the decision-making method, several challenges may arise and affect the outcome of a group decision. We would be remiss if we did not acknowledge that even the best of groups can be led astray. Three of these decision-making challenges include hidden agendas, groupthink, and diverse decision-making styles.

Hidden Agendas Most effective groups have a clear purpose. In addition, each member may have individual goals and plans for achieving those goals. There is, however, one type of individual goal—called a *hidden agenda*—that can jeopardize group success.

Hidden agendas occur when members' private, unspoken goals differ from the group's common and openly acknowledged goal. Hidden agendas represent what people really want, rather than what they say they want. When hidden agendas become more important than a group's goal, the result can be group frustration and failure. Here are two examples:

1. A group member who wants to make sure a friend is chosen for a prestigious award points out the flaws in other candidates while heaping praise on the friend.
2. A group member who knows why a plan won't work may remain silent to make sure that the person responsible for implementing the plan fails.

Although most conscientious and ethical group members do not pursue such hidden agendas, it would be naive to presume that all members care equally about achieving the group's shared goal. Unfortunately, hidden agendas may obscure real issues while pseudo-issues dominate the discussion. You can minimize the effects of hidden agendas by making sure that the group agrees on a common goal, strongly endorses the importance of quality content, and carefully selects and follows effective decision-making and problem-solving procedures.

Groupthink Although conforming to group norms and promoting group cohesiveness benefit groups in many ways, too much conformity and excessive cohesiveness can result in a phenomenon known as groupthink. **Groupthink**, according to Irving Janis, is the deterioration of group effectiveness as a consequence of in-group pressure.[8] By overemphasizing group unity and consistency, groupthink stifles the free flow of information, suppresses constructive disagreement, and erects nearly impenetrable barriers to effective communication.

DECISION-MAKING CHALLENGES

▶ Hidden Agendas
▶ Groupthink
▶ Diverse Decision-Making Styles

Figure 11.2	Symptoms of Groupthink

SYMPTOMS	DESCRIPTION	EXPRESSION
Invulnerability	Group is overconfident; willing to take big risks	"We're right. We've done this before and nothing's gone wrong."
Rationalization	Group makes excuses; discounts warnings	"What does he know? He's only been here three weeks."
Morality	Group ignores ethical and moral consequences	"Sometimes the ends justifies the means. Only results count."
Stereotyping Outsiders	Believes opponents are too weak or stupid to make trouble	"Let's not worry about them— they can't get their act together."
Self-Censorship	Members doubt their own reservations; are unwilling to disagree	"I guess it's okay if I'm the only one who disagrees."
Pressure on Dissent	Members are pressured to agree	"Why are you holding this up? You'll ruin the project."
Illusion of Unanimity	Group believes that everyone agrees	"Hearing no objections, the motion passes."
Mindguarding	Group shields members from adverse information or opposition	"Tamela wanted to come to this meeting, but I told her that it wasn't necessary."

Source: Irving L. Janis, *Groupthink*, 2nd ed. (Boston: Houghton Mifflin, 1982), p. 9.

Irving Janis developed the theory of groupthink after recognizing patterns in what he called policy-making fiascoes. Groupthink has been implicated as a significant factor in major policy decisions, including the Bay of Pigs invasion of Cuba, the escalation of both the Korean and Vietnam Wars, the Watergate burglary and coverup, the Challenger space shuttle disaster, and, in some analysts' opinions, the decision to invade Iraq in 2003. After investigating these kinds of decisions, Janis identified eight symptoms of groupthink, which are illustrated in Figure 11.2.[9]

The best way to deal with groupthink is to prevent it from happening in the first place. Fortunately, there are practical ways to minimize the potential for groupthink.[10] Choose the strategies that are most appropriate for you and your group.

- Ask each member to serve in the role of critical evaluator.
- If possible, have more than one group work on the same problem independently.
- Discuss the group's progress with someone outside the group. Report the feedback to the entire group.
- Periodically invite an expert to join your meeting, and encourage constructive criticism.
- Discuss the potential negative consequences of any decision or action.
- Encourage expression of disagreement and evaluation of ideas.
- Ask questions, offer reasons for positions, and demand justifications from others.
- Before finalizing the decision, give members a second chance to express doubts.

How did faulty decision making and groupthink principles contribute to the tragic explosion of the space shuttle *Challenger*?

The consequences of groupthink can be serious. Consider the tragic consequences that groupthink would have on a jury deliberating a death penalty case or a medical team diagnosing a patient. Spending the time and energy to work through differences will result in better decisions without sacrificing group cohesiveness.

Diverse Decision-Making Styles   Not everyone makes decisions in the same way. Your way of making decisions may be very different than the way others reach a decision. In Chapter 7, "Interpersonal Communication: Understanding Relationships" we describe the Myers-Briggs Type Indicator. Two traits—thinking and feeling—focus on how we make decisions. Thinkers, for example, are task-oriented members who prefer to use logic in making decisions. Feelers, on the other hand, are people-oriented members who want everyone to get along, even if it means spending more time socializing or giving in to members to avoid interpersonal problems. When thinkers and feelers work together in groups, there is a potential for misunderstanding. However, when thinkers and feelers appreciate their differences as decision makers, they can form an unbeatable team. Thinkers make decisions and move the group forward whereas feelers make sure the group is working harmoniously throughout the process.

In "Decision Making Style: The Development of a New Measure," Suzanne Scott and Reginald Bruce take a more detailed look at decision-making style.[11] They describe five styles, all of which have the potential to improve or impair group decision making:

- *Rational Decision Maker.* "I've carefully considered all the issues." Rational decision makers carefully weigh information and options before making a decision. They make decisions in a systematic way using logical reasons to justify final decisions. However, they must be careful not to analyze a problem for so long that they never actually make a decision.

- *Intuitive Decision Maker.* "It just feels like the right thing to do." Intuitive decision makers make decisions based on instincts, feelings, or hunches. They may not always be able to articulate specific reasons for decisions, but know that their decisions "feel" right.

- *Dependent Decision Maker.* "If you think it's okay, then I'll do it." Dependent decision makers solicit the advice and opinions of others before making a decision. They feel uncomfortable making decisions that others disapprove of

Regardless of how persuasively an idea is presented, group members must also strive to be ethical decision makers. Group members should keep in mind four ethical responsibilities: (1) the research responsibility, (2) the common good responsibility, (3) the reasoning responsibility, and (4) the social code responsibility.[1]

1. *The Research Responsibility.* Group members come to a discussion informed and prepared to discuss the issues. Information must be used honestly. To fulfill this responsibility, follow these guidelines:

   - Do not distort information.
   - Do not suppress important information.
   - Never fabricate or make up information.
   - Reveal the sources of information so others can evaluate them.

2. *The Common Good Responsibility.* Ethical group members look beyond their own needs and consider the circumstances of others. Members should be committed to achieving the group goal rather than merely winning an argument. The following two principles are important for preserving the common good responsibility:

   - Consider the interests of those affected by the decision.
   - Promote the group's goal as more important than winning an argument.

3. *The Reasoning Responsibility.* Members avoid presenting faulty arguments. Understanding critical thinking, methods of building a valid argument, and ways to recognize fallacies will help you fulfill this ethical responsibility, as will following these recommendations:

   - Do not misrepresent the views of others.
   - Use sound critical thinking supported by evidence.
   - Avoid making arguments containing fallacies.

4. *The Social Code Responsibility.* Group members promote an open and supportive climate for discussion. Follow these guidelines for fulfilling the social code responsibility:

   - Treat other group members as equals.
   - Give everyone, including those who disagree, the opportunity to respond to an issue.
   - Do not insult or attack the character of a group member.
   - Give the group an opportunity to review evidence and ideas.
   - Respect the established group norms.

[1]Adapted from Karyn C. Rybacki and Donald J. Rybacki, *Advocacy and Opposition: An Introduction to Argumentation*, 4th ed. (Boston: Allyn & Bacon, 2000), pp. 11–15.

---

or oppose. They may even make a decision they aren't happy with just to please others.

- *Avoidant Decision Maker.* "I just can't deal with this right now." Avoidant decision makers feel uncomfortable making decisions. As a result, they may not think about a problem at all or will make a final decision at the very last minute.

- *Spontaneous Decision Maker.* "Let's do it now and worry about the consequences later." Spontaneous decision makers tend to be impulsive and make quick decisions on the spur of the moment. They often make decisions they later regret.

Consider the ways in which different decision-making styles could cause disruption in a group. For example, what would happen if half the group were rational decision makers and the other half were intuitive decision makers? Also, consider the potential pitfalls of having only one type of decision-making style in a group, such as dependent or avoidant decision makers.

Effective Group Problem Solving

Although there are several problem-solving methods, there is no "best" model or magic formula that ensures effective problem solving in every group. However, as groups gain experience and success as problem solvers, they learn that some procedures work better than others and some need modification to suit group needs. Here

Directions: For each of the following statements, indicate the degree to which you agree or disagree by circling the appropriate number on the following scale: (1) strongly disagree, (2) disagree, (3) undecided (neither agree nor disagree), (4) agree, or (5) strongly agree. There are no right or wrong answers; answer as honestly as you can. Think carefully before choosing option 3 (undecided)—it may suggest you cannot make decisions.

Decision Styles Quiz

_____	1. When I have to make an important decision, I usually seek the opinions of others.	1 2 3 4 5
_____	2. I tend to put off decisions on issues that make me uncomfortable or that are unpleasant.	1 2 3 4 5
_____	3. I make decisions in a logical and systematic way.	1 2 3 4 5
_____	4. When making a decision, I usually trust feelings or gut instincts.	1 2 3 4 5
_____	5. When making a decision, I generally consider the advantages and disadvantages of many alternatives.	1 2 3 4 5
_____	6. I often avoid making important decisions until I absolutely have to.	1 2 3 4 5
_____	7. I often make impulsive decisions.	1 2 3 4 5
_____	8. When making a decision, I rely upon my instincts.	1 2 3 4 5
_____	9. It is easier for me to make important decisions when I know others approve or support them.	1 2 3 4 5
_____	10. I make decisions very quickly.	1 2 3 4 5

Scoring: To determine your score for each type of decision making, add the total of your responses to specific items as indicated below. Your higher scores identify your preferred decision-making styles.

Answers to items 3 and 5 = _____ (rational decision maker)

Answers to items 4 and 8 = _____ (intuitive decision maker)

Answers to items 1 and 9 = _____ (dependent decision maker)

Answers to items 2 and 6 = _____ (avoidant decision maker)

Answers to items 7 and 10 = _____ (spontaneous decision maker)

Sources: www.ucd.ie/careers/CMS/decision/student_skills_decision_styleex.html; www.acu.edu/campusoffices/ocad/students/exploration/assess/decision.html, updated August 24, 2005. Also see Suzanne Scott and Reginald Bruce, "Decision Making Style: The Development of a New Measure," _Educational and Psychological Measurement_ 55 (1995), pp. 818–831.

we offer four methods that can help groups through the problem-solving process: brainstorming, the Decreasing Options Technique (DOT), the Standard Agenda, and the Single Question Format.

BRAINSTORMING

In 1953, Alex Osborn introduced the concept of brainstorming in his book _Applied Imagination._[12] **Brainstorming** is a technique for generating as many ideas as possible in a short period. It works because deferring the evaluation of ideas improves the quality of participants' input and because the quantity of ideas breeds quality. The latter idea is based on the notion that creative ideas will come only after we have gotten the obvious suggestions out.[13]

Brainstorming is a fairly simple and widely used method. In fact, more than 70 percent of businesspeople claim that brainstorming is used in their organizations.[14] Unfortunately, many groups fail to use brainstorming effectively. The guidelines shown in Figure 11.3 explain the rules and nature of brainstorming.

PROBLEM-SOLVING METHODS

▶ Brainstorming

▶ The Decreasing Options Technique (DOT)

▶ The Standard Agenda

▶ The Single Question Format

Figure 11.3	Brainstorming Guidelines

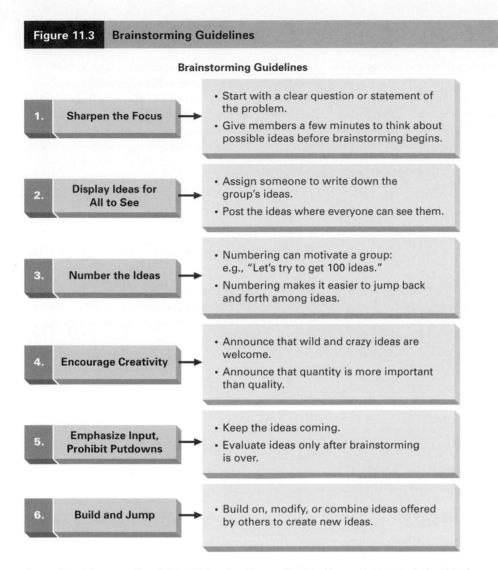

Brainstorming Guidelines

1. Sharpen the Focus
- Start with a clear question or statement of the problem.
- Give members a few minutes to think about possible ideas before brainstorming begins.

2. Display Ideas for All to See
- Assign someone to write down the group's ideas.
- Post the ideas where everyone can see them.

3. Number the Ideas
- Numbering can motivate a group: e.g., "Let's try to get 100 ideas."
- Numbering makes it easier to jump back and forth among ideas.

4. Encourage Creativity
- Announce that wild and crazy ideas are welcome.
- Announce that quantity is more important than quality.

5. Emphasize Input, Prohibit Putdowns
- Keep the ideas coming.
- Evaluate ideas only after brainstorming is over.

6. Build and Jump
- Build on, modify, or combine ideas offered by others to create new ideas.

Source: Based, in part, on Tom Kelley with Jonathan Littman, *The Art of Innovation: Lessons in Creativity from IDEO, America's Leading Design Firm* (New York: Currency, 2001), pp. 56–59. Also see Rodney W. Napier and Matti K. Gershenfeld, *Groups: Theory and Experience,* 7th ed. (Boston: Houghton Mifflin, 2004), p. 321.

Brainstorming is a great way to tackle open-ended, unclear, or broad problems. If you're looking for lots of ideas, it is a very useful technique. But if you need a formal plan of action or you have a critical problem to solve that requires a single "right" answer, try another method. Brainstorming may *not* be useful in the following situations:

- *Crises.* A crisis needs rapid decisions and clear leadership, not a fun-filled brainstorming session.
- *Repairs.* If you need to correct something, and you know what went wrong and how to fix it, it's better to organize an effective repair team.
- *Planning.* If you know where you are and where you want to be at a definite point in the future, you should hold a comprehensive planning session to map out details.

There are several sure-fire ways to prevent having a productive brainstorming session.[15] For example, if the boss is allowed to speak first, she or he can potentially influence and limit the direction of ideas. In an effort to be more democratic, some

The decision-making and problem-solving methods presented in this chapter were created with the assumption that group members would be meeting face-to-face. However, most of these methods also work well in virtual groups. Additionally, specialized computer software, or groupware, can facilitate group collaboration, decision making, and problem solving.

Successful virtual groups match their problem-solving or decision-making tasks to the appropriate technology. Usually, virtual groups engage in four types of interactive meetings: information sharing, discussion, decision making, and product producing. An information-sharing meeting could include a virtual presentation or an online exchange of information among members. A discussion meeting also shares information but promotes dialogue through the generation of ideas or options and discussions about issues or problems via e-mail or bulletin boards. In a decision-making meeting, virtual groups review the important issues and make decisions collaboratively. During product-producing meetings, virtual group members work on a project such as developing a design or drafting a new policy. These meetings require the most collaboration.[1]

All types of technology are not equally well suited to all types of group interaction. For example, when virtual groups share information, several types of technology work quite well: audio conferences, e-mail, video

conferences, and collaborative writing with audio/video. If, however, your group is engaged in brainstorming, using groupware with audio, text, and graphics is much more effective than using e-mail. When your virtual group has to make a decision, a videoconference or software voting feature would be more useful than an electronic bulletin board. In product production meetings, collaborative writing with audio and video is much more effective than voice mail, e-mail, and bulletin boards.[2]

Virtual groups have the advantage of "multiple monologues" that foster multiple conversations on a screen at the same time and, as a result, stimulate more ideas and overall productivity with fewer blocking behaviors. In fact, some studies have found that idea generation and consolidation using computers are more productive and satisfying than if done face-to-face.[3] However, computer groups require more time for task completion, and eventually members may feel dissatisfied.[4] In other words, eventually group members lose interest or want to see each other face-to-face.

[1]Deborah L. Duarte and Nancy Tennant Snyder, *Mastering Virtual Teams: Strategies, Tools, and Techniques That Succeed*, 3rd ed. (San Francisco: Jossey-Bass, 2007), p. 168.

[2]Ibid., p. 171.

[3]Rodney W. Napier and Matti K. Gershenfeld, *Groups: Theory and Practice* (Boston: Houghton Mifflin, 2004), p. 327.

[4]Ibid., p. 328.

groups have members speak in turn. This approach, however, will prevent the group from building momentum and will result in fewer ideas. Finally, some members may try to write down all of the group's ideas, but those members end up being so focused on note taking that they rarely contribute ideas. It is better to have one person record all the ideas contributed by the group members.

Although brainstorming is often used in groups, much depends on the nature of the group and the character of its members. If a group is self-conscious and sensitive to implied criticism, brainstorming can fail. However, if a group is comfortable with such a freewheeling process, brainstorming can enhance creativity and produce numerous ideas and suggestions.

DECREASING OPTIONS TECHNIQUE

The DOT, which stands for **Decreasing Options Technique**, is a decision-making tool that helps groups reduce and refine a large number of suggestions into a manageable number of ideas.[16] In our work as professional facilitators, we have used this technique to assist small and large groups facing a variety of decision-making tasks. We have enlisted the DOT strategy to write an identity statement for an academic discipline, to create an ethics credo for a professional association, to draft a vision statement for a college, and to create an academic curriculum for an emerging profession. The DOT method works best when a group must sort through a multitude of ideas and options. There are four basic steps to follow when using the DOT: (1) generate individual ideas, (2) post ideas for all to see, (3) sort the ideas, and (4) prioritize the ideas with "dots."

Generate Individual Ideas   At the beginning of the DOT process, group members are asked to generate ideas or suggestions related to the topic being discussed. Ideas can be single words or full-sentence suggestions. For example, when creating a professional association's ethics credo, participants contributed words such as *honesty, respect,* and *truth* for inclusion.[17] You can ask group members to generate and submit ideas *before* the group meets or ask them to contribute their ideas at the beginning of a meeting. Conference participants working on the ethics credo mailed and e-mailed key words to the conference chairperson several weeks in advance. These words were then sorted to avoid duplication, and prepared for posting at the upcoming meeting.

Post Ideas for All to See   Each idea should be written on a separate sheet of thick paper in large, easy-to-read letters—only one idea per page. Then, post the pages on the walls of the group's meeting room for all to see and consider. When members submit their ideas in advance, the postings can be done before the meeting begins. When members generate ideas during a meeting, postings should be displayed after all members have finished writing their ideas on separate sheets of paper.

Sort Ideas   Not surprisingly, many group members will contribute similar or overlapping ideas. When this happens, sort the ideas and post similar ideas close to one another. For example, when facilitating the development of a college's vision statement, phrases like *academic excellence, quality education,* and *high-quality instruction* were posted near one another. After everyone is comfortable with the manner in which postings have been sorted, give a title to each grouping of ideas. For example, in the vision statement session, the term *quality education* was used as an umbrella phrase for nearly a dozen similar concepts.

Prioritize Ideas   At this point, members must prioritize the ideas by choosing the ones they believe are most important: Which words *best* reflect the vision we have for our college? Which concepts *must* be included in our association's ethics credo? Which units are *essential* in the new curriculum?

To prioritize ideas efficiently, give every member a limited number of colored sticker dots and ask them to "dot" the most important ideas or options. For example, after giving ten dots to each member of the vision statement group, we instructed them to choose the most important concepts from among the twenty-five phrases posted on the walls. After everyone has finished walking around the room and posting dots, the most important ideas are usually very apparent. Some ideas will be covered with dots; others will be speckled with only three or four; some will remain blank. After a brief review of the outcome, the group can eliminate some ideas, decide whether marginal ideas should be included, and end up with a limited and manageable number of options to consider and discuss.

Advantages of the DOT Method   When a group generates dozens of ideas, valuable meeting time can be consumed by discussing each idea, regardless of its merit or relevance. The DOT method reduces the quantity of ideas to a manageable number. Often the DOT precedes an extended discussion of key ideas and suggestions. When the DOT approach is not used, the number of topics to be reviewed can overwhelm a group and discourage members from participating. Consider using the DOT when the group

- is so large that open discussion of individual ideas is unworkable
- has generated a significant number of competing ideas
- wants to ensure equal opportunities for input by all members

- wants to restrain dominant members from exerting too much influence
- does not have enough time to discuss multiple or controversial ideas

Although the examples we have used to describe the DOT process focus on face-to-face interaction, the DOT also works very well in virtual settings. Instead of writing ideas on sheets of paper, posting them on walls, and dotting preferences, a virtual group can follow the same steps by using e-mail or networked software designed for interactive group work. Ideas can be generated online, grouped by a moderator or committee, and then "dotted" electronically. Sophisticated software can tally members' preferences and rank ideas based on the number of dots given to each idea.

THE STANDARD AGENDA

The founding father of problem-solving procedures is a U.S. philosopher and educator named John Dewey. In 1910, Dewey wrote a book entitled *How We Think* in which he described a set of practical steps that a rational person should follow when solving a problem.[18] These guidelines have come to be known as Dewey's *reflective thinking process.*

Dewey's ideas have been adapted to the process of solving problems in groups. The reflective thinking process begins with a focus on the problem itself and then moves to a systematic consideration of possible solutions. We offer one approach to this process: the **Standard Agenda**.[19] The seven basic steps in the Standard Agenda are summarized in Figure 11.4.

As a way of appreciating how each step in the Standard Agenda functions, we provide an extended example. Although this example does not offer many details, it can demonstrate how a group can use the Standard Agenda method of problem solving.

Fallingstar State College

For three consecutive years Fallingstar State College has experienced declining enrollment and no increase in funding from the state. To balance the budget, the board of trustees has had to raise tuition every year. There are no prospects for more state funding in the near future. Even with significant tuition increases, there has been a drop in overall college revenue. The college's planning council, composed of representative vice presidents, deans,

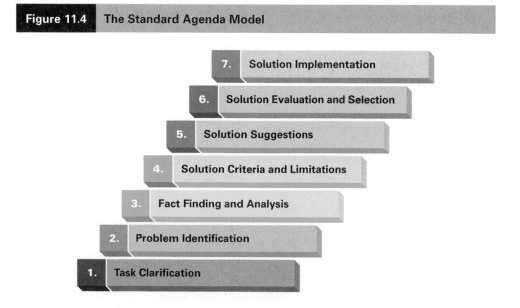

Figure 11.4   The Standard Agenda Model

7.   Solution Implementation

6.   Solution Evaluation and Selection

5.   Solution Suggestions

4.   Solution Criteria and Limitations

3.   Fact Finding and Analysis

2.   Problem Identification

1.   Task Clarification

faculty members, staff employees, and students, has been charged with answering the following question: Given severe budget constraints, what should the college do to continue providing high-quality instruction and student services?

Task Clarification   The goal of this initial phase is to make sure that everyone understands the group's assignment. For example, Fallingstar State College's planning council could dedicate the beginning of its first meeting to making sure that everyone is aware of the time frame in which to work and the need to produce a written set of recommendations. During this phase, group members can ask questions about their roles and responsibilities in the problem-solving process.

Problem Identification   Overlooking this second step can send a group in the wrong direction. In the case of Fallingstar State College, there may be several different ways to define the problem. Is the problem declining enrollment? Some may consider reduced enrollment an advantage rather than a disadvantage, because having fewer students can result in smaller classes, more individualized instruction, less chaos at registration, and easier parking. Is the problem a lack of money? Although lack of money seems to be a universal problem, an inefficiently run college may have enough money if it enhances productivity and becomes more businesslike.

The group's problem should be worded as an agreed-upon question. Whether it is a question of fact, conjecture, value, or policy determines the way the discussion will be focused. The question "What should the college do to continue providing high-quality instruction and student services?" is a question of policy that can only be answered by also considering subquestions of fact, value, and conjecture.

Fact Finding and Analysis   During the third step—fact finding—group members have several obligations, reflected in the following questions of fact and value:

- What are the facts of the situation?
- What additional information or expert opinion do we need?
- How serious or widespread is the problem?
- What are the causes of the problem?
- What prevents or inhibits us from solving the problem?

These questions require investigations of facts, conclusions about causes and effects, and value judgments about the seriousness of the problem.

Fallingstar State College's planning council could look at the rate of enrollment decline and future enrollment projections, the anticipated budgets for future years, the efficiency of existing services, the projected impact of inflation, salary increases, maintenance costs, and the likely causes for declining enrollment. It could take months to investigate such questions, and even then there may not be clear answers to all of them. Failing to search for such answers, however, is much more hazardous than ignoring them.

Although carefully evaluating facts and opinions is critical to effective problem solving, groups must also avoid analysis paralysis. **Analysis paralysis** occurs when groups are so focused on analyzing a problem that they fail to make a decision.[20] In other words, a college planning council could collect dozens of reports and identify ten possible causes of declining enrollment but still be unable to verify or settle on the most important reasons. Rather than spending months arguing about the issue or giving up on finding the correct answer, a group may have to move on and begin its search for solutions.

Solution Criteria and Limitations   Solution criteria are standards that should be met for an ideal resolution of a problem. The development of realistic criteria should also include an understanding of solution limitations, which can be financial, institutional, practical, political, and legal in scope. For a college planning council, criteria could include the cost of potential solutions, the goal of ensuring that all subgroups—administrators, faculty, staff, and students—accept the solution, a commitment to using fair and open procedures to assess existing programs, and considerations of the political and legal consequences of proposed actions.

Solution Suggestions At this point in a group's deliberations, some solutions are probably apparent. Even so, the group should concentrate on suggesting as many solutions as possible without criticizing them. Brainstorming is an effective method for generating suggestions. Having spent time understanding the task, identifying the problem, analyzing its consequences and causes, and establishing criteria, members should be able to offer numerous solutions.

Suggestions from the college's planning council could include a wide range of options: raising tuition, embarking on a new promotional campaign, seeking additional grants and corporate donations, forgoing raises, freezing promotions, requiring additional teaching by faculty, increasing class size, reducing the number of administrators and staff, eliminating expensive programs and services, lobbying the state for more funds, and charging students fees for special services. The list could double or triple, depending on the creativity and resourcefulness of the group.

Solution Evaluation and Selection This stage of the Standard Agenda may be the most difficult and controversial. Here, group members discuss the pros and cons of each suggestion in light of their agreed-upon criteria for a solution. Questions of conjecture—"What will happen if we decide to do X?" or "How long can we offer quality instruction if we don't do X?"—arise as the group considers the possible consequences of each suggestion. Discussion may become heated, and disagreements may grow fierce. In some groups, members may be so tired or frustrated by the time they get to this phase that they are tempted to jump to conclusions. If the group has been conscientious in analyzing the problem and establishing criteria for solutions, however, some solutions will be rejected quickly whereas others will swiftly rise to the top of the list.

The college's planning council may hear students argue against increasing tuition and fees, but faculty predict a decline in instructional quality if they are required to teach more courses or larger classes. Administrators and staff may cringe at freezing salaries, but faculty may support a reduction in administrative staff. In this phase, a group should remember its solution criteria and use them to evaluate the strengths and weaknesses of each suggested solution. At the end of this stage, a group should identify the solutions it wishes to endorse and implement.

Solution Implementation Having made a difficult decision, a group faces one more challenge: How should the decision be implemented? Should the group assume this responsibility, or will implementation be delegated to others? How will the group explain the wisdom or practicality of its decision to others? For all the time a group spends trying to solve a problem, it may take even more time to organize the task of implementing the solution. If a planning council wants a new promotional campaign to attract students, the campaign must be well planned and affordable if it is to achieve its goal. If a college wants to enhance its fund-raising efforts, a group or office must be given the authority and resources to seek such funds. Brilliant solutions can fail if no one takes responsibility or has the authority to implement a group's decision.

THE SINGLE QUESTION FORMAT

The **Single Question Format** is a problem-solving procedure in a seemingly simple format that approximates the way successful problem solvers and decision makers naturally think.[21] The five basic steps in the Single Question Format provide a sharp focus on an agreed-upon question that, if thoroughly analyzed and responsibly answered, should provide the solution to a problem[22]:

1. *Identify the problem.* What is the single question, the answer to which is all the group needs to know to accomplish its purpose? Although it may take many hours to reach agreement on the single question, the investment is essential if additional time and effort are to be well spent.[23]

2. *Create a collaborative setting.* The group agrees on a set of norms by generating a list of "we will" statements designed to promote open discussion and participation. We will

   - listen to and respect all points of view
   - ask for facts as well as opinions
   - be tough on issues but not on each other
   - put aside our personal agendas

   In addition, the group should identify any assumptions or biases that may influence the discussion: Have past approaches worked or do we need a new approach? Do we really understand the problem or do we need to take a fresh look at the situation?

3. *Analyze the issues.* What issues or subquestions must be addressed to understand the complexities of the overall problem? Here the group should ask the following:

   - Do we have accurate and relevant facts about each issue?
   - Given what we know, what is the best or *most reasonable* response to each issue?

4. *Identify possible solutions.* What are the two or three most reasonable solutions to the problem? In addition to identifying reasonable solutions to the overall single question, the group should discuss the advantages and disadvantages of each solution.

5. *Answer the single question.* Which is the most desirable solution? After group members have completed the previous four steps, they "proceed with sufficient confidence to their final decision and commit to it."[24]

Although the Single Question Format shares many characteristics with the Standard Agenda approach, two features make it both different and effective. First, it sharply focuses on goal clarity (a prerequisite for any work group) and issue analysis. Second, it cultivates a supportive group climate that helps members identify, raise, and resolve many interpersonal and process problems that can affect group success.

Effective Meetings

More than ten million business meetings occur daily in the United States.[25] Studies of managers show that they spend 30 to 80 percent of their time in meetings.[26] Odds are that you've already spent your share of time in meetings, and certainly you will be attending meetings in the future.

Unfortunately, many meetings fail to achieve their purpose—assuming they even *have* a purpose. Ninety percent of managers report that half the meetings they attend are "either unnecessary or a complete waste of time."[27] How bad is this problem? One company in California holds daylong meetings on boats so no one can leave early. The National Management Association reports that "too many meetings" is the second biggest employee complaint. Only "too much work" receives more criticism. One unusual strategy, called meetingwise, removes the chairs from a room on the premise that the meeting will end sooner if no one gets comfortable.[28]

CommFAQ   What's the Difference between a Meeting and a Group Discussion?

In a communication course or training seminar, you may be assigned the task of participating in or chairing a group discussion. Your instructor may specify assignment requirements, such as a thirty-minute time limit, the phrasing of a discussion question, the need for using researched supporting material, and fairly equal participation by all participants. The concept of a group discussion, however, has a broader meaning in business and professional settings. In these contexts, group discussion is the means used to conduct business and professional meetings. In most meetings, group members discuss a topic, issue, or problem, often in an order specified by an agenda and under the direction of a manager or officer. Classroom discussions are a way of simulating what happens in real-world meetings where participants share information, solve problems, and make decisions. The competencies used in both contexts require effective communication skills.

Effective leaders understand that their ability to conduct meetings significantly affects their reputation and ultimate success.[29] Before looking at the leader's responsibilities in a meeting, we should specify what we mean by a meeting. Merely having a gathering of people in one place is not a meeting. We define **meeting** as a scheduled gathering of group members for a structured discussion guided by a designated chairperson. Leaders who also chair meetings have a tremendous amount of influence over and responsibility for the success of the meeting. If you are in such a position, the following discussion may present some useful guidelines.

PLANNING THE MEETING

The success or failure of a meeting largely depends on proper planning. In fact, careful planning can prevent at least twenty minutes of wasted time for each hour of a group's meeting.[30] Before calling a meeting, ask yourself several planning questions that can make your meeting more efficient and effective and also help you decide whether a meeting is even needed: Why are we meeting? Who should attend? When should we meet? Where should we meet? What materials do we need?

Why Are We Meeting?   The most important step in planning a meeting is defining its purpose and setting clear goals. Purpose identifies the desired outcome of the meeting. For example, "employer-provided daycare" merely identifies the subject of a meeting; the purpose of the meeting is "to determine whether our employer-provided daycare system needs to be expanded."

Groups should be able to achieve their purpose by the end of the meeting. If an objective cannot be accomplished during a single meeting, the purpose statement should be revised to focus on a more specific outcome. If necessary, a series of meetings can be scheduled to achieve the final goal.

Who Should Attend?   The membership of many groups is predetermined. However, if a task does not require input from everyone or only needs the expertise of certain people, you should select participants who can make a significant contribution. Try to include members who will be affected directly by the group's decision. In addition, choose participants with special expertise, different opinions and approaches, and the power to implement decisions.

When Should We Meet?   Seek input and decide what day and time are best for the meeting. Determine what time the meeting should begin as well as what time it should end. For a time-consuming and difficult goal, you may discover that more than one meeting will be necessary. Contact group members to find out when they are avail-

MEETING PLANNING QUESTIONS

▶ *Why are we meeting?* If a meeting doesn't have a purpose, don't hold it.

▶ *Who should attend?* If a task doesn't need everyone, don't invite everyone.

▶ *When should we meet?* If the time's not convenient, change it.

▶ *Where should we meet?* If the location's unsuitable, modify it.

▶ *What materials do we need?* If the group needs materials, provide them.

able, and schedule the meeting when the most essential and productive participants are free. A meeting that only a few members can attend will not be productive and will waste the time of those who do show up.

Where Should We Meet? Choose a location that is appropriate for the purpose and size of the meeting. Do your best to find a comfortable setting, making sure that the meeting room is free of distractions such as ringing phones and noisy conversations. An attractive and quiet meeting location will help your group stay motivated and focused on the group's discussion.

What Materials Do We Need? The most important item to prepare and distribute to the group is the meeting's agenda. In addition to the agenda, it may be necessary to distribute reports or other reading material for review before the meeting. Distribute all materials far enough in advance of the meeting so that everyone has time to prepare. In addition, make sure that supplies and equipment such as markers, paper, or computers are available to participants.

PREPARING THE AGENDA

An **agenda** is the outline of items to be discussed and the tasks to be accomplished at a meeting. A well-prepared agenda can serve many purposes. First and foremost, the agenda is an organizational tool—a road map for the discussion that helps the group remain focused on their task. In *Meetings: Do's, Don'ts, and Donuts*, Sharon Lippincott uses a simile to explain why a well-planned agenda is the first key to conducting effective meetings:

> Starting a meeting without an agenda is like setting out on a journey over unfamiliar roads with no map and only a general idea of the route to your destination. You may get there, but only after lengthy detours. A good agenda defines the destination of the meeting, draws a map of the most direct route, and provides checkpoints along the way.[31]

When used properly, an agenda helps participants prepare for a meeting by telling them what to expect and even how to prepare. After a meeting, the agenda can be used to assess a meeting's success by determining the extent to which all items on the agenda were addressed.

Although a group's leader usually prepares and distributes an agenda in advance of the meeting, group input can ensure that the agenda covers topics important to the entire group. The customs of the group and the purpose of the meeting will determine the format of the agenda. For example, if the purpose of the meeting is to solve a problem, the agenda items may be in the form of questions rather than the key word format of a formal business agenda. The following suggestions will help you prepare an effective agenda to guide your group's discussion:

- Note the amount of time it should take to complete a discussion item or action.
- Identify how the group will deal with each item by noting whether information will be shared with the group, whether the group will discuss an issue, or whether a decision must be made. The phrases "For Information," "For Discussion," and "For Decision" can be placed next to appropriate agenda items.
- Include the name of any person responsible for reporting information on a particular item or facilitating a portion of the discussion. Such assignments remind members to prepare for a specific topic or role.
- Carefully consider the order in which topics should be discussed. When several different topics must be addressed within a single meeting, agenda items should be put in an order that will maximize productivity.
- Make sure that all the items on the agenda relate to the purpose of the meeting.

Figures 11.5 and 11.6 present two sample agendas. Figure 11.5 focuses on a discussion agenda for a group examining a specific issue: ways to improve a company's recycling program. Figure 11.6 provides a brief version of a standard business agenda that follows a traditional format for formal business meetings.

TAKING MINUTES

Most business and professional meetings require or benefit from a record of group progress and decision making. Responsible group leaders make sure that someone is assigned the important task of taking **minutes**—the written record of a group's discussion and activities. The minutes record discussion issues and decisions for those who attend the meeting, and provide a way to communicate with those who do not attend. Most important, minutes help prevent disagreement over what was said or decided in a meeting and what tasks individual members agreed to or were assigned to do. Groups may designate a recorder or secretary to take minutes at every meeting or have members take turns volunteering to do the minutes.

Figure 11.5	**Sample Meeting Agenda**

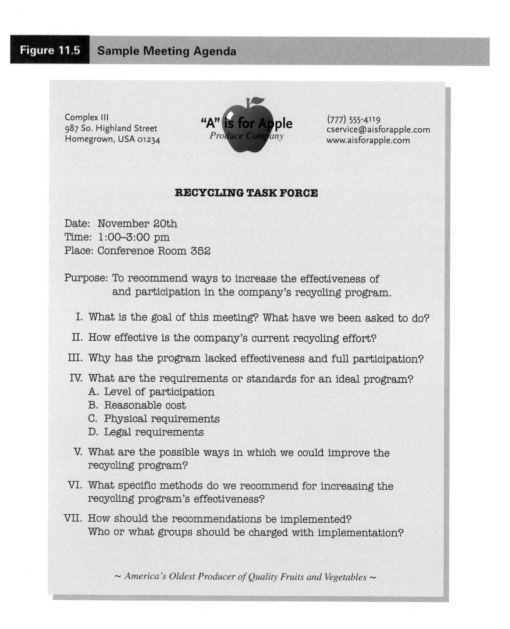

Complex III
987 So. Highland Street
Homegrown, USA 01234

"A" is for Apple
Produce Company

(777) 555-4119
cservice@aisforapple.com
www.aisforapple.com

RECYCLING TASK FORCE

Date: November 20th
Time: 1:00–3:00 pm
Place: Conference Room 352

Purpose: To recommend ways to increase the effectiveness of
          and participation in the company's recycling program.

  I. What is the goal of this meeting? What have we been asked to do?

  II. How effective is the company's current recycling effort?

  III. Why has the program lacked effectiveness and full participation?

  IV. What are the requirements or standards for an ideal program?
     A. Level of participation
     B. Reasonable cost
     C. Physical requirements
     D. Legal requirements

  V. What are the possible ways in which we could improve the
    recycling program?

  VI. What specific methods do we recommend for increasing the
    recycling program's effectiveness?

  VII. How should the recommendations be implemented?
     Who or what groups should be charged with implementation?

~ America's Oldest Producer of Quality Fruits and Vegetables ~

CommFAQ   How Can a Person Be a *Chair*?

The responsibilities of planning a meeting, preparing an agenda, and making sure that accurate and useful minutes are recorded belong to the person with the title of *chair*. Rather than worrying about whether to call someone a *chairman*, *chairwoman*, or *chairperson*, people have chosen the word *chair* for a one-size-fits-all title for the person who has "power" in meetings. Effective chairs move a group through an agreed-upon agenda, enforce group rules and regulations, and assign tasks when potential volunteers look away. The person who chairs a meeting may be the group leader, a designated facilitator, or a group member who usually assumes that role.

If you face the challenge of running a meeting, you have many responsibilities. Several guidelines can help you chair a meeting smoothly:

- Begin on time. Discourage chronic or inconsiderate late arrivals.
- Create a positive climate. Establish ground rules for member behavior.
- Delegate someone to take the minutes.
- Follow the agenda. Keep the group on track and aware of its progress.
- Facilitate the discussion. Ensure that all views are heard. Intervene when members ramble or discuss irrelevant topics. Clarify and summarize ideas and suggestions.
- Provide closure and stop on time.[1]

[1]Isa N. Engleberg and Dianna R. Wynn, *Working in Groups: Communication Principles and Strategies*, 4th ed. (Boston: Houghton Mifflin, 2007), pp. 335–337; Sharon M. Lippincott, *Meetings: Do's, Don'ts, and Donuts* (Pittsburgh, PA: Lighthouse Point Press, 1994), pp. 89–90.

Figure 11.6   Standard Business Agenda

Complex III
987 So. Highland Street
Homegrown, USA 01234

"A" is for Apple
Produce Company

(777) 555-4119
cservice@aisforapple.com
www.aisforapple.com

AGENDA

Date: September 15th
Time: 12:30–4:45 pm
Place: Presidential Ballroom

I.   Call to order by president

II. Approval of minutes and agenda

III. Reports by officers and committees

IV. Unfinished business

V.   New business

VI. Announcements

VII. Adjournment

~ America's Oldest Producer of Quality Fruits and Vegetables ~

For the most part, the format of the minutes should follow the format of the agenda. If you are responsible for taking minutes, you will probably include much of the following information:

- Name of the group
- Date and place of the meeting
- Names of those attending and absent
- Name of the person who chaired the meeting
- Exact time the meeting was called to order
- Exact time the meeting was adjourned
- Name of the person preparing the minutes
- Summary of the group's discussion and decisions, using agenda items as headings
- Specific action items, or tasks that individual members have been assigned to do after the meeting

Well-prepared minutes are brief and accurate. When summarizing a group's discussion, it is important to remember that the minutes are not a word-for-word record of everything that every member has said. Instead they summarize arguments, key ideas, actions, and votes. Immediately after a meeting, minutes should be prepared for distribution to group members. The longer the delay, the more difficult it will be for members to remember the details of the meeting and the individual task assignments made at the meeting.

Communication Challenge

Create a Standard Agenda

Directions: Your group has been assigned the task of discussing the question "What is the best way to reduce domestic violence in our community?" Use the Standard Agenda's seven steps to construct an agenda for this discussion:

1. Task Clarification

2. Problem Identification

3. Fact Finding

4. Solution Criteria and Limitations

5. Solution Suggestions

6. Solution Evaluation and Selection

7. Solution Implementation

Place each of the following questions under the appropriate step:

a. What criteria should we use to select a solution?

b. What are the causes of domestic violence?

c. What do we mean by "community"?

d. Is the solution affordable?

e. What are the possible solutions to the problem?

f. Which options best meet the solution criteria?

g. What are the different types of domestic abuse and violence?

h. Which is the best or most feasible solution?

i. What do we mean by "domestic violence"?

j. What resources are needed to implement the solution?

k. What services are available for victims and their families?

l. Is the solution legal?

m. Who are the victims?

n. Will the proposed solution be accepted by community members?

o. What tasks must be done to implement the solution?

p. Will the solution work—that is, reduce domestic violence?

q. Who will be responsible for implementing the solution?

r. How widespread and serious is the problem in our community?

s. How will we know whether the solution is effective?

Decision-Making and Problem-Solving Competencies

Directions: This assessment tool is designed to evaluate the performance of individual group members who participate in a problem-solving discussion. There are five competencies related to basic problem-solving steps and three competencies focused on task orientation, a supportive climate, and productive interaction. Rate individual group members on each item as well as the group as a whole by placing a check mark in the appropriate column, using the following scale: (1) excellent, (2) satisfactory, or (3) unsatisfactory.

Group Problem-Solving Competencies	1	2	3
1. *Identifies the problem.* Helps the group define the nature of the problem and the group's responsibilities.			
2. *Analyzes the issues.* Identifies and analyzes several of the issues that arise from the problem.			
3. *Establishes solution criteria.* Suggests criteria for assessing the workability, effectiveness, and value of a solution.			
4. *Generates solutions.* Identifies possible solutions that meet the criteria.			
5. *Evaluates solutions.* Evaluates the potential solutions.			
6. *Chooses solution and plans implementation.* Advocates appropriate solutions and plans for implementation.			
7. *Maintains task focus.* Stays on task and follows the agreed-upon agenda.			
8. *Maintains supportive climate.* Collaborates with and provides appropriate support to other group members.			
9. *Facilitates interaction.* Appropriately manages interaction and encourages others to participate.			

Key Terms

agenda
analysis paralysis
authority rule
brainstorming
consensus
decision making

Decreasing Options Technique
groupthink
hidden agenda
majority vote
meeting
minutes

problem solving
Single Question Format
Standard Agenda
two-thirds vote

Notes

1. Rodney W. Napier and Matti K. Gershenfeld, *Groups: Theory and Practice*, 7th ed. (Boston: Houghton Mifflin, 2004), p. 291.

2. *The American Heritage Dictionary*, 4th ed. (Boston: Houghton Mifflin, 2000), p. 484.

3. Peter R. Drucker, *The Effective Executive* (New York: HarperBusiness, 1967), p. 143.

4. Randy Y. Hirokawa, "Communication and Group Decision-Making Efficacy," in *Small Group Communication: Theory and Practice*, 7th ed., ed. Robert S. Cathcart, Larry A. Samovar, and Linda D. Henman (Madison, WI: Brown and Benchmark, 1996), p. 108.

5. Marshall Scott Poole, "Procedures for Managing Meetings: Social and Technological Innovation," in *Innovative Meeting Management*, ed. Richard A. Swanson and Bonnie Ogram Knapp (Austin, TX: 3M Meeting Management Institute, 1990), pp. 54–55.

6. Julia T. Wood, "Alternative Methods of Group Decision Making," in *Small Group Communication: A Reader*, 6th ed., ed. Robert S. Cathcart and Larry A. Samovar (Dubuque, IA: Wm. C. Brown, 1992), p. 159.

7. Napier and Gershenfeld, p. 337.

8. Irving L. Janis, *Groupthink*, 2nd ed. (Boston: Houghton Mifflin, 1982), p. 9.

9. Ibid.

10. See Janis; also Rebecca J.W. Cline, "Groupthink and the Watergate Cover-Up: The Illusion of Unanimity," in *Group Communication in Context: Studies of Natural Groups*, ed. Lawrence R. Frey (Hillsdale, NJ: Lawrence Erlbaum, 1994), pp. 199–223; 3M Meeting Management Team, *Mastering Meetings* (New York: McGraw-Hill, 1994), p. 58.

11. Suzanne Scott and Reginald Bruce "Decision Making Style: The Development of a New Measure." *Educational and Psychological Measurements* 55 (1995), pp. 818–831.

12. Alex F. Osborn, *Applied Imagination*, rev. ed. (New York: Scribner, 1957).

13. 3M Meeting Management Team with Jeannine Drew, *Mastering Meetings: Discovering the Hidden Potential of Effective Business Meetings* (New York: McGraw-Hill, 1994), p. 59.

14. Tom Kelly with Jonathan Littman, *The Art of Innovation: Lessons in Creativity from IDEO, America's Leading Design Firm* (New York: Currency, 2001), p. 55.

15. Kelley and Littman, pp. 64–66.

16. Isa N. Engleberg and Dianna R. Wynn, *Working in Groups: Communication Principles and Strategies*, 4th ed. (Boston: Houghton Mifflin, 2007), pp. 254–257. The DOT method combines useful features found in brainstorming, nominal group technique, and the Standard Agenda and Single Question Format.

17. See Kenneth E. Andersen, "Developments in Communication Ethics: The Ethics Commission, Code of Professional Responsibilities, and Credo for Ethical Communication," *Journal of the Association for Communication Administration* 29 (2000), pp. 131–144. The Credo for Ethical Communication is also posted on the NCA website (www.natcom.org).

18. John Dewey, *How We Think* (Boston: Heath, 1910).

19. Based on Kathryn Sue Young, Julia T. Wood, Gerald M. Phillips, and Douglas J. Pedersen, *Group Discussion: A Practical Guide to Participation and Leadership*, 3rd ed. (Prospect Heights, IL: Waveland Press, 2001), pp. 8–9. Also see Chapters 7 to 12. Young et al. present six steps in their Standard Agenda model by combining Solutions Suggestions and Solution Selection into one step. We have divided this step into separate functions given that the Solution Suggestion step may require creative thinking and brainstorming. Given that the Solution Evaluation and Selection step may be the most difficult and controversial, it requires a separate focus as well as different strategies and skills.

20. J. Dan Rothwell, *In Mixed Company: Small Group Communication*, 4th ed. (Fort Worth, TX: Harcourt College Publishers, 2001), p. 193.

21. Frank LaFasto and Carl Larson, *When Teams Work Best* (Thousand Oaks, CA: Sage, 2001), pp. 84–85.

22. Ibid., p. 85.

23. Ibid., p. 88.

24. Ibid., p. 90.

25. Edward D. McDonald, "Chaos or Communication: Technical Barriers to Effective Meetings," in *Innovative Meeting Management*, ed. Richard A. Swanson and Bonnie Ogram Knapp (Austin, TX: Minnesota Mining and Manufacturing, 1991), p. 177.

26. Marshall Scott Poole, "Procedures for Managing Meetings: Social and Technological Innovation," in *Innovative Meeting Management*, ed. Richard A. Swanson and Bonnie Ogram Knapp (Austin, TX: Minnesota Mining and Manufacturing, 1991), p. 53.

27. Dave Wiggins, "How to Have a Successful Meeting," *Journal of Environmental Health*, 60 (1998), p. 1, http://db.texshare.edu/ovidweb/ovidweb.cgi.

28. Shawn Hubler, "Don't Just Stand There, Hold a Meeting," *Baltimore Sun*, July 27, 1999, p. 11A.

29. Engleberg and Wynn, pp. 357–358.

30. Karen Anderson, *Making Meetings Work: How to Plan and Conduct Effective Meetings* (West Des Moines, IA: American Media Publishing, 1997), p. 17.

31. Sharon M. Lippincott, *Meetings: Do's, Don'ts, and Donuts* (Pittsburgh, PA: Lighthouse Point Press, 1994), p. 172.

Presentations: The Planning Process

Key Elements of Communication	Communication Axioms	Guiding Principles of Presentation Planning
Self	*Communication Is Personal*	Assess *your* speaking credibility by identifying your strengths and positive character traits.
Others	*Communication Is Relational*	Analyze and adapt to audience diversity, characteristics, knowledge, interests, attitudes, beliefs, and values.
Purpose	*Communication Is Intentional*	Determine what you want the audience to know, think, believe, or do as a result of your presentation.
Context	*Communication Is Contextual*	Analyze and adapt to the logistics of the place where you will be speaking as well as the occasion and psychosocial context.
Content	*Communication Is Symbolic*	Research and select appropriate information and valid supporting material. Choose content that generates audience interest.
Structure	*Communication Is Structured*	Organize the presentation content in a format that adapts to your purpose, audience, context, and content.
Expression	*Communication Is Irreversible*	Plan and practice appropriate verbal and nonverbal speaking skills.

The Challenge of Presentation Speaking

Effective presentations have enormous power. Famous speeches—President Abraham Lincoln's "Gettysburg Address" and Martin Luther King Jr.'s "I Have a Dream" speech—have shaped the nation in which we live. The best presentations can inform, persuade, delight, and inspire us. Effective presenters not only have good ideas, they also know how to share them.[1]

Presentation speaking is the process of using verbal and nonverbal messages to generate meaning with audience members, who are usually present at the delivery of a presentation. In addition to sharing a message, an effective presentation allows your knowledge, talents, and opinions to stand out. The person who speaks well is more likely to be noticed, believed, respected, and remembered. The benefits of learning how to speak effectively extend well beyond the few minutes you stand before an audience.

- *Personal Benefits.* You can develop self-awareness and self-confidence, improve listening and critical thinking skills, and enhance your ability to use verbal and nonverbal messages to generate meaning.

- *Professional Benefits.* You can analyze, adapt, and appeal to a variety of audiences; enhance your credibility as well as the likelihood of becoming a leader; and improve your chances of getting a job, keeping it, and advancing in your career.

- *Public Benefits.* You can understand, analyze, and critique public speeches; effectively participate in public discussions and decision making; and enrich your appreciation of effective and ethical public discourse.

Purpose and Topic

Students enrolled in a public or presentational speaking course often ask their instructors: What should I talk about? The question is a good one, but it may be unique to a speech class. Speakers outside the classroom rarely ask that question. Outside the classroom, speakers are invited to speak because they are experts on a subject, because events call for a particular topic, or because they are recognized celebrities. What they should talk about is rarely a concern. A noted scientist may present at an international conference; a candidate may speak at a political rally. In both cases, the speakers know their topic. Even more important, they know their purpose.

Identify your purpose by answering the following question: What do I want my audience to know, think, feel, or do as a result of my presentation? Purpose focuses on *why*: Why am I speaking and what outcome do I want? Having a clear purpose does not guarantee that you will achieve it. But without a purpose, it is difficult to decide what to say, what materials to include, and even how to deliver your presentation.

PRESENTATION GOALS

How do you convey your purpose to the audience? Begin by deciding whether you want to inform, persuade, entertain, inspire, or use a combination of all four goals as a strategy.

Speaking to Inform   An **informative presentation** instructs, enlightens, explains, describes, clarifies, corrects, reminds, and/or demonstrates. Teachers spend most of their lecture time informing students. Sometimes an informative presentation explains a complex concept, demonstrates a complicated process, or clears up misunderstandings. Informative presentations take the form of class reports, committee updates, or formal lectures. Chapter 15, "Presentations: Speaking to Inform," covers the theories, strategies, and skills of informative speaking.

Speaking to Persuade   A **persuasive presentation** seeks to change or influence audience opinions and/or behavior. These changes may be directed toward an idea, a person, an object, or an action.

Idea:	Do unto others as you would have them do unto you.
	FIRO theory best explains the nature of interpersonal relationship needs.
People:	Martin Luther King Jr. was the greatest speaker of the twentieth century.
	Our state's governor should be impeached.
Objects:	SUVs are dangerous vehicles.
	A healthy diet should include salmon, green tea, broccoli, and ground flax.
Action:	Register to vote.
	Get a flu shot in October.

Advertisements persuade customers to buy products. Political candidates persuade audiences to elect them. Persuasive presentations occur in courtroom trials, religious services, college classrooms, around the dinner table, and in daily conversations. Chapter 16, "Presentations: Speaking to Persuade," provides more details on the theories, strategies, and skills of persuasion.

PRESENTATION GOALS
▶ To Inform
▶ To Persuade
▶ To Entertain
▶ To Inspire

When Leslie Walker, the great-great-grandniece of Harriet Tubman—a fugitive slave, abolitionist, and Union spy active in the Underground Railroad—speaks to a third-grade class about her famous relative, is she speaking to inform or speaking to persuade?

Before identifying your presentation's purpose and topic, you should make a more basic decision: Should you speak or should you write? Presentations may be more appropriate than written messages when

- the situation calls for a presentation: a graduation speech, a wedding toast, an oral report at a staff meeting
- immediate action is needed: an unexpected and urgent problem arises, a crisis requires that everyone be told about a situation immediately
- the topic is controversial: a problem requires face-to-face communication to ensure understanding
- the audience may have questions: a news conference, following an explanation of a complex procedure or process
- *you* will make a difference: an emotional message needs a visible and sincere messenger, a topic in which your expertise adds credibility

Now look at the following situations. In your opinion, which form of communication—speaking or writing—is the best choice for sharing the following messages? Remember to apply the guidelines just listed and put a check mark in the appropriate column.

Speak	Write	
_____	_____	Describe how to assemble a computer system.

Speak	Write	
_____	_____	Warn preteens about the long-lasting effects of alcohol abuse.
_____	_____	Teach someone how to meditate.
_____	_____	Influence people to buy insurance from you.
_____	_____	Explain a new employee evaluation system.
_____	_____	Explain why you are the best candidate for a job.
_____	_____	Convince an interviewing committee to hire you.
_____	_____	Share a recipe for lemon poppyseed pound cake.
_____	_____	Persuade nonvoting friends to vote.
_____	_____	Coax a frightened group of students to speak.

Did certain types of topics lend themselves to speaking? Can you definitely say that one form is always better than another for certain kinds of messages? Deciding whether to speak or write is not a minor decision. It influences whether and how well you achieve your communication purpose.[1]

[1]John A. Daly and Isa N. Engleberg, *Presentations in Everyday Life: Strategies for Effective Speaking,* 2nd ed. (Boston: Houghton Mifflin, 2005), p. 14–15.

Speaking to Entertain **Entertainment speaking** amuses, interests, diverts, or "warms up" an audience. Standup comedy is a form of entertainment speaking. After-dinner speakers amuse audiences too full to move or absorb serious ideas and complex information. At a retirement party, friends may "roast" a retiree. Humorous speaking requires more than funny content. It requires comic timing—knowing when and how forcefully to say a line, when to pause, and when to look at the audience for reactions. Chapter 15, "Presentations: Speaking to Inform," discusses how to use humor effectively in a presentation.

Speaking to Inspire **Inspirational speaking** brings like-minded people together, creates social unity, builds goodwill, or celebrates by arousing audience emotions. Inspirational speaking occurs in special contexts, takes many forms, and can tap a wide range of emotions. Here are just a few examples:

- *Toasts*. To invoke joy and/or admiration for a person or persons
- *Eulogies*. To honor the dead and/or comfort the grieving
- *Motivational Presentations*. To rally and arouse the emotions and enthusiasm of an audience
- *Welcomes*. To help an audience feel appreciated and comfortable in a new situation or place
- *Introductions of a Speaker*. To arouse audience interest in a speaker and the speaker's message

Highly skilled speakers, regardless of their goal, often accomplish all four purposes of speaking—to inform, persuade, entertain, and inspire. A professor may lecture on cultural differences with the primary goal of informing students about Hofstede's cultural dimensions. At the same time, the professor may also try to persuade students that the information is important and applicable to their daily lives and careers, while using humorous examples of cultural misunderstandings to entertain students in the hope they will pay better attention to the lecture. In addition, a professor's stories about other cultures may inspire students to travel abroad. Presentations that only inform, persuade, entertain, or inspire are very rare. Make your presentation more interesting and compelling by including all four types of speaking goals.

Inspirational speaking also includes sermons, pep talks, commencement addresses, dedications, and tributes, as well as award presentations and acceptances. Chapter 16, "Presentations: Speaking to Persuade," explains how speakers can motivate listeners by arousing their emotions and appealing to societal and cultural values.

CHOOSE A GOOD TOPIC

Your topic is the subject matter of your presentation. A topic is often a simple word or phrase: *rap music.* Yet two presentations on the same topic can have very different purposes. Look at the differences between these two purpose statements:

> "I want my audience to understand and appreciate rap and hip-hop music."

> "I want my audience to boycott recording companies that promote rap music with violent and offensive lyrics."

Three questions help you find a topic that suits you, your audience, and your purpose: (1) What topics interest you? (2) What do you value? (3) What do you know?

QUESTIONS FOR CHOOSING A GOOD TOPIC

► What Topics Interest You?
► What Do You Value?
► What Do You Know?

What Topics Interest You? Many speakers have no trouble answering this question. They have fascinating hobbies, special expertise, or unusual jobs, backgrounds, beliefs, and causes. However, if you have difficulty identifying a topic, ask yourself some leading questions:

• I've always wanted to know more about . . .
• If I could make one new law, I would . . .
• I've always wanted to . . .
• If I won a fifty million-dollar lottery, I would . . .

If leading questions don't work, try creating a chart in which you list potential topics under broad headings—sports, food, hobbies, places and destinations, famous people, music, important events, personal goals, community issues. By the time you finish filling in your interests, you may have dozens of presentation topics.

What Do You Value? **Values** are beliefs that guide how you think about what is right or wrong, good or bad, just or unjust, correct or incorrect. Values also trigger emotions and guide your actions.[2] The Institute for Global Ethics identified eight universal values: love, truthfulness, fairness, freedom, unity, tolerance, responsibility, and respect for life. What emotional reaction do you have when these values are linked to the following issues?

• *Love*. Marital infidelity
• *Truthfulness*. Plagiarism
• *Fairness*. Race-based grants and scholarships

- *Freedom.* Gun control
- *Unity.* Labor unions
- *Tolerance.* Hate speech
- *Responsibility.* Parental accountability
- *Respect for Life.* Human cloning

Be cautious when you search your personal values for a topic. Your values may not be aligned with those of your audience. For example, you may strongly support gun control, but audience members may consider gun ownership a basic freedom. Also remember that cultures often differ in what they value. Although most Americans strongly value individualism, other cultures may place greater value on community and group goals.

What Do You Know? Everyone knows more about a few things than most other people. A fruitful source of topics is your work experience, personal experiences, and skills. Look at the following topics presented by student speakers who were either topic experts or who researched a topic that interested them:

Interpretation of dreams	Exercise and long life
Investment strategies	Editing a video
Closing a sale	Genealogy and your family tree
Wine tasting	Becoming a Big Brother/Big Sister
Afro-Cuban jazz	Restoring cars

NARROW YOUR TOPIC

Make sure that you appropriately narrow or modify your topic to achieve your purpose and adapt to listeners' needs and interests. Narrowing a topic involves selecting the most important and interesting ideas and information for your presentation, rather than telling your audience everything you know about a topic.

Although you may be an expert on your topic, your audience may be hearing about it for the first time. Don't bury them under mounds of information. Ask yourself: If I only have time to tell them one thing about my topic, what should it be? Chances are that conveying a single important idea is enough to achieve your purpose. To convey that single idea, use no more than two or three main points, not five or six. Consider the amount of time you have to speak, and narrow your topic to suit those limits. Look at how these speakers narrowed broad topic ideas into more specific speech topics:

Broad: A review of Greek mythology

Narrow: The origins of Aphrodite

Broad: Advances in semiconductor technology

Narrow: What is a semiconductor device?

DEVELOP A PURPOSE STATEMENT

When you know *why* you are speaking (your purpose) and *what* you are speaking about (your topic), you should develop a specific, achievable, and relevant **purpose statement** to guide your preparation. Ask yourself: What is the main idea I want to communicate to my listeners? Your reply to this question is your purpose statement. It identifies the main idea in your presentation or the position you are going to take on an issue. It is not enough to say, "My purpose is to tell my audience all about my job as a phone solicitor." This statement is too general and probably an impossible goal to achieve in a time-limited presentation. Instead, your purpose statement must convey the specific focus of your presentation, such as "I want my audience to rec-

The World Wide Web is a wonderful resource for finding presentation topics. Major search engines such as Google, Yahoo!, AltaVista, CNET, Excite, Galaxy, Lycos, and WebCrawler have directories that suggest topic areas.[1] The following categories represent a composite list of topic areas included in website directories. Within each of these areas are dozens of subtopics. For example, the Health and Fitness directory on one site begins with Alternative Medicine and ends with Women's Health. The Disease directory on that site begins with AIDS and ends with Thyroid Disease.

Here are some common topic categories to search:

Agriculture

Animals

Arts and entertainment

Automotive

Business and economy

Cities and towns

Computers and
    technology

Education

Geography

Health and fitness

History

Hobbies and games

Home and garden

Jobs and careers

Money

Music

News and media

Parenting and family

People and relationships

Philosophy

Recreation and sports

References

Religion and
    spirituality

Science

Shopping

Society and culture

Teens

Travel

Women's issues

World

[1]Robert Perrin, *Handbook for College Research* (Boston: Houghton Mifflin, 2005), pp. 65–66.

ognize two common strategies used by effective phone solicitors to overcome listener objections."

A purpose statement is similar to a writer's thesis statement, which asks, "What is the main idea you want to communicate to your reader in your writing?" Regardless of whether you are speaking or writing, a purpose statement guides how you research, organize, and present your message. In most speaking situations, effective purpose statements are specific, achievable, and relevant, as depicted in Figure 12.1.

Analyze and Adapt to Your Audience

Audience analysis refers to your ability to understand, respect, and adapt to listeners before and during a presentation. Audience analysis means researching your audience, interpreting those findings, and, as a result, selecting appropriate strategies to achieve your purpose. A thorough understanding of your audience helps you focus your presentation and decide how to narrow your topic. An audience-focused approach simplifies and shortens your preparation time by using the audience as a criterion for deciding what to include or exclude. The examples in your presentation, the words

Figure 12.1	**Characteristics of Effective Purpose Statements**

SPECIFIC	ACHIEVABLE	RELEVANT
Narrows a topic to content appropriate for the purpose and audience.	Purpose can be achieved in the given time limit.	Topic should be related to audience needs and interests.
✓ I want my audience to understand how to use the government's new food group recommendations as a diet guide. ✗ The benefits of good health.	✓ There are two preferred treatments for mental depression. ✗ You should learn all the causes, symptoms, treatments, and preventions of mental depression.	✓ Next time you witness an accident, you'll know what to do. ✗ Next time you encounter an exotic Australian tree toad, you'll appreciate its morphology.

315

What kind of audience adaptations does a park ranger have to make when guiding a diverse audience on a tour?

you choose, and even your delivery style should be adapted to your audience's interests and needs.

KNOW YOUR AUDIENCE

The answers to five basic questions about audience characteristics can help you understand, respect, and adapt to your listener: (1) Who are they? (2) Why are they here? (3) What do they know? (4) What are their interests? and (5) What are their attitudes?

AUDIENCE ANALYSIS QUESTIONS

▶ Who Are They?
▶ Why Are They Here?
▶ What Do They Know?
▶ What Are Their Interests?
▶ What Are Their Attitudes?

Who Are They? Gather as much **demographic information** (audience characteristics) as you can about the people who will be watching and listening to you. Consider the following general demographic characteristics:

Age	Race	Gender
Religion	Marital status	Cultural background
Occupation	Income level	Place of residence
Education	Parental status	Disabilities

If you know that your audience is composed of a particular group or is meeting for a special reason, gather more specific demographic information, such as the following:

Political affiliations	Professional memberships
Employment positions	Career goals
Military experience	Individual and group achievements

Avoid "one-size-fits-all" conclusions about people based on visible or obvious demographic characteristics such as age, race, gender, occupation, nationality, or religion. As you know from Chapter 3, "Understanding Others," these oversimplified conceptions, opinions, or images are stereotypes. Stereotyping allows your beliefs and biases about a particular group to distort your perceptions about audience members. Moreover, remember that *your* age, nationality, race, gender, educational level, and socioeconomic background may be just as critical in determining how well an audience listens to you.

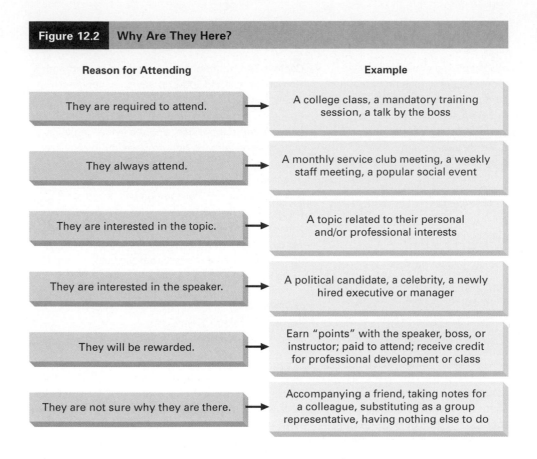

Figure 12.2 Why Are They Here?

Reason for Attending	Example
They are required to attend.	A college class, a mandatory training session, a talk by the boss
They always attend.	A monthly service club meeting, a weekly staff meeting, a popular social event
They are interested in the topic.	A topic related to their personal and/or professional interests
They are interested in the speaker.	A political candidate, a celebrity, a newly hired executive or manager
They will be rewarded.	Earn "points" with the speaker, boss, or instructor; paid to attend; receive credit for professional development or class
They are not sure why they are there.	Accompanying a friend, taking notes for a colleague, substituting as a group representative, having nothing else to do

Why Are They Here? Although you may want your audience to assemble because they are interested in you and your presentation, this is not always the case. Audiences attend meetings and presentations for many reasons, as Figure 12.2 illustrates.[3]

Audience members who are interested in your topic or who stand to benefit from attending a presentation will be different from those who don't know why they are there or who are required to attend. Each type of audience presents its own challenges for a speaker. A highly interested and well-informed audience demands a compelling, knowledgeable, well-prepared speaker. An audience required or reluctant to attend may be pleasantly surprised and influenced by a dynamic speaker who gives audience members a reason to listen. Entire audiences rarely fit into one type or group. Your audience may include people representing each reason for attending.

What Do They Know? Ask the following questions to assess audience knowledge:

- How much do they know about the topic?
- How much background material should I cover?
- Will they understand my vocabulary and specific, topic-related terminology or jargon?
- Have they heard any of this before?

Answering these questions is essential to matching your presentation to an audience's level of understanding and knowledge. Almost nothing is more boring to an audience than hearing a speaker talk about a subject they know well or listening to a speaker talk over their head.

What Are Their Interests? Find out if audience members have interests that match your purpose and topic. Consider two types of interests: self-centered interests and topic-centered interests.

Self-centered interests are aroused when a presentation can result in personal gain or loss. Some audience members are enthralled by a speaker who teaches them how to earn or save money. Others will be riveted by advice on career advancement strategies or ways to improve their appearance or health. A proposal to restructure a company or organization can result in more or less power for employees. In all these cases, the listener stands to gain or lose something as a result of the presentation and its outcome.

Audiences also have **topic-centered interests**—subjects they enjoy hearing and learning about. Topic-centered interests include hobbies, favorite sports or pastimes, or subjects loaded with intrigue and mystery. However, topic-centered interests tend to be personal. A detailed description of a Civil War battle may captivate Civil War history buffs in the audience but bore the other members. Whether self-centered or topic centered, listener interests have a significant effect on how well an audience pays attention to you and your message.[4]

What Are Their Attitudes? When assessing **audience attitudes**, you are asking about audience opinions—whether they agree or disagree with you as well as how strongly they agree and disagree. There can be as many opinions in your audience as there are people. Some audience members will already agree with you, others will disagree no matter what you say, whereas others will be undecided or have no opinion.

GATHER AUDIENCE INFORMATION

How do you gather information about your audience? It depends on how much time and energy you can devote to the audience analysis process. Two basic techniques can tell you a great deal about your audience: look and listen.

Look Observe your audience or imagine what they look like, and answer as many questions as you can on the basis of their appearance:

- What percent will be male or female?
- Will there be a wide age range?
- Will the audience be racially diverse?
- Will they be dressed formally, professionally or casually?

Under the right circumstances and with adequate lead time, you may be able to gather valuable information about your audience by surveying it. An **audience survey** is a series of written questions designed to gather information about audience characteristics and attitudes. Unfortunately, surveys can be difficult to write and interpret accurately. That's why corporations, nonprofit agencies, marketing companies, and politicians hire huge polling companies to prepare, administer, and interpret survey results for them. Here are a few suggestions for writing and administering a useful survey.

- Ask something you need to know, something you don't already know. Don't ask obvious questions: "Do you want to earn more money?" or "Should the United States oppose terrorism?"
- Ask for specific and useful information. If you ask a question that is too general, such as "Do you exercise regularly?" the answer may not tell you whether "regularly" means twice a day, twice a week, or twice a month.

- Use inclusive questions. Yes or no questions often leave out audience members who don't know the answer or who are undecided. A question such as "Are you against gun control?" doesn't leave room for answers such as "It depends on the circumstances" or "I haven't made up my mind." Allow respondents to answer, "I don't know" to eliminate guessing.
- Consider using an open-ended question to capture additional thoughts and feelings.
- Word your questions carefully to avoid bias and misunderstanding. Pretest your items to make sure people understand your questions.
- Keep information confidential. People are less likely to give you information about themselves, their opinions, and their behavior if you also ask for their names.
- Be brief. Most people won't fill out a long survey. Furthermore, a long questionnaire gives away too much about your speech and can ruin the effect you are trying to achieve.

Before and during your presentation, observe their behavior. Are they restless or do they appear to be eager to listen? Are they smiling or frowning? Based on your conclusions about their behavior, you may want to shorten your presentation or add more examples. You may want to inject more or less energy into your delivery. Your ultimate success may depend on how well you observe and adapt to audience reactions.

Listen   Ask questions about the people in your audience and listen to the answers. Interview the person who invited you to speak or someone who previously spoke to this group. If you can, arrange to talk to some audience members in advance. Listen for common characteristics and concerns. But be careful—one person's opinion may not represent most audience members.

ADAPT TO YOUR AUDIENCE

Everything you learn about your audience tells you something about how to prepare and deliver your presentation. Depending on the amount of audience research and analysis you do, you can adapt your presentation to your audience as you prepare it. In other cases, you may use audience feedback to modify your presentation as you speak.

Prepresentation Adaptation   After you research and analyze information about your audience's characteristics and attitudes, go back to your purpose statement and apply what you've learned. Note how the answers to the five basic audience questions discussed earlier in this chapter affect the ways in which you can modify your preliminary purpose into one that better suits your audience.

> *Preliminary Purpose.* To provide general information about how to grow tomatoes
>
> *Who Are They?* They are ten women and four men who are long-term members of the local garden club. Most are more than forty years old.

Why Are They Here? They attend monthly club meetings at which they discuss group-selected topics.

What Do They Know? They already know a lot about growing tomatoes, but want to improve the health and output of their plants.

What Are Their Interests? They are interested in many types of plants, but a few are more interested in flowers. Fortunately, the group picked the topic.

What Are Their Attitudes? They are avid gardeners who may be a bit wary about *my* ability to tell them something new and interesting about tomatoes.

Revised Purpose. To share the latest research on improving the health and output of a tomato plant in this growing region

Midpresentation Adaptation No matter how well you prepare for an audience, you may run into unexpected audience reactions. What if your presentation doesn't seem to be working? If your audience members seem restless or hostile, how can you adjust? What if your twenty-minute speech must be shortened to ten minutes to accommodate another speaker?

Adapting to your audience *during* a presentation requires you to do three things at once: deliver your presentation, correctly interpret audience feedback as you speak, and successfully modify your message. Interpreting audience responses requires that you look at your audience members, read their nonverbal signals, and sense their moods. If audience feedback suggests that you're not getting through, don't be afraid to stop and ask comprehension questions such as, "Would you like more detail on this point before I go on to the next one?"

Think about adjusting your presentation in the same way you would adjust your conversation with a friend. If your friend looks confused, you might ask what's wrong. If your friend interrupts with a question, you probably will answer it or ask if you can finish your thought before answering. If your friend tells you that he has a pressing appointment, you are likely to shorten what you have to say. The same adaptations work just as well when speaking to an audience.

ADAPT TO CULTURAL DIFFERENCES

The cultural diversity of audience members plays a critical role in audience analysis. Respecting and adapting to the cultures represented in your audience begins with understanding the nature and characteristics of various cultures. In Chapter 3, "Understanding Others," we examine many cultural dimensions and characteristics. Three of these dimensions stand out as critical to audience analysis and adaptation: power distance, individualism and collectivism, and masculinity and femininity. (See Chapter 3, "Understanding Others," for more detailed descriptions of these cultural dimensions.)

Power Distance As we indicate in Chapter 3, "Understanding Others," power distance refers to varying levels of equality and status among the members of a culture. Although the rich, famous, and powerful enjoy special perks and privileges, influential Americans may play down such expressions of power differences. U.S. presidents are often photographed wearing casual clothes, corporate executives may promote an open-door policy, and college freshmen and full professors may interact on a first-name basis.

If most audience members represent a low-power distance culture, you can ask them to challenge authority and make independent decisions. However, if most audience members embrace a high-power distance perspective *and* if you also command authority and influence, you can tell them exactly what you want them to do—and expect compliance.

Individualism and Collectivism When speaking to individualistic audiences (e.g., listeners from the United States and Australia) you can appeal to their sense of

Did you study French or Spanish in school? If so, what happens when you listen to a native speaker of that language? Do you understand every word? Probably not. Such an experience can be difficult and frustrating. Imagine what it must be like for a nonnative speaker of English to understand a presentation in English. The following guidelines are derived from general intercultural research and from observations of international audiences, both at home and abroad.

- *Speak slowly and clearly.* Many nonnative speakers of English need more time because they translate your words into their own language as you speak. But don't shout at them; they are not hearing impaired.
- *Use visual aids.* Most nonnative speakers of English are better readers than listeners. If you use slides or provide handouts, write important information on the visual aids. Give the audience time to read and take notes.
- *Be more formal.* In general, use a more formal style when speaking to international audiences. Dress professionally, consider using a manuscript, and adopt a more formal speaking style.
- *Adapt to contextual perspectives.* If you are addressing an audience from a high-context culture, be less direct. Let them draw their own conclusions. Give them time to get to know and trust you.
- *Avoid humor and clichés.* Humor rarely translates into another language and can backfire if misunderstood. In addition, avoid clichés—overused expressions familiar to a particular culture. Will a nonnative speaker of English understand "Cool as a cucumber," "That dog won't hunt," or even "Shop 'til you drop"?[1]

[1]Isa N. Engleberg and John A. Daly, *Presentations in Everyday Life: Strategies for Effective Speaking*, 2nd ed. (Boston: Houghton Mifflin, 2005), pp. 122–123.

adventure, their desire to achieve personal goals, and their defense of individual rights. When speaking to a collectivist audience (e.g., listeners from most Asian and Latin American countries), you may be more successful demonstrating how a particular course of action would benefit their company, family, or community. A collectivistic audience is more willing to make personal sacrifices for others. If you are a typical, individualistic American who feels comfortable boasting about your own or your organization's accomplishments, you may find a collectivist audience disturbed by your apparent arrogance and lack of concern for others.

Masculinity and Femininity   The masculine and feminine cultural dimension does not refer to the number of men or women in your audience. Instead, it focuses on the extent to which a culture embraces values considered masculine or feminine. When speaking to a masculine culture, you might focus on competitive goals and the glory of winning. For feminine cultures, focus on ways in which audience members can achieve social and interpersonal harmony. In the United States, values tend to be more masculine than feminine.

Speaker Credibility

The concept of speaker credibility is more than 2,000 years old. In his *Rhetoric*, Aristotle wrote about *ethos*, a Greek word meaning *character*. "The character [ethos] of the speaker is a cause of persuasion when the speech is so uttered as to make him worthy of belief. . . . His character [ethos] is the most potent of all the means to persuasion."[5] Aristotle's concept of **ethos** evolved into what we now call *speaker credibility*.

Speaker credibility represents the extent to which an audience believes the speaker and the speaker's message. The dictionary defines credibility as the "quality,

Two former ecstasy users—residents of a rehabilitation center—testify on drug abuse before the Senate Government Affairs committee in Washington, DC. How credible is the testimony of these speakers?

capability, or power to elicit belief."[6] In other words, the more credible you are in the eyes of your audience, the more likely you will achieve the purpose of your presentation. If your audience rates you as highly credible, they may excuse poor delivery. They are so ready to believe you that the presentation doesn't have to be perfect.[7]

COMPONENTS OF SPEAKER CREDIBILITY

Researchers identify three major components of speaker credibility that have a strong impact on the believability of a speaker: character, competence, and charisma.[8] Figure 12.3 presents distinct characteristics that personify each component of speaker credibility.

Character   **Character** relates to a speaker's honesty and good will. Are you a person of good character—trustworthy, sincere, and fair? Do you put the good of the audience above your own? When presenting an argument, is the evidence valid, the reservations acknowledged, and the claims warranted?

Of the three components of speaker credibility, character may be the most important. A speaker of good character is seen as a good person. In this case, "good" means being ethical: doing what is right and moral when you speak in front of an audience. If an audience doesn't trust you, it won't matter if you are an international expert or an electrifying performer.

Competence   **Competence** relates to a speaker's expertise and abilities. Proving that you are competent can be as simple as mentioning your credentials and experience. An audience is unlikely to question a recognized brain surgeon, a professional baseball player, or an internationally acclaimed dress designer, as long as they stick to brain surgery, baseball, and dress design. Fortunately, you don't have to be famous or a highly trained professional to be an expert. An auto mechanic, a waitress, a parent of six children, a nurse, and a government employee can all be experts. Such speakers can rely on their life experiences and opinions to demonstrate competence.

But what happens when you are not an expert? How can you demonstrate that you know what you're talking about? The answer lies in one word: research. As Chapter 13, "Presentations: Content and Structure," discusses, you must thoroughly research the ideas and information for your presentation. Thorough research arms you with enough up-to-date content to become a well-informed speaker. If you don't

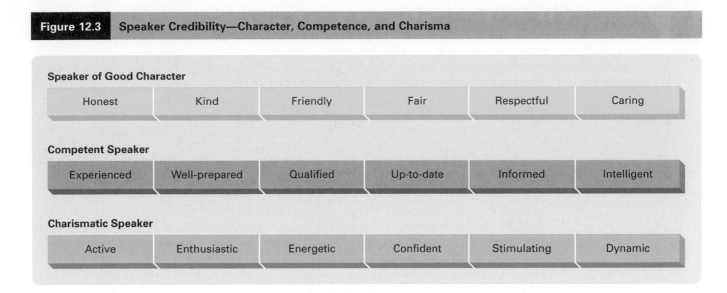

Figure 12.3 Speaker Credibility—Character, Competence, and Charisma

Speaker of Good Character

| Honest | Kind | Friendly | Fair | Respectful | Caring |

Competent Speaker

| Experienced | Well-prepared | Qualified | Up-to-date | Informed | Intelligent |

Charismatic Speaker

| Active | Enthusiastic | Energetic | Confident | Stimulating | Dynamic |

have first-hand experience or cannot claim to be an expert, let your audience know how well prepared you are: "We conducted a study of more than 2,000 individuals and found . . . ," "After reviewing every textbook on this subject written after 1995, I was surprised that the authors didn't address . . . ," "I have spoken, in person, to all five of our county commissioners. They all agree that . . . ."

Charisma **Charisma** is a quality reflected in your level of energy, enthusiasm, vigor, and commitment. A speaker with charisma is seen as dynamic, forceful, powerful, assertive, and intense. President John F. Kennedy and Martin Luther King Jr. were charismatic speakers who motivated and energized audiences. So was Adolph Hitler. People can disagree about a speaker's message yet still find that speaker charismatic. Charisma has more to do with how you deliver a presentation than with what you have to say. Speakers with strong and expressive voices are seen as more charismatic than speakers with hesitant or unexpressive voices. Speakers who gesture naturally and move gracefully are viewed as more charismatic than those who look uncomfortable and awkward in front of an audience. Speakers who look their audiences in the eye are thought of as more charismatic than those who avoid contact with members of the audience. Practicing and developing your performance skills enhances your charisma in the same way that preparation helps you to be seen as a competent speaker.

DEVELOPING SPEAKER CREDIBILITY

Only the audience decides whether you are believable. Credibility does not exist in an absolute sense; it is solely based on the attitudes and perceptions of the audience. Thus, even if you are the world's greatest expert on your topic and deliver your presentation with skill, the ultimate decision about your credibility lies with your audience. Credibility is "like the process of getting a grade in school. Only the teacher (or audience) can assign the grade to the student (or speaker), but the student can do all sorts of things—turn in homework, prepare for class, follow the rules—to influence what grade is assigned."[9] At the same time, there are things you can do to influence your audience's opinion of you and your presentation. Find out what you have to offer to your audience, prepare an interesting presentation, and show your audience why you're uniquely qualified to deliver it; in other words, do a personal inventory, and toot your own horn.

DEVELOPING SPEAKER CREDIBILITY

▶ Do a Personal Inventory
▶ Toot Your Own Horn

One of the best ways to strengthen your credibility is to have someone introduce you to the audience. The introducer usually tells the audience something about the speaker's background, experiences, achievements, and skills—qualities that demonstrate character, competence, and charisma. A well-delivered introduction can motivate an audience to listen to you and help you achieve your purpose. If the person who will be introducing you asks for information, don't be shy. Provide a list of your accomplishments. Or, write down what you want the person to say, choosing those items most relevant to your purpose and audience. A custom-made introduction can create an atmosphere that lets your character, competence, and charisma shine.

Do a Personal Inventory   To enhance your credibility, you have to believe you have something to offer an audience. Every person can do something that sets himself or herself apart from most other people. It's just a matter of discovering what that something is. A personal inventory is a way of identifying the unique gifts and talents that contribute to your credibility. Begin your self-inventory by answering three questions: (1) What are my experiences? (2) What are my achievements? and (3) What are my skills and traits?

An experience that seems routine to you may be a new experience for your listeners:

- Have you lived or worked in another town, city, state, or country?
- Do you or have you had an unusual job?
- What experiences have had a big impact on your life (meeting a famous person, childbirth, the illness or death of a friend or family member, physical disability, a visit to a foreign country, combat experience)?

You don't have to land on the moon to achieve something important. What seems like an everyday accomplishment to you may be an impressive achievement to your listeners. The following questions may help you identify your unique achievements:

- What can I do that most people cannot (play the cello, manage a swimming pool, reconstruct a computer, write a song or short story, raise money for charities, train a horse, design clothing, speak Turkish)?
- What awards or contests have I won (a scholarship, a prize in an art show, an award for public service, a sporting championship, a cooking contest, a TV or radio quiz, the lottery)?

Your unique qualities can enhance your credibility as a speaker. Take the opportunity of giving a presentation to use your experiences, accomplishments, and skills to your advantage.

Toot Your Own Horn   A presentation lets you show an audience that your ideas and opinions are based on more than good preparation. They are based on your experience, your accomplishments, and your special skills. There is nothing wrong with using words such as *I* and *my* and *me* if they are appropriate. But using too many *I*, *my*, and *me* words can sound overly boastful. For example, at an honors awards ceremony for students, two faculty members gave presentations that annoyed the audience. The faculty members talked more about themselves than about the student who was being honored: "As chairman of the department and an expert in this field of study, I decided . . ."; "As outgoing president of the association, I was the first person to . . . ." By using the awards presentation to spotlight themselves, the speakers undermined their credibility.

THE ETHICAL SPEAKER

The words *ethos* and *ethics* are very similar. Both come from the Greek word meaning *character*. As we indicate in our discussion of character as a component of credibility, the apparent "goodness" of a speaker is important in determining whether that speaker is believed by an audience. *Ethos*, Aristotle's term for speaker credibility, and *ethics*, however, are not the same. What makes them different is their source. Remember that the audience determines a speaker's credibility (*ethos*). A speaker's *ethics* is personal and embodies his or her beliefs about what is right or wrong, moral or immoral, good or bad (Figure 12.4). **Ethics** is a set of personal principles of right conduct, a system of moral values.[10] Only you can determine how ethical you are.

When audiences see you as an ethical speaker, they are more likely to believe you. Ethical decisions about your presentation should consider all seven guiding principles of human communication.

Elie Wiesel, a Holocaust survivor and winner of the Nobel Peace Prize, contends that it is the moral responsibility of all people to fight hatred, racism, and genocide because "to remain silent and indifferent is the greatest sin of all." Why is Elie Wiesel recognized as a highly ethical and credible speaker?

- *Ethical Decisions about Self.* Have you used your expertise or established a trustworthy image to deceive your audience in any way? Ethical speakers are liked and respected by their audiences because they are honest, fair, caring, informed, and justifiably confident.

- *Ethical Decisions about Others.* Are you using the information you gather about audience members to take advantage of them? You would question correctly the character of a politician who tells an audience of teachers and parents that education is the first priority, and then tells a group of builders and bankers that tax breaks for developers come first. Changing your message from group to group may be unethical if the messages conflict with one another.

- *Ethical Decisions about Purpose.* Who will benefit if you achieve your purpose—you, your audience, or you *and* your audience? If you would be embarrassed to

---

Figure 12.4   Ethos and Ethics

ETHOS Source: Audience	ETHICS Source: Speaker
Speakers ethos is determined by the audience	Speaker determines her/his ethics
Speaker	Speaker
Audience	Audience

CommEthics   Avoid the Perils of Plagiarism

The word **plagiarism** comes from the Latin, *plagium*, which means "kidnapping." Thus, when you plagiarize, you are stealing or kidnapping something that belongs to someone else. Simply put, when you plagiarize, you fail to document or give credit to the source of your information. Unfortunately, some speakers believe that prohibitions about plagiarism don't apply to them. Others know that they apply but think they can get away with it. Still others plagiarize without knowing they are doing it. Ignorance, however, is no excuse.

The key to avoiding plagiarism and its consequences is to identify the sources of your information in your presentation. Changing a few words of someone else's work is not enough to avoid plagiarism. If they're not your original ideas, and most of the words are not yours, you are ethically obligated to tell your audience who wrote or said them and where they came from. The bottom line is this: Plagiarism is not just unethical; it is illegal. If you include a quotation or idea from another source and pretend it's your idea and words, you are plagiarizing. The following guidelines are criteria for avoiding plagiarism:

- If you include an identifiable phrase or an idea that appears in someone else's work, always acknowledge and document your source orally.

- Do not use someone else's sequence of ideas and organization without acknowledging and citing the similarities in structure.
- Tell an audience exactly when you are citing someone else's exact words or ideas in your presentation.
- Never buy, find, or use someone else's speech or writing and claim it as your own work.

There are familiar phrases that can be used without concerns about "kidnapping" someone's work. For instance, politicians often use phrases borrowed from other sources. So do writers. Suppose you tell an audience that when it comes to friends and family, "there's no place like home." Anyone who's seen the film *The Wizard of Oz* knows that Dorothy used that magic phrase to get home to Kansas. Think how awkward the acknowledgment would be: "'There's no place like home' said Dorothy to her family and friends in the 1939 movie *The Wizard of Oz*, which is based on a book of the same title written by Frank Baum." Making an allusion to a famous quotation is not plagiarism as long as the phrase is well-known and is used to interest or inspire audience members who will recognize the phrase.[1]

[1]Isa N. Engleberg and John A. Daly, *Presentations in Everyday Life: Strategies for Effective Speaking*, 2nd ed. (Boston: Houghton Mifflin, 2005), pp. 185–186; Isa Engleberg and Ann Raimes, *Pocket Keys for Speakers* (Boston: Houghton Mifflin, 2004), pp. 21–22.

reveal your private purpose to an audience, you should question the honesty and fairness of your public purpose.

- *Ethical Decisions about Context.* Do you use time limits as an excuse to withhold important information? "If time allowed, I could explain this in more detail, but, trust me . . . ." Do you use excuses to make quick and uncritical decisions? "We've tried to get the air conditioner working but, because we can't, let's cut off debate and vote so we can get out of here."

- *Ethical Decisions about Content.* Are your ideas and information truthful? Have you identified and qualified your sources? Is your information recent, complete, consistent, and relevant? Ethical speakers learn as much as they can about their topics. They recognize that most controversial issues have good people and good arguments on both sides. They demonstrate respect for those who disagree with them.

- *Ethical Decisions about Structure.* Should you include both sides of an argument in a presentation or present only one side, even if the opposing view is reasonable and well supported? Should you organize your presentation by telling funny stories or sharing emotional examples to cover up the fact that you lack valid statistics? Emotional examples can be powerful forms of supporting material as long as they complement other types of valid supporting material.

- *Ethical Decisions about Expression.* Do you fake emotions to gain sympathy or incite an audience? Does your appearance or clothing deceive an audience about your background? An ethical speaker uses an honest communication style and avoids acting out a false role.

THE ETHICAL AUDIENCE

Ethical audience members listen for ideas and information with an open mind. They withhold evaluation until they comprehend what a speaker is saying. Ethical audiences are active listeners; they listen to understand, to empathize, to analyze, and to appreciate. They think critically about a speaker's message. Unfortunately, some audience members may lack these skills. Even worse, they may not listen because they have decided, even before the presentation begins, that they don't like the message or the speaker.

Your audience is more likely to appreciate and listen to you if they think you have character, competence, and charisma. The audience has the final say, and also an ethical responsibility to do unto the speaker as they would have the speaker do unto them. An audience with an open, unprejudiced mind is essential for a genuine transaction to occur between speakers and listeners.

Analyze and Adapt to the Context

Whether you prepare a presentation for a formal banquet or a family barbecue, a prayer meeting or a retirement party, take time to analyze the context of the situation before you decide what you want to say.

ANALYZE AND ADAPT TO THE LOGISTICS

Logistics refers to planning and adapting to the audience size, the physical location, the equipment, and the amount of time you have.[11] Proper attention to the logistics of your presentation helps to ensure its success. Logistical problems distract audience attention from you and your message.

ASK LOGISTICAL QUESTIONS ABOUT . . .
- ► Audience Size
- ► Facilities
- ► Equipment
- ► Time

Audience Size   If there are only fifteen people in your audience, you probably don't have to worry about whether they will be able to hear you. If there are hundreds or thousands of people in your audience, you should plan to use a microphone and make sure it's supported by a good sound system. Knowing the size of your audience also helps you figure out the kinds of visual aids to use. For example, if you expect five hundred people in your audience, projecting images onto a large screen is more effective than using a small chart or demonstrating a detailed procedure.

Facilities   Make sure you know as much as you can about the facility in which you will be speaking:

- What is the size, shape, and decor of the room?
- Does the room have good ventilation, comfortable seating, distracting sights or sounds?
- What are the seating arrangements (rows, tables)?
- What kind of lighting will there be? Can it be adjusted for the presentation?
- Will you speak from a stage or platform? Will you have a lectern and a table for materials or equipment?
- Is there a good sound system?

Ask questions about the seating arrangements. Will audience members be seated in a theater-style auditorium, around a long conference table, or at round tables scattered throughout a seminar room? If you are in an auditorium that seats eight hundred people and you only expect one hundred listeners to attend, consider closing off the balcony or side sections so that the audience will be seated in front of you.

Equipment   Computer-generated slide presentations are the norm in many speaking situations. Wireless microphones and sophisticated sound systems enable speakers to

CommFAQ How Long *Should* I Speak?

We often encounter two questions about staying within the time limit for a presentation: "What if I'm not given a time limit?" and "What if I have something *really* important to say and I have to talk longer?" In both cases, we urge you to rethink the planning process to answer these questions.

If you are not given a time limit, we recommend nothing longer than twenty minutes. Tony Buzan, famous for his work on adult learning, brain research, and mind mapping, found that people will listen to you for ninety minutes, but they will only retain what they hear for twenty minutes.[1] Peggy Noonan, President Reagan's speechwriter, also recommends a twenty-minute limit.[2] Granville Toogood, author of *The Articulate Executive*, reports the results of a study conducted by the U.S. Navy in which they tried to determine how long people can listen and retain information. The answer: eighteen minutes.[3]

Of course, there are times when the circumstances or content requires that you speak longer than twenty minutes. In such cases, we offer the following advice:

Change the medium to break the tedium. Cover the basics in twenty minutes and then set aside time for a question-and-answer session. Use presentation aids or a tape to break up your talk. Insert short personal stories or anecdotes to help drive home your point and give the audience a pleasant respite.[4]

Finally, don't fall into the ego trap of thinking that what you have to say is *so* important that it deserves more time. Your audience may not share this belief—no matter how long you take to convince them. Demonstrate respect for your audience's time and they will appreciate your self-discipline and kind consideration.

[1]Lily Walters, *Secrets of Successful Speakers* (New York: McGraw-Hill, 1993), p. 94.

[2]Peggy Noonan, *Simply Speaking* (New York: HarperCollins, 1998), p. x.

[3]Granville N. Toogood, *The Articulate Executive* (New York: McGraw-Hill, 1996), p. 93.

[4]Ibid., pp. 94–95.

---

address large audiences with ease. Make sure you know in advance what is—and what isn't—available at the location where you will be speaking so you can consider those factors when preparing:

- What equipment, if any, do you need to be seen and/or heard?
- What equipment, if any, do you need for your audio or visual aids?
- Is there a lectern (adjustable, with a built-in light or microphone, space enough to hold your notes)?
- Are there any special arrangements you need to make (a timer, water, special lighting, wireless microphone, a media technician)?

Arrive at least forty-five minutes before you speak. Check that everything you need is in the room, that the equipment works, and that you know how to dim or brighten the lights if needed. Allow enough time to find equipment if something is missing or to make last-minute changes.

Time Asking questions about the time and duration of a presentation is essential. Begin this process by answering the following questions:

- At what hour will you be speaking?
- For how long are you scheduled to speak?
- What comes before or after your presentation (other speakers, lunch, entertainment, questions and answers)?
- Is there anything significant about the date or time of your presentation (birthday, holiday, anniversary)?

The most important question about time is how long you are *scheduled* to speak. Most audiences become impatient if you exceed your allotted time. Plan your presentation so that it fits well within your time limit. Time yourself, keeping in mind that real presentations often take longer than the one you practiced. Put a watch next to you when you speak or ask someone to give you a signal when it's time to begin your conclusion. And when that signal comes, don't ignore it, even if it means skipping major sections of your presentation. Audiences rarely like, appreciate, or return to hear a long-winded speaker.

ANALYZE AND ADAPT TO THE OCCASION

What's the occasion of your presentation? Will you be speaking at a celebration? Or is the occasion an oral class assignment, a memorial service, a convention keynote address, or testimony before a government agency? Make sure that your presentation suits the **occasion**—the reason an audience has assembled at a particular place and time. As is the case with setting, there are important questions to respond to as you prepare a presentation.

What Is Your Relationship to the Occasion?   When you are invited to make a presentation, ask yourself: Why have *I* been invited to speak to *this* audience in *this* place on *this* occasion? Speakers are not picked randomly. They are chosen because they are the most knowledgeable, most able, most popular, most appropriate, or most available person to speak at a specific occasion. Make sure you understand how you are personally connected to the occasion.

What Does the Audience Expect?   The occasion raises audience expectations about the way a presentation will be prepared and delivered. Business audiences may expect well-qualified speakers to pepper their presentations with sophisticated, computer-generated graphics. Audiences at political events are accustomed to the sound bite on television and expect to hear short, crisp phrases. Think about what style of presentation you expect to hear at a particular occasion. Then match your speaking style and content to those expectations.

What Behavior Is Appropriate for the Occasion?   Special events often have specific rules of **protocol**, a term that refers to the expected format of a ceremony or the etiquette observed at a particular type of event. We expect an uplifting tone at a graduation ceremony and a more raucous tone at a pep rally. At a funeral, a eulogy may be touching or funny, but it's almost always very respectful and short.

Inquire about the protocol of an occasion. What customs or rules may require special adaptation? Understanding customs and rules of delivery style, timing, language, or appearance helps you plan what to say, how to organize your message, and how to choose the most appropriate delivery style.

What Should You Wear?   Long before an audience hears what you say, they will see you, so wear something that matches the purpose and tone of your presentation. Your clothes don't have to be expensive or make a fashion statement. What matters is that they are appropriate for the situation.

Common sense dictates our number one piece of advice: Wear comfortable clothes. Presentations are stressful enough without worrying about clothing. Brand-new clothes or shoes can be a source of irritation or embarrassment if they're not "broken in." If you perspire, wear cool fabrics and colors that mask wet stains. If you're not comfortable moving in constricting clothing or high heels, save them for less stressful occasions.

When selecting appropriate clothes for a presentation, dress as conservatively as key members of your audience. If you know in advance that everyone will be wearing cowboy boots or tropical wear, use your best judgment and consider joining them. However, if you've never worn cowboy boots or brightly colored clothing, stick with a comfortable and professional outfit.

Nothing on your body (clothes, grooming, accessories) should draw attention to itself. Clanging bracelets or earrings, or ties featuring big patterns or cartoon characters, may not be appropriate. Take items out of your pockets, whether they're pens in your shirt pocket or the change and keys in your pants pockets. Women can leave their purses with a friend or colleague. Remember, your presentation should be the center of an audience's attention. If something in your appearance could distract your listeners, fix it.

Linking Self, Others, Purpose, and Context

At this point in the preparation process you should have identified an appropriate speaking goal (*purpose*), analyzed your audience (*others*), developed your credibility (*self*), and decided how you will adapt to the occasion and place where you will be speaking (*context*). All these decisions should be made before preparing the content of your presentation. At the same time, we urge you to be flexible. As you do your research, you may discover that your purpose will change because of audience expectations or the time limit you've been given. As you organize your content and plan your speaking strategies, you may find that you need more presentation aids (or none) to make your point. If, as you practice your delivery, you discover that you are more comfortable using more notes, you may need to make sure a lectern will be available. When preparing a presentation, self, others, purpose, and context are linked. Devoting attention and critical thinking to all four will, in the long run, save you time and help you develop and deliver a more effective presentation.[12]

From Topic to Purpose Statement

Directions: Consider the broad topic areas listed in the left-hand column in the following table. Individually or as a group, compose a more narrow topic—one that can be covered in the amount of time you have for a class presentation. After narrowing the topic, write a specific, clear, achievable, and relevant purpose statement, as illustrated in the example.

Topic Area	Narrow Topic	Purpose Statement What is the main idea and key points you want to communicate?
Example: Tomatoes	*Growing healthy and productive tomato plants*	*To explain how to grow healthy and productive tomato plants by providing good soil, full sunlight, plenty of water, and a watchful eye for garden pests*
Birth control		
Weight loss		
Stock market		
Cell phones		
Immigration		
Global warming		
Other topic: _____		

Communication Assessment

What's Your Plan?

Directions: Before you begin selecting content, structuring your message, and practicing your delivery, make sure you have made intelligent decisions about the four elements involved in presentation planning: *self*, *others*, *purpose*, and *context*. The following checklist will help determine whether you are prepared to take the next steps in preparing your presentation

Self

_____ 1. Have you assessed your potential credibility by identifying your strengths, talents, achievements, and positive character traits?

_____ 2. Will you be able to demonstrate your competence and good character?

_____ 3. Have you made ethical decisions about self, others, purpose, context, content, structure, and expression?

Others

_____ 1. Have you researched, analyzed, and planned ways of adapting to audience characteristics, knowledge, and interests?

_____ 2. Have you researched, analyzed, and planned ways of adapting to audience attitudes?

_____ 3. Have you researched, analyzed, and planned ways of adapting to cultural differences in your audience?

Purpose

_____ 1. Have you decided whether your purpose will inform, persuade, entertain, and/or inspire?

_____ 2. Have you developed a specific, achievable, and relevant purpose statement?

_____ 3. Does your topic area reflect your interests, values, and/or knowledge?

Context

_____ 1. Have you researched, analyzed, and planned ways of adapting to the logistical context (audience size, facilities, equipment, time)?

_____ 2. Have you researched, analyzed, and planned ways of adapting to the psychosocial occasion?

_____ 3. Have you researched, analyzed, and planned ways of adapting to the cultural context?

Key Terms

audience analysis
audience attitude
audience survey
character
charisma
competence
demographic information
entertainment speaking

ethics
ethos
informative presentation
inspirational speaking
logistics
occasion
persuasive presentation
plagiarism

presentation speaking
protocol
purpose statement
self-centered interest
speaker credibility
topic-centered interest
values

Notes

1. Sections of Chapters 12 to 16 are based on Isa N. Engleberg and John A. Daly, *Presentations in Everyday Life: Strategies for Effective Speaking*, 2nd ed. (Boston: Houghton Mifflin, 2005); and Isa N. Engleberg and Ann Raimes, *Pocket Keys for Speakers* (Boston: Houghton Mifflin, 2004).

2. Milton Rokeach, *The Nature of Human Values* (New York: Free Press, 1973), p. 3.

3. Engleberg and Daly, p. 106.

4. Ibid., p. 107.

5. Lane Cooper, *The Rhetoric of Aristotle* (New York: Appleton-Century-Crofts, 1932), pp. 8, 9.

6. *The American Heritage Dictionary of the English Language*, 4th ed. (Boston: Houghton Mifflin, 2000), p. 427.

7. Malcolm Kushner, *Successful Presentations for Dummies* (Foster City, CA: IDG Books Worldwide, 1997), p. 21.

8. The earliest and most respected source describing the components of a speaker's credibility is Aristotle's *Rhetoric*, trans. Lane Cooper (New York: Appleton-Century-Crofts, 1932, p. 92). Aristotle identified "intelligence, character, and good will" as "three things that gain our belief." Aristotle's observations have been verified and expanded. In addition to those qualities identified by Aristotle, researchers have added variables such as objectivity, trustworthiness, co-orientation, dynamism, composure, likability, and extroversion. Research has consolidated these qualities into three well-accepted attributes: competence, character, and dynamism. We have used the term *charisma* in place of dynamism.

9. Kushner, p. 21.

10. *The American Heritage Dictionary of the English Language*, p. 611.

11. Based on material in Engleberg and Raimes, pp. 42–46.

12. Ibid.

Columbine High School teacher Patty Nielson, seated next to former Senate Minority Leader Tom Daschle, tells her story of surviving the fatal shooting incident at her school. Is her story an effective way of supporting a plea to control guns and gun violence?

Stories   Real stories about real people in the real world arouse attention, create an appropriate mood, and reinforce important ideas. **Stories** are accounts or reports about something that happened. Audiences often remember a good story even when they can't remember much else about a presentation. In addition to gaining and holding audience interest, a story reinforces your message. A detailed look at the art and craft of storytelling is provided in Chapter 15, "Presentations: Speaking to Inform."

In the following example, a successful attorney with an incapacitating physical disability uses her brief, personal story to emphasize the importance of hope, hard work, and determination:

> I was in an automobile accident just after high school, which left me in a wheelchair for life. I was trying to deal with that, a new marriage, and other personal problems, not the least of which was uncertainty about what I could do—about the extent of my own potential.[6]

DOCUMENT YOUR SOURCES

Documentation is the practice of citing the sources of your supporting material. You should document all supporting material (including information from Internet sources and interviews) in writing and then orally in your presentation. Documentation enhances your credibility as a researcher and speaker while informing listeners about the sources and validity of your ideas and information.

Always be prepared to provide a *written* list of the references you use in your presentation—just as you would for a written report. You should have complete, written citations for every reference you use, particularly if someone in your audience wants more information or if someone challenges your claims.

Unlike writers, speakers cannot display footnotes during a presentation. Nor should they recite every detail such as the publisher, publisher's city, and page number of a citation. In speaking situations, citations must be oral. Your spoken citation—sometimes called an **oral footnote**—should include enough information to allow an interested listener to find the original sources you're citing. Generally, it's a good idea to provide the name of the person (or people) whose work you are using, to say a word or two about that person's credentials, and to mention the source of the information. If you want the audience to have permanent access to the information you use, provide a handout listing your references with complete citations.

Hypothetical examples and stories ask audience members to imagine themselves in a relevant situation. Hypothetical examples are particularly useful when you can't find the perfect example or story to support a key idea or when you want the example to be tailor-made for your audience. When someone offers a hypothetical example or story, it usually begins with a phrase such as "Suppose you . . ." or "Imagine a situation in which you . . ." or "Picture this . . . ."

Examples and stories don't have to be real to be interesting and powerful.[1] They must, however, be believable and possible. And, as an ethical communicator, you must tell your audience that the example or story is hypothetical, rather than pretending it is true.

A hypothetical example can be short, as in "How would you feel if you called the police to report a robbery and, upon their arrival, they put *you* in jail along with the thief?" A hypothetical story can set the stage for serious contemplation by audience members, as in "Imagine this. You are well prepared and eager to present an important report at a major staff meeting. Minutes before the meeting begins, you learn that your speaking time has been shortened from thirty minutes to ten minutes and that you won't be able to use PowerPoint as planned. In addition, two of the company's vice presidents will be attending. What would you do? Throw in the towel? Plead for more time? Panic? Or would you remember to use the seven guiding principles of presentation speaking to adjust your presentation—and thus demonstrate your flexibility and talent as a speaker?"

[1]Thomas Leech, *How to Prepare, Stage, and Deliver Winning Presentations* (New York: AMACOM, 1993), p. 115.

One of the most effective ways to cite information from another source is to paraphrase. Remember paraphrasing from Chapter 4, "Understanding Listening and Critical Thinking"? A paraphrase captures someone else's ideas and feelings but does *not* use the same words or sentence structure. If you keep the sources out of sight as you write a paraphrase, you will not be tempted to use the sentence patterns or phrases of the original. Note how the content changes from the original source to a paraphrase:

Original Source. We cannot legislate the language of the home, the street, the bar, the club, unless we are willing to set up a cadre of language police who will ticket and arrest us if we speak something other than English. (Source: James C. Stalker, "Official English or English Only," *English Journal* 77 [March 1988], p. 21.)

Oral Paraphrase. In a 1988 *English Journal* article, Dr. James Stalker noted that in a democracy like ours, we cannot pass laws against the use of other languages. If nothing else, it would be impossible, even foolish, to enforce such laws in our homes and public places.

EVALUATE YOUR SUPPORTING MATERIAL

Speakers rely on researched information to enhance their credibility and to demonstrate their depth of knowledge. Evaluate every piece of supporting material before adding it to your presentation. Make sure your information is **valid**—that the ideas, opinions, and information you include are well founded, justified, and accurate.

Is the Source Identified and Credible?   How credible are your sources of information? Are the author and publisher identified? Are they reputable? Sources such as *The Information Please Almanac* and the *New York Times Almanac* have been in business for many years, and their continued success depends on their ability to collect and publish information that is accurate and up-to-date.

Also check newspapers and online news and information services. Their reputations depend on their ability to publish accurate information. There are, however, big differences among sources. The sensational and often bizarre *National Enquirer* may be fun to read, but the *Wall Street Journal* is more likely to contain reliable infor-

QUESTIONS TO TEST SUPPORTING MATERIAL

▶ Is the Source Identified and Credible?

▶ Is the Source Biased?

▶ Is the Information Recent?

▶ Is the Information Consistent?

▶ Are the Statistics Valid?

When conducting research and deciding which supporting materials to use, consider whether you need primary or secondary sources of information. A **primary source** is the document, testimony, or publication in which information first appears. For example, a journal article that contains the results of an author's original research is a primary source. A magazine or newspaper that reports on the original research or writing by someone else is a secondary source. A **secondary source** reports, repeats, or summarizes information from one or more other sources. Look carefully at secondary sources of information to determine, if possible, the primary source. Publications such as *Newsweek* and *Parade Magazine* as well as many websites may not conduct their own research. As secondary sources, they publish information they obtained from primary sources.[1]

[1] Isa N. Engleberg and John A. Daly, *Presentations in Everyday Life: Strategies for Effective Speaking*, 2nd ed. (Boston: Houghton Mifflin, 2005), p. 180.

mation. Ask yourself whether the source you are quoting is a recognized expert, a first-hand observer, or a respected journalist.

Is the Source Biased? A source can be **biased**, meaning that it states an opinion so slanted in one direction that it may not be objective or fair. If the source has a strong opinion or will gain from your agreement, be cautious. For years, tobacco companies publicly denied that cigarette smoking was harmful, even though their own research told them otherwise. Now we recognize that the tobacco companies' pronouncements were biased and untrue. Even not-for-profit special-interest groups such as the National Rifle Association, pro-choice or pro-life groups, or the American Association of Retired Persons have biases. The information they publish may be true, but the conclusions they draw from that information may be faulty.

Is the Information Recent? Always note the date of the information you want to use. When was the information collected? When was it published? In this rapidly changing information age, your information can become old news in a matter of hours. Books provide a wealth of background information and historical perspectives. For current events or scientific breakthroughs, use magazines, journals, newspaper articles, or reliable Web sources.

Is the Information Consistent? Check to ensure that the information you include reports facts and findings similar to other information on the same subject. Does the information make sense based on what you know about the topic? For example, if most doctors and medical experts agree that penicillin will *not* cure a common viral cold, why believe an obscure source that recommends it as a treatment?

Are the Statistics Valid? Good statistics can be informative, dramatic, and convincing. But statistics also can mislead, distort, and confuse. Make sure your statistics are valid—that they are well founded, justified, and accurate. Here are six questions that can help you assess the validity of statistics:

1. Who collected and analyzed the data?
2. Is the researcher a well-respected expert?
3. How was the information collected and analyzed?

Why was Secretary of State Colin Powell convincing when he presented the United Nations with what he claimed was evidence of poison found in Iraq during a search for weapons of mass destruction?

4. When was the information collected and analyzed?

5. Who is reporting the statistics—the researcher or a reporter?

6. Are the statistics believable?

Structure Your Content

Michael Kepper, a marketing communication specialist, compares the need for structuring content with the needs of a human body:

> A speech without structure is like a human body without a skeleton. It won't stand up. Spineless. Like a jellyfish. . . . Having structure won't make the speech a great one, but lacking structure will surely kill all the inspired thoughts . . . because listeners are too busy trying to find out where they are to pay attention.[7]

Clear **organization** of a presentation's content provides structure. It helps you focus on the purpose of your presentation while you decide what to include and how to put your content into an effective format.

As an audience member, you know that organization matters. A well-organized presentation is easier to listen to and remember than a poorly organized one. It is difficult to understand and remember the words of a speaker who rambles and doesn't connect ideas. In fact, you may never want to hear that speaker again. Research confirms that audiences react positively to well-organized presentations and negatively to poorly organized ones.[8]

SELECT YOUR KEY POINTS

The first step in organizing a presentation requires the answer to a single question: What are the key points that you want to cover in your presentation? **Key points** represent the most important issues or the main ideas in the message you want your audience to understand and remember. Finding and selecting key points are the first step in developing a clear organizational structure for your presentation.

Look for a pattern or natural groups of ideas and information. Depending on your purpose and topic area, this can be an easy task or a daunting puzzle. Inexperienced speakers often feel overwhelmed by what seems to be mountains of unrelated facts and figures. Don't give up! Finding a structure is similar to assembling a patchwork quilt or planting a flower garden. You have all the pieces or plants; now it is time to look for similarities in shape and color and to find out how the pieces can be combined to create a complete picture.

LINK YOUR KEY POINTS AND CENTRAL IDEA

Now, link the key points to a central idea that captures the essence of your purpose statement. Your **central idea** is a sentence that summarizes the key points of your presentation. The central idea provides a brief preview of the organizational pattern you will follow to achieve your purpose.

The following examples illustrate how topic area, purpose, and central idea are different but closely linked to one another:

Topic area	Mental depression
Purpose	To educate listeners about the significance of mental depression
Central idea	The many people who suffer from depression share similar causes, symptoms, and treatments.

Topic area	Refugee families
Purpose	To increase donations to the church's refugee assistance program
Central idea	Because the church's refugee families program is a blessing for all of us—the families, our church, and you—please make a financial contribution to our ministry.

SELECT AN ORGANIZATIONAL PATTERN

Even the most polished speakers sometimes find it difficult to see how their ideas and information fall into a clear structure. If you're in a similar position, do not despair. There are several commonly used organizational patterns that can help you clarify your central idea and find an effective format for your presentation: topical, time, space, problem–solution, causes and effects, stories and examples, and comparison–contrast.[9]

Arrange by Subtopics **Topical arrangement** involves dividing a large topic into smaller subtopics. Subtopics can describe reasons, characteristics, techniques, or procedures. Use a topical arrangement if your ideas and information can be divided into discrete categories of relatively equal importance. For example:

ORGANIZATIONAL PATTERNS
▶ Topical
▶ Time
▶ Space
▶ Problem–Solution
▶ Causes and Effects
▶ Stories and Examples
▶ Comparison–Contrast

Topic area	Facial expression in different cultures
Purpose	To appreciate that some facial expressions don't always translate between cultures
Central idea	Americans and native Japanese often misinterpret facial expressions depicting fear, sadness, and disgust.
Key points	A. Fear B. Sadness C. Disgust

Sequence in Time **Time arrangement** orders information according to time or calendar dates. Most step-by-step procedures begin with the first step and continue sequentially (or chronologically) through the last step. Use a time arrangement when your key points occur in time relative to each other, as in recipes, assembly instructions, technical procedures, and historical events. For example:

Topic area	Making vanilla ice cream
Purpose	To explain how to make traditional custard-based vanilla ice cream

What type of organizational format is used when a master chef teaches students how to properly whip egg whites?

Central idea	To make perfect homemade vanilla ice cream, make sure that you heat the ingredients properly, know when the custard is thick enough, and correctly churn the ice cream.
Key points	A. Warm up and whisk in the first ingredients.
	B. Cook the custard slowly.
	C. Cool and add final ingredients.
	D. Refrigerate before churning.

Position in Space   Use a **space arrangement** if your key points can be arranged in order of their location or physical relationship to one another. For example:

Topic area	Brain structure
Purpose	To explain how sections of the brain are responsible for different functions
Central idea	A guided tour of the brain begins in the hindbrain, moves through the midbrain, and ends in the forebrain, with side trips through the right and left hemispheres.
Key points	A. The hindbrain
	B. The midbrain
	C. The forebrain
	D. The right and left hemispheres

Present a Problem and a Solution   Use a **problem–solution arrangement** to describe a situation that is harmful or difficult (the problem) and then offer a plan to solve the problem (the solution). Problems can be as simple as a squeaky door or as significant as world famine. In the following example, each key point presents guidelines for dealing with a specific problem often found in group discussions:

Topic area	People problems in groups
Purpose	To provide suggestions for solving common people problems that occur in group discussions and meetings
Central idea	Learning how to deal with a few common behavioral problems in groups will improve a group's performance.

Key points	A. Dealing with nonparticipants
	B. Dealing with loudmouths
	C. Dealing with latecomers and early leavers

Show Causes and Effects   Use a **cause-and-effect arrangement** either to present a cause and its resulting effects or to detail the effects that result from a specific cause. Here is an example that identifies how watching too much television adversely affects children:

Topic area	Children and television
Purpose	To describe the harmful effects that television has on children
Central idea	Television has a negative influence on children and their families because it displaces time that could be spent on more important activities.
Key points	A. Television has a negative effect on children's physical fitness.
	B. Television has a negative effect on children's school achievement.
	C. Television watching may become a serious addiction.

In cause-and-effect presentations, speakers may claim that eating red meat causes disease or that lower taxes stimulate the economy. In effect-to-cause presentations, speakers may claim that sleepiness or lack of energy can be caused by an iron deficiency or that a decrease in lake fish is caused by acid rain.

Be careful with cause-and-effect arrangements. Just because one thing follows another does not mean that the first causes the second. Lack of sleep, not lack of iron, can be a cause of sleepiness.

Tell Stories and Share Examples   A series of well-told stories or dramatic examples can be so compelling and interesting that they easily become the organizational pattern for a presentation. For example, dramatic stories about successful individuals who escaped from poverty and prejudice or who triumphed with disabilities can be the key points of a presentation:

Topic area	Leaders and adversity
Purpose	To convince listeners that disabilities are not barriers to success
Central idea	Many noteworthy leaders have lived with disabilities.
Key points	A. Franklin D. Roosevelt, president of the United States, who lived with polio
	B. Jan Scruggs, disabled soldier and Vietnam Memorial founder
	C. Helen Keller, deaf and blind advocate

Compare and Contrast   Use a **comparison–contrast arrangement** to demonstrate how two things are similar or different. This pattern works well in two situations: (1) when an unfamiliar concept can be easily explained by comparing it with a familiar concept or (2) when you are demonstrating the advantages of one alternative over another. Comparisons can be real (comparing products or contrasting medical treatments) or fanciful (comparing student success to racehorse success). For example:

Topic area	Family sedans and SUVs
Purpose	To recommend a way of evaluating medium-size cars and SUVs
Central idea	Comparing performance, comfort, fuel economy, and reliability can help you decide whether to purchase a new mid-size car or an SUV for your family.
Key points	A. Performance
	B. Comfort
	C. Overall fuel economy
	D. Predicted reliability

Directions: Develop a purpose statement, central idea, and list of key points for one of the two presentation topics listed, using the subtopics provided. You may delete or add subtopics to create an effective organizational pattern.

Topic: Collecting Fossils

Identifying fossils	How fossils are useful
How fossils are formed	What are fossils?
Geologic time	Types of fossils
Myths about fossils	How to collect fossils
Where to collect fossils	Paleozoic era
Cenozoic era	Cambrian era
Mesozoic era	Jurassic period
Pleistocene period	Living fossils

Topic: Care and Treatment of Common Shoulder Problems

Need for early treatment	How the shoulder moves
Causes of shoulder injuries	Shoulder injury symptoms
Anatomy of the shoulder	Heat treatment
Diagnosing shoulder injuries	Cortisone injections
Role of physical therapy	Oral medication
Cold treatment	Shoulder sprains
Shoulder separations	Torn rotator cuff
Arthroscopic surgery	Shoulder exercises

Prepare to Outline Your Presentation

A good outline organizes your main ideas and information, and can be used to reject irrelevant or uninteresting material. Before producing a formal outline of your presentation, consider two techniques for structuring it: a preliminary outline and mind mapping.

PRELIMINARY OUTLINES

Outlines begin in a preliminary form with a few basic building blocks. A **preliminary outline** puts the major pieces of a presentation in order. Figure 13.1 illustrates the format of a preliminary outline.

You can use this model outline to organize almost any presentation, modifying it based on the number of key points and the types and amount of supporting material. Aim for at least two pieces of supporting material under each key point—fact, statistic, testimony, definition, description, analogies, example, or story.

MIND MAPPING

If a linear, logical progression of ideas is difficult to find or develop, then consider mind mapping. **Mind mapping** is an alternative method for identifying and organizing key points. It encourages the free flow of ideas and lets you define relationships among those ideas. Mind mapping harnesses the potential of your whole brain to generate ideas while your brain is in a highly creative mode of thought.[10]

Start with a clean piece of paper. Write your subject or central ideas in the middle of a blank page. Then write down the ideas you want to cover in your presentation. Don't be afraid to fill the page—neatness does not count. Initially, there are no bad ideas. What is important is that you have a one-page conglomeration of the ideas that you might include in your presentation. If possible, put related ideas near each other on the page and draw a circle around that group of ideas. If groups of ideas are related, let your circles overlap or draw lines between those circled.

Figure 13.2 shows a mind map for a presentation on Muzak, that ever-present background music you often hear in stores and offices. The mind map

Figure 13.1	Preliminary Outline Format

TOPIC AREA:

I. **Introduction**
   A. Purpose/Topic
   B. Central Idea
   C. Brief Preview of Key Points
      1. Key Point #1
      2. Key Point #2
      3. Key Point #3

II. **Body of the Presentation**
   A. Key Point #1
      1. Supporting Material
      2. Supporting Material
   B. Key Point #2
      1. Supporting Material
      2. Supporting Material
   C. Key Point #3
      1. Supporting Material
      2. Supporting Material

III. **Conclusion**

Figure 13.2 Mind Map

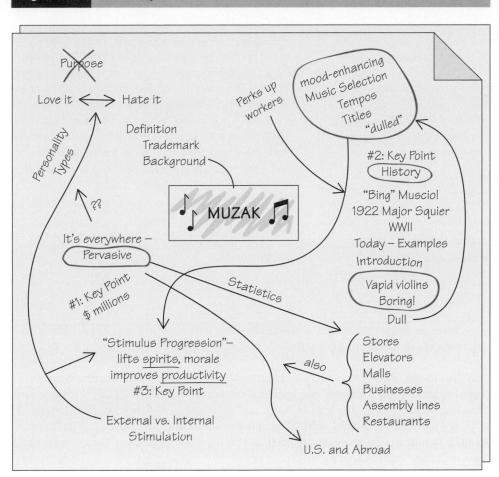

in Figure 13.2 is a hodgepodge of words, phrases, lists, circles, and arrows. Certainly it contains more concepts than should be included in a single presentation. After completing such a mind map, you can label circled ideas as key points and put them in a logical order.

Mind maps allow you to see your ideas without superimposing an organizational pattern on them. They also let you postpone the need to arrange your ideas in a pattern until you collect enough information to organize the content. Use mind mapping when you have lots of ideas and information but are having trouble deciding how to select and arrange your material for a presentation.

Comprehensive and Speaking Outlines

Refining preliminary outlines and mind maps into a complete presentation often requires the creation of two additional outlines: a comprehensive presentation outline and a speaking outline.

COMPREHENSIVE OUTLINE

A **comprehensive outline**—also referred to as a **formal outline**—provides an all-inclusive framework that follows established outlining conventions. A preliminary outline helps you plan your presentation, but a comprehensive outline creates the first draft of your presentation.

After you identify the key points that will support your central idea and after you choose an organizational pattern to structure your message, it's time to determine which key points go first, second, or last. In many cases, the organizational pattern you choose dictates the order. For example, if you use time arrangement, the first step in a procedure comes first. If your format does not dictate the order of key points, place your best ideas in strategic positions.

- *Strength and Familiarity.* Place your strongest points first and last, and your weakest or least familiar idea in the middle position, so that you start and end with strength.
- *Audience Needs.* If your audience needs current information, satisfy that need early. Background information can come later. If you anticipate that your audience may not be very interested in your topic, don't begin with your most technical, detailed point. If you are speaking about a controversial topic, begin with a point that focuses on the background of an issue or on the reasons for a change.
- *Logistics.* If you're one of a series of presenters, you may end up with less time to speak than was originally scheduled. Plan your presentation so that the key points come first in case you need to cut your presentation short.[1]

[1]Isa N. Engleberg and John A. Daly, *Presentations in Everyday Life: Strategies for Effective Speaking*, 2nd ed. (Boston: Houghton Mifflin, 2005), p. 206.

There are three basic rules of comprehensive outlining: use numbers, letters, *and* indentations; divide your subpoints logically; and keep the outline consistent.

Use Numbers, Letters, and Indentations   A comprehensive outline uses a system of indenting and numbers and letters. Roman numerals (I, II, III) signify the major divisions such as the introduction, body, and conclusion. Indented capital letters (A, B, C) are used for key points. Additional indents use Arabic numbers (1, 2, 3) for more specific points and supporting material. If you need a fourth level, indent again and use lowercase letters (a, b, c).

Divide Your Subpoints Logically   Each major point should include at least two subpoints indented under it, or none at all. If there is an A, there must be a B; for every 1, there must be a 2.

Wrong:	I.
	A.
	II.
Right:	I.
	A.
	B.
	II.

Keep the Outline Consistent   Use a topic, a phrase, or a full sentence for each key point in your outline, rather than a mix of styles. If you begin each subpoint with a verb, use a consistent grammatical form; don't switch to beginning with nouns halfway through the outline.

Wrong:	I. Consistent Style.
	II. Use a consistent grammatical form.
Right:	I. Keep the outline consistent in style.
	II. Use a consistent grammatical form.
Right:	I. Consistent style.
	II. Consistent grammatical form.

348

Figure 13.3	Speaking Outline

Presentation on the Importance of Customer Care

I. Introduction

   A. Question: What will be the most important factor for competitive business success in the first decade of the 21st Century? (Gallup Poll of CEOs, business owners, and company presidents)

   B. Answer: 18% said operating efficiency; 25% said product/service quality; and 27% said **customer service.**

   C. Central Idea: Become a service-centered business if you want to succeed.

II. Body

   A. Your job security and business success depends on how valuable you are to your customers. (Stories, statistics, and descriptions of successful employees and businesses)

   B. Customers will replace you with better service providers. (When product and price are the same, service is the only area in which you can be different from the competition. Ask audience for examples.)

   C. Develop a reputation for responsiveness. (Examples: Nordstrom, Saturn, Ritz Carlton Hotels, the local hospital)

III. Conclusion

Customers are the lifeblood of your business. Customers are not dependent on you; you are dependent on them. So remember the secret of keeping good customers: Exceed their expectations! That's how you succeed in business!

SPEAKING OUTLINE

The notes you use during a presentation may be based on a comprehensive outline, but they shouldn't look like one. A **speaking outline** can be a short outline that includes little more than a list of key points and reminders of supporting material. If your topic is complex and your presentation loaded with quotations and statistics, however, a highly detailed speaking outline may be needed. In Chapter 15, "Presentations: Speaking to Inform," we provide an example of a detailed speaking outline for a presentation on Internet marketing. In some cases, a speaking outline may include notes on when to introduce and remove a visual aid or provide a handout.

Figure 13.3 shows a speaking outline for a presentation on the importance of customer service. Note that the introduction, central idea, key points, and conclusions are written out, but the reminders about the type and substance of supporting material are in parentheses.

Connect Your Key Points

An outline shows how you structured and developed your key points, but it's missing the "glue" that attaches the key points to each other and makes your presentation a coherent whole. **Connectives** are this glue, and they include internal previews and summaries as well as transitions and signposts.[11]

INTERNAL PREVIEWS AND INTERNAL SUMMARIES

An **internal preview** reveals or suggests your key points to the audience. It tells them what you are going to cover and in what order. In the body of a presentation, an internal preview describes how you are going to approach a key point. For example:

> How do researchers and doctors explain obesity? Some offer genetic explanations; others psychological ones. Either or both factors can be responsible for your never-ending battle with the bathroom scale.

If you want your presentation to be both unique and memorable, try thinking creatively about its structure. Lee Towe, president of Innovators International, defines **creativity** as consisting of two parts: creative thinking and creative output.[1] Mind mapping is a good example of *creative thinking* in action. When you mind map, you begin with a blank page rather than with a predetermined organizational pattern. *Creative output* consists of connecting and combining previously unrelated elements. For example, the circles and arrows you draw on a mind map allow you to combine ideas from various places on the page.

As an example, a presentation on growing tomatoes can be ordered topically and creatively. How can you improve upon the following organization pattern: "You can grow healthy tomatoes by (1) planting them in a sunny place, (2) giving them plenty of fertilizer and water, and (3) keeping pests and weeds under control"? What about comparing tomatoes with caring for a newborn baby? "You can be the proud parent of healthy tomato plants by (1) making their garden 'nursery' safe and comfortable, (2) giving them special food and formula that helps them grow up strong and healthy, and (3) seeing that they don't come down with the usual diseases." The tomatoes/newborns analogy makes the organizational pattern more interesting and more memorable.

Patricia Phillips, a customer service expert, often uses excerpts from popular songs to begin each major section of her training seminar. Notice how the following song titles lend themselves to customer service: "I Can't Get No Satisfaction" by the Rolling Stones, "Help" by the Beatles, "Respect" by Aretha Franklin, "Don't Be Cruel" by Elvis, and "Don't You Come Back No More" by Ray Charles. These well-known songs provide an upbeat and creative way to move into each new section of the customer service seminar.

Creativity, however, runs some risks. Suppose some audience members are unfamiliar with the songs chosen by a speaker? What if the audience was expecting a more technical presentation? If you want to use creative patterns, make sure your audience will understand and appreciate your creativity.

[1]Lee Towe, *Why Didn't I Think of That? Creativity in the Workplace* (West Des Moines, IA: American Media, 1966), p. 7.

If your topic is straightforward and uncomplicated, you may need an internal preview only in your introduction. However, regardless of where you include them, audiences like internal previews because they prepare them for listening to and remembering important ideas.

Internal summaries are a useful way to end a major section and to reinforce important ideas. They also are an opportunity to repeat critical ideas or information. Internal summaries usually come at the end of major sections or key points to help the audience review and remember what you said. For example:

> So remember, before spending hundreds of dollars on diet books and exercise toys, make sure that your weight problem is not influenced by the number and size of your fat cells, your hormone level, your metabolism, or the amount of glucose in your bloodstream.

TRANSITIONS AND SIGNPOSTS

The most common type of connective is the **transition**—a word, number, brief phrase, or sentence that helps you move from one key point or section to another. Transitions act like lubricating oil to keep a presentation moving smoothly. In the following examples, the transitions are underlined:

> Yet it's important to remember . . .
>
> In addition to metabolism, there is . . .
>
> On the other hand, some people believe . . .
>
> Finally, a responsible parent should . . .

Transitions also function as mini previews and mini summaries that link the conclusion of one section to the beginning of another. For example:

> After you've eliminated these four genetic explanations for weight gain, it's time to consider several psychological factors.

A fourth type of connective is **signposts**—short phrases that, like signs on the highway, tell or remind listeners where you are in the organizational structure of a presentation. For example, if you are sharing four genetic explanations for weight gain, begin each explanation with numbers—first, second, third, and fourth: "Fourth and finally, make sure your glucose level has been tested and is within normal levels."

Signposts focus attention on an important idea or piece of information; they can highlight an eloquent phrase or special insight. Here are two examples:

> Even if you can't remember all of his accomplishments, please remember one thing: Alex Curry is the only candidate who has been endorsed by every newspaper and civic association in the county.

> As I read aloud this section of Toni Morrison's novel, listen carefully to how she uses simple metaphors to describe the cemetery scene.

Beginning Your Presentation

The best introductions capitalize on the power of first impressions. In Chapter 7, "Interpersonal Communication: Understanding Relationships," we describe the primacy effect, our tendency to base our impressions on the first thing we see or hear from a person. First impressions can create a positive, lasting impression and pave the way for a highly successful presentation. A weak beginning gives audience members a reason to tune out or remember you as a poor speaker.

GOALS OF THE INTRODUCTION

The best introductions give your audience time to adjust, to block out distractions, and to focus attention on you and your message. They also establish a relationship among three elements: you, your message, and your audience.[12] Figure 13.4 on page 352 presents five goals for an effective introduction.

How does this handwritten outline help the speaker preview the key points of her presentation on preventing depression to a Spanish-speaking audience?

WAYS TO BEGIN

The following methods represent only a few of the many strategies for beginning a presentation effectively. Use these methods separately or in combination.

Use a Statistic or Example Sometimes your research turns up a statistic or example that is unusual or dramatic. If you anticipate a problem in gaining and keeping audience attention, an interesting statistic or example can do it for you.

> The statistics are appalling: More than 5,000 juveniles and 35,000 adults die each year from gunshot wounds. Millions of latchkey kids come home to a house or apartment in which there is a gun. Since 1984, the homicide rate for males has tripled. This is an epidemic! An epidemic that is about 10 times as big in terms of lives lost as the great polio epidemic of the first half of the 20th century.[13]

Quote Someone A dramatic statement or eloquent phrase written by someone else may be ideal for beginning a presentation. A good quotation helps an audience overcome their doubts, especially when the quotation is from a writer or speaker who is highly respected or an expert source of information. Remember to give the writer or speaker of the quotation full credit. In the following example, a speaker quotes a columnist who thinks we need more than gun control to end gun violence:

> Syndicated columnist Don Feder began an article about an Arkansas murder with these words: "Blame the guns. Don't blame the wretched little monsters who murdered four children and a pregnant teacher because one of them had just been dumped by a girlfriend; blame the guns. Don't blame a culture where many parents spend more time watching televised sports than with their kids; blame the guns."[14]

Tell a Story Audiences will give you their undivided attention if you tell a good story and tell it well. Consider using a story about a personal hardship, a triumph, or even an embarrassment. Remember that the purpose of using a story is to illustrate a concept or idea. The story can be personal, well-known, or fictional.

> When I was fifteen, I was operated on to remove the deadliest form of skin cancer, a melanoma carcinoma. My doctors injected ten shots of steroids into each scar every three weeks to stop the scars from spreading. I now know that it wasn't worth a couple of summers of being tan to go through all that pain and suffering. Take steps now to protect yourself from the harmful effects of the sun. (Author's files)

Use a Metaphor Dr. Ralph Bunch, grandson of a former slave, earned a PhD from Harvard, was a member of the United Nations Secretariat, and later won the Nobel Peace Prize. In June 1949, Dr. Bunch began a speech at Brandeis University with a "road to peace" metaphor that explains what must be done to achieve a more peaceful world:

> There is no road in the world today more important than the road to peace. It is, to date, insufficiently traveled, and indeed, not at all clearly chartered. The United Nations is attempting both to chart it and to guide the nations and people of the world along it.[15]

Dr. Bunch compares peace with a road that is not well traveled. This metaphor is an eloquent way of beginning a presentation. In Chapter 5, "Understanding Verbal Communication," we define and provide additional examples of this powerful figure of speech.

Ask a Question Asking a question attracts your audience's attention because it challenges them to think about an answer. One of the best

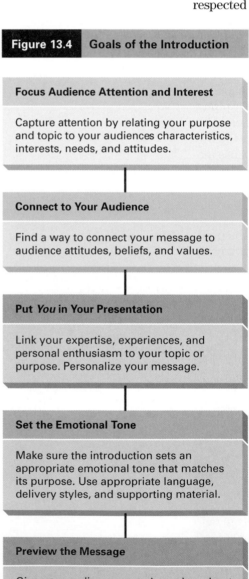

Figure 13.4 **Goals of the Introduction**

Focus Audience Attention and Interest

Capture attention by relating your purpose and topic to your audiences characteristics, interests, needs, and attitudes.

Connect to Your Audience

Find a way to connect your message to audience attitudes, beliefs, and values.

Put *You* in Your Presentation

Link your expertise, experiences, and personal enthusiasm to your topic or purpose. Personalize your message.

Set the Emotional Tone

Make sure the introduction sets an appropriate emotional tone that matches its purpose. Use appropriate language, delivery styles, and supporting material.

Preview the Message

Give your audience a sneak preview about the subject. State your central idea and briefly list the key points you will cover.

In their eagerness to get going, some speakers don't give their introductions enough attention. Rather than applying the time-honored introduction techniques described in this chapter, they may fall into one or more common traps. If you know what these are, you can avoid them—and start strong!

- *Plan the beginning at the end.* Don't plan your introduction before you develop the content of your presentation.

- *Don't apologize.* Don't use your introduction to offer excuses or apologize for poor preparation, weak delivery, or nervousness.
- *Avoid beginning with "My speech is about . . . ."* Boring beginnings do not capture audience attention or enhance a speaker's credibility. Be original and creative.

---

kinds of questions elicits a response such as "I had no idea!" In the following example, a student speaker used this technique in a series of questions:

> What do China, Iran, Saudi Arabia, and the United States have in common? Nuclear weapons? No. Abundant oil resource? No. What we have in common is this: Last year, these four countries accounted for nearly *all* the executions worldwide.[16]

Refer to the Place or Occasion   A simple way to begin a presentation is to refer to the place in which you are speaking or the occasion for the gathering. Your audience's memories and feelings about a specific place or occasion conjure up the emotions needed to capture their attention and interest.

When Dr. Martin Luther King Jr. made his famous "I Have a Dream" presentation on the steps of the Lincoln Memorial, his first few words echoed Abraham Lincoln's famous Gettysburg Address ("Four score and seven years ago"). Dr. King began:

> Five score years ago, a great American, in whose symbolic shadow we stand, signed the Emancipation Proclamation.[17]

Refer to a Well-Known Incident   Events that occurred shortly before your presentation or in the recent past will gain audience attention and interest. For example:

> Soon after the September 11 tragedy, I saw a proliferation of highway billboards that celebrated our country and citizen patriotism. One billboard stood out. It was both simple and eloquent. A stars-and-stripes ribbon sat on a plain white background. Three words declared its purpose: United We Stand. The same three words are just as relevant at this college. Immediately following the September 11 tragedy, we united to counsel our students. Today, we unite to recognize and celebrate the achievements of our colleagues at our annual convocation.

The "recent event" technique is frequently used for political speechmaking. If you listen carefully to the news or watch the president's State of the Union address, you are bound to hear references to well-known recent events. Much like references to place or occasion, memories and feelings about a recent event capture an appropriate mood for your introduction.

Address Audience Needs   When there is a crisis, address the problem at the outset. If budget cuts require salary reductions, audience members are not interested in clever questions or dramatic statistics.

> As you know, the state has reduced our operating budget by 2.7 million dollars. It is also just as important that you know this: All of you will have a job here next year—and the year after. There will be no layoffs. Instead there will be cutbacks on nonpersonnel budget lines, downsizing of programs, and possibly, short furloughs.

WAYS TO BEGIN A PRESENTATION

▶ Use a Statistic or Example
▶ Quote Someone
▶ Tell a Story
▶ Use a Metaphor
▶ Ask a Question
▶ Refer to the Place or Occasion
▶ Refer to a Well-Known Incident
▶ Address Audience Needs

Concluding Your Presentation

You know that audiences remember things that are presented first (the primacy effect). They also remember information that comes last. Much like the primacy effect, the recency effect suggests that the last information audiences see and hear also creates a lasting impression. Final words have a powerful and lasting effect on your audience and determine how your audience thinks and feels about you and your presentation.[18]

GOALS OF THE CONCLUSION

What are the goals for concluding a presentation? Like the introduction, a conclusion establishes a relationship among you, your topic, and your audience. Figure 13.5 presents three important goals for concluding a presentation.

WAYS TO CONCLUDE

Some methods of concluding your presentation reinforce your message; others strengthen the audience's final impression of you. As with introductions, use these approaches separately or in combination.

Summarize   Reinforcing your key points in a succinct summary is the most direct way to conclude a presentation. This is also the best way to review and repeat the key points in your presentation. Keep summaries memorable, clear, and brief. Here, a speaker uses questions to emphasize her central idea and key points:

> Now, if you hear someone ask whether more women should serve in the U.S. Congress, ask and then answer the two questions I discussed today: Can women and their issues attract big donors? And, are women too nice to be "tough" in politics? Now that you know how to answer these questions, don't let doubters stand in the way of making a woman's place in the House.

Quote Someone   What is true about quoting someone in your introduction is true about concluding with a quotation. Because quotations are memorable, clear, and brief, speakers often use them to conclude their presentations.

Good research can provide a quotation with a dramatic effect. For example, when Rudolph Giuliani gave his 2001 farewell speech as mayor of New York City, he ended by reciting the conclusion of Abraham Lincoln's Gettysburg Address as a tribute to those who died in the terrorist attack on the World Trade Center.

> " . . . that we here highly resolved that these dead shall not have died in vain—that this nation, under God, shall have a new birth of freedom—and that the government of the people, by the people, for the people, shall not perish from the earth." God bless New York and God bless America.[19]

Tell a Story   End with a story when you want the audience to visualize the central idea of your presentation. Marge Anderson, chief executive of the Mille Lacs Band of Ojibwe Indians, concluded a presentation with this story:

> Years ago, white settlers came to this area and built the first European–style homes. When Indian People walked by these homes and saw [windows], they looked through them to see what the strangers inside were doing. The settlers were shocked, but it made sense when you think about it: Windows are made to be looked through from both sides. Since then, my People have spent many years looking at the world through your window. I hope today I've given you a reason to look at it through ours.[20]

Figure 13.5	Goals of the Conclusion

Be Memorable

Give the audience a reason to remember you and your presentation. Show how your message affected you and how it affects them.

Be Clear

Repeat the one thing you want your audience to remember at the end of your presentation.

Be Brief

The announced ending of a presentation should never go beyond 2–3 minutes.

Knowing that you have a well-prepared and strong ending for your presentation can calm your nerves and inspire your audience. The most effective endings match the mood and style of the presentation, and make realistic assumptions about the audience.

- *Make sure the mood and style are consistent.* Don't tack on an irrelevant or inappropriate ending. Match the mood and method of your conclusion to the mood and style of your presentation.

- *Have realistic expectations.* Most audience members will not act when called upon unless the request is carefully worded, reasonable, and possible. Don't end by demanding something from your audience unless you are reasonably sure you can get it.

Use Poetic Language   Being poetic doesn't mean ending with a poem. Rather, it means using language that inspires and creates memorable images. A presentation about respecting older people ended with the following short but poetic phrases:

> For old wood best to burn, old wine to drink, old authors to read, old friends to trust, and old people to love.

Call for Action   A challenging but effective way to end a presentation is to call for action. Use a call for action when you want your audience to do more than merely listen—when you want them to *do* something.

A call to action might mean rallying an audience to remember something important, to think about the importance of a story you told, or to ask themselves a significant question. The Reverend Jesse Jackson began his conclusion to a presentation at the 1984 Democratic convention with a call to action:

> Young Americans, dream. Choose the human race over the nuclear race. Bury the weapons and don't burn the people. . . . Dream of lawyers more concerned with justice than a judgeship. Dream of doctors more concerned with public health than personal wealth. . . .[21]

Refer to the Beginning   Consider ending your presentation with the same technique you used to begin it. If you began with a quotation, end with the same or a similar quotation. If you began with a story, refer back to that story. Audiences like this concluding method because it returns to something familiar and "bookends" the content of your presentation. For example:

> Remember the story I told you about two-year-old Joey, a hole in his throat so he can breathe, a tube jutting out of his stomach so he can be fed. For Joey, an accidental poisoning was an excruciatingly painful and horrifying experience. For Joey's parents, it was a time of fear, panic, and helplessness. Thus, it is a time to be prepared for, and even better, a time to prevent.

The content and structure of a presentation depend on one another. Carefully selected, valid content needs a structure to create impact, generate meaning, and achieve a purpose. A highly creative and effective structure, however, needs appropriate content to justify its form and value. At the beginning of this chapter we offer a metaphor that compares constructing a presentation to constructing a building. No matter how well you collect the necessary materials for a building, they are useless without a frame or structure. And no matter how well you frame the structure of a building, it will be a virtual, bare-bones skeleton until you add the walls, roof, floors, rooms, doors, and windows. Your decisions about content and structure work hand-in-hand to achieve the purpose of your presentation.

WAYS TO CONCLUDE A PRESENTATION

▶ Summarize
▶ Quote Someone
▶ Tell a Story
▶ Use Poetic Language
▶ Call for Action
▶ Refer to the Beginning

Communication Challenge

Match the Organizational Pattern

Directions: Each of the following examples demonstrates how to use one (or more) of the organizational patterns listed below. Try to match each outline with a pattern.

A. Topical arrangement
B. Time arrangement
C. Space arrangement
D. Problem–solution
E. Causes and effects
F. Stories and examples
G. Comparison–contrast

_____ 1. The Three Stages of Pregnancy
    First trimester
    Second trimester
    Third trimester

_____ 2. Four Basic Techniques Used to Play Volleyball
    Setting
    Bumping
    Spiking
    Serving

_____ 3. The Richest Sources of Diamonds
    South Africa
    Tanzania
    Murfreesboro, Arkansas

_____ 4. The Legacies of Presidents Reagan, Bush Sr., and Clinton
    Domestic politics
    International politics
    Party politics

_____ 5. Homeless Shelters and Homeless Families
    The Khoo family
    The Taylor family
    The Arias family

_____ 6. The "Throw, Row, Then Go" Rules of Lifesaving
    Throw a life preserver to the victim.
    Row a boat or surfboard to the victim.
    Go (swim) to the victim as the last resort.

_____ 7. Slowing the AIDS Epidemic
    AIDS is a devastating disease.
    A cure has not been found.
    New drug "cocktails" can slow the onset of AIDS.

_____ 8. Aspirin and Heart Attacks
    Does research verify that aspirin prevents heart attacks?
    Who should follow the aspirin prescription?
    Are there potential, dangerous side effects of aspirin therapy?

Communication Assessment

Assessing Information from a Website

Directions: When testing the reliability of supporting material, use the criteria presented in this chapter. For website sources, you will need to apply additional criteria. These criteria are listed in this Website Assessment Checklist under "Assessment Criteria and Questions."

Use this checklist to assess the reliability of supporting material found on two websites of your choice. For website 1, select a site that is, in your opinion, a *good* site for researching valid supporting material. For website 2, select a site that is, in your opinion, a *questionable* or *poor* site that may not provide credible, recent, consistent, relevant, and/or valid information. Be prepared to present your assessment of both websites.

Website 1 URL: Host:	Website 2 URL: Host:	Assessment Criteria and Questions
Website Assessment Checklist			

Website 1 URL: Host:	Website 2 URL: Host:	Assessment Criteria and Questions
____ Acceptable ____ Unacceptable ____ Cannot determine Comments:	____ Acceptable ____ Unacceptable ____ Cannot determine Comments:	Criterion #1: Authority 1. Are the *sponsor's* identity and purpose clear? 2. Are the *author's* identity and qualifications evident? 3. If the material is protected by copyright, who is the copyright holder? 4. Can you verify the legitimacy of the page's sponsor (e.g., a phone number or postal address to contact for more information)? 5. Are you sure that the named source is actually operating the site? 6. Have you run the names of unfamiliar topics, sources, and authors through a search engine to learn more about them and what other people have said about them?
____ Acceptable ____ Unacceptable ____ Cannot determine Comments:	____ Acceptable ____ Unacceptable ____ Cannot determine Comments:	Criterion #2: Accuracy 1. Are the sources of factual information clearly listed so that you can verify them in another source? 2. Has the sponsor provided links that can be used to verify claims? 3. Are statistical data well labeled and easy to read? 4. Is the information free of grammatical, spelling, and typographical errors that indicate a lack of quality control?

(continues)

Communication Assessment (*continued*)

Website Assessment Checklist (*continued*)		
Website 1 URL: Host:	**Website 2** URL: Host:	**Assessment Criteria and Questions**
___ Acceptable ___ Unacceptable ___ Cannot determine Comments:	___ Acceptable ___ Unacceptable ___ Cannot determine Comments:	Criterion #3: Objectivity 1. Is it evident why the sponsor is providing each piece of information? 2. Is the information separate from advertising or opinion? 3. Is the sponsor's point of view presented clearly with well-supported arguments? 4. If the site is not objective, does it account for opposing points of view?
___ Acceptable ___ Unacceptable ___ Cannot determine Comments:	___ Acceptable ___ Unacceptable ___ Cannot determine Comments:	Criterion #4: Currency 1. Is the material recent enough to be accurate and relevant? 2. Are there any indications that the material is kept up-to-date? 3. Do you see statements indicating where data from charts and graphs were gathered? 4. Is there an indication that the site is complete and not still being developed?

Key Terms

analogy
bias
cause-and-effect arrangement
central idea
comparison–contrast arrangement
comprehensive outline
connective
content
creativity
definition
description
documentation
example

fact
formal outline
framing
internal preview
internal summary
key point
mind mapping
oral footnote
organization
preliminary outline
primary source
problem–solution arrangement
secondary source

signpost
space arrangement
speaking outline
statistics
story
structure
supporting material
testimony
time arrangement
topical arrangement
transition
valid

Notes

1. Sections of Chapters 12 through 16 are based on Isa N. Engleberg and John A. Daly, *Presentations in Everyday Life: Strategies for Effective Speaking*, 2nd ed. (Boston: Houghton Mifflin, 2005); and Isa N. Engleberg and Ann Raimes, *Pocket Keys for Speakers* (Boston: Houghton Mifflin, 2004).

2. Melvin Patrick Eli, *The Adventures of Amos 'n' Andy: A Social History of an American Phenomenon* (New York: Free Press, 1991). See inside cover.

3. American Association of Community Colleges, *Community College Fact Sheet*, 2006, www.nche.edu/Content/NavigationMenu?AboutCommunityColleges/Fast_Facts1/Fast_Facts.htm.

4. David Evans, *Big Road Blues: Tradition and Creativity in the Folk Blues* (New York: Da Capo Press, 1982), p. 22.

5. Jesse Jackson, Rainbow Coalition speech given at the 1984 Democratic Convention, July 17, 1984. For an analysis and complete text of the speech, see James R. Andrews and David Zarefsky, *Contemporary American Voices: Significant Speech in American History, 1945–Present* (New York: Longman, 1992), pp. 355–362.

6. Vivian Hobbs, Commencement Address at Prince George's Community College, Largo, Maryland, 1991. See full manuscript in Isa N. Engleberg, *The Principles of Public Presentations* (New York: HarperCollins, 1994), pp. 339–341.

7. Michael M. Kleeper with Robert E. Gunther, *I'd Rather Die Than Give a Speech* (Burr Ridge, IL: Irwin, 1994), p. 6.

8. Some of the best research on the value of organizing a presentation was conducted in the 1960s and '70s. See Ernest C. Thompson, "An Experimental Investigation of the Relative Effectiveness of Organizational Structure in Oral Communication," *Southern Speech Journal* 26 (1960), pp. 59–69; Ernest C. Thompson, "Some Effects of Message Structure on Listeners' Comprehension," *Speech Monographs* 34 (1967), pp. 51–57; James C. McCroskey and R. Samuel Mehrley, "The Effects of Disorganization and Nonfluency on Attitude Change and Source Credibility," *Communication Monographs* 36 (1969), pp. 13–21; Arlee Johnson, "A Preliminary Investigation of the Relationship between Organization and Listener Comprehension," *Central States Speech Journal* 21 (1970), pp. 104–107; and Christopher Spicer and Ronald E. Bassett, "The Effect of Organization on Learning from an Informative Message," *Southern Speech Communication Journal* 41 (1976), pp. 290–299.

9. Engleberg and Daly, pp. 199–207.

10. Tony Buzon, *Use Both Sides of Your Brain*, 3rd ed. (New York: Plume, 1989).

11. Engleberg and Daly, pp. 226–229.

12. Engleberg and Daly, pp. 238–251.

13. Bob Herbert, "Gun Violence Is Becoming an Epidemic," in *Guns and Violence: Current Controversies*, ed. Henry H. Kim (San Diego, CA: Greenhaven Press, 1999), p. 20.

14. Don Feder, "Guns Should Not Be Blamed for Violence" in *Guns and Violence: Current Controversies*, ed. Henry H. Kim (San Diego, CA: Greenhaven Press, 1999), p. 44.

15. Quoted in Isa N. Engleberg, *The Principles of Public Presentation* (New York: HarperCollins, 1994), p. 160.

16. Ann Quindlen, "The Failed Experiment," *Newsweek* (June 26, 2006), p. 64.

17. For the complete text of King's "I Have a Dream" speech plus commentary, see Andrews and Zarefsky, pp. 78–81.

18. Engleberg and Daly, pp. 251–256.

19. www.newsmax.com/archives/2001/12/27/15090.shtml.

20. See Chapter 16 in this book, "Presentations: Speaking to Persuade," for the complete text and commentary on this speech. Source: Marge Anderson, "Looking through Our Window: The Value of Indian Culture," *Vital Speeches of the Day* 65 (1999), pp. 633–634.

21. See Andrews and Zarefsky for complete text of Jesse Jackson's Rainbow Coalition speech, pp. 355–362.

Presentations: Language and Delivery

Key Elements of Communication	Communication Axioms	Guiding Principles of Presentation Language and Delivery
Self	*Communication Is Personal*	Identify your most natural and effective speaking style after analyzing your delivery strengths and weaknesses.
Others	*Communication Is Relational*	Adapt your language and delivery to the diverse characteristics and perspectives of your audience.
Purpose	*Communication Is Intentional*	Choose language and a speaking style appropriate to your purpose, topic, and audience.
Context	*Communication Is Contextual*	Use language, speaking style, and presentation aids appropriate for the presentation's context. Respect time limits.
Content	*Communication Is Symbolic*	Pronounce words correctly and clearly. Select presentation aids that directly support your content.
Structure	*Communication Is Structured*	Use clear and grammatically correct language. Integrate presentation aids into the structure of your presentation.
Expression	*Communication Is Irreversible*	Choose appropriate modes of expression. Practice your vocal and physical delivery as well as your use of presentation aids.

Expression: Language and Delivery

In this chapter we focus on two performance components of presentation speaking—language and delivery.[1] The key element at work here is *expression*. Expression is governed by the axiom *Communication Is Irreversible*. For example, if you use inappropriate words or speak in a voice that cannot be heard, you can't undo what you've said or how you've performed. If your language is bland and boring or your eye contact never strays from your notes, you can't recapture an audience to do a better job. **Presentation performance**—how you use words, your voice, your body, and presentation aids to express your message—is a significant and irreversible component in every presentation.

Language Style

Carefully chosen words can add power and authority to a presentation and transform good presentations into great presentations. The best words give presentations a unique flavor, emotional excitement, and brilliant clarity.

The most successful and memorable speakers work diligently to master an effective speaking style. **Speaking style** refers to how you use vocabulary, sentence structure and length, grammar and syntax, and language devices to express a message.[2] Effective presenters find their own unique style—the one that suits them best. Some speakers do best with a formal speaking style in which every sentence is carefully crafted and rehearsed. Other speakers prefer a more informal style in which key points are carefully worded but stories and personal observations are shared informally.

CLEAR STYLE

Clarity always comes first. If you aren't clear, your audience won't understand you and won't be impressed with how you express your message. Use simple and direct words. When possible, choose concrete rather than abstract words. Consider the connotative meanings of words. Don't let long, fancy words mask your message. As marketing expert Jerry Della Femina notes: "Nobody has time to try and figure out what you're trying to say, so you need to be direct. Most great advertising is direct. That's how people talk. That's the style they read. That's what sells products or services or ideas."[3]

ORAL STYLE

Chapter 5, "Understanding Verbal Communication," emphasizes the importance of using oral language when interacting with others. Review the features of oral style: short, familiar words; shorter, simpler, and even incomplete sentences; and more personal pronouns and informal colloquial expressions. To contrast the differences in written and oral styles, examine the student essay and the transcript of a presentation in Figure 14.1 (page 364). Although the essay and presentation use much of the same information, there are significant differences in their written and oral styles.[4]

THE CORE CHARACTERISTICS OF SPEAKING STYLE

▶ **C**lear Style
▶ **O**ral Style
▶ **R**hetorical Style
▶ **E**loquent Style

Chapter 5, "Understanding Verbal Communication," devotes a major section to improving your way with words. All the strategies and skills described in that section apply to presentation speaking. Reinforce the following suggestions by rereading portions of Chapter 5:

- Expand Your Vocabulary
- Use Oral Language
- Use Active Language
- Use *I*, *You*, and *We* Language
- Use Grammatical Language
- Use Metaphorical Language

Chapter 5 also explains why and how poor language choices can cause misunderstandings. We discuss the problems of bypassing, exclusionary language, and offensive language. Keep these problems in mind when addressing your audience. Remember, if you use exclusionary or offensive language, even unintentionally, you can't take it back. Such language can damage your credibility, offend your audience, defeat your purpose, and create a hostile environment.

RHETORICAL STYLE

A rhetorical style of speaking uses language designed to persuade and/or inspire. One way of achieving this goal is through the use of **rhetorical devices**, strategies designed to enhance a presentation's impact and persuasiveness. Two rhetorical devices work particularly well in most kinds of presentations: repetition and metaphors.

Repetition   Because your listeners can't rewind and immediately hear again what you just said, use repetition to highlight the sounds, words, ideas, and phrases you want your audience to remember. Repetition can be as simple as beginning a series of words (or words placed closely together) with the same sound. This type of repetition is called an **alliteration**. For example, the first part of Lincoln's "Gettysburg Address"—"*F*our score and seven years ago our *f*athers brought *f*orth"—includes three words beginning with the letter *f*.

Two contrasting examples of alliteration come from the Presidents Bush. In his 2003 State of the Union Address, President George W. Bush used a repetitive *d* sound to create a memorable line: "The *d*ictator of Iraq is not *d*isarming. To the contrary, he is *d*eceiving." His father, President George H. W. Bush, went a little too far with alliteration at the 1992 Republican National Convention: "[Congress] is a body caught in a hopeless tangle of PACs, perks, privileges, partisanship, and paralysis." Rather than adding impact and motivation, the sentence sounds a bit silly and is difficult to pronounce with dignity and style.

Repetition can be extended to a word, a phrase, or an entire sentence. Dr. Martin Luther King Jr. used the phrase "I have a dream" nine times in his famous 1963 speech in Washington, DC. He used "let freedom ring" ten times. Repetition can drive home an idea and evoke action. Audience members anticipate and remember repeated phrases.

| Figure 14.1 | Differences between Written and Oral Styles |

Excerpts from an *Essay* on Neuromusicology	Excerpts from a *Presentation* on Neuromusicology
I have n't understood a bar of music in my entire life, but I have felt it" (qtd. in Peter 350). These words were spoken by Igor Stravinsky, who composed some of the most complex and sophisticated music of his century. If the great Stravinsky can accept the elusive nature of music, and still love it, why can't we? Why are we analyzing it to try to make it useful? Ours is an age of information—an age that wishes to conquer all the mysteries of the human brain. Today there is a growing trend to study music's effects on our emotions, behavior, health, and intelligence. Journalist Alex Ross reports how the relatively new field of neuromusicology (the science of the nervous system and its response to music) has been developed to experiment with music as a tool and to shape it to the needs of society. Observations like these let us know that we are on the threshold of seeing music in a whole new way and using music to achieve measurable changes in behavior. However, this new approach carries dangers, and once we go in this direction, there can be no turning back. How far do we want to go in our study of musical science? What effects will it have on our listening pleasures? A short history lesson reveals that there has been an awareness that music affects us, even if the reasons are not clear. Around 900 B.C., David (late King David) played the harp "to cure Saul's derangement" (Gonzalez–Crussi 69). Quoted from Ann Raimes, *Keys for Writers: A Brief Handbook,* 3rd ed. (Boston: Houghton Mifflin, 2003), pp. 152–158.	[Note: As an opening, the speaker plays an excerpt from "God Bless America" followed by an excerpt from *Sesame Street*'s theme music.] What did you think of or feel when you heard "God Bless America"? What about the *Sesame Street* theme? I'm sure that you're not surprised to learn that "God Bless America" reminds many people of the September 11th tragedy, the War in Iraq, and patriotism. And the theme from good ol' *Sesame Street* probably put a smile on your face as you revisited the world of Kermit the Frog, Miss Piggy, and Big Bird. Why were your responses so predictable and so emotional? The answer lies in a new brain science—a science that threatens to control you by controlling the music you hear. Is resistance futile? In the next few minutes, we'll take a close look at the field of neuromusicology. What? *Neuro* meaning related to our brain and nervous system. And *musicology*—the historic and scientific study of music. Journalist Alex Ross put it this way. By understanding the nervous system and its response to music, neruomusicologists study music as a tool and shape it to the needs of society. As New Age as all this may sound, there's plenty of history to back up the claims of neuromusicologists. For example, those of you who know your Bible know that King David played the harp to "cure Saul's derangement." Quoted from Isa Engleberg and Ann Raimes, *Pocket Keys for Speakers,* (Boston: Houghton Mifflin, 2004), pp. 191–193.

Metaphors Metaphors and their cousins—similes and analogies—are powerful rhetorical devices. In Chapter 5, "Understanding Verbal Communication," we identify metaphors as the most powerful figure of speech. Review Chapter 5 for strategies that will help you find powerful images for your presentation.

President Bill Clinton's Inaugural Address in 1993 relied on several metaphors related to spring and the changing seasons. In his opening paragraph, Clinton introduced these metaphorical terms (noted in italics):

> My fellow citizens, today we celebrate the mystery of American *renewal*. This ceremony is held in the *depth of winter*, but by the words we speak and the faces we show the world,

Personal pronouns put *you* in your presentation, help establish a connection with your audience, and can enhance your credibility. Use the pronouns *you* and *your* frequently—and focus your attention on people in different parts of the room.

Also use pronouns such as *I, me,* and *my.* By taking responsibility for your message, you can enhance your credibility. First-person accounts engage an audience. Using pronouns such as *we, us,* and *ours* intensifies the connection between you and the audience. "We shall overcome" has significantly more power than "You shall overcome" or "I shall overcome."

One study by a group of psycholinguists found interesting results about the use of the word *I* in pre-sentations. Like many people, you may believe that frequent use of the word *I* is the mark of a self-centered speaker. Research, however, shows that the use of *I*—if used appropriately—can characterize a more vulnerable, personal, and honest style of speaking. For example, Rudolph Giuliani was fond of using the word *we* during his early years as mayor of New York. He switched to *I* after his marriage broke up and he learned he had cancer.[1]

[1]Study by psycholinguists James Pennebaker, Richard Slatcher, and Cindy Chung (University of Texas at Austin), quoted by John Tierney, "Positive Words, Negative Effect," *New York Times*, February 29, 2004, p. 18.

we force the spring. A *spring reborn* in the world's oldest democracy that brings forth the visions and courage to reinvest in America.[5]

ELOQUENT STYLE

Eloquence is the ability to phrase thoughts and feelings in a way that makes them clear *and* memorable. Eloquent language does not have to be flowery or grand; it can use an oral style, personal pronouns, and the power of repetition and metaphors. Statements such as Abraham Lincoln's "government of the people, by the people, for the people shall not perish from the earth" are memorable and inspiring because (in

Why is Martin Luther King's eloquent 1963 *I Have a Dream* speech often rated as the greatest speech ever delivered in the United States?

addition to the alliteration and despite myths to the contrary) Lincoln spent considerable time and effort searching for the best words to communicate his thoughts and feelings.[6] Several language strategies can help you achieve a more eloquent speaking style. These include intense language and poetic language.

Intense Language   A second way to add eloquence to a presentation is to vary the intensity of your language. **Language intensity** refers to the degree to which your language deviates from bland, neutral terms.[7] Effective speakers use intense language to get attention and signal importance. Instead of *nice*, try using *delightful* or *enchanting*. *Disaster* is more powerful than *mistake*. A *vile* meal sounds much worse than a *bad* one. Research suggests that audiences perceive a speaker as more credible (competent, of good character, and charismatic) as the speaker's language intensifies. However, speakers who are too intense or who don't vary their levels of intensity may lose credibility.[8]

Poetic Language   Good poetry has the remarkable ability to capture profound ideas and feelings in a few simple words. Chapter 13, "Presentations: Content and Structure," suggests the use of poetry as a method for concluding a presentation because it encompasses all three concluding goals: It's memorable, clear, and brief. When faced with making a eulogy or paying tribute to someone, speakers often turn to great poets whose words eloquently express deeply felt thoughts and feelings.

In addition to rhetorical devices, you might consider using a common poetic device: rhyme. **Rhyme** occurs when words correspond with one another in terms of final sounds. Rhyme can make a phrase easier to remember, even though it also gives the phrase a singsong quality. A study of rhyme by communication scholar Matthew McGlone concludes that rhyme makes ordinary statements more believable.[9] A statement such as "Woes unite foes" was deemed more credible than one like "Woes unite enemies."

Modes of Delivery

The term **delivery** is used to describe the ways in which a speaker expresses a message. If you think about the literal definition of the word *delivery*, it makes sense. When you deliver something, you send, transport, or convey it to a place or person. In this chapter, the terms *delivery* and *expression* are used interchangeably to describe how you use your voice, body, and presentation aids to convey your message.

Whether you rely on a few note cards or read from a manuscript, your decisions about delivery affect whether your audience responds positively or negatively to you and your message. Just as you made decisions about your self, others, purpose, context, content, and structure, you will make decisions about how to use your voice, body, and presentation aids to achieve your purpose.

One of the first decisions to make is which delivery mode will suit your purpose. You will need to decide which form of expression to use: impromptu, extemporaneous, manuscript, memorized, or a combination of forms.

IMPROMPTU

Impromptu speaking occurs when you give a presentation without advanced preparation or practice. For example, you may be called upon in class or at work to answer a question or share an opinion. You may be inspired to get up and speak on an important issue at a public meeting, religious gathering, or celebration.

Even though you don't have enough time to stop and give a lot of thought to all seven elements of human communication, you can very quickly think of a purpose and the ways in which you can organize and adapt your message to the audience. The more experience you have as a speaker, the more instinctive the "basics" become,

Figure 14.2	Advantages and Disadvantages of Impromptu Delivery

Advantages	Disadvantages
• Natural and conversational speaking style • Maximum eye contact • Freedom of movement • Easier to adjust to audience feedback • Demonstrates speaker's knowledge and skill	• Limited time for making basic decisions about purpose, audience adaptation, and organization • Speaking anxiety can be high • Delivery may be awkward and ineffective • Difficult to gauge speaking time • Limited or no supporting material • Speaker may have nothing to say on such short notice

even in impromptu speaking. Figure 14.2 lists the advantages and disadvantages of impromptu delivery.

EXTEMPORANEOUS

Extemporaneous speaking is the most common form of delivery and occurs when you use an outline or a set of notes to guide yourself through a prepared presentation. Your notes can be a few words on a card or a detailed outline that reflects the decisions you have made in the preparation process. Classroom lectures, business briefings, and courtroom arguments are usually delivered extemporaneously. Extemporaneous speaking also is the type of delivery that is easiest for beginners to do well and the method preferred by professionals. No other form of delivery gives you as much freedom and flexibility with preplanned material, as illustrated in Figure 14.3.

Notice, in Figure 14.3, that the advantages of extemporaneous speaking far outweigh the disadvantages. Extemporaneous speaking gives the audience the impression that you are speaking spontaneously. Because what you are saying is well planned and well rehearsed, you can change things around to adapt to the audience, the circumstances, and the setting. Because it's not restricted by a manuscript, a well-practiced extemporaneous presentation has an ease to it that makes both audience and speaker feel more comfortable.

MANUSCRIPT

Manuscript speaking involves writing your presentation in advance and reading it out loud. Using a manuscript allows you to choose each word carefully. You can plan and practice every detail. It also ensures that your presentation will fit within your allotted speaking time. For very nervous speakers, a manuscript can be a life-saving document.

However, manuscript presentations are difficult to deliver for all but the most skilled and practiced speakers. If you must use a manuscript, *write it as though you are speaking*. Use all

What delivery advantages does former Olympic athlete Mary Lou Retton have by delivering a presentation in an impromptu mode?

| Figure 14.3 | Advantages and Disadvantages of Extemporaneous Delivery |

Advantages	Disadvantages
• Allows more preparation time than impromptu delivery	• Speaker anxiety can increase for content not covered by notes
• Seems spontaneous but is actually well prepared	• Language may not be well chosen or eloquent
• Speaker can monitor and adapt to audience feedback	• Can be difficult to estimate speaking time
• Allows more eye contact and audience interaction than manuscript delivery	
• Audiences respond positively to extemporaneous delivery	
• Speaker can choose concise language for central idea and key points	
• With practice, it becomes the most powerful form of delivery	

the guidelines we provide about the difference between oral and written style. Like most instructors and consultants, we do not encourage our students or clients to use manuscript delivery. Yet there are occasions when a word-for-word manuscript is either necessary or very helpful. If the occasion is an important public event at which every word counts and time is strictly limited, you may have no choice but to use a manuscript. If you will be speaking "on the record" and do not want to be misunderstood or misinterpreted, you will want to make sure that you are quoted accurately. If the occasion is highly emotional (such as a funeral eulogy or a prestigious award presentation), you may need the support provided by a manuscript. As Figure 14.4 notes, the most significant disadvantages are inappropriate or too formal word choice, poor reading, and inflexibility.

| Figure 14.4 | Advantages and Disadvantages of Manuscript Delivery |

Advantages	Disadvantages
• Can pay careful attention to all the basic principles of effective speaking	• Delivery can be dull
• Can choose concise and eloquent language	• Sufficient eye contact is difficult to maintain
• Speaker anxiety may be eased by having a "script"	• Gestures and movement are limited
• Can rehearse the same presentation over and over	• Language can be too formal, lacking oral style
• Ensures accurate reporting of presentation content	• It is difficult to modify or adapt to the audience or situation
• Speaker can stay within time limit	

Figure 14.5	Advantages and Disadvantages of Memorized Delivery

Advantages	Disadvantages
• Incorporates the preparation advantages of manuscript delivery and the delivery advantages of impromptu speaking • Maximizes eye contact and freedom of movement	• Requires extensive time to memorize • Disaster awaits if memory fails • Can sound stilted and insincere • Very difficult to modify or adapt to the audience or situation • Can lack sense of spontaneity unless expertly delivered

MEMORIZED

A memorized presentation offers a speaker one major advantage and one major disadvantage when compared with the other three forms of delivery. The major advantage is physical freedom. You can gesture freely and look at your audience 100 percent of the time. The disadvantage, however, outweighs any and all advantages. If you forget the words you memorized, it is more difficult to recover your thoughts without creating an awkward moment for both you and your audience.

Rarely do speakers memorize an entire presentation. However, there's nothing wrong with trying to memorize your introduction or a few key sections, as long as you have your notes to fall back on. If you decide to memorize portions of a presentation, make sure you are well aware of the potential pitfalls, as illustrated in Figure 14.5.

USING NOTES EFFECTIVELY

Regardless of what form of delivery you select, be ready to use notes effectively. Even when you are speaking impromptu, you may use a few quick words jotted down just before the presentation. Remember to keep your notes nearby in case you lose track of your thoughts.

Using Index Cards and Outlines Extemporaneous speakers often use index cards to record key points and supporting material. Think of each index card as a visual aid. Provide yourself with just enough information to trigger an idea or to supply a vital piece of supporting information and its source.

If you put your notes on index cards, which works especially well for extemporaneous speaking, follow these guidelines:

- *Use key words.* Use key words rather than complete sentences on each card. Manuscripts do not fit and do not belong on note cards. If you can't fit your notes on a few index cards, consider using the presentation outline suggested in Chapter 13, "Presentations: Content and Structure."
- *Use fewer cards.* Use one for your introduction, one for each key point, and one for your conclusion. Fewer cards are much better than a huge stack.
- *Use only one side of a note card.* Fiddling with and flipping cards can distract and confuse you, particularly if you can't remember whether you have used the other side or not.

- *Number the cards.* This will keep your presentation organized and allows you to rearrange key points at the last minute. Make sure your cards are in the proper order before you begin speaking.

- *Practice using your notes.* You may discover that you have too many or too few cards.

Using a Manuscript   You face a delivery challenge if you decide to write portions of a presentation or an entire presentation in manuscript form. The disadvantages of manuscript speaking include difficulty maintaining sufficient eye contact as well as dull delivery. The following guidelines will help you use your manuscript more effectively:

- *Make it readable.* Use large fonts (fourteen to sixteen point) and double spacing.

- *Number your pages.* Make sure that they stay in order.

- *Type only on the top two-thirds of the page.* This way you don't have to bend your head to see the bottom of each page, a movement that will cause you to lose eye contact and will constrict your windpipe in such a way that your voice can sound muffled.[10]

- *Use page breaks.* Make sure that none of your sentences run over to a new page.

- *Use wide margins.* Wide margins give you a place to make last-minute changes or additions to your manuscript.

- *Do not staple the pages together.* Instead, place your manuscript to one side of the lectern and slide the pages to the other side when it's time to go on to the next page.

Marking up Your Notes and Manuscripts   If you are going to use a manuscript, you can make it easier to use by marking it up. Marking up your notes and manuscript provides additional "punctuation" that tells you which words or phrases to emphasize as well as when to pause, gesture, or move. The following list represents a few of the common graphics for presentation manuscripts that are available on most word processing programs:

/	Short pause
//	Medium pause
///	Long pause
◄	Speak louder
➤	Speak softer
▲	Speak faster
▼	Speak slower
★	Key point or important sentence follows
✖	Stop and look up for a reaction
☺	Smile
❒ ❶	Slide 1
❒ ❷	Slide 2

In addition to using these or other symbols, you can underline or **boldface** words that should be emphasized. Some speakers use a bright highlighting pen or similar computer feature to make important words and phrases stand out. Or you can increase the font size to indicate a very important word or series of words.

Learning how to deliver a presentation in impromptu, extemporaneous, manuscript, and memorized forms lets you select the method that works best for you and your purpose. It also allows you to vary your delivery style within a presentation. Don't hesitate to mix and match these delivery modes when appropriate. An impromptu speaker may recite a memorized statistic or a rehearsed argument in the same way that a politician responds to press questions. An extemporaneous speaker may read a lengthy quotation or a series of statistics and then deliver a memorized ending. For example, at the end of most political debates, candidates are given an opportunity to make a short state-ment. In most cases, statements are strategically devel-oped, written out, and then memorized well in advance of the debate. A manuscript reader may stop and tell an impromptu story or may deliver memorized sections that benefit from uninterrupted and direct eye contact with the audience. A speaker can pause in a memorized presentation to repeat a key phrase or to reexplain an idea. Your decision about which delivery form or forms to use is important, and, under most circumstances, it will be yours to make.[1]

[1]Isa N. Engleberg and John A. Daly, *Presentations in Everyday Life: Strategies for Effective Speaking*, 2nd ed. (Boston: Houghton Mifflin, 2005), p. 325.

Bullet points also provide a convenient way of breaking up a list or series of words. Bullet points in a manuscript do more than highlight a list or series of ideas; they also tell you when to take a breath and pause between those ideas.

Vocal Delivery

Only a few lucky speakers are born with beautiful voices. The majority of us must work at sounding clear and expressive. Fortunately, there are ways to improve the characteristics and quality of your voice.

Developing a more effective speaking voice requires the same time and effort that you would devote to mastering any skill. You don't learn to be an accomplished carpenter, pianist, swimmer, writer, or speaker overnight. You need to learn the basics first: breathing, volume, rate, pitch, fluency, articulation, and pronunciation.

BREATHING

All the sounds in spoken English are made during exhalation. In fact, we control and use air in much the same way that a trumpet player applies breath to the mouthpiece of the instrument. The key to effective breathing for presentation speaking is control-ling your outgoing breath, not just inhaling and holding more air in your lungs. Effec-tive breath control improves the sound of your voice in several ways:

- *Volume.* Effective breath control amplifies the loudness of your voice.
- *Duration.* Effective breath control lets you say more with a single breath.
- *Quality.* Effective breath control reduces the likelihood of vocal problems such as harshness or breathiness.

Voice coaches—whether they are teaching speakers or singers—always begin with breathing. Whether they call it *deep breathing*, *abdominal breathing*, or *dia-phragmatic breathing*, they insist that students learn how to breathe more efficiently and effectively. Thus, the first step in learning how to breathe for presentation speak-ing is to note the differences between the shallow, unconscious breathing you do all the time and the deeper breathing that produces strong, sustained sound quality.

IMPORTANT VOCAL CHARACTERISTICS

▶ Breathing
▶ Volume
▶ Rate
▶ Pitch
▶ Fluency
▶ Articulation
▶ Pronunciation

The following exercise demonstrates how to breathe properly for a presentation:

1. Lie flat on your back. Support the back of your knees with a pillow.
2. Place a moderately heavy, hard-bound book on your stomach, right over your navel.
3. Begin breathing through your mouth. The book should move up when you breathe in and sink down when you breathe out.
4. Place one of your hands on the upper part of your chest in a "Pledge of Allegiance" position. As you inhale and exhale, this area should *not* move in and out or up and down.
5. Take the book away and replace it with your other hand. You abdominal area should continue to move up when you breathe in and sink down when you breathe out.
6. After you're comfortable with step 5, try doing the same kind of breathing while sitting up or standing.
7. Add sound. Try sighing and sustaining the vowel *ahh* for five seconds with each exhalation. Then try counting or saying the alphabet.

Although your progress may be slow (it often takes singers years to perfect this kind of breathing), your efforts will reward you with a strong and more controllable voice.

VOLUME

Volume measures your voice's degree of loudness. The key to producing adequate volume is knowing the size of the audience you will be addressing and the dimensions of the room in which you will be speaking. Experienced speakers use these factors to adjust their volume automatically. You can do the same. If there are only five people in an audience and they are sitting close to you, then speak at a normal, everyday volume. If there are fifty people in your audience, you need more energy and force behind your voice. When your audience exceeds fifty—and you're going to speak for more than fifteen minutes, you may be more comfortable with a microphone. How-

How should a speaker rallying employees protesting a bill that limits their medical benefits adapt his delivery when speaking to a large crowd in an outdoor setting?

If the speaking situation requires a microphone or presents you with one, make the most out of this technology. Unless a sound technician is monitoring the presentation, your microphone will be preset for one volume. If you speak with too much volume, it may sound as though you are shouting at your audience. If you speak too softly, the microphone may not pick up everything you have to say. The trick is to go against your instincts. If you want to project a soft tone, speak closer to the microphone and lower your volume. Your voice will sound more intimate and will convey subtle emotions. If you want to be more forceful, speak farther away from the microphone and project your voice. This technique will make your presentation sound more powerful.

Most important, familiarize yourself with the specific microphone and system you will be using. For example, when placed on a lapel, the microphone faces outward rather than upward. As a result, it receives and sends a less direct sound. At the same time, it also hides inhalations and exhalations of breath as well as nose sniffles.[1] Here are some tips to follow for all microphones:

- Test the microphone ahead of time.
- Determine whether the microphone is sophisticated enough to capture your voice from several angles and distances or whether you will need to keep your mouth close to it.
- Place the microphone about five to ten inches from your mouth. If you are using a hand-held microphone, hold it below your mouth at chin level.
- Focus on your audience, not the microphone. Stay near the mike, but don't tap it, lean over it, keep readjusting it, or make the p-p-p-p-p "motorboat sounds" as a test. Experienced speakers make the adjustments they need during the first few seconds that they hear their own voice projected through an amplification system.
- Keep in mind that a microphone will do more than amplify your voice; it will also amplify other sounds—coughing, clearing your throat, shuffling papers, or tapping a pen.
- If your microphone is well adjusted, speak in a natural, conversational voice.

[1]Ty Ford, *Ty Ford's Audio Bootcamp Field Guide* (Baltimore, MD: Technique, Inc., 2004), p. 19.

---

ever, a strong speaking voice can project to an audience of a thousand people without any electronic amplification. Professional speakers, actors, and classical singers do it all the time, but they also spend years developing the power of their voices.

Practice your presentation in a room about the same size as the one in which you will be speaking, or, at least, imagine speaking in such a room. Ask a friend to sit in a far corner and report back on your volume and clarity. Also note that a room full of people absorbs sound; you will have to turn up your volume another notch. Speakers who cannot be heard are a common problem. It's very rare, though, for a speaker to be too loud.

To reach all audience members, learn to project. **Projection** is controlled vocal energy "that gives thrust, precision, and intelligibility to sound." It involves a deliberate concentration and a strong desire to communicate with your listeners. When you project, your voice "does more than reach them; it penetrates them."[11] Like many speakers, you may tend to speak to people sitting right in front of you. You don't need a loud voice to be heard by someone five feet away. It's the person in the back row who will strain to hear you. Simply looking at people in the back row and deliberately thinking about making them hear you can automatically increase your volume.

RATE

Your **rate** of presentation equals the number of words you say per minute (wpm). Generally, a rate less than 125 wpm is too slow, 125 to 145 wpm is acceptable, 145 to 180 wpm is better, and 180 wpm or more exceeds the speed limit. But do not carve these guidelines in stone. Your rate depends on you, the nature and mood of your message, and your audience. If you are explaining a highly technical process or expressing personal sorrow, your rate may slow to 125 wpm. On the other hand, if you are telling an exciting, amusing, or infuriating story, your rate may hit 200 wpm. For maximum effectiveness, speakers vary their rate. For example, Martin Luther King's "I Have a Dream" speech opened at approximately 90 wpm, but ended at 150 wpm.[12]

In most cases, it's better to speak a little too fast than too slowly. Listeners perceive presenters who speak quickly *and* clearly as energized, motivated, and interested. Given the choice, we'd rather be accused of speaking too fast than run the risk of boring an audience. Too slow a rate suggests that you are unsure of yourself or, even worse, that you are not very bright. Remember that audiences can listen faster than you can talk, so it's better to keep the pace up than speak at a crawl. Practice reading passages that contain 140 to 180 words to see if you can complete them with clarity and comfort in sixty seconds.

PITCH

Pitch refers to how high or low your voice sounds—just like the notes on a musical scale. Anatomy determines pitch (most men speak at a lower pitch than women and children). The key to an effective pitch is finding your natural or **optimum pitch**, the pitch at which you speak most easily and expressively. At your optimum pitch, your voice

- will be stronger and less likely to fade at the end of sentences
- will not tire easily
- will be less likely to sound harsh, hoarse, or breathy
- will be more expressive and energetic

One way to find your optimum pitch is to sing up the scale from the lowest note you can sing. When you reach the fifth or sixth note, you should be at your optimum pitch. Test your optimum pitch to see if you can increase its volume with minimal effort and if your voice is clear at that pitch.

Finding your optimum pitch does *not* mean using that pitch for everything you say. Think of your optimum pitch as "neutral," and use it as your baseline for increasing the expressiveness of your voice. Expressive speakers use inflection to vary their pitch. **Inflection** is the changing pitch within a syllable, word, or group of words. Inflection makes speech expressive; lack of it results in a monotone voice. A **monotone** voice occurs not because you use the wrong pitch or speak slowly, but because you don't change the pitch of sounds within words or the pitch of words within phrases and sentences.

Inflection helps you to avoid a monotone voice and allows you to emphasize an important or meaningful word or phrase. When speaking from a manuscript, we recommend underlining words that should receive extra stress or emphasis. More often than not, varying pitch sets a word apart from the rest of a sentence. A single change in inflection changes the entire meaning of a sentence:

I was born in New Jersey. You, on the other hand, were born in Iowa.

I *was* born in New Jersey. No doubt about it!

I was *born* in New Jersey. So I know my way around.

I was born in *New Jersey.* Not in New York.

Inflection may not seem important given that the change in pitch can be a fraction of a note. Yet, like the effects of any strong spice, a small increase or decrease in inflection can change the meaning of a sentence or the quality of your voice.

CommFAQ How Can I Prevent My Voice from Shaking?

An assistant superintendent of schools in New York told us: "My problem—my voice quivers!" When you speak louder and more forcefully, you may perceive the sound of any vocal variation more intensely because your speaking voice is amplified in your head. Most of the time, the audience does not hear anything distracting in your voice. However, if the shaking of your voice is obvious, you can take a few steps to minimize it:

- Make sure your breathing and volume are appropriate for the presentation, which in turn ensures a strong and steady stream of air.

- Make sure you are speaking at your optimum pitch.
- Review ways of reducing any presentation anxiety that may be responsible for your quavering voice.

FLUENCY

Fluency is the ability to speak smoothly without tripping over words or pausing at awkward moments. The more you practice your presentation, the more fluent you will become. Practice will alert you to words, phrases, and sentences that look good in your notes but sound awkward or choppy when spoken. You'll also find words that you have trouble pronouncing.

Too many filler phrases can impede a speaker's fluency. Annoying **filler phrases** such as *you know*, *uh*, *um*, *okay*, and *like* break up your fluency and can annoy your audience. There is nothing wrong with an occasional filler phrase, particularly when you're speaking informally or impromptu. What you want to avoid is excessive and unconscious use of these phrases. Try tape-recording your practice sessions and listen for filler phrases as you play the tape back. To break the filler phrase habit, slow down and listen to yourself as you practice and as you speak. Do the same when you're not giving a presentation. To break the habit, you must work on it all the time, not just when you are speaking in front of an audience.

ARTICULATION

A strong, well-paced, optimally pitched voice that is also fluent and expressive may not be enough to ensure the successful delivery of a presentation. Proper articulation is just as important as your volume, rate, pitch, and fluency. **Articulation** describes how clearly you make the sounds in the words of a language. Poor articulation is often described as sloppy speech, poor diction, or mumbling. Fortunately, you can improve and practice your articulation by speaking more slowly, speaking with a bit more volume, and opening your mouth wider when you speak.

Certain sounds account for most articulation problems: combined words, "-ing" endings, and final consonants. Many speakers combine words—"what's the matter" becomes "watsumata." Some speakers shorten the "ing" sound to an "in" sound: "sayin'" instead of "saying." The final consonants that get left off most often are the ones that pop out of your mouth. Because these consonants—*p, b, t, d, k, g*—cannot be hummed like an "m" or hissed like an "s," it's easy to lose them at the end of a word. Usually you can hear the difference between "Rome," and "rose," but poor articulation can make it difficult to hear the difference between "hit" and "hid" or "tap" and "tab."

If Standard American English is not your first language and you believe that audiences may have trouble understanding you, work on your articulation and keep checking your pronunciation. Here are specific suggestions:

- *Study and practice.* Identify and work on Standard American English sounds that are difficult for you to make. Consult a good pronunciation dictionary or a voice and diction textbook.
- *Slow down.* Slow down in your introduction so that audience members have time to become accustomed to your accent. Slow down when you state a key point or share a significant piece of supporting material.
- *Substitute.* If a particular word is very difficult to pronounce, find an equally good word as a substitute.

- *Listen to good speakers.* Use good speakers as models. Listen to them in person, on television and radio, or on tape. Try repeating short phrases and sentences using the same articulation, pronunciation, and style.
- *Ask for feedback.* Depending on the size and characteristics of your audience as well as the formality of the occasion, you can ask audience members for feedback. Ask if they understand a problematic word or phrase. In most cases, you will be perfectly understood.
- *Practice, practice, practice.* Practice in private, practice on tape, and practice in front of someone who speaks Standard English.

PRONUNCIATION

Pronunciation refers to whether you say a word correctly, whether you put all the correct sounds in the correct order with the correct stress. In a presentation speaking situation, poor pronunciation results in misunderstanding and embarrassment. One of us heard a speaker give a presentation on the importance of pronunciation, but she undermined her effectiveness by repeatedly saying the word *pronunciation* incorrectly. Over and over again, she said "pro*noun*ciation,"—pronouncing "noun" rather than "nun" in the middle of the word.

Pronunciations can and do change. For example, according to most dictionaries, the word *often* should be pronounced "awfen," but many people now put the "t" sound in the middle so it's pronounced the way it's spelled. The word *a* should be pronounced "uh," not rhyme with *hay*, but many people now use both versions. Even the word *the* is often mispronounced. When *the* appears before the sound of a consonant as in "the dog" or "the paper," it should be pronounced "thuh." When *the* comes before the sound of a vowel as in "the alligator," or "the article," it should be pronounced "thee."

Physical Delivery

The key to effective physical delivery is a natural delivery style. It tells your audience a great deal about who you are and how much you care about reaching them. However, being natural doesn't mean "letting it all hang out." Rather, it means being so well prepared and well practiced that your presentation is an authentic reflection of you.

Audience members jump to conclusions about speakers based on first impressions of their appearance and behavior. The way you stand, move, gesture, and make eye contact has a significant impact on your presentation.

EYE CONTACT

Eye contact may be the most important component of effective physical delivery. Quite simply, **eye contact** is establishing and maintaining direct, visual links with individual members of your audience. Eye contact does more than ensure that you are looking in the direction of your audience. Effective eye contact helps you initiate and control communication, enhances your credibility, and helps you to interpret valuable audience feedback.

Control   Effective eye contact can initiate and control communication. Have you ever noticed a teacher "catch the eye" of her students, or "give the eye" to inattentive students? When you establish initial eye contact with your audience, you indicate that you are ready to begin speaking and that they should get ready to listen. Lack of eye contact communicates a message too: It says that you don't care to connect with your audience. After all, if you don't look at your audience, why should they look at you?

Credibility   Eye contact communicates that you are competent, confident, and caring. It has the power to make people listen. Direct eye contact says, "I'm talking to *you*; I want *you* to hear this." Direct eye contact transforms the speaker from an impersonal messenger into someone worth listening to.

Eye contact also has a direct and positive effect on your credibility.[13] It says: I'm of good character (I care enough to share this important message with you), I'm competent (I know this subject so well I can leave my notes and look at you), and I'm charismatic (I want to energize and connect with everyone in this room). Looking directly at your audience shows your dedication to open and honest communication. At least in western cultures, people who seek and maintain eye contact while speaking, whether face-to-face or before an audience of thousands, tend to be more believable.

Feedback   Eye contact is the best way to gauge audience feedback during a presentation. At first, looking at audience members eye-to-eye may distract you. Some people smile, others may look bored or confused, and some will be looking around the room or passing a note to a friend. With all this going on in the audience, it's easy to become sidetracked, wondering why there are so many different reactions. Those different responses can be unsettling until you realize that those responses are the very reason you must establish and maintain eye contact. Looking at the individual members of your audience can tell you whether they are interested, bored, delighted, or displeased. Speakers who don't look at their audiences rarely have a clue about why their presentations succeed or fail. Eye contact gives you a wealth of information about you and your presentation. When you see that your audience is attentive and interested, you may gain more confidence and enthusiasm. When you speak to an audience

- talk to them and look at them the same way you would talk and look at a friend, coworker, or customer
- move your gaze around the room, settle on someone, and establish direct eye contact
- switch your eye contact to someone else—someone sitting near the person whom you just looked at or someone all the way across the room
- don't move your eyes in a rigid pattern; try to establish eye contact with as many individual people as you can

Generally, the more eye contact you have with your audience, the better. Try to maintain eye contact with your audience during most of your presentation. If you are using detailed notes or a manuscript, use a technique called *eye scan*. **Eye scan**

COMPONENTS OF PHYSICAL DELIVERY
▶ Eye Contact
▶ Facial Expression
▶ Gestures
▶ Posture and Movement

involves training your eyes to glance at a specific section of your notes or manuscript, to focus on a phrase or sentence, to look back up at your audience, and to speak. Begin by placing your thumb and index finger on one side of the page to frame the section of your notes you are using. Then, as you approach the end of a phrase or sentence within that section, glance down again and visually grasp the next phrase to be spoken. This allows you to maintain maximum eye contact without losing your place.

FACIAL EXPRESSION

Whether you are speaking to one person or to one hundred people, your audience will be interpreting your facial expression. According to Mark Knapp and Judith Hall, experts in nonverbal communication, your face reflects your attitudes and emotional states, provides nonverbal feedback, and, next to the words you speak, is the primary source of information about you.[14]

Despite the enormous consequences of facial expression, it is difficult to control. We tend to display a particular style of facial expression. Some people show little expression—they have a serious, poker face most of the time. Others are as open as a book—you have little doubt about how they feel. It's very difficult, therefore, to change a "poker face" into an "open book" or vice versa. Adding to the difficulty are the effects of nervousness. A nervous speaker may be too distracted to smile, too frightened to stop smiling, or too giddy to register displeasure or anger when appropriate.

Audiences will direct their eyes at your face, so unless your topic is very solemn or serious, try to smile. A smile shows your listeners that you are comfortable and eager to share your ideas and information. Audience members are more likely to smile if you smile. However, if you do not feel comfortable smiling, don't force it. Let your face communicate your feelings; let your face do what comes naturally. If you speak honestly and sincerely, your facial expression will be appropriate and effective.

GESTURES

A **gesture** is a body movement that conveys or reinforces a thought, an intention, or an emotion. Most gestures are made with the hands and arms, but shrugging a shoulder, bending a knee, and tapping a foot are gestures, too. Gestures can clarify and support your words, relieve nervous tension, and arouse audience attention.

A police chief talks about the department's proactive style and open system of communication at a meeting with police administrators. How does his physical delivery reinforce his message?

Eliminating distracting gestures is not easy. Repetitive movements such as constantly pushing your eyeglasses, tapping on a lectern, and jingling change or keys in your pocket can distract and eventually annoy an audience. One of the best ways to eliminate unwanted gestures is to videotape and then watch your practice session. When you see how often you fidget, you'll work even harder to correct your behavior.

POSTURE AND MOVEMENT

Posture and movement involve how you stand and move, and whether your movements add or detract from your presentation. Your posture communicates. If you stand comfortably and confidently, you will radiate alertness and control. If you stoop or look unsure on your feet, you will communicate anxiety or disinterest. Try to stand straight but not rigid. Your feet should be about one foot apart. If you stand tall, lean forward, and keep your chin up, you will open your airways and help make your voice both clear and loud.

In general, a movement can attract attention, channel nervous energy, or support and emphasize a point you are making. Movement gives you short pauses during which you can collect your thoughts or give the audience a moment to ponder what you have said.

If your presentation is formal or your audience large, you will probably have a lectern. The key is learning how to take advantage of a lectern without allowing it to act as a barrier. Two distracting lectern habits deserve mention. In your desire to connect with an audience, don't lean over your lectern. It may look as though you and the lectern are about to come crashing down into the audience. Second, avoid hitting the lectern or tapping it with a pen or pointer while you speak. Given that a microphone is often attached to the lectern, the tapping can become a deafening noise.

Although lecterns can become a crutch or a protective barrier between the speaker and the audience, they have many advantages if used well. Lecterns provide a place to put your notes, a spot to focus audience attention, and even an electrical outlet for a light and microphone.

When possible *and* appropriate, speak without a lectern or come out from behind the lectern and speak at its side. In this way, you can remain close to your notes but also get closer to the audience.

The National Speakers Association of nearly four thousand professional speakers asked its members for their top tips for a successful presentation. One tip received more than 35 percent of the vote for first in importance—practice![1] Even the simplest talk can become a simply terrific talk if you practice.

Practice requires more than repeating your presentation over and over again. Practice can tell you whether there are words that you have trouble pronouncing or sentences that are too long to say in one breath. In addition, it may help you discover that what you thought was a ten-minute talk takes thirty minutes to deliver. Practicing with presentation aids is critical, particularly if you've seen the embarrassing results when speakers don't have their visuals in order. It's not a question of whether you should practice; rather, it's deciding what aspects of your performance need the most practice. Practicing is the only way to make sure that you sound and look good in a presentation.[2] To put it another way, "give your speech *before* you give it."[3]

Practice can take many forms. It can be as simple as closing your door and rehearsing your presentation in private or as complex as a full, onstage, videotaped rehearsal in front of a volunteer audience. The ways in which you can practice range from a quick look at your notes to a major dress rehearsal. Here are some do's and don'ts that can help you get the most out of practicing:

- Do not memorize your presentation. Not only do memorized presentations sound memorized, you run the risk of forgetting. If you must memorize even a small portion of a presentation, practice so it sounds natural.
- Practice wherever and whenever you can. If you have a long commute to work or school, turn off the radio and practice portions of your presentation out loud. Practice while you exercise, while you shower, when there's no one around to interrupt or distract you.
- Time your practice session and understand that your actual presentation will take longer. So if you are scheduled for a ten-minute speech, make sure it only takes eight minutes in a practice session.
- Audio tape and, if possible, videotape your practice sessions.
- Practice in front of a friend or a small volunteer audience. Listen carefully to their comments and decide which ones can help you improve your presentation.

[1]Cyndi Maxey and Kevin E. O'Connor, *Present Like a Pro* (New York: St. Martin's Griffin, 2006), p. 50.
[2]Isa N. Engleberg and John A. Daly, *Presentations in Everyday Life: Strategies for Effective Speaking*, 2nd ed. (Boston: Houghton Mifflin, 2005), p. 328.
[3]Peggy Noonan, *Simply Speaking: How to Communicate Your Ideas with Style, Substance, and Clarity* (New York: HarperCollins, 1998), p. 9.

Presentation Aids

We use the term **presentation aids** to refer to the many supplementary resources—most often in visual form—available to speakers for highlighting key ideas and supporting material. Presentation aids are not only for presentations. They also have a strong presence in group meetings and individualized interactions, such as when explaining a medical procedure to a group of interns or making a sales pitch to a potential customer.

MyCommunicationLab Chapter B, "Effective Presentation Aids," builds on the basic information we provide here and offers hands-on advice about ways to prepare presentation aids that transform an acceptable talk into a memorable experience for everyone.

FUNCTIONS OF PRESENTATION AIDS

Presentation aids are more than a pretty picture or a set of exciting computer graphics. Presentation aids function to support you and your message by attracting audience attention and clarifying and reinforcing ideas. They also can compare statistics and illustrate a point. Presentation aids save you time and also help the audience learn and remember your message.

How well did this speaker design her presentation aids? How well is she presenting them to her audience?

Gain Attention   A clever cartoon, a soundtrack, or an attractive or shocking picture can gain and hold audience attention. Think of how photographs and videos of the 2005 tsunami in southern Asia helped us understand the magnitude of this tragedy. A plummeting line on a graph of company profits can drive home the urgency for a solution better than hours of talk. Attention can wane, however, if the visuals are poorly prepared or irrelevant to a presentation.

Clarify and Reinforce Ideas   Depending on the subject, presentation aids can be more effective than words in conveying meaning. Complicated directions to Jay Street in Anchorage are often easier to give if you can point to a map of Anchorage. The intricacies of a business plan can be better explained if the plan is charted, particularly if a series of slides builds the plan in stages.

    Presentation aids can even clarify and reinforce ideas for a speaker. For example, if your slides follow the outline of your presentation, they function as speaking notes. Instead of using paper notes, you can speak from the visuals. You won't forget what you want to say, and your audience can follow along as you speak.[15]

Enhance Comprehension   Common sense and academic research arrive at the same conclusion: Visual information enhances learning. Imagine the impossibility of learning human anatomy without lifelike illustrations of the heart and lungs, or the absurdity of studying American music history without listening to recordings of ragtime, jazz, and accompanying musical scores.

    In general, successful presentation aids enhance comprehension when you are

- presenting numbers and statistical data
- comparing and contrasting items or characteristics
- introducing or explaining a complicated process
- talking about something that is normally visual, like a map, an architectural design, or a fine art object such as a painting or sculpture
- giving complicated, step-by-step directions

FUNCTIONS OF PRESENTATION AIDS
- ▶ Gain Attention
- ▶ Clarify and Reinforce Ideas
- ▶ Enhance Comprehension
- ▶ Improve Efficiency

A student asked if she could do an in-class rehearsal of a presentation she was scheduled to give at work to an important group of clients. She had an absolutely stunning multimedia presentation filled with animation, bright colors, extraordinary sound effects, and delightful, even funny pictures. When it was over, the class had only one criticism. Most of her visuals had little to do with what she was talking about. She had fallen in love with her visuals and was committed to using them—even though they were not relevant.

Emotionally interesting but irrelevant pictures actually depress learning and comprehension among readers and listeners. **Seductive details** refers to the elements in a message that attract audience attention but do not support the writer's or speaker's key points.[1] Instead of learning, audience members are "seduced" and distracted by interesting scenes, dramatic graphics, vivid colors, and engaging motion. Even when images are relevant to the presentation topic, they can make the information seem too easy and effortless to understand. Moreover, seductive details can confuse audience members about the meaning or purpose of the presentation.[2]

Make sure that the images you use are directly relevant to the purpose and topic of your presentation. Time spent viewing relevant images helps audience members understand the concepts you are presenting.

Here are more ways to minimize the effects of seductive details:

- *Minimize the competition between pictures and written text*. If you have a vivid picture or dramatic graphic, display the slide accompanied by only the most important key words. Then follow the slide with a more detailed explanation.
- *Avoid using background sound effects or music*. They distract an audience from you and your message.
- *Encourage visualization*. When you want your audience to appreciate and learn a concept, give them just enough visual information so that they can construct or imagine their own version of the message. Just as radio shows and recorded books serve as a medium of the imagination, effective presentation aids encourage audience members to apply concepts and visualize consequences in their own lives, jobs, and world.

[1]See Ruth Clark, "Six Principles of Effective e-Learning: What Works and Why," *The e-Learning Developers' Journal* (September 10, 2002), www.e-LearningGuild.com; and Jennifer Wiley, *Cognitive Implications of Visually Rich Media: Images and Imagination*, paper supported by grants from the Paul G. Allen Virtual Education Foundation and the Office of Naval Research, Cognitive and Neural Science and Technology Program.

[2]www.vancouver.wsu.edu/fac/kendrick/loquent/eloquentjw.htm.

Improve Efficiency   Presentation aids save time when you use a graph, drawing, or chart to summarize a complex process or a set of statistics. As instructors and consultants, we often use overhead transparencies or computer-generated slides to highlight important ideas. This way, we don't need to spend time writing on a board or flip chart, and we also save time by pointing to the critical sections of a pie chart or the key variable on a graph.

If you give listeners copies of the visual aids, you save them the time it takes to write down what you say. But be forewarned: If you give your audience a manuscript or a comprehensive outline, they may read your handout rather than listen to you speak. Even worse, if your handout includes everything you will cover in your talk, they may leave the room before your presentation begins.

PRESENTATION AIDS ARE JUST THAT: AIDS

You and your presentation come first; your presentation aid helps you achieve your purpose. Don't let your aids and their technical razzle-dazzle steal the show. Keep in mind the most basic principle of all: *Presentation aids are aids*. Don't become one of those speakers who prepare a presentation by preparing a series of slide images. Begin with your ideas, not with computer software. Outstanding speakers thoroughly prepare their presentations *before* creating their presentation aids. Prepare visuals only after carefully considering what you want to say and what you want your audience members to understand and remember.

TYPES OF PRESENTATION AIDS

Preparing effective presentation aids requires strategic thinking. Which type of aid will best achieve your purpose? Which type will be best for gaining and maintaining audience attention, clarifying and reinforcing your message, and saving time? First, it is important to understand that certain types of aids work best for specific purposes. Figure 14.6 lists types of presentation aids and briefly describes how each functions to support a presentation. MyCommunicationLab Chapter B, "Effective Presentation Aids," provides examples of each type with more detailed advice about their effective use.

| **Figure 14.6** | **Types of Presentation Aids** |

Graphs

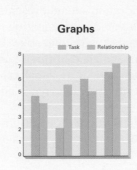

Graphs show *how much* but primarily are used to demonstrate comparisons. In addition, they can illustrate trends and clearly show increases or decreases. Graphs can be displayed using bars or lines and usually represent countable things like the number of responses to a survey question or the number of products produced over a period of time.

Tables

Tables *summarize* and *compare* data. When graphs aren't detailed enough and descriptions require too many words, tables are an effective alternative for showing numeric values. Tables also summarize and compare key features.

Pie Charts

Pie charts show *how much* by identifying proportions in relation to a whole or depicting relationships among related items. Each wedge of the pie usually represents a percentage. Most audiences comprehend pie charts quickly and easily.

Text Charts

Text charts *list* ideas or key phrases often under a title or headline. They depict goals, functions, types of formats, recommendations, and guidelines. Items listed on a text chart may be numbered, bulleted, or set apart on separate lines.

Maps

Maps show *where* by translating data into spatial patterns. Maps give directions, compare locations, or link statistical data to population characteristics.

Diagrams and Illustrations

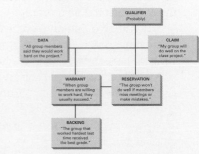

Diagrams and illustrations show *how things work*. They explain relationships or processes. They can be flow charts, organizational diagrams, or chart a process. Drawings also chart time lines, provide floor plans, and even enlarge a physical object so you can see the inside of an engine, a heart, or a flower.

Photographs and Other Aids

Photographs portray reality—a real face or place is easily recognized and can capture emotions. Other forms of presentation aids include audio recordings, objects, handouts, or physical demonstrations.

Regardless of the type, the key to selecting presentation aids is making sure that they are relevant to your topic and purpose and that they save time, gain attention, and clarify or reinforce content.

CHOOSING THE MEDIA

The first and most important decision to make in preparing presentation aids is selecting the right media for the message you are supporting. Consider your purpose, the audience, the setting, and the logistics of the situation. You may want to do a multimedia presentation, but the room where you're scheduled to speak cannot be darkened or the facility cannot provide the hardware you need for the presentation. Writing detailed notes on a board or flip chart for an audience of hundreds will frustrate listeners in the back rows. Figure 14.7 does not include all possible media, but it will help you understand how to select an appropriate medium for your audience.

Like all recommendations, there are exceptions. A corporation's team presentation to a small group of prospective clients may require a multimedia presentation to compete with other team presentations. A predesigned flip chart with huge, one- or two-word messages on each page would work in front of an audience of three hundred people whereas an overhead transparency with too much data or too-small type would not. But, in general, certain media are better suited for particular types and sizes of audiences.

The accompanying CommQuiz provides two examples that match a purpose statement with three different presentation aids that could be used to help a speaker achieve his or her purpose.

| **Figure 14.7** | **Selecting Appropriate Media** |

Media	Small Audience (50 or fewer)	Medium Audience (50–100)	Large Audience (150 or more)
Chalk/white board	✓		
Flip chart	✓		
Hand-held object	✓	✓	
Overhead transparencies	✓	✓	✓
Presentation software slides	✓	✓	✓
Videotapes/DVDs	✓	✓	✓
Multimedia	✓	✓	✓

Directions: What kinds of presentations aids do you recommend for the last two presentations?

Purpose	Presentation Aids
Purpose: To explain the parts of an internal combustion engine	• Drawing of an engine • Pieces of an engine • Animated cartoon of engine operation
Purpose: To compare rap music and blues	• Audio excerpts of each musical form • Live performance • Chart listing characteristics
Purpose: To demonstrate how to separate egg whites from egg yolks	• • •
Purpose: To learn the causes and symptoms of sickle cell anemia	• • •

DESIGN PRINCIPLES

Even with the best intentions, equipment, and cutting-edge software, presentation aids can fail to have an impact. They can be unattractive, distracting, and difficult to follow. Regardless of what type of supporting materials or which medium you choose to display them in, you can apply basic visual design principles to creating your presentation aids. Figure 14.8 (page 386) presents the most basic design principles. MyCommunicationLab Chapter B, "Effective Presentation Aids," adds additional principles and offers more detailed advice on how to improve the effectiveness of presentation aids.

HANDLING PRESENTATION AIDS

After you invest time, effort, and significant resources to plan and prepare presentation aids, make sure you handle your aids smoothly and professionally.

- *Focus on your audience, not on your aids.* Don't turn your back to the audience or stand in front of your screen or flip chart while speaking. Remember this memory aid: touch, turn, talk. Touch your aid (or refer to it with your hand or a pointer). Turn to your audience. Then talk.

- *Pick the right time to display your aids.* Decide when to introduce your aids, how long to leave them up, and when to remove them. Here is a rule of thumb: Display aids for at least the length of time it takes an average reader to read them twice. When you're finished talking about a presentation aid, get rid of it.

- *Begin with you, not your visual.* Establish rapport with your audience before you start using presentation aids. Even if you have numerous presentation aids to display, always start and end your presentation by making direct and personal contact with your audience.

- *Be prepared to do without.* Even if you are very well prepared, something can go wrong. To avoid presentation aid disasters, have a special practice session just to check your aids. Also, have a "Plan B." Can you deliver your presentation without your presentation aids? In many cases, you can. Remember that presentation aids are not the presentation; they are only there to assist you. You and your message should always come first.

Figure 14.8	Design Principles for Presentation Aids

Preview and Highlight

Presentation aids should preview your key points and highlight important facts and features.

Headline Your Visuals

Clear headlines reduce the risk that readers will misunderstand your message.

Exercise Restraint

Avoid using too many graphics, fonts, colors, and other visual elements and effects.

Choose Readable Type and Suitable Colors

Don't use more than two different fonts on a slide, a font size smaller than 24 points, or illegible colors.

Use Appropriate Graphics

Make sure your graphics are essential and support your purpose.

Communication Challenge

Customized Pronunciation Drill

Directions: Review the table of commonly mispronounced words. Use the blank boxes to add other words you hear that are frequently mispronounced. Place the mispronounced words in the appropriate category, such as substituting sounds, omitting sounds, and so on. Using the words on the list, write at least two sentences that use as many of these mispronounced words as possible. The sentences must be grammatically correct but will be unusual or nonsensical. Example: *Both Italian athletes were impotent once they were asked to take a picture of the wolf's larynx.*

Be prepared to read your sentences out loud. As a listener, identify mispronounced words while also paying attention to the speaker's volume, rate, pitch, fluency, and articulation. Pay careful attention to the pronunciation of *the* before consonants ("thuh") and vowels ("thee") as well as the pronunciation of the word *a* as "uh" rather than "ay."

Commonly Mispronounced Words				
Substituting Sounds	**Omitting Sounds**	**Adding Sounds**	**Misplacing Sounds**	**Reversing Sounds**
Anesthetist	Arctic	Accompanist	Applicable	Entrepreneur
Agile	Asphyxiate	Across	Epitome	E pluribus unum
Chasm	Berserk	Athlete	Guitar	Hundred
Et cetera	Caribbean	Corps	Impotent	Introduction
Genuine	Couldn't	Escape	Infamous	Irrelevant
Italian	February	Heir	Mischievous	Larynx
Pitcher	Library	Nuclear	Omnipotent	Perspiration
Pronunciation	Picture	Often	Preferable	Prescription
Strength	Recognize	Schism	Theater	Professor
Espresso	Miniature	Quiche	Mischievous	Entrepreneur

Sources: Lyle V. Mayer, *Fundamentals of Voice and Articulation*, 11th ed. (Madison, WI: Brown and Benchmark, 1996), pp. 154–263; Lyle V. Mayer, *Fundamentals of Voice and Articulation*, 12th ed. (Boston: McGraw-Hill, 1999), pp. 254–258; Lyle V. Mayer, *Fundamentals of Voice and Articulation*, 13th ed. (Boston: McGraw-Hill, 2004), pp. 254–260; Susan D. Miller, *Be Heard the First Time: A Woman's Guide to Powerful Speaking* (Herndon, VA: Capital Books, 2006), p. 106.

Communication Assessment

Performance Assessment

Speaker: _____

Evaluator: _____

Directions: Use the following ratings to assess each of the competencies on the performance assessment instrument: E = excellent, G = good, A = average, W = weak, M = missing, N/A = not applicable.

<u>COMMENTS</u>

Competencies	E	G	A	W	M	N/A
Preparation and Practice						
Extent of preparation and practice						
Use of limited notes and manuscript						
Vocal Delivery						
Volume						
Rate						
Pitch						
Fluency						
Variety						
Articulation						
Pronunciation						
Physical Delivery						
Eye contact						
Facial expression						
Gestures						
Posture and movement						
Modes of Delivery						
Memorized						
Manuscript						
Extemporaneous						
Impromptu						
Presentation aids						
Overall Assessment						

Key Terms

alliteration
articulation
delivery
eloquence
extemporaneous speaking
eye contact
eye scan
filler phrase
gesture

impromptu speaking
inflection
language intensity
manuscript speaking
monotone
optimum pitch
pitch
presentation aid
presentation performance

projection
pronunciation
rate
rhetorical device
rhyme
seductive detail
speaking style
volume

Notes

1. Sections of Chapters 12 through 16 are based on Isa N. Engleberg and John A. Daly, *Presentations in Everyday Life: Strategies for Effective Speaking*, 2nd ed. (Boston: Houghton Mifflin, 2005); and Isa N. Engleberg and Ann Raimes, *Pocket Keys for Speakers* (Boston: Houghton Mifflin, 2004).

2. Lani Arredondo, *The McGraw-Hill 36-Hour Course: Business Presentations* (New York: McGraw-Hill, 1994), p. 147.

3. Jerry Della Femina, in *Creative Strategies in Advertising*, 2nd ed., ed. A. Jerome Jewler (Belmont, CA: Wadsworth, 1985), p. 41.

4. Engleberg and Daly, p. 272.

5. For the complete text of President Clinton's 1993 Inaugural Address and a critique written by *New York Times* columnist William Saffire, see Isa N.

Engleberg, *The Principles of Public Presentation* (New York: HarperCollins, 1994), pp. 344–349.

6. Engleberg and Raimes, pp. 94–95.

7. John W. Bowers, "Some Correlates of Language Intensity," *Quarterly Journal of Speech* 50 (1964), pp. 415–420.

8. Lawrence A. Hosman, "Language and Persuasion," in *The Persuasion Handbook: Developments in Theory and Practice*, ed. James Price Dillard and Michael Pfau (Thousand Oaks, CA: Sage, 2002), pp. 376–377.

9. Matthew McGlone, *Forbes* (October 5, 1998), p. 45.

10. Laurie E. Rozakis, *The Complete Idiot's Guide to Speaking in Public with Confidence* (New York: Alpha Books, 1995), p. 222.

11. Lyle V. Mayer, *Fundamentals of Voice and Articulation*, 13th ed. (New York: McGraw-Hill, 2004), p. 66.

12. Susan D. Miller, *Be Heard the First Time: A Woman's Guide to Powerful Speaking* (Herndon, VA: Capital Books, 2006), p. 100.

13. Steven A. Beebe, "Eye Contact: A Nonverbal Determinant of Speaker Credibility," *The Speech Teacher* 23 (1974), pp. 21–25.

14. Mark L. Knapp and Judith A. Hall, *Nonverbal Communication in Human Interaction*, 5th ed. (Belmont, CA: Wadsworth/Thomson Learning, 2006), p. 295.

15. Malcolm Kushner, *Successful Presentations for Dummies* (Foster City, CA: IDG Books, 1997), p. 128.

Presentations: Speaking to Inform

Key Elements of Communication	Communication Axioms	Guiding Principles of Informative Speaking
Self	*Communication Is Personal*	Earn audience respect and interest by demonstrating your knowledge of and personal interest in them and the topic.
Others	*Communication Is Relational*	Adapt to audience knowledge, attention span, and listening ability. Demonstrate the information's value.
Purpose	*Communication Is Intentional*	Select appropriate informative strategies for reporting information or explaining difficult, complex, or misunderstood concepts and processes.
Context	*Communication Is Contextual*	Adapt your informative presentation to the psychosocial, physical, and situational context.
Content	*Communication Is Symbolic*	Select content appropriate for an informatory or explanatory purpose. Use storytelling, appropriate humor, and audience involvement to generate interest.
Structure	*Communication Is Structured*	Use organizational strategies appropriate for your informative purpose and topic.
Expression	*Communication Is Irreversible*	Practice expressive delivery to add vitality, variety, and naturalness. When possible, speak extemporaneously.

Informative Speaking

Informative speaking is the most common type of presentation. Students use informative speaking to present oral reports, to share research with classmates, and to explain group projects. Business executives use informative presentations to orient new employees, to present company reports, and to explain new policies. Administrators and teachers at colleges use informative presentations to advise new students, to teach classes, and to report to boards of trustees and funding agencies.

The primary purpose of an **informative presentation** is to instruct, explain, describe, enlighten, demonstrate, clarify, correct, or remind. An informative presentation can present new information, explain complex concepts and processes, and clarify and correct misunderstood information. You will be asked to prepare and deliver informative presentations throughout your lifetime and career, so learning how to do it well can give you a competitive edge.[1]

INFORMATIVE VERSUS PERSUASIVE SPEAKING

Most informative presentations contain an element of persuasion. An informative presentation explaining the causes of acid rain may convince an audience that the problem is serious and requires stricter air pollution laws. Even an informative presentation demonstrating the proper way to change a tire can persuade an audience member to forgo calling the local garage because changing a tire is not as difficult as it looks. Your purpose signifies the difference between informative and persuasive presentations. When you ask listeners to change their opinions or behavior, your presentation becomes persuasive. The dividing line between informing and persuading, however, can be blurry. For example, if your presentation compares brands of tires, it may slip over the boundary between informative and persuasive presentations if you manage a tire store that only sells Brand X and you "inform" your audience that Brand X is the best brand. Advertisers often use borderline techniques. Statements such as "Laboratory tests show . . . ," "Three out of four doctors recommend . . . ," or "America's Number One selling . . ." may present accurate information, but their primary purpose is persuasive, not informative.

THE CHALLENGES OF INFORMATIVE SPEAKING

In general, persuasive presentations can more easily capture audience interest. Controversy can arouse listeners and make them more alert (or even wary) when a speaker tries to change their opinions or behavior. Informative speaking often requires a concerted effort to gain and keep the audience's attention. To meet this challenge, we recommend explaining the value of your information to the audience and enhancing your credibility.

Include a Value Step   A **value step** in your presentation's introduction tells audience members why the information is of value to them and how it can affect their success or well-being. If there's a good reason for you to make a presentation, there should be a good reason for your audience to listen. Tell them how the information can increase happiness, wealth, safety, success, or popularity. Don't rely on your audience to figure out why they should listen. Tell them. A value step may not be necessary in all informative presentations, but it can motivate a disinterested audience to listen to you.

Enhance Your Credibility   Sometimes audience disinterest is really audience distrust in disguise. Review the credibility factors discussed in Chapter 12, "Presentations: The Planning Process"—character, competence, and charisma—that contribute to whether an audience believes you and your message. Think about ways to enhance

The long-winded infomercials on television are not presented for your education and enjoyment. They have only one purpose: to persuade you to buy a product. When a salesperson says (and yes, we've actually heard this line), "I'm not here to sell you anything. Trust me. I only want to give you the facts," we know the opposite is true. "Judged strictly on truth-telling criteria, advertising rarely makes product claims that are demonstrably false. However, it almost always exaggerates, puffs up products, and links products with intangible rewards."[1]

The first principle in the National Communication Association's Credo for Ethical Communication states,

"We advocate truthfulness, accuracy, honesty, and reason as essential to the integrity of communication."[2] Claiming to inform when you're real purpose is to persuade violates this ethical principle.

[1]Richard M. Perloff, *The Dynamics of Persuasion: Communication and Attitudes in the 21st Century*, 2nd ed. (Mahwah, NJ: Lawrence Erlbaum, 2003), pp. 299–300.

[2]www.natcom.org/aboutNCA/Policies/Platform.html.

your credibility. For example, let your audience know that you're an expert on the topic or that you've done considerable research. Show them that you care about them. Audiences are more likely to listen and learn from a speaker they respect, trust, and like.

Informative Communication Theory

Communication scholar Katherine Rowan offers a theoretical model that examines two types of informative communication—informatory and explanatory. The purpose of **informatory communication** is to increase audience awareness of some phenomenon. Much like news reporting, informatory communication creates awareness by presenting the latest information about a topic. **Explanatory communication** enhances or deepens an audience's understanding of some phenomenon. Explanatory communication goes beyond "the facts" and helps audiences understand, interpret, and evaluate. Good explanatory presentations answer questions such as "Why?" or "What does that mean?"[2]

When John Ghidiu, a skating instructor and rep for Rollerblade demonstrates a technique, what factors influence the class of would-be rollerbladers to respond as they do?

Just because *you* love opera, bowling, and bidding on eBay doesn't mean audience members share your enthusiasm. In most informative presentations, you know more and care more about your presentation than they do. So how do you motivate audience members to listen? What makes your presentation valuable?

Research on listening tells us that good listeners ask themselves a simple question when listening to a presentation: What's in it for me? In sales, the "What's in it for me?" question is called WIIFM. If you cannot demonstrate that there's something of value in your presentation or product, why should they listen to you? Why should they care?

Begin your search for a value step by making a list of the ways in which the information can benefit audience members. Ask yourself whether your presentation will provide the following:

- *Social Benefits.* Will your presentation help listeners interact with others more effectively, become more popular, resolve social problems, or even throw a great party?
- *Physical Benefits.* Will your presentation offer advice about improving their physical health, tips on treating common ailments, or expert recommendations on diet and exercise?
- *Psychological Benefits.* Will your presentation explain common and interesting psychological topics such as the causes and treatment of stress, depression, and anxiety or descriptions of interesting psychological disabilities? Will your presentation help audience members feel better about themselves?
- *Intellectual Benefits.* Will your presentation help your audience learn difficult concepts or explain intriguing and novel discoveries in science? Will you demonstrate the value of intellectual curiosity and creativity?
- *Economic Benefits.* Will your presentation help your audience make or save money? Will you explain or clarify monetary and economic concepts that may help them become more savvy investors? Does your presentation offer advice about employment opportunities?
- *Professional Benefits.* Will your presentation demonstrate ways in which audience members can succeed and prosper in a career field or profession? Will you provide expert instruction on mastering professional strategies and skills?

In addition to considering individual benefits, create a list of the interest factors. Audiences often find intriguing stories compelling and memorable. They are impressed with new ideas and breakthrough discoveries; they enjoy humor and remember funny stories. These interest factors—covered in detail later in this chapter—can transform a simple informative talk into an impressive presentation.

Rowan provides the following examples of each type of informative communication. Instruction on how to shift bicycle gears is an example of informatory communication, but an account of how the gears are constructed or why bicycles stay upright when pedaled are examples of explanatory communication. An announcement about the day on which the Jewish holiday of Hanukkah begins is informatory communication; a brief lecture explaining why Hanukkah is a minor holiday for Jews, rather than a major one, is explanatory.[3] Figure 15.1 provides additional examples of the differences between informatory and explanatory communication.

Effective speakers understand when they need to report information and when they need to explain a more complicated concept or process. Not surprisingly, different types of informative messages require different types of communication strategies.

REPORT NEW INFORMATION

Reporting new information is what most news reporters do when they answer basic *who, what, where, when, how,* and *why* questions. You can find new information in daily newspapers and popular magazines, in textbooks and classroom lectures, in reference books, and on the Internet.

Like news reporters and writers, you face two challenges when reporting new information. First, if your information is very new, an audience may have trouble grasping your central idea. Second, you may need to give an audience a reason to lis-

Figure 15.1   **Examples of Informatory and Explanatory Communication**

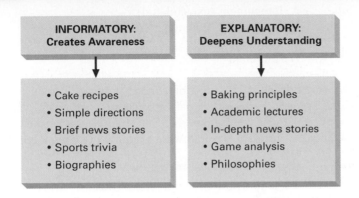

INFORMATORY: Creates Awareness	EXPLANATORY: Deepens Understanding
• Cake recipes • Simple directions • Brief news stories • Sports trivia • Biographies	• Baking principles • Academic lectures • In-depth news stories • Game analysis • Philosophies

ten, learn, and remember. Rowan suggests four strategies for overcoming the challenges of sharing new information with an audience, as outlined in Figure 15.2.

Informative presentations report new information that falls into several subcategories—informing about objects, people, procedures, and events. Choosing one of the subcategories can help you clarify your purpose, organize your presentation, and select appropriate supporting material.

Informing about Objects   Students in communication classes often choose objects as the topic of their informative presentations. Why? Because a tangible object can be described, touched, and even brought to the presentation, either in visual aid form or "in the flesh." The challenge of informing about objects, however, is that an object is not a purpose statement or central idea. It's a fishing lure, an exotic pet, a digital camera, or a full-dress uniform. Use the guiding principles of human communication to develop and focus your message. The following example provides the topic area, purpose, central idea, value step, organizational pattern, and key points for an informative presentation about fire ants:

Topic area	Fire ants
Purpose	To familiarize audience members with the external anatomy of a fire ant
Central idea	A tour of the fire ant's external anatomy will help you understand why these ants are so hard to exterminate.
Value step	Besides inflicting painful, sometimes deadly, stings, fire ants can eat up your garden, damage your home, and harm your pets and local wildlife.

Figure 15.2   **Strategies for Reporting New Information**

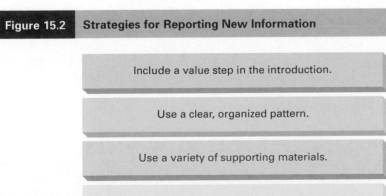

Include a value step in the introduction.

Use a clear, organized pattern.

Use a variety of supporting materials.

Relate the information to audience interests and needs.

Organization	Space arrangement—a visual tour of the fire ant's external anatomy
Key points	A. Integument (exoskeleton) B. Head and its components C. Thorax D. Abdomen

Informing about People   A presentation about a person can focus on a historical or literary figure, a famous living individual, or someone you know. Regardless of the "who," be selective and focus your remarks on the personal characteristics or achievements that match your purpose. The following example presents a focused plan:

Topic area	Early female blues singers
Purpose	To demonstrate the influence of three female blues singers of the 1920s on musicians in later eras
Central idea	In the 1920s, Sippie Wallace, Edith Wilson, and Victoria Spivey paved the way for other female blues singers.
Value step	To be able to call yourself an honest-to-goodness blues fan, you should know more about the major contributions made by the early *female* blues singers.
Organization	Stories and examples—brief biographies of three blues singers
Key points	A. Sippie Wallace B. Edith Wilson C. Victoria Spivey

Informing about Procedures   Presentations about procedures can be among the easiest to plan and present, or they can be the hardest. It depends on the topic and whether your communication purpose is informatory or explanatory. If you are describing a fairly simple procedure, an informatory demonstration may be all that is needed to achieve your purpose. Here are some sample topics well suited for an informatory presentation based on procedures:

- How to complete an evaluation form.
- How to build a safe campfire.
- How to prepare a meeting agenda.
- How to prune a tree.

Note the use of the word *how*. Procedures focus on *how* to do something rather than *what* or *why* to do it. Changing a tire, filling out a form, and sewing on a button are not necessarily easy procedures, but at least there are accepted steps for doing each of them. Transplanting a heart and docking a space shuttle are highly complex procedures. There is no do-it-yourself manual; there are no "simple tips" to follow. These topics require explanatory communication as well as information.

Make sure you know enough about your topic to explain it properly to your audience. If it's a simple procedure, then provide enough information to cover each step. For example, anyone who has tried to make a hard-boiled egg knows that the right procedure can make the difference between a perfect outcome and a mess of white albumen floating around in a pot of boiling water.

Topic area	Hard-boiled eggs
Purpose	To teach listeners how to make foolproof, hard-boiled eggs
Central idea	There are four steps to cooking perfect, hard-boiled eggs.
Value step	Rather than wasting or throwing away cracked eggs, you can have a perfect hard-boiled egg if you follow the proper procedure.

Organization	Time arrangement—step-by-step instructions
Key points	A. Cold water start
	B. Stopping the boil
	C. The fifteen-minute stand
	D. The cold-water rinse

Informing about Events   A presentation about current fluctuations in the stock market (recent) or the landing on the moon (historical) can form the basis for informatory presentations. History professors often center their lectures on an important event. Politicians are often invited to commemorate an event, such as the opening of a new museum. An event can be a single incident, such as an athlete winning an Olympic gold medal or the dedication and opening of a presidential library. An event can also be a series of incidents or milestones that become a historical phenomenon or institution, such as the Civil War, the race to the moon, or the founding of a company. Regardless of its date, size, or significance, the purpose of your informatory presentation determines how you will talk about an event.

Topic area	Our company's fiftieth anniversary
Purpose	To preview the events scheduled for the company's upcoming fiftieth anniversary
Central idea	The premiere events for our fiftieth anniversary have something for everyone.
Value step	Making our fiftieth anniversary celebration a success can bring more attention and, as a result, more business and profits to the company.
Organization	Topical—four major events
Key points	A. Dedication of the new office annex
	B. Employee picnic and baseball game
	C. Presentation by a nationally recognized speaker
	D. Fiftieth anniversary gala

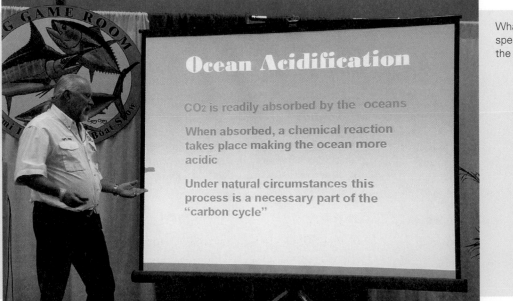

What explanatory strategies should a speaker use when trying to explain the effects of ocean acidification?

EXPLAIN DIFFICULT CONCEPTS

Explaining a difficult concept is a challenge. Abstract concepts can't be touched or demonstrated; there are no simple terms to define the concept. You may be perplexed and bewildered for days trying to discover the essence of a concept and the most effective ways to explain it to an audience. It is a difficult task for any speaker to explain, for example, a new scientific theory, the relationship between nutrition and chronic disease, or the distinguishing characteristics of Karl Marx's dialectic materialism.

Explaining a difficult concept requires more than reporting. It requires explanatory communication in which a speaker helps audience members understand and separate essential characteristics from nonessential features. For example, what is the difference between validity and reliability, blues and jazz, ethos and ethics? Why are corals classified as animals and not plants?[4] The strategies in Figure 15.3 focus on the unique challenges of explaining difficult concepts.

Learning a difficult concept is just that—difficult. It is a challenge to both speakers and listeners. By using some of the strategies we recommend, you are more likely to give your audience an accurate understanding of the concept. In the following example, the concept of heuristics (shortcut decision-making rules that are correct often enough to be useful) is explained in terms of its impact on persuasion:

Topic area	Heuristics
Purpose	To explain how an understanding of heuristics affects persuasion
Central idea	An understanding of the nature and uses of heuristics provides speakers with important persuasive tools.

Figure 15.3   Strategies for Explaining Difficult Concepts

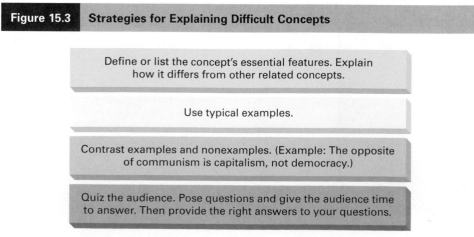

Define or list the concept's essential features. Explain how it differs from other related concepts.

Use typical examples.

Contrast examples and nonexamples. (Example: The opposite of communism is capitalism, not democracy.)

Quiz the audience. Pose questions and give the audience time to answer. Then provide the right answers to your questions.

Value step	Understanding heuristics can help you persuade others and reject invalid arguments.
Organization	Topical plus questions to audience
Key points	A. Definition of heuristic messages
	B. Examples of heuristic messages
	1. Use longer messages
	2. Trust the speaker
	3. Quote celebrities
	C. Contrast heuristic messages with valid arguments
	D. Quiz the audience about heuristic messages

When giving this talk, a speaker would provide examples of each type of heuristic message. For example, we know that celebrity endorsements are often highly persuasive in many situations. We also know that audiences often buy more expensive items because they believe that the quality of products often correlates with the price. Explaining that heuristics are not the same as using poor evidence or unjustified emotional appeals could pave the way for audience questions about arguments taken from political speeches, advertisements, and tabloid newspaper and magazine columns.

EXPLAIN COMPLEX PROCESSES

When you explain a complex process, you are asking audience members to unravel something that is complicated and multidimensional. You are trying to explain how something works or functions. Before you begin, make sure *you* understand the "big picture" and can break down that picture into its component parts, as suggested in Figure 15.4.

In the following example, the process of breathing for speech is outlined for a presentation designed to teach audience members how to improve the quality of their voices. By comparing something well-known (breathing for life) with something less well-known (breathing for speech), the speaker helps the audience understand the process. Within the presentation, the speaker explains the importance of breathing for speech by comparing it with playing a wind or brass instrument.

Topic area	Breathing for speech
Purpose	To explain how to breathe for speech to be a more effective and audible speaker
Central idea	The ability to produce a strong and expressive voice requires an understanding and control of the inhalation/exhalation process.

Figure 15.4   **Strategies for Explaining Complex Processes**

Provide clear key points.
Make sure you are very well organized.

Use analogies and metaphors. Compare the unfamiliar process to something the audience already understands.

Use presentation aids. Models and drawings can help your audience visualize the process.

Use connectives frequently. Help your audience understand the interrelationships among key components.

Value step	Learning to breathe for speech will make you a more effective, expressive, and confident speaker.
Organization	Compare/contrast—three components of the breathing process
Key points	A. Active versus passive exhalation
	B. Deep diaphragmatic versus shallow clavicular breathing
	C. Quick versus equal time for inhalation

OVERCOME CONFUSION AND MISUNDERSTANDING

Audience members often cling to strong beliefs, even when those beliefs have been proved false. Informative speakers often face the challenge of replacing old, erroneous beliefs with new, more accurate ones. A special organizational strategy can help speakers meet this challenge, as illustrated in Figure 15.5.

In the following example, the speaker dispels misconceptions about the fat content in our diets:

Topic area	Fat in food
Purpose	To explain that fat is an important element in everyone's diet
Central idea	Our health-conscious society has all but declared an unwinnable and unwise war on any and all food containing fat.
Value step	Eliminating all fat from your diet can hurt you rather than help you lose weight.
Organization	Problem (misinformation)—solution (accurate information)
Key points	A. Many people believe that eliminating all fat from their diet will make them thinner and healthier.
	B. This belief is understandable given that fat is the very thing we're trying to reduce in our bodies.
	C. Fat is an essential nutrient.
	D. Fats are naturally occurring components in all foods that, in appropriate quantities, make food tastier and bodies stronger.

If you're thinking that an explanatory presentation designed to overcome confusion and misunderstanding is more persuasive than informative, you may be right. At the same time, it clearly fits within our definition of an informative presentation: one that seeks to instruct, explain, enlighten, demonstrate, clarify, correct, remind, or describe. If it's successful, a presentation about fat in the diet will encourage an audi-

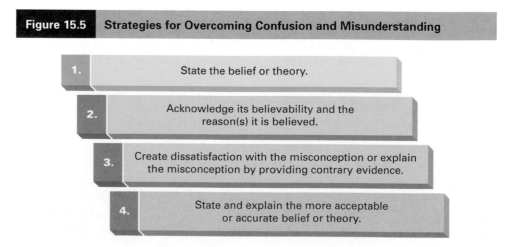

Figure 15.5 **Strategies for Overcoming Confusion and Misunderstanding**

1. State the belief or theory.

2. Acknowledge its believability and the reason(s) it is believed.

3. Create dissatisfaction with the misconception or explain the misconception by providing contrary evidence.

4. State and explain the more acceptable or accurate belief or theory.

ence to rethink what they believe. The primary purpose of such a presentation is to provide accurate information in the hope that an erroneous belief will be corrected.

Generating Interest

Several years ago, one of us collaborated on a national survey that asked working adults to identify the skills that are most important in becoming a better speaker. The study revealed that the number one concern was "keeping your audience interested."[5]

We frequently hear the following question from speakers: How can I be more interesting when I speak? Novice speakers often *assume* they're not interesting; they can't imagine why an audience would want to listen to them. Or they have heard lots of boring presentations and fear they are doomed to the same fate. Rarely is either assumption true. There is no reason a well-prepared, audience-focused speaker should be dull or boring. The key strategies for generating audience attention and interest work equally well in both informative *and* persuasive presentations.

OVERCOME DISINTEREST FACTORS

Audience analysis and adaptation are key to generating attention and interest. Effective speakers sense the audience's interest level and immediately adapt to any negative feedback. To develop an engaging presentation or to know when and how to improve a less-than-engaging one, you must figure out why audiences lose interest.

At the risk of simplifying a complex phenomenon, bored audiences are often victims of two bad habits: short attention span and poor listening skills. Two other bad habits can be laid at the feet of speakers: speaking too long and poor delivery. Learning to compensate for these habits is the first step in ensuring an interesting presentation.

Limited Attention Span   Even under the best circumstances, audience members drift in and out of presentations, paying more attention to some sections than others. They may be diverted for as little as half a second or as long as several minutes, thinking about personal or job problems, the need for sleep or food, or something you said earlier in the presentation. **Attention span**, the amount of time an audience member can be attentive to sensory stimulation, differs for each of us according to age, intelligence, health, past experience, and motivation.[6] How long do you think the average adult can sustain undivided attention? Fifteen minutes? No. Try fifteen seconds![7]

Poor Listening Habits   As noted in Chapter 4, "Understanding Listening and Critical Thinking," most people are not very good listeners. However, you can counteract the effects of poor listening by giving your audience more than one opportunity to listen to your ideas. That doesn't mean simply repeating them. Rather, look for more than one way to make and support your key points. For example, in addition to sharing a statistic, give an example or tell a relevant story. Try engaging the audience's senses. Use a presentation aid or provide a handout to reinforce your spoken message.

You can also help listeners by using a repetitive phrase to emphasize a point. For example, you may have heard politicians, clergy, or motivational speakers repeat a word or phrase for this purpose. In the following example, an elected county official shares information about the police force.

> Our crime rate? It's down. Car thefts? Down. Break-ins? Down. Assaults? Down. Rape and homicide? Down. And the number of complaints about police brutality? Down!

Length of Presentation   One reason audience members dread presentations is that many of them go on too long. In Chapter 12, "Presentations: The Planning

STRATEGIES FOR GENERATING AUDIENCE INTEREST
▶ Overcome Disinterest Factors
▶ Tell Stories
▶ Use Humor
▶ Involve the Audience

PRESENTATION DISINTEREST FACTORS
▶ Limited Attention Span
▶ Poor Listening Habits
▶ Length of Presentation
▶ Poor Delivery

Process," we recommended twenty minutes as the maximum length for most presentations. Peggy Noonan, President Ronald Reagan's speechwriter, emphasizes this time limit:

> Reagan knew that twenty minutes is more than enough time to say the biggest, most important thing in the world. The Gettysburg Address went three minutes or so, the Sermon on the Mount hardly more. . . . So keep in mind what [Senator] Hubert Humphrey's wife is said to have advised him: "Darling, for a speech to be immortal it need not be interminable."[8]

If you realize your presentation will run long, how do you shorten it? Alan M. Perlman, a professional speechwriter, recommends answering three questions:

1. Will the audience be able to reach this conclusion without my help? If the answer is *yes*, don't overburden an audience with unnecessary explanations, stories, visuals, or evidence.

2. Does the audience already know this information or is it inclined to believe this? Don't spend a lot of time on a point if the audience already knows or shares your opinion or belief.

3. Does the audience really need to know this? If the answer is *no*, delete or shorten any statement, idea, or piece of supporting material that isn't directly relevant to your purpose.[9]

If you learn to assess your material honestly in light of these three questions, controlling your presentation's length will be relatively easy.[10]

Poor Delivery Poor delivery can undermine even the best-prepared presentation. One performance component has a particularly strong impact on audience interest levels: expressiveness. **Expressiveness** describes the vitality, variety, and sincerity you put into your delivery. It is more than enthusiasm or energy. It is an extension of the speaker's personality and attitude.[11] If you feel good about yourself, are excited about your message, and are truly interested in sharing your ideas with an audience, you are well on your way to being expressive. Speakers who care about their topic and their audience are usually much more expressive than presenters who are struggling through a presentation they don't want to give.

You *can* become more expressive, although you may find it difficult if you are very self-conscious about showing your emotions. On the other hand, if you are comfortable injecting yourself and your feelings into your presentations, you will be rewarded with a more attentive and interested audience. Becoming expressive

How do you figure out how long a presentation will be during the preparation process? Depending on the complexity of the material, the mood of the message, and your natural speaking rate, five double-spaced pages of manuscript equals ten to fifteen minutes of speaking time. It's more difficult to gauge speaking time when using notes. The key is to practice your presentation repeatedly out loud while it is in the early stages of development. Time yourself and indicate the results right on your notes. Use a stopwatch to gauge the length of each section. You may discover that some sections go on too long whereas others are brief and clear. Before long, you'll be quite comfortable estimating how long it will take to deliver a presentation using notes.

requires you to know your material and to know yourself. And of course, it requires practice.

TELL STORIES

Throughout history, storytellers have acted as keepers of tradition. The ollahms and shanachies of Ireland, the African griots, the Navajo shamans, and the troubadours of medieval France were storytellers who held honored places in their societies.[12] All of us respond to stories, whether they are depicted in prehistoric cave paintings, written in a novel, or told to a child.[13]

Stories have the power to captivate and educate. Audiences remember stories because they create lasting images. Joanna Slan, author of *Using Stories and Humor*, claims that the ability to tell stories separates great presenters from mediocre ones.[14] Time after time, she contends, speakers who are invited to reappear before the same audience will be asked, "Are you going to tell us the story about . . . ?"

Successful politicians and their political consultants know that stories are much more powerful than facts and arguments when it comes to public persuasion.[15] Even corporations are learning the value of storytelling. The *New York Times* reports an increase in "executive storytelling" seminars, some of which can cost a business executive $3,000 to $4,000 for a personal, two-and-a-half-hour session. CEOs and corporate officers are mastering personal storytelling "as a way of enlivening speeches,

How does this traditional Aleut storyteller and environmental activist's use of drumming enliven the tales he tells young people on the Bering Sea coast in Alaska?

sales pitches, training sessions, and other presentations on otherwise dry or technical topics."[16]

Stories are accounts of real or imagined events. They can be success stories, personal stories, stories about famous people, humorous stories, and even startling stories. Members of the clergy use parables, or stories with a lesson or moral, to apply religious beliefs to everyday life. We read fables, fairy tales, and folk stories to children to demonstrate that "slow and steady win the race" or that "there's no place like home." Ancient peoples passed down stories—which we call *myths*—that commemorate famous events and people, explain natural and supernatural phenomena, and chronicle great adventures. Regardless of the type, stories must have a point that relates to your purpose, a reason for being told. Otherwise, you run the risk of annoying your audience with a pointless story.[17]

Stories also benefit speakers. If you're anxious, stories can reduce your nervousness. Most of us find it relatively easy to tell stories. And stories are easy to remember, particularly when they relate events that we experienced personally.

Where to Find Stories   You can find stories in children's books and religious books. Consider highlighting the exploits of heroes from mythology or movies to make a point. Sports celebrities and historical figures often have life stories that inspire and teach. Relate personal incidents from your childhood or tell tales about events that changed your life.

Keep your eyes and ears open for stories that can be used in a presentation. When you read a story in a newspaper, magazine, or book that can help you make a point, keep a copy of it. So how do you find the "right" story? There are at least four good sources: you, your values, your audience, and other people.

You are a living, breathing collection of stories. Storytelling experts Rives Collins and Pamela Cooper suggest that one of the best ways to find stories is to rediscover your family's stories. They offer four suggestions for "priming" your personal story pump[18]:

1. *The Story of Your Name.* Were you named for someone? Do you know how and why your name was chosen? Does your name have a meaning in another language? Does it reflect your ethnic background? Have you changed your name?

2. *When I Was Young in* _____. Fill in the blank. When I was a youngster up in Santa Rosa, at summer camp, in kindergarten, at the hospital, at my uncle's store, at my cousin's wedding, at the soccer finals. What happened? Why do you remember it so clearly? What did you learn?

3. *Your Family's "Roots."* Where does your family come from? How far back can you trace your family? Are there any unique customs in your family? What's the ethnic background of your family? Do you have a famous or eccentric family member?

4. *Your Special Place.* Most of us can find stories if we think about places that have been very special to us. Special places can be your childhood bedroom, the vacant lot where you played with childhood friends, the dance studio where you learned to stand tall, the farm where your family holds its annual reunion, the place where you were married, the first office where you worked, or the view from a nearby mountain top.

SOURCES OF STORIES
▶ You
▶ Your Values
▶ Your Audience
▶ Other People

What do you value? We're not talking about fur coats or fast cars, but personal principles and standards. Eating a great meal may delight and "fill" you, but volunteering at a soup kitchen can be much more satisfying and fulfilling. What are your deep-seated values—qualities such as justice, generosity, honesty? Do you have strong commitments to your family, the environment, or your profession? If you can identify something you strongly value, there's probably a story there. For example, if you value hard work, you can tell a story about someone who "gave all" as well as someone who "goofed off."

If you have spent time analyzing your audience, you may learn enough to find stories related to their interests, beliefs, and values. If your audience is deeply religious, you may share a story about a neighbor who gave up her worldly goods to work on a mission. If your audience loves sports, you may share a story about your own triumphs or trials as an athlete. If your audience is culturally diverse, you may share a story about how you, a friend, or colleagues succeeded in bridging cultural differences.

Finally, a great source of stories is people—people you know, people you have read about, or even people you interview to uncover wonderful stories about their life and knowledge. If you are going to tell a story about someone you know, make sure you have that person's permission. Don't embarrass a good friend or colleague by divulging a private story.

The Structure of a Story   Most good stories, no matter how short or how simple, follow an organizational pattern and share similar elements. Use the Story-Building Chart in Figure 15.6 to make sure that you have the right pieces in the right order.[19]

There are two additional features to note on the Story-Building Chart. The first is that the chart provides a space for your story's title. Titling a story can link it to your presentation's purpose. A title such as "The Big Bad Man in the Back of the Building" suggests a very different story than one titled "The Happy Haven behind Our House." At the bottom of the chart is a space for you to record the central point of your story. Make sure that the point supports your purpose. If it's just an entertaining story, save it for a friendly conversation and cut it from your presentation.

Figure 15.6	Story-Building Chart

TITLE OF THE STORY:

BACKGROUND INFORMATION:
- Where and when does the story take place?
- What is going on?
- Did anything important happen before the story began?
- Provide an initial buildup to the story.
- Use concrete details.
- Create a vivid image of the time, place, and occasion of the story.

CHARACTER DEVELOPMENT:
- Who is in the story?
- What are their backgrounds?
- What do they look and sound like?
- How do you want the audience to feel about them?
- Bring them to life with colorful and captivating words.

ACTION OR CONFLICT:
- What is happening?
- What did you or a character see, hear, feel, smell, or taste?
- How are the characters reacting to what's happening?
- Let the action build as you tell the story.

HIGH POINT OR CLIMAX:
- Whats the culmi nating event or moment of greatest intensity in the story?
- What's the turning point in the action?
- All action should lead to a discovery, decision, or outcome.
- Show the audience how the character has grown or has responded to a situation or problem.

PUNCH LINE:
- What's the punch line?
- Is there a sentence or phrase that communicates the climax of the story?
- The punch line pulls the other five elements together.
- If you leave out the punch line, the story won't make any sense.

CONCLUSION OR RESOLUTION:
- How is the situation resolved?
- How do the characters respond to the climax?
- Make sure that you don't leave the audience wondering about the fate of a character.
- In some cases, a story doesn't need a conclusion—the punch line may conclude it for you.

THE CENTRAL POINT OF THE STORY:

At the 2004 Democratic National Convention, Barack Obama began his keynote address by telling stories about his family. "My father was . . . born and raised in a small village in Kenya. He grew up herding goats, went to school in a tin-roof shack. His father, my grandfather, was a cook, a domestic servant to the British. But my grandfather had larger dreams for his son. Through hard work and perseverance, my father got a scholarship to study in a magical place, America . . . a beacon of freedom and opportunity to so many who had come before him." He then related that his parents gave him an African name, Barack, meaning "blessed"

because "in a tolerant America, your name is no barrier to success." He concluded his introductory story by saying, "I stand here knowing that my story is part of the larger American story, that I owe a debt to all of those who came before me, and that in no other country on Earth is my story even possible." Obama's eloquent and expressive speech and stories captivated his audience and launched his career into national politics.[1]

[1]*Washington Post*, E-Media, July 27, 2004.

Storytelling Tips   Crafting and telling a story for a presentation is not the same as describing the day's events. It requires attention to the features of a good story:

- *Simple Story Line.* Long stories with complex themes are hard to follow and difficult to tell. If you can't summarize your story in less than twenty-five words, don't tell it.

- *Limited Characters.* Unless you're an accomplished actor or storyteller, limit the number of characters in your story. If your story has more than three or four characters, look for another story.

- *Exaggeration.* You can exaggerate both content and delivery when telling a story. Exaggeration makes a story more vivid and helps you highlight its message. The tone of your voice, the sweep of your gestures, and your facial expression add a layer of meaning and emphasis to your story.

- *Audience Links.* Stories won't work if the audience can't relate to the setting, characters, or topic. Make sure that your story is appropriate for your audience.

- *Practice.* Practice telling your story to others—your friends, colleagues, or family members. Practice until you can tell it without notes. Storytelling skills come from lots of practice.

USE HUMOR

Interjecting humor into a presentation can capture an audience's attention and help them remember your presentation. Audience members tend to remember humorous speakers positively, even when they are not enthusiastic about the speaker's message. Humor also encourages listeners to have a good time while learning. Gene Perret, author of *Using Humor for Effective Business Speaking*, claims that humor can generate audience respect for the speaker, hold listeners' attention, clarify obscure or complicated issues, and help an audience remember your main points.[20]

How does a Grammy-award–winning comedian like Lewis Black use stategies such as personal storytelling, self-effacing humor, and frenetic delivery to engage his audiences?

Types of Humor   Presenting humor is difficult. Most listeners will give you the benefit of the doubt and forgive you if your joke or a humorous story doesn't come out as funny as it was intended. There are, however, some approaches to humor that an audience will not and should not forgive. Offensive humor—swearing, jokes that make fun of any group of people, references to private body functions—tops the list because it insults your audience and seriously damages your credibility. Irrelevant humor wastes the audience's time and makes you appear poorly organized. Stale, prepackaged humor is often irrelevant *and* offensive or just plain boring.

You are your own best source of humor. **Self-effacing humor**—your ability to direct humor at yourself—is usually much more effective than funny stories you've made up or borrowed from a book. But be careful that you don't poke too much fun at yourself. If you begin to look foolish or less than competent, you will damage your credibility and weaken the power of your message. President Ronald Reagan was well known for making fun of his age, an approach that also defused campaign controversy about him being the oldest president in U.S. history:

> There was a very prominent Democrat who reportedly told a large group, "Don't worry. I've seen Ronald Reagan, and he looks like a million." He was talking about my age.[21]

Tips for Using Humor   Just about everyone loves humor when it's related to your message and doesn't offend anyone. Here are seven tips for using humor in a presentation[22]:

1. *Focus your humor on the message.* Make sure that your humorous stories, jokes, puns, and gags support the central ideas and key points of your presentation.

2. *Make sure the humor suits you.* Decide which types of humor you do well— jokes, stories, puns, imitations, and so on. Don't contort yourself to fit your material; adapt the material to fit your personality and style.

3. *Practice, practice, practice.* Humorous speaking requires more than knowing the witty content of your presentation. It requires humorous delivery and comic timing—knowing when and how forcefully to say a line, when to pause, and when to look at the audience for their reactions.

4. *Tiptoe around body functions.* The point is not what *you* think is acceptable, but what your audience thinks is acceptable. Although body functions are a normal part of everyone's life, audiences may not appreciate hearing you talk about bodily fluids and private body parts.

5. *Don't tease anyone in your audience.* Unless you are speaking at a roast—an event at which a series of speakers warmheartedly tease an honored guest— avoid singling out audience members for ridicule.

6. *Never ever do ethnic or religious humor, unless you are making fun of yourself.* Even if everyone in the audience shares your ethnicity and religion, don't assume they will appreciate your humor.

7. *Don't go overboard.* You are a presenter, not a comedian. Humor counts, but too much humor can be counterproductive. One study found that award-winning teachers use humor *less often* than average instructors.[23] Don't let the prospect of arousing audience laughter distract you from your purpose.

INVOLVE THE AUDIENCE

AUDIENCE INVOLVEMENT STRATEGIES

▶ Ask Questions
▶ Encourage Interaction
▶ Do an Exercise
▶ Ask for Volunteers
▶ Invite Feedback

One of the most powerful ways to keep audience members alert and interested is to ask them to participate actively in your presentation. When audience members are encouraged to speak, raise their hands, write, or interact with one another, they become involved in the speechmaking process. Involve the audience by using several strategies: ask questions, encourage interaction, do an exercise, ask for volunteers, and invite feedback.

The differences between appropriate and inappropriate humor can be subtle. Analyze the following pairs of jokes.[1] Which of the jokes have the potential to hurt someone's feelings?

Age

- Old? At Ruth's last birthday the candles cost more than the cake.
- There are three signs of old age. The first is lost memory. . . . The other two I forget.

Banks

- A banker is just a pawnbroker in a three-piece suit.
- I think the reason banks have drive-up tellers is so the cars can see their real owners.

Computers

- One of our clerks was let go because of a new software package that enabled a computer to do everything he used to do. The odd part was that his wife went out and bought one.
- We had a tough day at the office. The computers went down and everyone had to learn to think all over again.

[1]Michael Iapoce, *A Funny Thing Happened to Me on the Way to the Boardroom: Using Humor in Business Speaking* (New York: John Wiley, 1988), pp. 120, 135, 131.

Ask Questions   Involve audience members by asking questions, posing riddles, or asking for reactions before, during, or after your presentation. Even if your listeners do little more than nod their heads in response, they will be involved in your presentation. Audience members will be more alert and interested if they know that they will be quizzed or questioned during or after a presentation.

Encourage Interaction   Something as simple as asking audience members to shake hands with each other or to introduce themselves to the people sitting on either side of them generates more audience attention and interest. Depending on the purpose of your presentation, add something beyond a handshake that relates directly to the content of your presentation. For example, in a talk to a business audience, ask members to exchange business cards. If you're addressing young college students, ask them to identify their majors or career aspirations.

Do an Exercise   Simple games or complex training exercises can involve audience members in your presentation and with each other. Most large bookstores sell training manuals describing ways to involve groups in games and exercises. Interrupting a presentation for a group exercise gives the audience and the speaker a break during which they can interact in a different but effective way.

Ask for Volunteers   If you ask for volunteers from the audience, someone will usually offer to participate. Volunteers can help you demonstrate how to perform a skill or how to use a piece of equipment. Some can even be persuaded to participate in a funny exercise or game. Most audiences love to watch a volunteer in action. If possible, find a way to reward volunteers—with a small prize or special thanks. As long as everyone is involved and feeling safe, most audiences will go along with what they're asked to do.

What do children's hands in the air tell you about the way this speaker has involved them in his presentation?

409

From an audience's perspective, informative presentations are learning experiences. The most effective speakers understand that audience members differ in terms of how they learn. Each of us has a unique **learning style**—that is, our strengths and preferences that characterize the way we take in and process information. If you understand the ways in which audience members learn, you can adapt your message and its delivery to three basic learning styles: visual, auditory, and kinesthetic/tactile.

Visual learners prefer reading and seeing. They learn by reading about a concept, seeing information displayed on a word chart, and using flash cards or note summaries to study. If they can't see it, they won't learn it well. Auditory learners learn by listening. In class, they may ask if they can audiotape an instructor's lecture. Books on tape delight auditory learners.

The third type of learning style, kinesthetic/tactile, is a hands-on approach. These learners may squirm in their seats if someone talks too long. They want to "do it," rather than listen or read.

As an informative speaker, take your audience's styles into account. Auditory learners may need nothing more than your spoken words, but visual learners may need diagrams, graphics, and physical demonstrations. Consider breaking up a presentation with audience questions or activities for those who learn by doing. A variety of approaches can make your presentation more dynamic and accommodate the range of learning styles in an audience.[1]

[1]Isa N. Engleberg and John A. Daly, *Presentations in Everyday Life: Strategies for Effective Speaking*, 2nd ed. (Boston: Houghton Mifflin, 2005), pp. 110–111.

Invite Feedback   Invite questions and comments from your audience either during your presentation or at the end. Encouraging audience participation requires skill and sensitivity. It takes a skillful presenter to allow this kind of interaction without losing track of a prepared presentation. Respect any feedback from your audience. If audience members seem reluctant to participate, don't badger or embarrass them. If no one responds, then continue your presentation without such involvement.

Informative Speaking in Action

In this section, two informative presentation outlines demonstrate how to integrate chapter strategies and skills into an informative presentation that achieves its purpose and enhances your credibility. The first is an outline of a presentation on marketing to women delivered to a group of marketing professionals. The second outline is a student's informative speech on *Cliffs Notes*.

MARKETING TO WOMEN OVER FIFTY ON THE INTERNET

Most informative presentations are prepared for extemporaneous delivery, a format that lends itself to using an outline as speaking notes. "Marketing to Women over Fifty on the Internet" by marketing expert Candace Corlett offers a comprehensive outline that functions as speaking notes.[24]

Because Ms. Corlett was addressing an audience of marketing professionals interested in her topic, she did not spend time addressing audience needs. Nor did she need a value step or a section devoted to establishing her credibility. However, she did prepare a well-organized presentation to cover the wealth of information she wanted to share with her audience. Given her credibility as president of 50+ Marketing

Directions, a division of WSL Strategic Retail, she did not identify the sources of her information.

The presentation is organized around two key points. Her introduction uses a song lyric as an attention getter, helps her listeners visualize a foot-stamping group of demanding consumers, and identifies why it's important for the audience to understand the 50-plus consumer. Ms. Corlett uses various types of supporting material: facts, statistics, testimony, definitions, analogies, descriptions, examples, and stories.

Although the presentation is well organized, the supporting material and subpoints do not always address its purpose and central idea. Very often, Ms. Corlett's supporting material applies to *all* consumers older than fifty (not just women) and their overall buying habits (not just on the Internet). Yet, to the extent that women belong to these groups, the speaker implies that the research and advice can be applied to the needs and interests of 50+ women who use the Internet.

The informal style and clever use of terms lend the presentation vigor and a sense of humor. Key words or phrases in parentheses provide reminders of how to explain or describe each point.

Notice how the presentation incorporates many informative speaking strategies: clear organizational pattern and key points, various types of supporting material, definitions of essential features, typical and contrasting examples, audience quizzes, appropriate transitional phrases, and information that overcomes misinformation.

Marketing to Women 50+ on the Internet: Promote the Upside of Aging
Address by Candace Corlett, President, 50+ Marketing Division
Delivered to the World Research Group Conference,
Orlando, Florida
May 27, 1999

I. Introduction. Baby boomers are not a generation to be ignored. What's that song, "I know what I want and I want it now." You can almost see them stamping their feet and demanding new products and services: skin creams to erase lines, medications to manage menopause, biotechnology to replace damaged body parts. That is why we are all here today, because the 50-plus population, even before the onslaught of the baby boomers, is a significant target audience that is getting attention. Why?

II. Central idea and preview
   A. Strategies that can help you approach women over 50 with products and services on the Internet
   B. Key points
      1. Understand 50+ consumer demographics.
      2. Follow the steps to successful Internet marketing to women over 50.
         a. Define your target audience.
         b. Get to know them.
         c. Speak to them in a voice they will hear.

III. Demographics: too compelling to ignore any longer.
   A. Characteristics of 50+ consumers.
      1. They represent 38 percent of the total U.S. adult population.
      2. They are 70 million people strong.
      3. They control 55 percent of the discretionary spending in our economy.
      4. 77 percent of U.S. assets and 80 percent of U.S. savings dollars are in their name.
      5. Because women live longer than men, the over-50 population skews 52 percent women vs. 48 percent men.
      6. 68 percent of online buyers are over 40 and they spend 38 hours a month online, more than any other demographic.

B. "Test Your Assumptions" quiz about consumers over 50.
  1. What percent of baby boomers expect to work at least part-time during retirement? (Answer: 80 percent)
  2. What percent of people 50-plus use a computer at home? (Answer: 40 percent)
  3. What percent of 50-plus computer owners access the Internet? (Answer: 25 percent)
  4. What percent of people over 50 feel these years are the best years of their lives? (Answer: 54 percent)

IV. Three steps to successful Internet marketing to women over 50
  A. Define your target audience.
    1. World War II generation of women
      a. 74+ years old
      b. Housekeepers, dependent on husband-providers, traditional roles and values
      c. Most not computer users
    2. The anything-but-silent generation
      a. 54–73 years old (22 million women)
      b. Caught between homemakers and the liberation of women
      c. Many users of computers and the Internet
    3. The boomers—the demanding, demanding, demanding generation
      a. 40–53 years old (26 million women)
      b. Business adjustments to this large market
      c. Majority users of computers and the Internet
  B. Get to know them (women consumers between 40 and 73 years old)
    1. Characterized by
      a. The liberation of women
      b. Identities apart from family and children
    2. Five indicators of the mature market consumer
      a. Lifestyle changes (children have left home and we're not retired)
      b. Renewed importance of the self ("Now it's time for me")
      c. New dimensions to money (no mortgage, no tuition, more spending)
      d. New messages from bodies (want products to help compensate for an aging body)
      e. Purchases viewed with new perspective (released from peer pressure; have more time to comparison-shop)
  C. Speak to them in a voice they will hear.
    1. Talk about what interests them.
      a. You can talk about hush-hush topics on the Internet. (Example: menopause.)
      b. Offer information about how to make the most of aging.
    2. Promote the upside of aging.
      (Transition: People are all too familiar with the downside of aging. You don't need to remind them. Sell to them with the promise of the second stage of life!)
      a. Vitality (how to live a long, fulfilling life). (Example: Club Med.)
      b. Glow (everything good will glow: glow of good health, glow of skin)
      c. Growth (personal, financial, muscle, and hair growth—not weight)
      d. Advertising copy
        i. *First* will replace *new* (people want to experience firsts).
        ii. Use call-to-action words—*begin, start, fast, instantly.*

    iii. Use good graphics (small tightly spaced type is illegible—LARGE
     BOLD TYPE IS OFFENSIVE).
    iv. Use "ageless," 45+-year-old models.
    v. Use active symbols (replace golf carts with sailboats, bicycles, hiking
     boots, carpentry tools, exercise).

 V. Conclusion.

  Will it be fun to get old? Of course not; but if advertising can make it appear
  fun to be a teenager or starting out young and single in your twenties, then why
  not the fifties, sixties, or seventies?

CLIFFS NOTES

John Sullivan, a former student and now director of information technology at a large
nonprofit organization, translated his very personable speaking style into a delightful
and memorable presentation about *Cliffs Notes*. The presentation included most types
of supporting material: facts, statistics, testimony, descriptions, analogies and metaphors (as in "Reading *Cliffs Notes* is like letting someone else eat your dinner"), examples, and stories from a variety of sources: self, interviews, and published materials.
Because John knew his material very well, he only needed a simple outline with supporting material reminders in brackets to guide him through the entire presentation.

Cliffs Notes
John Sullivan, student

 I. Introduction
  A. Personal story: using *Cliffs Notes* to study the *Iliad* the night before an exam
  B. The *Cliffs Notes* success story [more than 50 million sold annually]
  C. Preview
   1. History of *Cliffs Notes*
   2. Changes in *Cliffs Notes*
   3. Controversies about *Cliffs Notes*

 II. Body
  A. History of *Cliffs Notes*
   1. Cliff Hillegass [story]
   2. Original titles [facts]
   3. Sales figures [facts and statistics]
  B. Changes in *Cliffs Notes*
   1. Expanded to international markets [examples]
   2. Bought by IDG Publishers ["dummies" books]
   3. Expands into new disciplines [examples]
  C. Controversies about *Cliffs Notes*
   1. Writers: scholars and educators [description]
   2. Copyright issues [testimony]
   3. Plot summaries + critical analysis [testimony and metaphor]

 III. Conclusion
  A. Personal story: passed the exam
  B. *Cliffs Notes* success story: racks of yellow and black booklets here to stay

Communication Challenge

The Year of Ideas

Directions: Different kinds of informative topics require different explanatory communication strategies. The topics on this worksheet come from the *New York Times* annual feature "Year in Ideas" in which reporters investigate the latest thinking in a variety of subjects. Read the brief descriptions of each idea and decide which of the following explanatory communication strategies would best match each topic:

1. Strategies for explaining difficult concepts
2. Strategies for explaining complex processes
3. Strategies for overcoming confusion and misunderstanding

Topics

Coincidence Theory. Two researchers claim that coincidences may result from a type of information exchange between the unconscious and the intangible, that the unconscious mind may have the ability to subtly alter the physical world.

Hit Song Science. A new software is used to determine, with mathematical precision, whether a song is going to be a Top 40 hit by "clustering" algorithms that locate acoustic similarities among popular songs like common bits of rhythm, harmonies, or keys.

Junk Food Is Good for You. Kentucky Fried Chicken, Pizza Hut, Burger King, Hardee's, McDonald's, and light beer now claim that their products are part of a healthy, balanced diet.

Young Success Means Early Death. Researchers analyzed the lives of 1,672 U.S. governors and found that those who were elected at relatively tender ages generally died earlier than their less precocious counterparts. The same holds true for other young achievers. The cause may be competitiveness, aggressiveness, and a sense of urgency that takes a toll on their health, or that those who achieve early lose their incentive to stay healthy.

Bicycle Helmets Put You at Risk. After rigging a bicycle with an ultrasound sensor that could detect how close cars came to bicycles, a researcher hit the roads, alternatively wearing a helmet and not wearing a helmet until he had been passed by some 2,500 cars. When wearing the helmet, cars passed 3.35 inches closer than when he didn't wear a helmet. So helmets may be more risky because drivers approach helmeted riders with less caution.

Cohabitation Is Bad for Women's Health. Nutrition researchers found that women tend to gain weight once they move in with male partners. Apparently living with a male seems to put pressure on females to consume more of the fatty, less healthy foods.

Workplace Rumors Are True. Two researchers have concluded that workplace rumors tend to be substantially true because in a stable organizational setting people are very good at figuring out the truth. In organizations, the network connections are so dense that it's easy to cross-check information. There is, however, a difference between rumors and gossip in that gossip is usually less reliable as well as more personal and derogatory.

Source: Topics 1–4 from "The 3rd Annual Year in Ideas," *New York Times Magazine* (December 14, 2003) pp. 51, 105. Topics 5–7 from "The 6th Annual Year in Ideas," *New York Times Magazine* (December 10, 2006), pp. 36, 40, 86.

Communication Assessment

Informative Presentation Assessment

Speaker: _____

Topic: _____

Evaluator: _____

Directions: Use the following ratings to assess each of the competencies on the informative presentation assessment instrument: E = excellent, G = good, A = average, W = weak, M = missing, N/A = not applicable.

<u>COMMENTS</u>

COMPETENCIES	E	G	A	W	M	N/A
Preparation and Content						
Purpose and topic						
Audience adaptation						
Adaptation to context						
Introduction						
Organization						
Supporting material						
Transitions						
Conclusion						
Oral language/style						
Interest factors						
Informative strategies						
Expression						
Extemporaneous mode						
Vocal delivery						
Physical delivery						
Presentation aids						
Miscellaneous						
Outline/written work						
Bibliography						
Other: _____						
Overall Assessment						

Key Terms

attention span
briefing
explanatory communication
expressiveness

information overload
informative presentation
informatory communication
learning style

punch line
self-effacing humor
value step

Notes

1. Sections of Chapters 12 through 16 are based on Isa N. Engleberg and John A. Daly, *Presentations in Everyday Life: Strategies for Effective Speaking*, 2nd ed. (Boston: Houghton Mifflin, 2005); and Isa N. Engleberg and Ann Raimes, *Pocket Keys for Speakers* (Boston: Houghton Mifflin, 2004).

2. This section is based on the research and theory building of Katherine E. Rowan, professor of communication at George Mason University. See Katherine E. Rowan, "Informing and Explaining Skills: Theory and Research on Informative Communication," in *Handbook of Communication and Social Interaction Skills*, ed. John O. Greene and Brant R. Burleson (Mahwah, NJ: Lawrence Erlbaum Associates, 2003), pp. 403–438; and Katherine E. Rowan, "A New Pedagogy for Explanatory Public Speaking: Why Arrangement Should Not Substitute for Invention," *Communication Education* 44 (1995), pp. 236–250.

3. Rowan, 1995, p. 242; Rowan, 2003, p. 411.

4. Rowan, 1995, p. 241.

5. Engleberg and Daly, pp. 3–4.

6. Florence I. Wolff and Nadine C. Marsnik, *Perceptive Listening*, 2nd ed. (Fort Worth, TX: Harcourt Brace Jovanovich, 1992), p. 176.

7. Ibid.

8. Peggy Noonan, *Simply Speaking: How to Communication Your Ideas with Style, Substance, and Clarity* (New York: HarperCollins, 1998), p. 9.

9. Alan M. Perlman, *Writing Great Speeches: Professional Techniques You Can Use* (Boston: Allyn & Bacon, 1998), p. 52.

10. Ibid., p. 53.

11. Thomas Leech, *How to Prepare, Stage, and Deliver Winning Presentations* (New York: AMACOM, 1993), p. 242.

12. Rives Collins and Pamela J. Cooper, *The Power of Story: Teaching through Storytelling*, 2nd ed. (Boston: Allyn & Bacon, 1997), p. 2.

13. Walter R. Fisher, *Human Communication as Narration: Toward a Philosophy of Reason, Value, and Action* (Columbia, SC: University of South Carolina Press, 1987), pp. 64, 65.

14. Joanna Slan, *Using Stories and Humor: Grab Your Audience* (Boston: Allyn & Bacon, 1998), pp. 5–6.

15. Frank Rich, "Truthiness 101: From Frey to Alito," *New York Times Week in Review*, January 22, 2006, p. WK16.

16. Eric Quinones, "Companies Learn the Value of Storytelling," *New York Times*, August 1, 1999, p. 4.

17. Malcolm Kushner, *Successful Presentations for Dummies* (Foster City: CA: IDG Books, 1997), p. 79.

18. Collins and Cooper, pp. 24–28.

19. Based on Slan, pp. 116, 89–95.

20. Gene Perret, *Using Humor for Effective Business Speaking* (New York: Sterling, 1989), pp. 19–26.

21. Malcolm Kushner, *Success Presentations for Dummies* (Foster City, CA: IDG Books, 1997), p. 350.

22. We have added four guidelines to those recommended by Slan, pp. 170–172.

23. Valerie C. Downs, Manoochehr "Mitch" Javidi, and Jon F. Nussbaum, "An Analysis of Teachers' Verbal Communication within the College Classroom: Use of Humor, Self-Disclosure, and Narratives," *Communication Education* 37 (1988), pp. 127–141.

24. This presentation outline is based on an address by Candace Corlett that appeared in *Vital Speeches of the Day* 66 (October 15, 1999), pp. 24–27. As a subsidiary of WSL Strategic Retail, 50+ Marketing Directions specializes in marketing to fifty-plus target audiences. The World Research Group sponsors business conferences that often specialize in marketing.

Presentations: Speaking to Persuade

16 chapter

Key Elements of Communication	Communication Axioms	Guiding Principles of Persuasive Speaking
Self	*Communication Is Personal*	Choose a purpose and topic you care about to enhance your credibility and persuasiveness.
Others	*Communication Is Relational*	Adapt to audience attitudes. Seek common ground. Adapt to the audience's level of involvement and ability to think critically.
Purpose	*Communication Is Intentional*	Pursue reasonable persuasive goals based on audience characteristics, attitudes, interests, and abilities.
Context	*Communication Is Contextual*	Adapt to how the psychosocial, physical, and situational contexts affect audience attitudes.
Content	*Communication Is Symbolic*	Select appropriate forms of proof and persuasive strategies. Use sound claims, evidence, and warrants to construct valid arguments.
Structure	*Communication Is Structured*	Use organizational patterns appropriate for your persuasive purpose and content.
Expression	*Communication Is Irreversible*	Be prepared to adjust your speaking style to audience expectations and feedback.

The Nature of Persuasion

Persuasive messages bombard us from the moment we wake up in the morning to the moment we fall asleep. Sometimes the persuasion is obvious—a television commercial, a sales call, a political campaign speech. Other times it is less obvious—an inspirational sermon, an investment newsletter, a product sample in the mail. Businesses use persuasion to sell products. The armed forces use persuasion to justify military budgets. Colleges use persuasion to recruit students and faculty.[1]

Persuasion encourages audience members to change their opinions (what they think) or behavior (what they do). Figure 16.1 illustrates the relationship between opinions and behavior.

During informative presentations, you *tell* an audience something by *giving* them something—directions, advice, explanations. During persuasive presentations, you *ask* for something *from* your audience—their agreement or a change in their opinions or behavior. What determines the difference is your purpose. When you ask others to change their opinions or behavior, your presentation becomes persuasive.

In addition to having a clear persuasive purpose, make sure it's worth pursuing. Ask yourself why *you* are trying to persuade others. Are you making a persuasive presentation because you believe the audience would benefit or because you have been asked to give a persuasive speech? If you believe that taking a CPR course saves lives, you can justify the time needed to prepare a good talk on this topic. If you make a presentation on the need for CPR training because you think it is easy to research, you may not be very convincing.

Theories of Persuasion

Researchers in many disciplines—communication, philosophy, psychology, political science, and marketing—have devoted significant attention to developing theories that explain how persuasion works and why it works in some situations and not in others. Here we offer three schools of thought about the nature of persuasion. Each one explains why and how particular persuasive strategies work in different contexts.

ARISTOTLE'S FORMS OF PROOF

PERSUASION THEORIES

▶ Aristotle's Forms of Proof

▶ The Elaboration Likelihood Model of Persuasion

▶ Psychological Reactance Theory

Like lawyers before a jury, persuasive speakers must prove their case. Lawyers decide what proof to use when they argue a case, but it's up to the jury to determine the outcome. When you try to persuade an audience, your success depends on whether the audience believes what you say. **Proof** consists of the arguments you select and use to persuade a particular audience in a particular context. Because audiences and persuasive situations differ, so should your proof.[2]

Figure 16.1	Persuasion Changes Opinions and Behavior

Opinion	Behavior
• Your family is more important than your job.	• Eat dinner with your family at least five times a week.
• Japan makes the best automobiles.	• Buy a Japanese-made car.
• Vegetarian diets are good for your body and good for the planet.	• Stop eating meat.

During the early fourth century BC, Aristotle developed a multidimensional theory of persuasion based on observations of speakers in the courts, government, and marketplace. More than 2,000 years later, his conclusions continue to influence the way we study persuasion. In *Rhetoric*, Aristotle identifies three major types of proof: *logos* (message logic and arguments), *pathos* (audience emotions), and *ethos* (the personal nature of the speaker). To that list we add a fourth type of proof—*mythos* (social and cultural values often expressed through narratives).

Logos: Logical Proof *Logos* or **logical proof** addresses whether your arguments are reasonable and whether your presentation makes rational sense. Logical arguments appeal to listeners' intellect—that is, their ability to think critically to arrive at a justified conclusion or decision. Note how the following speaker uses facts and statistics to prove logically that health care is too expensive for many Americans:

> Many hard-working Americans cannot afford the most basic forms of health care and health insurance. Some 41 million Americans, 15.5 percent of the population, most of them lower income workers or their families, live without health insurance—a necessity of modern American life. In New Mexico and Texas, 25 percent of the population is not covered by any form of health insurance. And contrary to popular belief, most of the uninsured are jobholders or their family members—the working poor.[3]

FOUR FORMS OF PROOF
- ► *Logos*: Logical Proof
- ► *Pathos*: Emotional Proof
- ► *Ethos*: Personal Proof
- ► *Mythos*: Narrative Proof

Facts and statistics drive home the speaker's conclusion that the high cost of health insurance seriously affects the health and prosperity of many working Americans.

Logical proof, however, does not have to depend on supporting material. Often, appealing to common sense is the best way to prove your point. For example, most people accept the argument that everyone needs good health care, whether you are rich or poor. Reasonable people will agree with reasonable arguments.

Pathos: Emotional Proof *Pathos* or **emotional proof** touches audience emotions—anger, fear, pride, envy, love, regret, or jealousy. Persuasion can be aimed at deep-seated, emotional feelings about justice, generosity, courage, forgiveness, and wisdom.[4] Notice how a student speaker uses testimony to touch the audience's emotions:

> Kevin was twenty-seven years old and only two months into a new sales job when he began to lose weight and feel ill. After five weeks of testing and finally surgery, he was found to have colon cancer. The bills were more than $100,000. But after his release from the hospital, he found out that his insurance benefits had run out. Kevin's reaction: "Five weeks into the chemotherapy, I walk into my doctor's office, and he sits me down, puts his hand on my knee and tells me there's been no payment. . . . Then he said the hospital could no longer bankroll my treatment. At one point in the middle of the whole thing, I hit bottom; between having cancer and being told I had no insurance, I tried to commit suicide." (Author's files)

Rather than using logos to prove that many Americans suffer because they do not have dependable health insurance, the speaker tells a story of one person's suffering. Stories such as this one can persuade an audience that lack of health insurance can seriously affect the health and prosperity of many Americans in situations like Kevin's. Audiences are more likely to agree with such arguments because they know that the same thing *could* happen to them or someone they love. Many

How could this speaker use logos, pathos, ethos, and mythos as persuasive proof in a presentation about the value and impact of The AIDS Memorial Quilt?

Logical proof can be divided into two major categories: deductive logic and inductive logic. Understanding each form will help you develop stronger arguments for your persuasive presentation.

Deductive logic moves from accepted, general premises (All accredited colleges have libraries. This college is accredited.) to a specific conclusion (Therefore, this college must have a library.). A valid **deductive argument** is an argument in which it is impossible for the conclusion to be false *if* the premises are true.[1] Consider the following deductive argument for improving a company's customer service program:

> *Premise:* All successful companies in our industry provide high-quality customer service.
> *Premise:* Our customer service is rated poorly compared with our competitors.
> *Conclusion:* We should improve the quality of our customer service if we want to be a successful company.

Note that the word *all* often appears in the first premise of a deductive argument. If *x* is true of all— then *x* is also true of members of that group.

Whereas deductive logic moves from the general to the specific, **inductive logic** does the opposite, moving from specific instances (The communication professors we observed are good speakers. This instructor is a communication professor.) to a general conclusion (Therefore, this communication professor is *probably* a good speaker.). An **inductive argument** is an argument in which it is *possible* for the conclusion to be false even if the premises are true.[2]

When using inductive logic, you build your argument piece by piece. You find out what is true by researching or observing the characteristics and qualities of a group (such as communication instructors). But unless you carefully examine every possible example, you cannot claim your conclusion is absolutely true. The key to understanding inductive logic is the term *probably*—there can always be an exception. Here is another example:

> Johns Hopkins University Hospital is consistently rated as the best hospital in the United States.
> My doctor practices medicine at Johns Hopkins University.
> Therefore, my doctor is *probably* a very good doctor.

[1]Patrick J. Hurley, *A Concise Introduction to Logic*, 4th ed. (Belmont, CA: Wadsworth/Thomson Learning, 2003), p. 41.

[2]Ibid., p. 41.

television commercials appeal to audience emotions. Telephone companies and fast-food restaurants use human interest stories and gentle humor. Insurance companies may dramatize human tragedies to persuade you to buy more insurance protection. Like it or not, commercials work because they understand the power of emotional proof.

Ethos: Personal Proof As we noted in Chapter 12, ***ethos*** has three major dimensions: competence, character, and charisma. Each of these dimensions can serve as a form of **personal proof** in a persuasive presentation. To demonstrate that you are a competent speaker and of good character, deliver your presentation with conviction. Audiences are more likely to be persuaded when a speaker seems committed to the cause.

Mythos: Narrative Proof During the second half of the twentieth century, *mythos*, or narrative proof, emerged as a fourth and significant form of persuasive proof. According to communication scholars Michael and Suzanne Osborn, ***mythos*** is a form of proof that addresses the values, faith, and feelings that make up our social character and that is most often expressed in traditional stories, sayings, and symbols.[5] Mythos can connect your message with your audience's social and cultural identity, and give them a reason to listen carefully to your ideas.[6]

In the United States, we are raised on mythic stories that teach us about patriotism, freedom, honesty, and national pride. President George Washington's "I cannot tell a lie" after cutting down the family's cherry tree may be a myth, but it helped

Many advertisements, public service announcements, political ads, and magazine articles "go negative" by using fear as a persuasive tool. Persuasion scholar Richard Perloff writes, "Appealing to people's fears is, to a considerable degree, a negative communication strategy. The communicator must arouse a little pain in the individual, hoping it will produce gain."[1] Fear appeals work because they try to scare listeners into changing their attitudes or behavior by suggesting how bad things will be if they fail to take the speaker's advice.

Kathleen Hall Jamieson studies political campaign ads with a special focus on attack ads. She concludes that these ads have a bad reputation because most reporters and the public believe that candidates use them to spread deceptions about a rival. Ironically, the ads that *brag* about the candidate running for office often contain more distorted information than the ads that blast the opponents. Like it or not, attack ads designed to arouse negative emotions succeed in changing opinions and behavior.[2]

Fear appeals directed toward people we care about also work. Think of how many advertisements use this approach. Life insurance ads suggest that you invest not for yourself but for those you love. Political ads tell you to vote for particular candidates because they will make the world safer for you and your family.

[1]Richard M. Perloff, *The Dynamics of Persuasion: Communication and Attitudes in the 21st Century*, 2nd ed. (Mahwah, NJ: Lawrence Erlbaum, 2003), p. 186.

[2]Kathleen Hall Jamieson, "Shooting to Win," *Washington Post*, September 26, 2004, pp. B1, B2.

teach millions of young Americans about the value of honesty. The following phrases are also part of American beliefs and values: "Give me your tired, your poor" from Emma Lazarus's poem inscribed on the base of the Statue of Liberty, and the civil rights refrain "We shall overcome." Speakers who tap into the mythos of an audience form a powerful identification with their listeners.

One of the best ways to enlist mythos in persuasion is through storytelling. Religions teach many values through parables. Families bond through stories shared across generations. Effective leaders who inspire others are almost always excellent storytellers. Review the guidelines in Chapter 15, "Presentations: Speaking to Inform," for telling coherent and believable stories.

THE ELABORATION LIKELIHOOD MODEL OF PERSUASION

In the **Elaboration Likelihood Model of Persuasion**, social psychologists Richard Petty and John Cacioppo identify two "routes" to persuasion that depend on how motivated and able an audience is to process a message.[7] The term *elaboration* refers to whether audience members can engage in elaboration—that is, think critically about the arguments in a communication. How motivated are they to listen comprehensively and analytically to your message? Do they see the issues as relevant to their lives? The answers to these questions help determine which route or persuasive strategy to follow.

Routes to Persuasion   Persuasion can take a central route or a peripheral route. When people are highly involved in an issue and when they are capable of thinking critically about arguments, the **central route to persuasion** is best. Highly involved critical thinkers do a lot of counterarguing when listening to a persuader. They may think, "I just read an article that says the opposite" or "That may be fine in Arkansas, but it won't work in South Dakota." Thus, logic backed by strong and believable evidence is the best form of proof. When audiences are highly involved, persuasion using the central route tends to be enduring, resistant to counterpersuasion, and predictive of future behavior.

In *Rhetoric*, Aristotle claims that the speaker's personal "character may almost be called the most effective means of persuasion he possesses."[1]

Think about Aristotle's claim about the persuasiveness of *ethos* and how it operates in everyday life. Do you believe what your favorite professors tell you? If, in your opinion, your professors are of good character (honorable and reliable) and are experts in their field of study, you probably do. Do you believe what a respected member of the clergy preaches? Again, if you trust the integrity and expertise of that person, you probably believe what you hear. And, if your two or three best friends have always been trustworthy and well informed, you probably believe what they say. *Ethos* is a powerful form of proof—but you have to *earn* it from your audience if you expect it to help you achieve your persuasive purpose.

[1]Aristotle, *Rhetoric*, in *The Complete Works of Aristotle: The Revised Oxford Translation*, vol. 2, ed. Jonathan Barnes (Princeton, NJ: Princeton University Press, 1995), p. 2155.

When audience members are less involved or are not interested in an issue, take the **peripheral route to persuasion**. "Rather than examining issue-relevant arguments, these listeners examine the message quickly and allow simple cues to influence their decisions."[8] These types of listeners are highly influenced by whether they like the speaker and whether they think the speaker is credible.[9] The peripheral route focuses on cues that aren't directly related to the substance of a message—catchy phrases, dramatic stories, the quantity of arguments and evidence (rather than quality), the credibility and attractiveness of the speaker, and even the nature of background visuals and music. Unlike the central route, persuasion achieved through the peripheral route tends to be less enduring, less resistant to counterpersuasion, and less predictive of future behavior. Figure 16.2 shows key points about both routes to persuasion.

Consider the Elaboration Likelihood Model of Persuasion from the listener's perspective. Suppose you are very concerned about the traffic patterns in your neighborhood. You're tired of long waits at lights and slow-moving traffic. You attend a meeting during which a county official tries to convince the audience that traffic will not get worse in the future and that money would be better spent on parks and recreation. Because you're a good critical thinker and care about this issue, you're listening carefully and probably generating a lot of counterarguments: Traffic is awful, it's going to get worse, we need to spend money where it affects us right now. If the presenter wants to persuade you, she is going to have to come up with logical arguments that take the central route to persuasion. Why? Because you're questioning almost everything she says. The only way she can create a lasting change in your opinion is to present logically persuasive arguments that directly address your counterarguments.

Now imagine that the person sitting next to you doesn't care that much about the traffic. He works at his home and rarely drives during the busiest commuting hours. He's not very involved and is unlikely to do much critical thinking about this issue. The Elaboration Likelihood Model of Persuasion suggests that a peripheral route would be more effective. Although logic and good evidence may be useful, the uninvolved listener might be more attuned to the speaker's emotional appeals as well as her credibility and attractiveness ("She seems like a nice person"; "She looks like she knows what she's talking about"). But remember, you often get only a short-term attitude change when you use the peripheral route.

Applying the Elaboration Likelihood Model of Persuasion   Using the Elaboration Likelihood Model of Persuasion requires a deep understanding of your audi-

Figure 16.2   Routes to Persuasion

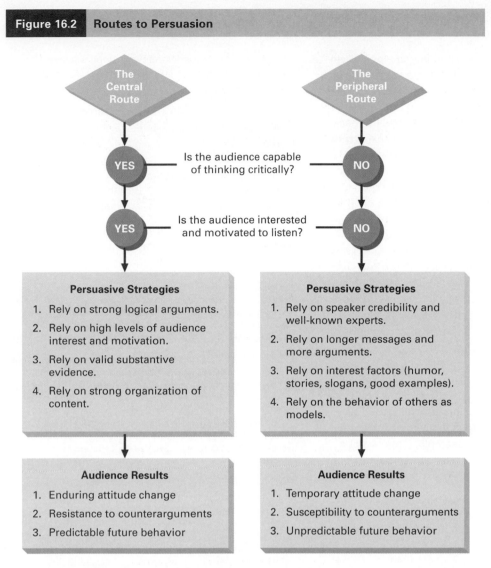

Source: Isa N. Engleberg and John A. Daly, *Presentations in Everyday Life: Strategies for Effective Speaking*, 2nd ed. (Boston: Houghton Mifflin, 2005), p. 440.

ence. Begin by assessing their level of personal involvement and their ability to think critically. If you think the majority of people in your audience are highly involved and will respond to the central route, develop a well-organized presentation with strong arguments buttressed by good evidence and sound reasoning. Imagine the objections and reservations that audience members might raise as they think critically about your message. If you address these reservations, you are more likely to persuade your audience.

If you think audience members are far less involved and thus more responsive to the peripheral route to persuasion, concentrate on your credibility, emotional appeals, and the power of stories and traditions. Demonstrate how and why the issue affects each audience member.

Many audiences are composed of people with different levels of interest in a topic or issue, as well as with a variety of critical thinking and listening abilities. Therefore, using both routes to persuasion may be necessary in a single presentation, even though highly involved, critical thinkers may become impatient with peripheral strategies whereas less involved audience members may become lost or bored with detailed argumentation. If you need to take both routes, carefully balance the strategies.

If you are in doubt about whether audience members are motivated to listen and able to think critically, what types of proof should you use to support your argu-

Understanding the nature of heuristics helps explain why and how persuasion works in everyday life as well as in persuasive presentations. **Heuristics** are shortcut decision-making rules that are correct often enough to be useful. For example, listeners often use simple decision rules such as "Experts can be trusted" or "Consensus implies correctness" to reach a conclusion without carefully scrutinizing the quality of persuasive arguments. Unfortunately, because some heuristics are widely believed, unethical persuaders use them to gain compliance even though their arguments are flawed.[1]

Here's an example. An article titled "A New Twist on Tuition Games, Popularity Rises with the Price," in *The New York Times* notes that families associate price with quality[2] and, as a result, apply to colleges that have higher tuition because they erroneously believe that "the higher the price, the better the education" or "you get what you pay for." As a result, some colleges have raised their tuition to compete with their more expensive counterparts.

The peripheral route to persuasion in the Elaboration Likelihood Model of Persuasion often relies on heuristic arguments that aren't directly related to the substance of a message; for example, it may emphasize the quantity (rather than quality) of arguments or the credibility of the speaker. Here we provide a brief list of common heuristics relevant to persuasive messages:

- Longer messages are strong messages.
- The quality of an item correlates with its price.
- We should trust those whom we like.
- The behavior of others is a good clue as to how we should behave.
- Confident speakers probably know what they are talking about.
- Something that is scarce is also valuable.[3]

Be cautious when you hear a message loaded with heuristics. Analyze the arguments carefully before you succumb to their persuasive power.

[1]See Alexander Todorov, Shelley Chaiken, and Marlone D. Henderson, "The Heuristic–Systematic Model of Social Information Processing," in *The Persuasion Handbook: Developments in Theory and Practice,* ed. James Price Dillard and Michael Pfau (Thousand Oaks, CA: Sage, 2002), pp. 195–211; James Price Dillard and Linda J. Marshall, "Persuasion as a Social Skill," in *Handbook of Communication and Social Interaction Skills,* ed. John. O. Green and Brant C. Burleson (Mahwah: NJ: Lawrence Erlbaum, 2003), pp. 494–495; and Isa N. Engleberg and John A. Daly, *Presentations in Everyday Life: Strategies for Effective Speaking*, 2nd ed. (Boston: Houghton Mifflin, 2005), p. 441.

[2]Jonathan D. Glater and Alan Finder, "In New Twist on Tuition Game, Popularity Rises with the Price," *The New York Times,* December 12, 2006, pp. A1, A26. Also see Letters to the Editor responses, *The New York Times,* December 17, 2006, p. WK 11.

[3]Dillard and Marshall, p. 495.

ments? We strongly recommend that you use logically sound arguments supported by valid evidence. Research by Hee Sun Park and colleagues shows that regardless of an audience's motivation and ability, strong arguments produce "greater attitude change in the direction of message recommendations than weak arguments."[10] Their research also finds that weak or flawed arguments may generate counterarguments. When an audience believes that your arguments are inept or flawed, they may suspect the same about you and your message. As a result, they resist persuasion.[11] Therefore, we urge you to make sure that all your arguments are valid, that they are supported by sound evidence, and that your conclusions are reasonable and fully warranted.

Effective speakers often use heuristics such as storytelling, memorable phrases, high-quality visuals, and their personal credibility to generate audience interest and encourage persuasion. Ultimately, they rely on strong arguments to make their case. Valid arguments are not a shortcut to persuasion; they are the heart of persuasion.

PSYCHOLOGICAL REACTANCE THEORY

How would you feel if a speaker got up and shouted, "Listen up! I'm here to tell you exactly what you should think and how you should behave." "Oh yeah?" you might

Banner ads on the Internet can block copy you want to see or lurk behind your working document. The number of banner ads is increasing, and they're becoming more aggravating and difficult to get rid of. If they're so annoying and universally disliked, why are they there? The answer should be obvious: They persuade! Banner ads successfully sell products and services. At least, that's what banner ad developers and agencies want advertisers to believe. Depending on whose statistics you read, only 0.5 to 5 percent of people who view a banner ad actually click on it—and only a small percentage of those people purchase or subscribe to the product.[1] At the same time, think of the many commercials you see on television. Do you rush right out and buy these products? Probably not. Yet, unlike television, the Web is a user-driven experience in which *you* decide to click or not to click. Most people watching TV put up with commercial interruptions in programs. Not so with Web users (and those who record television programs or use TiVo to avoid such sales pitches).

Although there aren't foolproof guidelines that separate effective from ineffective banner ads, several features characterize the ones that are more successful.

Effective banner ads

- are posted on pages with related Web content
- advertise a particular product or service, not the features of a site
- sit at the top of pages, rather than farther down. One study that compared different ad placements concluded that "advertisers on the Web should do everything they can to purchase ads on the top of the page."[2]
- use simple messages rather than complicated ones
- use animated ads rather than static ones
- stimulate curiosity
- are small and do not take long to load[3]

Note how these banner ads characterize an indirect route to persuasion and use many of the design features we recommend for presentation aids.

[1] Tom Harris, "How Banner Ads Work," http://money.howstuffworks.com/banner-ad/htm.

[2] Ibid.

[3] Sheree Josephson, "Eye Tracking Methodology and the Internet," in *Handbook of Visual Communication: Theory, Methods, and Media,* ed. Ken Smith et al. (Mahwah, NJ: Lawrence Erlbaum, 2005), p. 78.

think. "Go ahead and try!" In addition to understanding why persuasion works, it's important to understand what happens when persuasion fails to work or even backfires.

Psychologist Jack W. Brehm provides a theory that helps explain why telling an audience what *not* to do can produce the exact opposite reaction. **Psychological Reactance Theory** suggests that when you perceive a threat to your freedom to believe or behave as you wish, you may go out of your way to *do* the forbidden behavior or rebel against the prohibiting authority.[12]

In 1984, President Ronald Reagan signed the National Minimum Drinking Act that raised the legal drinking age to twenty-one throughout the country. Those who supported the new law believed that it would decrease the number of drunk driving casualties among sixteen- to twenty-year-olds. Unfortunately, this well-intended law may have boomeranged: Underage drinking and incidents of driving while intoxicated continued at high levels across the country, particularly at resident colleges and universities. When drinking was made a "don't," it became a "do" for many students. A study of college student drinking concluded that when underage students have the opportunity to drink, they do so in an irresponsible manner because drinking is seen as an enticing "forbidden fruit," a "badge of rebellion against authority," and a "symbol of adulthood."[13]

Kids react this way all the time. "Don't snack before dinner." "Don't hit your brother." "Get off the Internet, now!" The reaction? Hidden snacks, surreptitious punches, and even longer stays in a chat room. Consider this interesting fact. Even though designated "coffee shops" in Amsterdam are allowed to sell marijuana, only about 15 percent of Dutch people older than twelve years old have ever used marijuana, whereas 33 percent of Americans have. Because the drug is strictly prohibited by law in the United States, it may be more attractive as an outlet of rebellion.[14]

If you tell an audience "Do this" or "Don't believe that," you may run into strong resistance. After years of telling young people to "Just say no," we have learned that preaching abstinence (from alcohol, drugs, premarital and unprotected sex, junk food) doesn't work very well. Instead, we should recommend behaviors that reduce harm. For example, messages advocating the use of designated drivers and seat belts avoid saying, "Don't drink." Instead, these messages suggest moderation and responsible behavior to avoid the harms of drunk driving.

An effective persuasive message is one that does not give the impression of threatening the audience or constraining their choices.[15] If you believe that your audience may react negatively to your advice or directions, consider the following strategies to reduce the likelihood of a reactance response:

- Avoid strong, direct commands such as "don't," "stop," and "you *must*."
- Avoid extreme statements depicting terrible consequences such as "You will die," or "You will fail," or "You will be punished."
- Avoid finger pointing—literally and figuratively. Don't single out specific audience members for condemnation or harsh criticism.
- Advocate a middle ground that preserves the audience's freedom and dignity while moving them toward attitude or behavior change.
- Use strategies (described later in this chapter) that are appropriate for audience members who disagree with you.
- Respect your audience's perspectives, needs, and lifestyles.

Persuading Others

If your goal is to persuade audience members to change their opinions or behavior, you need to understand why they may resist. Why don't you vote for the first candidate who asks you for your support? Why don't you buy the cereal that a sports hero recommends? Why don't you change your job to one that offers more money? There are good answers to all these questions, and that's the problem. Most audience members can give you a reason why they *won't* vote, buy, quit, or do any of the things you ask them to do. It's up to you to address those reasons.

CLASSIFY AUDIENCE ATTITUDES

The more you know about your audience, the more effectively you can adapt your message to them. Begin this process by classifying expected audience attitudes along a continuum such as this:

Strongly agree with me	Agree	Undecided	Disagree	Strongly disagree with me

An audience of homeowners may strongly agree that their property taxes are too high, but a group of local college students may support more taxes for higher education. If you're scheduled to talk to a group of avid gun collectors or hunters, you can probably assume that they are resistant to stricter gun control legislation.

In what ways should this elected official adapt his message to the attitudes, needs, and listening ability of his older adult audience at the Barton W. Stone Christian Home in Jacksonville, FL?

Review what you know about your audience's demographic characteristics and attitudes. Then place your audience along a continuum that measures the extent to which *most* members will agree or disagree with you. When you understand where audience members stand, then you can select strategies adapted to the people you're trying to persuade.

WHEN AUDIENCE MEMBERS AGREE WITH YOU

When an audience agrees with you, you don't have to change their way of thinking. Instead, strengthen those attitudes and encourage behavioral change. Several persuasive strategies will help you achieve your purpose with an audience that agrees with you:

- *Present new information.* New information reminds them why they agree and reinforces their agreement.
- *Strengthen audience resistance to opposing arguments.* Prepare them to answer questions asked by those who disagree.
- *Excite the audience's emotions.* Use examples and stories that show them why they should feel pride, anger, happiness, or excitement.
- *Provide a personal role model.* Tell them what *you* have seen or done.
- *Advocate a course of action.* Explain why and how they should pursue a specific course of action (such as sign a petition, change their eating habits).

WHEN AUDIENCE MEMBERS DISAGREE WITH YOU

Disagreement does not mean that audience members will be hostile or rude. It does mean, however, that changing their opinions is more challenging. In the face of disagreement, it is best to attempt to change only what can be changed. Consider the following strategies carefully, and choose the ones that best adapt to your audience:

- *Set reasonable goals.* Do not expect audience members to change their opinions or behavior radically. Even a small step taken in your direction can eventually add up to a big change. In the most challenging cases, getting an audience to listen to you is a victory.

People often use the expression "preach to the choir" to imply that speakers don't need to persuade friendly, supportive audiences. Yet members of the clergy preach to the choir all the time. In fact, choir members are often a congregation's truest believers. Every time a member of the clergy delivers a sermon, he or she speaks to an audience that shares many of the same beliefs and values. So why preach? It's because the strength and survival of a religious institution and its

values lie with the faithful—members who already believe. A preacher strengthens that bond by reassuring loyal members that their faith is well founded, encouraging them to stand by their religious beliefs, and advocating good works. In much the same way, a persuasive presentation to an audience of "true believers" can build even stronger agreement and bonds with the speaker.

- *Find common ground.* Find a belief, value, attitude, or opinion that you and your audience have in common. Identify with your audience by beginning on common ground before moving into areas of disagreement.

- *Accept and adapt to differences of opinion.* Acknowledge the legitimacy of audience opinions and give them credit for defending their principles. Demonstrate respect for their viewpoint before asking them to respect yours.

- *Use fair and respected evidence.* Your supporting material must be flawless. Choose evidence from respected, unbiased sources.

- *Build your personal credibility.* Positive feelings about you may rub off on your arguments and help you achieve your persuasive purpose.

Finding common ground with your audience may be the key to persuading an audience that disagrees with you. Even many pro-life and pro-choice opponents often agree that abortions should be allowed to save the life of the mother. Smokers and nonsmokers may agree that smoking should be prohibited in and around schools. If you can find areas of agreement, your audience is more likely to listen to you when you move into less friendly territory.

WHEN AUDIENCE MEMBERS ARE UNDECIDED

Some audience members may not have an opinion about your topic, or they may not be able to decide whether they agree or disagree with you. Some listeners may be uninformed, some unconcerned, and others adamantly undecided. Persuasive strategies differ depending on the source of indecision. Here are some strategies to use with undecided audience members:

- *Persuade the uninformed by* (1) gaining their attention and interest and (2) providing information.

- *Persuade the unconcerned by* (1) gaining their attention and interest, (2) giving them a reason to care, and (3) presenting relevant information and evidence.

- *Persuade the adamantly undecided by* (1) acknowledging the legitimacy of different viewpoints, (2) providing new information, and (3) emphasizing or reinforcing the strength of arguments on one side of the issue.

In the following example, a college student addressed a group of undecided students by opening her presentation on the importance of voting with a strategy designed to get their attention and give them a reason to care:

You find **common ground** by identifying a belief or behavior that you share with your audience—a place where you both can stand without disagreement. Listed below are several controversial topics. Complete each sentence by stating an issue on which a speaker and audience would find common ground. For example, "Free speech advocates and antipornography groups would *probably* agree that . . . pornography should not be available to young children." Note that the word *probably* is written in italics. Audience members at extreme ends of any position or belief may not make exceptions and may not be willing to stand on common ground with you.

1. Pro-capital punishment and anti-capital punishment groups would probably agree that

   _____.

2. The National Rifle Association and gun control advocates would probably agree that

   _____.

3. Opera lovers and rap music fans would probably agree that

   _____.

4. Citizens without health insurance and health insurance companies would probably agree that

   _____.

The next time you anticipate audience disagreement, write a similar fill-in-the-blank statement representing your position and your audience's viewpoint. Then generate as many endings for the sentence as you can to help you find common ground.

How many of you applied for some form of financial aid for college? [More than half the class raised their hand.] How many of you got the full amount you applied for or needed? [Less than one-fourth of the class raised their hand.] I have some bad news for you. Financial aid may be even more difficult to get in the future. But the good news is that there's something you can do about it.

In the real world, you are likely to face audiences with some members who agree, others who don't, and still others who are neutral. In such cases you have several options. You can focus your persuasive efforts on just one group—the largest, most influential, or easiest to persuade—or you can seek common ground among all three types of audiences by providing new information from highly respected sources.

Building Persuasive Arguments

After giving considerable thought to your self, others, your purpose, and the persuasive context, turn your attention to the content of your message. Now is the time to develop and clarify your arguments in light of their persuasive potential. Remember, an **argument** consists of a claim supported by evidence and reasons for accepting it. Good arguments explain and justify why audience members should change their attitudes or behavior. Good speakers develop and select the arguments most likely to achieve their purpose.

In Chapter 4, "Understanding Listening and Critical Thinking," we introduce and explain Toulmin's model of an argument as a way to understand the components of critical thinking. Here we take a closer look at two key elements in Toulmin's model—claims and data (or evidence)—as critical components of persuasion.

When you get a flu shot, you are being inoculated against a harmful illness. According to social psychologist William McGuire, protecting audience attitudes from counterpersuasion by the "other side" is like inoculating the body against disease.[1] By exposing the flaws in the arguments that oppose your persuasive message, you increase audience resistance to those arguments. So present the arguments of the opposition *and* show your audience how to refute them. This builds up their resistance to counterpersuasion and creates a more enduring change of attitude or behavior.

Inoculation is most effective when audience members are highly involved critical thinkers because it makes them aware that their attitudes are vulnerable to attack and then provides ammunition against or resistance to the attack.[2]

[1]William J. McGuire, "Inducing Resistance to Persuasion: Some Contemporary Approaches," in *Advances in Experimental Psychology*, ed. Leonard Berkowitz (New York: Academic Press, 1964), pp. 192–229.

[2]Robert H. Gass and John S. Seiter, *Persuasion, Social Influence, and Compliance Gaining*, 3rd ed. (Boston: Allyn and Bacon, 2007), p. 198.

USE RELEVANT CLAIMS

First, list all the possible claims you could use—all the reasons why the audience should agree with you. For example, a speaker planning a presentation on hunting as a means of controlling the growing deer population could list several reasons:

The enormous deer population . . .

   . . . is starving and dying of disease.

   . . . is eating up crops, gardens, and forest seedlings.

   . . . is carrying deer ticks that cause Lyme disease in people.

   . . . is causing an increase in the number of highway accidents.

   . . . is consuming the food needed by other forest animals.

Although there may be several arguments for advocating hunting to reduce the deer population, a speaker would only use the arguments that, based on an analysis of the audience, would most likely persuade that audience.

Whatever arguments you choose, ask yourself whether you are making a claim of fact, conjecture, value, or policy. Your answers will help determine how best to "make your case." In Chapter 4, "Understanding Listening and Critical Thinking," we took a brief look at these four types of claims. Here we expand our discussion to examine the ways in which these claims affect the choices you make when developing a persuasive message.

Claims of Fact   Claims of fact can be difficult to prove, particularly when audience members are undecided or disagree with your position. Most friendly audiences will accept what you say as fact. Skeptical audience members will want you to demonstrate that your facts are accurate and true. When developing a factual claim, look for the best evidence, and subject that information to close scrutiny. Use the tests of evidence we provide in Chapter 13, "Presentations: Content and Structure," to make sure that your facts are accurate, credible, and relevant.

Claims of Conjecture   Instead of focusing on *what is true*, you are asking the audience to consider possibilities: *what could be* or *what will be*. Even though it's impossible to know what the future will bring, you can make claims of conjecture based on statistical trends, past history, and expert opinion.[16] When making a claim of conjecture, consider the values held by audience members. A stockbroker trying to convince an audience to invest in mutual funds or in a particular company presents facts about

USE RELEVANT CLAIMS

▶ **Claims of Fact**. Assert that something is true or false, whether an event did or did not happen, whether something was caused by this or that.

▶ **Claims of Conjecture**. Assert that something will or will not happen.

▶ **Claims of Value**. Assert that something is good or bad; right or wrong; moral or immoral; best, average, or worst.

▶ **Claims of Policy**. Assert that a particular course of action should be taken.

Many effective speakers use all four types of claims—fact, conjecture, value, and policy—in a single presentation. For example, a persuasive presentation on capital punishment—regardless of your position on the issue—might start with facts that answer questions such as: How many people are executed in the United States each year? What crimes are punishable by the death penalty? Which state leads the nation in executions? Then you might move on to value claims that answer questions such as: Is it right for a state to take the life of a prisoner regardless of the seriousness of the crime? Is capital punishment cruel? Is a-life-for-a-life a moral position? Claims of conjecture require predictions about the future: Will the number of executions increase in the future? Will criminals be deterred from committing crimes if all states have mandatory capital punishment laws for similar crimes? Finally, you may ask listeners to support a policy claim: "Capital punishment should be expanded [or curtailed or abolished]." Most persuasive presentations include more than one type of claim. If you fail to prove related claims of facts, value, conjecture, and policy, you may be headed for a disappointing reaction to your persuasive presentation.

the past and present, and acknowledges the audience's hopes and fears about the future.

Claims of Value   It can be difficult to make value claims because success hinges on your ability to modify well-established attitudes and beliefs among audience members. When addressing a claim related to audience values, remember to say, "It depends." Are public colleges a better place to begin higher education than a prestigious private university? It depends on a student's financial situation, professional goals, academic achievement record, work and family situation, and beliefs about the quality of an education at each type of institution. Changing listeners' perceptions about strongly held values requires an understanding and respect for your audience and, depending on their critical thinking ability and motivation, either a central or peripheral route to persuasion.

Claims of Policy   A persuasive presentation that looks at a policy claim focuses on the issues that arise when people are asked to change how things are or should be done. We often argue about policy claims when trying to make difficult decisions. We weigh the pros and cons of choosing a particular college, accepting a new job, or making a major purchase.[17] When used for a persuasive presentation, arguments based on claims of policy ask audiences to do something or support a course of action. Vote for Jane Doe. Speak out against the college's proposed tuition increase. Exercise regularly. When supporting a policy claim, try to determine whether your listeners are able and willing to think critically about your arguments. If they are, a central route to persuasion is more likely to produce long-lasting behavior change. For less critical and less motivated audience members, a peripheral route to persuasion may be the only way to induce even a temporary change in their behavior.

USE PERSUASIVE EVIDENCE

In Chapter 4, "Understanding Listening and Critical Thinking," we define evidence as the information, data, or audience beliefs that support and prove the claim of an argument. In Chapter 13, "Presentations: Content and Structure," we describe why and how to use valid supporting material to explain and/or advance your central idea and key points. In this chapter we examine how evidence is used to strengthen the persuasive claim of an argument.

In persuasive speaking, evidence verifies and strengthens the proof you use to secure belief in an argument. Evidence answers the questions "How do you know that?" and "What do you have to go on?" If you claim that millions of Americans cannot afford health insurance, a statistic from a reputable source can help justify your claim. If you argue that responsible environmentalists support deer hunting, use a highly reputable quotation or survey to prove your point. If you are demonstrating the benefits of early diagnosis of diabetes, tell two contrasting stories—one about a person who was diagnosed early and one who wasn't diagnosed until the disease had ravaged her body. Be strategic. Select your evidence based on the types of argument you are trying to prove, the attitudes and needs of your audience, and whether you're seeking a central or peripheral route to persuasion. You will also succeed if your evidence is novel, believable, and dramatic.

NOVEL EVIDENCE

Effective persuaders look for new evidence to support their arguments. Overly familiar evidence just doesn't work that well. This is one of the reasons TV advertisements keep changing: If an ad is familiar, we don't pay as much attention to it.

When speaking to a friendly audience, new evidence can strengthen their resolve and provide answers to the questions asked by those who disagree. When audience members are undecided, new evidence can tip the balance in favor of your position. And if you are seeking a central route to persuasion, audiences will expect to hear new, well-researched evidence to support your arguments.

BELIEVABLE EVIDENCE

Even if your evidence is completely accurate, easily understood, and novel, it will not be persuasive if people don't believe it. If your audience may doubt the believability of your evidence, take time to explain why it's true, or provide other sources of evidence that reach the same conclusion. If the source of your evidence has high credibility, mention the source *before* presenting your evidence. On the other hand, if naming the source will not add to the evidence's believability, mention it *after* you present the evidence.

**PERSUASIVE EVIDENCE
IS . . .**
▶ Novel
▶ Believable
▶ Dramatic

When, in 1995, Senator Tom Harkin of Iowa learned that the federal government paid $2.32 for surgical gauze that could be bought wholesale for 19 cents, how well did he dramatize his evidence?

In Chapter 4, "Understanding Listening and Critical Thinking," we identify six common fallacies that impair critical thinking. These six fallacies only represent the "tip of the iceberg." There are, in fact, hundreds of potential fallacies waiting to distort persuasive messages. Fallacies can mislead and misinform listeners, rob audiences of their precious time and well-founded convictions, and permanently damage a speaker's reputation and credibility.

Every communicator has an ethical obligation to recognize and reject the fallacies in persuasive arguments. Three factors lead to most mistakes in reasoning[1]:

- *Intentional Fallacies.* Unethical speakers may intentionally use fallacies to deceive or mislead audience members. Ethical, well-intentioned speakers may use fallacious reasoning without knowing it. Ignorance— as the old saying goes—is no excuse. Every speaker has an ethical obligation to avoid fallacies.
- *Careless Reasoning.* Inattentive listeners can fall prey to deceptive arguments and claims that evoke strong emotions. Unchecked emotions are an open invitation to illogical reasoning, and they can lead a person, blindly, to accept fallacies as true.
- *Different Worldviews.* Cultural differences affect how people view arguments. Prejudices may allow someone to interpret misbehavior by a handful of immigrants, police officers, or basketball players as typical of everyone in that population. A politically conservative speaker or listener may ignore or dismiss an argument made by a liberal speaker. Your worldview—developed over many years of life experiences and teachings in a particular culture—affects how you size up the world and determines what you believe is reasonable and unreasonable. Ethical communicators consider how culture, language, gender, religion, politics, and social and economic status affect the way they and their audiences see the world.

[1] Based on Patrick J. Hurley, *A Concise Introduction to Logic*, 8th ed. (Belmont, CA: Wadsworth Thomson Learning, 2003), pp. 172–174.

Statistical evidence can be highly persuasive. Several studies claim that messages using statistical evidence are *more* persuasive than messages using narratives (storytelling).[18] How is this possible, given the power of storytelling? The answer is that it depends on how you use the statistics.

Lisa Massi Lindsey and Kimo Ah Yun claim that three factors affect the persuasiveness of statistics: sample size, perceived validity, and message credibility.[19] When statistics are based on large sample sizes, they are more believable. For example, if statistics report that 90 percent of doctors recommend, 75 percent of Americans believe, or 89 percent of college professors claim, we are more likely to believe the results—and be persuaded. Perceived validity refers to the fact that statistics are the product of extensive surveys and careful observations whereas a story can be manipulated to support a point. Therefore, we believe that statistics are more valid—and more persuasive. Finally, statistical appeals enhance message credibility because they supposedly represent conditions that exist in the real world. These three factors make statistics highly believable and therefore persuasive.

DRAMATIC EVIDENCE

When using evidence, especially statistics, for a persuasive presentation, find ways to make it memorable. Rather than saying that your proposal will save the organization $250,000 in the next year, say that it will save a quarter of a million dollars next year, the equivalent of the entire travel budgets of the three largest divisions of the company.

Statistics are more dramatic when they are used in attention-getting comparisons. Consider the comparison offered by Robert Reich, former secretary of labor in the Clinton administration. Writing about the increasing income disparity between the rich and the poor in the United States, Reich noted that Bill Gates's net worth roughly equals the combined net worth of the least wealthy, or 40 percent of American households.[20] This comparison brings home the point far better than relying solely on statistical evidence. Presenting such statistical comparisons visually heightens their impact. Imagine the chart or graph Reich could have used to dramatize his evidence!

The Structure of Persuasive Presentations

You have a topic you care about; a list of potential arguments; an understanding of how your arguments present claims of fact, value, conjecture, and policy; and good evidence to support your arguments. You've reached a key decision-making point. It's time to put these elements together into an effective persuasive message. In addition to the organizational patterns discussed in Chapter 13, "Presentations: Content and Structure," there are some formats particularly suited to persuasive presentations.

PROBLEM/CAUSE/SOLUTION

As its name implies, the **problem/cause/solution organizational pattern** describes a serious problem, explains why the problem continues (the cause), and offers a solution. This organizational pattern works best when you are proposing a specific course of action.

The basic outline for a problem/cause/solution presentation looks like this:

A. There is a serious and/or widespread problem.
B. The problem is caused by . . . .
C. There is a solution to the problem.

In the following outline, the speaker uses a problem/cause/solution organizational pattern to propose a national health care system for all U.S. citizens:

A. Americans are not getting needed medical care.
    1. Serious diseases such as cancer, heart disease, and diabetes go undetected and untreated.
    2. Millions of Americans do not get regular checkups.
B. The high costs of health care and health insurance prevent a solution.
C. A national health care system can guarantee medical care by providing free care for those in need without eliminating private care for those who want it.
    1. This plan works well in other modern countries.
    2. This plan will not result in low-quality care or long waiting lines.

A BETTER PLAN

If a problem is complex and difficult to solve, a **better plan organizational pattern** may be a more appropriate way to structure a persuasive speech. In this pattern, you present a plan that will improve a situation and help to solve a problem while acknowledging that a total solution may not be possible.

The basic outline for a better plan follows:

A. There is a good, workable plan.
B. This plan will be better than current plans.

In the following outline, the speaker contends that increased deer hunting is a better plan for alleviating the serious problems caused by the growing deer population.

A. There is a plan that will help reduce the deer population.
  1. The deer-hunting season should be extended.
  2. States should allow hunters to kill more female than male deer.
B. This plan will reduce the severity of the problem.
  1. It will reduce the number of deer deaths from starvation and disease.
  2. It will save millions of dollars now lost from crop, garden, and forest seedling damage.
  3. It will reduce the number of deer ticks carrying Lyme disease.
  4. It will reduce the number of automobile deaths and injuries caused by deer crossing highways.

OVERCOMING OBJECTIONS

Sometimes audience members agree that there is a problem and even know what should be done to solve it; yet they do not act because the solution is frightening, expensive, or difficult to implement. In other situations, an audience disagrees with a speaker and comes prepared to reject the message even before hearing it. With both types of audiences, you should try to overcome these objections by selecting appropriate forms of proof and persuasive evidence.

The basic outline for an **overcoming objections organizational pattern** has three sections:

1. People should do X.
2. There are several reasons people don't do X.
3. These reasons can and should be overcome.

This organizational pattern takes a central route to persuasion by addressing audience reservations head-on.

In the following example, the speaker uses the overcoming objections organizational pattern to encourage listeners to donate blood:

A. People should give blood but often don't.
  1. Most people think that giving blood is a good idea.
  2. Most people don't give blood.
B. There are several reasons people don't give blood.
  1. They're afraid of pain and needles.
  2. They're afraid that they could get a disease from giving blood.
  3. They claim that they don't have time or know where to give blood.
C. These reasons can and should be overcome.
  1. There is little or no pain in giving blood.
  2. You can't *get* a disease by *giving* blood.
  3. The Red Cross makes it easy and convenient to give the gift of life by scheduling blood donation clinics in many locations.

MONROE'S MOTIVATED SEQUENCE

In the mid 1930s, communication professor Alan Monroe took the basic functions of a sales presentation (attention, interest, desire, and action) and transformed them into a step-by-step method for organizing speeches. Many persuasive speakers use the five basic steps in **Monroe's Motivated Sequence**, as shown in Figure 16.3, quite successfully.[21]

In the following example, a speaker uses Monroe's Motivated Sequence to point out Americans' lack of knowledge about geography and to urge listeners to support the teaching of geography in public schools.

A. The Attention Step. Half of all Americans don't know where Columbus landed.

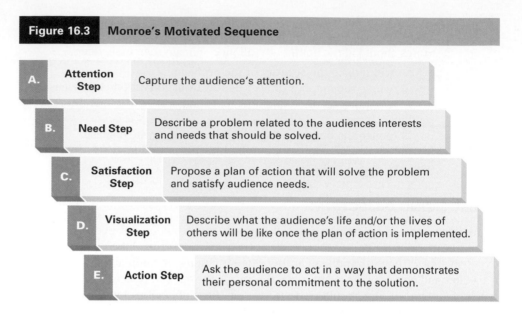

Figure 16.3 Monroe's Motivated Sequence

A. **Attention Step** — Capture the audience's attention.

B. **Need Step** — Describe a problem related to the audiences interests and needs that should be solved.

C. **Satisfaction Step** — Propose a plan of action that will solve the problem and satisfy audience needs.

D. **Visualization Step** — Describe what the audience's life and/or the lives of others will be like once the plan of action is implemented.

E. **Action Step** — Ask the audience to act in a way that demonstrates their personal commitment to the solution.

   B. The Need Step
      1. Americans need to know more about geography for environmental, economic, and political reasons.
      2. Citizens in other countries are much more literate about the world than Americans.
   C. The Satisfaction Step
      1. Integrate geography into the curriculum.
      2. Reinstate geography as a separate subject.
   D. The Visualization Step
      1. Heather Hill Elementary School will have successful geography classes.
      2. U.S. students will know as much about geography as students in other nations now do.
   E. The Action Step
      1. Increase parental involvement.
      2. Put more pressure on local and national education agencies.

The unique visualization step (D) in Monroe's Motivated Sequence makes this organizational pattern useful for audience members who are uninformed, unconcerned, and unmotivated to listen or for listeners who are skeptical of or opposed to the proposed course of actions. You can strengthen the impact of your message by encouraging listeners to "see" the results of taking or failing to take action.

PERSUASIVE STORIES

Stories capture and hold an audience's interest and serve as a persuasive form of proof. Stories can also be used as the key points in a persuasive presentation. When using the **persuasive stories organizational pattern**, rely on narrative and emotional proof to show how people, events, and objects are affected by the change you are seeking.

   A. The following stories (story 1, story 2, story 3) show why people should change their opinions and/or behavior about X.
   B. Unless people change their opinions and/or behavior about X, there will be more (or fewer) stories like stories 1, 2, and 3.

Note how a speaker uses a series of stories to convince an audience to support programs designed to help political refugees:

A. The stories of three refugee families demonstrate the need for and the value of migration ministries.
   1. Story of Letai Teku and her family (Cambodia)
   2. Story of Peter Musooli and his sister (Ethiopia)
   3. Story of Nasir Rugova and his family (Kosovo)

B. More support for migration ministries can save even more families who are fleeing foreign tyranny and persecution.

The persuasive stories organizational pattern can be a very effective way to present a persuasive speech to neutral audience members who are uninformed or are unable or unwilling to listen critically.

Persuasion in Action

In this section we present the manuscript of a persuasive presentation for your review and analysis. "Looking through Our Window: The Value of Indian Culture" by Ms. Marge Anderson, chief executive of the Mille Lacs Band of Ojibwe Indians, includes both informative strategies for generating audience interest *and* persuasive strategies that use different types of proof and a peripheral route to persuasion.[22] As you read Ms. Anderson's words, notice how she does the following:

- Adapts to her audience's level of motivation and ability to process message arguments

- Enlists powerful language

- Tells two stories—one real, one mythic

Ms. Anderson relies on novel, believable, and dramatic evidence to achieve the purpose of her persuasive speech. By explaining "what it means to be Indian," "how my people experience the world," and "the ways in which our culture differs from yours," she uses carefully selected information to take a peripheral route to persuasion. Thus, she informs her audience about her culture and helps them understand why they "should care about all this." For example, note how she enlists the following persuasive strategies:

- Relies on her competence, character, and charisma to enhance her credibility

- Uses St. Thomas Aquinas and the story of Jacob wrestling with the angel as a theme and a form of narrative proof

- Avoids alienating her audience with a "laundry list" of Indian problems and complaints

- Lists examples of the ways in which Indians have "given back"

- Uses logical, emotional, personal, and narrative persuasive proof

- Acknowledges and respects differences between Indians and non-Indians

After reading "Looking through Our Window: The Value of Indian Culture" by Ms. Marge Anderson, chief executive of the Mille Lacs Band of Ojibwe Indians, has your opinion or attitude about gambling casinos on Native American reservations changed in any way?

Looking through Our Window: The Value of Indian Culture

Address by Marge Anderson, Chief Executive, Mille Lacs Band of Ojibwe

Delivered to the First Friday Club of the Twin Cities, March 5, 1999

Sponsored by St. Thomas Alumni Association, St. Paul, Minnesota

▶ The presentation begins with an Indian greeting, a thank you, and an acknowledgment of audience interest. Chief Anderson acknowledges the audience's interest in issues related to Indian casino income and claims pride in their achievements.

Aaniin. Thank you for inviting me here today. When I was asked to speak to you, I was told you are interested in hearing about the improvements we are making on the Mille Lacs Reservation, and about our investment of casino dollars back into our community through schools, health care facilities, and other services. And I do want to talk to you about these things, because they are tremendously important, and I am very proud of them.

But before I do, I want to take a few minutes to talk to you about something else, something I'm not asked about very often. I want to talk to you about what it means to be Indian. About how my People experience the world. About the fundamental way in which our culture differs from yours. And about why you should care about all this.

▶ The speaker gently explains that she will pursue a somewhat different topic than the one requested by the audience. She then identifies her central idea: Non-Indians should care about what it means to be Indian in the United States. She also acknowledges that differences between Indians and non-Indians have created controversy. Note how she effectively uses an oral style in this section—simple words, short sentences, active voice, personal pronouns, and repetition of the word *about*.

The differences between Indians and non-Indians have created a lot of controversy lately. Casinos, treaty rights, tribal sovereignty—these issues have stirred such anger and bitterness.

I believe the accusations against us are made out of ignorance. The vast majority of non-Indians do not understand how my People view the world, what we value, what motivates us.

▶ Anderson uses the word *they* to refer to people who do not understand Indians, rather than using the word *you,* which could be seen as accusing the audience of ignorance. She then explains why *they* gave *you* (this audience) a distorted picture of Indians.

They do not know these things for one simple reason: They've never heard us talk about them. For many years the only stories that non-Indians heard about my People came from other non-Indians. As a result, the picture you got of us was fanciful or distorted or so shadowy it hardly existed at all.

It's time for *Indian* voices to tell *Indian* stories.

▶ Anderson acknowledges that some audience members may be reluctant to listen to an Indian talk about Indians. She attempts to overcome audience resistance through identification with St. Thomas Aquinas, a European and namesake of the university alumni association she is addressing.

Now, I'm sure at least a few of you are wondering, "Why do I need to hear these stories? Why should I care about what Indian People think, and feel, and believe?"

I think the most eloquent answer I can give you comes from the namesake for this university, St. Thomas Aquinas. St. Thomas wrote that dialogue is the struggle to learn from each other. This struggle, he said, is like Jacob wrestling the angel—it leaves one wounded and blessed at the same time.

▶ Note how the words *dialogue, struggle, learn, wrestle, wounded,* and *blessed* reappear throughout the presentation. The Aquinas quotation becomes an eloquent reference throughout the address. To counter negative expectations, Anderson assures the audience that she will not read a long list of complaints about the mistreatment of Indians. She also seeks common ground by describing Indian efforts to take the best of American culture into their own.

Indian People know this struggle very well. The wounds we've suffered in our dialogue with non-Indians are well documented; I don't need to give you a laundry list of complaints.

We also know some of the blessings of this struggle. As *American* Indians, we live in two worlds—ours and yours. In the five hundred years since you first came to our lands, we have struggled to learn how to take the best of what your culture has to offer in arts, science, technology, and more, and then weave them into the fabric of our traditional ways.

▶ This short transition attempts to transfer Indian struggles to the audience's attempt to wrestle with understanding that struggle. Anderson repeats a variation of her central idea that the audience will benefit if they care about what it means to be Indian.

But for non-Indians, the struggle is new. Now that our People have begun to achieve success, now that we are in business and in the headlines, you are starting to wrestle with understanding us.

Your wounds from this struggle are fresh, and the pain might make it hard for you to see beyond them. But if you try, you'll begin to see the blessings as well—the blessings of what a deepened knowledge of Indian culture can bring you. I'd like to share a few of those blessings with you today.

Earlier I mentioned that there is a fundamental difference between the way Indians and non-Indians experience the world. This difference goes all the way back to the Bible, and Genesis.

In Genesis, the first book of the Old Testament, God creates man in his own image. Then God says, "Be fruitful, multiply, fill the earth and conquer it. Be masters of the fish and the sea, the birds of the heaven, and all living animals on the earth."

Masters. Conquer. Nothing, *nothing* could be further from the way Indian People view the world and our place in it. Here are the words of the great nineteenth-century Chief Seattle:

"You are a part of the earth, and the earth is a part of you. You did not weave the web of life, you are merely a strand in it. *Whatever you do to the web, you do to yourself.*"

In our tradition, there is no mastery. There is no conquering. Instead, there is kinship among all creation—humans, animals, birds, plants, even rocks. We are all part of the sacred hoop of the world, and we must all live in harmony with each other if that hoop is to remain unbroken.

When you begin to see the world this way—through Indian eyes—you will begin to understand our view of land, and treaties, very differently. You will begin to understand that when we speak of Father Sun and Mother Earth, these are not New Age catchwords—they are very real terms of respect for very real beings.

And when you understand this, then you will understand that our fight for treaty rights is not just about hunting deer or catching fish. It is about teaching our children to honor Mother Earth and Father Sun. It is about teaching them to respectfully receive the gifts these loving parents offer us in return for the care we give them. And it is about teaching this generation and the generations yet to come about their place in the web of life. Our culture and the fish, our values and the deer, the lessons we learn and the rice we harvest—everything is tied together. You can no more separate one from the other than you can divide a person's spirit from his body.

When you understand how we view the world and our place in it, it's easy to appreciate why our casinos are so important to us. The reason we defend our businesses so fiercely isn't because we want to have something that others don't. The reason is because these businesses allow us to give back to others—to our People, our communities, and the Creator.

I'd like to take a minute and mention just a few of the ways we've already given back:

- We've opened new schools, new health care facilities, and new community centers where our children get a better education, where our elders get better medical care, and where our families can gather to socialize and keep our traditions alive.
- We've built new ceremonial buildings, and new powwow and celebration grounds.
- We've renovated an elderly center, and plan to build three culturally sensitive assisted living facilities for our elders.
- We've created programs to teach and preserve our language and cultural traditions.
- We've created a small Business Development Program to help band members start their own businesses.

► This section compares and contrasts non-Indian and Indian perspectives by using a familiar quotation from Genesis (a non-Indian source) and a quotation from Chief Seattle (an Indian source). The universal and respectful nature of Seattle's quotation should not offend her non-Indian listeners. The two quotations provide a basis for contrasting the differences between a European emphasis on *mastery* and an Indian focus on integration with nature.

► Anderson begins the process of linking the Indian worldview with Indian struggles for treaty rights. Although listeners may not believe in Father Sun and Mother Earth, they may share a respect for and concern about the environment. By understanding that Indians are intertwined in the web of life, non-Indians may better understand their worldview and their subsequent actions.

► Anderson addresses the casino issue in context by linking it to a better understanding of the Indian worldview. Casinos are described as a means of preserving the Indian way of life *and* as a way of giving back to non-Indians—the group represented in her audience.

► Chief Anderson provides multiple examples (factual and statistical) of the ways in which casino income allows Indians to "give back" to Indians and non-Indians. This is not a "laundry list" of complaints, but a list of benefits. Note how the examples begin with the word *we*, a stylistic device that helps Anderson focus on Indian contributions.

- We've created more than twenty-eight hundred jobs for band members, People from other tribes, and non-Indians.
- We've spurred the development of more than one thousand jobs in other local businesses.
- We've generated more than fifty million dollars in federal taxes, and more than fifteen million dollars in state taxes through wages paid to employees.
- And we've given back more than two million dollars in charitable donations.

The list goes on and on. But rather than flood you with more numbers, I'll tell you a story that sums up how my People view business through the lens of our traditional values.

Last year, the Woodlands National Bank, which is owned and operated by the Mille Lacs Band, was approached by the city of Onamia and asked to forgive a mortgage on a building in the downtown area. The building had been abandoned and was an eyesore on Main Street. The city planned to renovate and sell the building, and return it to the tax rolls.

Although the band would lose money by forgiving the mortgage, our business leaders could see the wisdom in improving the community. The opportunity to help our neighbors was an opportunity to strengthen the web of life. So we forgave the mortgage.

Now, I know this is not a decision everyone would agree with. Some people feel that in business, you have to look out for number one. But my People feel that in business—and in life—you have to look out for *every* one.

And this, I believe, is one of the blessings that Indian culture has to offer you and other non-Indians. We have a different perspective on so many things, from caring for the environment to healing the body, mind, and soul.

But if our culture disappears, if the Indian ways are swallowed up by the dominant American culture, no one will be able to learn from them. Not Indian children. Not your children. No one. All that knowledge, all that wisdom, will be lost forever.

The struggle of dialogue will be over. Yes, there will be no more wounds. But there will also be no more blessings.

There is still so much we have to learn from each other, and we have already wasted so much time. Our world grows smaller every day. And every day, more of our unsettling, surprising, wonderful differences vanish. And when that happens, part of each of us vanishes too.

I'd like to end with one of my favorite stories. It's a funny little story about Indians and non-Indians, but its message is serious: You can see something differently if you are willing to learn from those around you.

This is the story: Years ago, white settlers came to this area and built the first European-style homes. When Indian People walked by these homes and saw see-through things in the walls, they looked through them to see what the strangers inside were doing. The settlers were shocked, but it makes sense when you think about it: Windows are made to be looked through from both sides.

Since then, my People have spent many years looking at the world through your window. I hope today I've given you a reason to look at it through ours.

Mii gwetch.

▶ Andersen concludes her list with a factual story (narrative proof) that describes how the Mille Lacs Band forgave a city's mortgage—a decision that reflects Indian values such as caring for others and the environment in which they live.

▶ Anderson begins her conclusion by claiming that non-Indians will also "lose" if Indian ways are overshadowed by the dominant American culture. She resumes using words from the Aquinas quote—*struggle, dialogue, wounds, blessing.* Also note how she repeats the words *no, not,* and *all* in the second paragraph.

▶ Here Anderson's message becomes more urgent. She talks about wasting time, a world growing smaller, and the risk that Indian culture will vanish.

▶ Anderson's final story is more mythic than factual. She previews the story's moral: You can see something differently if you are willing to learn from those around you. This moral lets her return to the central idea that non-Indians will benefit if they learn from and understand Indians.

Communication Challenge

When *Don't* Means *Do*

Directions: Psychological Reactance Theory contends that effective persuasive messages do not give the impression of pressuring the audience or constraining their freedom of choice. The following message urges college students to limit their alcohol consumption. Use this book's strategies for reducing negative reactance to rewrite this message. Try to create a climate conducive for change by granting the listeners more options and freedom to make their own decisions. Give your message a title as well.[23]

Title: *Responsible Drinking: You Have to Do It!*

The conclusion is crystal clear: There is unequivocal evidence that overconsumption of alcohol is implicated in reducing school performance, sexual violence, secondary effects on others, and physical harm to the drinker. In fact, any reasonable person has to agree that overconsumption of alcohol is a serious campus problem that demands immediate attention. No other conclusion makes any sense. Stop the denial. There is a problem, and you have to be part of the solution. So: If you drink, drink responsibly. Three drinks is a safe, reasonable, and responsible limit and it's the limit that you need to stick to. Do it!

Title: _____

_____

_____

_____

_____

_____

_____

_____

_____

_____

_____

_____

_____

_____

_____

_____

_____

_____

_____

_____

_____

_____

_____

Communication Assessment

Persuasive Presentation Assessment

Directions: Use the following ratings to assess each of the competencies on the persuasive presentation assessment instrument: E = excellent; G = good; A = average; W = weak; M = missing; N/A = not applicable.

Speaker: _____

Topic: _____

Evaluator: _____

<u>COMMENTS</u>

COMPETENCIES	E	G	A	W	M	N/A
Preparation and Content						
Purpose and topic						
Audience adaptation						
Logistics and occasion						
Introduction						
Organization						
Supporting material						
Transitions						
Conclusion						
Language						
Persuasive strategies						
Performance and Practice						
Delivery mode						
Vocal delivery						
Physical delivery						
Presentation aids, if used						
Other Criteria						
Outline or manuscript						
Bibliography						
Other: _____						
Overall Assessment						

Key Terms

argument
better plan organizational pattern
central route to persuasion
claim of conjecture
claim of fact
claim of policy
claim of value
common ground
deductive argument
deductive logic
Elaboration Likelihood Model of
  Persuasion

emotional proof
ethos
heuristics
inductive argument
inductive logic
logos
logical proof
Monroe's Motivated Sequence
mythos
overcoming objections organizational
  pattern
pathos

peripheral route to persuasion
personal proof
persuasion
persuasive stories organizational pattern
problem/cause/solution organizational
  pattern
proof
Psychological Reactance Theory

Notes

1. Sections of this chapter are based on Isa N. Engleberg and John A. Daly, *Presentations in Everyday Life: Strategies for Effective Speaking*, 2nd ed. (Boston: Houghton Mifflin, 2005), Chapters 18 and 19; and Isa N. Engleberg and Ann Raimes, *Pocket Keys for Speakers* (Boston: Houghton Mifflin, 2004), Part 8: Sections 25 and 26.

2. Charles U. Larson, *Persuasion: Reception and Responsibility*, 11th ed. (Belmont, CA: Thomson/Wadsworth, 2007), p. 185.

3. U.S. Bureau of the Census, *Statistical Abstract of the United States: 1997*, 117th ed. (Washington, DC: U.S. Bureau of the Census, 1997).

4. Larson, p. 58.

5. Michael Osborn and Suzanne Osborn, *Public Speaking*, 7th ed. (Boston: Houghton Mifflin, 2006), p. 444.

6. Ibid., p. 441.

7. Richard Petty and John Cacioppo, *Communication and Persuasion: Central and Peripheral Routes to Attitude Change* (New York: Springer-Verlag, 1986). For a detailed explanation of the Elaboration Likelihood Model of Persuasion, see Daniel J. O'Keefe, *Persuasion: Theory and Research* (Newbury Park, CA: Sage, 1990), Chapter 6.

8. Richard M. Perloff, *The Dynamics of Persuasion: Communication and Attitudes in the 21st Century*, 2nd ed. (Mahwah, NJ: Lawrence Erlbaum, 2003), p. 129.

9. O'Keefe, p. 97.

10. Hee Sun Park et al., "The Effect of Argument Quality and Involvement Type on Attitude Formation and Attitude Change: A Test of Dual-Process and Social Judgment Predictions," *Human Communication Research* 33 (2007), p. 98.

11. Ibid., p. 96.

12. Jack W. Brehm, *A Theory of Psychological Reactance* (New York: Academic Press, 1966). Also see Michael Burgoon et al., "Revisiting the Theory of Psychological Reactance," in *The Persuasion Handbook: Development in Theory and Practice*, ed. James Price Dillard and Michael Pfau (Thousand Oaks, CA: Sage, 2002), pp. 213–232; and James Price Dillard and Linda J. Marshall, "Persuasion as a Social Skill," in *Handbook of Communication and Social Interaction Skills*, John O. Greene and Brant R. Burleson (Mahwah, NJ: Lawrence Erlbaum, 2003), pp. 500–501.

13. Don Levine, "Booze Barriers," *Boulder Weekly*, September 7, 2000, www.boulder weekly.com/archive/090700/coverstory .html. Also see Ruth C. Engs and David J. Hanson, "Reactance Theory: A Test with Collegiate Drinking," *Psychological Reports* 64 (1989), pp. 1083–1086.

14. Levine, p. 4

15. Dillard and Marshall, p. 501.

16. Dennis S. Gouran, "Effective versus Ineffective Group Decision Making," in *Managing Group Life: Communicating in Decision-Making Groups*, ed. Lawrence R. Frey and J. Kevin Barge (Boston: Houghton Mifflin, 1997), p. 139.

17. David L. Vancil, *Rhetoric and Argumentation* (Boston: Allyn & Bacon, 1993), p. 26.

18. Mike Allen and Raymond W. Preiss, "Comparing the Persuasiveness of Narrative and Statistical Evidence Using Meta-Analysis," *Communication Research Reports* 14 (1997), pp. 125–131.

19. Lisa L. Massi Lindsey and Kimo Ah Yun, "Examining the Persuasive Effects of Statistical Messages: A Test of Mediating Relationships," *Communication Studies* 54 (2003), pp. 306–321.

20. Robert B. Reich, "The Talk of the Town," *The New Yorker* (November 30, 1998), vol. 74(37), p. 32.

21. Alan H. Monroe, *Principles and Types of Speech* (Chicago: Scott, Foresman, 1935).

22. This presentation appeared in *Vital Speeches of the Day* 65 (August 1, 1999), pp. 633–634.

23. Dillard and Marshall, 2003, p. 501. See the Instructor's Manual for an example of a revised message.

Glossary

abdicrat   A person who wants or needs control but is reluctant to pursue it and therefore is often submissive

abstract word   An idea or concept that usually cannot be observed or touched because it is a generality that covers many examples or concepts

accent   The sound of one language imposed on another language

accenting nonverbal behavior   Nonverbal behavior that emphasizes important elements in a message by highlighting its focus or emotional content

accommodating conflict style   Giving in to others to preserve harmony even when the relationship could benefit from further discussion

active voice   When the subject of a sentence performs the action

adaptor   A gesture that helps us manage and express our emotions

adjourning stage   The final group development stage in which a group's goal has been achieved and members begin to disassociate or disband the group

A-E-I-O-U model   A conflict resolution model that focuses on communicating personal concerns and suggesting alternative actions to resolve a conflict

Affection   The need to feel liked by others; see Fundamental Interpersonal Relationship Orientation Theory

agenda   The outline of items to be discussed and the tasks to be accomplished at a meeting

aggression   Putting personal needs first often at the expense of someone else's needs

aggressor   A negative group role in which a person puts down other members, is sarcastic and critical, or takes credit for someone else's work or ideas

alliteration   Using repetition to highlight the sounds, words, ideas, and phrases you want your audience to remember

analogy   Identifies similarities in things that are alike as well as things that are not really alike

analysis paralysis   When groups are so focused on analyzing a problem that they fail to make a decision

analytical listening   A type of listening that focuses on evaluating a message

anger   An emotional response to unmet expectations that ranges from minor irritation to intense rage

appeal to authority   A fallacious claim based on the views of a supposed expert who has no relevant experience or authority on the issues

appeal to popularity   A fallacious claim that an idea or action is acceptable or excusable because many people believe it or are doing it

appeal to tradition   A fallacious claim that a certain course of action should be followed because it was done that way in the past

appraisal interview   An interview to evaluate an employee's job performance

appreciative listening   A type of listening that focuses on how well someone thinks, performs, or speaks

argument   A claim supported by evidence or reasons for accepting it

argumentativeness   The willingness to argue controversial issues with others; a constructive trait that avoids hostility or personal attacks

articulation   How clearly you make the sounds in the words of a language

assertiveness   Promoting your own needs and rights while also respecting the needs and rights of others

attacking the person   An argument that makes irrelevant attacks against a person rather than against the content of a person's message

attention span   The amount of time an audience member is attentive to sensory stimulation

audience analysis   Your ability to understand, respect, and adapt to listeners before and during a presentation

audience attitude   Audience opinion; whether they agree or disagree with you as well as how strongly they agree and disagree

audience survey   A series of written questions designed to gather information about audience characteristics and attitudes

authoritarian/coercive parenting   A parenting style in which children are expected to follow a set of rigid rules that may not account for their individual characteristics and needs

authoritative parenting   A parenting style that adapts to the individual characteristics and needs of children by being both compassionate and firm

authority rule   When groups gather information for and recommend decisions to another person or larger group who makes the final decisions

autocrat   A person who wants control and tries to take over or dominate others

autocratic leader   A leader who tries to control the direction and outcome of a discussion, makes many of the group's decisions, gives orders, expects followers to obey orders, focuses on achieving the group's task, and takes credit for successful results

avoidance conflict style   Changing the subject, avoiding bringing up a controversial issue, and denying that a conflict exists

axiom   A self-evident or universally recognized truth or belief

backing   Support for an argument's warrant

basic term   A word that immediately comes to mind when you see an object that exemplifies a superordinate term, such as *car, van, truck; cat, chicken, mouse*

better plan organizational pattern   The persuasive organization arrangement of key points that presents a plan that will improve a situation and help solve a problem while acknowledging that a total solution may not be possible

biased   An opinion so slanted in one direction that it may not be objective or fair

blocker   A negative group role in which a person continuously stands in the way of group progress, presents uncompromising positions, uses delay tactics to derail an idea or proposal

Boolean logic   A method of referring to the relationship among search terms

boundary turbulence   When two people cannot jointly develop and follow compatible rules about the boundaries of self-disclosure, either because they do not understand each other's boundaries or because they are well aware of the boundaries but do not respect them

brainstorming   A group discussion technique for generating as many ideas as possible in a short period

briefing   A type of informative presentation during which a speaker delivers a short report about the status of an upcoming or past event or project in an organizational setting

bypassing   A form of miscommunication that occurs when people miss each other with their meanings

cause-and-effect arrangement   An organizational pattern that presents a cause and its resulting effects or details the effects that result from a specific cause

central idea   A sentence that summarizes the key points of a presentation

central route to persuasion   The most direct route for persuading people who are highly involved in an issue and who are capable of thinking critically about arguments; see Elaboration Likelihood Model of Persuasion

channel   A physical or electronic media through which messages are transmitted

character   A personal quality reflected in audience perceptions of a speaker's honesty, sincerity, and goodwill

charisma   A personal quality reflected in audience perceptions of a speaker's energy, enthusiasm, vigor, and commitment

claim   A statement that identifies your belief or position on a particular issue or topic

claim of conjecture   An assertion that something will or will not happen

claim of fact   An assertion that something is true or false, that an event did or did not happen, that something was caused by this or that

claim of policy   An assertion that a particular course of action should be taken

claim of value   An assertion that something is good or bad; right or wrong; moral or immoral; best, average, or worst

cliché   A trite or overused expression

closed-ended question   A question that requires only a short and direct response

closure principle   When you fill in missing elements to form a more complete impression of an object, person, or event

clown   A negative group member who injects inappropriate humor, seems more interested in goofing off than working, or distracts the group from its task

co-cultures   Groups of people within a mainstream society who remain connected to one another through their cultural heritage

code switching   How, depending on the context, we often modify how we use verbal and nonverbal communication to generate meaning

coercive power   The power to punish, discipline, demote, or dismiss group members

cognitive restructuring   A method for reducing anxiety by replacing negative, irrational thoughts with more realistic, positive self-talk

cohesion   The mutual attraction that holds members of a group together

collaborative conflict style   Searching for new solutions that will achieve both your goals and the goals of others

collectivism   A cultural dimension in which members value interdependence and believe that "we" is much more important than "I"

committee   A group of people created by a larger group or by a person in a position of authority to take on specific tasks such as those required by social committees, budget committees, and awards committees

common ground   Beliefs, attitudes, or experiences that people share

communication   The process of using verbal and nonverbal messages to generate meaning within and across various contexts, cultures, and channels

Communication Accommodation Theory   A theory that in every communication situation, we compare ourselves with and may try to emulate speakers from other groups

communication apprehension   An individual's level of fear or anxiety associated with either real or anticipated communication with another person or persons

communication model   A model or illustration that simplifies and presents the basic elements of and interaction patterns in the communication process

Communication Privacy Management Theory   A theory that uses the metaphor of boundaries to describe the disclosure process; establishing boundaries or borders that we do not want others to cross when we interact with them

comparison–contrast arrangement   An organizational pattern that demonstrates how two things are similar or different

competence   A personal quality reflected in audience perceptions of a speaker's expertise and abilities

competitive conflict style   When you are more concerned with fulfilling your own needs than with meeting mutual needs in a relationship or group

complementary nonverbal behavior   Nonverbal behavior that is consistent with the verbal message being expressed at the same time

comprehensive listening   A type of listening that focuses on accurately understanding the meaning of another person's spoken and nonverbal messages

comprehensive outline   An all-inclusive framework that follows established outlining conventions

compromising conflict style   A "middle ground" approach to conflict resolution that involves conceding some goals to achieve others

concrete word   A word that refers to specific things that can be perceived by your senses; something you can smell, taste, touch, feel, or hear

confessor   A negative group role in which a member shares very personal feelings and problems, or uses the group for emotional support in inappropriate ways that distract members from the group's task

conflict   Disagreement that occurs in relationships when differences are expressed

connective   A word or phrase that highlights or joins the key points of a presentation to one another and helps make the presentation a coherent whole

connotation   The emotional response or personal thoughts connected to the meaning of a word

consensus   When all group members agree to support a group decision

constructive conflict   When you express disagreement in a way that respects others' perspectives and promotes problem solving

constructive deviation   When resistance to a norm helps a group achieve its goal

content   The ideas, information, and opinions you collect and select for inclusion in a message

context   The circumstances and setting in which communication takes place

contradictory nonverbal behavior   Nonverbal behavior that conflicts with the spoken words

control   The need to feel competent and confident; see Fundamental Interpersonal Relationship Orientation Theory

conversation   An interaction, often informal, in which two people exchange speaking and listening roles as they discuss information, thoughts, or feelings

conversational dilemma   When you or another person violate expectations about acceptable conversational behavior

coworker relationship   A relationship that involves interacting with people who have little or no official authority over one another but who must work together to accomplish the goals of an organization

creativity   Characterized by originality and imagination, creativity has two parts: creative thinking and creative output

critical thinking   The kind of thinking you use to analyze what you read, see, or hear to arrive at a justified conclusion or decision

culture   A learned set of shared interpretations about beliefs, values, norms, and social practices that affect the behaviors of a relatively large group of people

customer relationship   A relationship between someone communicating on behalf of an organization with an individual who is external to the organization

cybersex   The exchange of real-time sexually explicit messages through the Internet

data   The evidence you provide to support your claim

decision making   The passing of judgment on an issue under consideration; the act of reaching a conclusion or making up one's mind

decoding   Converts a "code" or message sent by someone else into a form you can understand and use; the decision-making process used to interpret, evaluate, and respond to the meaning of verbal and nonverbal messages

decreasing options technique   A decision-making tool that helps groups reduce and refine a large number of suggestions into a manageable number of ideas

deductive argument   An argument in which it is impossible for the conclusion to be false if the premises are true

deductive logic   Reasoning that moves from accepted, general premises to a specific conclusion

defensive behavior   Behavior that reflects our instinct to protect ourselves when we are being physically or verbally attacked by someone

definition   An explanation or clarification of the meaning of a word, phrase, or concept

delivery The way in which a speaker expresses a message

democratic leader A leader who promotes the social equality and task interests of group members

democratic person Someone who has no problems with power and control and who feels just as comfortable giving orders as taking them

demographic information Information about a group of people that may include data about age, race, gender, and cultural background

denotation The objective, dictionary-based meaning of a word

description Content that offers causes, effects, historical background information, and characteristics about a person, object, event, idea, or behavior

DESC scripting A four-step process that addresses another person's objectionable behavior: describe, express, specify, and consequences

deserter A negative group role in which a member withdraws from the group, appears "above it all" and annoyed or bored with the discussion, or stops contributing

destructive conflict The result of behaviors that create hostility or prevent problem solving

destructive deviation Resistance to conformity without regard for the best interests of the group and its goal

diagram A presentational aid that shows how things work; also used to explain relationships or processes

dialect Regional and cultural difference within the same language; different from accents

dialogue A conversation in which two people interact in order to understand, respect, and appropriately adapt to one another

disciplinary interview An interview to discuss and correct problematic behavior

discrimination The act of excluding groups of people from opportunities granted to others

discriminative listening A type of listening that relies on your ability to distinguish auditory and/or visual stimuli

documentation The practice of citing the sources of supporting material

dominator A negative group role in which a member prevents others from participating, interrupts others, or tries to manipulate others

Elaboration Likelihood Model of Persuasion Proposes two alternate "routes" to persuasion that depend on how motivated and able an audience is to process a message

eloquence The ability to phrase thoughts and feelings in a way that makes them clear and memorable

emblem A gesture that has the same meaning as a word and has a meaning that is clear to most members of a group or culture

emoticon A typographical character that is used to convey a nonverbal expression

emotion A transitory positive or negative experience that is felt as it is happening, is generated in part by a cognitive appraisal of a situation, and is accompanied by both learned and reflexive physical responses

emotional intelligence The capacity for recognizing your own feelings and those of others, for motivating yourself, and for managing emotions well in yourself and in your relationships

emotional proof Persuasive proof that appeals to audience emotions such as anger, fear, pride, envy, love, regret, and jealousy; see pathos

emotional support Specific communicative behaviors enacted by one party with the intent of helping another cope effectively with emotional distress

empathic listening A type of listening that focuses on understanding and identifying with a person's situation, feelings, or motives

encoding The decision-making process by which you create and send messages that evoke meaning

entertainment speaking A form of speaking that amuses, interests, diverts, or "warms up" an audience

ethics An understanding of whether communication behaviors meet agreed-upon standards of right and wrong; a set of personal principles of right conduct, a system of moral values

ethnocentrism The belief that your culture is superior to others

ethos Speaker credibility and a form of persuasive proof; consists of three major dimensions: competence, character, and charisma

euphemism When you substitute a mild, indirect, or vague term for a harsh, blunt, or offensive one

example A specific case or instance

exclusionary language Words that reinforce stereotypes, belittle other people, or exclude others from understanding an in-group's message

exemplification When you offer yourself as a good example or model of behavior

exit interview An interview to solicit information about why an employee is leaving an organization and whether any problems contributed to the decision

Expectancy Violation Theory A theory that explains how expectations about nonverbal behavior have a significant effect on how you interact with others and how you interpret the meaning of nonverbal messages

expert power The power associated with having a particular skill or special knowledge

explanatory communication A form of informative communication that enhances or deepens a person's or audience's understanding of some phenomenon

expression How a message is conveyed to others

expression–privacy dialectic A conflicting desire to *both* reveal personal information openly and honestly to another person *and* also to protect your privacy

expressiveness   The vitality, variety, and sincerity you put into your delivery of a message

extemporaneous speaking   The most common form of delivery; occurs when you use an outline or a set of notes to guide yourself through a prepared presentation

external noise   Elements in the environment or communication context that interfere with effective communication

extrovert   A person who is outgoing; talks more, gestures more, and can become enthusiastic during a discussion; A Myers-Briggs personality trait

eye contact   Establishing and maintaining direct, visual links with individual members of your audience

eye scan   Using your eyes to glance at a specific section of your notes or manuscript, to focus on a phrase or sentence, to look back up at your audience, and to speak with confidence

4-M Model of Leadership Effectiveness   Divides leadership tasks into four interdependent leadership functions: (1) **m**odeling leadership behavior, (2) **m**otivating members, (3) **m**anaging group processes, and (4) **m**aking decisions

face   The positive image that you wish to create or preserve when interacting with others

fact   A verifiable observation, experience, or event known to be true

fallacy   An error in thinking that has the potential to mislead or deceive others

family   A self-defined group of intimates who create and maintain themselves through their own interactions and their interactions with others

faulty cause   A fallacious claim that a particular situation or event is the cause of another event

feedback   Any verbal or nonverbal response you can see or hear from others

feeler   A people-oriented person who helps others and wants everyone to get along; a basic Myers-Briggs personality trait

feminine society   A society in which gender roles overlap; both men and women are supposed to be modest, tender, and concerned with the quality of life

figure–ground principle   Focusing on certain features while deemphasizing less relevant background stimuli

filler phrase   A word or phrase such as *you know, uh, um, okay,* or *like* that, when overused, breaks up your fluency and may annoy or distract listeners

formal outline   An all-inclusive framework that follows established outlining conventions

forming stage   An early phase of group development in which members may be more focused and worried about themselves than about the group as a whole

forum   A meeting that provides an opportunity for audience members to comment or ask questions

framing   The organizational process of giving structure to a message

Fundamental Interpersonal Relationship Orientation (FIRO) Theory   A theory that claims there are three basic interpersonal needs: the needs for inclusion, control, and affection

gesture   A body movement that communicates an idea or feeling

gobbledygook   Using several words in place of one good word or using a multi-syllable word when a simpler, single syllable word would suffice

Golden Listening Rule   Listen to others as you would have them listen to you

gossip   Information, usually unverified, regarding an organization, its employees, or personal relationships that is communicated through informal organizational channels

governance group   A group that makes policy decisions in public settings

graph   A presentational aid that shows how much, but is primarily used to demonstrate comparisons; illustrates trends and clearly shows increases or decreases

group communication   The interaction of three or more interdependent people who interact for the purpose of achieving a common goal

groupthink   The deterioration of group effectiveness and responsible decision making as a consequence of excessive cohesiveness and resulting in-group pressure

guiding principle   Answers questions about how to communicate and why certain communication strategies succeed or fail; used to help select and apply the best strategies and skills for specific communication situations

habit   Something you do so frequently and for so long that you've stopped thinking about why, when, how, and whether you do it; something that is second nature to you; requires knowledge, skills, and desire

hasty generalization   A fallacious claim in which a speaker jumps to a conclusion based on too little evidence or too few experiences

heuristic   A shortcut decision-making rule that is correct often enough to be useful

hidden agenda   When members' private, unspoken goals differ from the group's common and openly acknowledged goal

high-context culture   A cultural dimension in which people primarily rely on nonverbal communication and the nature of interpersonal relationships to generate meaning; less meaning is expressed through words

high power distance   A cultural dimension in which individuals accept differences in power as normal and may believe that all people are not created equal

high uncertainty avoidance   A cultural dimension in which the members of a particular culture feel threatened by uncertain or unknown situations

hypothetical question   A question that describes a set of circumstances and asks how you would respond

iceberg statement   A comment or piece of information in which most of the meaning is hidden under the surface waiting to be revealed

ideal personal type   A person who wants to be liked but who also is secure enough to function effectively in situations where social interaction and affection are not high priorities

ideal social person   A person who enjoys being with others but is also comfortable being alone

illustrator   A nonverbal sign that is used with verbal messages but does not have any meaning without the words

immediacy   The degree to which a person seems approachable or likable

impersonal relationships   Occasional interactions with people in predictable social or business roles, or in random encounters

impression management   The strategies people use to shape others' impressions of them to gain influence, power, sympathy, or approval

impromptu speaking   When you give a presentation without advanced preparation or practice

inclusion   The need to belong, to be involved, and to be accepted; see Fundamental Interpersonal Relationship Orientation Theory

individualism   A cultural dimension in which members value independence and believe that each individual is unique, important, and deserving of personal success

inductive argument   An argument in which it is possible for the conclusion to be false even if the premises are true

inductive logic   Reasoning that moves from specific instances to a general conclusion

inference   A conclusion based on valid claims of fact

inflection   The changing pitch within a syllable, word, or group of words

information-gathering interview   An interview to obtain facts, opinions, data, feelings, attitudes, beliefs, reactions, and feedback from others

information overload   The inability to extract needed knowledge from a huge quantity of information

informative presentation   A presentation that instructs, enlightens, explains, describes, clarifies, corrects, reminds, and/or demonstrates

informatory communication   A form of informative communication used to increase awareness of some phenomenon

ingratiation   When you agree, give compliments, and do favors so another person will like you

inspirational speaking   A form of speaking that brings like-minded people together, creates social unity, builds goodwill, or celebrates by arousing audience emotions

integration–separation dialectic   The desire for *both* connection *and* independence in a relationship

interactional context   The composition of the interaction; whether communication occurs one-to-one, in groups, or between a speaker and an audience

interactive communication model   A model that includes the concepts of noise and feedback: each communicator becomes both the source and receiver of messages and every component of communication becomes susceptible to disruption

intercultural dimension   An aspect of a culture that can be measured relative to other cultures

internal noise   Thoughts, feelings, and attitudes that interfere with your ability to communicate and understand a message as it was intended

internal preview   A connective that reveals or suggests the key points of a presentation

internal summary   A connective that sums up a major section of a presentation, reinforces important ideas, and reiterates critical ideas or information

interpersonal communication   Interaction between a limited number of people (usually two) for the purpose of sharing information, accomplishing a specific goal, or maintaining a relationship

interview   An interpersonal interaction between two parties, at least one of which has a predetermined and serious purpose, that involves asking and answering questions to share information, solve a problem, or influence one another

intimacy   The feeling or state of knowing someone deeply in physical, psychological, emotional, and/or collaborative ways because that person is significant in your life

intimidation   Occurs when communicators indicate they are willing and able to cause harm, but not by using violence or brutality

intrapersonal communication   The way in which you communicate within yourself about yourself to yourself

introvert   A person who thinks before speaking and usually is not very talkative; A basic Myer-Briggs personality trait

intuitive   A person who looks for connections, the "big picture" concept, and basic assumptions rather than focusing on details, procedures, and potential flaws; a basic Myers-Briggs personality trait

jargon   The specialized or technical language of a profession or homogenous group

jealousy   An intense feeling caused by a perceived threat to a relationship

Johari Window   A model that looks at two interpersonal dimensions: willingness to self-disclose and receptivity to feedback

judger   A highly structured person who plans ahead, is very punctual, and becomes impatient with others who show up late or waste time; a basic Myers-Briggs personality trait

key element   A fundamental building block of human communication

key point   An important issue or main idea in a presentation

laissez-faire leader   A leader who lets the group take charge of all decisions and actions

language   A system of arbitrary signs and symbols used to communicate thoughts and feelings

language intensity   The degree to which your language deviates from bland, neutral terms

leader–member relations   A leader's interactions with group members that can be positive, neutral, or negative

leadership   The ability to make strategic decisions and use communication to mobilize group members toward achieving a shared goal

leading question   A question that suggests or implies the desired response

leakage cue   Unintentional nonverbal behavior that may reveal deceptive intentions

learning style   Strengths and preferences that characterize the way people take in and process information

legitimate power   The official power that comes with a particular job, position, or assignment

linear communication model   The earliest type of communication model; functions in only one direction: a source creates a message and sends it through a channel to reach a receiver

linguist   A scholar who studies the nature and structure of speech

linguistics   An academic discipline that studies the nature and structure of human speech

listening   The ability to understand, analyze, respect, and respond appropriately to the meaning of another person's spoken and nonverbal messages

logical proof   Proof that addresses whether your arguments are reasonable and whether your presentation makes rational sense; logos

logistical context   The physical characteristics of a particular communication situation; focuses on a specific time, place, setting, and occasion

logistics   Planning and adapting to the audience size, the physical location, the equipment, and the amount of time you have in a communication context

logos   Proof that addresses whether your arguments are reasonable and whether your presentation makes rational sense; logical proof

low-context culture   A cultural dimension characterized by people who primarily express meaning through language

low power distance   A cultural dimension in which people believe that power distinctions among groups should be minimal

low uncertainty avoidance   A cultural dimension in which people accept change as part of life, tolerate nonconformity, take risks, and view rules and regulations as restricting and counterproductive

maintenance role   A group role expressed in behavior affecting how group members get along with each other while pursuing a common goal: maintenance roles include encourager/supporter, harmonizer, compromiser, tension releaser, gatekeeper, standard monitor, observer/interpreter, and follower

majority vote   When more than half the members of a group vote in favor of a proposal

manuscript speaking   When you write your presentation in advance and read it out loud

map   A presentational aid that shows where; translates data into spatial patterns; also used to give directions or compare locations

marker   The placement of an object to establish nonverbal "ownership" of an area or space

masculine society   A society in which men are supposed to be assertive, tough, and focused on material success whereas women are supposed to be more modest, tender, and concerned with the quality of life

mass communication   Mediated communication between a person and a large, often unknown, audience; radio, television, film, newspapers, magazines, and books

mediated communication   Any communication in which something exists between communicators; telephones, email

meeting   A scheduled gathering of group members for a structured discussion guided by a designated chairperson

message   Verbal and nonverbal content that generates meaning within and across various contexts, cultures, and channels

metamessage   A message about a message

metaphor   A word or phrase that ordinarily designates one thing but is used to designate another thing by making an implicit comparison

mindfulness   Being fully aware of the present moment without making hasty judgments

mindlessness   Allowing rigid categories and false distinctions to become habits of thought and behavior

mind mapping   An alternative method for identifying and organizing a presentation's key points; encourages the free flow of ideas and defines relationships among those ideas

minutes   The written record of a group's discussion, activities, and decisions

mixed message   A contradiction between verbal and nonverbal meanings

monochronic time   A cultural dimension in which people schedule events as separate items; one thing at a time; time is viewed as a valuable commodity

monologue   An interaction in which one person is doing all or almost all of the talking with another person or group of people

monotone   When you don't change the pitch of sounds within words or the pitch of words within phrases and sentences

Monroe's Motivated Sequence   A step-by-step method for organizing persuasive presentations that consists of five basic steps: Attention, Need, Satisfaction, Visualization, and Action

Muted Group Theory   A theory that explores how and why powerful, wealthy groups at the top of a society determine who will communicate and be listened to while messages from less powerful groups are suppressed or ignored

Myers-Briggs Type Indicator   A personality type theory that identifies preferred way of thinking and behaving with two opposite preferences in each of four personality traits: extrovert-introvert, sensor-intuitive, thinker-feeler, and judger-perceiver

mythos   A form of proof that addresses the values, faith, and feelings that make up our social character and that is most often expressed in traditional stories, sayings, and symbols

negotiation   A process of bargaining to settle differences or reach solutions

noise   Obstacles that can prevent a message from reaching its receivers as intended

nonverbal communication   Message components other than words that generate meaning

nonverbal deintensification   When you reduce the amount of emotion you display

nonverbal intensification   When you exaggerate your facial expressions

nonverbal masking   When you conceal your true emotions by displaying facial expressions considered more appropriate in a particular situation

nonverbal neutralization   When you make an effort to eliminate any display of emotions

norm   A set of expectations held by group members concerning the kinds of behavior or opinions that are acceptable or unacceptable, good or bad, right or wrong, appropriate or inappropriate

norming stage   A group development stage in which members define their roles and determine group procedures

occasion   The reasons that a group or an audience has assembled at a particular place and time

open-ended question   A question that encourages detailed responses

optimum pitch   The pitch at which you speak most easily and expressively

oral footnote   A spoken citation in an oral report or presentation that includes enough information to allow an interested listener to find the original source

organization   The structure of a presentation that helps you focus on your purpose by arranging your content in an effective pattern or format

organizational culture   The shared symbols, beliefs, values, and norms that affect the behavior of people working in and with an organization

organizational subculture   A group of individuals who engage in behavior and share values that are different from the larger organizational culture

other   One person or a large audience engaged in a communication activity; listeners, readers, or observers

other orientation   Giving serious attention to, concern for, and interest in other communicators

overcoming objections organizational pattern   A persuasive organizational pattern that takes a central route to persuasion by addressing audience reservations head-on with relevant and effective counterpersuasion

overpersonal type   A person who tries to get close to everyone

oversocial person   A person who feels unworthy and undervalued but tries to attract attention to compensate for feelings of inadequacy

panel discussion   Several people who interact about a common topic to educate, influence, or entertain an audience

paraphrasing   The ability to restate what others say in a way that indicates you understand them and relate to their feelings and the underlying meanings that accompany their words

parenting style   A stable sets of behaviors that characterize the psychosocial climate of parent–child interactions in a wide range of situations

passive aggressiveness   Communication that only *appears* to accommodate another person's needs, but actually represents subtle aggressive behavior; also referred to as hidden aggression.

passive voice   When the subject of a sentence receives the action

passivity   Giving in to others at the expense of your own needs or avoiding conflict and disagreement altogether

pathos   A form of persuasive proof that appeals to audience emotions such as anger, fear, pride, envy, love, regret, and jealousy; see emotional proof

perceiver   A person who is flexible and adaptive as well as less concerned about rules and punctuality; a basic Myers-Briggs personality trait

perception   The process through which you select, organize, and interpret sensory stimuli in the world around you

perception checking   An awareness of how you select, organize, and interpret sensory stimuli; whether you consider alternative interpretations; and whether you try to verify your perceptions with others

performing stage   A group development stage in which most conflict has been resolved and members concentrate on performing the tasks necessary to accomplish the group's common goal

peripheral route to persuasion   A route to persuasion that focuses on cues that are not directly related to the substance of a message—catchy phrases, dramatic stories, the quantity of arguments and evidence (rather than quality), the credibility and attractiveness of the speaker, and even the nature of background visuals and music; see Elaboration Likelihood Model of Persuasion

permissive parenting   A parenting style in which parents are often less involved in their children's lives and may overindulge or neglect them

personal integrity   Behaving in ways that are consistent with your values and beliefs

personal proof   A form of persuasive proof that relies on listener or audience perceptions of a speaker's competence, character, and charisma; see *ethos*

personal relationship   A relationship characterized by a high level of emotional connection and commitment

person-centered message   The degree to which a helper validates a distressed person's feelings and encourages him or her to talk about the upsetting event

persuasion   The art of discovering and skillfully using effective communication strategies to change people's opinions (what they think) or behavior (what they do)

persuasive presentation   A presentation that seeks to change or influence audience opinions and/or behavior

persuasive stories organizational pattern   A persuasive arrangement of the key points in a presentation that relies on narrative and emotional proof to show how people, events, and objects are affected by the change you are seeking

phatic language   Socially predictable small talk used in everyday conversations, such as "Hi," "Have a nice day," and "See ya' around"

photograph   A presentational aid used to portray reality

pie chart   A presentational aid that shows how much; shows proportions in relation to a whole or depicts relationships among related items

pitch   How high or low your voice sounds

plagiarism   Failing to document or give credit to the source of researched information or falsifying information used in a message

polychronic time   A cultural dimension in which people do many things at once, are easily distracted, change plans easily, and do not put great importance on time schedules or deadlines

power   The ability or authority to influence and motivate others

power distance   A cultural dimension which reflects the physical and psychological distance between those who have power and those who do not have power in relationships, institutions, and organizations

prejudice   A positive or negative attitude about an individual or cultural group based on little or no direct experience with that person or group

preliminary outline   A short outline that puts the major pieces of a presentation on paper

presentation aid   A supplementary resource—most often in visual form—available to speakers for highlighting key ideas and supporting material

presentational communication   A form of communication that occurs when speakers generate meaning with audience members, who are usually present at the delivery of a presentation

presentation performance   How you use words, your voice, your body, and presentation aids to express your message; a significant and irreversible component in every presentation

presentation speaking   The process of using verbal and nonverbal messages to generate meaning with audience members, who are usually present at the delivery of a presentation

primacy effect   The notion that the first information you perceive about someone is highly influential in forming an enduring impression

primary source   The document, testimony, or publication in which information first appears

primary tension   The social unease and inhibitions that accompany the getting-acquainted period in a new group

probing question   A question used to follow up another question and/or a response that encourages clarification and elaboration

problem/cause/solution organizational pattern   A persuasive arrangement of key points in a presentation that describes a serious problem, explains why the problem continues (the cause), and offers a solution

problem–solution arrangement   An organizational pattern that describes a situation that is harmful or difficult (the problem) and then offers a plan to solve the problem (the solution)

problem solving   A complex process in which groups make multiple decisions as they analyze a problem and develop a plan of action for solving the problem or reducing its harmful effects

process   A set of constantly changing actions, elements, and functions that bring about a result

professional relationship   A connection with people you associate and work with to accomplish a goal or perform a task

projection   Controlled vocal energy that gives thrust, precision, and intelligibility to the sound of your voice

pronunciation   Whether you say a word correctly; whether you put all the correct sounds in the correct order with the correct stress

proof   The arguments you select and use to persuade a particular audience in a particular context

protocol   The expected format of a ceremony or the etiquette observed at a particular type of event

proxemics   The study of spatial relationships and how the distance between people communicates information about their relationship

proximity principle   The closer objects, events, or people are to each other, the more likely you will perceive them as belonging together

Psychoevolutionary Emotion Theory   A theory that helps explain the development and meaning of emotions

Psychological Reactance Theory   A theory that explains why, when you perceive a threat to your freedom to believe or behave as you wish, you may go out of your way to do the forbidden behavior or rebel against the prohibiting authority

psychosocial context   The overall psychological and cultural environment in which you live and communicate

public group   A group that discusses issues in front of or for the benefit of the public

punch line   A sentence or phrase that communicates the climax of the story

purpose   What you and others are trying to accomplish by communicating; a key element when deciding what and how to communicate

purposeful living   Identifying short-term and long-term goals and developing an action plan to achieve those goals

purpose statement   The main idea in your presentation or the position you are going to take on an issue

qualifier   The degree to which a claim appears to be true characterized by terms such as *possible, likely* or *unlikely,* and *possibly*

race   A socially constructed concept that classifies people into separate value-based categories

racism   Practicing ethnocentrism, stereotyping, prejudice, and discrimination

rate   The speed at which you speak

receiver   Another person or group of people who interpret and evaluate your message

recency effect   The notion that the last information you receive creates a lasting impression

receptivity to feedback   Your awareness, interpretation, and response to someone else's disclosures about you

recognition seeker   A negative group role in which a member boasts about personal accomplishments, tries to be the center of attention, pouts if not getting enough attention

reference group   A group to which you closely identify and enjoy membership

referent power   The power and influence that result from others' respect and admiration

reflected appraisal   Accepting the opinions that others have about you

regulating nonverbal behavior   Nonverbal behavior that manages the flow of a conversation

Relational Dialectics Theory   A theory that focuses on the ongoing tensions between contradictory impulses in personal relationships

relationship-motivated leader   A leader who gains satisfaction from working well with other people even if the cost is neglecting or failing to complete a task

religious illiteracy   The inability to understand and use the religious terms, symbols, images, beliefs, practices, scripture, heroes, themes, and stories that are used in American public life

repetitive nonverbal behavior   Nonverbal behavior that visually repeats a verbal message

research   The search for and analysis of information to support a message

reservation   An exception to an argument; acknowledgement that a claim may not be true under certain circumstances

reward power   The power to give others something they value

rhetorical device   A technique designed to enhance a presentation's impact and persuasiveness through the use of specific language strategies

rhyme   When words correspond with one another in terms of final sounds

role   A pattern of behaviors associated with an expected function in a specific context or relationship

secondary source   A source that reports, repeats, or summarizes information from one or more other sources

secondary tension   The frustrations and personality conflicts experienced by group members as members compete for social acceptance, status, and achievement

seductive detail   The element in a message—particularly when visual aids are used as a form of support—that attracts audience attention but does not support a writer's or speaker's key points

selection interview   An interview to evaluate and choose candidates for a job

self   Part of an invisible and unique inner sphere in which your unique characteristics and attitudes influence how effectively and ethically you communicate

self-acceptance   The willingness to acknowledge and "own" your thoughts, feelings, and behaviors

self-appraisal   Evaluation of your self-concept in terms of your abilities and behaviors

self-assertiveness   Knowing your needs and goals and being willing to pursue them

self-awareness   The ability to be conscious of your own traits, thoughts, and feelings; a personal understanding of your identity

self-centered interest   When a presentation can result in personal gain or loss

self-centered role   A group member whose behavior adversely affects member relationships and the group's ability to achieve its common goal

self-concept   The relatively stable sum total of beliefs you have about yourself

self-disclosure   The process of sharing personal information, opinions, and emotions with others that would not normally be known to them

self-effacing humor   Your ability to direct humor at yourself

self-esteem   Your judgments about yourself

self-fulfilling prophecy   An impression formation process in which an expressed impression of another person elicits behavior that conforms to the impression

self-monitoring   The ability to monitor your thoughts and feelings; a combination of introspection (thinking about yourself), careful observation (noting how others react to you), and adaptation (modifying how you present yourself)

self-promotion   Telling others about your successes and the things you do well

self-responsibility   The realization that you are largely responsible for your own happiness and the fulfillment of your goals

self-talk   The silent statements you make to yourself about yourself

semantics   Understanding the various meanings of words and phrases

sensor   A person who focuses on details and prefers to concentrate on one task at a time; a basic Myers-Briggs personality trait

sexual harassment   Unwelcome sexual advances for sexual favors, and other verbal or physical conduct of a sexual nature

sign   Something that stands for or represents something specific and often looks like or depicts the thing it represents

significant other   An individual whose opinions you value, such as a family member, best friend, valued coworker, or respected mentor

signpost   A connective that consists of a short phrase that, like a sign on the highway, tells or reminds listeners where you are in the organizational structure of a presentation

skill   Your acquired ability to accomplish communication goals during the course of an interaction

similarity principle   Organizing information so that similar elements or people are often perceived as part of a group

simile   A phrase that makes a direct comparison between two things or ideas by using the words *like* or *as*

simplicity principle   Organizing information in a way that provides the simplest interpretation

single question format   A group problem-solving procedure in a seemingly simple format that approximates the way successful problem solvers and decision makers naturally think

Situational Theory of Leadership   Seeks an ideal fit between leader characteristics and leadership roles

social comparison   The process of evaluating yourself in relation to the others in your reference groups

social dimension   Focuses on the interpersonal relationships among group members

social identity   Your self-concept as derived from the social categories to which you see yourself belonging

Social Penetration Theory   A theory that examines how, in the process of relationship bonding, individuals move from superficial communication to deeper, more intimate communication

source   A person or group of people who create a message intended to produce a particular response

space arrangement   An organizational pattern in which the key points are put in order of their location or physical relationship to one another

speaker credibility   The extent to which an audience believes a speaker and the speaker's message; components include character, charisma, and competence; see *ethos*

speaking outline   A short outline used during a presentation that includes little more than a list of key points and reminders of supporting material

speaking style   How you use vocabulary, sentence structure and length, grammar and syntax, and language devices to express a message

stability–change dialectic   A desire for *both* the security of a stable relationship *and* the novelty and excitement of change, the predictability of day-after-day interactions *and* an occasional change in routine

standard agenda   A seven-step problem solving method that begins with a focus on the problem itself and then moves to a systematic consideration of possible solutions

statistics   Data that organizes, summarizes, and analyzes numerical information; often used to predict human behavior and events ranging from economic trends to the winners of football games

stereotype   A generalization about a group of people that oversimplifies their characteristics

storming stage   A group development stage in which members are more argumentative and emotional as they discuss important issues and vie for leadership

story   An account or report about something that happened

storyboard   A visual plan for your presentation that combines words and pictures to create a coherent message

strategy   The specific plan of action you select to help you communicate

structure   The organization of appropriate content into a coherent and purposeful message

Styles Theory of Leadership   A theory that examines a collection of specific behaviors that constitute three distinct styles: autocratic, democratic, and laissez-faire leadership

subordinate term   A word that is very concrete and specialized such as a 1987 Toyota 4×4 long-bed truck rather than a vehicle

substituting nonverbal behavior   Nonverbal behavior that substitutes for language such as waving goodbye or holding two fingers up in a victory sign

superior–subordinate relationship   A relationship that is characterized by the authority one person has over another person's work and behavior

superordinate term   A word that groups objects and ideas together very generally, such as vehicle, animal, or location

supplication   Behavior that makes others feel resourceful and helpful

supporting material   Ideas, opinions, and information that explain and/or advance a presentation's main ideas and purpose

supportive behavior   Behavior that creates a climate in which sincere self-disclosure and responsiveness to feedback benefit both parties

symbol   A grouping of letters or words used to represent an object, idea, quantity, quality, concept, relationship, element, or function

symposium   A session in which group members present short, uninterrupted presentations on different aspects of a topic for the benefit of an audience

systematic desensitization   A relaxation and visualization technique that helps reduce the anxiety associated with stressful situations

table   A presentational aid that summarizes and compares data

task dimension   Focuses on getting a job done, achieving a goal, or producing a product through group effort

task force   A group that has some authority and power, is appointed for a short term, develops its own procedures, and expects recommendations to be taken seriously

task-motivated leader   A leader who wants to get the job done

task role   A group role expressed in behavior that helps get a job one, achieve a goal, or produce a product; task roles include initiator/contributor, information seeker, information giver, opinion seeker, opinion giver, clarifier/summarizer, evaluator/critic, energizer, procedural technician, and recorder/secretary

task structure   The nature of a task's structure that ranges from disorganized and chaotic to highly organized and rule driven

territoriality   The sense of personal ownership attached to a particular space

testimony   Statements or opinions that someone has said or written

text chart   A presentational aid that lists ideas or key phrases often under a title or headline

theory   A statement that explains how the world works; describes, explains, and predicts events and behavior

thinker   A person who is analytical and task oriented; takes pride in their ability to think objectively and logically; a basic Myers-Briggs personality trait

thought speed   The speed (words per minute) at which most people can think compared with the speed at which they can speak

time arrangement   An organizational pattern that puts information in an order according to time or calendar dates

topical arrangement   An organizational pattern that divides a large topic into smaller subtopics

topic-centered interest   A subject that audience members enjoy hearing and learning about

touch approacher   A person who generally feels comfortable with touch and often initiates touch with others

touch avoider   A person who is less comfortable initiating touch or being touched

Toulmin Model of Argument   A framework for developing and analyzing arguments that includes the following components: data, claim, warrant, backing, reservation, and qualifier

Trait Theory of Leadership   A theory that attempts to identify individual characteristics associated with leadership

transactional communication models   Models in which we send and receive messages at the same time within specific contexts

transition   A connective consisting of a word, number, brief phrase, or sentence that helps you move from one key point or section in a presentation to another

turn-requesting cues   Verbal and nonverbal messages that signal a desire to speak, such as leaning forward, providing direct eye contact, and lifting one hand as if beginning to gesture

turn-yielding cues   Verbal and nonverbal messages that signal that you are completing your comments and are preparing to listen, such as slowing down your speaking rate, relaxing your posture or gestures, and leaning slightly away

two-thirds vote   When at least twice as many group members vote for a proposal as against it

uncertainty avoidance   A cultural dimension that represents the extent to which people within a culture are made nervous by situations that they perceive as unstructured, unclear, or unpredictable

underpersonal type   A person who believes he or she is not liked; establishes only superficial relationships with others

undersocial person   A person who feels unworthy or undervalued

upward distortion   The hesitancy of some subordinates to communicate negative news up the chain of command and their tendency to distort such news to place it in a more positive light

valid   Ideas, opinions, and information that are well founded, justified, and accurate

values   Beliefs that guide how you think about what is right or wrong, good or bad, just or unjust, correct or incorrect

value step   Part of a presentation's introduction that tells audience members why the information is of value to them and how it can affect their success or well-being

verbal communication   The ways in which you use the words in a language to generate meaning

visualization   The process of imagining what it would be like to experience an entire communication act

volume   The loudness level of your voice

warrant   An explanation of how and why the data support the claim

whistle-blower   A person who reports wrongdoing in a workplace or organization to another individual or organization that has the power to expose publicly, correct, or punish the behavior

Whorf hypothesis   The hypothesis that language reflects cultural models of the world, which then influences how the speakers of a language think, act, and behave

willingness to self-disclose   The extent to which you are prepared to disclose personal information and feelings

word stress   The degree of prominence given to a syllable within a word or words within a phrase or sentence

workgroup   A group that assumes primary responsibility for making decisions, solving problems, and implementing projects in organizations

work team   A group that is usually given full responsibility and resources for its performance

Index

Page numbers in italics refer to the online chapters available on *MyCommunicationLab* (www.mycommunicationlab.com), which requires a passcode. Page numbers followed by a *f* or *t* indicates a figure or table.

Photo Credits